Nicholas Wiseman

AND THE TRANSFORMATION OF ENGLISH CATHOLICISM

Nicholas Wiseman

AND THE TRANSFORMATION OF ENGLISH CATHOLICISM

Richard J. Schiefen

THE PATMOS PRESS   SHEPHERDSTOWN

1984

Library of Congress Cataloging in Publication Data

Schiefen, Richard J., 1932–
  Nicholas Wiseman and the transformation of English
Catholicism.

  Bibliography: p.
  Includes index.
  1. Wiseman, Nicholas Patrick, 1802–1865. 2. Cardinals—
England—Biography. 3. Catholic Church—England—History
—19th century. 4. England—Church history—19th century.
I. Title.
BX4705.W6S34 1984   282'.092'4 [B]   84-7763
ISBN 0-915762-15-3

Manufactured in the United States of America

In memory of John F. and Lois Lasater Maher

Preface

WHEN THE ROMAN CATHOLIC HIERARCHY IN ENGLAND AND WALES celebrated its centenary in 1950, many articles and some books were written to commemorate the event. Few of these studies were, in themselves, of major significance, but they indicated the vast field of research that promised a fruitful harvest for ecclesiastical historians interested in nineteenth-century England. Numerous letters and manuscripts of every description had been gathering dust in ecclesiastical archives for a century and more; in some cases, their very existence was unknown. I have in my possession, for example, a letter written by the late Monsignor Philip Hughes on June 27, 1967, in which he stated that when he assumed the duties of archivist for the archdiocese of Westminster in 1933, he was "startled" to discover that the latest paper in his care was a letter written in 1849 by the future Cardinal Wiseman. He was told that the Wiseman and Manning papers had been burned at the turn of the century, although he recalled that Wiseman's "private papers" were preserved at Ushaw College and that Manning's could be found at the residence of the Oblates of St. Charles, Bayswater.

Through no fault of his own, Hughes was unaware of masses of manuscripts, many unsorted, preserved in the basement of the archbishop's house, Westminster. For many years now, Miss Elisabeth Poyser, archdiocesan archivist, has been putting them in order to make them accessible to those who may wish to consult them. Hughes was correct in stating that many of Wiseman's personal papers could be found at Ushaw College, although it is not always clear whether correspondence should be considered as "personal" or "official," and the various collections, there and elsewhere, are not easy to designate in that way.

This book is the result of a continuing interest which first developed in the 1960s when I was preparing a Ph.D. thesis for the University of London on "The Organisation and Administration of Roman Catholic Dioceses in England and Wales in the Mid-Nineteenth Century." Since then, I have made a number of return visits to archives in England and Rome, partially made possible by grants from the American Philosophical Society and the Canada Council, for which I am extremely grateful. Although I am not satisfied that my efforts have been exhaustive, there comes a point at which any historian must stop gathering data in order to write. Among the archives in England, I have devoted least attention to that of the diocese of Clifton, as the notes will indicate. These manuscripts, now transferred from the bishop's house to the Bristol City Records Office, were examined carefully and used by Bishop Bernard Ward and Dom Cuthbert Butler, upon whose works I have often depended.

Historians will always be indebted to the outstanding studies by Bernard and Wilfrid Ward, unsurpassed by any similar works since their day. They were sons of W. G. Ward, however, a partisan if ever there was one, and although their books are remarkably unbiased, these authors were not entirely unaffected by their father's influence. They, and Cuthbert Butler as well, were also limited by the inaccessibility of certain manuscripts. The Holy See, for example, was unwilling, until recent years, to admit scholars to the enormous quantities of nineteenth-century archival materials in Rome. Bernard Ward was permitted to consult some specific papers in the possession of the Sacred Congregation for the Propagation of the Faith, but he was not allowed free access and seems to have been further hampered by a lack of fluency in Italian.

There are no doubt errors of fact and interpretation in a work that has been based upon scattered primary sources of various kinds, even personal notes and diaries. I accept, of course, full responsibility for mistakes. Where it seems to clarify a quoted passage, I have sometimes expanded abbreviations and altered the original punctuation and spelling, but I have never consciously changed the wording of a text. All translations from Latin and Italian are my own, unless otherwise indicated. In many instances, finally, there are multiple copies of particular manuscripts. Most often I cite only the source that I have consulted or can be located most conveniently. It has been virtually impossible to acknowledge all of the authors who have made use of the same sources. To them I express my apologies if they have been overlooked.

I owe much to the archivists who have assisted me in working through the manuscripts in their custody. Above all, Miss Elisabeth Poyser of Westminster has helped and encouraged me to a degree beyond the call of duty. Others who have been extremely helpful include

Fathers G. T. Bradley of Leeds, James McGettrick of Southwark, and the late J. Denis McEvilly of Birmingham; the late Monsignor Bernard Payne, and Fathers David Milburn, J. Derek Holmes, and Michael Sharratt of Ushaw College; Dom Placid Spearitt of Ampleforth Abbey; the abbé Alphonse Chapeau, who in 1969 allowed me to consult many manuscripts among the Manning papers at Bayswater; and Bishop Patrick J. Casey, then provost of the Westminster Chapter, who obtained the necessary permission for me to see the relevant chapter records; the various archivists of the Venerable English College and the Sacred Congregation for the Propagation of the Faith, and Father Charles Burns of the Vatican Archives; and the Franciscan Friars of the Atonement, who, along with my good friend, Mrs. Mary Buck, offered me every courtesy and assistance during my frequent visits to the Catholic Central Library, London. I am grateful to the ecclesiastical authorities for permission to use the manuscripts for which they are responsible. To the National Portrait Gallery (London) I am indebted for permission to reproduce the sketch of Wiseman by Richard Doyle.

A special expression of gratitude should be offered to Professor J. B. Conacher of the University of Toronto and Professor Emeritus C. W. Dugmore of King's College, London, whose direction when I was their student and unflagging interest throughout many subsequent years have meant much to me. Among others who, I hope, will recall their particular contributions to my work, I am grateful to J. L. Altholz, F. J. Cwiekowski, David J. Dooley, Sheridan Gilley, Mark Miller, Raymond H. Schmandt, Nancy Vesey, and Beryl Wells. Mrs. Eileen Dumas typed the entire final manuscript with her customary skill and patience, and Ann Hofstra Grogg, copyeditor, has demonstrated care and an eye for detail. James C. and Mary G. Holland, codirectors of The Patmos Press, have shown interest in my work since 1976 and have been faithful and supportive in waiting for its completion.

Finally, for almost thirty-five years, my confrères of the Basilian Fathers have provided me with every conceivable means of support. To all of them, most especially to those of the University of St. Michael's College, Toronto, and the University of St. Thomas, Houston, I must state that I am very proud to be one of them.

February 1984   Houston, Texas   R. J. SCHIEFEN, CSB

Introduction

NOT SINCE THE FUNERAL OF THE DUKE OF WELLINGTON IN 1852 HAD so much public interest been accorded the passing of a prominent Englishman, reported the *Times*, when Cardinal Nicholas Wiseman was buried on February 23, 1865. The *Hull Advertiser* noted, "The greatest among the present generation of England's great men has ceased to be numbered with the living." More than thirty years later, when Wilfrid Ward's biography of the cardinal was published, a reviewer contended that however much others had done for English Catholics, it was to the first archbishop of Westminster that "humanly speaking, the Church in this country owes her existence and her strength."[1] If the tributes seem exaggerated today, it is because Wiseman's human failings and undeniable eccentricities, along with the numerous controversies in which he was engaged throughout much of his life, have tended to cloud a proper assessment of his contribution, which was unquestioned by the vast majority of his contemporaries, even those with whom he was engaged in verbal combat.

In November 1850 Cardinal Wiseman returned to England from Rome as archbishop of the newly established hierarchy. He was then confronted by crowds whose sentiment little resembled that of the thousands upon thousands of men and women who would gather to pay their last respects as his funeral cortège made its way to the Roman Catholic cemetery of St. Mary's, Kensal Green. When it was announced that Pope Pius IX had restored a Catholic hierarchy to England and Wales, mobs moved into street and field to burn the pontiff in effigy, along with his emissary the first archbishop. Few at the time, even among Catholics, understood the significance of the papal gesture or the long and sometimes painful process by which it had been achieved. Fewer still fully realized the unique service for English Catholics performed by Nicholas Wiseman and the role that he would continue to exercise in the development of the church in his country. "The cause of religion, I am convinced, is thrown back at least a century by this proceeding," complained one of his priests.[2]

Roman Catholics were still on the defensive in 1850, though with less reason than most of them thought.[3] Wiseman's apparent flamboyance, his Roman ways and attitudes, his outspoken criticism of the English clergy, and the stubborn vigor with which he promoted his views were subject to much ridicule and to many harsh judgments both before and after 1840, when he took up permanent residence in England. Sometimes he encountered mistrust and open hostility from quarters where he had every reason to expect support. It was indicative of his strength of character that he set himself to the task to which he considered himself called with such determination that the announcement of his death was received with almost universal sympathy. "The angry feelings evidenced in 1850 are in truth past and done with long ago," wrote one observer.[4]

The purpose of this book is to examine Nicholas Wiseman's contribution in the light of the documentation now available. Long before Wiseman left Rome and throughout the rest of his life, his writings, his public activities, and his administrative and pastoral endeavors were all motivated primarily by his wish to advance the cause of English Catholics. He was remarkably successful, although his objectives and the impetuous manner in which he often pursued them led him into constant controversy. The impression has been normally conveyed that only Wiseman's final years were characterized by disagreeable battles. Such was not the case, although certainly his failing health and the opposition of many who had been his intimate friends and associates, including the majority of his fellow bishops, made his last struggles particularly hard to bear.

To dwell upon so many controversial episodes may tend to provide readers with an unbalanced picture not only of Wiseman's achievement but also of the character and purpose of those who sometimes opposed him. It is not possible to avoid the risk. Wiseman's stature can hardly be assessed without an understanding of the difficulties that he had to overcome and even the defeats that he suffered. His judgments were sometimes wrong, but he was a man of action as well as vision and extraordinary talent. None of his contemporaries possessed the combination of ability, education, social and ecclesiastical connections, character, and energy necessary to rival his achievements.

Wilfrid Ward's *Life and Times of Cardinal Wiseman* (1897) is a masterful, detailed study in the tradition, now considered by some to be "idiosyncratic," of much nineteenth-century biography. In this century Brian Fothergill's more modest but admirable study has provided us with a much-needed updated biography.[5] The present book is an attempt to offer, in some instances, further explanation of matters discussed by both authors, more thorough documentation of sources than has hitherto been possible, and, where called for, reinterpretation of Wiseman's career as he sought to carry England into the orbit of the Catholic revival that, he was convinced, characterized the life of the church on the Continent and promised a new and splendid future for English Catholics as well.

Contents

Nicholas Wiseman

AND THE TRANSFORMATION OF
ENGLISH CATHOLICISM

1. Spain – Ireland – England – Rome

NICHOLAS PATRICK STEPHEN WISEMAN WAS BORN IN SEVILLE ON August 2, 1802.[1] His paternal grandfather, James, seems to have belonged to a new class of Irish Catholic merchants who carried on direct trade with France, Spain, and England. He settled in Seville during the second half of the eighteenth century. The future cardinal's father, also named James, first married Mariana Dunphy, the daughter, according to contemporaries, of a Spanish general.[2] Their union produced four daughters, one of whom died in infancy. On April 18, 1800, some years after the death of Mariana, James Wiseman married Xaviera Strange of Aylwardstown Castle, County Kilkenny. The nuptials were solemnized in the Church of Saints Mary and Michael in the Commercial Road, London, while James was on a prolonged visit to England. Nicholas was their second son. His older brother James had been born in February 1801, before the family returned to Spain. Francesca, called Frasquita by the family, was born in August 1804. Five months later Xaviera Wiseman was widowed when her husband, while dining with family and friends to celebrate the birthday of his eldest daughter, was stricken by a fatal apoplectic seizure. The distraught young widow, alone with three small children, soon returned to Ireland, where for approximately two years she resided at the home of her father.

According to those who knew the family, Nicholas was remarkably quiet as a child. In view of the sudden loss of his father, the distress of his mother, their subsequent departure for new surroundings, and the fact that Spanish was the first language to which he had been introduced, it is no wonder that the child was shy. Shyness was a characteristic that Nicholas maintained throughout his life; it was mistaken by some as aloofness or even arrogance. After his death a relative recalled how young Nicholas, along with his brother and their playmates, had gone to see his grandfather's new threshing machine. Quiet though intensely observant, the lad watched while the others inquired, "Grandpapa what is this for? grandpapa what is this wheel for?" Colat, as Nicholas was called, finally spoke up, "Can't you look and you'll see what they are for."[3] The incident was completely in character.

James and Nicholas were eventually placed in a boarding school in Waterford. In March 1810, however, both boys were taken to England, where they were enrolled in St. Cuthbert's College, Ushaw, about four miles to the west of Durham City. The college, like St. Edmund's, Old Hall, near Ware in the South, descended from Douai, which had been forced to close during the Reign of Terror in 1793. The new buildings in which the boys were housed had been occupied only since 1808. In 1815 Frasquita was placed in a convent school at York in which her "cousin" Fanny Tucker had already been enrolled for three years.[4] It then became customary for the boys to spend their holidays with their mother and sister in York.[5]

"The traditional picture of young Wiseman's external appearance which remains at Ushaw," according to Wilfrid Ward, "is that of a somewhat gawky youth, with limbs ill knit together, betokening the absence of all aptitude for athletics, sauntering about with a book under his arm, oftener alone than in company." The description was a caricature based on some verses prepared by Wiseman himself six months before his death. Printed privately, they were — quite mercifully — never published. Ward, however, would have read the following:

> Thirsty panting after knowledge,
>   With the zest of unseen joy,
> May depict the life in college,
>   Of a lone unmurmuring boy;
> To whom pastime gave no pleasure,
>   Nor to run, or row, or climb;
> For whom book, or thought, the measure,
>   Filled, of fragmentary time.
>
> . . . .
>
> For, wan features, frame ill-knitted,
>   Wrung compassion from the strong:
> Oh! how many, who then pitied,
>   In their tombs have slumbered long![6]

In 1848 Bishop Wiseman described his experiences at school for his favorite nephew.

When I look back on my own school companions, & others whom I have known at College, I do not by any means find that their success in life, or their usefulness, which is more important, has been in proportion to their brilliancy at College, but rather the contrary. I can speak from experience, since as a boy at College I was always considered stupid & dull by my companions (when out of class) and made hardly an [*sic*] friend there & particularly never got the least notice or favour from superiors. But I knew that I was reading a great deal more than others without saying a word about it, both in study time & out of it, & I made myself happy enough. I am sure I never said a witty or clever thing all the time I was at College, but I used to *think* a good deal. . . . The great lesson which I learnt during my desolate years of College life is the one I should wish you to learn—self-reliance; not vanity or presumption, but the determination to work *for yourself,* and by steadily doing your duty, without minding what others may say, gain for yourself character and respect. One result which I soon found was this: that while no one would ever have thought of asking me to join him in playing or amusement, neither would any have proposed to me to be a party to the violation of any rule, or the playing of any trick; & I learnt when I left the house, & only then, that though I had never received any favour from superiors, nor half the notice which more agreeable, but ill-behaved boys had, I received, & had enjoyed as high a character & more esteem & real regard than usually falls to the lot of boys at school.[7]

Even allowing for a certain romanticizing on Wiseman's part, there is no reason to question the general accuracy of his recollection.

Nicholas, in fact, was singled out for special attention by John Lingard, vice-president of Ushaw when the Wiseman boys arrived and acting president from May 1810 to June 1811. Many years later Wiseman recalled Lingard's "specific acts of thoughtful and delicate kindness, which showed a tender heart mindful of its duties, amidst the many harassing occupations just devolved on him, through the death of the president, and his own literary engagements; for he was reconducting his first great work through the press."[8] The renowned historian left the college in 1811. His successor, John Gillow, president until 1828, assured Mrs. Wiseman "that Nicholas had more judgment than he (Mr G) had ever found in a young man of his age."[9] The boy was at the head of his class at the end of his final year at Ushaw.

Wiseman remained at Ushaw for almost nine years. Although he was thoughtful and impressionable, the isolation of the college and the rigid routine to which the students were subjected would have precluded his obtaining a fully accurate view of the state of English Catholicism or its needs. It is not farfetched to conjecture that Lingard, during the short period in which Wiseman knew him, would have conveyed the need for English Catholics of talent and education to present the history and doctrine of the church in their true light and to defend them from the attacks of opponents.

There is no clear indication that Nicholas, aside from his early desire to be a priest, foresaw the significant role that he would play in the church, although his mother must have told him of the remark made by the Irish Capuchin who baptized him in 1802: "Now, Madam, it shall be my prayer that this child become one of the brightest ornaments of the Church." Comments of this kind, even if accurately reported, become relevant only with hindsight, nor should too much be made of the report that Mrs. Wiseman laid her infant son upon the altar of the cathedral in Seville "and consecrated him to the service of the Church."[10]

In later years Wiseman recalled an anti-Catholic demonstration that he had observed in Durham when he was ten or eleven years old. His mother and superiors would have told him that Catholics were still a persecuted minority in England, subject to disabilities or restrictions that set them apart from their fellow citizens. He would have been warned, moreover, that they were obliged to be on guard against various forms of attack and that it was necessary to avoid undue ostentation. Catholics were objects of sporadic demonstrations of hostile feeling, especially during periods prior to parliamentary elections, like that recalled by Wiseman, when their religious disabilities were becoming an increasingly volatile issue. They were, however, neither as isolated nor as persecuted as popular accounts indicate.[11]

The cardinal also recalled the festivities marking a visit to London in 1814 of the king of Prussia and the emperor of Russia, England's allies against Napoleon. He described the fêtes as "splendid but somewhat childish." He noted that it was on this occasion that Cardinal Ercole Consalvi, shrewd negotiator for the Holy See at the Congress of Vienna and Pius VII's secretary of state, had been received by the prince regent and made a favorable impression in England.[12] Consalvi was the first cardinal to land in England for more than two hundred years. Wiseman himself would be the second.

The Northern District, the ecclesiastical area in which Durham was situated, was one of four vicariates into which England had been divided by the Holy See in 1688.[13] Each was placed under the direction of a vicar apostolic of episcopal rank, appointed by Rome, who exercised delegated jurisdiction only. These bishops were guided and controlled directly by the Sacred Congregation for the Propagation of the Faith, often referred to as "Propaganda," composed of cardinals who were responsible for directing the church in mission areas. A constitution issued by Pope Benedict XIV in 1753 had laid down directives for English Catholics, but there were no dioceses, cathedrals, or chapters of canons, and ecclesiastical law was suspended as in all mission territories.[14] The bishops held foreign titles, strange to English ears, *in partibus infidelium*, that is, sees, normally in Africa or Asia, no longer in practical existence.

Since the Reformation, Roman Catholic priests had been assigned as chaplains to the gentry or to foreign ambassadors. In this capacity they served the needs of a relatively small Catholic community. By the nineteenth century they were taking on the functions of parish priests, but they continued to speak of serving particular missions rather than parishes, chapels instead of churches. They would do so for some time to come. Priests were normally addressed as "Mister" or, when appropriate, "Doctor," not as "Reverend" or "Father."

Chapels and mission stations were springing up throughout England, especially in the increasingly populated cities, where Irish immigration helped to account for the development.[15] Priests still functioned without any formal ecclesiastical framework, however, since no canonically established parishes could be provided for. Even the distinction between rector and curate was not defined, a situation sometimes resulting in unhappy squabbles. Since there were no irremovable pastors, an office provided for by canon law under certain specific circumstances, priests frequently objected to the ease with which they were transferred from one post to another by their bishops. Members of religious orders, finally, accustomed to the independence from episcopal control deemed necessary during penal times, attempted to establish themselves as they had always done, much to the resentment of the bishops and secular priests.

A number of attempts had been made to substitute bishops-in-ordinary for vicars apostolic — in short, to restore a proper hierarchy — but such efforts were premature and motivated chiefly by the desire for greater independence from Rome.[16] In the late eighteenth century it was widely felt that only by establishing canonical government and clearly defined laws could non-Catholic prejudice be dissolved. Protestants commonly considered Roman Catholics to be completely subservient to the pope in matters political as well as spiritual, and it was the aim of some Catholics to demonstrate that such was not the case.

It was not, however, the state of English Catholics that would preoccupy Nicholas Wiseman during the years of early manhood. In the autumn of 1818 he and nine other English students set out on the long journey to Rome, where they entered the Venerable English College, often called the "Venerabile." They were the first English inhabitants of the college since the invasion of the French revolutionary army that had ransacked it early in 1798. George Brown, vice-president of Ushaw, wrote with pride to Robert Gradwell, sent from England to prepare the college for the students and to serve as its rector, that Wiseman was "above all praise." He continued: "His talents are unrivalled in Ushaw College, his piety fervent, and solid, and his character as a Christian scholar quite without a fault. He is of a good family, and though quite independent in his circumstances, has voluntarily devoted himself to the English mission." Wiseman's financial independence was not as complete as Brown implied, but the priest offered a further observation that was sound: "When they [the students] become a little accustomed to the Roman schools, I think Mr. Wiseman will not fear to enter the lists with any Italian that can stand forth against him."[17]

The previous year James Wiseman had left Ushaw for Spain, where he settled in Madrid with his Uncle Patrick and his family.[18] Later Mrs. Wiseman, plagued by financial worries, withdrew Frasquita from school and established their home in Paris. She wrote to Nicholas of how "miserably uncomfortable" she was: "More wretched days than those I have spent in Paris I never have passed." She may have been attempting to ease the pain of separation for her son, who was on the verge of leaving for Rome. "I'm sure," she wrote, "you would be wretched were you here."[19]

There is no doubt that Mrs. Wiseman's financial concerns were real. A month earlier James had written from Madrid: "I should regret very much to see you deprived of Ann's services. I certainly should think it very hard that you should not have a servant, & much more should I feel at seeing you take the last step that you say you will take. I mean that of putting yourself *en pension* with a *country priest.*" James continued somewhat dramatically: "I think this would *be degrading* yourself, & did I see things come to such an extremity as that you should be obliged to dismiss your servant, or shut yourself up with a person so much beneath you as a country curate, I apprehend that I should not be able to contain myself but that I should come to a clear explanation with my uncle."[20]

Uncle Patrick, in fact, was generous in assisting his brother's widow, although he suffered financial losses himself the following year. When he died in 1822, he had been sending Xaviera 3,000 francs every six months, although she wrote that the last payment had been only 2,500 francs.[21] The subject of their financial distress was raised again and again in the letters that Xaviera and Frasquita wrote to young Nicholas. Mrs. Wiseman managed, nevertheless, to provide hospitality for those who visited her and to maintain the appearance of genteel respectability.

Nicholas had been ill during his last days at Ushaw, but he recovered in time to embark from Liverpool with his nine companions on October 2, 1818. In 1858 Wiseman pointed out that the voyage alone was "thrice the length of one to America at present, and, with its additional land-journey, about as long as a circular sail, in a clipper, to New Zealand!" After a strenuous voyage, the young travelers arrived at Leghorn. Six of them completed their uncomfortable overland trip on December 18, when they entered the Eternal City. The four others, proceeding at a slightly more leisurely pace, appeared the following day.[22]

Hurried preparations were made for the students to be received by Pope Pius VII, the venerated pontiff who had stood up to Napoleon and returned from exile in France to Rome in the spring of 1814. Wiseman, forty years later, recalled the audience, taking advantage of the opportunity to convey his personal reflections upon the Holy Father and describe the papal quarters that he visited often in subsequent years.[23]

The six students who could be attired properly accompanied their rector into the papal presence on Christmas Eve. They would have startled one accustomed to the practice of the English clergy, who, seeking to be inconspicuous, simply adopted the lay dress of their day. The youngest of the students, George Heptonstall, wrote to his mother:

> Our dress is a very good one, in the first place a cassock reaching down to our feet, of the finest black French cloth; over this is a gown of the same material, with the two wings behind — under these we have all black instead of cravats — we have a collar turned down with white — but as for our hats — it is a wonderful one — an immence tryangular one so that if you were to meet me I doubt whether you would dare to look at me or not, thinking me some great Cardinal.

The Holy Father, according to a memorandum made by Gradwell to record the event, "received them standing, shook hands with each, and welcomed them to Rome." He then "praised the English clergy for their good and peaceful conduct, and their fidelity to the Holy See." There may have been a note of irony and a mild warning in the pontiff's comment. He urged the young men to "learning and piety," before concluding, "I hope you will do honour both to Rome and to your own country."[24]

Wiseman's spirit and genius blossomed in Rome. In the verses prepared shortly before his death, he described himself while at Ushaw as "poring, plodding, slow, industrious, without soar of wit, or will":

> Till Rome's mighty spirit beckoned,
>   Not as though 'gainst him it strove;
> For its signal did but second
>   Hidden claims of early love.

The "hidden claims of early love," Wiseman explained in a footnote, referred to the fact that some years before leaving Ushaw he and James Sharples, a fellow student, had formed a society of two to study Roman antiquities, "by the aid of a wretched old plan." The other boys called them "the Romans." Sharples was among those who went to Rome in 1818; later, as a bishop, he would be Wiseman's companion on an important mission. As youths the two wrote a "little book or story," which they called "Fabius." The cardinal added that he had not thought about that story when he later wrote his novel, *Fabiola*.[25]

The newcomers were delighted with what they found at the Venerabile. Wiseman wrote that "it seemed incredible that we should have fallen upon such pleasant places as the seat of future life and occupation." There was much to be done before the necessary repairs could be finished, furniture added, and the library put in order. The boys were provided, however, with "just the right number of rooms for their party, clean and speckless, with every article of furniture, simple and collegiate though it was, yet spic-and-span new and manifestly prepared for their expected arrival." Wiseman continued, "One felt at once at home; it was nobody else's house; it was English ground, a part of fatherland, a restored inheritance." He concluded that "one could not but feel that we had been transported to the scene of better men and greater things than were likely to arise in the new era that day opened."[26]

Wiseman was especially fascinated, then and throughout his life, by the study of antiquities, pagan as well as Christian. He was enthralled by Italian art, architecture, and music. Although able to give free rein to these interests only with the greater freedom that followed his ordination to the priesthood, daily walks and weekly tours with the other students at the Venerabile provided him with ample opportunity to develop his tastes. Some, however, objected to the fact that when they left the college grounds they were required to walk in *camerata*, that is, in procession, all together, two by two.

Because the young men arrived in Rome in the middle of the academic year, their first lessons were provided within the college. After the late summer holiday, or *villegiatura*, as it was called, at Monte Porzio—site of the college villa in Tusculum, purchased early in the eighteenth century—they attended lectures, in spite of protests, at the Roman (now the Gregorian) University. In 1824, when the Roman University was again put under the control of the Jesuits, the English students were transferred to the Apollinare, Rome's own diocesan seminary. The health of a number of the students suffered, whether because of the difficulty in adjusting to Rome's climate or, less likely, from the diet, which "was necessarily meagre in those days." One of them died in September 1820, a victim of fever. There would be similar fatalities in the future. Wiseman's name was included among those who were ill, but in his case the indisposition was attributed to overwork.[27]

The English students acquitted themselves with distinction in the *concorso*, or examination, at the end of their first year. Wiseman tied with a fellow Englishman for the medal in "Physico-Mathematics" and received the second medal in "Physico-Chemistry." His sister consoled him at not having placed first: "We are sorry you experienced any mortification at not having had the first prize. We certainly should have been glad to hear that you had had it but assure yourself dear Nicholas had you been crowned at the Capital or had you not had a prize at all you could not have either gained or lost in our opinion." Wiseman soon developed into an outstanding student, although Wilfrid Ward noted that his tastes were not primarily in the direction of philosophy and theology.[28] This seems to have been the case. Wiseman did not excel in the speculative sciences, which may account for the impression of superficiality left with some who have read his works. He was outstanding, however, in languages and in those studies essential for literary and biblical criticism.

There seems to have been a practical purpose in everything that Wiseman set himself to execute. His interests were exceptionally varied, and if, as many have stated, the extremely active life to which he was later called was a loss to the world of scholarship, he was able to put his attainments to a purpose that won the admiration of his countrymen and others. In 1848, while offering advice to his nephew who was a student at Oscott College in Birmingham, he outlined his philosophy of education. The relevant passages are well worth quoting.

> There is not a single thing that I do which I do not consider that many others do much better; there is nothing that I know, which hundreds in my office don't know better. What I have aimed at, and what I recommend to you, is the cultivation of *all* your faculties. The best and most successful abilities consist of a well balanced state of the different powers of mind. Mere dry reason & judgment, however solid, has little power to influence, because it does not please; mere feeling becomes morbid and useless; imagination if too prevalent leads to the unreal & impractical; memory if excessive leads to unexactness and negligence; & so of every other mental power. The just cultivation of each is the object of a *complete* education. Boys grumble, & ask of what use can this study, or that, be to me, who am not going to be an engineer, or a lawyer, or a priest, or perhaps anything? But the course of education is intended *mainly* to bring out & strengthen, one by one, each latent power, in proper order, & at a fitting age.

Wiseman outlined the lessons to be gained by studying the various disciplines and concluded:

> You will see from what I have written, that I want you to read a variety of things, history for instance, and poetry; something of each; not long histories but such as will make you well acquainted with the great facts & leading characters of every period of history. These form great points on which a great deal of matter will afterwards hang. And so in poetry, try to see, & learn the characteristics of each author, try to penetrate into them & to feel their beauties. . . . Think & reflect on what you read and take occasionally

notes of what strikes you. Probably later you will be tempted to throw them into the fire; but no matter, you will have formed your judgment, as you go on, & got into a good practice.[29]

Almost five years later, when John Henry Newman prepared his lectures on liberal education, he treated the subject in a spirit not unlike Wiseman's.

There is reason to believe that Wiseman's advice to Willy Burke was not based solely on the reflections of a man in his middle years. In the summer of 1820 Nicholas's brother wrote to him from Madrid, "I was well pleased to read your observations on the system of education followed in Ushaw, & perfectly coincide with your ideas." James complained that important "branches of modern science" had been neglected there, including "Geography, Modern History, the Laws of Nations and Political Economy." He considered these areas of study to be "so intimately interwoven with the events which we daily observe in the political vicissitudes of Europe, that the knowledge of them is indispensably necessary to the statesman, to the merchant, to the man of learning, and to the gentleman." He concluded by lamenting the fact that the superiors of Ushaw attached little importance to these subjects.[30]

James, in the same letter, described for Nicholas the revolution in Spain, which had recently reestablished the liberal constitution of 1812. Similar events in Italy resulted in the temporary ascendancy of the revolutionary society of the Carbonari over the king of Naples. It was the significance of such events and the state of European society in general that led James to write of the deficiencies of the education which, he felt, ill equipped young men to cope with the tumultuous times in which they were living.

Late in 1820 Nicholas received minor orders, known today as "ministries." It was then that the young clerics were told to prepare to take an oath by which they would be bound to serve the English mission, which, of course, was under the direct control of Propaganda. Nicholas evidently had scruples about taking the oath, fearing his freedom of action might be restricted by superiors who could send him anywhere in the world they wished. Frasquita warned him that their mother disapproved: "It is in my opinion (pardon me the expression) shocking for two reasons: first because you are a great deal too young and secondly because you received them [the orders] without Mamma's permission." She added, "You had I know her permission to receive them but certainly not for some time."[31] Nicholas had been in Rome only two years, and he was just eighteen.

Mrs. Wiseman penned an angry letter to Wiseman's rector: "I have this day received a letter from my son, the contents of which have not only surprised but agitated me. You will not be at a loss to discover that it alluded to the regulations about to be imposed on the students." Xaviera argued that the parents of the young men should have been consulted, and she condemned the oath "about to be forced upon my son" as both "unfair" and "tyrannical."

First, Nicholas was not of age, so that no oath could be binding. Second, it would make him unhappy throughout his student days. "It never was a wish of mine that he should enter into holy orders," wrote Xaviera, but she had given permission due to the recommendation of the president of Ushaw. She had not wanted to stand in the way of her son's happiness but had hoped to keep him near the family. Xaviera continued: "I felt much hurt that he should have taken the minor orders without consulting me, for which he is under age. . . . I have been his only parent since he was three years old. I have in every respect fulfiled [sic] my duty towards my children & it is not too much to expect from them a reasonable submission until they are old enough to judge for themselves." She excused her harsh letter to Gradwell by noting that "the feelings of a mother cannot be subdued when she considers that her child is not dealt fairly with."

Mrs. Wiseman wisely sent her letter, unsealed, to Nicholas, leaving it to his discretion whether or not to deliver it: "Put but a small bit of wax on the letter & let it dry. It is rather strong but no matter, he deserves it all. I hope you will deliver it to him." She suggested that rather than take the oath, Nicholas might be permitted to remain at the college as a boarder until she had the opportunity to consult relatives as to the course she should take and concluded that she would rather earn her daily bread to support him than have him take an oath for life. Her reaction does not entirely fit the picture of the lady who hastened to lay her infant son on the altar of the Seville cathedral in order to consecrate him to God's service. The letter was never sealed, in any case, and since it is to be found among Wiseman's papers rather than Gradwell's, we may safely conclude that it never reached its intended destination.[32]

In the meantime, at Mrs. Wiseman's urgent request, Joseph Shee, a relative who was a lawyer in London, consulted the vicar apostolic there and wrote to Nicholas to calm his scruples. "My dear Nicholas," wrote Shee, "you have I think permitted the nicety of your conscience to supersede the goodness of your judgment, a fault if one at all quite on the safe side, & if I am able to convince you that this has been the case, I am persuaded you will feel no less pleased with me than if I had helped to fortify your scruples by concurring in them." Nicholas would be obliged to keep the college rules, no addition to his present practice. "There are very few states of life in which we are not accountable to others," wrote Shee. He would not be obliged to take major orders upon the sole command of the college rector, nor would he be prevented from visiting his family. The jurisdiction of Propaganda would not be a personal problem because "in the first place you are not subject to be sent out of Europe or out of England against your will."

Shee sent the letter, unsealed, to Xaviera and added a note concerning the authority of Propaganda, which, to Nicholas, "appeared the greatest [difficulty] of any." "He may rely on it," wrote Shee, "he will never be troubled by the command of the Congregation until he become a Bishop, & very little even then unless he should happen to preside over the London District, in good time far from impossible." Xaviera added to the letter the assurance that she would support Nicholas in whatever decision he might reach, and no further maternal objections were recorded.[33]

Following his four-year undergraduate program, Nicholas remained in Rome and proceeded to advanced studies. When he took his examinations for the degree of doctor of divinity on July 7, 1824, he was not quite twenty-two years old. The grueling defense or "Public Act," as it was called, took place in the presence of a large audience of prelates, professors, and students. Gradwell, himself the recipient of an honorary doctorate in divinity as a reward for his achievement in reopening the Venerabile, was elated by Wiseman's performance: "On Wednesday Mr. Wiseman defended at the Roman College his 400 theses of divinity. It is universally admitted that it was the most arduous, most able and most splendid defension [sic] that the Roman College has seen for many years, and has redounded very much to the honour of the Roman College as well as our own."[34]

Among those who witnessed the event were two men whose paths would cross again in less fortuitous circumstances; both would be influential in the life of young Wiseman. The first was Dom Mauro Cappellari, the future Pope Gregory XVI, not yet a cardinal. In 1799 he had published *Il trionfo della Santa Sede*, in which he had defended not only papal infallibility but the temporal sovereignty of the papacy as well. The second observer was the man whose views would lead to his unqualified condemnation by Gregory, Félicité Robert de Lamennais. His most recent work, *Essai sur l'indifférence en matière de religion* (1817–23), with its ultramontane principles and attack on rationalism, had made him a favorite of Pope Leo XII, crowned as Supreme Pontiff on October 5, 1823. It was the first time that Lamennais had visited Rome. His writings had already created sufficient controversy to earn him a great deal of displeasure at home. Two years later Gradwell wrote that "the Pope is surfeited with him [Lamennais] since he and his party have raised such a stir in France about the Gallican principles."[35]

Soon after his triumphant examination, Wiseman set out for France, where he visited his mother and sister, who by then had resettled in Versailles. The permission to visit the family must have been unusual, as Mrs. Wiseman wrote to thank Gradwell, explaining that she was unable to travel to Rome as she would have preferred.[36] It was the first reunion of mother and son since she had moved to France in 1818.

When Xaviera thanked Gradwell for allowing Nicholas to visit her, she explained that she would soon travel to Spain in order to manage house for James since, as she wrote, he had formed a banking establishment in Madrid. She never made the trip, and on September 5, 1825, she wrote to Nicholas to say that James was with a printing company in Spain.[37]

James, undoubtedly talented, showed clear signs of instability. He had not been happy while living with his uncle's family and later moved from one venture to another, disappointing both his mother and sister by his inability to contribute adequately toward their support. The year after Nicholas visited Versailles, Frasquita complained that James could not send them money because his own affairs were going so badly: "It is dreadful. You cannot imagine in what a state we are and upon my word I do not exaggerate when I say we have not one hundred franks [sic] by us." A few days later, however, James sent them one thousand francs "which I hope will get you out of present difficulties." He wrote that he had confidence in his own resources and that he expected "to retrieve the ground that has been lost." He added: "You mention my Dear Mama something of Frassi becoming a nun. Such a rash step let her not take in the name of heaven. It would drive me into despair, and embitter my existence to its very last day."[38]

Frasquita's letters are not those of a girl who was seriously considering life in a convent. In 1824 she wrote to Nicholas of a French officer whom she had known and liked for several months. They had quarreled, and "after having had the folly of throwing away my heart upon him I have the vexation to find he was not worth even a thought." She hoped to find a "balm" for her sorrow in one of her brother's "delightful epistles." She continued: "I have, you must know, been occupied for some time in mounting into *fool's paradise*, if you know what that is, occasioned by the love and attention (don't be frightened) of an old Irish gentleman who is worth about 25,000£ a year and as he has no children he always says he will adopt me. He is always making me presents to the amount of 25 *sous* but at least it shows that he thinks of me and perhaps will do so in a more important case."[39]

In the autumn of 1828 James paid a visit to his mother and sister. At first they were delighted, and Frasquita reported that his religious opinions were "not so free as we have been led to suppose, but he has that manner so prevalent avec la jeunesse d'aujourd'hui of blaming the clergy and finding fault with every thing they do." She added, however, that "he keeps within bounds as Mama you know does not like to hear any thing of that sort blamed and he is both dutiful and polite."

The visit soon proved to be a mixed blessing. Frasquita lamented the fact that James was without means of livelihood. He drained what little capital their mother had, and they wondered whether they might be able to secure a place for him with an Italian commercial house.[40]

James arrived at a difficult time. Several months earlier the Wiseman women, finding Versailles too expensive, had moved to Blois, where they could rent a furnished house for 650 francs a year. They had hoped to return to England to live with relatives but discovered that the MacCarthys, the family with whom they thought they might stay, were themselves experiencing serious financial embarrassment. Shortly afterward, Nicholas sent his mother 400 francs, double the amount that she had expected from him.[41]

Throughout Wiseman's life his family made demands upon him of various kinds. It is not possible, from the sources now available, to determine precisely his own means of income. There seem to have been some small legacies left him by relatives, and he would have been provided with a salary for his services at the college. He also received a stipend for the professorship that he later held. There were probably occasional gifts from visitors to Rome, and his publications were successful enough to guarantee some profit. Clearly, however, Wiseman was never a wealthy man.

Following his holiday with his mother and sister in 1824, Nicholas returned to Rome, stopping along the way to sightsee, to visit those to whom he was recommended, and to execute a number of commissions. The young traveler was somewhat bold in expressing his judgments of what he observed. "I think the French are the greatest political hypocrites in the world," he wrote from Paris; "Two thirds of them are Liberals, and pretend to be Royalists."[42]

Wiseman became the pride of the English College. He was ordained to the priesthood on March 10, 1825, at the age of twenty-two. In 1827 he was named vice-rector of the college, and in the same year his *Horae Syriacae* was published. The work was divided into three parts. The first was a defense of the literal meaning of the words "Hoc est enim corpus meum." The other two, called "Philological Contributions to the History of the Syriac Versions of the Old Testament," included an account of a manuscript version of the Old Testament, the Karkaphensian Codex, previously known only by name. "His accurate description and analysis of its chief features," wrote one contemporary, "exhibit his high critical faculty and his familiarity, as an expert, with Syriac MSS."[43]

Wiseman's reputation as an orientalist was established, and letters of congratulation poured in from scholars throughout Europe. It is significant, however, that he had not published the book as an end in itself. He had been hoping for a professorship in the Roman University, and when it appeared that another would be appointed, Wiseman was told that a clear indication of his scholarship would be necessary to compete for the position. He then set himself to the task of gathering and publishing the data included in the volume.

Wiseman had been encouraged by Monsignor Angelo Mai of the Vatican Library, who took a special interest in him. Thus supported, Wiseman sought and obtained two interviews with the pope himself, who intervened to guarantee that the young scholar would be given an opportunity to compete fairly. Wiseman was awarded the professorship.[44] His achievement resulted in his election to the Royal Asiatic Society, and in 1831 he was made an honorary member of the Royal Society of Literature. The Anglican bishop of Salisbury, Thomas Burgess, assisted in promoting Wiseman's reputation in England. Burgess corresponded with the younger man, and in 1829 he urged on him the publication of a second volume of the *Horae Syriacae*.[45] By then, however, there were indications that his life would not be confined to scholarly pursuits.

In 1827 Wiseman was assigned by Pope Leo XII, at the recommendation of Gradwell, as special preacher for the many English visitors in Rome who welcomed an opportunity to listen to sermons in their own language. Wiseman found the task difficult, but his success was immediate. It was then also that he began work on the subject of the Eucharist as well as studies directed toward lectures on science and revealed religion. "Without this training I could not have thrown myself into the Puseyite controversy at a later period," he wrote in 1858.[46]

In spite of his obvious successes, these years were not entirely happy for Wiseman. He described them in verse in 1864.

> Nights of anguish, days of labour,
>   Then bright flashings of God's sun,
> Made Gethsemani, and Thabor,
>   Blend their mountains into one.

"Many and many an hour have I passed alone, in bitter tears, on the *loggia* of the English College," he wrote to his nephew in 1848. He explained that he "was fighting with subtle thoughts and venomous suggestions of a fiendlike infidelity which I durst not confide to anyone, for there was no one that could have sympathised with me."[47]

Ten years later Wiseman wrote to the same correspondent:

Such a course of years! Oh, my dearest Willy, may you never experience them! Years of solitude, of dereliction, without an encouraging word from superior or companion, denounced even, more than once by unseen enemies; years of shattered nerves, dread often of instant insanity, consumptive weakness, enfeebled frame, sinking energy, of sleepless nights and weary days, and hours of tears, which no one ever witnessed. For years & years this went on, till a crisis came in my life and character, and I was drawn into a new condition where all was changed.

Since Wiseman identified the period as that during which he wrote the *Horae Syriacae*, Wilfrid Ward concluded that the "mental trials appear to have passed away about the year 1829, when he settled down to a state of resolute conviction."[48]

As he prepared his lectures on the Eucharist and on the relation between science and religion, Wiseman had been reading the rationalists in order to arm himself against their attacks on the credibility of the Scriptures. This may account for his temptations against faith. If these were mitigated at the time Ward suggested, however, it is difficult to account for the "denunciations" mentioned by Wiseman, since he experienced few of these until after he took up the duties of rector. The "crisis" to which he referred and which, he said, drew him into a changed condition may well have been the determination to work wholeheartedly for the church in England. Wiseman's was a volatile temperament, and throughout his life periods of elation over apparent successes were followed by severe depression, sometimes prolonged, when he was next subjected to disappointment.

After his ordination Wiseman was more and more in contact with English affairs, partially through correspondence and also through his many occupations at the college. "My uncouth and half-barbarous English pen hardly knows how to address your refined, elegant, Roman and classical Eminence," wrote George Brown, a future bishop, in 1826. Brown had spent some time in Rome for reasons of health. He now went on to discuss the progress of religion in England as well as non-Catholic opposition there: "In the meantime our congregation continues increasing in numbers notwithstanding the ravages that have been made in it since I came." He continued: "For the last two years the chapel has been fuller than I ever saw it before and since my return from Rome I have reconciled six converts, one of whom was a Quaker whom I baptized on H. Saturday. . . . I have continual applications on behalf of others and when the days are a little longer I mean to give lectures in the evening."

In discussing the possible admission of Catholics to Parliament, Brown gave a graphic description of the extent of anti-Catholic prejudice.

When I arrived in England I found the nation apparently on the brink of being thrown furiously into a No Popery phrenzy. It is truly pitiful to know the base acts and the cool deliberate malignity which many persons have showed themselves capable of who have lived all their lives in habits of intimacy with Catholics and had previously expressed honourable sentiments in their regard. Others again there are who are strangely ignorant of our principles and tho' men of information on other points are so weak as really to believe that we hold all *imputed* doctrines laid to our charge. However since Xmas there has been a decided change and there is now a reaction going on in our favour.[49]

Reports of an increase in conversions, lectures to explain the true beliefs of Catholics, and evidence of goodwill on the part of non-Catholics would all have made an impact on the young, still impressionable man who was pondering his own future and the role that he might play in the so-called Catholic Revival.

In November 1827 the London vicar apostolic, Bishop William Poynter, died. He was succeeded by his coadjutor, James Yorke Bramston, and Gradwell was appointed to serve as coadjutor in London. After hearing of his selection, Gradwell immediately recommended Wiseman to succeed him as rector of the English College. He described the younger man as "a person of excellent character, the most amiable dispositions, and first rate talents" who "loves Rome and the college, and understands perfectly every part of the administration." Gradwell acknowledged that Wiseman was young and that he had weaknesses: "He has so much sensibility that if any thing happens wrong or teasing, he is apt to fret himself into illness and despondency; and so good natured that he would find it difficult to say *no*, or resist and censure on every proper occasion."

To counteract the drawbacks in appointing Wiseman to the position, Gradwell recommended, as vice-rector, George Errington, who "has most of the same good qualities for a Vice-Rector; but though he has more firmness in resisting acute sensibility, he is younger still, and perhaps still less convinced of the necessity of the austerer parts of college discipline."[50]

Errington, two years younger than Wiseman, had also been a student at Ushaw. Although the youths had not been intimate companions at that time, their families were very close indeed. The year before Mrs. Wiseman and Frasquita moved to Paris, in fact, they had stayed with the Erringtons, and their letters are filled with references to them. This may explain the fact that some considered the two men to have been related. After referring to the first marriage of Wiseman's father and the children born of that union, a correspondent wrote, "I think Mrs. Errington was one of them. Mrs. Errington was the cardinal's step sister, and either her daughter or her sister was a Mrs. Burke, whose son is now a priest in London." The information was incorrect, although in view of the later estrangement between Wiseman and Errington, it would have had a special appeal for the lover of gossip.[51]

George Errington had arrived in Rome in 1821. His brother Michael wrote to Wiseman, "I hope that Rome, Roman climate, Roman studies may agree with George so as to allow him to stay." He continued, "I think he has distinguished himself perhaps more than any one before him; they consider him a great loss, and I suspect that I shall have many harsh thanks as they know that I did every thing in my power to forward his going to Rome."[52]

A contemporary, whose information and judgments were frequently unreliable, wrote with snobbish relish that Errington, whom she nevertheless admired, "had uncouth Ushaw manners and lacked social training." In his letter to Wiseman, Michael Errington issued a word of warning that seems to substantiate the general accuracy of this assertion.

> One thing there is wanting in George — some degree of polish, and gentlemanliness, and perhaps I may beg of you when you come to be acquainted with him to endeavour to give him something of that kind; I am fully convinced that I could not apply on this subject to any one more capable or more willing than yourself; you will soon see how it may be prudent to act in this respect, only never let George know that any thing was said to you upon the subject.

Errington was, in fact, a great success in Rome. On August 22, 1827, he presented himself for the public examination for the doctor of divinity degree, and, like Wiseman, he was an unqualified success. "His answers," wrote Gradwell, ". . . excited the astonishment and admiration of the whole assembly." The rector concluded that he "did not yield to the celebrated performance of Wiseman . . . three years ago."[53]

By June 1828 Gradwell wrote that he, on his own authority, would recommend Wiseman to the Holy Father as pro-rector "while the Bishops can be informed of my leaving the rectorship and have time to write to your [his] holiness recommending in form the man of their choice as my successor. I am persuaded," he concluded, "they will be unanimous for the appointment of Dr. Wiseman."[54] Wiseman's appointment was confirmed by December, and Errington was named as his vice-rector. Gradwell, then, was responsible for the first of the three occasions that the two men would work together. If his analysis of their characters was accurate, as it seems to have been, the very qualities that made them complementary to one another could easily lead them on a collision course, the ultimate result of their association.

Cardinal Francis Aidan Gasquet wrote that the twelve years of Wiseman's rectorship "may be regarded as the golden age of the English College," and Michael E. Williams has recently stated that "the figure of Wiseman dominates the history of the Venerabile in the early years of the nineteenth century." Wiseman's European reputation for scholarship, his preaching at the Church of Gesù e Maria on the Corso, the lectures that he delivered to packed audiences of English visitors, and the professorship to which he had been appointed all added to the prestige of the college. As rector, he also served as Roman agent for the English bishops. His duties brought him into increasing contact with ecclesiastical affairs in England, and there were those who soon began to urge him to put his talents to use there. When Frasquita heard that Bishop Poynter had died, she wrote to Nicholas and asked whether a coadjutor would be appointed to assist Bramston: "I thought perhaps they might nominate you and how nice that would be but on second thought I think it better you should remain in Rome and be created a Cardinal which cannot fail to happen."[55] More than twenty years later, Frasquita's premonition would be more than realized when Wiseman was elevated to the dignity of the cardinalate, not to remain in Rome, but to serve English Catholics as archbishop of Westminster.

2. Bishop Baines

OON AFTER WISEMAN'S APPOINTMENT AS RECTOR OF THE ENGLISH
College had been confirmed, and George Errington had been
named as vice-rector, Bishop Thomas Smith of the Northern District threatened to recall Errington to work in England. The prospect
caused Wiseman what he described as "serious anxiety and pain." He
observed that there was nobody to replace his assistant, since they were
the only two priests living at the college. Errington, moreover, had "all
the minute but important details of domestic expenditure and discipline to attend to." He was thoroughly familiar with the complicated
financial details related to college property and in addition was responsible for instructing students in both moral philosophy and Hebrew.
Wiseman urged Smith to consult Bishop Gradwell, who would not
have recommended him as rector had he not counted upon Errington's
appointment as well: "Dr. G. is perfectly acquainted with the state of
the house and with my disposition; he knows how much is wanting in
my character for any situation of authority, and I am sure his kindness
for me will not interfere with his declaration where the interests of the
College are concerned." Errington, finally, was known personally and
respected by the Holy Father and by Cardinal Giacinto Placido Zurla,
protector of the college, a factor that would have been of some consequence to the vicars apostolic.[1] Wiseman's arguments were convincing,
and Errington remained at his post.

Years later, Wiseman recalled how much he had appreciated "the
invaluable assistance" of Errington, who had been "stern, inflexible
and minutely accurate in looking into every bill, every book and every
employment of money." He wrote, "Depend upon it that if he had discovered any cooking of accounts, or fraud, or peculation or excessive
profits or gain, he would never have rested till it was cured."[2]

It was Wiseman's privilege in 1829 to inform the newly elected Pope Pius VIII of the successful passage into law of the Catholic Emancipation Bill, which after a long struggle at last admitted Roman Catholics to Parliament.[3] Wiseman had not been involved directly in the controversies leading up to the momentous event, a fact that, he later claimed, freed him and his companions from the bitter feelings toward its opponents which persisted among many English Catholics: "We had left our country young, and hardly conscious of the wrongs which galled our elders, we should return to it in possession of our rights; and thus have hardly experienced more sense of injury than they who have been born since that happy era."[4]

Bernard Ward pointed out that Catholic Emancipation was a "layman's Act," with few implications for the clergy.[5] Its provisions, however, explicitly provided for the eventual exclusion of male religious orders from the United Kingdom, specifying the Jesuits by name, and there were those who anticipated that Rome would not accept such an insult without protest. Wiseman received a letter from Charles Butler, longtime advocate of Catholic rights but typical, as well, of those who defended "the importance of national customs, the role of the laity, and [ecclesiastical] decentralization." Butler was delighted with the new law. He admitted that the exclusion of religious orders was regrettable but concluded that "in this respect, it is a mere dead letter and I am sure it is for their interest to say nothing upon the subject, and to take no step whatever respecting it."[6] Whether or not Butler's own prejudice against the regulars was a factor in his judgment, his advice in this case was sound and his prediction accurate.

The pope raised no objection to the clauses in the Emancipation Act that dealt with religious orders, but he was concerned, according to Wiseman, with another provision of the new law. The oath that Catholics were required to take before being admitted to Parliament denied any temporal power, "even indirect," to the Holy See with respect to English Catholics. The Holy Father pointed out that even "marriage cases exert a temporal influence," and he sought assurance that the oath would not be taken "in a sense that interferes with such powers." The same reservation had been expressed among the vicars apostolic, but ultimately they agreed unanimously that Catholics were free to take the oath.[7]

Although Wiseman had not been in a position to exercise any significant role in the steps leading to Catholic Emancipation, he was becoming increasingly involved in matters of ecclesiastical importance in England. As Gradwell's vice-rector, he must have heard his superior discuss the business that, as agent for the vicars apostolic, he had been required to transact. Gradwell, of course, would have prepared his successor for his work on behalf of the English bishops. Moreover, when former classmates and students returned to England, they often wrote to describe for him the state of religion there. If, then, his analysis of the situation at home was sometimes less than accurate, an explanation may be found in the fact that he had not been there himself since the age of sixteen, nor had he ever been required to take sides in the controversial questions that tended to divide English Catholics. Wiseman did not create the battles into which he was drawn. Less than thirty years old in 1829, he was still a neophyte in matters of ecclesiastical politics. Through no fault of his own he was unprepared either for the bitterness of the vicars apostolic, who felt that the Holy See did not understand their circumstances, or for their resentment when Rome's policies seemed to undermine their authority.

Perhaps the most significant of Wiseman's associations in Rome was that with Peter Augustine Baines, bishop of Siga and coadjutor to the bishop of the Western District. Bernard Ward concluded, with good reason, that Bishop Baines "was by far the strongest personality among the English bishops, and exercised a greater activity than any one of his brethren."[8] Baines had been one of the first four novices professed at Ampleforth Abbey, near York, in 1804. The Benedictines of St. Lawrence's, Dieuleward, had established their institution there in 1802. Baines, as director of studies, had contributed to the development of the school at Ampleforth before he was transferred, in 1817, to the important Benedictine mission in Bath. After his elevation to the episcopate in 1823 at the age of thirty-six, his primary aim, overshadowing all other considerations, was the establishment of a suitable seminary and a school for boys in the Western District. Each of the other districts had such an institution. In the North there was Ushaw College; in the Midland District, Oscott College; and London had St. Edmund's College. The Western District was the most barren of all in terms of the number of Catholics and the very few secular priests serving them. Baines looked to the founding of a first-rate educational establishment as a means to remedy the situation and to provide prestige for the church as well.

Only a powerful leader, prepared to do battle against incredible odds, could hope to achieve the kind of success Baines pursued. Twenty years later John Lingard described the great hopes he had once placed in Bishop Baines.

> For you must know that I have long had the notion, a very presumptuous one probably, that the revolution in the protestant mind as to the doctrines of popery was owing to my history. Young and inquisitive minds in the universities were induced to examine my authorities contradicting their favourite religious opinions; and, finding me correct began to doubt of their previous convictions and so forth. . . . But what has that to do with Doctor Baines? Why, in consequence of the Catholic emancipation, I trusted that the Cath-

olic Church in England would throw open its portals to draw within it men of influence and education, which I thought could never take place if we insisted on practices calculated to enforce on the minds of protestants that much of our religion consisted in superstitious or fanatical practices. But of the then bishops there was not one who could be persuaded to see the matter in this light excepting Dr. Baines.[9]

Baines, like Lingard, was convinced that only through education could English Catholics gain sufficient stature in the community to eradicate the prejudice against them. Wiseman and Newman were among those who came to share the same conviction, but Lingard never appreciated either man. He blamed Wiseman for introducing into England a type of spirituality that was foreign to English tastes and led to "superstitious" and "fanatical practices." He positively disliked Newman: "I don't like Newman. Too much fancy or enthusiasm."[10] Yet Baines was ultimately the least successful of all. He lacked tact and found it impossible to cooperate with any except his staunchest supporters.

Soon after he became bishop, Baines approached the monks of Downside Abbey in Somerset with the suggestion that they should place themselves directly under the jurisdiction of the western vicar apostolic and that their monastery should serve as the seminary for the district. This would have made it necessary for the Downside monks, founded there in 1814, to break their ties with the English Benedictines. Not surprisingly, their response was negative. Baines, undaunted, then turned to Ampleforth, where his plan met with a better reception, although it would have required the monks of Ampleforth and those of Downside to exchange properties. The obstacles were insuperable, and no little bitterness resulted from the forcefulness with which he persisted in his efforts.[11] The crisis was postponed when his health broke down, and he was advised to seek a more favorable climate. The bishop left for Italy where he remained from the summer of 1826 to that of 1829. The pressing needs of his own district and his ambitious plans were never forgotten, as subsequent events would demonstrate.

As he regained his strength, Bishop Baines became more and more active, sharing with Wiseman the responsibility, imposed on them by the Holy Father, of preaching to English-speaking residents of Rome. His eloquence attracted large crowds. Baines was also a frequent visitor at the English College and seems to have exercised considerable influence over the students there. He was often consulted by Roman authorities, moreover, concerning matters related to England.

In his *Recollections of the Last Four Popes*, Wiseman described Baines as having had "a power of fascinating all who approached him, in spite of a positive tone and manner which scarcely admitted of differences from him in opinion." Wiseman's assessment, though appreciative, was somewhat less than flattering.

> He [Baines] had sometimes original views upon a certain class of subjects; but on every topic he had a command of language, and a clear manner of expressing his sentiments, which commanded attention, and generally won assent. Hence his acquaintances were always willing listeners, and soon became sincere admirers, then warm partisans. Unfortunately, this proved to him a fatal gift. When he undertook great and even magnificent works, he would stand alone: assent to his plans was the condition of being near him; any one that did not agree, or that ventured to suggest deliberation, or provoke discussion, was soon at a distance; he isolated himself with his own genius, he had no counsellor but himself; and he who had, at one time, surrounded himself with men of learning, of prudence, and of devotedness to him, found himself at last alone, and fretted a noble heart to a solitary death.[12]

Wiseman and Baines shared a similar genius and vision, but both men found it difficult to work with those who failed to appreciate fully their designs. Robert Whitty, at one time Wiseman's vicar general in Westminster, wrote of the cardinal: "He had much more talent for devising plans than for executing them. He hardly ever tried *to get round* a supervening difficulty and was too often inclined to throw up a good work merely because one or two of his agents objected or did not enter into his views."[13] The end result was not unlike that which Wiseman described in the case of Baines. Both men were caught up in a great deal of controversy and ended their lives somewhat isolated because of their apparent inability to tolerate opposition.

Wiseman was among those who were attracted by the grand ideas and powerful personality of Bishop Baines, although at this point he had not become, in spite of Denis Gwynn's assertion to the contrary, "one of the Bishop's most enthusiastic supporters." The new rector had been under the influence of his predecessor, and Gradwell and Baines were not on the best of terms. The bishop claimed that Gradwell was ambitious, with a "passion for intrigue." Gradwell, moreover, was known to mistrust the Jesuits, who had governed the English College for almost two hundred years prior to their suppression by Pope Clement XIV in 1773. The future London bishop suspected that they were scheming to regain control of the college.[14] Baines, on the other hand, was considered to be a strong supporter of the regular clergy, in spite of his dispute with the monks of Downside. When the pope confirmed Gradwell's appointment, he warned him to avoid in the future his opposition to the regulars. Wiseman, Gradwell's handpicked successor, must have been aware of the tensions between his predecessor and the outspoken western bishop.

The Society of Jesus had been restored throughout the world by the papal bull *Sollicitudo omnium Ecclesiarum*, issued on August 7, 1814. The English vicars apostolic had opposed the enactment of the measure in their districts, fearing that it would reopen old wounds between the secular and religious clergy and that the publicity would hinder the efforts of those working for Catholic Emancipation. By the late 1820s, however, the opposition of the vicars was weakening. Within their own houses, in fact, Jesuits lived according to their own rule and under their own religious superiors, although in matters relating to the missions they were under the jurisdiction, at least in theory, of the vicars apostolic. Even Bishop Bramston of London, considered to be an anti-regular on principle, acknowledged that the situation made little sense. "I must say," he wrote to Gradwell in 1828, "that the present anomaly is to be deplored, that Rome should send Jesuits to our missions, whilst we cannot acknowledge them."[15] On January 1, 1829, the Holy See issued a rescript that restored the Jesuits to full canonical status in England, permitting members to be ordained under the title of poverty, that is, subject to their own religious superiors rather than to the vicars apostolic. Bishop Baines had played an active role in promoting the step and had even prepared a petition asking for it.

A decade earlier Gradwell had written to the London vicar apostolic to assure him that although the papal bull restoring the Jesuits had been published to the whole world in 1814, "such Governments as choose may adopt it; but it is not to be forced on any."[16] Now Wiseman lost no time in writing to Gradwell to express his judgment on the latest move and to offer assurances similar to those which Gradwell had once made. He told the bishop that "the Holy See would not take any steps upon the delicate point of the restoration of the society without consulting the Vicars Apostolic," although he acknowledged that the spirit of recent events indicated the contrary. He said that the rescript of January 1 was merely "declaratory" and did not impose any obligation. The bishops, he advised, should prepare a memorial in which they might explain their motives if, in fact, they considered it inopportune to accept the Holy See's directive. Wiseman was sure that this "would be the best way of bringing the question once more fairly before the consideration of his Holiness who has certainly not followed the rule of 'audi alterum partem' [listen to the other side], but is surrounded by persons who are daily interesting themselves on one side." A joint memorial from the vicars apostolic, he continued, would also have "the effect of suggesting to him [the pope] the propriety & necessity of consulting the wishes of the vicars & taking the opinion of their experience, *before* deciding such delicate & momentous questions" and would also demonstrate "that the opinion of one individual is not to be identified with that of all the Bishops, for I am not without apprehensions that, if what I understand be true, it may be soon necessary to make this declaration plainly."

Baines, of course, was the "one individual" to whom Wiseman referred. Wiseman pointed out that the bishop had shown "a tendency . . . to form a separate interest from the rest of his Episcopal brethren & to act independently." The accusation was based on the fact that Baines alone had "declined putting his name to the papers which the vicars apostolic did me the honor of sending me in order to [support] my appointment to the Rectorship and agency," although, wrote Wiseman, "I am willing fully to do justice to his motives, and have great gratitude in owning that he went personally to Card. Zurla & to the Pope, & spoke most handsomely of me & my capacity as Rector & as Agent for such of the Bishops as might employ me, but he reserved to himself the power of nominating a separate agent, on the ground that however desirable, it would be hardly possible for all the Vicars to be of one mind in affairs."

Wiseman acknowledged that there had been no "rupture" between Baines and himself and that the bishop treated him "with the same kindness as before." He added: "I feel the same respect for his virtues, talents and character as ever; nor should I have entered into this disagreable detail had I not felt it due to the confidential relation which your Lordships have, in your goodness, established between yourselves & me." He then described the manner in which Baines had acted on behalf of the Jesuits and warned Gradwell that the western coadjutor had great influence in Rome, even receiving a monthly pension from the Holy Father. "Of this I am confident," concluded Wiseman, "that every measure in favor of the regulars will have in him [Baines] a steady, fearless, & influential supporter whether here or in England, & that he sees the probability of his line of action being distinct from that of the other vicars, his declaration on declining to employ the same agent proves I think sufficiently."[17]

The vicars apostolic had no choice but to accept the decision of the Holy See with respect to the Jesuits. The restrictive clauses of the Catholic Emancipation Act made their position difficult, however, and hard feelings continued for some time to come. One of the bishops complained "that the clandestine acceptance of them [the Jesuits] would destroy the credit both of Rome and of the Catholics in general in this kingdom."[18]

Wiseman continued to warn Bishop Gradwell of the independent spirit exhibited by Bishop Baines. In the autumn of 1829 he wrote to account for rumors of insubordination and unrest among the students at the college. He attributed any discontent to the influence of Baines, who "had made it a point to chime in with every whim and complaint of the students, whether it was, at one time, that they did not learn sufficient, or at another that they were put to learn too much." Obviously irritated, the young rector concluded that "it would be impossible for any English establishment to meet Dr. Baines's approbation as long as it is in the hands of secular Clergy. His declamations against Ushaw and St. Edmund's have always been as violent as those against us. Oscott has more of his esteem, but Ampleforth is the *ne plus ultra;* he always quotes that as the model on which others should be formed."[19]

By this time Baines had moved back to England. Bishop Peter Collingridge had died on March 31, 1829, a few weeks after Pope Leo XII, and at the end of August, Baines returned home prepared to assume full responsibility over the Western District. Before returning to England, Baines had taken preliminary steps that, he hoped, would assist him in pursuing his plans for the Benedictines there. He spoke with Cardinal Cappellari, prefect of Propaganda since 1826. His arguments were sufficiently convincing for the prefect, himself a Camaldolese Benedictine, to urge the prior of Downside to cooperate with his bishop, although the cardinal did not attempt to decide the points at issue in the controversy. Baines argued that the order had not been canonically established in England and that the validity of the vows taken by its members was questionable. Wiseman, aware of what was going on, wrote, "Before leaving he [Baines] seems determined to put an end to the Downside monks, with whom he has always been at variance." The Benedictines, however, also had informers in Rome, and they prepared their self-defense.[20]

Had Baines limited his efforts on behalf of the Western District to matters touching upon education and his relationship to the Benedictines, he might have gained the support of the other vicars apostolic. Before leaving Rome, however, he proposed a measure bound to antagonize his episcopal brethren and indicating that Wiseman was not mistaken when he observed that Baines tended to pursue an independent policy. Baines prepared a plan for redistributing the four vicariates in such a way that each bishop would have approximately the same number of Catholics under his jurisdiction. The scheme would have been primarily at the expense of the Northern District, although only the Western District would gain by it. Wiseman wrote to calm the fears of the coadjutor bishop of the Northern District, Thomas Penswick, assuring him "that no scheme of that sort can now be carried into effect without the Vicars Apostolic being heard." He informed Penswick that Baines did not have the ear of the new pope, Pius VIII, as he had that of Leo XII: "His Holiness refers all proposals to the Congregations."[21] Baines, in this case, was unsuccessful, and he endangered his relationship with the other bishops, whose support he desperately needed.

It is clear that Pope Leo XII intended to make Baines a cardinal. He would have done so at the next consistory, according to Wiseman, had the Holy Father not died in February 1829. The honor would not have been entirely due to the pope's admiration for Baines. Wiseman wrote, "It is quite certain that had the late Pope lived, Dr. B. would have had the cardinal's hat; the restoration of the hat to the Benedictine order was a point of etiquette to which he was bound, in consequence of the Pontiff, who gave him his [i.e., Pius VII], having been of that order." Wiseman doubted whether Baines knew the whole story but said that his own information was received "at first hand, from the individuals to whom Leo XII addressed these conversations." He concluded, "The thing is now at an end, & therefore I should suppose it will be better that nothing should be said upon the matter, the more as Dr. B. is now preparing to set out for England."[22]

Baines, it seems, knew more than Wiseman. He declared that within a week of his coronation the new pope offered him a position at court which would have led, as he understood it, to his reception of the cardinal's hat, "for which dignity I confidently believed Leo XII had intended me." Baines respectfully declined the offer: "My predecessor had just died; I felt in better health and spirits; I was home-sick and anxious to return to friends and native air; I preferred just then the position of an English Vicar Apostolic, immeasurably though it was beneath the Cardinalitial dignity, and I was eager to found the Seminary for the Western District, and to promote by my presence the interests of religion in that part of England."[23]

As soon as he reached England, Baines plunged into battle with the Benedictines. Cardinal Cappellari, after talking with Baines in Rome, had not only written to the prior of Downside but also sought the advice of the vicars apostolic. They gathered in Wolverhampton in the autumn, a meeting that Baines attended, and framed a reply to the cardinal's letter. The vicars apostolic deplored the desolate state of the Western District and promised to work together so that it might flourish as the others. Bishop Thomas Walsh of the Midland District was commissioned to write to the president general of the English Benedictines to express the "heartfelt respect and veneration" of the vicars apostolic toward "the illustrious order of St. Benedict." He then stated their desire "that no impediment should arise to the establishment in that district of an Episcopal Seminary which appears necessary for the hallowed purposes of providing Missionaries, of propagating our Holy Religion, and promoting the salvation of souls."[24]

The monks were prepared to argue that they were certainly placing no impediment in the way of Bishop Baines or the interests of the district by maintaining their own monastery and school as they had done for years. When Baines saw that he could hope for no success in obtaining their services as he wished, he used his trump card by depriving them of their faculties to preach and hear confessions, putting forward the argument which he had hit upon before leaving Rome, that the Benedictine establishment had never received the formal approbation of the Holy See and that the validity of the vows of its members was in doubt. The monks were therefore completely subject to him. Convinced of the rightness of their cause and of the fact that within their own monastery they were exempt from episcopal control, they defied the bishop by ignoring his directive within their own establishment, although they had to accept his order as it touched them elsewhere. They sent two of their members to Rome to present their case to the authorities there.[25]

The Ampleforth monks, in the meantime, were no longer united in wishing to cooperate with Baines. He then purchased the property of Prior Park, outside of Bath, and succeeded in attracting several prominent members of that monastery to join him there. They asked for release from their vows as Benedictines. Their departure, along with a number of students whose parents were attracted by the promise of what Baines hoped to achieve at Prior Park, seriously jeopardized the school at Ampleforth as well as that at Downside, which also suffered the loss of students to Prior Park.[26] An additional complication developed when the survivors at Ampleforth accused those who left of alienating property that they had carried off to their new home.

Although Cardinal Cappellari had given Baines a favorable hearing before the bishop left Rome, he was shocked when he heard that the Downside Benedictines had been deprived of their faculties. His sentiment was shared by Thomas Weld, formerly of Lulworth, a widower who had been ordained to the priesthood in 1821 and raised to the episcopate in 1826. Elevated to the cardinalate by Pius VIII in the winter of 1830, Weld was consulted, along with Wiseman, as to the means of settling the disputes between Baines and the Benedictines. It seems to have been Wiseman who provided a solution to the question of the validity of the Benedictine vows by suggesting a *sanatio*, that is, a declaration of "healing," which would overlook any possible defect in the past by the assertion that the vows were, from that point on, to be considered as certainly valid. Weld wrote to Bishop Bramston of London that he had put forward the plan, which he hoped would bring peace between Baines and his Benedictine brethren. "If I have contributed towards it God be praised," wrote Weld. He added, however, that it was Wiseman who deserved credit for the plan. It was this proposal that led Cardinal Cappellari to seek the advice of the vicars apostolic. Baines circumvented the spirit of Propaganda's wishes, at the very least, by refusing to restore the faculties of the Benedictines until the monks were prepared to admit that their vows had been previously invalid.[27]

On December 1, 1830, Pope Pius VIII died. His successor was none other than Cardinal Cappellari, who now became Gregory XVI. In addition to his interest in England as prefect of Propaganda, Cappellari had been of assistance to Wiseman's scholarly pursuits. "You must now revise your own proofs. I fear I shall not have much time in future to correct them," warned the new pope when greeted by Wiseman. The Holy Father was by now convinced that Bishop Baines was guilty of acting in a high-handed manner. In March 1831 Wiseman wrote that the Holy Father "complained strongly of Dr. B[aines]," and that "he had directed Mgr. [Castruccio] Castracane [secretary of Propaganda] to write in *his* name to order the faculties of the Regulars to be restored, & if this failed, he should proceed to extremities." Gregory criticized Baines also for the alienation of missionary funds to support his new college and for the "secular nature of his plan of education." Wiseman concluded by stating that he himself knew nothing of all these points since he had not heard from Baines for about a year. The Holy Father, however "did not seem pleased."[28]

The following summer Wiseman's health failed. He wrote to Bishop Gradwell that he had been spitting blood and that he suffered from a violent cough and "oppression of the chest." The remedies proposed were "copious bleeding, iced acid drinks, diet and suspension of every occupation." In his letter he said that he was about to summon Errington, who was visiting his family, although the vice-rector was also "recuperating from disagreeable symptoms." Wiseman urged Gradwell not to be alarmed: "I do not see any cause to apprehend, & I place myself in God's hands to do whatever it shall please him with me."[29]

Both Wiseman and Errington were told by their doctors to seek relaxation from their duties and engagements, and the practical administration of the college fell to Charles Baggs, ordained in November 1830, two months after he had distinguished himself in his doctoral examination. In August, Baggs wrote that the doctors had decided "that the blood which I am sorry to say he [Wiseman] still continues to spit, comes from the chest, and not from the stomach, they think that scorbutic humours in the blood, to which it appears he had been long subject, have at last affected his breast . . . and caused the present malady." He continued by informing Bishop Gradwell that "Dr. Wiseman unfortunately is not a good subject." There were signs, however, of improvement, according to the latest reports from Monte Porzio, where Wiseman had gone to rest. Errington, in the meantime, was unfit to travel, but he, too, was recuperating, and two months later was back in Rome. From there he reported that Wiseman was recovering: "We will endeavour to make such arrangements for the winter as will enable him to lead an unanxious quiet life, in his rooms, which are favorable for an invalid from their exposition."[30]

Bishop Baines, perhaps unaware that Wiseman had been critical of his line of action in the past, urged him to travel to England. He offered him the hospitality of Prior Park, which, he wrote, "has been favourable to several who came hither with delicate health." Baines continued earnestly: "If you are not better in the spring, I hope you will do this. You will give me great pleasure and if I succeed in restoring your health, it will make me very proud." Baines was not the only bishop who wrote to invite Wiseman to England. Bishop Walsh of the Midland District wrote, "I am much concerned, my dear sir, about your valuable health." His proposal was not unlike that of Baines: "I am told by many who have been in Italy that Rome is the worst climate for pulmonary affections. Which is more use to the Church, a zealous priest in England, or a learned doctor in Rome? Come to the healthy Midland country of England."[31]

Neither invitation was without self-interest. Of course Baines was anxious for all of the assistance he could obtain in establishing his new college, for which he had extravagant plans. Walsh, at the same time, was in process of constructing a new Oscott College in the heart of Birmingham. Their attention must have been flattering to Wiseman in any case, and he traveled to England in the autumn of 1832. It was his first visit since he had set out for Rome fourteen years earlier.

Wiseman remained in England for only a very short time, returning to the college by December. The authorities in Rome had appointed him as arbiter in the disputes between Baines and the Benedictines. His solution of the disputed question concerning the validity of the Benedictine vows was accepted generally. A *sanatio* was issued and the matter settled. This, however, was the extent of his success. The controversies over the property that the Ampleforth monks claimed to have been taken unlawfully would not be settled for some time to come, and additional disputes would soon develop as well. Nevertheless Wiseman was won over completely by the zeal with which Baines was striving to meet the needs of the church in England, and he returned to Rome as a firm supporter and advocate of the bishop of Siga's cause.

3. Scholar — Rector — English Agent

S WISEMAN'S CONTACTS WITH EUROPEAN SCHOLARS AND HIS OWN reputation grew, so did his determination to apply his talents to advance the cause of English Catholics. He was never a man to underestimate his own potential, nor would it have been to his credit had he done so. Among the scholars with whom he corresponded were J. M. A. Scholz, professor of exegesis at Bonn, and Karl Joseph Windischmann, professor of philosophy and medicine at the same university. Wiseman was later in contact with the two great leaders of the Catholic revival in Munich, Joseph Görres, appointed to his professorship in 1827, and Johann Joseph Ignaz von Döllinger, named professor of church history in the same year. A lifelong friendship and correspondence was also established between Wiseman and Alexis-François Rio, erudite historian of Christian art, who in 1828 published his *Essai sur l'histoire de l'esprit humain dans l'antiquite.*

The success of Wiseman's *Horae Syriacae* resulted in high praise from Friedrich Augustus Tholuck, Protestant theologian at Berlin from 1820 to 1826 and then professor at Halle until his death in 1877. Tholuck is said to have made the future cardinal's name known in Germany much as Bishop Burgess of Salisbury did in England. Father Leopold Ackermann, professor of exegesis in Vienna, wrote in 1828, "I wondered at your erudition, and I blushed at recognising the slenderness of my own knowledge; we are greedily awaiting the second volume."[1]

With this kind of encouragement and at the urging of Burgess, Wiseman prepared a second treatise on biblical philology, in which he defended the authenticity of what is sometimes called the Johannine Comma, a passage on the Trinity in the final chapter of the first Epistle of St. John, where reference is made to the "three witnesses." Although modern biblical scholarship does not support Wiseman's position, he amassed a great deal of information and demonstrated evident familiarity with his sources. Seventy years afterward Wilfrid Ward cited a number of eminent scholars who supported Wiseman and concluded that his work "still holds the field as a masterpiece of judgment and criticism."[2]

Years later Wiseman acknowledged that l'abbé de Lamennais was another of those who had exercised a profound influence upon him. The Frenchman was a frequent visitor at the English College in the 1820s, when he first visited Rome. In 1832 he visited there again, this time accompanied by Charles Forbes de Montalembert and Jean Baptiste Henri Lacordaire. The three travelers were seeking the pope's blessing on the liberal positions that they had been expressing in their journal, L'Avenir, including the desirability of the separation of church and state and the identification of the church with the principles of 1789. Under fire from the French government as well as the Gallican hierarchy, they turned to the papacy, the ultimate authority that they considered to be the mainstay of European society.

Since Lamennais had not been popular with Gradwell, Wiseman must have been somewhat guarded in his own first associations as rector with the three liberal Frenchmen. In 1825–26 Lamennais had published De la religion considérée dans ses rapports avec l'ordre politique et civil. Although still clinging to his earlier ultramontanism, the work showed him to be increasingly radical. It was his "last attempt to cling to monarchy as a workable system of society." The author condemned French society as atheistic, and he was openly critical of the church for having submitted "to the tyrannical demands of the state." He justified the right of a people to overthrow a monarch under certain circumstances. In defending papal authority Lamennais maintained that the pope could "use spiritual sanctions against transgressors" and even "absolve subjects from their oath of allegiance," a position that would have been an embarrassment to those English Catholics who, struggling to achieve emancipation, were denying that such was the official teaching of the church.[3]

In 1826 Frasquita wrote to Nicholas from Versailles, where Lamennais was visiting: "We are very curious to know what the Pope and the clergy of Rome think of his last work. For my part I think he is very much to be blamed for it, for to say the best of it, it was certainly useless, and in England it certainly must have done great mischief to the Catholick cause." She complained that "the protestants seize with such avidity on any thing which is injurious to the Caths," and concluded, "I own in this point of view I feel quite incensed against the little abbé (for such a shabby diminutive little thing I never saw)."[4]

Wiseman was more favorably impressed by Lamennais than was

his sister, although he agreed that the Frenchman "was truly in look and presence almost contemptible; small, weakly, without pride of countenance or mastery of eye, without any external grace." He concluded his description by stating that "his tongue seemed to be the organ by which, unaided, he gave marvellous utterance to thoughts clear, deep, and strong."[5]

Partly through the influence of his cousin Charles MacCarthy, a boarder at the English College and an intimate friend of Lamennais, Wiseman discovered how convincing the leader of France's liberal Catholics could be. Surely English Catholics could learn much from so brilliant a man whose ultimate aim was the elevation of the French church to a place of dignified independence from the state. If the contents of MacCarthy's letters to Lamennais are to be trusted, Wiseman continued to express sympathy for the Frenchman even when the Holy Father made it clear that his principles were not acceptable to the Holy See.[6]

In later years Wiseman attributed Lamennais's ultimate defection from the church to pride. He described, at the same time, one of their conversations in which he had asked Lamennais what weapons English Catholics could use in order to overcome the prejudice against them. "They do not exist as yet," replied the abbé; "You must begin there by making the implements with which your work has to be performed. It is what we are doing in France."[7] Wiseman interpreted the response as a recommendation to form intellectuals within the Catholic community who might present the church's teaching in its true light and answer intelligently the prejudiced attacks of Protestant critics. He was in a unique position to carry out the advice. Not only was he directly in charge of a college of young men who were preparing to exercise the priestly ministry in England, but his contacts with non-Catholics could be used effectively to alter the traditional view of the church that many of them would have shared with the vast majority of their fellow countrymen.

Those who met Wiseman during his rectorship were struck not only by his erudition but also by his appearance. One who knew him in 1830 described him as "tall, slight, apparently long-necked, with features rather pointed and pale, and demeanour very grave." In 1838 Thomas Babington Macaulay recorded a visit to the English College: "We found the principal, Dr. Wiseman, a young ecclesiastic full of health and vigour . . . in purple vestments standing in the cloister."[8]

In 1833 John Henry Newman and Richard Hurrell Froude visited the college in Rome. Although disappointed that Wiseman insisted upon the necessity of unqualified acceptance of the decrees of the Council of Trent before one could be admitted into Roman communion, Froude concluded, "We mean to make as much as we can out of our acquaintance with Monsignor Wiseman, who is really too nice a person to talk nonsense about." Among other Anglicans to meet Wiseman in Rome were Charles Marriott, Henry Edward Manning, and William Gladstone—all, like Newman and Froude, identified with high church views within their communion; Julius Charles Hare, prominent among broad churchmen; and Richard Trench, later to become archbishop of Dublin. Newman later wrote of Wiseman, "He can speak with readiness and point in half a dozen languages, without being detected for a foreigner in any of them, and at ten minutes notice can address a congregation from a French pulpit or the select audience of an Italian academy."[9]

It was to men of learning such as those mentioned above that Wiseman wanted to appeal, yet there were few English Catholics capable of assisting in such an effort. In 1830 he wrote to Frederick C. Husenbeth, well-known antiquarian and Roman Catholic apologist, then serving as a missioner in the Midland District. He praised the older man for "defending God's truth from the assaults of its opponents and our enemies," and added, "There is no part of this field in which I envy your facilities so much, as in meeting—which you have done with such decided success, the calumnies of the apostate Blanco White."

White was a Spanish-born, apostate priest and scholar who had settled in Oxford, where he was received into the Oriel common room. He had actively sought to influence the views of the fellows there, including John Henry Newman.[10] Wiseman regretted the fact that he was not on the spot to answer White's attacks upon the church, since he was in a unique position to do so: "Were it not that my distance from the field of action precludes me from seeing any thing which he publishes, I should think myself particularly called to take up his glove, from the former connection between our families, and the similarity of our situations—in all thank God but in the dreadful step which he has taken. Our parents were both English commercial settlers in Seville, and our families very intimate."

Although Wiseman could claim kinship to a prominent English family of that name, it is interesting that he identified his parents simply as "English," rather than Irish or even Anglo-Irish, indicative, perhaps, of his wish to be associated as closely as possible with the cause of English Catholics. Blanco White's parents, like his own, originated in Ireland.

After further discussing White's background, Wiseman concluded his long letter to Husenbeth: "I trust soon, my dear Sir, to hear from you, as I should be sorry to lose the advantage of a correspondence, so agreably begun as far as my wishes are concerned. My long absence abroad, and my previously secluded life at Ushaw have not permitted me to make a single acquaintance among my confrères except Roman schoolfellows, and of course I must be equally a stranger to them. An acquaintance with them could not have been opened more to their advantage or to my profit than by a correspondence with you."[11] Wiseman, then, was clearly willing, and even anxious, to make his mark by promoting the cause of Catholicism in England, and the opportunity soon presented itself.

Early in 1831 several priests of the Midland District established the *Catholic Magazine*. They were convinced that emancipation had placed Catholics in a political situation that demanded new approaches "for the propagation of Catholic truth in all areas of life." Wiseman took advantage of his correspondence with Husenbeth to express his enthusiastic support for the venture: "I have heard with ineffable delight of a new catholic journal being established in the Midland district; it is a thing I have long and earnestly desired, and shall beg to be allowed to contribute my humble mite to its success." He doubted whether he could offer anything "of very general interest" but hoped to "furnish an occasional article, which may show that the undertaking interests even such secluded and unserviceable members of the clergy as myself."[12]

The elderly John Kirk, the last student to be received by the Jesuits at the English College before their suppression in 1773, was coeditor of the *Catholic Magazine*. He had heard from Henry Weedall, president of Oscott College, that Wiseman "was very desirous that a respectable periodical should be established here for the communication of Catholic intelligence" and that he was willing to contribute to the work. Weedall had added that "no one could do it more powerfully, or from more ample resource of authentic information [than Wiseman]." Kirk wrote immediately that he and the other editors "would be obliged to you for any communication you might think proper to favour us with" and that they "looked for it with no small degree of eagerness & anxiety." Wiseman, in fact, had already sent off a learned article on the chair of St. Peter, which appeared in the fourth number of the journal. Kirk thanked him and urged "a continuance of such communications," even on a monthly basis, if possible.[13]

When Wiseman paid his brief visit to England in 1832, he discovered that even those Catholics who saw a promising new era opening up for the church in their country were far from united as to the best means of responding. The *Catholic Magazine* illustrated their divisions, and in 1833 Wiseman found it necessary to withdraw his services. Joseph P. Chinnici has made a good case for the fact that the basic disagreement was between those who, educated in the enlightenment tradition of the eighteenth century, saw the need for the church to adapt to the times in a clear, well-reasoned manner, especially suitable to the English temperament, and those who, influenced by the romantic revival, stressed the emotional appeal of Catholic devotional life, advocating Latin forms as ideal, while emphasizing organic development in the church and the strictest adherence to the directives of the Holy See. Kirk and Lingard represented the older model, Wiseman the newer and, it may be argued plausibly, that which represented the wave of the immediate future. The division was evident when Henry Weedall published in the *Catholic Magazine* an article on the liquefaction of the blood of St. Januarius, which he accepted as an authentic miracle. Lingard questioned the validity of the "miracle" and insisted that scientific evidence of a respectable kind was necessary to test it.[14]

A second debate in the pages of the journal was the occasion of Wiseman's decision to break with it. Lingard sparked the controversy by writing against the suitability of including the Litany of Loreto in an English Catholic prayer book. He concluded that "every rational man will deem it preferable to put his petitions in language which he can understand, than to employ for that purpose a jargon of mysterious, unintelligible, aye, even 'portentous sounds.'"[15]

Wiseman explained to one of his former students, William Tandy, now a professor at Oscott, that it would be impossible for him to continue writing for the *Catholic Magazine.* The editors, he said, allowed matters to be discussed without taking into account the scandal that might be generated. Such a policy would incur the displeasure of the Holy See, "where propositions are often condemned not because heretical but as *subversive of piety, offensive to pious ears,* &c." He continued, "Now I am *part of Rome,* as a professor in its university, and still more as a consultor of the Index and can allow myself to judge by no principles which could not be approved here." He mentioned specifically the treatment of the Litany of the Blessed Virgin: "What could give greater offense at Rome or in any Catholic country than to denounce the Litany of the B. Virgin as unfit for public use and as mere unintelligible nonsense." He concluded, "God knows devotion towards her is sufficiently cold in England without the clergy throwing water upon it."[16]

It is no wonder that there were those who would judge Wiseman to be a young upstart, little familiar with the English scene and hardly in a position to judge his fellow Catholics there. Kirk responded sensitively, however: "Were I in your situation, & under the same circumstances, I have no doubt I should have acted in the same manner." He suggested that Wiseman might still send communications from Rome to his friend William Tandy, who then could submit them to the journal as his own.[17]

John Lingard questioned Rome's apparent reluctance to assist Englishmen in defending the church.

To me it has sometimes appeared extraordinary that some of the thousand ecclesiastics at Rome do not undertake to refute the works that are published for the purpose of disgracing the Holy See, but leave that office to us strangers at a distance, who have not the facilities that they have, nor access like them to original documents. At least there should be some officer appointed, whose duty it should be to make extracts and furnish assistance to Catholic writers in foreign countries, whose object it is to defend religion and the pope from the disgrace and charges heaped upon them by their adversaries.[18]

Lingard's letter was something of a rebuke to Wiseman, who was in a position to fill the role that the historian suggested. In fact, Wiseman seems to have followed Kirk's suggestion by continuing to provide Tandy with information on Roman affairs, especially concerning the revolutionary movements that had spread to the papal states themselves upon the accession of Gregory XVI.

In March 1834 Wiseman wrote:

I have felt myself for some months gradually passing into a new state of mind and heart which I can hardly describe, but which I trust is the last stage of mental progress, in which I hope I may yet much improve, but out of which I trust I may never pass. . . . I think I could make an interesting history of my mind's religious progress, if I may use a word shockingly perverted by modern fanatics, from the hard dry struggles I used to have when first I commenced to study on my own account, to the settling down into a state of stern conviction, and so after some years to the nobler and more soothing evidences furnished by the grand harmonies and beautiful features of religion, whether considered in contact with lower objects or viewed in her own crystal mirror.[19]

Wiseman had become increasingly convinced that his mission was to the English, and if he experienced minor setbacks and disappointments, as in his hopes for the *Catholic Magazine,* there were other signs that there was a great work for him to perform in the country he now considered his own. It was Bishop Baines who offered him the most probable means of success.

Even before his return to England in 1829, Baines had dreamed of establishing there a university that, he hoped, would be affiliated with the Roman University but would work closely with the "seminary-college" he planned to found in his district.[20] Wiseman, while not yet a firm devotee of the bishop of Siga, suggested names of those who might contribute their services to Prior Park, upon which Baines soon centered his ambitious schemes.

Among the first whom Wiseman proposed was Luigi Gentili, a member of the Institute of Charity founded in 1828 by Antonio Rosmini-Serbati. Baines already knew Gentili, not yet thirty years old in 1830, when Wiseman mentioned him as a possible assistant to the bishop at Prior Park. Some years earlier, in fact, the bishop of Siga had refused Gentili's request to marry Anna de Mendoza y Rios, a ward of Baines after her father's death. The bishop was aware of the ability and piety that led the disappointed suitor to offer himself to Rosmini, and now he welcomed Wiseman's idea: "Many thanks for your suggestion respecting Gentili. He is the very man I want, and as I know him so well & like him so much I have no hesitation in begging you to urge my proposal to him." Baines, however, wanted nothing short of total commitment: "He has only to make himself over to this District and I will try to make him comfortable, which I think I can do full as well as any of the other Bishops — nay for such a person as him, I think much more so." The allurement of comfort was the last thing that would attract Gentili, who was as passionately earnest in his asceticism as he had been in his early love. He dreamed of cooperating in the work of converting England, but that endeavor was not even mentioned in the invitation. The offer was refused.[21]

In 1830 H. F. C. Logan, a Cambridge convert, settled at Prior Park following two years of study in Rome. He had been received into the church by Baines, who had recommended him to Wiseman in 1828. When returning him to the bishop, Wiseman described Logan as "one of the most precious acquirements which the Church has made in our days." He was "equal to the chair of any University, whether in metaphysics, the most abstruse parts of mathematics, or their application to other branches of Sciences." After commenting on the breadth of Logan's reading "in every department of literature," his college rector concluded, "To me he is a serious loss, for he was of the greatest use to me in many parts of my studies."[22]

The loss of Logan was made somewhat less serious for Wiseman by the acquisition, in 1830, of another Cambridge convert, George Spencer, son of Lord Spencer and brother of Lord Althorp. Three years older than Wiseman, he later joined the Passionists, where he was known as Father Ignatius. Spencer was instrumental in shaping his superior's future. "He told Wiseman bluntly," according to Wilfrid Ward, "'that he should apply his mind to something more practical than Syrian MSS. or treatises on geology, and that he would rather see him take up with what suited a priest on the English mission as it then was.'"[23]

Spencer's advice was reminiscent of that which Bishop Walsh had offered to Wiseman in 1829: "What we want in England are zealous, laborious ecclesiastics, full of the spirit of their holy state, burning with hunger & thirst for the conversion of souls, *good preachers & good catechists*, without which talent, Latin & Greek will be of comparatively little use."[24] Wiseman, already known as an erudite author, distinguished preacher, and convincing lecturer, felt increasingly isolated from the work to be done in England. His desire to participate in the activity there became more urgent as those to whose intellectual and spiritual formation he had contributed returned home to commence their pastoral mission.

Early in 1834 Bishop Baines returned to Rome to present his side of the controversies, old and new, in which he was involved. His struggles with the Benedictines continued. An added dimension was a dispute with the order over control of the mission in Bath, which according to the bishop belonged to the local congregation attending services there rather than to the Benedictines. Baines also battled with the Benedictine sisters who had a convent at Cannington, near Bridgwater. He found fault with the financial state of their establishment and especially antagonized them by appointing as their confessor one of the former Benedictines who had followed him to Prior Park. The sisters appealed to Rome. Finally Baines was now challenging his former allies, the Jesuits, for control of a church in Bristol that had been constructed by members of the society earlier in the century but that he now refused to acknowledge as belonging to them, since in fact they had been suppressed at the time.[25]

Shortly after Baines arrived in Rome, Wiseman wrote to his friend Tandy that the bishop was living at the college and that the two of them engaged in "much talk on the state and prospects of the Catholic body." The younger man was falling under the spell of the bishop of Siga: "I find our ideas coincide greatly upon the matter. He will do much through his College to rouse the slumbering energies of the Catholic spirit amongst us; and I trust every other will second his efforts and emulate his zeal."[26]

A month later Baines had won Wiseman completely to his cause. The latter told Tandy: "You will be anxious to hear about Dr. Baines, as doubtless many rumours will be abroad, and I shall be glad if you give all possible publicity to what I say, that he has been received by every one who knew him with the most marked kindness and affection." The pope had received Baines "with peculiar friendship" and "was greatly delighted with Prior Park and has since expressed himself highly interested in its success on the largest scale." Wiseman had read over the documentation that Baines had provided as explanation of the various struggles in which he was engaged and stated his "honest conscientious opinion . . . that never was a Christian Bishop so shamefully and so unjustly treated." Wiseman expected to visit England the following year to have some of his lectures published, and it was his hope that he and Tandy would then visit Prior Park together.[27]

The fact that Baines included Wiseman in his plans for Prior Park was a matter of some consequence in the relationship of the two men. Baines had proposed to Propaganda that Wiseman, only thirty-two years old, should be made his coadjutor bishop. When the cardinals discussed the matter, however, they decided to delay any decision, as Wiseman told Tandy.

> Monsignor Mai [Propaganda secretary] assured me that not a word was said in opposition; that all the cardinals without exception spoke in the highest terms of me; that the only thing like an objection raised was the ages of both; but that the fact was, it was brought on late, the cardinals were tired, someone suggested that we were both young [Baines was forty-seven], the matter would not spoil by keeping, and hence arose the delay. He has taken great pains to assure me in private that the thing will certainly be done, but advised that nothing more should be urged about it for the present.

Wiseman concluded, however, that even though Mai's description of the meeting was accurate, "the delay was not accidental." He wrote, "Something must have been dropt in conversation intimating the Pope's unwillingness, and hence the decision."

Baines had assured Wiseman that even aside from his other business, he would have come to Rome to make the proposal that he had set his heart upon.

> His [Baines's] object is manifestly to have me at the head of Prior Park, *when a university,* and I own that what induced me to accede to his proposal was the same motive. I have so long deplored, as you know, the defects of our education, and the want of a literary centre and institution, I have so long wished for a good journal, and a power to lead the Catholic mind, which necessarily requires station, that I felt I was called in duty to make a sacrifice of worldly comfort, peace, and interest, and accept a situation, the *only one* which would have enabled me to carry my views into execution. I say the only one, for every other College is too old, too shackled by custom & rule to *begin* this reformation.

Wiseman had reflected upon his own motivation and concluded that it was not ambition that led him to concur in the plan of Bishop Baines. His sole desire was "to aid God and religion's cause," and he added that he would have refused the offer had any other bishop sought his assistance as coadjutor.

Wiseman continued his account by stating that Baines had anticipated Propaganda's decision but had urged him, in any case, to put himself "at the head of Prior Park [university] leaving it to time to effect the other project [the coadjutorship]." The younger man refused, however, arguing that as a simple priest he would have insufficient power to effect his plans. In addition, he wrote, "I could not in justice to myself leave an honourable, happy and permanent situation for one full of risks and uncertainty." Finally he pointed out that he did not belong to the Western District and that the northern vicar apostolic might complain were he to abandon his post for a district other than his own. Newman's experience in establishing the Catholic University in Dublin nearly twenty years later would show that the first of Wiseman's arguments was realistic.

Bishop Baines had persisted by approaching the Holy Father directly. The pope approved of the establishment of a university at Prior Park, stating that he would act as he had in the case of Louvain in Belgium by providing a rescript approving of the plan and that when "it was organized and ready, he would erect it and endow it with all the privileges and power of a university; but he wished the other Bishops to concur in the plan." When Baines went on to raise the question of the coadjutorship for Wiseman, however, Gregory "positively refused, assigning as his reason . . . that he [Baines] must first settle his dispute with the Benedictines."

Wiseman wrote that the pope was willing to allow him to leave Rome, "for a time," so that he could assist in organizing the university at Prior Park. He could retain his position as rector of the Venerabile in the meantime and return whenever he might wish. Baines accepted the plan, as did Wiseman. The main problem, however, was to obtain someone to replace him in Rome. George Errington was the only person whom he could conceive of, but "how unpleasantly situated should I be," he observed, "if out of kindness to me he took it [the rectorship] even in this way, and I had to dispossess him of it after 2 or 3 years."

In spite of the difficulties, Wiseman concluded that it would be "wrong to throw away at once the opportunity opened me of exciting a new spirit, and rousing the energies of latent catholic feeling." He decided, therefore, "to tell the Bp. [Baines] that I will go over to England in the spring as I proposed, and stay a year or a year & a half; if he finds my services of value, he may then take his measure to secure them to his District." Two years would be sufficient to determine whether the plan would work and whether the Holy See might then be willing to elevate him to the episcopate. If that obstacle remained, he wrote, "I will return to Rome before I am become a stranger to it." He saw clearly that he would experience opposition and added, "The more I reflect the more I see the impossibility of carrying my views into execution without a firm stable position, placing me above the sneers of the Clergy and the grave opinion of the Bishops."[28] While Wiseman may have been an idealist in his dreams for Catholicism in England, his eyes were wide open to the divisions that might result as he tried to execute his plans.

Wiseman claimed that the proposal was to remain a secret, but it soon leaked out. John Maguire, later to be one of his vicars general in London, wrote to him, "I am delighted to hear that you are coming to settle in England & to direct the projected establishment at Bath." Maguire added: "The church party are taking the alarm at the 'churches' that we are raising in every District; when they see a University founded they will become furious. But happily, mischief is out of their power; they can only foam & fret & do us the honour of railing at us in sermons & after dinner speeches." Baines, in the meantime, attributed the pope's refusal to grant Wiseman a coadjutorship to "the influence of the Jesuits," who, he thought, "would cease to oppose when they saw that nothing was to be gained by opposition."[29]

Both Wiseman and Errington were theoretically subject to the vicar apostolic of the Northern District, Thomas Penswick. Wiseman wrote to his bishop to explain the plan that he and Baines had framed with the approval of the Holy Father himself: "I had previously determined on a journey to England next year on business which my run through the country two years ago did not allow me to discharge, and the only change in my plan is the extension of its period." Since Errington was still unwell, Wiseman added, "To take my place during my absence, I have cast my eyes on my dear friend Dr. Errington, whose health may allow him later to undertake duty in England, but hardly I should think as yet, though I fancy Italy would not disagree with him." He concluded, "If I go to England on this errand, be assured, my Lord, that no spirit of rivalry or ambition shall actuate me in any way; the good of religion and the glory of God shall be my only aims."[30]

Bishop Penswick was by no means prepared to acquiesce in the proposal. He wrote to the London vicar apostolic:

If Dr. Baines had been satisfied with asking for Dr. Wiseman for his Coadjutor, no fault, I suspect, would have been found with him; he would, in that case, have been doing no more than another might have done; but to solicit the pope to give him a bishopric in partibus for the purpose of attaching him to himself will, I think, make me listen with great caution to proposals which he tells me he is preparing to make to the Bishops for their cooperation in his projects for the aggrandizement of Prior Park. Of course, we are to hear of the advantages which religion will derive from the circumstances of education being in the hands of Bishops and not of their opponents. The argument when fully developed may appear more convincing than was the passing mention of it.

Penswick refused to free Errington to replace Wiseman in Rome. Moreover, two months later he wrote that he did not approve of the rector of the English College being absent from his post for any length of time.[31]

The fact that his bishop disapproved of the plan disturbed Wiseman as much as the veto that was exercised. It was a somewhat chastened man, then, who declared that neither he nor Errington had any intention of acting without full episcopal approval. He went on to stress the fact that "no allurements" had been offered to entice him to Prior Park and that he had only agreed to the proposal after Bishop Baines had arranged matters with the Holy Father, "subject according to my stipulation to the Bishop's [Penswick's] approval." Wiseman also insisted that leaving Rome would be "a decided sacrifice of interest, comfort, ease & enjoyment of the highest order, for Rome is now to me what no other place can ever become." He told the bishop, finally, that he had not entered into the plan merely to serve the interests of Prior Park.

> All my studies for years have been directed for England, with a feeling that the day would come when with God's blessing they might be useful there. I have several works some nearly ready, others far advanced, and I thought this a fair opening for trying the experiment which, with several able & zealous young men, I had long planned, of giving a push to the energies of our body towards higher feelings on religious literature than have yet been exhibited to the public. If I failed, my retreat was secured to my own peaceful occupations.

Wiseman repeated to Penswick that he would have to travel to England soon for reasons of business, but that his absence from Rome would be no longer than necessary.[32]

Soon after Wiseman had incurred the anger of his own bishop because of the arrangements with Baines, he was made to realize, as never before, that serving as Roman agent for the English vicars apostolic could be a painful and sobering experience. Bishop Baines was not the only member of the episcopate who was at odds with the English regular clergy. Unlike recusant times, by the 1830s the secular priests formed about 70 percent of the English clergy. The papal constitution of 1763 had been an attempt to settle the long-standing controversies between the two divisions of priests. From then until the restoration of the hierarchy in 1850, wrote Canon E. H. Burton, "the 'Rules of the Mission' remained the chief constitutional regulations for the Church in England, and the gradual cessation of the ancient differences, and absence of very serious difficulties during that period is sufficient testimony to the large wisdom and statesmanship with which Benedict XIV solved the problem."[33] By the third decade of the nineteenth century, however, the document to which the author referred had been outdated for many years, and a series of disputes had resulted in much hard feeling.

Early in the century the Jesuits appealed successfully to Rome when the vicar apostolic of the Northern District refused them permission to build a new chapel at Wigan. In fact he had made plans to build one of his own on a site about three hundred yards from their existing structure. When both chapels were completed, a pamphlet war broke out between the members of the respective congregations. By the 1830s it was the Benedictines whose plans for expansion in the Northern District met with the bishop's disapproval.[34]

In London, in the meantime, two maiden ladies, the Misses Louisa and Jesse Gallini, wished to construct a chapel in St. John's Wood. They had the bishop's grateful blessing on their generous work, but, unknown to him, they offered the chapel to the Jesuits. Bishop Bramston opposed the arrangement, insisting that he had sufficient secular clergy to staff the new church. He was losing patience when the Jesuits appealed their claim to the Holy See. "We ought to know, and I trust do know the interests of our Districts, and ought not to have set over us monks or friars of any kind," he wrote to Penswick. Bramston concluded with a warning: "Surely this intriguing must be put a stop to, or else of what possible use are vicars apostolic in England. Are they to be directed and governed by any religious order or society? If so, then indeed I should say 'the Church is in danger.'"[35]

Bishop Baines wrote from Rome that Wiseman was anxious for the vicars apostolic to exercise their joint influence in opposing the regulars. He addressed the letter to Thomas Griffiths, former president of St. Edmund's College, who had been made coadjutor to Bishop Bramston in October 1833, after the death of Gradwell in March of that year.[36] The views of Bramston and Griffiths coincided perfectly in their attitude toward the regulars.

Baines persisted in urging the necessity of action: "One thing is quite evident, that when the Bishops act in a body, they will *always* be an even match even for the Jesuits, but *never* when they act singly." He recommended that they should meet as soon as possible to settle upon "some uniform mode of acting," and he concluded: "The remedy is in our hands. If we refuse to use it, ourselves or our successors will have cause to repent our neglect." He was convinced that "the Jesuits are using all their efforts . . . to get into London and all the great towns, & will succeed if not soon & effectively checked."[37]

Wiseman foresaw the same danger when he wrote to Bishop Bramston that "the Pope in the strongest terms expressed his conviction that there was a conspiracy among the Bps. to crush the regulars." The Holy Father had used the instance of St. John's Wood to illustrate the accusation, considering it to be "the counterpart to Dr. Baines's transactions in the West." Wiseman echoed Baines by warning that the Jesuits considered the affair of St. John's Wood to be "but a beginning of a plan to get all the London chapels into their hands." The assertion was absurd, but the vicars apostolic agreed that a joint petition was needed. As Bishop Penswick declared, "Tho' no great attention may be paid to the communication of a single Bishop at Rome, it has always been held a maxim that resistance is not to be offered to the wishes of the whole prelacy." He continued, "It is pretty evident that reasons pass for nothing, but if it is discovered that a spirit of disapprobation pervades the whole of the Bishops of this Island the religious will not be allowed to tease us as they are doing."[38]

John Lingard was selected to prepare the petition. At his suggestion it was addressed directly to the Holy Father for, as he said, "if to Propaganda, you may depend upon it, the instrument will be cushioned and forgotten." He also urged that the Scottish vicars apostolic should be asked to attach their names to the letter, since they, too, had objected to the independence of the regulars.[39]

When the petition was prepared, it was sent to all of the vicars apostolic for their suggestions and signatures. Three specific examples were cited to demonstrate the problems that had arisen because of the claim to independent jurisdiction by the religious orders: the affair of the Cannington sisters, the chapel at St. John's Wood, and a dispute between the vicars apostolic of the Northern District with the Benedictines. Lingard was optimistic: "You will be victorious," he wrote to Bramston. "If they find that the VV.AA. come forth in one body and express their dissatisfaction, the Romans will be alarmed. They may wear bas rouges but they are cowards at the bottom."[40]

All of the prelates signed the petition with the single exception of Bishop Walsh, who pointed out that none of the matters discussed had taken place in the Midland District and that he had no complaint with the regulars.[41] Lingard wrote, "I had always my fears of Dr. Walsh, for Mr. Kirk has often represented him to me as a complete Jesuit, at least so far as to scruple doing anything disapproved by the Padri [the Jesuits]."[42]

When he sent the petition to Wiseman with instructions as to how it should be presented, Bishop Bramston stressed that no time should be lost in placing it before the pope. The urgency was great because Bishop Walsh had kept the document for so long while making up his mind whether or not to add his signature and, in addition, had shown it to others while seeking their advice. Bramston wanted a trusted agent to be present in order to provide further information for the pope, should such be necessary. "You know all the circumstances of the cases mentioned," he wrote, and so "can give to his Holiness all the requisite explanations respecting them." He also suggested that Wiseman should be accompanied by the Reverend Paul Macpherson, former agent of the English vicars apostolic and now exercising that role on behalf of the Scottish bishops. The proposal had originated with one of the Scottish vicars, who wrote, "I know the old Abbé [Macpherson] stands well with his Holiness, who lately paid his expences to go to the Apennines for the good of his health." Even more to the point was his next observation: "I know the Abbé is sufficiently anti-Jesuit to do all in his power to thwart their plans. I know he has some considerable influence in Rome."[43]

Wiseman failed to follow instructions. He did not secure the services of Macpherson, nor did he present the petition in person. He explained that he had misgivings about sending the petition to the pope at all, but that he was "duty bound" to do so. He wrote that "after much mature deliberation I thought it better that he [the pope] should read it alone, without having any one on whom to vent his first feelings, which I feared would be violent." His fears, he continued, were justified. The pope immediately called for Cardinal Weld and "expressed his most marked anger and displeasure." He planned on taking no notice of the joint letter but would write directly to Bishop Baines, who, he was convinced, had been responsible for originating the petition. Wiseman said that the pope intended to "express himself in the strongest terms and say that now he saw how he [Baines] had deceived him from the beginning, and must expect no favour or kindness from him in future." Two weeks later, however, Wiseman informed Bramston that the pope had "undergone some change of feeling in consequence of a letter received from Dr. Baines, which seems to have opened his eyes upon some points of his controversy."[44]

The English bishops did not receive Wiseman's news kindly. They were already annoyed with him for his failure to inform them promptly of the death of the cardinal protector of the English College and the appointment of Cardinal Weld to that position. Weld's father had provided Stonyhurst for the former Jesuits after their suppression, and the cardinal was known to be their supporter. As a boy he had been tutored by Charles Plowden, one of the former Jesuits who was a close friend of the Weld family.

Weld now wrote to Bramston that he had Wiseman's assurance that his appointment as protector of the college would be agreeable to the vicars apostolic. Wiseman, in fact, had been presumptuous and naive. Baines, above all, had reason to complain of Cardinal Weld, who had been selected to intervene in the controversy between the bishop and the Cannington sisters. He had removed them from the jurisdiction of the western bishop and had appointed for them the very confessor whom Baines had withdrawn. The bishop, of course, was utterly humiliated, convinced that "his Eminence believes the evidence of the subject rather than that of the superior, having laid it down as a general rule that in all disputes between Bishops and regulars, 'the former are always wrong & the latter always right.'"[45]

When Weld's appointment was made, Wiseman explained to the vicars apostolic that there was no cause for concern. Bishop Bramston called Wiseman's letter a "flippant performance," and concluded, "It seems extraordinary that he sent no information himself respecting the death of Cardinal Zurla [the previous protector of the college] & that he merely supposes I am informed of Cardinal Weld's appointment." John Lingard was outraged: "I am . . . jealous of *Card. Weld's appointment.* Both he and his son-in-law, Lord Clifford, are Jesuits to the backbone, and an incapable rector may open to them a door for the re-introduction of the Jesuits [as administrators of the English College]."[46] Since it was the special responsibility of the cardinal protector to represent English interests to the pope and to offer advice on the government of the college, it is no wonder that the vicars apostolic were uneasy as a result of the appointment. The very fact that it was Weld to whom the pope turned to complain of the petition concerning the regulars was now a confirmation of their worst fears.

Wiseman's explanation of the pope's response to the petition of the bishops and of his own failure to present it personally evoked an angry outburst from the vicars apostolic. Bishop Penswick was positively indignant. "What childish work do the letters of which yr. Lp. has been so good as to furnish copies exhibit," he wrote; "H[is] H[oliness] cannot be known; it is impossible that he should be the violent man who cannot be approached by an accredited agent, until time is given for wrath to subside." He added, "Neither do I wish to believe that he entertains the opinion that his vicars in Britain, with their coadjutors, are mere puppets that can be made to dance when a single mastermind among them [Baines] thinks proper to pull the wires." Griffiths suggested that if Wiseman had done as he was told, the Holy Father's reaction might well have been different. Baines, finally, was understandably excited when he heard that Cardinal Weld had observed "that if the Benedictines had paid Dr. Lingard for writing that letter, he could not have served their cause more effectually."[47]

Bishop Penswick severely reprimanded Wiseman for having failed to serve the interests of the vicars apostolic properly. The rebuke was not well received, and Wiseman defended himself vigorously. The petition had come at an unpropitious time, he noted, and its "plain" wording was hardly the kind that would "soothe" the pope, who recently "had been brought once more into a state of almost hostile feelings towards Dr. Baines." With little attempt at subtlety, Wiseman pointed out that those familiar with the transaction of business in Rome were better able to judge such matters than those at a distance from the scene.[48]

Wiseman also wrote frankly to Bishop Bramston.

I am not conscious of having taken a single imprudent step in the business, and I am sure that there was nothing in my power to do beyond what I did. I have certainly suffered as much as anyone, in character and influence, by boldly identifying myself with the Bishops and their cause since my return to Rome [after his 1832 visit to England]; the other party have spared neither vexations nor slanderous annoyances till my peace & health have been disturbed in no inconsiderable degree, and I cannot but think it hard that from those I have done my best conscientiously to serve, I should meet no better encouragement than reproaches and suspicions.

Convinced that his conduct had been correct, Wiseman again wrote to Bishop Penswick, "Of course I will not presume to place my judgment against that of my superiors, but when an emergency occurs in which I cannot take their opinion I must depend upon my own, and I trust there is no danger of my forming it other than upon the most upright and conscientious grounds."[49]

Wiseman had consulted Cardinal Weld before deciding on the best way to present the petition. His grievance at the reaction of the vicars apostolic is as understandable as their criticism of his conduct. He was clearly overworked, and he had been suffering from poor health, at least a partial excuse, surely, for his neglecting to keep the English bishops as well informed as they considered proper and even necessary. They resented the Holy See's inability to interpret the English scene accurately, but they should have understood that Wiseman, on the spot and with a number of years of experience, was truly in a better position than they to assess the situation in Rome. Since the death of Bishop Gradwell, Baines was the only one of their body who could claim any familiarity with the manner of conducting business in Rome, and his judgment was questionable at its best. If Wiseman was imprudent in following the advice of Cardinal Weld, the bishops were no less so for depending too much upon the views of Lingard, notoriously antiregular and always critical of Roman authoritarianism.

The bishops, nevertheless, were dissatisfied with Wiseman's explanation, and they concluded that his letters were evidence of the fact that he was, in the words of Penswick, "very sensitive and, I fear, very silly." Wiseman was expected in England soon, and the bishop suggested that this would be the time for them to express their opinions more fully. He further noted that the joint petition had been unduly identified in Rome with the various controversies in which Bishop Baines was involved. In addition to Wiseman, Penswick blamed Lord Clifford, Cardinal Weld's son-in-law, and John Talbot, the earl of Shrewsbury. Both men had been "sadly too meddling in ecclesiastical matters."[50]

The Holy Father responded to the joint petition in June 1835. He did so by writing directly to Bishop Baines alone, with the order that copies of his letter should be sent to the other vicars apostolic. The pope made it abundantly clear that the complaints of the bishops were, in his judgment, without foundation. With respect to the specific concerns mentioned by the bishops, he stated that the Benedictines were planning no new foundations in the Northern District, and in fact no crisis developed there between the order and the bishops. The pope reserved for later a decision on the St. John's Wood Chapel, although within two months it was secured for the secular clergy.[51] Finally, the Cannington sisters ended their disagreement with Bishop Baines by moving to the Midland District, where they were received by Bishop Walsh. It should be noted that Bishop Baines failed to win possession either of the Jesuit chapel in Bristol or that of the Benedictines in Bath.

Wiseman suggested that the vicars apostolic should respond to the pope's letter. Bishop Bramston tended to agree, as he wrote to his northern counterpart, "You and I have no very great respect for his [Wiseman's] judgment, but I am half inclined to think that later some notice might be taken of this letter; but your Lordship's determination will settle mine."[52]

Two years later, according to Wiseman, the pope lamented the fact that neither Bramston nor Penswick had replied to his letter.[53] If the report was accurate, as it seems to have been, the pontiff's sensitivity was somewhat curious, considering that he had answered the joint petition of the bishops with a letter addressed to Bishop Baines alone. Moreover, both Bramston and Penswick were already suffering from the illnesses that would end their lives in the following year.

By the spring of 1835, then, Wiseman had incurred the displeasure and mistrust of the English vicars apostolic for his tentative arrangements with Bishop Baines, his support of Cardinal Weld as protector of the Venerabile, and his inept handling, as the bishops unjustly felt, of their business. It must have been with a certain amount of apprehension that he pursued his plan of setting out for England. He arrived in the summer of 1835 and was there for more than a year. The visit changed his life more radically than anything that he had yet experienced.

4. "Loss and Gain" in England

BEFORE SETTING OUT FOR ENGLAND, WISEMAN, ON THE LAST DAY OF May 1835, went with his mother to visit his sister and her husband. On May 5 he had written to his faithful friend, William Tandy, that Frasquita was to marry Count Andrea Gabrielli of Fano on the following day. The match, he said, "has given us all great satisfaction." He described Gabrielli as "a very accomplished and religious person, of a very noble family."[1] Xaviera was delighted that her daughter, approaching her thirty-first birthday, had secured a husband. *"He came, he saw,* and *she* conquered," wrote the mother of the bride in a boastful letter to her sister. The wedding had taken place in Rome, where Cardinal Weld had officiated in the private chapel of his own palace and afterward provided "a most elegant breakfast." Wiseman's mother went on to describe the gifts presented by Lord and Lady Shrewsbury, who, with their two daughters, spent the greater part of each year living in Rome. "As for Nicholas," continued his mother, "he is almost one of the family, for he might walk into dinner there every day if he chose to do so, and at least dines there three or four times a week."

Mrs. Wiseman reported that her own future was undecided but that probably she would live in Milan where her elder son, James, had established himself. He had been urged to join his family in Fano, but Xaviera wrote that his "delicate health" would prevent him from doing so. Nicholas and James had not seen each other since their student days at Ushaw. Two months later Wiseman's mother again wrote and described the pleasant days that she and Nicholas had spent at Fano. They then traveled in a leisurely way to Milan, where they discovered that James was no longer ill. Xaviera reported that "the brothers cordially embraced each other after a separation of 18 years" and that "had they met elsewhere, they would have passed each other unknown." Nicholas then continued his journey alone.

Mrs. Wiseman's own material status had not been improved by Frasquita's marriage: "I feel now as though I were beginning the world again. I am without house or home for the present, lodged in a single bed chamber at an hotel, all alone without knowing a single creature." She stayed with James, who was away for hours each day and evening, engaged in teaching French, Spanish, and English. "He had met many disappointments this time past," wrote his mother, "and every thing went wrong with him, poor fellow." His prospects were now promising, but in the meantime they could not afford furnished lodging, nor did they have the means to equip an unfurnished apartment. Xaviera complained that she felt "lonely and isolated . . . without any thing to occupy or interest me, whereas if I had a place of my own, with servants and something to do, the case would be quite otherwise."

In the same letter she wrote that Nicholas had delivered a series of lectures in Rome which were so well-received that he was on his way to have them published in London. Before leaving the Continent, he had traveled through Germany, "as there are many literary correspondents who are most anxious to make his acquaintance."[2]

Among those whom Wiseman wanted to meet was Ignaz von Döllinger, who had just completed the second volume of his ecclesiastical history. When sending a copy to Wiseman in April, he had written, "The first volume of my Ecclesiastical History having met from you with such a favourable reception, I feel emboldened to send you the second too, and I shall continue to send you the succeeding volumes." He had heard that Wiseman was to be "a member of the College of Dr. Baines at Prior Park," and he added, "I hope you recollect the promise you made me in your letter of passing through Munich, and spending at least some days with us; you will find there not only Görres, but also Möhler, who has of late consented to lecture henceforth on Divinity at our University." Johann Adam Möhler had been at Tübingen in 1832 when he published his famous *Symbolik*. Wiseman was anxious that the fruits of Catholic scholarship in Germany might be enjoyed in England as well. Döllinger shared the hope: "What you say respecting a closer connexion between the Catholic clergy of England and Germany has my fullest approbation and it seems to me 'a consummation devoutly to be wished.'"[3]

Wiseman paid the promised visit to Munich, where he was stimulated by conversations with the leaders of the Catholic intellectual movement there. Döllinger was sufficiently encouraged by the meetings to travel to England the following year, where he developed contacts and interests that would last throughout his life.

Wiseman finally arrived in London on July 14, 1835.[4] He stopped there to visit with Bishops Bramston and Griffiths. Bramston had only one year to live. He died on July 11, 1836, not quite six months after the death of Bishop Penswick on January 28, 1836. Both men were succeeded by their coadjutors, Thomas Griffiths in London and John Briggs, former president of Ushaw, in the North. By the time that Wiseman left England, then, none of the vicars apostolic had coadjutors to assist them, although all four had served their predecessors in that capacity.

Bishop Griffiths wrote to Briggs on August 3, 1835, and informed him that Wiseman had been staying with the London bishops for three weeks and was "in very good health." Bramston, on the same day, wrote to Bishop Penswick:

> I understand he [Wiseman] leaves London tomorrow for Prior Park. I had a very long conversation with him respecting his conduct with regard to our petition. I made him distinctly understand, not I think much to his satisfaction, though I spoke as mildly as the subject would permit, that I was entirely of the same opinion as your Lordship respecting his conduct with regard to our petition, and that I conceive that such conduct was the cause of His Holiness's displeasure, and of the unbecoming, because ill-tempered, answer of H. Holiness to our petition, written in his own hand and of which I presume Dr. Baines has, as he was commanded to do, sent a copy to your Lordship and the other prelates.[5]

Wiseman then set out for Prior Park, aware of the fact that both Bramston and Penswick were dissatisfied with his past conduct. Upon reaching the college, he found that Luigi Gentili had arrived a month ahead of him, having traveled to England in June, prepared now, with the blessing of Rosmini, his superior, to undertake the work that Baines had asked him to do earlier. He later became president of St. Paul's College at Prior Park, the position that the bishop had intended to offer Wiseman.

The visit also provided the occasion for a reunion of Wiseman with his friend Logan, who was no longer satisfied with conditions at the college. He had fallen out with Bishop Baines, who, he now concluded, failed to grasp the obstacles to be overcome in attempting to establish a university at Prior Park. In November 1834 Logan had written to Wiseman: "I am sorry to say and I do so with reluctance & sorrow that Dr. Baines is utterly unfit to project an efficient university & more so to carry any scheme into execution which requires the co-operation of other heads and hands. The former he will never trouble; the latter must work at his beck and nod or they will be placed under the ban of holy obedience." Wiseman, however, was still eager to work with Baines and unwilling to accept the unfavorable reports about the bishop that were rampant. He had written to Tandy in March, "Do not allow yourself to be drawn into any opinion about Dr. Baines; I am fully satisfied that he is in every particular a calumniated and shamefully injured man."[6] In his enthusiasm Wiseman himself soon crossed swords with Bishop Baines, innocently ignoring the fact that his station and reputation were insufficient to win him the right to express his opinions when they conflicted with those of the vicars apostolic and, above all, the bishop of Siga.

Bernard Ward concluded that the basis of their disagreement was Wiseman's resentment at being asked to take up his work at the college tentatively, without resigning his position in Rome.[7] The explanation is certainly an oversimplification, since both men understood that their original plan had been rejected not only by the Holy Father but by Bishop Penswick as well. It does seem to have been the case, however, that Baines judged Wiseman to have been irked when he discovered that the bishop was no longer prepared to follow through with his initial intention of pressing for the coadjutorship for the thirty-three-year-old rector.

Years later Wiseman described the occasion of their quarrel, recalling that he had been "devoted" to Baines "heart and soul" and that he had "lost favour at Rome by the manner in which I espoused his cause." He then explained:

> I saw in Prior Park the beginning of a new era for Catholic affairs, in education, in literature, in public position, and in many things which are now realities, and then were hopes. How was all this broken off? One cause of our separation is too painful for me to recite; but the decisive one was my unfortunately presuming on what I thought confidence, and offering advice when I thought it would be most useful. This produced such a rebuff as I had never received before, and never have since. It was by letter; but if my answer was preserved among the Bishop's papers, I should not mind all the world seeing it.[8]

Most probably the cause of separation that was "too painful" for Wiseman to discuss was based on the supposed or real alteration in the bishop's plans for him. The second may be pieced together easily by means of available documentation.

After stopping at Prior Park, Wiseman had visited the estate of John Talbot, sixteenth earl of Shrewsbury, at Alton Towers in North Staffordshire. His lordship was the most outstanding benefactor of the church in the 1830s and 1840s. He was always interested, and even meddlesome, when it came to the affairs of the vicars apostolic. While staying with Lord and Lady Shrewsbury, Wiseman was critical of much that he had found at Prior Park, and when this was reported to Baines, the bishop responded angrily.

Wiseman was prepared to defend himself and wrote to Bishop

Baines that he had always taken his side in previous disputes and that even before visiting Prior Park he had considered negotiations between them to be at an end. He was convinced that the bishop no longer intended to make use of him in the way that had been proposed initially. The younger man then acknowledged that he had observed a lack of order, discipline, and spirituality at Prior Park and that he had also noted the inadequate financial basis on which the institution had been established. He made it clear, moreover, that he sided with Logan, whose disagreement with Baines was reaching its climax. He went on to list more specific criticisms of religious practice at Prior Park, and his observations provide a good picture of what reforms he considered to be necessary.

> Now my own observation was this. I was at Prior Park seven Sundays (I believe) & one holiday, Aug. 15 [feast of the Assumption of the Blessed Virgin Mary], & every time said the comm[unity] mass. the number of students at the 1st about thirty & increased by the end to 80; from the 1st Sunday to the last there was not one single com[munion] except on the last day when 3 communicated. You will acknowledge that three communicants in the 8 feasts from an average of 50 students is not what wd. be expected in a college under ecclesiastical management; if Your Lordship doubts this statement I beg you will ask Gentili about it. I was at Oscott & there were about 40 communicants. I asked if there had been more than usual & was answered negatively. At Ushaw there had been the [sic] a general communion so that one of the superiors remarked to me casually on the Sat. night he wd. not have much to do; yet next day there were from 40 to 50 at communion and the Sunday following there were 90. On enquiry I was told that it was only as usual & at both places the number included every age down to the young boys & secular as well as church students.

Wiseman continued in this forthright manner, demonstrating, perhaps, more nerve than sense.[9]

Baines was not the man to take criticism lightly, much less from one inferior to himself in station and just thirty-three years old. Considering, moreover, the unfavorable impression that his conflicts with the regulars had created in Rome, he was unlikely to tolerate the interference of one whom he had personally invited to the college but who, for whatever reasons, now seemed to be proceeding as a Roman inquisitor.

Bishop Baines responded on November 10, and it was this letter, preserved in the archive of the Venerabile, that Wiseman said contained "a rebuff as I had never received before, and never have since." The bishop began as one hurt, rather than angry, by expressing his regret that Wiseman had written as he had, especially in view of "the high value I set upon and the pride I felt in the friendship of one of the most talented & most distinguished men of his day." Wiseman's comments were those, "I do not say of an enemy, but of an irritated man." He admitted proposing when Wiseman was at Prior Park that he be head of one of its colleges rather than the whole institution. In addition to St. Peter's College for the primary branches of education, Baines had established St. Paul's, intended for higher studies, ecclesiastical and secular, to supply for the lack of a Catholic university in England. He had proposed that Wiseman should be president of the latter.[10]

The bishop was convinced that his friend was hurt by what he considered a lesser offer than he had expected: "I am aware that to omit the conferring of an expected favour, and to inflict an injury are too often considered in the same light." He was not surprised, therefore, that the altered plan had been a disappointment, but it had been the Holy See's decision, not his own. Upon hearing that Wiseman was coming to England, the bishop had investigated whether Rome might have relented and whether the question of the coadjutorship might be reopened. When told that further application, at the time, would be "not only . . . vain, but injudicious," he had taken up a suggestion made by the Holy Father himself, by offering Wiseman the management of the new college, St. Paul's, expecting that he would retain, as well, the Roman rectorship: "It was with this view I made you the offer I did at Prior Park, being well aware at the time that in the event of your accepting the offer and accomplishing your predictions, it would be impossible for me to avoid, even if I had wished it, to endeavour to make you my coadjutor." Baines insisted, in fact, that he had decided that he would "retire altogether from Prior Park should I find the establishment succeeding in your hands, and that my presence was no longer wanted."

After offering his own defense, Baines moved on to his attack. It was Wiseman, he wrote, who had failed to carry out his promises and who had cooled in his earlier enthusiasm.

> Though I had not changed in my "earlier intentions" you had changed most strikingly your earlier conduct. You had formerly acted & I persuaded myself, felt towards me as a friend. Latterly you had not acted, nor I think, felt as such. You had lost no opportunity of letting me know how much you could do for me, although without an effort, but you also gave me very clearly to understand that the fulfilment of my "earlier intentions" was the only condition on which you would do it. You could raise 25,000 pounds in France any day — but you would not do it. You could do more in Germany but you would not do it. You could procure professors, and I requested you as a favour to do it as you came through Germany, but you did not do it. I requested from you some trifling assistance at Prior Park, which you acknowledged you could easily give but you would not give it. To every application I fancied that I recd. the same answer: "Fulfill your earlier intentions & then I will help you but not till then. Let me be sure of my reward before I merit it, because I have no confidence in your honor or your friendship."

Baines said that he had been willing to overlook all of this and to attribute it "to an ill-judged ardour in the pursuit of an object," but he had miscalculated. Wiseman, he claimed, "left Prior Park angry & disappointed," and "represented to some of those whose good opinion I valued most highly that my new college was deplorably conducted — in spirituals, in studies, in temporals." Many of the criticisms, wrote Baines, were without justification. Still others "were distorted & exaggerated in a way which is never used by a friendly or perhaps I ought rather to say by a dispassionate narrator."

All of this was strongly worded, but it was not all. Baines then asked Wiseman to consider himself in a similar situation in order to reflect on how he might respond: "Suppose that when I was last in Rome I had collected reports from your own disenchanted subjects & had told some distinguished family in Rome, (I will suppose the Shrewsbury family themselves) the following story." He then proceeded with a narrative that, although outrageously exaggerated, contained a number of observations which Wiseman would have recognized as having a basis in his administration of the English College.

I have been residing in the English College by Dr. W's obliging invitation, & therefore I speak from knowledge, as well as from authority. There is a deplorable want of discipline in the Eng. college. Some of the young men do not communicate at all regularly & none of them so often as they do in such and such colleges. There have been so many disorders that Dr. W. was obliged to expel I don't know how many, & the remainder, though he thinks otherwise, are by no means united or so satisfied with him as he imagines. Some of his best friends have had serious apprehensions that philosophy is more attended to in his college than piety. I have heard that the studies are ill managed, that the students are dispensed with half what the Italian students have and that instead of seeing that they learn the rest, Dr. W. is constantly engaged in giving them lectures on subjects which are little to the purpose, which few of them understand & which produce very little effect but to make them conceited — that it is much to be feared that their principles may be shaken by the new learning and the quantities of heterodox books which he puts into their hands, that as to rules, the college has literally none, those they had being lost, so that all is left to the absolute will of the rector who is not always of the same mind, and constantly out of the way — nay it not infrequently happens that the college is left without either rector or vice-rector, both being out at some dinner or evening party from which they do not return till a late hour at night, that of all the rectors in Rome, Dr. W. is the only one that is seen . . . at all the gay assemblies, that of course his expences are much increased by them and similar means, which may account for the college not maintaining more than two-thirds the numbers it did in Dr. Gradwell's time, that Dr. W. pretends that he has improved the farms, but the only improvement which can be seen is in his own apartments (which are very much improved) and in some of the galleries in adorning which he has spent great sums of money which "can make no return." Nay it has been whispered, to the great regret of some of his best friends, that certain of his own relatives have been somehow or other supported or endowed by him, and that he is making a private purse out of the means of the college by keeping in it a number of secular young men. But *this of course* is false.

It would not have been lost on Wiseman that his own cousin, Charles MacCarthy, had been among the small number of lay students who had resided at the college.

Baines continued:

> It is also regretted "by some of his best friends" that he allows the college to be inundated with ladies, several dashing young ladies having been seen strolling about the galleries and even coming from his own private apartments. There is not the smallest suspicion that Dr. W. himself means any harm by this, but it is a pity the ladies, if he admits any at all, should not be of a more matronly character, &c. &c. &c. But of all this say nothing till you get back to Alton. Then write to him a friendly letter of serious warning.

Lord Shrewsbury, in fact, had written such a letter to Baines with reference to Wiseman's charges. Now the bishop told Wiseman that if he had engaged in similar gossip with reference to the English College, he would have considered the rector to have had good reason to be angry: "In me such conduct would have made me despise myself as the basest of men, & therefore I have acted very differently, rejecting all such vile charges with indignation. In you a similar conduct, I am quite sure, is not base. Though what you have said of Prior Park is as injurious in itself & infinitely more so in its effects than the account given above of the English College. It is certainly not more true, nor in itself more friendly."

Baines concluded his letter by urging Wiseman to call upon him again so that they could "examine on the spot into the bulk of the statements given to you, and into the accuracy of the opinions you have formed." He would be happy, he said, to have the opportunity of convincing him of "my perfect forgiveness, as far as this is necessary, & of . . . [my] continued esteem & regard."

In a postscript Baines added that the students at Prior Park received communion about once a month, and that those in holy orders, not yet ordained to the priesthood, communicated weekly. During the vacation period, however, when their confessor was away, they were less regular. There were only four students at Prior Park who were in orders, and only one of these was there during Wiseman's visit. "In the other colleges which you visited, the vacations were over," he wrote, and then pointed out: "The number of advanced ecclesiastical students is much greater & their customs may be different. I said the community mass two Sundays ago and gave communion to almost all the boys & to all the others. I hope you will correct your statements by this information. If not you will wrong us grievously." He added that he had never "claimed a universal superiority for Prior Park over the other colleges. Dr. Briggs and Dr. Weedall [both having been college presidents, the first of Ushaw and the second of Oscott] can testify to this fact. In many respects I aspire only to become equal when I have been established as long." [11]

Wiseman did not return to Prior Park, nor is their evidence that he ever acknowledged that either his observations or his conduct had been incorrect. There was some further correspondence, and Baines, in fact, wrote graciously: "Your kind note of the 25th ult. gave me more pleasure than you will perhaps believe. I felt like a man who has recovered a treasure which he had lost and almost given up hopes of finding." He continued to criticize Wiseman, however, until his own death in 1843. It should be noted that by the time of Wiseman's arrival in England, the altercation between Bishop Baines and the Benedictines had been settled by arbitration, with a clear and unanimous verdict on the part of the judges that neither party was guilty of deliberate wrongdoing. [12]

Both Wiseman and Baines were responsible for their estrangement. It is unfortunate that the two men, both of them brilliant, and even farsighted, should have been unable to work together in a complementary way. In spite of his failings and the controversies in which he was chronically embroiled, Baines was the most talented of the vicars apostolic. He met more than his match, however, in Wiseman. The younger man was not single-handedly responsible for the interest in Catholic practice and doctrine that was already evident during his visit to England. He capitalized on it, however, and responded as no contemporary English Catholic could have done. Baines, less sanguine in his vision of the future prospect of the church there, but equally convinced of the necessity of nurturing a Catholic intellectual community, failed to take advantage, as Wiseman was willing to do, of the work already begun by others.

Baines, moreover, never appreciated the significance of the Oxford Movement, which began in 1833. It embraced characteristics of doctrine and devotion among Anglicans that could provide a basis for better understanding with Roman Catholics. Above all, like others of a previous generation, he rejected what he considered to be excessively emotional devotions, savoring, as he thought, too much of a Latin flavor. Yet this was the very time, as Wiseman understood, that a number of Anglicans were expressing interest in Catholic practices. It was the visit to the English College of John Henry Newman and Richard Hurrell Froude in 1833 that, according to Wiseman, first inspired his interest in the potential significance of a Catholic movement among a small group of Anglicans at Oxford: "From that moment it took the uppermost place in my thoughts, and became the object of their intensest interest."[13]

The first three *Tracts for the Times* were published in September 1833. By the time that Wiseman left England in 1836 to return to his duties in Rome, seventy-five tracts had been published, dealing with such topics as the apostolical succession, the obligation of primitive practice, the priesthood and episcopate, the liturgy, the visible church, mortification, the catholicity of the church, and the justification of Anglicanism as a *via media* between Rome and Protestantism. Wiseman later referred to Tractarianism as "that wonderful movement which, originating at Oxford, was destined to pervade and agitate the Anglican Establishment, till it should give up many of its most loving and gifted sons to the Catholic Church." He added that he "had been surprised, on visiting England in 1835, to find how little attention it had yet excited among Catholics, though many *Tracts for the Times* had already appeared."[14] Although one of his purposes in visiting England had ended in disappointment when it became painfully clear that he could no longer be of service to Bishop Baines, he continued enthusiastically and without apparent bitterness to investigate the state and prospects of religion throughout the country and to make his presence widely known.

After visiting Prior Park, Wiseman returned to London for a short time before setting out on a tour of the country. On the eve of his departure he wrote to Richard Monckton Milnes, later first Baron Houghton:

> My projects are as follows: in a few days, after I have made some further arrangements . . . about my publication, I set out on a species of tour, or rather *progress*, through England and Ireland, having made a resolution never to sleep in an inn or hostelry the whole way; but I intend to quarter myself upon such of the nobility or gentry of these realms as can sufficiently appreciate such an honour. My first station will be in the neighbourhood of Birmingham, and other Midland Cyclopean towns, where I have several short calls to make. Thence I proceed to the princely towers and enchanted gardens of Alton, and so forward to Sir E. Vavasour's where, if you are in the neighbourhood, I hope I may have the pleasure of seeing you. If you think this practicable, and any preliminary arrangements are necessary, you could let me know by a few lines under cover to Lord Shrewsbury at Alton, Ashbourne.[15]

It was during this trip, while staying at Alton, that Wiseman engaged in the conversations concerning Prior Park that so offended Bishop Baines. He had not yet returned again to London when he received the bishop's reproachful letter. Lord Shrewsbury's family estate attracted a number of those interested in furthering the cause of English Catholicism, some of whom Wiseman had come to know in Rome and who now found in him a ready and encouraging listener. Among them was Augustus Welby Pugin, gifted but intolerantly eccentric architect and avid promoter of the gothic revival, who had converted to Rome in 1834. Pugin was still an Anglican when Shrewsbury first met him, and the earl made use of the architect's talents not only in remodeling Alton Towers but also in the construction of a number of churches for which he provided the necessary funds.

In 1836 Pugin published the first edition of his most famous work, *Contrasts*, and, initially at least, he won the admiration of Wiseman, who later made use of him not only in designing chapels but also as professor of ecclesiastical art at Oscott. Wiseman was too devoted to Rome and its monuments, however, to endorse wholeheartedly Pugin's conviction that "every church that has been erected from St. Peter's at Rome downwards, are [sic] so many striking examples of the departure from pure Christian ideas and Architecture."[16]

Wiseman's visit to Alton Towers was also the occasion of a reunion with Daniel Rock, a former student at the Venerabile who in 1833 had become known as an able ecclesiologist when he published his *Hierurgia*. Rock was chaplain to Lord Shrewsbury and his family. His work did much to educate Englishmen on the mass and Roman liturgy.

Previously, while still in Rome, Wiseman had met Ambrose Phillipps, whose acquaintance he was now able to renew through the Shrewsburys. Known after 1862 as Phillipps de Lisle, this unusual young man had converted from Anglicanism to Roman Catholicism in 1824 when he was only fifteen. Two years later he went into residence at Trinity College, Cambridge, where, as a Catholic, he was unable to take his degree. While there, however, he became closely associated with Kenelm Digby, also a convert, who in 1831 published the first of eleven volumes of *Mores Catholici, or Ages of Faith* (1831–40).

Phillipps became one of the foremost proponents of gothic architecture. His father had given him the old family manor of Grace Dieu in Leicestershire, and he later called upon Pugin to decorate his domestic chapel. Phillipps also established the Cistercian Abbey of Mount St. Bernard on his property, and, in fact, it was in 1835 that the first members of that order arrived in England. In 1844, through the munificence (somewhat reluctant in this case) of Lord Shrewsbury, a new Pugin monastery was opened there. Phillipps, finally, was a lifelong advocate of the cause of Christian unity.[17]

There was much to encourage the observant visitor, then, as he looked for means of fostering the Catholic revival in England. Even at Prior Park, although Wiseman could not cooperate personally in what was being achieved, Luigi Gentili was not idle. His biographer has described his ultimate contribution.

In spite of all his difficulties, Gentili had transformed the religious outlook of Prior Park; he had introduced, against fierce opposition, many Catholic practices that were universally approved outside England; he had done much to raise the outlook and spirituality of those who were studying for the priesthood; he had cultivated devotion to our Lady and shown it to be an integral part of Catholic life, private and public, and he had encouraged frequent Communion and frequent confession.[18]

Gentili was later critical of Wiseman, whom he considered to be a showman, but the two men, while at Prior Park, must have discussed the needs of the church in England. Their ultimate goals were not dissimilar.

Much of the religious activity that attracted Wiseman was centered in the Midland District. He was clearly interested, therefore, when, after his disagreement with Baines, Bishop Thomas Walsh began a long series of overtures to attract him to his district. In the spring of 1836, while Wiseman was still in England, Walsh wrote to him: "I must once more request you to tell me most candidly whether I am *quite free to* make application to Rome for you as coadjutor in the Midland District & whether Doctor Baines has distinctly signified to you that he has quite resigned all claim to you from a prior postulation."[19]

Walsh had reason to be cautious, since all of the vicar apostolics, especially Baines, tended to resent him for the encouragement that he gave to religious orders and for his willingness to pursue an independent course of action. The Midland bishop, however, while anxious to avoid antagonizing his episcopal brethren, was equally concerned with grasping every opportunity to advance religion in his district. He had the advantage of Lord Shrewsbury's presence there and so benefited, more than the others, from a generous source of income. In 1835 Walsh had begun building a new Oscott College in Birmingham to serve both as a seminary and as a school for lay students. His plans were less elaborate than those of Baines at Prior Park, but his prospects were more promising. Both Cambridge and Oxford were in the Midland District, moreover, making the new college an excellent center for the work that more and more attracted Wiseman to England. Walsh was more open to devotional innovation than Baines was; he was also a self-effacing man, less likely to upstage Wiseman than was the case with the vicar apostolic of the Western District. Wiseman was unprepared to rush into another commitment, however. There were other possibilities to be tested.

After his round of visits, Wiseman returned to London where he stayed with his friend Henry Bagshawe, a prominent Catholic lawyer. Wiseman contributed his services to the Sardinian Chapel in Lincoln's Inn Fields, one of the embassy chapels serving the Catholics of the area and beyond. He preached in Italian each Sunday to the immigrant congregation that lived nearby. During Advent, moreover, he experimented by giving a series of lectures on the Catholic faith to an audience of Protestants as well as Catholics. The effect of these talks exceeded his most optimistic expectations. He described his London activities in a letter to Tandy.

I was meditating an epistle to you when I received yours. I have also been thinking of paying Dr. Walsh my visit during the holidays, as the museum is then closed [Tandy was at Oscott]. At present I am there writing from 10 till 4, and hope to be soon in print. . . . I have two lectures every week; and I am there trying what I have so long wished to try, to bring into the pulpit & try the effect of close hermeneutical examination, and the strict methods of philological criticism which I have so long followed, though censured by many for it. The effect has been 1000 times beyond my expectations. The chapel is crowded to suffocation, every seat is occupied half an hour before the compline and if it were 3 times as large it would be full. I have never preached less than an hour & a half, generally 1 & 3/4, yet no one has found it long, nor has attention once flagged. Last week I treated of church authority, and this of the real presence, next week, the supremacy & indulgences &c. The common people say they can follow every word & that I "make them quite sensible." The priests come in shoals & they & all the congregation tell me that the whole system & the form of argument throughout is quite new to them all. Indeed they insist that I should stay till Lent & give a fuller course, but this is out of the question. Nay, *entre nous* for I write to you as a friend, they say I ought not to go back. But I am thus *vainly* full with you, because it will convince you of what I have often said, that the method I have followed in school was as applicable to a congregation, if simplified & reduced to a popular form, & in this I always thought I could succeed. Every one agrees that a most successful experiment has been made, and that proof has been given of the interest which may be thrown round the Catholic doctrines, by a little exertion.

At the request of Bishop Bramston, Wiseman did repeat the lectures, during Lent, at St. Mary's Moorfields, a church that served as "cathedral" for London Catholics. As predicted, the church was packed for each lecture.[20]

In the fall of 1835 Döllinger wrote to Wiseman and expressed his regret that Lingard and other English scholars had not learned German and so were unable to profit by the historical works in that language. English Catholics, he observed, were suffering from "a sort of literary apathy and inactivity." Yet they were continually under attack, "and, if I mistake not, your numerous adversaries take too much advantage of your silence." He asked, "Are there no persons of literary pursuits among your Catholic clergy who are capable and inclined to study our theological literature of the last years?"[21]

Wiseman saw himself as able to achieve what Döllinger suggested. With this in mind, he arranged for the publication of two series of lectures that he had delivered in Rome, one on the real presence in the Eucharist, the second on the connection between science and revealed religion.[22] Wiseman anticipated that the books might draw criticism. His readiness to make use of the then available tools of biblical criticism and his presentation of unfamiliar illustrations to substantiate his arguments might well be misunderstood by more traditional Catholic apologists in England. "His [the author's] studies have, perhaps, led him into a different view of the arguments from what is popularly taken," wrote Wiseman in one preface, "and he may be found to have sought illustrations from sources not commonly consulted; but he will leave it to his reader to determine whether he has thereby weakened the cause which he has undertaken."[23]

In his first lecture on the Eucharist, Wiseman explained his understanding of the science of hermeneutics and its significance.

> The sum of all these remarks is, that, if we wish to understand an author — for instance, the New Testament — we must transport ourselves from our age and country, and place ourselves in the position of those whom our Saviour or his disciples addressed. We must understand each phrase just as they must have done; we must invest ourselves with their knowledge, their feelings, habits, opinions, if we wish to understand the discourses which were addressed primarily and immediately to them. This we will attempt in the lectures which will be addressed to you on the Real Presence. We will sift every phrase, when necessary, till we discover the exact ideas which it must have conveyed to the Jews or the Apostles; and for this purpose, we must enter into minute and detailed reasoning — from parallel passages, from the genius of the language used, from the context, and every other philological source within our reach. . . . Proceeding thus by a perfectly analytical method, when we have discovered a signification for a text, which alone can be reconciled with all these data, I shall feel justified in concluding that signification to be the *only* true one.[24]

Modern exegetes may well smile at the ambitious goal that Wiseman claimed to be his. Even though his work was marked by self-confidence, however, it lacked the polemical overtones that characterized so much of the writing of English Catholics in his day. Consequently his books and articles were received favorably in many quarters. For example, John Henry Newman concluded a review of Wiseman's work in the *British Critic* (December 1836) by stating, "Romanism has great truths in it, which we of this day have almost forgotten, and its preachers will recall numbers of Churchmen and Dissenters to an acknowledgment of them."[25]

Although many of Wiseman's conclusions and even his methodology are outdated today, his contribution was of immense value. He presented his material positively and, in spite of his unmistakable erudition, clearly. Catholic truth, he was convinced, would sell itself by its consistency and reasonableness, if put forward in the manner that he chose as his own. London Catholics, especially appreciative of his achievement, had a medal struck in his honor. On one side was his own likeness; on the other were a papal tiara, St. Peter's keys, a chalice, and other objects of devotion, all placed before a shining cross. The legend around the design was an acknowledgment of Wiseman's eloquence in strongly yet gently vindicating the ancient religion.[26]

Nevertheless, Wiseman was accurate in predicting that there might be those who would fail to appreciate his procedure. When his lectures on the Real Presence were published in 1836, he sought a critique from Frederick Husenbeth, who replied, "I may say that a careful perusal of it [the book] has given me very great satisfaction." He continued, "It is not easy after all that the erudition and ingenuity of three centuries have poured out upon that adorable mystery, to find any thing new to say upon it; but you have certainly treated it in a new manner, I think, with marked success and have found some novel corroborating arguments of great value."[27]

Husenbeth was less than enthusiastic in his appreciation of Wiseman's methodology, however, and a week later, writing to an acquaintance of his impressions of the *Lectures on the Principal Doctrines and Practices of the Catholic Church*, he said that he had read the first three and last three lectures.

> They do not please me by a great deal. His [Wiseman's] explanation of the Catholic Rule of Faith [the first lecture] is not only very encumbered and unsatisfactory; but it appears to me to lay him open to the very objection which he exposes in the Protestant Rule, — he makes our only certainty of the authority of the Church depend upon our interpretation of certain parts of Scripture which we believe to establish that authority. It is not the old vicious circle, because he takes the Bible first as a mere human, but true book: still the objection remains. A Protestant would tell him that he had no means of proving the authority of his Church but his own arbitrary interpretation of certain tracts of Scripture. But on other grounds these Lectures have displeased and disappointed me. The style is artificial, stultified and obscure; the language harsh and unintelligible to the multitude. Popular Lectures cannot be rendered too plain and easy, consistently with correct and respectable language. I question if these will do any extensive good.[28]

There was justification for Husenbeth's criticism of Wiseman's literary style, although it improved after he had lived in England for some years. Wilfrid Ward wrote that Wiseman's "style was at times florid and overcharged with imagery. This defect was little noticed in

Rome, but it became the theme of hostile criticism in later years when he had taken up his residence in England." Ward attributed the defect to the fact that Wiseman was in the habit of speaking and writing in a number of languages and that this "inevitably damaged both the force and the correctness of his English."[29]

Husenbeth was less justified in his view of Wiseman's method. The Roman authorities, ready enough to seize upon passages of questionable orthodoxy, joined in praising his achievement, an indication, surely, that his procedure was, at the very least, acceptable. Wiseman himself doubted the orthodoxy of much of John Lingard's *New Versions of the Four Gospels*, which was published the same year as his own lectures on the Eucharist. The historian, influenced by the enlightenment and the principle of historicity, tended to presume too much on the basis of reason alone, including the limitations of Christ's human knowledge. While both men hoped to elucidate the Scriptures, making them more understandable for English Catholics, Wiseman was more prepared than Lingard to draw his conclusions from tradition.[30]

Wiseman responded to Husenbeth's criticism by denying that his lectures were beyond the comprehension of those who had listened to them: "They were addressed to an audience on the whole highly respectable, and to all appearance able to understand them, and therefore I did not feel it necessary to take so simple a manner as I otherwise should have done. But at the same time I had a large proportion of poor, who yet stood out the longest of the Discourses, apparently without much fatigue." From across the Atlantic, Wiseman received the commendation of the future archbishop of St. Louis, Peter Kenrick: "I must candidly tell you that the reading of your various writings has revived a desire I once was possessed of — of acquiring an acquaintance with oriental literature, and of using my little influence to have Hebrew, at least, taught in our Seminaries."[31]

Wiseman was as convinced as ever that a journal was needed with a wider appeal than the *Catholic Magazine*, which, according to Bernard Ward, "was never meant to be read by others than Catholics, and never in fact penetrated beyond that body."[32] Moreover the editorial policy of that journal represented the Anglo-Catholic, or as it was often called, the Cisalpine attitude, of another generation, in spite of the learned articles that the editors were sometimes willing to include within its pages.

During his extended visit to London, Wiseman was approached by Michael Quin, originally of Thurles, Ireland, who now practiced law in England. Quin invited him to enter into an arrangement as joint proprietor of a new journal. The two men, along with Daniel O'Connell, founded the *Dublin Review*, and two issues were published in May and July 1836, before Wiseman returned to Rome. This was the opportunity that Wiseman had been waiting for. His aim was, according to Wilfrid Ward, "to depict both for English Catholics themselves and for an inquiring age the 'genius of Christianity' in its Catholic form" as well as "to exhibit to the more candid representatives of English thought the variety and elasticity of Catholicism (as he viewed it), and the power of its organisation." He wanted to avoid controversies, especially among Catholics, an obvious challenge because of O'Connell's radical views in promoting the repeal of the union between England and Ireland. Wiseman's one condition, therefore, before entering into the project, was that the journal should refrain from taking up "extreme political views."[33]

Wiseman contributed a short, perceptive article to the first issue in which he treated the Oxford controversy surrounding the appointment of R. D. Hampden as Regius Professor of Divinity. To those who opposed Hampden, considering him to be an exponent of the antidogmatic principle associated with religious liberalism, Wiseman argued that, within the Established Church, Hampden's views were as acceptable as their own. The fact that the appointment evoked little episcopal opposition lent weight to the observation. Wiseman then wrote:

> We [Catholics] are not chimerical in our views, nor over sanguine in our expectations; but we are confident that if the divines who have censured Dr. Hampden would calmly look upon their principles, without the dread of popery in their hearts to stifle better feeling, if they would fearlessly pursue their own doctrines to their furthest consistent conclusions, they would surely find that they have unguardedly, perhaps unknowingly, rejected the principles of the Reformation, and returned to thoughts and feelings which belong to other times, or at least to another Church.

Wiseman invited discussion between Roman Catholics and members of the so-called High Church party: "Let us . . . gird up our loins, and contend together in a friendly spirit."[34]

It was this "friendly spirit," in fact characteristic of Wiseman's treatment of Tractarian principles, that made his writings more acceptable to the Oxford divines than those of the vast majority of his fellow Catholics. When his articles on the Oxford Movement were republished in 1853 in the second of his three volumes of *Essays on Various Subjects*, a reviewer in the *Rambler* wrote, "Intellectual good nature, that kindliness which is generally found in combination with the highest order of mind, extreme fairness to the adversary, even to the extent here and there, at least to the unpractised eye, of risking too much, and, above all, sincere and genuine charity and zeal for souls, pervade every page of these volumes."[35] While rejecting Wiseman's arguments, Anglicans would not fail to see that the tone of his writings was unlike that of most Catholic polemicists.

By cooperating in the establishment of the *Dublin Review*, Wiseman lost the support of the editors of the *Catholic Magazine*, who, in fact, discontinued publication of their journal. They refused to accept a complimentary copy of the new review, a rudeness that Wiseman said was "quite unprecedented in the profession, as the most hostile journals exchange without any compromise being thereby implied or any approbation." "I should be sorry to think," he wrote to Husenbeth, "that any pique should have arisen from the establishment of the Dublin R. as the Magazine had formally declared that it would give way the moment a more extensive periodical should appear in London. Indeed, I do not see how one should interfere with the other."[36]

At first the *Dublin Review* was plagued with financial problems as well as those involved in securing and maintaining a suitable editor.[37] Soon after its foundation, Quin retired from the editorship. The third number of the journal was brought out by Mark Tierney, chaplain, since 1824, to the duke of Norfolk and recognized as a gifted historian. Tierney was a friend of Lingard's and shared his views. Beginning in 1837 Wiseman's friend Henry Bagshawe served as editor. His work was primarily managerial. Charles Russell of Maynooth served as *de facto* literary editor, without the formal title, while contributing a number of articles.

In addition to alienating the editors of the *Catholic Magazine*, Wiseman also offended Mark Tierney, who, it seems, had hoped for the permanent editorship of the new journal. Tierney's close friend, Father Thomas Doyle, complained that Bagshawe was little qualified for the editorship.[38] Wiseman, back in Rome, also received a long letter from J. Chisholm Anstey, a recent convert who was on the threshold of a legal and political career in London. Anstey was himself a frequent contributor to the *Dublin Review*. In March 1837 he informed Wiseman of Doyle's attempts to secure the editorship for Tierney. Doyle had "declared . . . that without a priest at its head he had no confidence in the Review and would take measures to 'put it down,' and that he always lamented that you [Wiseman] had ever been connected with it." Anstey described what he called *"a phalanx of the clergy"* in London who shared that same view.[39]

Finally, J. B. Robertson, the historian and a regular contributor to the *Dublin Review*, also wrote to plead Tierney's cause. He was less sure of his fellow antiquarian's qualifications than others, however, and he suggested that Wiseman, even while living in Rome, should be practical editor: "I frankly declare, I do not think the Dublin Review will obtain a high literary eminence, a very extensive circulation, or the entire confidence of the Catholic clergy, unless you be associated with him [Tierney] in the editorship of that journal."[40]

Tierney was, nevertheless, rejected. The wisdom of the decision ought not to be questioned. He had little sympathy, then or later, with the pro-Roman spirit that Wiseman hoped to instill into English Catholicism. The failure to make use of him in some capacity, however, may have been a tactical blunder. Until Tierney died in 1862, he was one of Wiseman's most vocal opponents in the ranks of the English clergy.

Immediately after his return to Italy in September 1836, Wiseman went to the college villa at Monte Porzio for a few days of rest. He then visited his sister at Fano and, as he wrote to Tandy, found her "happy, and expecting to increase the number of the inhabitants of this earth in the course of a few weeks." His stay at Fano was very brief. There had been tales of laxity at the college as a result of his absence, and it was imperative that he resume his duties immediately.

Wiseman found college affairs "terribly neglected," although not to the extent that some had claimed. He knew that the students were well disposed, but he complained that "unfortunately there is hardly one whose abilities give me any hope of distinction." He continued his letter to Tandy by stating that he could not rid himself of the desire to return to England.

> For my part I am almost sick of going perpetually over the same round with so little profit or fruit in return for the trouble I take. England has done not a little to spoil me for Rome. After having seen nothing around me for so many months but faces that welcomed me, and met such unvarying kindness and cordiality on every side, so much friendship from Catholics and so much respect from Protestants, but still more, after having seen the immense good that is to be done there and feeling a consciousness that it is in my power to cooperate towards it, you will imagine it must be a painful change, to return to the society of discontented young men, and suspicious Italians, the former at least *in posse*, and the latter *in esse*.

He concluded, "However for the present I must do my duty, but every day makes me feel more & more that *I must* return to England."[41]

Wiseman had been severely rebuked by the vicar apostolic of London; quarreled with Bishop Baines, to whom he had looked previously as a patron; antagonized a number of others, including the editors of the *Catholic Magazine*; and alarmed still others through his promotion of devotions that were viewed as too Italian for English sensibilities. He had good reason, nevertheless, to congratulate himself for his successes. He had established friendships with the leading Roman Catholics in the country, many of whom entered fully into his views; he had preached and lectured with noteworthy success; he had seen to the publication of three series of lectures, which, he anticipated, would do much good; he had earned the goodwill of a number of non-Catholics; he had cooperated in the establishment of a journal, a dream that he had cherished for many years; and he had secured the support of the vicar apostolic of the Midland District, who intended to make every effort to obtain him as coadjutor. Wiseman, in August 1836, had just turned thirty-four years of age.

5. The Vicars Apostolic and the Holy See

A FTER HIS LONG VISIT TO ENGLAND, WISEMAN NEVER AGAIN DOUBTED that it was there he was meant to offer his talents in the service of the church. Although unfriendly criticisms were reported to him from time to time, they failed to dampen his enthusiasm or self-confidence. Of course he could not have failed to realize that the vicars apostolic, with the exception of Bishop Walsh, were dissatisfied with his performance as their Roman agent. Soon after he returned to Rome, he received a letter from William Riddell, formerly a student at the English College and later to be a bishop, who wrote that John Briggs, the vicar apostolic of the Northern District, seemed "very uneasy or dissatisfied at present with the state of Roman affairs, both as to the college & the agency." Briggs had heard rumors of insubordination among the students, and he was afraid that the college, if badly managed, would be turned over to the Jesuits. "I partially satisfied Dr. B. (I believe) that your personal weight in Rome would prevent the evil consequences he apprehended," wrote Riddell, but he went on to warn Wiseman that the bishop was not satisfied that the students were receiving sufficient practical instruction to prepare them for work in England. He was concerned, moreover, with the delays in transacting business with the Holy See, a problem that he attributed to Wiseman's neglect of his office. Briggs himself wrote to Bishop Griffiths at the end of the year to suggest that at their next meeting the vicars apostolic should discuss the possibility of communicating more directly with the pope, thus "restricting the manner in which we are situated as to our employing an agent at Rome."[1]

The previous summer, Cardinal Giacomo Fransoni, prefect of Propaganda, had complained of the manner in which the English bishops carried on their business with the Holy See. He told them that they should deal directly with the Sacred Congregation for the Propagation of the Faith, not through an intermediary or a procurator. When the vicars sought a clarification of the directive, they were informed that they were not forbidden to have a procurator or agent in Rome, but that his duty was to amplify and clarify their correspondence with Propaganda.[2] Wiseman, in fact, continued to act as agent, but never to the universal satisfaction of the bishops.

Among the matters that had to be negotiated between the vicars apostolic and the Holy See, none was more pressing than the necessity of reorganizing ecclesiastical structures in England. The bishops were clearly overworked, and their priests were increasingly expressing dissatisfaction. The *Catholic Magazine*, in the autumn of 1833, published a letter proposing that the time was ripe for the restoration of a Roman Catholic hierarchy. The correspondent stated that in his travels throughout the country he had met many priests who longed for the step. The following month the principal article in the journal asserted that with a properly constituted hierarchy for the three kingdoms, "uniformity might be established throughout, as to discipline and to practices of devotion and instruction, the want of which is severely felt through this part of the empire."[3]

Not everyone agreed that the move was expedient. More than a year later another correspondent in the *Catholic Magazine* argued that it would increase bigotry throughout the country: "Protestant England is certainly not prepared for an event, which many zealous Catholics have contemplated; and, while the hostile impression last, any effort to induce the apostolic See to close with the proposal would unquestionably fail." He offered an alternative proposal, recommending that the number of bishops should be increased. Each district might be divided into three parts, so that instead of four bishops, there would be twelve, who "might not inaptly be called the Twelve Apostles of England." The discussion was still going on when Wiseman arrived in England in 1835, one man expressing his hope that he might "live to see the happy day, when the ancient discipline of the Catholic church shall be again established in this country, consisting of bishops in ordinary, with their respective chapters, grand vicars, and archdeacons."[4]

In the autumn of 1837 the clergy of Northumberland and Durham sent a petition to Bishop Briggs asking that all future candidates to the episcopate might be elected by the clergy whom they would govern. They also sought the division of the Northern District, "that the interests of religion may be more immediately under the eye of the Bishop, who would thereby be freed from labour universally acknowledged at present to be too great." Two months later a meeting of fourteen clergymen in Leeds prepared a series of resolutions that they sent to Briggs, asking for a change in their ecclesiastical administration. They, too, said that it was expedient that the number of bishops should be increased and that the clergy should have a voice in the election of their bishops. Finally, in February 1837 a similar petition was addressed to the pope and a copy sent to Briggs.[5]

The northern vicar apostolic was under pressure. It is not surprising that the first united demands for ecclesiastical reorganization should have originated in his district. Since its establishment in the seventeenth century, cities and towns such as Manchester, Liverpool, Leeds, and Newcastle had become increasingly important, and the number of Catholics was growing rapidly. With industrialization and population growth, the clergy found themselves dealing with problems unlike those of any previous period.[6] To compound the difficulty, the religious orders, better organized and equipped than the secular clergy, were taking initiatives that seemed to be threatening the control of the vicars apostolic.

The bishops met in January 1837 and agreed to prepare a plan for reorganizing their districts. They decided to discuss it at their next scheduled meeting in April 1838. Almost immediately afterward, however, Wiseman wrote to Bishop Griffiths to state that there were those in Rome who wondered whether the vicariates would be divided. Propaganda, reported Wiseman, wanted any proposal to come from the bishops themselves. He added that there was reason to believe that the pope was even prepared to support the restoration of a hierarchy, although the Propaganda secretary said that the sacred congregation had never discussed the step and that it would have to be considered very seriously because of possible opposition from the British government. He assured Wiseman, however, that "it would meet with no opposition here, as Rome ever considered Vicars Apostolic only in the light of a temporary arrangement when Bishops could not be established, but a hierarchy as the true normal government of the Church."

Wiseman continued by stating that he had gone to see the Holy Father, who spoke with him for an hour about the Church in England, including the proposal to increase the districts. Bishop Walsh was on the point of visiting Rome, a fact that pleased the Holy Father, who expressed the wish that every English bishop would make it his regular practice to visit the Holy See as the Irish and Americans did. Wiseman suggested that the pope would be pleased were the London vicar apostolic to accompany Bishop Walsh on his visit.[7]

The following month Cardinal Weld wrote to Bishop Briggs, "We have heard much here from England on the necessity of dividing some of the Districts in that country, but nothing has come officially on the subject before the Sacred Congregation de Propaganda fide." The Roman authorities were anxiously awaiting the visit of Walsh and Griffiths, the latter having decided to take Wiseman's advice, but Weld concluded that there was "no immediate propsect of the arrival of either." He said, finally, that Briggs also should travel to Rome: "It would not be right to make a division of your District, till you had had an opportunity of fully expressing your sentiments upon it."[8]

The vicars apostolic were prepared for changes. They did not approve, however, of the nature of the petitions that were being circulated. Bishop Briggs complained of the one that had been addressed to the pope: "Who has heard of vicars ap. being elective? Has not His Holiness the sole power of appointing his vicars? Can he safely consent to this proposed assignment and divide with the missioners of England this power of appointing his vicars?" He added, "Who can tell how this plan would work, especially as the electors, being missionaries only, could not be protected from annoyance as parish priests who are movable only for a canonical fault."[9]

Bishop Walsh, like Briggs, was overwhelmed with the demands made upon him. He wrote to the vicar apostolic of the Northern District in January 1837: "I shall probably propose a greater number than five districts. I am inclined to apply for a division of my district into two, to be called the Midland & the Eastern District. I have had no application to this effect from my clergy, but I am of opinion that religion would be much promoted by such division." Walsh added, "There seems so much ignorance at Rome of our difficulties & labour on the English mission that it appears to me quite evident we should have an English ecclesiastic for our agent at Rome."[10]

Bishop Griffiths, nearly three months later, wrote to Walsh, "They have no knowledge in Rome of our numerous occupations, and of the little assistance we can command." The implication of his remark, of course, was that their agent in Rome, Wiseman, was not providing the authorities with adequate information. Griffiths urged Walsh to obtain the services of a secretary, adding that he himself "could not get through business in any way without one."[11]

Walsh and Griffiths agreed that by visiting Rome they would be able to provide the authorities with an accurate picture of the state of Catholicism in England. Prior to their departure Griffiths warned, "An attempt to change the ecclesiastical government in this country is beginning at the wrong end and may lead to confusion and divisions among the English Catholics." By going to Rome, the two bishops "would place the affair in the proper hands."[12] Together they left England on April 13, 1837.

It had become evident to Bishop Walsh that it would not be wise for the bishops to wait another full year before meeting, in some way, the demands of those who were proposing changes. He suggested that if his own district were to be divided, he would turn over to Wiseman the

Midland, "or flourishing part, containing the new college, all the convents, &c." It was imperative, he wrote, that Wiseman should be *"in the neighbourhood of the new College* [Oscott]." He opposed the establishment of a hierarchy, however, since "it would be quite inexpedient to have parish priests with the immunities of regular parish priests in the barren parts of ecclesiastical England." Walsh was sensitive to the complaints of priests who resented the ease with which they could be transferred from one mission to another. In areas where hierarchical government was established, church law provided for the appointment of irremovable pastors, that is, those whose transfer could take place only for serious and specific canonical offense. Frequent changes, some members of the clergy argued, often resulted in poverty for the priests themselves, an inability to know and understand their congregations, the interruption of important work, and even scandal among the laity, who considered removal of their priests to be the result of wrongdoing.[13] On the other hand, in a period characterized by rapidly changing population patterns, as Walsh understood, there were advantages in being able to transfer priests as current circumstances might demand.

By 1837 Bishop Baines was even more anxious than his colleagues for ecclesiastical changes. He told Griffiths that the immediate addition of a single district was desirable. Although he recognized that certain problems would have to be discussed, especially those relating to the division of students and temporalities belonging to the colleges, Baines did not consider the difficulties to be "either insuperable or very difficult to overcome." In any case they were "not at all commensurate with the immense advantages which would result to religion in England *generally* from a better division of the Districts, which the addition of a fifth would, I trust, occasion." He was prepared for the immediate restoration of the hierarchy and thought that the measure should "be strongly pressed upon His Holiness, now that he seems disposed to receive the application favorably." It was his conviction that the Holy See should only allow the vicars apostolic to determine "the *manner how*, not the *time when*, for if left to ourselves I think we might be more sluggish in the business than is desirable." By May, however, Baines warned Griffiths, "I do not expect that you will find the Pope so prepared for the changes in our ecclesiastical government as Dr. Wiseman's letter to you to suppose."[14]

In the course of their journey to Rome, Bishops Walsh and Griffiths received word that Cardinal Weld had died. The loss was serious. Only Wiseman remained to accompany them in their various interviews and to serve as interpreter. They arrived in Rome on May 13 and soon afterward met both the prefect and secretary of Propaganda. They were received briefly by the Holy Father on May 20, but it was not until June 12 that they were able to discuss their affairs with him.[15]

His Holiness received the English bishops warmly and supported the prefect and secretary of Propaganda in the view that the vicars apostolic should meet in the spring to plan for the division of their districts. It would be left to them, wrote Griffiths, "to make whatever other arrangements relative to the election of future VV.A. & the government of the clergy they may judge necessary." The London bishop continued this letter to Bishop Briggs: "I hope our visit will tend to quiet any movement in your Lordship's district." He concluded, "The affair is now, as it ought to be, between His Holiness and the vicars apostolic." Bishop Baines had been correct, however, in his fear that the pope would not approve the restoration of the hierarchy at that time.[16]

While in Rome, Bishop Walsh formally requested the assistance of Wiseman as his coadjutor.[17] Griffiths warned Briggs of the request and added a detail that was bound to confirm the suspicion with which the other bishops viewed Walsh.

> The circumstance which you should know is that he [Walsh] has deemed it necessary to exculpate Dr. Wiseman from the *fault* of having presented the petition of the VV.A. of England to His Holiness, and if he has followed the same line of argument with them as he mentioned to me, he has effected it by observing that though the authorized agent of the VV.AA., Dr. Wiseman delayed its presentation for some days — did not present it in person — & was blamed by his Bishop for his behaviour in the whole affair. I want your Lordship to be aware of this circumstance *for your own guidance only*, and therefore write this letter in strict confidence.

Griffiths, as a matter of fact, had discussed with the Holy Father the petition that had so offended the pontiff: "The Pope complained of the joint letter of the Vicars Apostolic on the subject of St. John's Wood, etc., but particularly of the silence of Bishops Bramston and Penswick when he had answered it." The bishop explained that Bramston had been suffering his final illness and added that the vicars apostolic had never been guilty of complaining of "private acts of His Holiness." Griffiths concluded that Gregory XVI "appeared satisfied."[18]

It became clear to Bishop Walsh that he would not succeed in obtaining Wiseman as his coadjutor at that time, and he withdrew his petition.[19] A year later, still eager to have Wiseman in the Midland District, Walsh wrote to him.

> This day of the month last year I was preparing to leave Rome after a two months' visit, which, from the disappointments I met with, was far from being gratifying. *My object* in undertaking the journey was to see Cardinal Weld, to benefit the New College, but chiefly to obtain you for coadjutor. It pleased the Almighty to remove the dear Cardinal from this state of trial before I entered the Eternal City. I obtained nothing for the

New College. I was unable to obtain you for my coadjutor. On this latter point I was so intent that my visits to the Pope & to the Cardinals were mainly for the purpose. I was as urgent on the subject without succeeding that I left Rome with the impression that His Holiness & the Cardinals in general were not for some cause or other so very favorably inclined to me.

Walsh remained persistent, adding, "With you, my dear Dr. Wiseman, to assist me & to give lectures at the New College, all would go on well. What have I done to displease His Holiness or the Cardinals which prevented me from carrying my points?"[20]

It was most unlikely that the good bishop had done anything to offend the Roman authorities. It is far more probable that the pope and cardinals, fully aware of the unsettled state of the church in England and the obvious need for reorganization and cognizant, too, that Wiseman was unpopular in some quarters, decided to defer any final decisions until the vicars apostolic themselves were able to reach more substantial agreement on the course to be followed. No new bishops were appointed until 1840, in spite of the fact that previous vicars apostolic had customarily been assigned coadjutors of their own choosing. Since the coadjutors normally succeeded their superiors, it was this very procedure which the priests found so objectionable and led them to request that they might participate in the selection of vicars apostolic.

Bishops Walsh and Griffiths arrived home in August. They decided it would be best to avoid any undue speculation that might arise if the vicars apostolic were to assemble prior to the time already announced for their next meeting, to be held at York in April. After they left Rome, Wiseman wrote to Briggs, "I think all agitation must come to an end even if the results of the Bishops' journey to Rome should not become publicly known. At any rate," he continued, "any appeal to Rome will do no good to the parties that make it, as nothing will be listened to that does not come through the Vicars Apostolic."[21]

The vicars apostolic moved slowly in preparing the plans that they were expected to discuss at their spring meeting. Bishop Briggs was losing patience when, in November, he wrote to Griffiths for further information than he had received from Rome. Two months later Griffiths finally responded, but he wrote nothing that Briggs did not know already. He concluded by stating "that the Holy See wishes the arrangement for the future ecclesiastical government of England to originate with the VV.A., whose situation & responsibility best qualify them for the office of forming those arrangements."[22]

After another two months Griffiths wrote that he had consulted several of his clergy "under secrecy" and that "no two have thought alike, though most agree that a change of some kind is desirable." The bishop himself was of the opinion that there should be bishops-in-ordinary with an archbishop at their head "because clergy & laity desire it, regulations & duties could be more easily enforced, religion would gain in splendor & notoriety, and if deferred, government may perhaps interfere later in the nomination of our Bishops." The pope, of course, was opposed to the measure, but Griffiths concluded that the Holy Father's "reasons, . . . with all respect, should prompt us to adopt the change at present, as every thing would be quietly arranged whilst the government pays no attention to our names or duties."

Griffiths proposed that they should retain the title of vicars apostolic but do everything possible to assimilate the government of their districts to that of bishops-in-ordinary. He prepared detailed suggestions for organization, including, in addition to an archbishop, a vicar general and eight or ten deaneries for each district. He also outlined a method of selecting future bishops that would have included some voice on the part of the vicar general and deans.[23]

The vicars apostolic met in York, at the home of Bishop Briggs, from April 23 to May 4, 1838. They passed a resolution in favor of increasing the number of the vicariates but stated that the step "must needs be postponed for a time until certain obstacles have either been removed or come to an end." The major difficulty, not mentioned specifically in the minutes, seems to have been the lack of funds necessary to support new bishops and the administrative machinery that the change would entail.[24]

The vicars apostolic then proceeded to draw up what have come to be known as "Statuta Provisoria," statutes to be submitted for the approval of the Holy See concerning their ecclesiastical government. The document affirmed the right of the vicars apostolic to nominate men for ecclesiastical offices in their districts and provided for a vicar general, vicars forane (i.e., rural deans), rectors, with curates to assist them, and finally, a plan for the selection of new vicars apostolic. Upon the death or retirement of a bishop, the chapter of the district was to elect a vicar capitular, whose role it would be to govern the vacant district until the chapter selected three names to be sent to the pope. The Holy Father, it was suggested, would be free to choose a new bishop from either the chapter list or the one drawn up by the surviving vicars apostolic. The "Statuta Provisoria" indicated the wish of the bishops to maintain control over the church in England. The regulations, if implemented, would also have gone far toward meeting the clergy's demands.[25]

At the end of their meeting, the vicars apostolic prepared a "Monita et Statuta" to be distributed to their clergy. It contained regulations that Bernard Ward later described as "simple and practical." The document demanded uniform practice throughout the country in the use of English prayers that were customarily said before or after the celebration of mass on Sundays; it prohibited singing English vespers, which had become common toward the end of the eighteenth century; it provided details on the law of abstinence; and finally, it limited the granting of indulgences by members of religious orders in favor of restricting the privilege to the vicars apostolic. When the bishops sent the "Statuta Provisoria" to Rome, however, they failed to forward a copy of the "Monita et Statuta" for approval, an omission that left the authorities there with the further conviction that the vicars apostolic acted with undue independence.[26]

At this point Wiseman again entered the picture. When consulted by the secretary of Propaganda in mid-June regarding the decisions reached by the vicars apostolic at their spring meeting, he had to admit that he had still received no information from the bishops. He wrote immediately to all four vicars. "I could not give them the slightest information," he complained to Briggs, "not having had a letter from any of the Vicars, so that application to me was useless." He continued:

> Mgr. [Ignazio] Cadolini [Propaganda secretary] then told me that a *strong* letter was lying before the Pope for approbation, urging your Lordships to an immediate decision, if one is not come to, upon the two points of division of Districts and episcopal election. The Secretary proceeded to inform me that if this was not done, Propaganda would itself undertake the matter, & originate a plan, and warned me that I should be called on to afford such information as it is in my power to give. This would place me in a most delicate situation, as your Lordship will easily see. I therefore entreat you, as I have the other Vicars Ap., in case information have not been sent to the S. Cong., that no time be lost in writing. I am most willing to exert all my power to serve your Lordships' views, but of course can do nothing without some information.[27]

Considering the expectations of the vicars apostolic concerning the Roman agency, Wiseman's complaint was justified. When the results of the bishops' meeting finally reached Rome, moreover, they did not meet with approval.

In July 1838 Wiseman wrote to Griffiths that Propaganda and the Holy Father wanted matters to be "pushed on." They were not pleased with the decision to postpone the division of the vicariates. One of the consultors of the Sacred Congregation for the Propagation of the Faith had been told to prepare a plan to be sent to the English bishops for their opinion. The secretary of Propaganda, wrote Wiseman, spoke of six vicariates, although it was possible that a plan for dividing England into eight districts would also be proposed. "The basis on which the division will be regulated," he said, "seems to be number of missions and distances, the latter however being considered secondary in importance for England." He concluded:

On the whole there is some soreness, and an idea that sufficient energy has not been brought to the discussion & definition of the new arrangements, evidently much taken to heart by the Holy Father. The delay of at least another year seems a grievous disappointment. I do not think it necessary to write all this to each of the Vicars Ap., trusting that your Lordship being in close communication with them, will use your discretion in acting as you judge best.[28]

The fact that Wiseman was privy to Propaganda's plan and his outspokenness in reporting Rome's displeasure led to further mistrust on the part of the bishops. They were more convinced than ever that he was not defending their interests adequately.

In the autumn of 1838 the vicars apostolic received copies of a plan of government, called the "Statuta Proposita," drawn up by Cardinal Antonino De Luca, consultor for Propaganda. It was intended to provoke action on the part of the bishops.[29] While acknowledging the inexpediency of restoring the hierarchy, the "Statuta Proposita" suggested that the vicariates should be divided immediately into eight. The bishops were asked to comment upon the boundaries proposed, the means of support for additional bishops, the methods to be followed in settling affairs common to two or more districts, and a plan to assign the proposed Welsh District to the Benedictines as a means of promoting harmony between the secular and regular clergy. The document, in fact, mentioned the Midland rather than the Welsh District to be assigned to the Benedictines, but Wiseman stated that this was an error, although his clarification did not arrive before the bishops lodged a complaint.[30]

A plan for selecting future vicars apostolic, almost identical with the one suggested by the bishops themselves in the "Statuta Provisoria," intimated in addition that the regular clergy should have a voice in the selection. Provision was also made for the appointment of vicars general and rural deans, as well as chapters composed of twelve priests in each district. The "Statuta Proposita," finally, contained the suggestion that a special seminary should be established in England for training priests to labor in the mission areas of the British colonies.

The Holy See can hardly be blamed for taking the initiative. The vicars apostolic had themselves insisted that reorganization was demanded. However, they were understandably distressed by the expressed wish of the Holy See that they should prepare priests to work outside of England. Several months earlier Bishop Walsh had complained to Wiseman of the desperate shortage of priests in England: "I am still in great distress from the want of priests." A large number of the clergy in the Northern District had died: "Our priests are too hard worked. If Propaganda wish to preserve Catholicity in this country, they must not call for any more English priests from England for these two or three years to come." It was "the incessant labor amongst the poor, wretched Irish" that was ruining the health of priests and had given them "the fever which has, within the last 18 months, been so fatal." Walsh noted that the majority of the congregations in London, Manchester, and Liverpool were composed "of the poorest Irish," and he added, "This ought to be known at Rome where probably when the hundreds of thousands of Catholics in England are spoken of, His Holiness & the cardinals imagine they are English."

Walsh continued by describing the "horrid opposition to our holy religion & persecution of the poorer Catholics" in England and the need for more priests to engage in the battle raging there.[31] His concern was commendable, but the authorities might well have wondered why, if conditions were so pitiful, the vicars apostolic were opposed to the efforts of the regulars and jealous of their attempts to build churches. Others, moreover, had argued that Catholics were at peace with the country and that the time for a hierarchy had arrived. Griffiths and Walsh, finally, had insisted upon the urgent necessity of redefining the districts for the good of religion. Now all the bishops considered the step to be inexpedient.

The fact of the matter was that the bishops could not make up their own minds or agree upon an acceptable plan. Even after Walsh and Griffiths returned from Rome, their two colleagues in the West and North found it difficult to obtain a full report of their trip.[32] In 1838 Bishop Briggs, commissioned by the others to draw up a tentative plan of government, requested Griffiths to take on the job. He concluded his letter by advising that Walsh should not be informed of the work until the rest of the bishops had seen it, lest it be "shown to the regulars and their opinion . . . sought upon it." Even when they were later called upon to recommend new candidates for the episcopate, Briggs preferred that Walsh should be omitted from any consultation, since "all the world says he is about to join the Jesuits."[33]

With respect to the nature of the plan to be devised, there was no consistent agreement. Baines, as we have seen, at first favored the addition of a single district. In 1837 he went so far as to support the immediate establishment of a hierarchy, but he then changed his mind. By 1840 he concluded that even if the appointment of bishops-in-ordinary were made within two years, the measure would be "premature." Walsh, on the other hand, opposed the hierarchy, but he was desperately anxious for the division of his district. He agreed, however, with the others in the spring of 1838 when they voted to postpone the measure. Almost immediately he regretted his decision, convinced that his district was beyond his control. "I see little reason now for the delay," he wrote to Wiseman in July 1838.[34]

Griffiths was in favor of a hierarchy, even when faced with Rome's opposition. He consulted a number of his priests, including Mark Tierney, and received advice that he incorporated into a plan of reorganization. Yet it was Griffiths who now reported to Wiseman that action should be deferred for a year, since the bishops, when they met at York, were all so concerned with their own districts that they could reach no general agreement.[35] With the best of intentions, these men were themselves responsible for Wiseman's inability to determine their wishes and to support them in Rome, where the authorities were prepared for immediate changes. The Holy See wanted them to agree on specific procedural matters. When they failed to do so, Propaganda took on the task.

In their response to the "Statuta Proposita," the vicars apostolic stated quite simply that it was impractical for them to establish a special seminary for missionary priests. They replied briefly, however, to all the other suggestions, asking for several minor changes in the boundaries suggested by Rome for the new vicariates. They saw no immediate means of maintaining new bishops in the proposed Eastern and Northern districts but agreed that funds could be found, provided that Wales be assigned to the Benedictines. They made no practical suggestions for settling affairs common to several districts, stating that this would have to be left for later negotiations among the vicars apostolic. They opposed any plan to include regulars on episcopal chapters and doubted, finally, whether it would be possible to find twelve suitable priests to serve as chapter members in some of the districts. They proposed that a reasonable compromise might specify six and no more than twelve.[36]

The vicars apostolic had received the "Statuta Proposita" when they were in London, where they gathered on November 20, 1838, to discuss two decrees issued by the Holy See, and sent to them in September, concerning the regular clergy in England. The first of these gave a special privilege to priests belonging to religious orders to grant certain indulgences independent of the vicars apostolic. Such a right, common in Catholic countries, had been abrogated in England in the eighteenth century, and the bishops had repeated the prohibition the previous spring without informing Rome. Their action seems to have been responsible for the new decree. The second was even more offensive. It gave the regulars the right to establish chapels whenever and wherever they wished, even without the approval of the vicars apostolic.

The vicars apostolic now prepared a memorial, which was signed by all of them and sent to the pope on November 28, 1838. They resolved, as stated in the minutes, "that these decrees had been surreptitiously obtained; that the first, respecting indulgences, was uncalled for, not adapted to the present state of Religion in England, & would be the source of discord between the Regular & Secular clergy." The second "was subversive of Episcopal jurisdiction, & would give rise to dissensions & scandals." They decided "to remonstrate respectfully but firmly against them, and to request His Holiness to annull them." In the meantime the bishops asked the heads of religious orders in England not to let any of their members act upon the decrees until they had a reply from Rome.[37] Even Bishop Walsh initially joined the other bishops in their protest, but, characteristically, he later changed his views and withdrew his support.

The Holy See, in fact, clarified its position in a way acceptable to the bishops, but the damage was, to a certain extent, irreversible. Wiseman wrote to Bishop Griffiths on February 16 that the pope had spoken "with tears in his eyes" of the manner in which the vicars apostolic had opposed the two rescripts concerning the regulars. He complained "that he never had any communication from the vicars that would console him, as of the progress of religion, the state of the districts, etc., but that he had to learn what he could from newspapers, etc., while all correspondence was of a disagreeable nature." His Holiness finally stated that the brief replies to the "Statuta Proposita" were not satisfactory because the bishops had responded "in the dry authoritative form of a decision, *affirmative* and *negative*, which is the way definitive replies are given in Congregations."[38]

The vicars apostolic tended to blame Wiseman for the misunderstandings, convinced, not unreasonably, that he must have been aware of the nature of Rome's proposals even before they were sent to the bishops. At their next meeting they resolved to send a special agent to Rome "to supply Propaganda with information connected with the present ecclesiastical state of England." Even more significant was their resolution "that the future agent of the Bishops at Rome be unconnected with the English College, and not employed in any other office." Bernard Ward concluded that they were guilty of a tactical error: "The tone as well as the substance of this Resolution shows that the Bishops underrated the strength of Dr. Wiseman's position in Rome, and the confidence which was reposed in him by the authorities there. In point of fact, their opposition to him tended not to allay, but to increase the misunderstandings with which the situation had become surrounded."[39] Another interpretation is of course possible and perhaps more likely. The vicars apostolic understood full well the extent of Wiseman's influence, and they were convinced that he was responsible, to a great extent, for the mistrust with which they were viewed by the Roman authorities.

It seems that Wiseman was now convinced of the value of religious orders in England. "It is said, & I believe the report, that Dr. Wiseman is to be coadjutor to Dr. Walsh before the end of the year," reported the Roman procurator for the English Benedictines in August 1837. He continued, "I think Dr. Wiseman's prejudices are a good deal softened down, & that he will not be hostile to the regulars."[40] The same man, in December 1838, described the contents of the "Statuta Proposita" and, aware of the fact that the document had originally suggested that the central counties be given to the Benedictines, objected to the plan. The major problem, he said, was that of "equalizing the property we give up with the property we receive," and he also anticipated the opposition of the congregations of the faithful that would be affected. It was his understanding that the order would have to give up all of the missions it served outside of the new district in order to displace the secular missionaries there.

Although the procurator was not pleased with the principle of limiting the Benedictines to a specific district, he concluded, "Nevertheless we must not overlook the situation in which we now are placed amidst the secular clergy; we are pressed on every side by their encroachments, & we are yearly & almost daily losing, by that means, the extent of our jurisdiction." He said that the religious orders provided one-seventh or one-eighth of the total number of clergy in the country, but that unless the vicars apostolic changed their attitude toward them, they would soon form only one-seventeenth or one-eighteenth of the whole. He took seriously the proposition that the order was to be given the central counties. It is possible, in fact, that contrary to Wiseman's assurances, such had been Propaganda's original intention. The Benedictine procurator claimed that it had been the plan of the cardinals to give the Benedictines the western counties of Hereford, Monmouthshire, and Shropshire, as well as Wales, but that they soon saw "the absurdity of the plan," and only then determined on giving them the new Central District instead.[41] Faced with the immediate and vehement opposition of the vicars apostolic, however, Propaganda was most likely realistic enough to back off, only then assuring the bishops that a mistake had been made and that it was the West which would be assigned to the Benedictine order.

By the 1830s the regulars considered themselves to be losing ground with respect to the secular clergy. Whereas in 1803 the religious orders provided 40 percent of the priests engaged in parochial work, and were still 37 percent of the total number in 1815, by 1837 they accounted for only 26 percent of the English priests on the mission.[42] They were as jealous of the gains being made by their secular counterparts as the latter were of what was considered to be unwarranted independence on the part of the regulars. The two decrees issued by Propaganda added to the hard feelings, even though they were effectively withdrawn.

In 1839 Bishop Briggs explained to Wiseman the reasons that led him to oppose construction of a chapel in Liverpool by the regular clergy. He provided, at the same time, information on the state of

Catholicism in that part of England, little understood, he felt, by the cardinal prefect of Propaganda.

> The means of the support and propagation of our Holy Religion, particularly in this manufacturing and commercial country, partake so much of speculation, and depend so much on the goodness and badness of trade, that we are here particularly circumstanced. This I venture to say only those who are on the spot and who watch narrowly the state of our various trades, their movements from one part of the country to another, the sudden rising of one town, and the depression of another, the influx of Catholics from Ireland to some parts of the country, their desertion of that part when trade is depressed; it is only those who can look with the priest of the place at the prospect of raising a new mission, who can calculate with him the chances of success, who can see the resources upon which he can prudently reckon, both for the meeting of the interest of the debt to be incurred in the erection of a new chapel, and for the support of the incumbent, for many years of difficulty under which the chapel must labour; it is only they who do this that can fully understand the peculiar circumstances in which we are placed.

He then cited an instance in which a chapel had been constructed but the priest left with an enormous debt as a result of a local financial depression.

Briggs also observed that several letters from Rome had stated that missionary houses and chapels in the possession of regulars ought to be considered as monasteries, with privileges making them independent of the vicars apostolic. He pointed out that such establishments had been built "by the contributions of the faithful" and that they were "as much parish or parochial chapels as any served by the secular priests."

The northern bishop insisted that he was by no means opposed to the construction of chapels by the regular clergy where they were needed.

> But for the regulars to be allowed and proceed to build chapels in the district in quasi parishes of the secular priests, when either a chapel is not there wanted or could and would be built by the seculars, if wanted, this as has already appeared in Liverpool must produce great disorder, great dissentions [sic] amongst priests & people, and cause great scandal to the faithful, but great exultation to our enemies.

Briggs pointed out that the church was under attack from its enemies, who "would exult in triumph did they hear that dissentions have arisen amongst us."

The bishop concluded his letter by discussing Protestant prejudice in England and the ridicule from which Catholics suffered. He repeated the fact that the principal reason for the increased number of Catholics in England was Irish immigration, contrary to the reports of those who provided Propaganda with information of a different nature, presumably of the large number of conversions that were taking place. "Would to God those representations were correct," he wrote. Unfortunately, those making them, "with the best of intentions," had provided "an interesting and enchanting, but faithless picture of the very extraordinary and very rapid growing prosperity of the Catholic religion in England."[43] There was no one whose reports on the prospects of the English Catholics were more enthusiastic than Wiseman's. Briggs was not unaware of the fact.

Among the suggestions included in Propaganda's "Statuta Proposita" was one that promoted a means of collecting funds throughout the country for the benefit of the colonial missions. The model was the Oeuvre pour la Propagation de la Foi, or the Society for the Propagation of the Faith, established with its headquarters in Lyons in 1822. Late in 1838 Bishop Walsh agreed to be president of an English branch of the association, considering the annual collection to be the "expressed wish" of the pope and Propaganda.[44]

The response of the other vicars apostolic was less than encouraging. Bishop Griffiths wrote to Walsh stating that when he consulted with his own advisers and deemed the time right for recommending "this pious work" within his own district, he would give his approbation. In the meantime, however, it did not have his sanction. Walsh, by placing himself at the head of the society's council in London, was interfering in a district not his own. Griffiths observed, "I should certainly condemn myself if I named myself President of a similar council in Birmingham."[45]

All the districts had annual collections for general missionary purposes. The money collected was distributed at the discretion of the vicars apostolic. It was the conviction of Griffiths, as he wrote to Briggs, that "each bishop should organize the system of collection in the manner best adapted to his own district."[46]

One priest of the Northern District voiced the concern of the majority of vicars apostolic: "There is much reason to fear that any *general* scheme for raising money for the benefit of the colonies may deprive this country of means which our wants cannot spare, unless it comprise the object of supplying our numerous & urgent demands at home. Many will contribute for a remote object, while they overlook that at their own doors."[47] This kind of response was still an added cause for displeasure on the part of the Roman authorities. The Holy Father intended that the English bishops should establish an organization related to that in France, and when it became clear that they were not interpreting his will in this way, he considered them to be disobedient.

When Wiseman wrote to Bishop Griffiths in February 1839 to describe the Holy Father's dissatisfaction with the vicars apostolic, he said that the pope complained that the English bishops had "resisted or opposed" the rescripts on the regulars issued in September, that they had drawn up and distributed their "Monita" without obtaining the permission of the Holy See, and that they paid insufficient attention to proper forms in drawing up their letters to Rome. Wiseman had already informed the vicars apostolic that the secretary of Propaganda was "in a state of considerable irritation at the suppression of the Association, which the Pope has so much at heart."[48]

In fact the Society for the Propagation of the Faith had not been suppressed in England. It was simply not being supported by any of the bishops except Walsh, the others not understanding clearly that its establishment was the direct wish of the pope himself. Ultimately they all became patrons of an English branch of the society, and Walsh resigned as president. He was succeeded in that position by a layman, the earl of Shrewsbury.

The correspondence of the vicars apostolic leaves no doubt that they blamed Wiseman for the misunderstanding of their situation which, they were convinced, prevailed in Rome. To Briggs, Wiseman vehemently denied the accusation.

> I understand that in a letter received by Lord Clifford from your Lordship, you state an opinion that the disagreeable differences which have lately arisen between the Holy See and some of the VV.A. are owing (in part at least) to the latters' not having been supported here; which has been interpreted as applying to me, as though I ought in some way to have further explained the Bishops' views or supported them. I can hardly bring myself to believe that this interpretation of your Lordship's expressions is correct, when I consider the following circumstances.

He then pointed out that when it was evident that Propaganda would consult him on certain matters related to England, he had written to the vicars apostolic asking for instructions. He had received no reply from any of them: "I was left utterly in the dark as to their wishes." No copy of the "Monita," drawn up in York, had been sent to him, and, until he read it in a French journal, the *Univers Religieux*, he knew nothing about it. By the end of February 1839, when Wiseman wrote the letter to Briggs, he had still seen no copy of the reply the bishops made to the "Statuta Proposita" or to the two rescripts relating to the regulars. The letter to the pope was sent to him sealed: "I could not be expected to think myself called on to support or explain documents which I have never been allowed to see and of which I was never furnished with copies." He added, "On the contrary, it seemed evidently the wish of the VV.A. that I should be kept in ignorance of their contents and consequently debarred from all right to act as their agent concerning them."

Wiseman reminded Briggs that when he had once failed to follow instructions, he had received a severe reprimand from Bishops Penswick and Bramston. He was then warned "that, as agent, I had no discretion allowed me to follow my own judgment, but was bound literally to obey the Bishops' commands, without presuming to act on my own behalf. After such positive limitations of my powers," he declared, "I could not consistently, with what I owe to myself, expose myself to a similar rebuke by taking any active steps in a matter whereon I had no authority." He insisted that he had been faithful in reporting to the London vicar apostolic, for transmission to the others, all conversations concerning English affairs that he had with church authorities, and that when the pope "found fault with the tone and form of the letters and answers sent to him and the Holy Congregation, I immediately assured him . . . that nothing was further from your Lordships' minds than intentional disrespect, and that any departure from conventional form must be attributed entirely to want of practice in such, my acquaintance with the VV.A.'s sentiments towards the Holy See being such as authorised me to remove, as far as I could, an erroneous impression made regarding them." He admitted that he had not opposed the rescripts that had so offended the bishops because they contained nothing that was not common practice in Catholic countries, and he finally concluded, "I flatter myself that the above considerations will be sufficient to satisfy your Lordship that I have not neglected my duty on the present occasion, & that situated as I am, I could not have taken a more active part in supporting any opinions which I may have indirectly *learnt* that your Lordship or any other of the Vicars Ap. may entertain regarding the points under discussion."[49]

Wiseman had reason for protesting to the vicars apostolic. At the same time, they can hardly be blamed for not understanding procedures in Catholic countries or for insisting that their own circumstances warranted special consideration. By this time, in any case, the days of Wiseman's agency on behalf of the vicars apostolic were drawing to an end. Broader issues and more momentous decisions concerned him than the specific, practical, but narrow concerns of the English vicars apostolic. Wiseman had a vision of the future prospects of Catholicism in England that little resembled the view of the vast majority of his contemporaries. He had been working to fulfill his dream since his return to Rome in 1836. He wrote, "The age wants doctors and apostles, men devoted to the cause they have embraced at the altar; with the zeal which our excellent clergy have displayed till now, and with those additional energies which the increasing demands of circumstances will doubtless require at their hands."[50] He was firmly convinced of the rightness of his view and his own ability to meet the challenges of the age.

6. A New Vocation

URING HIS LAST FOUR YEARS IN ROME, WISEMAN DEVOTED HIM-
self more and more to what he perceived as the needs of the
church in England. After his memorable lectures in London,
according to Bernard Ward, English Catholics came to view him "as
the one possible leader who would command the respect of all, non-
Catholics as well as Catholics." Whether or not the young lecturer had
made as deep an impression as Ward implied, there were, without
doubt, those who considered his ultimate presence among them to be
far more important than anything that he might achieve by remaining
in Rome. A. W. Pugin wrote to him in 1838, "Of what service would
your great talents and eloquence be in this contry [sic] where unfortunately the great body of those who profess the true faith are lamen-
tably deficient in this respect."[1]

Pugin's view was shared by Charles Newsham, president of Ushaw
College, who also encouraged Wiseman to turn his attention exclusively to England. Wiseman responded warmly, "Ever since my return
to Rome, one only subject has been uppermost in my mind: my prayers,
meditations, studies and ordinary thoughts have been centred upon
England." While there, he had been "busy with eyes and ears collecting all the information within my reach, towards forming for myself a
just estimate of the state of religion, catholic and protestant, of our
wants and their remedies." It was Wiseman's conviction that a new
order of priests was needed, one in which both "intellectual culture and
very warm piety should be combined as much as possible in the highest
degree." He was convinced that the religious state of England had
reached a crisis requiring "great learning, both to keep down infidelity
and to combat the Church of England, which has now really learned

champions." He hoped, therefore, to inculcate into the Catholic clergy "the active power of research, and a practice in laying hold of and destroying any new error."

Wiseman continued his letter to Newsham by comparing religion in England with that in Catholic countries, observing that there was an "immense difference . . . between the part which the affections and heart have in it in both, whether among clergy or laity." He explained, "The warm cordial attachment which we here [in Rome] see to all the duties and practices of religion, the familiarity so to speak, between the militant and triumphant portions of the Church of God, the devotion, corporal as well as spiritual, of many to charitable practices contrast in the strongest manner with the measured and almost cold standard of positive obligation which seemed to me to predominate in England." He suggested that the introduction of Lenten preaching, retreats, missions, and other devotions would "preserve piety from coldness and decay."

Warming to his subject, Wiseman then described the benefits derived at the English College after he called upon a Jesuit priest to guide its members through the Institutes of St. Ignatius, a series of meditations and practical steps designed to lead souls to closer intimacy with God. He assured Newsham "that if either at Ushaw or elsewhere, for the students *or the clergy*, the retreat *in this form*, strictly according to rule, were tried, you would not believe the effects it must produce." He had also scheduled a three-day retreat before Easter, and in May had established the *Mese Mariano*, or dedication of the entire month of May to the Blessed Virgin. After outlining the specific religious practices followed throughout the month, Wiseman wrote, "I think I can say that there was only one common feeling in the house: every one regretted when it was over, and all longed to see such a beautiful and profitable devotion transplanted to England." He was convinced that there would be no spiritual change among Englishmen until they had "a certain number of zealous, learned and devoted priests," who would be prepared to deliver "earnest, impressive, & moving discourses." Missions of ten days, or even a fortnight, might be given in any English chapel: "It is by this that conversions are made of obstinate sinners, & foundation laid for virtuous lives."

Returning to his own future, Wiseman told Newsham that he wanted to settle in England. His purposes could not be realized, however, if he were confined to one place. A certain amount of freedom would be necessary, for example, were he to oversee the *Dublin Review*, published in London, and other publications that he hoped to begin: "Of such a manner of living I see no prospect, as I suppose the idea would be considered extravagant, though I think I could do more work myself, and direct others towards introducing many of the institutions of Catholic countries better, than if I were fast in one place." Within a year or two he could easily "run over to England before Lent, give a complete Lent course, say at London, Liverpool, or any large town, spend the next month in giving a retreat, for example, to the clergy, and trying the plan of missions, and then give the Month of May at a College, as at Ushaw, delivering at the same time a course of lectures 3 or 4 times a week, so as to form a complete course on some leading point." He acknowledged that it would be presumptuous for him to propose this himself, since "such a plan should come from above." There was a note of urgency in his final appeal: "If something of this sort does not present itself, I fear it will be long before I am in England."[2]

Newsham responded positively to all that Wiseman proposed: "I firmly believe that unless God in his mercy raise up some means of counteracting the present spirit of both clergy & laity, some great catastrophe will before long befal [sic] us." The Ushaw president added, "Remember I am speaking *confidentially*, for one of the worst features of the case is that if I were known to have spoken as I am now doing, I should have the clamour & confusion of Babel ringing in my ears."

Newsham complained that there was "a very great want of a spirit of piety, faith & religion" among the Catholic clergy in England, due to the youth of many priests, the lack of control exercised by the bishops, and "the spirit of the times, which is incessantly infused into the minds of our young men by our abominable newspapers." These, he noted, were the greatest "pest" and the most "efficient weapon of the devil" in the world: "Their pernicious effects in the minds of our young ecclesiastics has [sic] been observed & lamented by many others as well as myself." He continued:

> If you speak the common language of piety, if you inculcate maxims that are to [be] found in every good book, if you require from young men what the gospel itself manifestly dictates, you are attacked by even priests on the mission, & cried down as a tory (for this is a favourite mode of attacking anything like discipline), a monk, a man who has no feeling of compassion for human nature. This is the spirit & you need not be told what the consequences must be. Now this spirit cannot be attacked or put down in a direct manner. Too violent an opposition would be raised by the attempt. It must be subdued & conquered by *indirect means* — by exciting a spirit of faith & religion, & for the accomplishing of this there is no other way than ecclesiastical retreats. If such be the spirit of the clergy, you easily see what the laity must be. In fact, you have in what I have said the key of what excited your surprise & regret when in England. . . . The truth is, we have not a man fully qualified for this task. Our priests, you know, are hurried through their studies & then placed on the mission, where they have neither no [sic]

time or inclination to pursue study. The consequence is an ignorance of church history, of antiquities, of the fathers, of oriental languages, & even of the modern mode of disputation adopted by our opponents. To read the defences of religion that occasionally appear, perfectly sickens me.

Newsham then arrived at the conclusion that Wiseman himself had already reached: "We want a man to give a *new turn* to controversy & you are that man. I am sure, then, you ought to return to England."

The Ushaw president stated that his bishop would promote the plans that they were discussing, an obviously uninformed observation, since Bishop Briggs was far from being a supporter of Wiseman. Newsham added that he would himself "leave no stone unturned to accomplish an object so dear to me." The major difficulty of the plan that Wiseman had suggested, however, was the means of supporting him if he were not to be attached to a particular district. Newsham proposed that Wiseman might make Ushaw his headquarters. In any case he hoped that his friend would be attached to the Northern District: "I see in this no clog, no impediment to your exertions & usefulness. But write soon; I will proceed to work immediately with full hopes of complete success." [3]

Bernard Ward wrote that Wiseman had hoped to persuade an existing religious community to establish itself in England, free of normal parochial duties and so able to preach retreats and missions throughout the entire country. [4] This, however, was certainly not the original plan. It was an entirely new kind of community that Wiseman had in mind, composed of secular priests but not bound to a particular district.

In October 1838 Wiseman again wrote to Newsham that there was nothing he had "so much at heart as cooperating with you and others in advancing the cause of religion in England, and especially by stirring up the spirit of the clergy." Fresh proposals had come to him since their previous correspondence, he noted, a reference, no doubt, to the plan of dividing the existing vicariates and Bishop Walsh's desire to make him coadjutor, or even vicar apostolic of a new division to be carved out of the Midland District: "Anyhow, I think it cannot be long before England is my residence."

Wiseman then described the kind of community that he hoped to establish, a small group of priests who would have a common home but who would "go bini [two by two] from place to place giving lectures, retreats, &c. in different dioceses, so as to be out several months at a time, and then repose, so that those at home would be engaged in conducting, at certain intervals, retreats for laymen or clergy in the house." Six or eight such men would suffice as a start, "but they must be truly filled with the spirit of devotion and piety, as well as learned and fluent, not to say eloquent." The young men at the college were aware of his plan, he wrote, and he had already begun the necessary training of the students.[5]

By the spring of 1839, when it was becoming clear that Wiseman was most attracted to the Midlands where he could best respond to the Oxford divines and where Bishop Walsh was prepared to welcome him with open arms, Newsham urged that George Errington might establish himself at Ushaw: "For my part, I am perfectly convinced that Dr. Errington will have it in his power to do infinitely more good if placed at Ushaw, than if he select any other place or station for the exercise of his talents & industry." Newsham understood that Wiseman was destined for the Midland District: "I am sure you will see at one glance that mighty things might be effected by you in the Midland District (a thing I expect to see before long) & Dr. Errington at Ushaw, supported and backed by me." Neither man could expect to be effective were they to live at a distance from one of the colleges: "That general system of combined energy, which you so beautifully describe in your letter, will never be produced, except through the colleges; nor even there without a constantly acting stimulus for several years, viz. for one generation, as we term it."[6] Wiseman must have been convinced that he had a firm ally in Newsham, a remarkable man who served as president of Ushaw from 1837 to 1863.

Newsham was surely aware, then, that Bishop Walsh had been doing all in his power to obtain Wiseman for the Midland District. "Bear in mind that I have the first claim on you," wrote the bishop; "I want you immediately. Do then in all sincerity & friendly candour tell how you think I can best succeed in obtaining you for my coadjutor." He made it clear that Oscott should be Wiseman's home, although he did not specify any particular role that he might exercise in that institution.[7]

Wiseman knew well, however, that there were those who would not welcome his elevation to the episcopate. His friend Logan had written: "I hope there are no obstacles thrown in the way of your coming to England, for those who do not wish it are very busy in affirming there are. The most industrious circulation of these reports is [by] Dr. Baines who assured me that His Holiness had positively declared that you never should be Bishop. Of course I knew his statement to be untrue and more founded upon his wishes than upon facts." Logan wrote from Oscott, where he was staying after departing forever from Prior Park. He noted that construction of the new college was nearly completed: "I long to see you in it and hear a pontifical high mass in the chapel sung by yourself as bishop."[8] When Wiseman went back to Rome in 1836, Logan accompanied him, although he soon returned to take up a post at Oscott.

While formulating concrete proposals on behalf of English Catholics and preparing the students to assist him in the work to be done, Wiseman continued to demonstrate his interest in the Oxford Movement. Of the vicars apostolic, only Bishop Walsh appreciated his efforts. Early in 1840 Walsh wrote to Monsignor Charles Acton, adviser and friend of Gregory XVI, to describe "the talented, zealous Oxford divines whose influence seems to be daily increasing & who in so many points seem to be approaching towards the Catholic religion, though at the present moment they are so decidedly hostile to it." Able and learned men were needed "to meet these learned & acute ecclesiastics." For this purpose he singled out Wiseman as one "respected by them" and "most qualified to meet them & to train others for the same purpose." If located at Oscott, "he would derive peculiar advantages for that object." [9]

Years later, when he published his articles on the Tractarian Movement in a single volume, Wiseman described the opposition with which they had been received, even by his friends. He had been treated "as an enthusiast, or rather a fanatic, who was digging a pit of bitter disappointment for his own feet." He had even been warned by "the most learned of our historians" (obviously Lingard) that "vain hopes" had been raised among Catholics in an earlier age, that of Bishop William Laud and the nonconformists, and he had been asked "what he saw in the present moment that gave better grounds of reliance than experience had proved to exist then." [10] In spite of those who advised him that his efforts would be futile, Wiseman produced a series of thoughtful articles for the *Dublin Review*. Little escaped his notice with reference to the Oxford Movement, and though his views were rejected by the majority of both Catholics and Protestants, the Tractarians themselves appreciated him as a formidable, though sympathetic, critic.

In his *Apologia pro Vita Sua* (1864), Newman described the impact of one of Wiseman's articles, in which he had proposed St. Augustine's appeal to the faith of the church universal as a simpler test in deciding authentic Catholic doctrine than that of antiquity. At the time Newman's position was that Protestants had subtracted from the Christian revelation, while Roman Catholics had added to it. It was his purpose to contribute toward the formation of a recognized Anglican theology, one that he described as a *via media*. [11]

In responding to Newman's arguments, Wiseman quoted from St. Augustine's "golden sentence" against the Donatists: "Wherefore, the entire world judges WITH SECURITY, that they are not good, who separate themselves from the entire world, in whatever part of the entire world." [12] Newman later wrote: "For a mere sentence, the words of St. Augustine, struck me with a power which I never had felt from any words before. By those great words of the ancient Father, interpreting and summing up the long and varied course of ecclesiastical history, the theory of the Via Media was absolutely pulverized."[13]

In describing this period in his life, Wiseman later wrote, "My studies changed their course, the bent of my mind was altered, in the strong desire to co-operate with the new mercies of Providence." He may not have appreciated, even then, the depth of his own influence. He anticipated, for example, the theory of doctrinal development, most commonly associated with Newman. Wilfrid Ward quoted from a sermon that Wiseman preached at the opening of St. Mary's Church, Derby, when visiting England in 1839; it contained the principal theme of Newman's famous work.[14] Among Wiseman's retreat notes, preserved at Ushaw, a passage relating to the Eucharist is a striking parallel to Newman's theme.

> It is absurd to consider the first record of anything as its origin, or to consider that a doctrine began to prevail in proportion as its monuments appear in history. Examples: If we look back at our own lives for proofs or instances of our power of memory, or even reasoning, we should not find distinct evidences before 9 or perhaps 12 yrs. How active the memory has been before in learning languages &c. & this judgment in forming grammar, generalizing, forming opinions of men & things &c. It is not the first period of the life of *anything* that produces records, or reflects back upon itself; the silent operation has always gone on for a period, before it is looked back upon & analyzed & described.

He concluded, "The first period of the Ch[urch] was that of organisation & growth, also of external combat: it was not engaged in writing its own history."[15]

Wiseman, as no other Catholic of his time, understood the Tractarians. His view of Anglicanism was less kind than that expressed in a later, more ecumenically minded age, but for his time his approach was moderate. It was with some disappointment, then, that he found it necessary to respond in a more controversial manner to a critic like Thomas Turton, Regius Professor of Divinity at Cambridge, who wrote of Wiseman's lectures on the Real Presence in the Eucharist: "The author is subtle but not sagacious; he is dexterous but not circumspect; he is learned after the manner of a controversialist, not after that of a student. It would have afforded me great pleasure if I could have pointed out a single instance of fair manly investigation in the course of his lectures, and I sincerely regret that he has not enabled me to pay him the compliment."[16]

Such a criticism was especially insulting to Wiseman, since he prided himself on the care with which he used his sources. He described Turton's attack as "intemperate and ill-judged" but acknowledged the difficulty in answering it: "He takes three or four pages to comment on one of mine; and if I keep the same proportion there will be no end of my answer. This I could afford neither time nor money for." [17]

A year later one of Wiseman's friends wrote: "I am right glad that you are taking Turton to task, and sorry only that you did not do so much sooner. It has been the boast of the parsons that you could not answer the book, and the lament of the Catholics that you have not done it." It was almost another year, nevertheless, before Wiseman's reply was published. He responded point by point to Turton's arguments, allowing his supporting evidence, for the most part, to speak for itself. Only the first chapter was personal, warranted, surely, by Turton's own remarks. He applied to the Cambridge professor (and future bishop of Ely) the Arabic proverb, "The learned man knows the unlearned, because he himself has once been unlearned; but the unlearned knows not the learned, because he has never himself been learned." [18] The approach was unlike the one to which he was accustomed to take in his controversial writings.

A student who began his studies at the English College in October 1836, right after Wiseman's return from England, later recalled:

> When I first knew him he was, I think, at the crisis of his career, at the close of his student life, and about to commence the important part he took in the religious movement and the ecclesiastical politics of his day. He may — I think, he must, have applied much to study (at an earlier time), but I never saw anything like continuous application on his part while I was at the English College. What he wrote was thrown off rapidly and at a single effort. Indeed, what with his daily lectures at the University, his weekly sermons, his duties as agent to the bishops of England, his multifarious correspondence, his visitors and his visits, he was too busy to be able to read much.

At that time, of course, Wiseman was busily serving as editor of the *Dublin Review* (in fact, if not in name), writing articles, and drawing up a plan for the missionary community that he hoped to establish.

"He was never idle for a moment," continued the same man; "Even recreation he made subservient to a useful purpose. On each Thursday (the weekly holiday) it was his habit to take us all to one of the Catacombs, or churches, or antiquities, or picture galleries, or the museums, or the studios of artists, and on such occasions we were often accompanied by some German scholar or other friend of his interested in Christian art." He continued by pointing to Wiseman's versatility. The rector served as college organist, having "a critical appreciation of music as well of the other fine arts." He "painted the scenes for the first play which we acted in 1837," and in fact wrote one such play himself, "the scene of which was America." The students who managed the production were forbidden "to divulge even to the other students the fact that he had written it." [19]

Ushaw College has preserved two copies of a play called, "Extracting a Secret, An After Piece," originally called, "Drawing a Secret." According to the manuscript, in Wiseman's handwriting, it was composed in 1838. The action takes place in a small country town in the North of England and involves the stale, but amusingly told, story of the discovery of a long-lost son who had been to America. Among the characters are Sir Philip Worshipful, a justice of the peace; Dashwood, afterward recognized as young Worshipful; Mr. Seargeant Nonplus, a barrister; and Frank Hurricane, servant to Dashwood. [20] There was a playful streak in Wiseman, especially evident in his relationships with young people. He always seemed to be more at home with them than with his peers.

After Wiseman's long visit to England, his new interests seem to have been accompanied by an alteration in his appearance. He was recalled as having been, in 1835, "a tall thin priest, with a stoop and a rather frowning brow and black hair, and gold spectacles." Wiseman was more than six feet tall. By 1836 "the pale thin student had passed . . . into the ruddy-faced and somewhat corpulent man of action." About fifteen years afterward, a Jesuit priest first saw him standing between his secretary Monsignor Francis Searle, and the Jesuit provincial, Father Randall Lythgoe, and later wrote: "I thought, Is this, then, the effect of prayer and fasting? Three such mountains of flesh I had never before seen." He went on, "Dr. Wiseman's aspect was at first sight forbidding, his shaggy eyebrows . . . and wide, thick-lipped mouth, being neither handsome nor attractive." He then described the warmth with which Wiseman received him and added that "however young one might be, frankness even to familiarity, instead of meeting with the rebuff it might seem to deserve, only placed him completely at his ease, and was responded to with unaffected expansiveness." As a cardinal, Wiseman seems to have been delighted when addressed by one poor lady as "your Immense." [21]

Still another observer recalled Wiseman when, as a young man, he visited his mother and sister at Versailles. He had been "a thin, delicate-looking youth, who even then, when he must have come straight from Ushaw [in fact, he had left Ushaw six years earlier], was made much of by the Catholics as a young man of extraordinary ability and promise." The lady saw Wiseman again when he was a cardinal and wrote, "At that time he was hugely stout and coarse-looking, bearing a strong resemblance to his good and kind mother." [22]

Even Wiseman's spirituality underwent a change not too long after his visit to England, occasioned by the retreat he and the students made in the autumn of 1837, under the direction of a Jesuit. "Previously to that time," wrote one of the students, "my impression had been that the relations between Dr. Wiseman and the Society [the Jesuits] were not very cordial." More significant, Wiseman now "came out indeed in a new light, viz. as a spiritual counsellor. Many of the students chose him for their director." It was then, also, that Wiseman determined to devote himself to assisting the poor. "Towards the poor I will do all I can to aid them," he wrote, "and particularly I will seek out occasions of serving them and assisting them personally, either in the hospitals or in other ways." In 1838 he added a note to the effect that he had "found out a way of serving the poor in the hospitals, as I promised, for which God be praised."[23]

"I cannot tell you how anxious I am to quit Rome," wrote Wiseman to his sister in April 1839. Only her presence in Italy and his work at the college stood in the way of his returning permanently to England.

> But consider: I have been 20 years in Rome, and I have not formed one single friendship in it. I have no family in which I am welcome, or where I find any comfort in going — you know well enough the heartless and cold ac- quaintances which the system of society leads to in Rome, (I do not speak of the provinces); all is so full of mere frivolity and envy; those who are climb- ing up the ladder of ambition are so selfish and have so little true friendship or attachment, there is so much intrigue, and so little encouragement to any one who merely seeks to do his duty, that I can assure you I am heartily sick of it all. On the other hand I was but months in England and I have friends there that are pressing my return among them, with all the sincerity of friendship, whose arms will be open to welcome me, who I know will sym- pathise with me, and value any little thing I can do. But this is a trifle. What good do I at Rome? Excepting in the College, nothing to the purpose; while England is in the most interesting condition, and calls for all the exer- tions of those that wish her well.[24]

The explanation for this curious letter must be seen in its final state- ment.

Wiseman craved the activity that England offered him. He suffered from periods of depression throughout his life, of course, but the pic- ture of life in Rome as described for his sister little resembled that which he drew in his *Recollections of the Last Four Popes* some twenty years later. By then he had discovered, no doubt, that envy, ambition, and intrigue are confined to no particular place or people. He never un- derstood, however, that he demanded too much from his friends. The loyalty, support, and confidence that he expected of them tolerated no exceptional circumstance. He could withstand opposition, provided that his close associates offered him encouragement. When that was lacking, he considered himself to be abandoned, a nobly righteous war- rior battling alone against a veritable army of opponents.

Wiseman spent the summer and autumn of 1839 in England, where he did everything within his power to demonstrate the good that could be accomplished there. He wrote to his mother in October:

> I am quite strong and fit for work, though when I have finished my engagements, which will be before the end of the month, I shall not be sorry. By that time I shall have preached about 90 times in six weeks, averaging an hour each time, which I think you will say is pretty well. I have travelled, chiefly by railroad, 1600 miles since I came to England and have the satisfaction of being able to say that not five of them have been travelled for the sake of amusement or temporal interest of any sort, but entirely to promote, as much as was in my power, the interests of God and his holy religion.[25]

So rigorous a schedule would have caused the collapse of a lesser man. Wiseman's exertions were rewarded by a great deal of praise, however, and seemed to draw forth energies that were surprising even to him. One prominent Lancashire priest wrote to Edmund Winstanley, president of the English College in Lisbon: "He [Wiseman] is, at present, most fully engaged amongst us till his return to Rome. He gives, next week, a retreat at Oscott; thence to Manc[heste]r for 10 or 12 days of lecturing. He is, undoubtedly, a great genius."[26]

Wiseman, then, had tried the experiment that he was convinced would do so much good for English Catholics. He had traveled widely, lecturing and preaching in a variety of circumstances, and he had been received warmly. When writing to his mother, he stated that even Bishop Griffiths wanted him to return to London to preach during Lent, "but this would, indeed, be too soon, and I should hardly have had rest enough after this year's campaign." He hoped to return the following year, however, "if not for good, at least for a visit."[27]

While in England, Wiseman discussed with a number of acquaintances his plan for a special community of secular priests to preach throughout the country. There were already those, most notably Ambrose Phillipps, who had been urging that established orders should be brought from the Continent to England. Phillipps turned to Lord Shrewsbury, who was less than enthusiastic in supporting the proposal. The earl described an interview with Father Dominic Barberi, the saintly Passionist who later received Newman into the Catholic church: "Father Dominic spoke a little broken English but could not understand a word of what I said to him. You will only bring yourself and others into trouble with these good people, and do no good. We must work in the *large* towns, with *large* churches, in which we can influence the people by the splendour, etc. of our service." He added, "We must have a new race of zealous English missionaries, such as are now bringing up at Oscott, under the good Bishop and Pugin."

Lord Shrewsbury agreed that there was a need for "perambulating preachers." He argued, however, that it was "of no use preaching among people whom you must leave without any means of practising their religion. If we have supernumeraries this might be tried, but there is still so much to do where Catholicity has a footing, that I am sure we have no spare means as yet, for places where not even a Chapel can be built." He warned: "You will get nothing but stupid Methodists to frequent meeting houses. We must have chapels. These are not times which bear any analogy to those of Saint Augustine, and I think no parallel can be made between them." Shrewsbury was not unwilling to assist the orders financially, although it had been his hope that they might have obtained assistance from abroad: "I thought the Rosminians would bring their means with them—they must be rich in Italy." It was also his fear that an income tax would soon be instituted in England, "and then we shall not have a shilling to spare for anything, and I shall be too glad to get my £50 a year."[28]

Upon returning to Rome, Wiseman wrote that he had reported to the pope: "I have had the satisfaction of hearing His Holiness approve of all I have done in England & of the points I have there chiefly inculcated."[29] The time was right, he decided, to submit to the pope the plan that he had formulated for a special community or institute of priests. He called his written document, "Supplex Libellus, An Humble Address Submitted to His Holiness Pope Gregory XVIth, with a view to the Reformation of the State of the English Mission, A.D. 1839."

In his address Wiseman noted that having traveled "over almost the whole length and breadth of the island" and ascertained "the universal feeling and opinion of the Catholic clergy and laity" and "the unanimous consent of all the Vicars Apostolic," he had become convinced of the need for a special body of missionaries. The community would be charged, first of all, with visiting those areas where "the principles of the Catholic religion are either imperfectly understood, or entirely unknown." It would not be difficult to "insinuate the truths of faith into the minds of the people," he argued, "for the English run with great avidity to public orations; an avidity, of which your petitioner has had frequent evidence."

Members, second, would give "missionary exhortations" where Catholics already existed, "with a view to excite them to greater zeal and fervour." He claimed that missions of this kind were virtually unknown in England, "whence it arises, that *accustomed to the voice of their ordinary pastors, sinners are lulled asleep, and the good often become tepid; never hearing the word that would arouse them.*" Third, the mission band would preach during Lent and Advent "in the larger towns," where the clergy were too overworked by their ordinary duties "to undertake this extraordinary fatigue; from which cause those immense cities are *entirely destitute of an energetic announcement of the word of God*, both in its dogmatical and its moral bearing."

The group, finally, would provide spiritual retreats in colleges and monasteries and for the secular clergy, "a thing of which the necessity is every day becoming more evident: for, *among the clergy, these retreats have never been established;* and, even in communities, the custom is, to substitute the reading of some book, and this without any regular method for the meditations prescribed by the spiritual exercises." He concluded by advising the pope that he had been considering the matter for three years and that he was "ready, at a nod, to devote himself to this great undertaking, and dedicate to it all the influence or ability, which he may ever possess."

Some years after the death of Gregory XVI, a copy of the address, printed in England, was circulated. In a preface it was noted that the pope had sent copies to the vicars apostolic, "with a request that they would signify their opinion of it." The bishops replied "that they knew nothing of the scheme proposed by Dr. Wiseman; that they had *not* therefore given to it their 'unanimous,' or indeed, *any*, 'consent;' and that most, if not all, of the statements contained in the Petition were opposed to the truth!"[30]

Wiseman clearly *thought* that he had obtained the support of the vicars apostolic for his project. In January 1840 he wrote to Bishop Griffiths, in a forthright manner, to state that one of the students at the college, under no persuasive pressures, had offered "to devote himself to the missionary life in the sense in which I took the liberty of explaining it to your Ldp. in London, a plan which my own thoughts and the concurrent approbation of every person of piety and ability to whom I have opened it, convince me every day more & more would do great good both with protestants and catholics." He went on to say that he was anxious to devote himself to it, "if my ecclesiastical superiors think fit, for I will undertake nothing on my own judgment."[31]

Bishop Griffiths was by no means pleased with Wiseman's plan. He wrote to Briggs to describe the memorial, which, he guessed correctly, the pope would "probably send for our opinions on the subject." Griffiths continued: "Should our recognized agent act in this manner without consulting us? Is there not danger of confusion in our government from these unauthorized applications? Does not this show the danger of persons, whose prudence is not guided by experience, having authority in this country?" A few weeks later Griffiths informed Briggs that he intended to write to Propaganda that he and his predecessors had contemplated establishing a missionary house in the London District for the past twenty years, but "that it is not so much wanted as the memorial insinuates; that its establishment would be injurious to religion, if it withdrew necessary missioners from the congregations;

that I have not any subject whom I can spare for such a House, & that I purpose conferring with the VV.A. at our next meeting." He continued by telling Briggs that he had already written to let Wiseman know that the memorial had been presented without authorization.[32]

Bishop Briggs consulted the priests of his district on Wiseman's proposal. Thomas Youens, Newsham's predecessor at Ushaw, admitted "that the existence of some such society as Dr. Wiseman is contemplating would be of incalculable benefit to the English mission," but he nevertheless expressed his disapproval. It would withdraw some of the most promising priests from the jurisdiction of their own bishops; the young men proposed for the work were too inexperienced; and Wiseman, finally, had no right to propose such a plan without the approval of the vicars apostolic: "Looking at the whole affair, I must say that it appears to me much rather like a whim of the Doctor's, than a work dictated by the spirit of God, & moreover a whim in which there is a wonderful deal of self-confidence coupled with a corresponding degree of disregard for others."[33]

Robert Tate, formerly vice-president of Ushaw and later to be its president, sent a similar reply. He feared that Wiseman's presentation would make "an unfavourable & a groundless impression on the mind of His Holiness." Wiseman seemed to have forgotten, complained Tate, the obstacles that made it difficult for the clergy to gather for retreats, nor did he take into account that most of them, insofar as possible, did, in fact, make them annually. He concluded by observing that Wiseman's novel opinions made him a dangerous man to head the kind of community proposed. He cited the sermon that Wiseman had preached in Derby on the subject of doctrinal development, a theme considered by many to deviate from theological orthodoxy: "It is much to be doubted whether his German notions of theology be suited to the meridian of England. I should feel more confidence in one who has lived in the country, who has observed & studied the feelings of the people, & whose zeal has been tempered by the cool climate of missionary experience."[34]

Charles Newsham, above all, should have understood what Wiseman had in mind. In writing to his friend in Rome he had expressed his own strong views on the inadequacies of the English clergy. Now, however, he wrote to Bishop Briggs:

We all lament the tone & manner of Dr. Wiseman's petition, as calculated to lower the English Catholic clergy in the opinion of the Holy See. As to the plan itself, & the objects proposed, Mr. [Thomas] Cookson [Ushaw's vice-president] sees little to object to, unless, as we all are inclined [to] suspect, it be Dr. Wiseman's intention that the Institution, if I may so call it, is meant to receive its powers & authority directly from the pope, & thus become entirely independent of the Vicars Ap. of this country. If this be meant we are all opposed to the measure *in toto*. For by that means young men, not always the most prudent, might travel through any district in spite of the bishop or clergy of the district, take everything over the heads of the bishops & the clergy, & thus spread confusion everywhere.

Newsham continued by stating that Wiseman was "something of a zealot . . . far too sanguine, & I fear, a little too self sufficient. He is not well acquainted with England. His mind is full of golden dreams, which I fear he will never see realized." He thought, in fact, that the rector of the Venerabile might do more harm than good, so that he urged Briggs to inform the prefect of Propaganda "that Wiseman is much mistaken as to the very flattering prospect of the conversion of this country; in fact, that he can have nothing better than a very cursery [*sic*] superficial knowledge of the feelings & prejudices of English protestants."[35] The Ushaw president could hardly have been faulted for his fears regarding the possible independence of the proposed community from the jurisdiction of the vicars apostolic. Considering that Wiseman had confided in him as in few others and that he himself had been an important source of information on the state of the church in England, however, it is hard to avoid the conclusion that Newsham, for whatever reason, was playing a double game.

Unaware, it seems, of the extent of his opposition, Wiseman wrote to Newsham, while the storm was brewing, in order to comment on the deficiencies in the young men sent from Ushaw to Rome.

> George [Errington] and myself find, from the observation of the latest comers from Ushaw, that what is principally to be aimed at, is accustoming them, from the early part of their course to think & judge, of which they seem to have little idea. They do not seem to know how to make things out for themselves, or to make one bear upon another; whatever they learn they seem to put up in their heads, and not to have it at hand when wanted for some other purpose. This is I think a faculty which may be acquired by early cultivation, and makes up much for want of great memory or great abilities. It gives that *sagacity* in research, and that power of combination in application, which makes very moderate talents to effect what great powers without it seldom do. And where these exist, it gives them a tenfold value & efficacy.[36]

The observation may have been justified and the objective praiseworthy, but the letter was poorly timed, considering the criticism that Wiseman was then receiving in England.

Bishop Baines, of all people, provided qualified encouragement for Wiseman's plan. The western bishop wrote, "I think the project respecting the missionary association or Institute deserves serious consideration; but I would strongly recommend to you not to obtain its establishment till the VV.A. have given it their approval." He said that until he had received a letter from Wiseman on the subject, he had heard nothing about it, "except certain vague rumours to which I paid no attention, convinced that if the affair were seriously contemplated it would be brought before me in a regular and authoritative form." Baines was most certainly aware of Wiseman's memorial by this time. Under the circumstances, his warning was probably intended as a somewhat subtle rebuke. Bishop Walsh, on the other hand, when consulted by Propaganda, lent his full support to Wiseman's proposal.[37]

The Sacred Congregation for the Propagation of the Faith met in August 1839 to discuss the reorganization of the English ecclesiastical system at a time when, as we have seen, various misunderstandings and controversies were causing mistrust between the Holy See and the vicars apostolic. One cannot fail to be impressed by the thoroughness with which the sacred congregation examined the various problems. As in all major questions to be decided, a summary of the letters and documents pertinent to the case was printed and distributed to the members of the congregation prior to their general meeting. Along with this *ponenza* or *ristretto*, as it was called, prepared by Cardinal Angelo Mai, each was given a printed copy of the relevant documents themselves. In cases involving a specialized knowledge, consultors were asked to submit a dissertation or *votum*, and in this instance Cardinal De Luca was assigned the major task. Each cardinal then made his private study in consultation with specialists. When they finally met, one served as *relator* or *ponente*. It was his role to present the case to the assembled prelates and to lead the discussion. Cardinal Mai served in this capacity. Then the assembled fathers voted on specific questions, and the results were presented to the pope, who either approved them or referred particular matters for further study.[38]

The restoration of the hierarchy had been opposed by Monsignor, later Cardinal, Acton, whose judgment carried much weight. He admitted that the eventual reestablishment of a hierarchy would be a good thing, but he considered the immediate obstacles to be too great, including the clause of the Catholic Emancipation Act forbidding the assumption of titles held by bishops of the Established Church.[39]

Acton's position was opposed by Cardinal De Luca, who claimed that for two centuries the English clergy, the nobility, and the greater part of the Catholic body had been longing for a hierarchy. He quoted Lingard, who the previous February had complained that bishops *in partibus* were considered both by Catholics and Protestants as an inferior class of persons, merely subalterns, revocable *ad nutum*, without authority or will of their own. The historian had insisted that he had no personal stake in the decision, since he did not aspire to a mitre, although one had been offered to him twenty years before.[40]

Monsignor Acton's judgment prevailed in spite of the strong case made by Cardinal De Luca. Among those who opposed the restoration of the hierarchy were Luigi Gentili and his Rosminian confrère Giovanni Battista Pagani. They had prepared a *votum*, at the request of Propaganda, that arrived in Rome too late to be included among the documents formally considered by the sacred congregation. Its contents were known, however. The two men did not support the step because, as they said, "the English clergy are infected with Gallicanism and are dominated by a spirit of ambition and national independence. The result is that the bishops, as vicars apostolic, do not show the respectful submission and dependence on the Holy See that their duty requires." They acknowledged that Bishop Walsh was an exception to their observation.[41]

The Roman authorities were dissatisfied with the vicars apostolic for a number of reasons: their brief replies to the "Statuta Proposita"; their failure to support wholeheartedly the international Society for the Propagation of the Faith; their refusal to consult the Holy See as desired; and their inability to arrive at agreement with respect to the organization of the districts or even the expediency of restoring the hierarchy. Propaganda was ill disposed toward the prospect of allowing the greater independence that would result from the establishment of the hierarchy.

When the cardinals assembled in August, they discussed a number of questions systematically. If, first of all, the hierarchy were to be restored, they had to deal with the question of whether bishops should be placed over sees that had existed prior to the Reformation or whether new, more modern cities should be the diocesan centers. Since they decided at the outset not to appoint bishops-in-ordinary, however, they proceeded to the questions involved in dividing the existing districts. Possible boundaries had to be determined. In addition they considered the financing of the new vicars apostolic, the means of distributing the temporalities of the old districts, the role of the Benedictines in the reorganization, the establishment of episcopal chapters, the method of selecting new vicars apostolic, the possible means of curtailing their jurisdiction, and measures for increasing the zeal of the English clergy. They noted, moreover, that Cardinal De Luca, in his *votum*, had suggested that English seminaries should be subject to official visitations, that a new translation of the Bible into English should be undertaken, and that the English clergy should be prevented from taking too active a part in political discussions. No major decisions were made, but on September 28, 1839, Cardinal Fransoni wrote to Bishop Griffiths to inform him that although the erection of dioceses would be postponed, the number of districts was to be raised immediately to eight.[42]

Wiseman wrote to Bishop Griffiths on January 3 and told him that he had spoken with both the prefect and secretary of Propaganda, but that neither had entered into the details of the sacred congregation's decisions. He added that "there appear . . . to be better feelings with regard to England than there have been before, and a desire to have a good understanding about matters." He understood that the question of the hierarchy had been discussed: "The Cong[regation], with which the Pope agreed, thought that this measure wd. be premature, & that it would be better to make the changes gradually, first increasing the number of the bishops, then making them bishops in ordinary." The Propaganda secretary hoped that the final step would be taken within two or three years. The districts would be divided, finally, according to the plan of the "Statuta Proposita," "with such corrections as shall be thought necessary by the Card. Prefect and Mgr. Acton." In February, Wiseman wrote to Lingard: "They [the Roman authorities] hope to appoint our new bishops in a month or two, and their intention seems to be to give us a hierarchy in three or four years. They wish to see how an increased number of bishops works before taking that decided step." [43]

The selection of new bishops was not an easy matter. Acceptable candidates were limited by the fact that England was expected to provide bishops for the British colonies as well as administrative officials, of nonepiscopal rank, for the various colleges at home and abroad. Moreover, no one whose devotion to the Holy See was doubtful would be selected, nor would any man who was known to oppose the regulars.

On January 4 Cardinal Fransoni wrote to the vicars apostolic to ask for suggestions. Three weeks later, impatient at not having had a reply, he sent a list of names, drawn from those recommended in Rome (presumably by Wiseman and Acton) to each bishop, seeking comment on the suitability of each for the episcopate. [44] Bishop Walsh wrote to Wiseman, "I am puzzled what names to send to Rome in addition to that of Revd. Mr. Husenbeth." He was considering Henry Weedall of Oscott but was convinced that the college president would refuse. Walsh did not see, moreover, how Weedall could be replaced, "Unless your influence comes in his place." He added, "If, however, His Holiness will appoint you my coadjutor, I am prepared to make the sacrifice." [45]

The vicars apostolic were unable to agree on the suitability of the various candidates proposed. Bishop Briggs was offended when Griffiths presumed to recommend a priest from the Northern District. Griffiths attempted to soothe the sensibilities of his offended colleague: "The tone of my letter to Propaganda was designedly sent as to give it no weight." [46] If known in Rome, such a response would have done little to alter the conviction of the authorities that the English bishops were themselves responsible for the Holy See's inability to assess the state of the church in England.

Although Bishop Walsh was especially anxious to have Wiseman as coadjutor, others were far from favorable to the candidacy of their agent in Rome. Bishop Baines was most outspoken. He argued that Wiseman's ideas were divisive, especially regarding seminaries, and that although his zeal was beyond question, he would never be able to confine his efforts to a single district. The previous year Baines had written to Bishop Griffiths: "It is quite clear to me that that gentleman [Wiseman] is playing his own game, and proving to the authorities in Rome and to our noble countrymen there how absolutely necessary it is that a Bishop should be sent to England who may enlighten our ignorance and keep us out of mischief."[47]

Baines was not the only bishop who opposed Wiseman's elevation to the episcopate. Bishop Briggs was of the same mind as his western colleague. In February 1840 Charles Newsham, whom, of course, Wiseman considered to be his ally, wrote to Briggs: "I have often told you, & you may rely on its truth, that you [the vicars apostolic of England] have no secrets at Rome. Everything you say has been all along, & will continue to be, made known to the regulars & through them to the public." He continued, "I agree with you in all you say about Dr. Wiseman." Newsham considered the rector of the English College to be an enthusiast and, in addition, "much devoted to the regulars." Under no circumstances would Wiseman do for the Northern District, wrote Newsham.

Since Wiseman had left for Rome from the Northern District, the only one in which he had actually resided, it was arguable that he was still under the jurisdiction of Bishop Briggs. Newsham, however, continued his letter to the northern vicar apostolic by urging him not to press the matter.

> Again I think, if you claimed him you would do no good, but harm. *He* would deny your right to claim him: he would refuse to be V.A. in the North; for I happen to know that he is quite bent on residing near London, if he reside in England at all. He expressly said so to Mr. [Ralph] Platt [a northern priest] last summer. This fact did not occur to me when I wrote about him before. I think, then, you should not claim him. Will you recommend him? You cannot. You do not think him the fittest person. I am of opinion, then, that your own suggestion is the best: viz. Propose him as the *only* person (as I am inclined to think he is) for a more important work even than the office of V.A. Tell Fransoni that Dr. Wiseman is the *only* man likely to succeed in that undertaking. Then 2ndly you may, but softly, state any other objections you please.

Newsham continued: "I would not object to Wiseman as over-zealous

& a Spencerite. They are all at Rome, through ignorance of this country, Spencerites. They would think worse of *you*, & elect *him*, for that very reason. Neither can you with any advantage object to him as a bookworm or as biased to the regulars."[48] "Spencerite" was the name applied to those who were viewed as unduly enthusiastic and optimistic with reference to the prospects of Catholicism in England, a label implying a lack of prudence, associated with George Spencer, now at Oscott. It bore the same connotation for Roman Catholics as "Puseyite" did for Anglicans. Newsham, at least at this point, seems to have been willing to admit the good that Wiseman could do were he free to move about the country for purposes of preaching and lecturing.

Lingard advised Briggs not to oppose Wiseman's candidacy to the episcopate if, in fact, it were as coadjutor to Bishop Walsh. He could not understand why Baines and Newsham should object to Wiseman's presence at Oscott: "Do they suppose that his reputation would attract students? If it did, it would be but for a short time." He warned Briggs: "If Dr. Walsh approve, will your objections have much weight, particularly if the card[inals] wish to get rid of him at Rome? Will it not be said that you three object through jealousy?" Lingard offered a possible objection, however, to Wiseman's leaving Rome: "I should fear that, if he leave, the college at Rome will be put under the Padri [the Jesuits]." He advised, finally, that Briggs might object, but that he should do so "without seeming to attach much importance to the objection," and he added: "Whatever you write, be assured of this, that he will either see your letter or learn what is said of him in it. Of that I saw plenty at Rome."[49]

Lingard prepared the letter that Briggs would include with the list of the nominees for the episcopate. When writing to the bishop, however, the historian warned: "If your Lordship look over the list again you will find that there is not one of the whole number of 15 against whom you do not make some objection, actual or implied. Will not the Card. [Fransoni] remark this? Will he not attribute it to pique? Will it not deprive you of all authority with him?" He noted that Briggs had been most positive in his objections to the secular clergy proposed, while commenting with a simple negative on the regulars: "If then you have authority with him [Fransoni], that authority will act in favour of the monks and Jesuits. I wish I could prevail on you to withdraw some of your objections, such as to Wiseman, Weedall, and Tate."[50] Briggs, in fact, followed Lingard's advice.

When Propaganda met to discuss the nominees for the office of vicar apostolic, the cardinals were presented with a list of those suggested by the sacred congregation itself as well as the names of those offered by the vicars apostolic. Several were eliminated because of their "anti-Roman principles"; and another was said to be opposed to the regulars. One candidate was judged to be too old, while another was too young. Henry Weedall was thought to be excellent, especially by Monsignor Acton. Thomas Brindle, a former Benedictine, was nominated by Bishop Baines, but he was considered to have "doubtful principles" and little learning. George Spencer, included by Propaganda, was insufficiently grounded in knowledge and prudence. Thomas Joseph Brown, prior of Downside, was praised highly, as was William Wareing, vice-president of Oscott. Bishop Baines opposed Wiseman's nomination, as we have seen, but Cardinal Fransoni concluded that the reasons behind the incompatibility of the two men were more to Wiseman's credit than to that of Baines.[51]

Bishop Baines was again in trouble, and Wiseman was clearly identified as one of his opponents. For several years the younger man had been supporting a movement to encourage public prayers for the conversion of England. With the Holy See's explicit approval, he had initiated the practice of reciting such prayers with his students at the college and was actively encouraging that it be extended throughout England. In so doing, he had been influenced by George Spencer, to whom he wrote that "a new system in many things" was urgently needed in England: "One of the points on which I insisted was the want of systematic prayers for the conversion of England, and, at the same time, of *reparation* for her defection."[52]

Baines went so far as to devote his Lenten pastoral letter in 1840 to the subject of such prayers. As he explained to Wiseman:

> With respect to the Prayers for the conversion of England, whilst they are offered privately and no public parade is made about them, I have no objection to them. I therefore do not presume to express any opinion upon the approbation given to such private prayers by the late indulgences. I regret, however, that the authorities did not content themselves with granting your petition & restraining the indulgences to your own college, as I fear that some of our hotheads here will be publishing them. As to the *public* prayer about which Mr. Spencer is making such a stir, I have expressed my sentiments, which are in accordance with two of the other VV.A. — of Dr. Walsh's I know nothing.[53]

Bishops Griffiths and Briggs were careful to restrain themselves from any public criticism of the prayers, however, unlike the impulsive bishop of the Western District.

In May 1840 Baines was summoned to Rome to answer for the violence of his opposition to a movement that seemed destined to do so much good and had the support of the Holy See.[54] There is no doubt that the whole affair embittered the already unfriendly relationship between Wiseman and Baines.

Rome's selection of the new vicars apostolic was made known in the spring, and, as anticipated, Wiseman was named coadjutor to Bishop Walsh and president of Oscott College. He was to be titular bishop of Melipotamus, a see chosen by himself in commemoration of the martyrdom of a vicar apostolic of Tonquin who had held the same title.[55]

Bishop Walsh, while welcoming the appointment, was saddened to lose Weedall, who was assigned to the Northern vicariate, and Wareing, who was to be vicar apostolic of the new Eastern District. Walsh wrote to Lord Shrewsbury, "Both my dear friends feel exceedingly the responsibility imposed on them, & their separation from the college." He added: "I cannot but feel the stroke for many reasons. Doctor Wiseman must be my comfort and support. I must write to him to come to England soon. His chief residence must undoubtedly be in the college." Thomas Joseph Brown was to leave Downside to take up his duties as vicar apostolic of the new Welsh District. George Brown, in spite of poor health, was given the Lancashire District.[56]

"I presume your Lordship has heard of the *extraordinary Roman* appointments of the new vicars apostolic," wrote Bishop Briggs; "May heaven, in its greatest mercy avert what I fear must be the very sad consequences resulting from these appointments."[57] Briggs, along with many of the northern clergy, disapproved of Weedall's appointment, convinced that only a native of their district could understand their problems. All of those chosen, in fact, were among those whom Bishop Briggs had judged to be "unfit." He had suggested six candidates, all from his own district; none was appointed.

Weedall hurried to Rome and successfully persuaded the authorities to relieve him of the burden of a bishopric. Since Wiseman was to replace him at Oscott, where he had lived for thirty-six years, Weedall was forced to seek a position elsewhere, until he returned, thirteen years later, to take up again the presidency of that institution.[58] He was replaced among the new vicars apostolic by Francis Mostyn, who had been in charge of the mission at Wolverhampton and so, like Weedall, attached to the Midland District. By then the northern clergy may well have understood that it would not do to antagonize the Holy See any further. One of their priests wrote to Wiseman's successor in Rome: "We have heard lately from a very reputable source that it is confidently reported at Rome & probably *believed* by the sacred congregation that the *clergy of the north* have set up a *claim of right* to have a Bishop from their own Diocese. We are anxious to disclaim the *fact* of our having set up any *such* claim." He said that they had never set up a claim of any kind: "We merely expressed our *wishes* & gave our *reasons* for those *wishes*, without claiming *any right* whatever."[59]

The northern clergy had earlier feared that a bishop might be chosen for them from a religious order. They had protested against such a possibility, and Bishop Briggs had sent their petition to Rome. The procurator for the Anglo-Benedictines had been negotiating, in fact, for *two* of the new districts. He had written to Monsignor Acton:

> In increasing the Episcopacy from four to eight, it will be necessary, I conceive, to give some support to Religious Orders. This may be done by appointing out of the four new Bishops two Regulars. It is known how much the Religious Orders suffer in England, and at the same time how much they are attached to the Holy See. Among the *four* existing Bishops, *three* are enemies to all Religious Orders; they persecute them and would gladly see them all suppressed. But who are those three? Precisely those who are most reluctant to submit to the supreme decisions of Rome. In England there is only one Bishop who is the friend of Regulars, but though his support be felt and appreciated as it ought to be, yet it is only the support of *one* against the hostility of *three*. There is, moreover, reason to fear that on account of Dr. Walsh's advanced age, the Regulars will not enjoy his support for any great number of years.[60]

It was his wish that the districts named might be put completely in the hands of the regulars. Although this was not done, Bishop Brown of Wales was, of course, a Benedictine, and he depended to a great extent upon the support of his order. No other regular was appointed in 1840. Baines, though also a Benedictine, could hardly have been considered friendly to his own or to any other order. There is every reason to believe, however, that the Benedictine procurator found a ready listener in Monsignor Acton, who also seems to have communicated to him all the complaints of the vicars apostolic, in order that the Benedictines might anticipate any unfavorable action on the part of the bishops.

Wiseman was consecrated as bishop by Cardinal Fransoni on June 8, 1840. Bishop Baines, who was in Rome, wrote, "Dr. Wiseman has worked his way to his present station and influence by sacrificing the views & authority of the VV.A. — and by flattering the prejudices and confirming the errors of the authorities here." He continued: "At the dinner given at Dr. Wiseman's consecration, Cardl. Fransoni being present, it was said publicly & seriously, that another Gregory was sending another Augustine for the conversion of England! The Pope expressed to me his extreme dissatisfaction with the English VV.A. whom he considered on the brink of schism."[61]

Baines attempted to place one more obstacle in the way of Wiseman's appointment to the Midland District and therefore, the presidency of Oscott, by suggesting that the new bishop might be assigned to the North in place of Weedall. Wiseman, when he heard of the report, wrote to Monsignor Acton, "My great desire was simply to go to England for the purpose of carrying out practical plans respecting education, missions, controversy, all which I saw I could be enabled to do in residence at Oscott & Birmingham, a most central situation, better than any where else." He concluded, "If I be removed to the North, I must necessarily quit the field, at any rate, my long nourished hopes of being able by personal intercourse to win some of those learned men must be completely abandoned."[62] No more was heard of the suggestion.

Ten years after the English vicariates had been increased to eight, Pope Pius IX referred to the division and said that it had been accomplished in order to "prepare the way for the future restoration of the ordinary hierarchy."[63] The fact remains that the changes of 1840 achieved very little in themselves. The status of priests was not altered; no provision was made for chapters or deaneries; bishops were to be selected as before, normally upon the recommendation of their predecessors; parishes were not erected; nothing was specified about consulting the Holy See; and no explicit intention of restoring the hierarchy was expressed. The vicars apostolic were no more likely to agree on policies than before, since no system of precedence was established among them, although presumably they would continue to rely upon the London bishop to represent their common interests when corresponding with the Holy See, as had been the case previously. The vicariates were now smaller, of course, and it might have been hoped that the burden upon the bishops would be less strenuous.

The most noteworthy change in the new scheme of things, perhaps, was the presence of Wiseman in England. He was now in a position, as never before, to demonstrate the soundness of his ideas. His opposition was formidable, but he had more support than he seems to have realized or ever acknowledged. His achievement was extraordinary, nor does there seem to have been any other man who could have done so much.

7. Titular Bishop of Melipotamus

ON SEPTEMBER 9, 1840, WISEMAN WAS RECEIVED AT OSCOTT IN A formal ceremony, similar to that normally accorded to an ordinary about to be installed in his diocese. He was greeted by Bishop Walsh, the staff and students of the college, and a number of priests attached to the district, including John Kirk, "a veritable link with the past," who more than sixty-five years earlier had been a student at the English College in Rome, prior to the suppression of the Jesuits who had charge of it.[1] The new bishop had reason for optimism. Elevated to the episcopate, well known throughout Europe, president of a college with a promising staff, and in control of a journal that had already made its mark among intellectuals, he was very much aware of the opportunities now opening up for him.

Bishop Walsh soon demonstrated that he had been sincere in expressing his desire to turn over to his coadjutor the major responsibility for administering the district. In a pastoral letter to his flock, the older man wrote that his new assistant was invested with "full power" in governing Oscott and in nominating to all offices in the college. In addition, he was to serve as vicar general of the Central District, "with full communication, so far as in us lies, of all the powers, ordinary and extraordinary, which we possess, including such as require special deputation, or the episcopal character." Wiseman was also to take charge of all matters requiring direct communication with the Holy See, since his previous role as agent for the vicars apostolic especially qualified him for the task. "Wherefore," wrote Walsh, "those cases of dispensation, or others, which require application to the Apostolic See, you are at full liberty at once, in every instance, to refer to our Aforesaid Venerable Brother." Influenced, no doubt, by his coadjutor,

Walsh concluded by urging his priests to pray for England's return "to the unity of Faith and the bond of Peace, which are only to be found in the church of God, the chaste spouse of the Lamb."[2]

The new bishop was frequently accused of neglecting the discipline and the day-to-day management of the college. Even before he moved to England, however, it had been understood that his concerns and activities were such that he would not be able to confine them to his own district. His readiness to embrace the many demands made upon him would not have been subject to so much criticism, perhaps, had he been able to rely more completely upon those whom he delegated to assist him and upon whose help he counted. More than six years after his arrival in Birmingham, Wiseman wrote a personal memorandum to explain the problems he encountered: "I came to England and into this district and college without a claim upon anyone's kindness or indulgence, with overrated abilities, exaggerated reputation for learning, over-estimated character in every respect. I was placed in a position of heavy responsibility and arduous labour. No one on earth knows what I went through in head & heart, during my years of silent and salutary sorrow. In the house I have reason now to know that *not one* was working with me, thought with me or felt with me."

Wiseman's complaint was that too much was expected of him personally, but too little of the institution over which he had been placed: "How seldom has a word been spoken which intimated that those who worked the College considered it as more than a mere place of boys' education or worked it as a great engine employed in England's conversion and regeneration. What a different place it would be if all had laboured with this view, and for this purpose!" By 1847, nevertheless, it was clear that his efforts were bearing fruit: "But thank God! it [the college] has done its work, in spite of us; in spite of our miserable strifes and petty jealousies, and narrow views, and cold, almost sarcastic valuation of what a higher and better Power was working through it."[3]

Wiseman was not without blame for the lack of encouragement that he experienced. Like many men and women of strong character and views, he often lacked sensitivity toward the position of others, while enthusiastically pursuing his own objectives. He would embark impetuously upon particular projects without laying sufficient groundwork. His presumption seemed to be that the success of his policies would gain him the necessary support. Such had been the case when he had sought to establish a missionary community, obtaining the interest of some of his students but failing to communicate adequately his intention to the vicars apostolic, upon whom, of course, the success of his plan would depend. When opposed under circumstances of this kind, he was shocked and hurt. The problem was all the more serious because of his basic shyness, especially apparent when he had to confront those who disagreed with him. A convert who lived with him at Oscott for several years described an occasion on which he had opposed him: "His embarrassment was so great when I appeared that he sat silent for some three or four minutes before he could bring himself to enter on the subject."[4] Throughout Wiseman's life, he found it extremely difficult to deal with those who were not completely behind him.

Once established at Oscott, Wiseman immediately joined forces with those who anticipated, as a result of the Oxford Movement, an extraordinary Catholic revival. He was somewhat more modest in his expectations, however, than his critics would have admitted. Shortly before moving to England he had written: "That fanaticism has greatly exaggerated the views taken by many Protestants of our increase, we are sorry to be obliged to admit; we wish we were as numerous and powerful without being as terrible — as our adversaries would wish to represent us. Still it is a cheering and encouraging thing to us, to see ourselves acknowledged as growing and a strengthening body."[5]

Early in 1839 Wiseman had submitted an optimistic report to Propaganda concerning the prospects of Catholicism in England. It was based, to a great extent, upon letters that he had received from his friends. Pugin, first of all, had described the construction of new churches and chapels throughout the country; Phillipps had pointed to the conversions resulting from the special prayers offered for that intention; George Spencer had stressed the Anglo-Catholic interests of Newman, Edward Pusey, and John Keble, as had Daniel Rock. "It is quite possible," a modern commentator has written, "in view of the lack of other information, that this letter shaped the attitude of the Vatican toward the Oxford Movement."[6]

As a matter of fact, Wiseman was only one among a number of sources of information upon whom the authorities in Rome depended.[7] Among the most important was Monsignor Acton, who, in the same year that Wiseman prepared his report, wrote a similar one to describe the rapidly developing interest in Catholic doctrine among Protestant clergymen. He described the Tractarians as a new theological school that was stressing the importance of tradition and the necessity of authority in determining matters of faith. These Oxford divines encouraged practices such as prayers for the dead, in spite of opposition from those who considered devotions of that kind to be superstitious. Acton criticized a portion of the Catholic clergy for moving away from the very principles that were attractive to the Oxford divines, although he singled out Bishop Walsh as the only vicar apostolic who encouraged the regulars and took the lead in constructing chapels and schools in response to the demands of the times. Acton rejoiced, finally, in his conviction that the Oxford Movement would ultimately destroy the very foundations of the Anglican church.[8]

Newman, years after his conversion, wrote in his journal that "the Church must be prepared for converts, as well as converts prepared for the Church."[9] Wiseman, on more than one occasion, expressed the same concern. Shortly after his arrival at Oscott, he wrote to Charles Baggs, his successor as rector of the English College, and urged him to maintain the goals that had been established there under his own rectorship. He prefaced his remarks by warning Baggs to avoid taking sides in disputes among the vicars apostolic, wise advice based on bitter experience. He then continued by pressing for a continuation of his own policies, which, he feared, were being undermined: "I have laboured for some years to infuse into it [the college] all that I could of an apostolic spirit and ardent desire to promote or hasten the conversion of England & am I to fear that these feelings have been proscribed or checked as chimerical or enthusiastic?"

When Wiseman left for England, Bishop Baines was still in Rome, defending his opposition to public prayers for the conversion of the country and his conviction that enthusiasts were damaging the Catholic cause by implying, without justification, that there would soon be a massive conversion. It is likely that he had been exercising some influence on Baggs, who, in fact, eventually succeeded Baines as vicar apostolic of the Western district. Wiseman warned: "Believe me, my dear Dr. Baggs, that independently of all other considerations, you will not keep up great efforts without great objects in view, and that if the ardour of elevated hopes is cooled, the execution which they alone can call for will be damped with them. Every day & every hour convinces me more that we cannot look for too great things in England. . . . Even now, could we double the learning & piety of the clergy, we might do wonders."[10]

A year later Baines continued to criticize Wiseman. He described, in a letter to Baggs, some of the extreme devotional innovations that were being introduced into England, citing, as an example, an illustration in a book on the Sacred Heart that "gives an *eye* like a Cyclops to a large painted heart." He viewed the picture as "mawkish nonsense," designed by an "ambitious and avaricious association" to subject the intellects of "weak men and weak women."[11] Although Wiseman promoted devotional practices unfamiliar to most Englishmen, there is no evidence that he identified himself with the more extravagent examples cited by Bishop Baines.

Several months after Wiseman had settled at Oscott, Newman published his famous Tract 90. Its argument was that the Thirty-nine Articles admitted of a Catholic sense and that, in any case, they were never intended as an Anglican "rule of faith." Newman's position, unacceptable to the majority of Anglicans (including the bishops), was an encouraging sign for Wiseman, who wrote: "I see no insurmountable difficulties in Oxford against the return of unity. The passions of men, and the gross prejudices of the mass of the people are our real adversaries. The latter *they* [the Oxford men] are more likely to remove than we. The portion of the former which belongs to our own body we must study to remove." [12]

Two weeks earlier Wiseman had told the same correspondent that the Tractarians "are every day becoming more & more disgusted with Anglicanism, its barrenness, its shallowness, and its 'stammering' teaching. Their advance is so steady, regular, and unanimous, that one of two things must follow — either they will bring or push on their church with them, or they will leave her behind. The first is their great object, the second may be their gain." He by no means supported those who thought that Anglicans, even though convinced of the truth of Roman doctrine, should remain in their place in order to reunite corporately at a later time.

> In the meantime many of them are as yet terribly in the dark as to their *in-dividual* duty in their present state of feeling, & it seems to me that if consulted by any *one* as to what *he* should do, I should of course tell him to go forth from his father's house & kindred and go into the land which God's grace shows him, by *at once* yielding to his convictions & securing his *own* salvation. But when, as in every case I yet know of them, they have not been so far enlightened by faith & grace as to feel that it is a risk to their own salvation to remain united to the Anglican church, though they consider it a duty of *that church* to bring itself into communion with the Cath. church, all we can do is to push them forward in their views so as to make them diffuse it in every direction; and to invite them towards us rather than repulse them, as some seem inclined to do. I should like to see them become catholics at once, & one by one, but if they will not do that, I should be sorry to check them in their present course.

Wiseman was especially confident with respect to Newman: "I have recd. every explanation, & perfectly understand the course he is pursuing. He has, I feel assured, no other end but *Rome*." [13]

Wiseman was premature in his judgment, relying upon reports from unduly optimistic Catholics, like Phillipps and Spencer, as well as devotees of Newman within the Anglican communion who tended to race ahead of their leader and whose ardor he, in fact, attempted to subdue. When planning to travel to Oxford for a confirmation, Bishop Wiseman offered to meet privately with the Oxford divines. Although his proposal was rejected, he responded with tact: "I can have nothing of course to lose by not meeting any one there, but I should have been sorry to have had to decide for myself between placing others in any awkward position by my offering to see them, and my neglect of any courtesy on the other hand by my keeping aloof." [14]

There were those who were simplistic in their conviction that corporate reunion between the Anglican and Roman churches was an immediate probability. In some cases the enthusiasm of Catholics far exceeded any intention on the part of their Anglican friends. George Spencer, for example, has been described as possessing "almost childish innocence of historical and theological subtleties." He was a professor at Oscott and spiritual director for the students when Wiseman arrived. In 1840, while attempting what today would be considered a "dialogue" with some of the Oxford men, he had to report, "I was brought during the first days of fight to the most astonishing point not only of having my battery regularly silenced but of being in a complete maze in my own mind." [15]

Bishop Walsh wrote to inform Wiseman that Spencer's embarrassment at Oxford showed how dangerous it would be "to raise him at present to the episcopal responsibility, for if when more left to himself he should again indulge his enthusiastic schemes, again commit himself with the acute, learned Oxford divines and fall, the scandal & injury to our holy religion would be the more to be lamented." Walsh confined Spencer to the role of spiritual adviser at the college, encouraging him, at the same time, to improve himself "in the knowledge of ecclesiastical history, particularly in that of his own country, in which he is very deficient, and which gave a triumph to the Oxford divines over him." Walsh concluded, "If this dear saintly man be permitted to remain usefully employed in the college, as I have described, he will be much better prepared for higher employment in the church than he is now." [16]

It had been thought, some years earlier, that Spencer was surely destined for the episcopate. He was rejected, of course, in 1840. As a result of his experience at Oxford, Bishop Briggs wrote next to his name on the list of candidates, "unfit — an enthusiast — no prudence." [17] Wiseman, in spite of his erudition, was not inclined to rush into the kind of situation that caused Spencer so much distress.

In August 1841, however, Wiseman responded to Newman's Tract 90 in the pages of the Dublin Review. When writing for publication, he was far less inclined to express his harsh views of Anglican claims than in his private correspondence. He noted Newman's principal argument: "We feel ourselves, however unwillingly, compelled to think that, consoling as the new views of the Articles may be to our feelings, they cannot justify subscription so long as the subscribers are *supposed* to bind themselves to an interpretation of them incompatible with what is held by Catholics." [18] His appeal was to fact rather than theory. Newman, within a short time, would arrive at the same conclusion.

When Newman explained that Tract 90 had not been written to support the authoritative teaching of the Roman Catholic church but only to show that the Thirty-nine Articles were not directed against the decrees of the Council of Trent, and that he was unwilling to accept the teaching of Roman authorities on such matters as worship of the saints and the Blessed Virgin, the doctrine of purgatory, and indulgences, Wiseman again took up his pen to respond. He did so kindly, beginning by explaining that Newman had misinterpreted Catholic teaching, the major point later scored by the great Oratorian himself, when answering Gladstone's attack upon the achievement of the First Vatican Council.[19]

Wiseman went on to observe that he was eminently qualified to interpret Catholic doctrine as taught in Rome. He had lived there for twenty-two years and for five of these had "attended 'the Roman Schools' in the Roman College"; he had pursued "the entire theological course, and publicly maintained it in a thesis"; after that time, he had been engaged constantly in teaching theology at the English College; and finally he had been a professor in the Roman University: "I ought therefore to be tolerably acquainted with the doctrines of the Roman Schools." He continued, "Now I solemnly assure you that, throughout the entire course of studies, I never heard a word that could lead me to suppose, that our Blessed Lady and the Saints are, or ought to be, the 'prominent objects of regard,' or *could* be 'dispensers of mercy': or that 'Purgatory or Indulgences are the means of obtaining it, &c.'"[20]

In the same year Wiseman addressed a public *Letter on Catholic Unity* to the earl of Shrewsbury. Even today its sentiments appear strikingly enlightened. Anyone consulting the works of the Oxford divines, he wrote, could not fail to see that they were moving toward the Catholic church, "both in doctrine and in affectionate feeling." He continued, "Our saints, our popes, have become dear to them by little and little; our rites and ceremonies, our offices, nay our very rubrics, are precious in their eyes, far, alas! beyond what many of us consider them: our monastic institutions, our charitable and educational provisions have become more and more objects with them of earnest study; and everything, in fine, that concerns our religion, deeply interests their attention."

Although he argued that many Anglicans were dissatisfied with their church, Wiseman did not gloat. He warned Catholics, in fact, that it was their duty "to offer cheerfully and honestly every explanation in our power, and point out where our real doctrines are mistaken [i.e., misunderstood], where they are confounded with mere permissive practices, and where they may be liable to abuse." He added, "The sooner a clear and distinct understanding can be come to upon these matters, whether by personal conference, or by writing, the better for the cause," He offered a second imperative for Catholics, "that of self-improvement, and, where necessary, self reformation."[21]

Wiseman was encouraged by the steady stream of Anglican visitors who came to Oscott, interested not only in meeting him but seriously wishing to receive further enlightenment on the doctrines and practices of his religion. He always received them warmly. The summer after his arrival William George Ward and Frederick Oakeley, both belonging to the later and more enthusiastically inclined devotees of Tractarian doctrine and devotion, visited the college. They were not the most reliable informants of the position held by their associates, tending to exaggerate the readiness of others, like Newman, to accept the teachings of Rome. Wiseman was away when they first came, but he wrote to Lord Shrewsbury to inform him that they had been there and to describe the activity of Pusey, who was in Ireland at the time: "Dr. Pusey literally lives with the priests, and in the convents at Dublin. He often calls on Dr. [Daniel] Murray [the archbishop], and has dined with him. Things are looking very well."[22]

Ward soon returned to Oscott, where, according to Wiseman's account, he "was most unreserved in his communications, authorized in fact by Mr. Newman." Wiseman concluded: "Their minds are now quite made up, that either their church must *very soon* make a great move towards us (of which they see no likelihood at present) or they must abandon her, and do what they can for her from without. I must beg your Lordship not to speak on this subject, for an imprudent word might ruin every thing, and a good deal of candid but most gentle management will be required with at least some."[23] Ward's report to Wiseman was based on wishful thinking. He had certainly not been commissioned by Newman in the manner understood by the bishop.

During the previous spring Wiseman had described for Ambrose Phillipps the approach that he was taking: "I think there is evidence enough in every direction that a hopeful, inviting, encouraging and mild tone and manner are not only the most Christian, but the most prudent and promising of success. I have received a letter from the Propaganda approving in the highest terms of the course I have pursued respecting Oxford. This cheers and encourages me." A month later, writing to Lord Shrewsbury, Wiseman described the progress that was being made: "I have hardly any doubt that in a short time we shall have many joining us, and I know that they look to us as the persons through and by whom their return to the Catholic Church will be effected." It would be a "glorious thing," he said, to have "a dozen or 20 Oxford men established at St. Mary's [Oscott] pursuing their ecclesiastical studies! I will not despair of seeing such a happy event, and then I should begin to hope more sanguinely still for England's conversion."[24]

There were evident signs of dissatisfaction among Anglo-Catholics, and Wiseman was quick to seize upon them. He made no attempt to hide his delight when Christian Karl von Bunsen, Prussian diplomat and scholar whom he had known in Rome, entered into negotiations in England on behalf of the Prussian king to set up a Jerusalem bishopric that might be acceptable to the established churches of both England and Prussia. Wiseman reported to Lord Shrewsbury that Bunsen was, in fact, making a "mess" as a result of the negotiations: "He is evidently come to get up a politico-religious intrigue, & the King is coming to follow it up. But they are only hastening the crisis and bringing about a most hopeful consummation." The "coalition between Lutheran-Calvinism & Anglicanism" was "disgusting" to many who deplored such a compromise, wrote the bishop, and a number of "very able pamphlets" had been circulated to condemn the plan. It would only take official condemnation of Tractarian doctrine by the Anglican establishment "to force many from the Church into our arms." He added, "There are several whose minds are made up and who will not be long held back." [25] Wiseman was not incorrect in his prediction.

Not long afterward Wiseman described for Cardinal Acton the conversions that were taking place: "On the second Sunday of Advent, I had the consolation of receiving the abjuration of 36 respectable people in the cathedral, before High Mass, & in a few weeks we shall have upwards of 50 more." He was soon going to receive 20 Wolverhampton converts into the church: "In many other places much is doing. Your Eminence will I am sure be delighted to hear that the other day one of the leading Oxford men said to a friend of mine that for his part, he did not find anything in St. Alphonsus Liguori's 'Glorii di Maria' that went at all too far. These things must be kept very quiet, as great prudence & caution are requisite in dealing with these persons." [26]

Among the many Anglicans who came to know Wiseman, then, a large number converted to Rome. Some of these remained closely associated with him throughout his life. George Talbot, nephew of Lord Talbot of Malahide, was among them. He converted in 1843 and later worked as a priest in the London District, until called to Rome as papal chamberlain and consultor to Propaganda. Although he was not among the best known of the converts, nobody would be more influential in Wiseman's affairs in later years than Monsignor George Talbot.

There were many Roman Catholics who denied that the Oxford Movement offered any reason for optimism. One clergyman went so far as to describe the Tractarians, including Newman, as "wily and crafty, though unskilful guides." He concluded by stating his conviction that "the embrace of Mr. Newman is the kiss that would betray us." Another Catholic explained the grounds of his mistrust: "For three hundred years they [the Anglicans] have looked quietly on while we were the victims of cruel laws. They even aided in the capture of our priests. A word from them, a declaration of their present opinions, would have extinguished the burning faggot and sheathed the bloody knife; yet they were silent. Can we now believe them sincere when they declare that their Church has always taught the doctrines which they now teach?" The feisty editor of the *Tablet*, himself a convert from Quakerism, criticized those who, like Wiseman, had diverted "the channel of Catholic exertion from those to whom it was first due—our own poor." He questioned the intentions of those who devoted themselves to encouraging the Tractarians, which had as its result "to cocker up the silken vanity of respectable conversions, and a few barren, noisy, windy triumphs."[27]

Before Newman's conversion it was rumored that he had experienced a vision assuring him that he should remain within the Anglican communion and from there make efforts toward the realization of corporate reunion with Rome. William George Ward, who converted shortly before Newman, seems to have spread the gossip, as did Ambrose Phillipps. When confronted with the allegation, Phillipps wrote a denial to Cardinal Acton, although he acknowledged that certain individuals considered themselves "justified in remaining in the Church of England only in order to bring Her back to Unity." Lord Shrewsbury, informed of Newman's supposed vision and the rumors concerning his intentions, asked, "Does not this sufficiently prove Newman's vision to be an illusion of the Father of Lies?"[28]

Bishop Walsh defended the approach of his valued coadjutor. Wiseman's exertions, he wrote, "have surpassed the expectations I had entertained of him and several splendid conversions have been, under the Divine blessing, the happy result." Walsh lamented the fact that Wiseman had "his opponents," and added, "We have both of us had to suffer of late from calumnious reports." In the summer of 1842, when Walsh wrote his letter, Wiseman was on his way to Rome to defend his conduct toward non-Catholics. Walsh urged Cardinal Acton to suspend judgment until he had heard the defense.[29]

Those who questioned Wiseman's policies were provided with ammunition when one of his converts, Richard Waldo Sibthorpe, rejoined the Anglican communion after his ordination as a Roman Catholic priest. Wiseman had been proud of Sibthorpe, former fellow of Magdalen College, who possessed the intellectual stature so much needed in the Catholic body. Moreover, the convert had been a generous benefactor on behalf of the bishop's projects. His defection in October 1843 was such a blow that Wiseman, quite overcome, took to his bed. Bishop Walsh tried gently to lift his spirits by some sound advice: "Why do you allow adversity to depress you to the injury of your health, and render your friends almost afraid to give you notice of what is going on wrong? The sooner such matters are made known to Superiors the better that a remedy may the more speedily be applied to the evil." He concluded: "My dear Lord, a Bishop, in this country more particularly, must be prepared for many difficulties, & trials. But is not the secure way to Heaven the way of the cross? And are not those crosses which happen in the way of our ministry the most valuable?"[30]

Wiseman was fully aware of the validity of his superior's observations. He was under constant pressure, however, from those who doubted the wisdom of his policies, and if his strong emotions made it possible for him to carry on enthusiastically in spite of opposition, they also contributed to the degree of depression that he experienced when confronted with reverses. He later recorded what he had gone through.

> How few sympathised (Mr. S[pencer] did certainly) with the tone of soothing & inviting kindness which from the beginning Roman education had taught me to adopt — the voice of compassion & charity; & who needed these more? Newspaper assaults, remonstrances by letter (& from some of our most gifted Catholics) sharp rebuke by word of mouth, and resisting to the face, were indeed my portion, as though I compromised the truth and palliated error; as though I narrowed the distance between the two, by trying to throw a bridge over the hideous chasm, that men might pass from one to the other! Hence, when one (& thank God! the only one) of our good converts fell back, after receiving orders, & I was publicly taunted with it in newspapers and privately in every way, and when struck down & almost heart-broken by it, I was told by a friend that he was glad of it; because it would open my eyes to the false plan on which I had gone, about converts, of hurrying them on. And yet I had been careful to consult the Holy See, through Propaganda, before acting in this case.

It had been to seek Rome's approval that Wiseman had gone there in 1842: "It had been usual to keep converts long under instruction & probation, even when prepared by previous study, fully convinced, & painfully anxious to escape from the meshes of error. The practice of Rome was entirely opposed to this cold system, and I felt that I could not go wrong in adopting it [Rome's policy] at once. But with I think one only exception (good Mr. S[pencer]) I do not remember any one approved of it, but many blamed it."

Wiseman then described an incident which confirmed him in the conviction that his policy had been correct. While visiting Rome in 1842, he visited a paralytic to whom he had ministered previously: "He was a poor, ignorant, uneducated man of the lowest class, and could not know or hear much, where he was, of what was going on in England." Yet he advised Wiseman to remain steadfast in his "mode of acting, . . . without minding what people said." The bishop left the hospital "quite amazed," he wrote, "for I had not said a word that could have suggested his speech on my leaving him, yet the impression on my mind was that he clearly alluded to my dealings with converts

. . . and that it thus pleased God to console and encourage me through the mouth of one of his poor to whom I had shown some little charity."[31] The episode is indicative of the simplicity of Wiseman's faith.

Thus encouraged, then, Wiseman returned to England only to witness the loss of one of his most treasured converts. "Alas! Poor Mr. Sibthorpe! I fear I have no comfort to send further than my conviction that the fall which he had at Skipton, by which his spine & the back of his head were certainly injured, hurt his mental powers," he wrote to Lord Shrewsbury, and added: "We, who were in intercourse with him, observed it then most painfully. He was never the same man after." Wiseman noted that the Anglicans were "not disposed to welcome him with joy," fearful that Sibthorpe would follow the course of Blanco White, who had abandoned the Roman Catholic priesthood to become an Anglican but who later abandoned that communion as well. Wiseman concluded: "God grant that this may help to open his eyes and make him return. His defection has given me a severe blow, and for the time quite made me unwell."[32]

The most famous convert to find a haven in Birmingham was John Henry Newman, who on October 9, 1845, finally submitted to Rome. Three weeks later Wiseman confirmed him at Oscott, where for the occasion there were "*ten* quondam Anglican clergymen" in the chapel. Wiseman asked one correspondent, "Has this ever happened before since the Reformation?" Newman, he continued, "opened his mind completely to me, & I assure you the Church has not received at anytime a convert who had joined her in more docility & simplicity of faith."[33]

Wiseman offered Newman the old Oscott College building to house the community of converts that had gathered around their leader at Littlemore, outside of Oxford. Newman christened his new home "Mary Vale." Wiseman reported, "we have given up the premises at Maryvale, without rent or consideration, after putting them in thorough repair — repainting &c. & have paid all the taxes &c. though we have no assistance from the establishment, in the way of teaching or otherwise. We keep a priest for them & defray all chapel expences &c. & we have given up our preparatory school, which has been a loss to us." His remarks were not meant as a complaint. He was proud, in fact, of the contribution that Oscott made to the converts because, without it, "some would have had to sell valuable libraries, others would not have lived at Maryvale, & some would have been reduced to starvation."[34]

Wiseman hoped that Newman and his brethren would form the kind of community that he had earlier urged upon the vicars apostolic: "They are to form a community devoted to literature, & in time it is to be a missionary College, the members to go out & preach &c. Please to keep all this to yourselves." Newman, too, described the plan in December 1845, stating that Wiseman had written "so kindly and confidingly that I hardly know how to accept his offer from its very amplitude." Wiseman, wrote Newman, was carrying out a scheme that he had been considering for seven years and had received "the clearly expressed approbation of the Holy See, as well as of many learned and pious persons." The bishop considered it "the best chance for the conversion of the country."[35]

It soon became apparent to Newman, however, that Wiseman's ideas were not supported by the other vicars apostolic. While visiting York in January 1846, Newman discovered that Bishop Briggs was less than encouraging. The bishop claimed that only a religious order could be anything other than "local." The community that Wiseman had in mind would have to be subject to the Bishop in whose district it was located: "There was no medium between entering religion, and being subject to the local Bishop, *as things were* — that is, the Old College *might* be bought of the Central District by the body of Bishops, and the body of Bishops constituted its visitors or directors, and thus have equal rights and an equal interest in it." Any such action, however, was still "premature."[36] Newman would have known little, at the time, of the relations between Wiseman and the other bishops or of their extreme caution concerning both his desire for a special community of secular priests and their own relations with the regulars.

Briggs, nevertheless, told Newman that there would be no difficulty if he wished to enter a religious congregation. He praised the Rosminians in particular, stating that "they, as all orders, are subject to no local Bishop, but were open to serve all equally." Newman was faced with a dilemma. "If we continue seculars," he wrote, "then Dr. Wiseman can claim us by virtue of our position in his district — if we all consent to become regulars, then we at once lose all claim to continue at Old Oscott; — but this is a question for the future."[37]

In 1863 Newman recalled his first year at Maryvale as "dreary" and complained of having been placed under "the gaze of so many eyes at Oscott, as if some wild incomprehensible beast, caught by the hunter, and a spectacle for Dr. Wiseman to exhibit to strangers, as himself being the hunter who captured it!" He continued this entry in his journal, "I did not realize this at the time except in its discomfort; but also, what I did realize, was the strangeness of ways, habits, religious observances, to which, however, I was urged on to conform without any delicacy towards my feelings."[38] Newman had been physically unwell when he wrote those lines. Moreover, he had experienced a number of major disappointments for which Wiseman, at the very least, had to share the blame.

It is doubtful whether Newman ever understood fully all that Wiseman had endured as he struggled to maintain the trust of the participants in the Anglo-Catholic movement and to welcome those who converted to Rome. His lack of sensitivity to Newman at the time, if founded on fact, was less the wish to take any personal credit for the conversion than the understandable hope that others might see and acknowledge the merits of his approach.

Wiseman continued his open-door policy at Oscott in spite of reverses and obstacles. By 1847 he calculated that over a two-year period the college had maintained continuously at least fifteen converts who would otherwise have found themselves without any means of support. He estimated the cost at £200 each per year, that is, a total of £6,000 during the two years. The care of converts had cost the Central District £75,000 in all.[39]

In an undated letter to Lord Shrewsbury, probably written in 1847, Wiseman proudly claimed that Oscott was "the centre of the great religious movement" in England. He did not take all of the credit for the phenomenon, acknowledging that "the impulse given from the col-lege to ecclesiastical reforms had begun before I was connected with it." He had taken advantage of what others had started, however, and he rejoiced that the college was known throughout France, Germany, and Italy: "It has become a place of some importance to the Church." He was most hopeful regarding the future: "I may mention that some of our Oxford friends are sanguine enough to think I sometimes say, that we might form the nucleus of a Catholic university—& certainly have now the flower of one of the English universities [Oxford] gathered round us." In the same letter he boasted that in spite of the cost of all that had been achieved, the debt on the college had been reduced from £8,000 to £5,000 in the course of a few years.[40]

Wiseman knew that he could not oversee the day-to-day management of the college effectively. He therefore appointed Logan as vice-president, confident that there would be no conflict with one whom he had known and trusted for so long. George Spencer was also at Oscott when Wiseman arrived, and Pugin graced the college by frequent visits, having accepted the impressive title of Professor of Ecclesiastical Architecture and Antiquities. The president, in fact, was surrounded by those from whom he expected support and encouragement.

In 1843 Wiseman secured the services of George Errington as prefect of studies. He admired his former assistant's abilities as administrator and disciplinarian, although he was sorry that Errington was somewhat skeptical concerning the prospect of England's conversion. Anticipating imagery that Newman later made famous, Wiseman wrote:

One may truly say "apparuerunt flores in terra nostra [the flowers have appeared in our land]." What a spring is opening upon us! & yet there are many who say, "you dream, it is as much winter as ever, no green, no blossom, no new sign of life, no blue skies, no balmy breeze to be seen or felt." These sounds have just reached me from Rome, from the infidel, incredulous George Errington. He tells me Bps. Griffiths & [George] Brown think so [they had been in Rome]. What sign shall we give to the incredulous generation? Shall it be the parable of the vineyard given to other husbandmen? I often fear so.[41]

Wiseman was self-assured enough to feel that Errington, once in England, would be won to the cause. His services were not wanted for any project more ambitious than that of overseeing and organizing the studies at the college, in any case, and Wiseman had ample evidence from the past to be confident that his old friend would execute his office with skill.

John Acton, a student at Oscott from 1843 to the end of 1848, left an account of the character of Wiseman's presidency. After stating that the coadjutor's strength was not to be found in administration, Acton concluded: "He was thinking of other things, and looking far afield, and these other things were what characterised him. We used to see him with Lord Shrewsbury, with O'Connell, with Father [Theobald] Mathew [the famous preacher of total abstinence from alcohol], with a Mesopotamian patriarch, with Newman, with Pugin, and we had a feeling that Oscott, next to Pekin, was a centre of the world. I think that this was stimulating and encouraging, and certainly made for his authority."[42]

This was precisely the impression that Wiseman wanted to create. "Never, never for an instant," he wrote, "did I waver in my full conviction that a new era had commenced in England. . . . To the promotion of this grand object of England's hopes I had devoted myself." The college was one of "the providential agencies that seemed justly timed, and even necessary for it." He concluded: "No, it was not to educate a few boys that this was erected, but to be the rallying-point of the yet silent but vast movement towards the Catholic Church, which has commenced and must prosper. I felt as assured of this as if the word of prophecy had spoken it."[43]

In view of Wiseman's objectives, his presidency was not unsuccessful, although its deficiencies were apparent. In this century his effectiveness has been judged somewhat harshly. "Wiseman, of course, brought much *éclat* to the college, but he was not a good President," wrote Arthur S. Barnes, who continued: "Both discipline and studies suffered under his rule. He was not a schoolmaster by temperament or training and was naturally much occupied with larger schemes. At the same time he retained the reins in his own hands too much to allow the necessary work being done by others."[44]

There is no doubt that Wiseman viewed Oscott through rose-colored glasses. In 1842, after his coadjutor had left Oscott to visit Rome, Bishop Walsh wrote to Lord Shrewsbury that his assistant was "easily depressed in spirits" and that it was "of the utmost importance to encourage so valuable a man to allow nothing to dishearten him, but, as his motives are all so pure, rather to derive strength from opposition." Walsh was not blind to the problems of the college, as he confided to his noble friend. Wiseman, he noted, "left the College for Italy under the impression that all was going on beautifully there, and that the number of students would be still greater after the vacation." In fact, the number of students was eleven or twelve less than anticipated, "and this in some degree owing to his great good nature in allowing too many indulgences to the boys, permitting them to have expensive clothes, and to what some have been pleased to call favouritism."

In Wiseman's absence, studies had commenced under Logan, considered by Walsh to be "an excellent disciplinarian." The bishop urged Shrewsbury to assist in persuading Wiseman "to allow Dr. Logan to manage in great measure the discipline of the college, and to attend himself more particularly to the moral and religious instruction of the students in which he excells." Walsh added: "He [Wiseman] is too great a man not to have enemies. His friends and admirers must exert to animate and encourage him not to allow any degree of opposition to damp his ardour in the good cause."[45]

More than two years later Walsh was still not satisfied with the state of the college. He wrote to Errington in order to complain "of the collapsed state of discipline." The bishop explained his intention in urging Wiseman to turn over to Logan the management of discipline, "and to confine himself more particularly to the spiritual department, in which he excelled, and which would give him frequent opportunities of animating the boys to attend to their studies from a motive of religion." He asked Errington "to cheer him [Wiseman], and to keep up his spirits." Walsh still hoped that the college would flourish, but he warned that "for that purpose . . . the bills must be kept down as Oscott is considered a very expensive place, more so certainly than Stonyhurst & Ushaw." Regarding the students, he added: "Much attention must be paid to *spelling correctly their own language*, to writing & ciphering, which the Mammas more particularly look to. It is . . . necessary that St. Mary's should have the character *now* of being a well disciplined college, for of late it has been considered far otherwise."[46]

In the summer of 1846, shortly before departing for studies in Rome, Newman described his impression of Oscott.

This letter is quite in confidence as you will see — but the fact is, Oscott is losing its Divines fast. They slip away. It cannot keep them. . . . The place has no bottom. St. Edmund's and Ushaw are long established places — they have a succession, but Oscott is the creation of this generation . . . and it depends *on one man*. That man, Dr. Wiseman, has far too much to do, to be able to do what comes on him. He is Bishop — he is fond of boys; he is every thing to the boys, but the divines suffer. They complain they don't see him once in three months. They don't like Errington. Again a school is a bustling place — divines require something more quiet, more strict, more monastic. Oscott is a place of dissipation. Tribes of women, and hosts of visitors. The want of *rule* is felt, even at St. Edmund's, I suspect, but all is disorder at Oscott — hurry, unpunctuality. I may exaggerate. Dr. W[iseman] is a punctual precise man — and at Rome made the English College semi-monastic, the students visited the hospitals, — but Oscott is a bustling thoroughfare. Consequently the divines are leaving it, and I don't see *how* he will set matters right. Decidedly he ought to make Maryvale the *Seminary* and Divinity School.[47]

Newman, as he himself admitted, may well have exaggerated in describing the situation, although there is almost universal agreement that Wiseman was not interested in administrative details.

Yet, as already noted, Wiseman claimed to have reduced the debt of the college and stated, at the same time, that there was "ample security" to cover what was still to be paid: "I am at this moment engaged with deeds which will make over to me (for the College) an Estate at Sheffield worth £3000 towards ecclesiastical education." In fact, Bernard Ward was not entirely justified when he implied that it was Wiseman's extravagance which caused the enormous debts for the college and the district, although he was certainly correct in stating that Wiseman's "large ideas . . . could not be carried out without a corresponding expenditure of money." He also acknowledged that Wiseman was generous in advancing large sums of money from his private means, "but he afterwards claimed payment of these, and in view of the free way in which he administered the College money, it was popularly said that financially the College far from prospered under his *régime*."[48]

In fact, the finances of the old Midland District were in deplorable condition well before Wiseman moved there. At the end of 1839 Bishop Walsh wrote to beg for financial assistance from Lord Shrewsbury, describing in detail the dire financial straits in which he found himself. Should the earl not be able to help, wrote Walsh, "I do not know what I should do. Every kind of misery would stare me in the face."[49]

Under such circumstances it is interesting to note a description of Oscott offered by a visitor less than a year before Bishop Walsh turned to Lord Shrewsbury: "It is really a magnificent place. The whole is built in the Gothic style & the same style is preserved down to the minutest objects, even to the common articles of furniture, such as chairs and tables. The decorations of the church are most splendid; the patriarchate does not possess richer ornaments." He commented on other aspects of the college as well: "The dinners were equal to the rest in splendour, wine (Lisbon) and ale without any restriction, three courses, that is boiled, roast, and pastry, fruit after dinner & coffee, not exceeded in elegance in many gentlemen's houses . . . all this every day."[50] It seems that others shared with Wiseman the responsibility for the reputed extravagance at Oscott.

The college was fortunate in not having suffered serious loss when Wrights Bank failed in the autumn of 1840. "Our procurator here had drawn out his balance a few days before," wrote Wiseman, "so that £150 will cover all our loss. In a few days more the Bishop would have had £25,000 in the Bank; his loss is nothing." The London District was not so fortunate. Its church fund, including a large sum intended for the construction of the future St. George's, Southwark, was wiped out.[51]

Bishop Walsh did suffer a severe financial blow, however, as a result of an unfavorable decision by an arbitration board that had been formed to settle a dispute between him and Bishop Griffiths. The litigation had its roots in the legal prohibitions that rendered it virtually impossible for Catholics to make bequests directly to their church. To circumvent the letter of the law, it was customary to designate specific persons as beneficiaries, in this case, Bishops Walsh and Bramston, vicars apostolic of the Midland and London districts. Before the death of Mr. Charles Blundell, the testator, Bramston himself died, and his successor, understandably, claimed the share intended for the London District. Bishop Walsh was disposed initially to share the legacy, but in the summer of 1840 Bishop Baines wrote from Rome to the London vicar apostolic: "Dr. Baggs tells me that Mgr. Wiseman lately asserted that Dr. Walsh was not justified in giving up to yr. Ldp. a portion of the Blundell property. Dr. Baggs thinks with me that Dr. Wiseman will try to set aside Dr. Walsh's dispositions in this matter."[52]

Whether, in fact, Wiseman was instrumental in the subsequent action, Walsh changed his mind, pointing out that Blundell was fully aware of the intended disposition of his estate, yet had failed to alter his will after Bramston's death. Since Griffiths had not been mentioned by name, it was argued that all should revert to Bishop Walsh for his own district.

The case dragged on until 1841, when it was decided against Bishop Walsh. The commissioners awarded £28,000 to Griffiths, although Wiseman wrote to Lord Shrewsbury that they had "declined giving the grounds of their award." He added, "I leave your Lordship to judge the severe blow which the award inflicts upon our capabilities and intentions for the District."[53]

After Wiseman was transferred from the Central District in 1847, Bishop Walsh complained that its finances were "in a deplorable state." He told Lord Shrewsbury that the situation would result in "the most disastrous consequences to religion," unless additional funds were forthcoming. Walsh accepted his own share of the blame, but he stated that only recently had he discovered the seriousness of the problem, since management of the district's finances had been turned over to Bishop Wiseman.[54]

For many years to come there would be claims and counterclaims between Wiseman and the bishop of the Central District and, later, of the Birmingham Diocese. It is difficult to assess the degree to which Wiseman contributed toward the financial chaos in the district. Forty years later his secretary Monsignor Searle admitted that the first archbishop of Westminster had seldom kept copies of his letters or papers and that before leaving the Central District he had ordered "the whole of the miscellaneous letters which he had received during the nearly seven years of his residence there" to be burned. Searle concluded that "there was undoubtedly much that might have been useful for his biography which he deliberately destroyed."[55]

Perhaps the missing papers contained further details of his financial transactions, but Wiseman, when quesitoned, was quick to explain his administration of funds. For example, when accused of appropriating, for the use of Oscott, funds intended for the clergy, he responded: "What Dr. Kirk states respecting Johnson's Fund having been appropriated to the College may be easily misunderstood. There is a provision in the original foundation of the Charity that any surplus is at the disposal of the Bishop for ecclesiastical education."[56]

As was the case with his alleged extravagance, the poor financial management in the district predated Wiseman's arrival. In March 1840, in fact, the clergy voted on a proposal demanding that Bishop Walsh provide for their inspection "a statement of all monies and other property belonging to the Clergy, or over which the Clergy have a right of control; together with the sources, from which they have been derived, the conditions attached to them, the actual application of them, and the management, to which they are committed."[57] Wiseman inherited as many problems as he created. Although he was insufficiently careful in maintaining records, it is significant that those who were in a position to judge with confidence, even when demanding an account of his administration, never called into question his integrity, and there were very few who intimated that he squandered what was entrusted to him.

In fairness to Bishop Walsh, it should be noted that Thomas M. McDonnell, the priest responsible for demanding that he should provide the clergy with a financial report, had been engaged in litigation with his vicar apostolic since 1834. McDonnell, a strong-willed man who was extremely popular with his congregation, had been in charge of St. Peter's Chapel, in the heart of Birmingham, for ten years when Walsh began to prepare for the construction of St. Chad's, designed by Pugin and eventually to become the diocesan cathedral. McDonnell voiced many of the objections that the vicars apostolic used when the building plans of religious orders threatened existing chapels. He even refused to leave St. Peter's when Walsh assigned him to a new mission.

Upon his arrival in England, Wiseman was assigned to negotiate with the recalcitrant priest. The fact that McDonnell was among those who blamed Wiseman for the demise of the *Catholic Magazine*, with which the priest had been involved, did not help the situation. McDonnell described the new bishop as "this 'celebrated' personage, this polyglot prelate, this acquaintance of the learned." When an arbitration board decided that an extraordinarily high monetary claim by McDonnell was without merit, the disgruntled missioner moved to the Western District, where Bishop Baines gave him an assignment. A perusal of the correspondence related to the whole unhappy episode makes depressing reading and is only of peripheral interest with relation to Wiseman. It is clear, however, that Walsh and Wiseman were more gracious in responding to McDonnell's intemperate and unwarranted attacks than even Christian charity would have demanded.[58]

While busily engaging himself in literary and social contacts with Anglo-Catholics, receiving converts, overseeing a young college, and coping with the financial problems of the Central District, Wiseman continued to work toward bringing new warmth into Catholic devotional life by his own widespread preaching and the encouragement he gave to others. In 1841, after describing the reverence of a non-Catholic visitor who had knelt before a relic of the true cross at Oscott, Wiseman wrote, "Such emotions as these shame our cold faith." He predicted "that if God unite these men to his Church they will bring back much of the strength & lively devotional spirit of which we have unhappily lost too much." It was in this spirit that he insisted upon special attention to detail in the execution of religious ceremonial.[59]

Wiseman also encouraged Pugin's promotion of a Gothic revival, though he was too Roman in his taste to give unqualified support. Bishop Walsh, in fact, had been more enthusiastic than Wiseman: "By his [Pugin's] beautiful churches & chapels in the Gothic style, his vestments according to the form of those used up to the time of the reformation by our Catholic ancestors in England, he has impressed the clergy & laity in general with a holy zeal to erect churches and chapels more worthy of their holy religion, and which are producing a power-ful effect on the Protestant mind." A year later Wiseman suggested that the rood screen planned for St. Chad's might have to be altered, "as at present, the view of the altar will be entirely shut out from many, and any function could be but partially seen by any one out of the Sanc-tuary." It was the younger bishop's conviction that the church's ceremonies had to be thrown open to all, so that Protestants might be "attracted by their splendour to the understanding of their meaning." Pugin, on the other hand, insisted with his usual, vehement hyperbole, "If any man says he loves pointed architecture and hates screens . . . that man is a liar — avoid that man, my dear Sir." [60] Wiseman, in this case, conceded, and the rood screen in St. Chad's remained until the liturgical changes following the Second Vatican Council led to its dismantlement.

After Wiseman's visit to England in 1839, he was reported by Lord Shrewsbury to have disapproved of some of the views expressed by Daniel Rock, the earl's chaplain at Alton Towers. Rock presumed that the basis of the criticism was the fact that the well-known antiquarian and liturgist had expressed his dislike of the architecture of St. Peter's in Rome. Wiseman soon informed him otherwise: "Any judgment on that subject can only involve a matter of taste, and as I have always stood up for toleration in these matters, and have wished that admirers of Gothic architecture to [sic] allow others to admire something besides, without being declaimed against for it, so I never expect others to sacrifice their opinions on such matters to mine, but wish each one to think for himself and let others do the same."

Wiseman's complaint was that Rock had referred to the Holy Father as "patriarch of the West" and had asserted "that no more authority should be allowed him [the pope] than what was barely necessary for keeping up communion, so that there should be no inter-course with, or recurrence to the Holy See." Wiseman went on:

> Such opinions if acted on would lead directly to schism, and in fact would at once place the church in England in the position of the schismatical church of Utrecht, where the chapter merely communicates to the Pope the election of each successive bishop. I must own that I was seriously pained, not to say alarmed, at finding such an idea prevail in any one ecclesiastic, especially one who has studied his theology in Rome; still more at the idea that such dangerous, not to say erroneous sentiments might prevail more extensively through the clerical body — sentiments which I think it would be the duty of any bishop to root out at any risk.

With reference to the churches being built in England and those already constructed, Wiseman added, "For my part, I would rather see all the splendid cathedrals on earth levelled to the ground, than a jot or a tittle of catholic truth allowed to pass away: & I would rather hear the pure doctrine of the church preached in barns than dangerous theories or principles that would weaken unity proclaimed under richly fretted and gilded vaults." He concluded his letter by informing Rock that he had just "received intimation of my appointment to the Coadjutorship of the Midland District," a word of warning, perhaps, that he was prepared to do battle with any and all opponents of Roman doctrine and customs.[61]

Even though he temporarily abandoned his plan of establishing a congregation of secular priests, Wiseman did all in his power to encourage established religious orders to expand their work in England. They were now his major hope of achieving the reforms that he had in mind. He had been instrumental in bringing the Fathers of Charity to the country, and he was delighted to have them in the Central District. He and Bishop Walsh visited Belgium in the summer of 1841, where they took preliminary steps to bring the Passionists as well. Father Dominic Barberi and three companions soon established their first house at Aston Hall, near Stone, in the Central District. By the mid-1840s the effects of these congregations were undeniable. Their efforts were supported by those of the Redemptorists and also by the Jesuits, who now began to preach missions and retreats throughout the country.

Some of the older clergy resented these newcomers who, with their strange ways, seemed to disparage the zeal of those who had worked tirelessly on the English mission in past years. Lingard summed up the position well when he responded to a friend who had been critical of Gentili:

> Whether you have been too hard upon Gentili or not, I cannot tell — but it appears to me to require a face of brass, and a quantum sufficit of spiritual pride for a man, a foreigner, to come forward and constitute himself the teacher and reformer of a whole national clergy, and in short, of all, both clergy and laity. What can he know of our people, their habits, their circumstance and wants, and the peculiar conduct to be observed by them, mixed as they are, few in number among a multitude of acatholics and anticatholics? Would he make us Italians?

He objected to the fact that Gentili was allowed to give retreats: "I should think that an old missionary could do it much better." He blamed Wiseman for encouraging him: "If we are to have new religious orders here, let them be such as are adapted to our habits and our circumstances. This is not the time or place for dirty or idle saints."[62]

Lingard, and many who agreed with him, mistrusted religious orders in general. They tended to identify their preaching with the most outrageous examples of excess that they could uncover. Lingard described a sermon preached by the Jesuit provincial, "who one day at Preston surprised his audience by a display of his knowledge of the obstetric art." The man had spoken of the Blessed Virgin Mary, a favorite theme of continental Catholics, not to mention Wiseman, but one that an earlier generation of Catholics recognized as especially liable to extravagant language. Lingard said that the Jesuit had informed his congregation of "how our B. Lady was delivered of our Saviour in the stable, not in bed, but standing on her feet with the aid of an unmarried girl hired for the purpose in Bethlehem. The ladies covered their faces, the gentlemen laughed, and he went through the whole process most intrepidly."

Lingard's concluding explanation of the flights of fancy behind this kind of preaching was questionable, to say the least: "I explain it thus: regulars are obliged daily to spend much time in mental prayer; a new idea strikes them. They pursue it and become habituated to it, unconscious of its indelicacy and absurdity, and at length detail it to others as a great discovery in the economy of religion. Many of them must be mad, in the strange ways they pursue."[63]

It should be noted that John Lingard himself wrote a popular hymn dedicated to the Blessed Virgin, "Hail Queen of Heaven, the Ocean Star." He and many others, however, opposed external practices that, they feared, were "making religion ridiculous in the eyes of Protestants." Among the innovations that they considered objectionable were devotions to the Sacred Heart, use of the rosary, the scapular, the introduction of sanctuary lamps where the Blessed Sacrament was reserved, May devotions in honor of Mary, and indulgences attached to membership in confraternities. Those who opposed what they considered to be an alien form of spirituality were fighting a losing battle, however. As Chinnici has shown, Lingard's generation, more influenced by the eighteenth-century enlightenment than by the romanticism of the nineteenth century, was out of step with what was happening.[64] Religious orders were experiencing extraordinary success, and their preaching was successful in spite of the criticisms of those who managed to dredge up a few outlandish or ridiculous examples to support their own opposition.

A large number of vocations to the religious life among both converts and old Catholics led, in a short time, to the full acceptance of the orders as a significant element in English Catholic life. George Spencer, for example, entered the Passionists, where he was known as Father Ignatius. It was Wiseman's presence in the Central District that led to the foundation of Newman's Oratorians there. First attracted to London, Newman later explained, "Dr. Griffiths is suspicious and unpleasant, wants to have us, yet is afraid of us." In fact, when Newman and his companions rejected the idea of entering any of the religious orders already established in England, it was Wiseman's idea that they should found an Oratory of St. Philip Neri. "It is curious and very pleasant that, after all the thought we can give the matter, we come round to your Lordship's original idea," wrote Newman, "and feel we cannot do better than be Oratorians."[65]

Bishop Wiseman took advantage of his office to lead his fellow Catholics in what Wilfrid Ward described as "a systematic exposure of injustice done to Catholics, resented on the ground of its violation of evenhanded justice to the principle of liberty." Typical of his effort was his response to a bill for educational reform, proposed on March 8, 1843, by Sir James Graham, home secretary in the government of Sir Robert Peel. The measure was intended to regulate the employment of children in factories. It provided that government grants would be available for schools in manufacturing districts and that no child could be employed unless he produced a certificate of school attendance. One of the trustees for each school was to be a clergyman of the Church of England, and the schoolmaster and his assistants were to be selected by the Anglican bishop of the diocese. The trustees were to select the books to be used, and religious instruction would consist of reading the Scriptures in the Anglican authorized version. Attendance at the Scripture class was to be required of all, and the liturgy and catechism of the Established Church were to be followed.[66]

In an interview with Graham in the winter of 1843, Wiseman pointed out that the bill was prejudicial to the interests of Catholics. He then prepared a memorial and form of petition to be circulated in the Central District, in which he argued that the bill placed a Catholic "in the alternative of either violating the principles of his religion or of suffering privation." There was no provision for Catholic education, and where schools attended by Catholics qualified as factory schools, children were faced with the alternatives of studying the Bible in a version not approved by their church or not being allowed to work. Parents could cast aside the obedience due to their pastors, "and with that probably the restraints of conscience," or they could obey, depriving their children of both work and education, so that "starvation and ignorance will increase together."[67]

Catholics were themselves divided. The earl of Arundel and Surrey stated that "as a Roman Catholic, he felt bound to declare it as his opinion that as long as there was a Church establishment, it must be predominant, and must also of necessity be administrative in any system of general or national education which Parliament might establish."[68] Protestant dissenters joined Catholics in opposing the bill, however, and numerous petitions were drawn up on the pattern of Wiseman's. Protest meetings throughout the country gave added weight to the objections that led Graham to drop the education clauses in his bill. Wiseman learned well the techniques that proved to be effective in pressuring the government.

In the spring of 1846 Wiseman used similar tactics against a bill "for securing the due administration of charitable trusts in England." When the measure was about to come up for its second reading in the House of Lords, he sent a printed letter to the clergy of his district and pointed out that it was "fraught with serious dangers to Catholic Charities, besides introducing a system of most arbitrary and oppressive interference with their administration." He noted that the bill gave "almost unlimited power to three irresponsible Commissioners and two Inspectors, to be appointed by the Lord Chancellor, over all the Property in the Kingdom, held upon charitable Trusts, which includes all Institutions for the Promotion of Religion or Education."

On the first page of his letter, Wiseman included a form of petition to the House of Lords, objecting to the "arbitrary and irresponsible power" which the commissioners would have and pointing out "that in the Religion which your Lordships' Petitioners profess there are special laws and principles for the administration of religious and charitable endowments, which administration is essentially connected with the exercise of spiritual jurisdiction, which cannot be communicated to any lay person, or commission." The law had for so long discountenanced and discouraged trusts for Roman Catholics, argued Wiseman, that there was sufficient reason to administer them differently from those held by others. There was no proof, or even charge, of misappropriation or maladministration of Roman Catholic trusts to justify such interference.[69] Catholics again won the battle, and no action was taken to jeopardize their trusts. The question arose a number of times during the next decade and a half, however, and Wiseman continued to take an active part in the debate.

Considering the variety of Wiseman's interests and activities and the extent of his opposition, it is not surprising that by the autumn of 1844, his health broke down. He was overworked and often distraught. Bishop Walsh supported the doctors who insisted that he should leave England for a rest. In November, Wiseman traveled to Spain for a holiday of several months. "We all believe," wrote Walsh to Lord Shrewsbury, "that he will return to England quite renovated in health and as efficient as ever. He must then strictly follow certain regulations prescribed for his continuing in health under the divine blessing." Lingard was less optimistic when he wrote, "I trust the ailment is only in body." He said that Wiseman, on one recent occasion, had "assumed an importance, which showed some infirmity of mind. But I hope it is not so."[70]

The trip was less successful than Walsh had hoped. Wiseman informed his friend Charles Russell that "the sources of fretfulness &

discomfort" remained after his return to England. He later wrote to the same correspondent: "I know it will give you pain to hear that for some time back my health (which I begin to think is not worth so much trouble) has been very uncomfortable to my friends — i.e. symptoms of an unpleasant nature have again shown themselves that they think threaten something serious." He described "the worst effect" as "a total prostration for the time of all mental as well as physical energy." Under such circumstances, "I cannot take up business, and things stagnate about me." He was unable to sleep: "Last night, for instance, I did not get to sleep till five this morning. This wears me out." He feared the consequences of his illness or death upon the works in which he had been engaged, most especially among converts: "You would be surprised how few can even understand their wants. This throws a weight upon me and a most serious responsibility."[71] Wiseman was not exaggerating the role he played in the lives of the converts.

Immediately after the number of districts was doubled in 1840, there were expressions of dissatisfaction from some of the clergy. A group of London priests, for example, complained of the lack of information and consultation that had characterized the changes proposed by the Holy See. They resented the situation of the secular, parochial clergy, as compared, especially, with the regular clergy, and circulated widely a pamphlet to that effect.[72] Toward the end of the same year the *Tablet* published a letter from a Yorkshire priest who demanded that further alterations in ecclesiastical government should be made. Then, in 1842, Daniel Rock addressed a circular to the clergy of the London District, in consequence of which about twenty priests gathered to hear him discuss the advantages that would follow upon the restoration of a hierarchy in England. A brotherhood was formed to work toward that end, and clergy throughout the country were invited to join. It was proposed that annual meetings should be held in each of the provincial centers in turn.[73]

The vicars apostolic were more determined than ever to maintain control of English ecclesiastical affairs. Wiseman now took the lead in opposing a movement that had its roots in clerical dissatisfaction, writing to Bishop Griffiths, "I should have wished to hear from your Lordship about the 'Brotherhood' which is sending out a circular to the clergy about the hierarchy, and the proposed meetings of deputies at Birmingham, among other places, without the slightest hint that the wishes of the vicars apostolic would in the least be taken into consideration." He warned the London bishop, "I think your Lordship will find at Rome that the course taken (which too closely resembles the Anti-Corn Law League) is more likely to injure than to forward the proposed object."[74]

Wiseman was not opposed to the establishment of the hierarchy.

The previous year, in fact, he had published an article on the subject in the *Dublin Review*, in which he maintained that Englishmen should begin immediately to prepare for the regular application of canon law in their country in order to show the Holy See that they were ready for a hierarchy. He asked that a national council might be set up to "sift canon law immediately," in order to discover what might apply to England. He suggested that the vicars apostolic should summon district synods, so that statutes could be framed to "secure to each district, at least, decision, uniformity, and clearness of proceeding upon points now left vague, doubtful, or of private judgment." In this manner, he wrote, "there would be a compact ecclesiastical organisation in each district, and it would not be difficult afterwards to bring all these well-ordered parts into a homogeneous and harmonious unity."

In the same article Wiseman pointed out that it would be unbecoming for the Holy See to appoint bishops who could not support themselves without constant appeals to the generosity of the laity. "Without a proper, at least a decent provision for the necessary exigencies of a hierarchy," he wrote, "it is folly, we think, to expect it." Instead of restoring bishops-in-ordinary who would be responsible for instituting canonical organization in their dioceses, Wiseman advised that the latter should be accomplished as a prelude to the former. As he later wrote to a friend: "For my part, I intend, with the divine blessing, to lose no time in so organising the [Central] district as to be able to say 'we are ready.'" [75]

The vicars apostolic agreed that they would have to regain control over the situation. Bishop Griffiths proposed in 1845 that they should discuss the feasibility of immediately restoring the hierarchy. During their annual Low Week meeting it was resolved "that it is desirable that the hierarchy should be restored, as far as changing vicars apostolic into titular bishops of England." They further agreed that a memorial should be sent to the Holy See with a full statement of the reasons supporting a change. [76]

Wiseman was charged with the task of drawing up the document, assisted by his successor as rector of the English College, Charles Baggs, now bishop of the Western District in succession to Bishop Baines, who had died in 1843. Baggs later offered to travel to Rome in order to present the case for the bishops, but he died two months after making the suggestion, and nothing was done. [77]

The following year it was decided that Bishop Thomas Joseph Brown of Wales should work with Wiseman in drawing up the statement to be presented to the Holy Father. [78] This time action was suspended when Pope Gregory XVI died on June 1, 1846. Still another year later, finally, Bishops Wiseman and Sharples, George Brown's coadjutor, were appointed to travel to Rome. It is understandable that the vicars apostolic should have selected the two coadjutors for the purpose, avoiding the otherwise necessary expedient of leaving one or two districts without a bishop for a number of months. In Wiseman's case, as we have seen, reasons of health were an added incentive for the trip. Bishop Walsh told Lord Shrewsbury that his coadjutor's "serious illness" had led to his "sudden departure from England at the urgent request of his medical adviser." [79] Wiseman's weakened health did not curtail his activity in Rome. Such visits always tended to reinvigorate him. When he left Birmingham, however, he did not know that he would never again return to live there.

8. Ambassador without Portfolio

WHEN BISHOPS WALSH AND GRIFFITHS WERE ON THEIR WAY TO
Rome in 1837, they learned of the death of their cardinal
protector, Thomas Weld. Before Bishops Wiseman and
Sharples reached their destination in the summer of 1847, they received
word that Cardinal Acton had died suddenly at the age of forty-four.
When Propaganda met later in the year to discuss the questions related
to the establishment of an English hierarchy, Cardinal Angelo Mai,
who was responsible for preparing the background paper, said that it
had been Acton's opposition which had led the sacred congregation to
oppose the step in 1839.[1] The two coadjutor bishops might well have
thought that a major obstacle to their objective had been removed by
the unexpected death of one who, while widely admired for his personal qualities, could have been a formidable opponent to their proposals.

The bishops discovered, however, that other voices had been raised
in opposition to the policies of the vicars apostolic. The complaints
were varied in nature and could be traced to several laymen who had
been busily engaged in reporting their grievances to the ecclesiastical
authorities, at the same time discrediting the bishops and, in fact, the
clergy in general.[2] The Holy See, moreover, was irked by the fact that
the vicars apostolic had been discussing the need for further changes in
their status since 1845 but had provided no more information than
before.

In March 1847 Cardinal Fransoni, prefect of Propaganda, wrote to
Luigi Gentili and informed him that the Holy See had "received convincing information which has made it necessary that it should turn its
urgent attention to England, which could be the most fertile field at

this moment for development or for harvest for the Catholic Church, unless the Catholic clergy itself becomes an obstacle for this end." He enlisted the aid of the Italian preacher, telling him that in the course of his travels throughout the English vicariates, he should "note carefully the actual state of affairs, study the conduct of the secular and regular clergy, and send me this information as you obtain it, or even a little at a time, noting the abuses that have crept in and suggesting what you think would be the remedy."[3] Gentili was scrupulously conscientious, and between May 3, 1847 and September 7, 1848 (the month of his death), he provided Propaganda with his impressions on a wide range of subjects.

Gentili did not appreciate Wiseman's achievement. The president of Oscott, he wrote, "had tried to keep under his control as many as possible of those who came over to the Church with Newman." Wiseman, moreover, was responsible for dissuading some of the converts from entering religious orders and was too anxious to alter existing congregations to suit his own purposes. The Rosminian opposed, for example, the alterations in the Oratorian rule that Newman and Wiseman considered necessary to adapt the community to English conditions. He also complained that the English Catholics had been lax by failing to establish a missionary community to counteract the efforts of Protestant preachers: "Is there a missionary or group of missionaries that goes round England preaching the gospel to Protestants, while there are so many preachers of every sect, who go into every corner of this kingdom without break or rest, adding darkness to darkness, spreading every kind of error?" Wiseman, of course, had wanted to introduce the kind of community suggested by Gentili, but the priest now concluded that the bishop was not the man to establish new orders, "nor should he be allowed to modify existing ones."

The bishops, according to Gentili, were clearly deficient in learning. Only Wiseman and Brown of Wales, he wrote, "have had a complete education," nor was there a single vicar apostolic who knew more than many of his clergy. He was specific:

> Griffiths cannot preach without reading his sermons, and when he reads them they are so poor that they say almost nothing. Riddell and Briggs preach with such a monotonous voice, and are so dull that people will not listen; Mostyn and Brown of Lancashire never preach because of their health. You never hear of Wareing preaching, and his pastorals are poor stuff; [William Bernard] Ullathorne and Sharples are the best after the first two, but Sharples begins to suffer from headaches and rarely preaches, and the former has not more eloquence than some of his clergy. Walsh, though inferior in learning and talents to many of the others, preaches very sensible sermons that are full of unction, and so are the best sermons of all; just as there is no other bishop who has done or does now as much as he. He is a

holy man and as such blessed by God. He has given a good example, and it is from his District that has come nearly all the good that now flows into the others, like retreats, building of churches and convents, the conversion of Protestant ministers, the wearing of a more clerical garb, the reviving of the liturgy, and if the preaching of missions did not start in his District, both the Passionists and our missionaries belong to his District.

Gentili should have added that in spite of the sterling qualities which no doubt characterized Bishop Walsh, Wiseman, even before moving to England, had exercised influence on the bishop of the Central District and deserved much of the credit for what had been achieved there.

In addition to his letters Gentili sent two reports, both dated June 28, 1847, in which he warned Propaganda against telling the two English bishops too much, "for in England, if anything is planned, it at once gets into the papers. . . . It is one of the weaknesses of this nation that they cannot keep a secret." He also suggested that it would be best for the Holy See to do no more than divide the existing districts and to settle upon titles for the new dioceses, leaving administrative details and the implementation of canon law for a later time. He observed, finally, that Wiseman did not like religious and "would never allow Jesuits to give a retreat when he was Rector of the English College in Rome."[4] The accusation was false, since Wiseman, as noted above, brought a Jesuit to the college in 1837 to lead him and the students through the Ignatian spiritual exercises. It is true that the former rector, as agent of the vicars apostolic, had been critical of the regulars, like Gradwell before him, but Gentili, of all people, should have known that, by 1847, he had changed his views and did his best to encourage the religious orders.

Bishop William Bernard Ullathorne of Birmingham later claimed that Gentili lived to modify his harsh judgments. The many missions that he had given "convinced him that the English priests knew best how to manage the English mind and to make their work secure by avoiding that haste, precipitancy and public excitement which defeated itself by awakening the adversary to vigilance and to counteracting efforts."[5] As a matter of fact, Gentili died only a little over a year after making some of his most critical statements concerning Wiseman. Since he had been preaching missions for several years, it is doubtful whether he ever altered substantially his opinion of the one bishop who had not only supported him personally for many years but whose understanding of the needs of the English mission most nearly coincided with his own. Although Gentili's reports would not have reached Rome when Wiseman and Sharples arrived there in July, they are indicative of the kinds of criticism that the vicars apostolic would have to counteract if their own assessment of the situation in England was to carry weight with the authorities.

Wiseman and Sharples were encouraged to discover that Monsignor Alessandro Barnabò, the new secretary of Propaganda, was in favor of the immediate restoration of a Roman Catholic hierarchy in England. They prepared a report, addressed to the Holy Father, in which they described the progress of religion there. The document was Wiseman's work, and it was the kind of effort in which he excelled.

After the customary expressions of loyalty to the Holy Father, Wiseman provided statistics to illustrate the internal growth of the church between 1840 and 1846. During that time the number of priests had risen from 537 to 714, and while there were 446 churches or chapels in England in 1840, there were 540 in 1846. At least 23 were under construction, not including those being enlarged or beautified. There was also a marked growth in the number of "colleges," as well as houses of both religious women and men.

Thirty thousand children were receiving free instruction due to the generosity of Catholics, wrote Wiseman, and between May 1842 (when a Catholic printing house had been established) and May 1847, 5,800,000 volumes of various kinds had been sold. The devotional life of the Catholic population was also changing. In 1840 there had been no special retreats for the clergy, whereas all the districts now provided for them on an annual basis. The first mission for the laity had been preached in 1842, and now there was no church or chapel in the major cities that had not offered at least one such religious exercise. Popular devotion toward the Holy Eucharist and the Blessed Virgin was now evident, and pious exercises, such as the stations of the cross, previously unknown in England, had multiplied.

The charity of the faithful had increased immensely, seen by the donation, disproportionate to their means, which they had sent to famine-stricken Ireland in 1847. At least 20,000 lire in sterling had been provided already. All of the expenses incurred in building so many new churches and other foundations, not to mention the maintenance of the clergy, provision for worship, and the necessary funds for the education of the poor, came from the contributions of the faithful. The claim was technically true, but somewhat misleading in view of the enormous benefactions of a relatively small number of Catholics like Lord Shrewsbury.

As for the clergy, it was not possible to praise sufficiently the zeal that was developing from year to year. Conversions were multiplying, not only among the well educated (a fact well known throughout Europe) but, even more, among the middle classes and the youth of the country. Many of the clergy now wore ecclesiastical garb of some sort and were treated with respect when they appeared in public. As proof of the dedication of the clergy, the report stated that in that year alone at least twelve priests had died of fever, contracted while assisting the poor Irish in England, and that many others were on the point of dying. Wiseman claimed, finally, that the ancient jealousies which had existed between the secular and regular clergy were a thing of the past and that peace and perfect harmony now reigned. The observation may have been accurate with reference to the Central District, but it was not universally valid.

Wiseman concluded by pointing out that Catholicism in England was unlike that of six years earlier. It would have been observed that he confined his description of the progress of. the church to the years in which he had been living in England. The obvious reason for the selection of that period alone, however, was that the number of vicariates had been doubled in 1840. He and Sharples wanted to stress the benefits that had resulted from that action and to convince the authorities that more extensive changes in the constitution of the church in England were now demanded.[6]

Wiseman wrote to the vicars apostolic to describe what he and Sharples had discovered in Rome and what they were proposing there. They were faced with the options of requesting a revision of the constitution issued by Benedict XIV in 1753 or of asking that the hierarchy might be restored. The promulgation of a new constitution "would either perpetuate for many years to come the state of vicariate government, or would have to be only for a limited period, while the study and trouble for it would be as great as for one granting and at once erecting the Hierarchy." Wiseman and Sharples had concluded that "many matters would be better decided by a Provincial Synod, approved by the Holy See, than by their being merely embodied in a Constitution," so that it would be best to establish a hierarchy at once. He added, "But we should feel naturally strengthened in these views were we to know that our course meets with the approbation of our Right Rev. Brethren; and this we shall be in time to receive before the next general Congregation of Propaganda."[7]

The other vicars apostolic responded immediately, some of them with reservations as to the expedience of a hierarchy at that time. Bishop Walsh raised two "serious objections." He was afraid that funds were lacking for additional bishops, and he thought that the erection of canonical parishes, "at least in country missions," would result in "the serious injury of religion." He reminded Wiseman "how much religion is injured by nonefficient priests whom we have such difficulty to remove," and asked, "What if a tepid, worldly, pleasure seeking priest can only be removed for a canonical fault?" His view was that "the present system is the best as we are now circumstanced." He added, however, that he would accept whatever Wiseman and Sharples thought best.[8]

Several days later Walsh again wrote to stress the financial difficulty of further dividing the ecclesiastical districts in England, "unless a considerable sum of money come from Rome to carry out the plan." Four days later he sent another letter, insisting, almost frantically, that "want of money" was "the grand obstacle that is in the way of the further progress of religion in this country." He was still opposed to additional territorial divisions: "I am decidedly of opinion that your Lordship and my self are quite equal to the work of the Central District." The next day Wiseman's secretary wrote from Birmingham: "Dr. Walsh is v[er]y anxious for your return. He finds the weight of the Dist[rict] too much."[9]

Bishop Wareing of the Eastern District doubted whether Rome would be willing to establish a hierarchy because of the false reports that had been made regarding the church in England.

> What I think of infinite importance is that the Holy See should be thoroughly informed of the real state and condition and means of Religion throughout England; and whereas it seems that the presentations of so many English bishops as have latterly been at Rome have not been attended to, would it not be well that Rome should send some authorized agent here, to spend a twelvemonth in England and make a close and searching inspection of all our spiritual and temporal affairs? The extraordinary and mistaken notions of Propaganda in our regard have often been matter of surprise to me, and have well nigh made me entertain but an humble opinion of their judgment or impartiality.

He agreed with Walsh that it would be "quite out of the question" to increase the number of bishops, "unless means of decent support can be devised." In 1840 there had been those opposed to the division of districts because of the lack of funds: "I think the Propaganda ought to be made aware of the existence of this feeling in some quarters on a former occasion, and of its probable revival in case of any addition of *unendowed* bishops."[10]

Bishop William Riddell, coadjutor to Bishop Francis Mostyn of the Northern District, wrote that they both supported Wiseman and Sharples in the plan to petition for a hierarchy. "Of course it will depend upon the kind of Hierarchy which we get whether it will work well or not," he wrote, "but I think great care must be taken lest anything be done to render it offensive to the clergy." He also noted the lack of money and suggested, as had Wareing, that the pope might "send over some one to look into the state of things." The Holy See complained that there were insufficient churches and priests, and he admitted that such was the case, "but I can't make out how this can be laid to the charge of the Bishops." In the Northern District there were few "monied men," wrote Riddell: "Then again, how can the Bishops do much with their own slender means? If Dr. M[ostyn] & myself had not something of our own, we could not live, for all that we get is the int[erest] of £2000 left by a lady for the support of the Bishop." [11]

Since Griffiths was ill, he had his friend Edward Cox, president of St. Edmund's College, reply for him: "He [Griffiths] has desired me to thank you for your kind letter and to state that he perfectly coincides with your Lordship & with Bishop Sharples in your view of the question of the Hierarchy, that it should be entered upon at once." Nine days later, however, Cox again wrote, this time with sad news: "A few words will suffice to express to you our calamitous loss. We have lost our dear Bishop. He expired a short time before mid-day this morning, dying as he had lived, a saint." [12] Bishop Mostyn had died the previous day, and three months later, in November 1847, Bishop Riddell also died, having contracted a fever while ministering to the sick of Newcastle.

The loss of these men underlined still another major problem if territorial divisions were to be increased. Finding suitable candidates for the episcopate would be as difficult as, if not more than, it had been in 1840. The English bishops and clergy had been hard hit by sickness and death throughout the decade. Bishop Baines had died suddenly in 1843 and was succeeded by Charles Baggs, who died prematurely in 1845. William Bernard Ullathorne was then named vicar apostolic of the Western District. He had earned a reputation for his administrative talent while serving as vicar general in Australia, where he drew up plans for the establishment of the hierarchy there. In 1843 George Brown, suffering from very poor health, was given James Sharples as his coadjutor. Sharples died in 1850, on the eve of the restoration of the hierarchy. It was the situation in the Northern District itself, however, that was most disastrous. The first bishop appointed in 1840, Henry Weedall, refused the office. Mostyn accepted it, in spite of his frail constitution, and William Riddell was soon named his coadjutor. Both of them died in 1847. By the end of the decade, then, every district, with the exceptions of the Eastern and Welsh vicariates, governed by William Wareing and Thomas Joseph Brown, had lost either its vicar apostolic or his coadjutor. It is not surprising that the more timid should have expressed hesitation at the prospect of further subdividing the districts, a step that would require the appointment of an even larger number of bishops.

Not for the first or last time, the Holy See was again confronted with contradictory reports. Gentili was preparing a complicated suggestion that would have demanded the appointment of at least twenty bishops! He did not see the difficulty of finances as insurmountable. Each bishop could easily find at least £100 a year on which to live: "They receive legacies, and the more people they convert, the more they will get!" Bishop Brown of Wales had £120–30 a year: "Why cannot the bishops live as poorly as the Bishop of Wales? The money would soon increase: surely they do not need carriages and splendid apartments 'as some of them begin to have.'" Gentili became simplistic: "As for the present vicars, they may complain, but they do quite well." He continued:

> Mgr. Brown of Lancashire has a fine country house near Liverpool and a carriage, servants male and female. Mgr. Sharples has money of his own. Mgr. Wiseman has a carriage and fine horses. Mgr. Briggs has a magnificent house in the country near York. Mgr. Riddell has money in his own right. Mgr. Ullathorne lives like a poor man, and is content with very little. London is well off. Mgr. Wareing seems to be well off, for he has a rich brother in Birmingham, but even if he lacked funds, we must think of the eternal salvation of thousands.[13]

It is no wonder that Rome tended to move slowly when called upon to solve the problems posed by the state of Catholicism in England. Even the facts were difficult to determine.

The Holy Father, nevertheless, took seriously the arguments presented by Wiseman and Sharples, and after a period of reflection in which he "offered up Mass three times for light to guide him in his decision," he decided to grant the request for a hierarchy. He asked that both Wiseman and Sharples should prepare further reports in order to respond to the specific objections that Cardinal Acton had raised previously. Sharples wrote to Bishop Briggs of Yorkshire on August 18: "Dr. Wiseman was with his Holiness day before yesterday. . . . His Holiness spoke privately to Dr. W. at great length on the subject of our Memorial, and most decidedly in favour of establishing the Hierarchy." Monsignor Barnabò informed the two bishops that Propaganda was preparing for a meeting to discuss the state of England and the memorial that had been presented: "We may now therefore almost take it for granted that our Hierarchy will be established immediately."[14]

Wiseman, at this point, had to cut short his stay in Rome and return to England. He was assigned an important mission on behalf of the Holy See and, at the same time, was named pro-vicar apostolic of the London District. According to his own interpretation, the appointment did not release him from his coadjutorship, but, as he wrote to Lord Shrewsbury, it "suspends its action for a time, as I cannot possibly attend to both." Wiseman arrived in London on September 11, 1847, and two days later he wrote to the other bishops to inform them formally of his new position and to urge them all to sign a petition requesting a hierarchy.[15]

On his way back to England, Wiseman stopped briefly at Fano, where he visited his mother and sister. While there, he prepared the further report that the pope had requested. He addressed specifically and at length the objections that the hierarchy would arouse the animosity of the church's enemies and lessen, rather than strengthen, the ties of the bishops to the Holy See. Prejudice was more and more breaking down, he argued, and English Catholics were prepared in every way for the proposed step. He defended the loyalty of the vicars apostolic, pointing out that the objection might have been more appropriately made regarding the Americans, who espoused republicanism, rather than the English. Yet a hierarchy had been instituted in the United States with fruitful results, as it had been in Australia and New Zealand.[16]

While Wiseman was still negotiating in Rome, his favorite nephew, Willy Burke, a student at Oscott, wrote to him playfully:

> Dearest Uncle,
>
> Is it really true that you are going to become a Cardinal? ah! ah! ah! His most gracious excellency, Reverrendissimo, Signore Dr. Wiseman with Bishop of Melipotannus to keep up the rear. Why your address would alone require a sheet of foolscap paper. Will you not come back to Oscott, should you be created Cardinal? What shall I do without you, for though perhaps you do not think so, & few people indeed, I fancy, would judge well or rightly of my feelings by appearances & expressions, yet I assure you that there is no one under the face of this beautiful creation, that loves you more sincerely & truly than I do, & who would not love such a noble relation! However you are not one of those who likes these courtly words & I am not the person as you well know that likes saying them.

Burke then became more serious: "Who cares for me, what am I to anyone? Oh! poor me! You indeed are almost the only person that cares for *poor Willy Burke*." Young people were instinctively drawn to Wiseman, and he to them. It is noteworthy that all of the reminiscences of his former students were devoted and loyal. "We would all have said that our impressions of Dr. Wiseman were pleasant," wrote one who had lived at Oscott from 1843 to the end of 1848; "We were proud of him; we were not afraid of him; he was approachable and gracious, and no great friend of discipline, and I heard him boast that he never assigned punishment."[17] The "boast" would not have endeared Wiseman to those more immediately involved in the day-to-day management of the boys and their studies.

Willy Burke was premature in suggesting that the cardinalitial dignity would soon be awarded to his uncle. Wiseman, however, was about to enter upon a new phase of his career, first as diplomatic emissary on behalf of the Holy See and second as acting bishop of England's metropolis. For the first time since boyhood, when he had been enrolled in boarding school, he would be denied the daily contact with young people, whose association he relished. The future would offer him few opportunities for the lighthearted activities that had been available to him in the past.

The specific reason for Wiseman's immediate return to England was a diplomatic one. At the beginning of his long pontificate, Pope Pius IX was faced with a situation that was critical for the future of the papal states. In 1831 his predecessor Gregory XVI had been urged by the European powers, including Britain, to reform the administration of his states. Neither the personal inclinations of that pontiff nor the revolutionary movements with which he was surrounded made it probable that he would accede to the advice, and his pontificate has been generally viewed as reactionary. In 1846 Pius IX had been hailed as a liberal. One of his earliest acts was to grant amnesty to political prisoners within his states, and he prepared for more far-reaching measures as well. He was caught, however, between those who were uncompromising in their promotion of Italian unification at any cost and those who, for various reasons, resisted the tide of nationalism.

The pope's position was at first moderate, but when Austria established a garrison of fifteen hundred soldiers in the papal states in order to obstruct the forces of national unification, he found himself, to say the least, awkwardly situated. His Holiness could not condone the Austrian incursion, but neither could he declare war upon a Catholic nation. He had no intention of sacrificing his own states to the cause of Italian nationalism, but in 1847 he saw the Austrian threat as most dangerous, so he looked abroad, to Great Britain, for support.

Lord Palmerston, British foreign secretary, had made known his opposition to Austrian intervention in Italy. The lack of formal diplomatic relations between Britain and the Holy See made the pope's appeal difficult to answer, however. There had been discussions in the past concerning the possibility of establishing formal diplomatic relations. In fact, Wiseman described an interview which he had with Gregory XVI in 1835, when the pontiff had stated that it was the duty of the Court of St. James to make the first overtures: "We have no laws to repeal on this subject, but could enter on such intercourse to-morrow. But England has a law, most discreditable to itself, and insulting to the Holy See, which prohibits it."[18]

Wiseman was now assigned the task of informing the British government of the liberal reforms that the Holy Father had executed in his states and of bringing it up to date on the current situation in Rome. As soon as he reached London, he called at the Foreign Office. Since Lord Palmerston was not in town, the bishop was advised to prepare a memorandum for the foreign minister's information. The task was completed two days later. In a covering letter to Palmerston, Wiseman wrote that he had engaged in several long conversations with the pope while in Rome and it was with the Holy Father's full knowledge and approval that he now presented his memorandum: "I will also add, that I feel sure His Holiness will receive with perfect confidence any communication which it may please your Lordship to transmit through my means."

The document was a careful explanation of the reforms that the pope had made in his states and the situation that now threatened them. In his attempt to broaden the base of government, to extend personal liberties, and to institute new economic policies, the pope had encountered opposition on two sides. The liberals were impatient with any delays in the execution of programs that they promoted. Reactionaries, on the other hand, relied on Austria's opposition to reforms in the papal states and interfered with all that Pius proposed. It was this group that had been involved in a plot, uncovered during the summer, against the papal government.

France no longer had the confidence of the Holy See and could not be counted on to check Austrian interference. The invasion of Ferrara by Austrian troops "put an end to all conjectures, and manifested to all the world the views and intentions of the Imperial Cabinet." Although the pope had no intention of entering into armed conflict, it was difficult to control "the excited population." Wiseman had been sent to convey the pope's appeal for support to the British government: "The return of the Imperial ascendancy is impossible except by force of arms, and Italy cannot again be Austrian except as a conquered country." The pope was looking toward unification of the peninsula along federal lines. His liberal reforms were a step in that direction, and Austrian interference would undermine all that had been achieved. Relief from Austrian constraint would make it possible for the Holy See to "carry out a policy which would eventually lead to Italian unity without revolution."[19]

The British ministry responded positively to Wiseman's appeal. Lord Minto, lord privy seal and Prime Minister John Russell's father-in-law, was about to visit several European states in an attempt to urge liberal policies on their governments. He was now directed to include Rome in his itinerary and to serve "as an authentic organ of the British Government, enabled to declare its views and explain its sentiments upon events which are now passing in Italy, and which, both from their local importance and from their bearing on the general interest of Europe, Her Majesty's Government are watching with great attention and anxiety." The foreign minister told Wiseman that he could assume "the entire credit of all that her Majesty's Govt. had done," and that it was his memorandum which had guided the government in sending

Lord Minto to Rome.[20] Unfortunately, Minto became an embarrassment to the pope by appearing in public with the more vocal exponents
of the liberal cause in Rome. Austria, nevertheless, signed a formal
agreement to limit strictly its use of troops to what had been earlier
agreed upon in the Treaty of Vienna, and the papal government declared itself satisfied. Italian revolutionaries were far from agreeable,
however, and conditions worsened steadily. The pope tried, for another year, to steer a middle course, but his efforts were nonavailing.

A few months after Wiseman arrived in London, Lord Lansdowne,
a member of Lord Russell's cabinet, introduced in the House of Lords a
bill to establish diplomatic relations between the British government
and tha' of the Holy See. The debates were less heated than might have
been expected, but in committee two changes were made in the wording of the measure. The duke of Wellington proposed that the pope
should be referred to as "the Sovereign of the Roman States," not as
"the Sovereign Pontiff," an attempt to make it clear that the relationship would have no religious implications. A second and more important alteration resulted from an amendment declaring that the pope's
nuncio to the Court of St. James could not be an ecclesiastic. Lord
Shrewsbury published a pamphlet objecting to the provision: "Is it not
. . . a most ungracious deed, whilst repealing a statute [prohibiting
such diplomatic relations], of which all the wrong is on our side, to
leave ourselves unfettered, but by that very act to shackle her?"[21] The
restrictive amendment passed by a narrow margin.

While deploring the amendment opposed by Lord Shrewsbury,
Wiseman supported the legislation, viewing it as a means of improving
the status of English Catholics. He had not anticipated the hostile response of the Irish bishops, who considered the bill to be a ploy on the
part of the government to interfere in their ecclesiastical affairs, even
to the point of controlling nominations to the episcopate. The British
government had accused the clergy of fomenting rebellion and of inciting Catholics to violence, a charge that the bishops had consistently
denied. It now seemed that the government was looking for a means of
enlisting the Holy See's support in stifling dissent.

A memorial was circulated for the signatures of the archbishops
and bishops of Ireland, as well as those of the vicars apostolic of England
and Scotland, which stated "that British diplomacy has been every
where inimical to our Holy Religion." It condemned those members of
Parliament who charged Irish priests "with being the abettors of the
horrible crime of murder whilst as kind Pastors they are striving to uphold & console their deeply afflicted & perishing people & like good
shepherds are in the midst of pestilence giving their lives for their
flocks."[22]

Similar sentiments were expressed in the *Tablet,* where Frederick

Lucas, its founding editor, had been condemning for years the prejudice of Englishmen, including Catholics, against the Irish clergy. He drew up a memorial of his own and presented it for signatures to the Westminster Association of St. Thomas of Canterbury for the Vindication of Catholic Rights, an organization established the previous June. There was, at first, a "formidable demonstration" against the memorial, instigated, according to Lucas, by "the highest authority," namely, Bishop Wiseman.[23] When brought before the association a second time, however, it received the support that its author wanted.

Lucas, quoting public statements made by members of Parliament, sought to demonstrate that the bill, if passed, would be used to limit the freedom of the church: "The Catholic subjects of the British Crown are proud of the independence of the Church within these realms, of their immediate spiritual connection with, and dependence on, the Holy See; of the absence of every pretence for interposition by the Civil Power between the humblest laymen and the Vicar of Jesus Christ." He contended "that nothing could be more fatal to the interests of religion in Ireland and to the influence of the Church over the people, than the belief generally entertained that Irish Ecclesiastical affairs were in any degree affected by English influence and exposed to the baneful effects of English intrigue."[24]

Wiseman, convinced that Catholics should present a united front where their interests were at stake, prepared a pamphlet in which he lamented the scandal that would arise from their division. When the Diplomatic Relations Bill had been proposed, he had written to the papal secretary of state and had included, with his letter, a copy of the bill. He was informed of "how agreeable an impression it had produced on the mind of His Holiness." He had to admit, however, that this was before the restrictive clause had been added.

Wiseman objected to the memorial prepared by Lucas, insisting that its underlying principle was "that the Pope must not allow himself to be drawn into diplomatic relations with England; because if so, the Memorialists feel no confidence but that (not he but) his successors will betray the interests of religion to a Protestant government, that can overreach him in cunning, and overmatch him in strength." He concluded by stating that the laity should leave purely ecclesiastical matters to those whose responsibility it was to execute them: "The Church does indeed often want your zealous co-operation, your social influence, your learned or ready pen, your skilful pencil, your brilliant talents, your weighty name, your abundant means. But the direction, the rule, belongs to us."[25]

Whatever the technical appropriateness of Wiseman's view of the laity's role in the church, shared by the majority of nineteenth-century ecclesiastics, it might have evoked the reasonable response that the matter under consideration would have effects transcending the purely religious sphere and that there was ample reason for the faithful to express their opinions. It was with the pope as temporal ruler, after all, that the government proposed to negotiate.

Wiseman also prepared a memorial to the pope in which he expressed complete confidence in any decision reached in Rome. He gave free rein to a somewhat simplistic, ultramontane view of papal authority:

> We believe that to you is given the fullest share of the Spirit of wisdom and of knowledge, of counsel and of fortitude, far beyond what belongs to us collectively. That Holy Spirit, who was seen ever at the ear of your glorious predecessor, the great St. Gregory, suggesting to him holy counsels, and amongst them doubtless the conversion of our nation, hovers, we sincerely hold, over your Holiness, and no less inspires, directs, and informs your wise and holy counsels. And while you are thus guided, we fear not that the subtleties or wiles of statesmen will deceive you, nor the frauds of covert enemies circumvent you.

The entire document was a clear indictment of those who, unsolicited, took it upon themselves to urge the Holy Father to reject the measure proposed by the British government.[26]

Wiseman became indignant when he learned that only certain bishops had been asked to sign the protest against the bill and that Bishop Briggs, along with an Irish prelate, was on his way to Rome to plead their cause. He wrote immediately to Ullathorne: "If some of the Bishops are asked to sign papers, without the others not [sic] being informed of the intention to do so, & without being allowed any voice in the matter, will not mistrust come in? Is it not like party spirit? & will it not tell in Rome strongly against us? I own I fear it much." He asked Ullathorne to cooperate in preventing any petition from being delivered to the Holy Father.[27]

Ullathorne replied that Bishop Briggs had indeed signed the petition, as had the Irish prelates, but that he himself had not done so. He noted, however, that these bishops were no more guilty of a lack of communication than Wiseman had been by failing to inform them of his own involvement in negotiations respecting the bill. He added: "On the subject of lay interference, your Lordship must allow me to speak very plainly, or we shall never come to the point. The most glaring cases have been ascribed to your Lordship's friends, to those over whom you have been supposed to have sufficient influence to have been able to guide them." He cited, as an example, a rumor to the effect that Catholic members of the aristocracy, led by Lord Shrewsbury, had petitioned the Holy See "to place a particular bishop in the archiepiscopal See of Westminster." Ullathorne knew nothing further on the subject, "but it was complained of to me as of a fact of strong lay interference with the Bishops, they themselves being unconsulted." Ullathorne concluded, "Thus whilst your Lordship lays open the supposed errors of other Bps., others consider these facts as mere reactions upon the action & omissions of your Ldp." The observation was solidly based, and Wiseman must have felt it. The forthright Yorkshireman urged him to communicate with Briggs directly: "A shyness has grown up on both sides which I feel satisfied might be broken through satisfactorily to both sides by letter."[28]

In late summer of 1848 the bill, with its offensive amendment, was passed by the lower house of Parliament and received the royal assent two days later. It was a dead letter from the start. The Holy See would not accept the restriction imposed on its freedom of appointment, and revolutionary developments in Rome made further negotiations impossible. The entire episode was an illustration of Wiseman's boldness and perhaps, as some might have argued, his farsightedness. It was also an example, however, of his unwillingness to draw others into his plans and his impetuosity in acting without due consultation. The other bishops admired him, as did the majority of English Catholics. His talents and zeal were undeniable. Yet he did not win the complete trust that he coveted and felt he deserved. He did not understand, in spite of warnings from those who, like Ullathorne, were prepared to express themselves, that he was frequently responsible for the rejection that he experienced. Rather than risk opposition, he would act without seeking the advice of others, even in matters of interest to them. His fellow bishops, from time to time, responded in a similar fashion by excluding him from their informal discussions.

Although Wiseman was still, in theory, coadjutor to the vicar apostolic of the Central District, Bishop Walsh was under no delusion when he wrote to Lord Shrewsbury that "virtually he [Wiseman] will be able to do little in that capacity, and I fully expect that he will be appointed Bishop of the London District." Walsh complained of losing his coadjutor's service, "more particularly when my health is not so good, and any thing like agitation is injurious to me." He concluded by stating that he would have asked immediately for another assistant, but that nothing could be expected in that regard until the hierarchy was established.[29]

Walsh's problem was greater than he had realized. Bishop Sharples returned from Rome on October 25, 1847, and Wiseman immediately wrote to the other bishops to inform them of the fact. Sharples brought the news that Propaganda had reached its decision and that the vicariates were "at once to be converted into Dioceses." The bishops were to "meet as soon as possible and propose a scheme for increasing the number of the Dioceses to at *least* twelve." The Holy Father had confirmed the plan, and the sacred congregation had been preparing the official documents when Sharples left Rome. Wiseman failed to add in his letter (although it soon became common knowledge) that Sharples had recommended to Propaganda that Bishop Walsh, as senior vicar apostolic, should be moved to London and that Wiseman should return to Birmingham. Propaganda accepted the recommendation.[30]

When informed of Propaganda's decision, Bishop Walsh begged to be relieved of the burden of moving to London on the grounds of his poor health and advanced age. He sought Wiseman's assistance: "You have it in your power to befriend me with very powerful sway which must eventually be as much for your comfort as my own." The bishop's pleas seemed to have been successful when the Holy Father reversed Propaganda's recommendation. He reassigned Wiseman to London, now to become the archdiocese of Westminster.[31]

The selection of the first archbishop was critical, and the London clergy were far from indifferent to the nomination. On October 8 there was a meeting at St. Mary's Chapel, Chelsea, where a motion was unanimously adopted by twenty-seven clergymen who declared their "unbounded confidence in the Right Rev. Dr. Wiseman D.D. the Pro-Vicar Apostolic of the London District." However, a different kind of document was also circulated among the priests of the district, and it was signed by some of the same men who had supported the first. It was addressed to the Holy Father and asked that since the hierarchy was about to be restored, the clergy might "have a canonical voice in the nomination of their bishop." It also sought an alteration to the power exercised by the vicars apostolic in transferring their clergy at will. Among the twenty-two priests who signed the petition were Daniel Rock, former chaplain to the earl of Shrewsbury, now living in the London District; Edward Cox, president of St. Edmund's; Mark Tierney, chaplain to the duke of Norfolk and Wiseman's future adversary; Richard Boyle, who would also oppose Wiseman; as well as others who later supported him and even served on his archdiocesan chapter: William Weathers, George Last, and James O'Neal.[32]

The earl of Shrewsbury severely reprimanded Rock and wrote to Wiseman of the "absurd Petition." He ridiculed "the inconsistency of asking for a Bishop in Ordinary, and at the same time, soliciting a voice in his nomination, as if the Pope were to abdicate his right of nominating the first Bishop for a new See." He supported the movement for a hierarchy, however, and agreed that the "inferior clergy" should be provided with canonical status: "Without this, . . . I fancy that no Hierarchy could beneficially exist in this country." He insisted, finally, that absolutely nothing should be done which might "indicate the slightest opposition to the will & wishes of His Holiness, who had, no doubt, appointed you [Wiseman] to London not only as his vicar apostolic, but as a medium of communication, having the confidence of both parties, between the Holy See & the government."[33]

The situation became more complex when, on October 19, still another group of London clergy prepared a counterpetition, agreeing with Shrewsbury's assessment and deploring the statement of their brethren. The future of ecclesiastical affairs, they wrote, should be submitted to the judgment of the Holy Father. This document, also with twenty-two signatures, expressed satisfaction at the appointment of Wiseman to the London District.[34]

A week later Wiseman received a delegation of those who had sought a voice in the nomination of the archbishop. He received them courteously, as they explained in a letter to their fellow clergy. He agreed that there was little that was offensive in their request, but advised that they ought not forward it to Rome, since it had been decided that the hierarchy would be restored and that Bishop Walsh would be transferred to London.[35]

The polarization of the clergy did not end here. On November 3 still another petition was prepared and sent to Bishop Briggs: "The Archbishopric of Westminster has been declined by Dr. Walsh, on account of his increasing years and infirmities. We have reason to suppose that it was offered to him on account of his seniority amongst the vicars apostolic of England, and we fervently hope, that on the same grounds, it will soon be offered to your Lordship."[36]

The day before the petition favoring Briggs was drawn up, Wiseman discovered what was happening. He now lost his patience, venting his feelings in an excited letter to Lord Shrewsbury. He acknowledged that Rome had been "following etiquette" in offering the archbishopric to Walsh, the senior vicar apostolic, "But I have not heard a word of Dr. Briggs." According to Wiseman, Briggs "was the intimate friend of Dr. Griffiths and his admirer in everything, and most intimate with the non-movement or 'status quo' party here, as they have been called." He added that all of the bishops, with the exception of Briggs, had "expressed to me his strong wish that I should be in London." He concluded by outlining what he had accomplished for the district in the very short time since his arrival: "I can assure you that within a few weeks, a change of tone, visible to all, has taken place here, in the clergy; all now want a new and more active system and a *development*." He planned an extensive building program: "But there are many other matters which are equally important and which I have planned but which I fear would all drop through, in the event of a change."[37]

One of the priests who had supported Briggs wrote to Wiseman complaining of the factions among the clergy. The major problem, he insisted, was that a group "called the Friends & admirers of your Lordship, most indelicately (pending the resignation of Dr. Walsh, & contrary to the long established order of seniority amongst the Bishops) put themselves forward & endeavoured by *every means* to persuade the Revd. Brethren to sign a petition to the Pope praying for the translation of your Lordship from the see of Birmingham to the Archbishopric of Westminster." He asked Wiseman to declare that he would not countenance any petition relative to himself. All would then obediently abide by the decision of the Holy See, "but depend upon it, my Lord, whoever obtains the mitre of Westminster by party petition, will, during his pontificate, find himself little more than the chief of a party." [38] Wiseman was not one to back off when presented with threats of this kind.

By the end of November, when the documents restoring the hierarchy and naming the new archbishop had not yet been released, even those living in Rome were still unaware of the pope's decision with respect to the appointment. Rumors abounded: "The general opinion is that Dr. W[iseman] will ultimately be appointed to the Primacy," wrote a student at the English College, "but the Propaganda assured Mr. Newman the other day that all reports were quite premature." Propaganda considered its dignity to have been "somewhat compromised by the premature discovering of the appointment." In fact when the petition in favor of Wiseman's nomination to Westminster reached the Holy Father, he said, "Dr. W. may be a very appropriate person, but it is my duty to receive the appointment from the Sacred College & then approve or disapprove, not to nominate." The student continued, "It was thought at one time that Newman would have received the compliment of bearing the first pallium to England, and I should have rejoiced had it been so." [39] It was clear that Newman, who returned to England after his studies in Rome in November 1847, would not bear the insignia of the office of archbishop to either Wiseman or to Walsh.

Before the year was out, Wiseman wrote to Propaganda in order to express his fears that there might be legal difficulties if the new sees were established outright, as had been intended. He doubted whether the bishops, if assigned new titles, could claim the property which they had held as vicars apostolic, and he suggested that it might be better for them to retain their old titles, along with the new, in order to avoid legal problems of ownership. Faced with this difficulty and the news that the British government was again planning to propose legislation concerning charitable trusts, the Holy See aborted the plan that had been drawn up to restore the hierarchy. [40]

As instructed, the vicars apostolic had met in November to prepare a scheme for the hierarchy based on a division of the country into twelve sees. Bishop George Brown objected to the plan of dividing Lancashire, and Wiseman took a similar position with respect to the London District. Nevertheless, the other bishops asked Wiseman, as vicar apostolic of London, to prepare a report of their meeting for the Holy See. They told him to incorporate the reasons for and against their proposals.[41]

By the spring of 1848, nothing had been heard from Rome. The death of Bishop Riddell and Wiseman's presence in London had left the Northern District without a bishop and Walsh of the Central District without a coadjutor. Moreover, critics of the vicars apostolic were again active in Rome. It was decided to send Bishop Ullathorne to Rome to explain what had been accomplished in England and to continue the negotiations that might lead to the establishment of the hierarchy.

Ullathorne arrived there on May 25. He was at first mystified to discover that the authorities knew nothing of the plans formed by the bishops the previous autumn. Wiseman, it seems, had never sent the report. It is doubtful whether his fears regarding legal difficulties were the reason for his negligence, since his concern had not been a secret. The other vicars apostolic, with the exception of Briggs, shared similar apprehensions. Ullathorne concluded that it was Wiseman's opposition to the division of London that had led him to neglect the commission he had been given. Wiseman continued to oppose the plan, even when it became clear that his protests would be ignored. He argued that the debt on the new Pugin church, St. George's, situated on the south side of the Thames, was partially his responsibility. "Now if Southwark and St. George's be separated from this side of London," he warned, "how is this debt to be discharged?" He continued: "While I can work on this side for *that*, I can manage it; separate the two, and it will be impossible. The debt will be in one diocese, the means in another."[42] The division of London raised questions that haunted Wiseman throughout the rest of his life.

A number of questions were raised and discussed by Propaganda, including the titles of the sees, the lack of clergy, legal problems involved in transferring funds, and diocesan boundaries. It was decided to create additional districts and to place the vicars apostolic over them before establishing the hierarchy formally. According to Ullathorne's plan, there would be twelve such districts.

At this point the pope again changed his mind, and it was decided that Bishop Walsh should be appointed to London, in spite of his aversion to the move. When it was clear that the decision was firm, Ullathorne urged that Wiseman should be left in London as coadjutor with the right of succession. Against his will, Ullathorne was himself appointed to replace Walsh in the Central District. His successor in the Western District would be Joseph William Hendren, formerly vicar general there. William Hogarth, vicar general in the Northern District and highly recommended by Ullathorne, would be named bishop of that vicariate.[43]

The stage was set at last. It seemed clear that Roman Catholics in England would soon have their own hierarchy. Reports circulated widely, although they were not always accurate. Aubrey de Vere, the Irish poet, still an Anglican although within a few years a convert to Rome, wrote, "Did you know that Dr. Wiseman is secretly Archbishop of Westminster, Primate of England, and that he has only to lift up his hand, open his commission, and appoint twenty-six bishops in England when he pleases?"[44]

At this point, however, events in Rome further postponed the step. In November 1848 the pope fled the Eternal City, which fell under the control of republican revolutionaries opposed to his temporal power. In the meantime Bishop Walsh obediently moved to London, preliminary to his promotion to the archbishopric of Westminster. He wrote to Lord Shrewsbury that Pius IX "had impressed on me *sacratissimum preceptum* to accede to the appointment." He noted pathetically: "Thus in my old age am I banished from the midst of many dear kind friends & as it were into a strange country! God's holy will be done!" He added, "The Holy See, aware of my infirmities, required from me to take no more of church government than I feel disposed to do."[45]

Wiseman, in fact, continued to govern the district of London. Walsh died on February 18, 1849, six months after his appointment had been announced. Bernard Ward wrote of him:

> He was not indeed a great leader, nor a very successful administrator. . . . But he was in many ways a remarkable man. Though personally retiring and self-effacing, he nevertheless identified himself with all the forward movements of those stirring times, and carried out several great projects, such as the building of Oscott College and St. Chad's Cathedral, not to mention also the churches at Derby and Nottingham, with which he was chiefly concerned. The Gothic monument which surmounts his grave, no less than the Pugin chasuble in which his portrait is always painted, are characteristic testimonials to one who took so large a share in the Gothic revival.[46]

Ward might have added that Walsh, while recognizing the defects in constitution and character of his coadjutor, was the only vicar apostolic who initially appreciated his worth. He supported him wholeheartedly, even when finding fault with his administrative deficiencies. Wiseman's career would have been extremely different had it not been for his self-effacing patron, Bishop Thomas Walsh.

The pope's flight from Rome resulted in Wiseman's further involvement with Lord Palmerston. In December he wrote to seek the protection of the British government over "the property of R[oman] Catholic Establishments at Rome, founded by British subjects, and devoted to the education of such, under exclusively British administrators." There were well-grounded fears that the revolutionary government would "lose little time in laying heavy imposts, perhaps confiscating, ecclesiastical property." Wiseman urged that the government send instructions to its agents in Rome, stating that the college was the property of British subjects and that it was guaranteed the protection of the British Crown. By now a familiar correspondent with the Foreign Office, Wiseman received the assurance he sought. He was promised that British establishments in Rome, belonging to the church, would be given "the same privileges in regard to property held by them as are allowed to similar establishments at Rome belonging to the subjects of other countries." [47]

Bishop Wiseman had become a public figure in a new way. His negotiations with the British government, while not always popular with all of his fellow Catholics, encouraged him to undertake bolder endeavors. Even if his welcome in London by the clergy was at first less wholehearted than he might have wished, and even if his initial appointment had been only temporary, he had a position like no other bishop. As never before, he now had the opportunity to pursue his ambitious objectives for English Catholics and to show others how it could be done. When he began his work in London, it had been as pro-vicar apostolic. A year later it was announced that he would remain there permanently when he was appointed coadjutor with the right of succession to Bishop Walsh. Within a matter of months, he was vicar apostolic in his own right and the most obvious choice as archbishop, when it became possible to restore the hierarchy. The success or failure of his efforts might well determine his future and that of the Roman Catholic church in England as well. He rose to the challenge.

9. Vicar Apostolic of the London District

W ISEMAN ATTRIBUTED HIS LONDON OPPOSITION TO THE "IRISH
party" which, he said, feared that "I might interfere or have
weight in Irish affairs, which certainly I have no wish or intention to burn my fingers with." More than ten years earlier, while
boldly associating with Daniel O'Connell in founding the *Dublin Review*, he had insisted that the journal should not be used to promote the
political views of the great Irish leader. Aside from his wish to avoid
topics that might divide Catholics, Wiseman was fully aware of the
fact that Newman and his friends abhorred the principles espoused, as
they were convinced, by O'Connell. "It is quite painful to see how they
are hand in glove with O'Connell and Co.," wrote Newman of Wiseman and another Catholic priest in 1835. He later explained:

> I had an unspeakable aversion to the policy and acts of Mr. O'Connell, be-
> cause, as I thought, he associated himself with men of all religions and no
> religion against the Anglican Church, and advanced Catholicism by vio-
> lence and intrigue. When then I found him taken up by the English Catho-
> lics, and, as I supposed, at Rome, I considered I had fulfilment before my
> eyes how the Court of Rome played fast and loose, and justified the serious
> charges which I had seen put down in books against it. Here we saw what
> Rome was in action, whatever she might be when quiescent. Her conduct
> was simply secular and political.

Wiseman, then, had played a dangerous game by associating with
those who were a stumbling block in his plan to attract Anglo-Catholic
sympathies. His wish to reconcile opposing parties left him little choice.
He tried to exercise caution, however, as he told Frederick Lucas in

1842: "I have avoided in any way taking part in the political questions of the day, especially such as divide Catholics, to the great detriment of a better cause."[1] Compromise was not a word that Lucas understood, however, and his intemperate attacks upon those who claimed Wiseman's loyalty led to public controversies, which the bishop had earnestly hoped to avoid.

Lucas was as eager as Wiseman to overcome the injustices that had been the lot of British Catholics. As he wrote in 1840:

> With the exception of the Irish . . . the world has exhibited hardly an instance of long-enduring passive courage to be compared with that of British Catholics. Every class has displayed this quality most admirably in the manner which its peculiar position required. There has been but one thing wanting, and that is that they should know when and how to lay aside the defensive tactics which their situation compelled them to adopt; when and how to take the offensive; content no longer with warding off the barbed arrow and the poisonous shaft of their cowardly and treacherous assailants, but choosing the point of attack, making the most of every vulnerable part; placing the foot forward; resolutely pressing on; deterred by no obstacles; discouraged by no absence of temporary success; if thrown to the ground, rising; if thrust back renewing the onset; calmly, resolutely, perseveringly, with steady eye, quick hand, stout heart, turning defeats into victories and doubling every success by the resolution with which it is followed up.[2]

He was himself a master in discharging "the barbed arrow and the poisonous shaft," always prepared to attack anyone with whom he disagreed, Catholic or Protestant.

The Catholic aristocracy was especially vulnerable to abuse in the *Tablet:* "'Good society,'" wrote Lucas, "owes us no gratitude, and we owe it no allegiance. On the contrary, we regard it as a corrupt heap of religious indifference, of half faith, of cowardice, of selfishness, of unmanly impotence."[3] Identifying himself completely with the cause of the Irish tenants, he scorned landowners, no matter their religious persuasion.

Wiseman understood how seriously divisive the questions related to Ireland might become. O'Connell's promotion of the repeal of the union of Ireland with Britain was especially contentious. Hoping to avert unnecessary bitterness, the bishop wrote to his friend Lord Shrewsbury, offering to serve "as mediator in any unkind feelings which might have sprung up between your Lordship and him [O'Connell]." Lack of union among Catholics could only weaken their power of doing good, and he argued that there was no reason why they could not be divided in politics, while "being thoroughly united in all points bearing upon the progress of religion, the removal of its difficulties, and the interests of the Catholic body." Wiseman asked, "May not religion be a neutral ground for us all, at which we may rally at any moment, without any political feelings being allowed to interfere?"[4]

Wiseman himself opposed repeal: "I can see no Catholicity in the repeal movement; I fear it is thoroughly of this world. . . . All this, of course, I say in friendly confidence, for we live in times when almost any statement of views which does not go to extremes is sure to be misrepresented."[5] Even Lucas had initially opposed the repeal movement, but when he changed his mind and threw himself into the debates, Wiseman's observation was shown to be justified.

Lord Shrewsbury had already fallen victim to attacks by Lucas when, in 1842, there was a bitter struggle over the *Tablet* that resulted, temporarily, in a change in its ownership. After a series of skirmishes, which today appear comical, Lucas established a rival paper called the *True Tablet*. Wiseman subscribed to both the new and the old papers, typically hoping to steer a course that would not lead him into conflict. His friend Lord Shrewsbury, however, failed to support Lucas and continued to receive the *Tablet*. Lucas accused Shrewsbury of being his enemy and attacked him mercilessly. Wiseman found it necessary to support his noble friend, and he informed Lucas that the accusations made against Shrewsbury clashed with all of his own ideas "of what is due to Catholic interest, to Christian charity or to personal character."[6] Within a few months Lucas's rivals ceased publication, and he resumed the title under which he had begun his paper. Wiseman was now identified as Shrewsbury's supporter, however, and there were some who, failing to make the necessary distinctions, considered this to mean that the bishop shared the anti-Irish prejudice that, however unjustly, was attributed to the Catholic earl.

Between 1841 and 1851, approximately 400,000 Irish emigrated to England, so that by the latter date, at least 3 percent of the population of England and Wales had been born in Ireland, with 108,548 of that number living in London.[7] Bishop Wiseman was not unmindful of the pastoral problems thus created. He understood, too, that his own public statements would be scrutinized to determine his position on questions related to Ireland. The deplorable conditions resulting from the famine, beginning in 1846, and the conviction of many, voiced in the newspapers and in Parliament, that the Irish clergy were inciting the faithful to violence, made the need for prudence even more imperative.

In late November 1846 the earl of Arundel and Surrey, a Catholic, wrote an open letter to Archbishop John MacHale of Tuam, in which he cited the denunciations, published in the *Times* and other newspapers, of the Irish priests who were accused of inciting their people against the landlords. Lord Arundel clearly believed the reports. He was prepared to accept excuses for the outraged peasantry, he wrote, "But that which completely overpowers me and deprives me of all defence is the conduct of some members of the priesthood. Denunciations from the altar, followed by the speedy death of the denounced, and public speeches of the most dangerous tendency to an inflammatory people are the melancholy accusations to which I am unable to reply."[8]

MacHale answered in an open letter to Lord John Russell, published, as was Arundel and Surrey's, in the *Morning Chronicle*. He began, "To the Catholic clergy of Ireland, who have been mainly instrumental in preserving the public peace, and keeping the frame of society through three successive seasons of famine as afflicting as ever zeal and piety were tried in, it must be a consoling requital to be held up in the high places as the preachers of sedition and founders of crime." Answering Lord Arundel and Surrey directly, he asserted that the accusations against the clergy were "*mostly* calumnies."[9]

At this point Lord Shrewsbury entered the picture by writing to the bishop of Elphin, G. J. Brown, in whose diocese a notorious murder had taken place. He demanded that an investigation should be launched to determine whether the priest charged with denouncing the victim, prior to the killing, was indeed guilty. When no reply was forthcoming, Shrewsbury wrote to the archbishop of Tuam, finding fault with the denials that His Grace had made to Lord Arundel's accusations. Shrewsbury's letter to MacHale crossed the reply sent by the bishop of Elphin, which was duly published in the *Tablet*.[10]

Frederick Lucas, needless to say, eagerly attacked the two English lords in the most vitriolic language of which he was capable. Wiseman, in London for no more than a few months, was in an extremely delicate position. Even if aware of the imprudence of Lords Arundel and Shrewsbury in jumping to dubious conclusions, he knew both men well enough to be convinced that their intentions had been honest. He could hardly be expected to condone harsh attacks against two of the most generous benefactors of the church in England.

Matters were further complicated, however, when Wiseman received word that the authorities in Rome were somehow identifying *him* with the editorial policies of the *Tablet*. Ecclesiastical officials, moreover, were far from happy that two eminent peers, well known for their loyalty to the church, were under attack in an avowedly Catholic publication. The bishop was warned to disassociate himself from the *Tablet*, and he did so by writing a letter to the cardinal secretary of state, disclaiming any responsibility for the statements made by the paper's editor. His letter was immediately published in an Italian newspaper. Lucas viewed Wiseman's letter as an act of war, and he publicly attacked the bishop himself. "I am really glad that Lucas has attacked you," wrote Lord Shrewsbury, "because I trust it will finish him up. The Bishops shd. agree amongst themselves to withdraw all countenance from him."[11]

Wiseman immediately wrote to the other vicars apostolic to explain his course of action and to seek their advice.

I shall be glad to receive from your Lordship such counsel as your kindness and wisdom may suggest, in this to me most painful matter. Your Lordship will, perhaps, take into your prudent consideration, whether each of us had better submit in silence and patience to any attack which a newspaper, reckoned a Catholic organ, may choose to lay upon him, in the face of his clergy and people; or whether such an ungrounded and calumnious assault, as I have laid open should be left to the individual *bishop* attacked, to be repelled as a personal offence, or taken up by his brethren, as an injury to the episcopal office and dignity, however humble he may be who bears them.

Bishop Wareing responded by agreeing that "if something be not done, he [Lucas] will ride rough shod over us all."[12] Wiseman, however, was unable to obtain the kind of support that he had hoped might harness the editorial policy of the *Tablet*.

Lucas again accused the bishop of trying to destroy him and his paper, so that Wiseman had his explanation to the bishops printed and circulated widely. Ambrose Phillipps wrote to congratulate him: "The Tablet is indeed a cruel thorn in the sides of all those who care for *England's* conversion," he wrote, and concluded that "its unfeeling and abominable assault on your Lordship and its disgraceful betrayal to the publick of the miserable jealousies that prevailed amongst some of the clergy of your Lordship's own archdiocese [*sic*] is perhaps the cruelest stab that our holy church has received for some time."[13]

Informed of Wiseman's printed circular, Lucas wrote to ask for a copy, stating, "I do not for a moment believe that such a document, if in existence, was meant to be a secret from me." The matter had gone far enough. Wiseman had his secretary reply: "I am desired by the Right Rev. Dr. Wiseman to acknowledge the receipt of your letter of yesterday, and to say that, after mature deliberation, his Lordship considers it his duty to decline entering into any correspondence on the subject to which it refers." Lucas printed and circulated all of the relevant correspondence between Wiseman and himself.[14]

Wiseman's dilemma was a difficult one. Lucas had won his support when the *Tablet* had been launched in 1840. The two men agreed that Catholics should be well informed on matters of concern to their interests and that they should openly struggle for justice. The bishop knew, at the same time, that Catholics were indebted to the benefactions of men like Lord Shrewsbury, himself outspoken, and he felt obliged to vindicate his friend's good name. Shrewsbury was not easily pacified: "*Now* Lucas is out & out Irish, & puts it forth that all who do not go *his* lengths are anti-*Irish*." There was truth in the assertion. The earl continued, "In fine there is no mischief he is not doing, as Yr. Lp. sees (if you are paying any attention to his effusions as I hope you are) as well as I do." Shrewsbury concluded that Lucas was a *communist*, that is, that he held the position "that the people of Ireland should live on the *soil* of Ireland — that they shd. live by honest *labour* on the *lands* on which they were *born, the lands rendered productive by* their labour & the labour of their fathers." He concluded, "This is *their* notion of tenant right — of fixity of tenure."[15]

Shrewsbury was not anti-Irish as such. His humanitarianism was too deep for that, and, in fact, his wife was Irish. He was typical of his class, however, and failed to grasp the justifiable fury of the poor Irish tenants, threatened by eviction and ultimate starvation. Wiseman was more understanding, recalling, perhaps, his own origins and the tales of injustice that he had heard as a boy. With Shrewsbury, he abhorred the menace of communism that, some years before, he had described as "a frightening enemy of religion" which was "erecting its hydra heads, and vomiting forth its blasphemies against the Christian religion." It was "the last monster birth, we hope, of the sectarian fecundity of the Reformation." Wiseman was not so simplistic, however, as to identify this threatening ideology with the claims of Irish tenant farmers. Its seat, rather, was in the manufacturing districts, "where it has a reading, semi-educated population to work upon."[16]

The bishop was also sufficiently bold to warn those who were blessed with the comforts of life that the advance of communism would be the result of their own selfish neglect, not to mention a legal system that appeared to recognize a double standard, one for the wealthy, another for the poor: "If one day we find these long neglected masses issuing forth from their desolate or squalid homes, to make war on property, whom shall we have to thank, but those who knew not what was for their country's peace, in the days of merciful visitation? It is not wonderful, that this class, who know so little of their betters, as the world calls them, should not have any great confidence in their administration of law."[17]

The neglected poor, whether in Ireland or England, had a friend in Wiseman, and his eventual popularity among them was clear evidence that they appreciated the fact. It was the harshness and injustice of the accusations made by Lucas, not the cause for which he struggled, that led the bishop to take public issue with him, in spite of the misunderstanding and criticism of a strong minority of the London clergy whose support Wiseman desperately wanted.

For years, sometimes from a distance, Shrewsbury had maintained a policy of interference in English church affairs that, in spite of his beneficence, sometimes irked the vicars apostolic. In 1838 he suggested that St. Edmund's should be closed down so that its students might attend Prior Park. Bishop Griffiths responded angrily at the time and, a year later, attributed to Shrewsbury "erroneous ideas" concerning the London District held by the secretary of Propaganda: "Because we do not publish every thing that is done in this District, some persons suppose we are idle. During the last two years I have expended more than £10,000 in building or enlarging chapels &c, and I am accused of hoarding up money, and so of other things."[18]

John Bossy has pointed out that in the eighteenth century, "the [Catholic] community was still dominated by its secular aristocracy," but that "in 1850 it was dominated by its clergy." The transfer of power was not achieved without a struggle, and Shrewsbury's constant meddling was sometimes reminiscent of an earlier age. Wiseman, though loyal to his old friend, was by no means under his control. Before leaving the Central District in 1847, the overworked coadjutor was rebuked by his noble benefactor for tardiness in answering letters, particularly those relating to important business matters. Wiseman was willing to defer to Shrewsbury "to the utmost that duty will permit," and he was certainly mindful of all that the earl had done for religion: "I have ever been ready to explain, discuss and yield on ecclesiastical matters, of an indifferent character, that is, when duty would not be compromised." He pointed out, however, that it was impossible "for the bishops to respond in detail to any layman who might find fault." As it was, the English bishops were not respected and were called to account in a way unlike that in Catholic countries: "I fear that with us, the Bishop, instead of being looked upon as 'the Angel' of his Church or considered as St. Ignatius M[artyr] tells the faithful he ought to be, is held for little more than a public officer or functionary of the Catholics; at least he is so treated very generally." He concluded, "I have now unburthened my mind freely and honestly, as becomes my station (however unworthily held) in God's Church: and I am sure your Lordship will not take it ill that I should have done so."[19] Whether he took it well or ill, Shrewsbury could not have failed to understand the message.

Although Wiseman consistently defended Lord Shrewsbury against the charges made by Lucas, he was exasperated by 1849 when, as vicar apostolic of the London District in his own right, he was again called upon to take sides with the earl. Shrewsbury's son-in-law, Prince Doria, had been war minister in Rome and had gone into exile with the pope in 1848. It was reported, however, that he was one of those who had pressured the Holy Father to govern the papal states as a constitutional monarch and that he had urged His Holiness to wage war on Austria, the one power capable of preventing Rome's fall. Lucas, in the *Tablet*, found in the affair a new pretext for attacking his old adversary, Lord Shrewsbury, that is, through his son-in-law.

On June 23, 1849, Lucas wrote in the *Tablet* that "a constitutional

Pope is a solecism in nature; a sheer and total impossibility. Temporal authority is lodged in the Pope, not to give him power or to make him one of the princes of the earth, but to secure his perfect independence." He asserted that the proposal made to the pope carried "the condition that he shall be a ruler only in name, and that some miserable Doria, or Mazzini, or Canino, shall be true Sovereign under the fiction of a Prime Minister elected by a constitutional majority." The very idea of associating Doria with Giuseppe Mazzini, leading member of the triumvirate that had replaced the pope in Rome, or Prince Canino (Charles Lucien, Napoleon's nephew), at one time the pope's ally, but in 1848 a member of the radical party in control of Rome, struck Shrewsbury as near blasphemy. Thomas Doyle, chief priest of St. George's, Southwark, in the London District, had even referred to Doria and to Shrewsbury's other son-in-law, the duke of Borghese, as "the Gaeta runaways," implying that their abandonment of Rome had been an act of cowardice.[20]

When one correspondent took Lucas to task for the injustice of the accusations, he heatedly defended the insulting assertions. Shrewsbury was furious at what he considered to be libelous charges, and he demanded that Wiseman should obtain a retraction from Doyle. The bishop responded sympathetically but admitted that he had not read the offensive article. He was reluctant to enter into still another contest with the editor of the *Tablet*, and said that he did not consider it his role to employ ecclesiastical authority in defending Prince Doria, especially since the earl had already vindicated his son-in-law's good name in an article published in another journal.[21]

Shrewsbury then became unreasonable and threatened to prepare a printed account of the entire affair and personally to distribute it "at the door of every chapel in London; by which it will run into much the same course of circulation as the slander itself; & thus follow it up as an antidote." When it seemed likely that he would carry out his threat, Wiseman responded: "It is not usual for a Bishop to be called on to throw his weight & authoritative decision into one side of what has been made by the representative of *this*, a newspaper controversy." He argued that the controversy had ended. Assuring Shrewsbury that he personally admired Prince Doria, considering him to have been "loyal & honourable in his conduct," he added, "But upon the private conviction, I cannot & will not, with God's grace, ever demand and exact, what is the most serious penalty that an official & judicial investigation into such a case could impose." It was this kind of inquiry, with the possible penalty of suspension from his priestly faculties for Thomas Doyle, that Shrewsbury was demanding. Wiseman condemned the earl's plan to distribute literature outside of the churches: "My Lord this would be revenge, not vindication—a scandal, but not satisfaction." Such a step would be a direct act of disobedience: "I hope there is not a Bishop in England, or elsewhere in the church, who would not indignantly rise against such a menace, & set it at defiance. No consideration of personal regard, or private intimacy would sway him in his decision." [22]

To his credit, Shrewsbury bowed to the bishop's will and agreed not to take further action. Wiseman was magnanimous upon receiving the earl's assurance: "I trust there will be no occasion for again alluding to it [Shrewsbury's threat] though I shall receive with respect & hence with attention your Lordship's further remarks." In the same letter Wiseman included the consoling news that Lucas was moving the office of the *Tablet* to Ireland and urged that another Catholic paper should be established immediately to replace it: "No time should be lost in determining, so as to stop the gap, the moment Lucas leaves the field, or some other violent man may take possession." [23]

The London vicar apostolic had been, in the past, the ordinary spokesman for his episcopal colleagues in negotiations with the government, as he normally was in dealing with the Holy See, and Wiseman assumed the same responsibility. When he arrived in London, for example, he sought from the government the assurance that Catholic convicts in Bermuda would be placed under the spiritual charge of a chaplain of their own religion. The reply was immediate and positive. In fact a stipend of £200 per year was set aside by the ministry for the man appointed. It was left to the bishops to name the specific clergyman for the post. The following year Wiseman received a request from the Colonial Office advising him that when a Roman Catholic priest was appointed to a British colony or when a diocese was created there, the secretary of state should be notified in a formal way, so that the governor of the colony might be free from doubt as to the propriety of the appointment and also as "a token of additional respect to the clergymen who may be so honored." [24]

Wiseman continued to demand that Catholics should be accorded the same benefits as other citizens. It was in this spirit that he and the other vicars apostolic had supported the Education Committee, which set out in 1845, under the chairmanship of Charles Langdale, to agitate for the right of Catholics to benefit from the public grants that, for more than a decade, had been distributed for purposes of elementary education. In the spring of 1847, Wiseman seconded the following resolution, moved by Langdale:

> That this meeting, deeply impressed with the outrage offered to the rights of conscience by the declaration of her Majesty's present Government that Catholics are to be excluded from the participation in a grant of £100,000 to be voted by Parliament for all other religious communions, call

upon all classes of their fellow-Catholics to unite in one cry of indignant reprobation at this insulting exception from a public grant, paid out of a public fund, under the administration of a Ministry who have appropriated to themselves the title of Liberal, but whose shrinking policy at the cry of a bigoted sect, has countenanced the worst features of religious intolerance.

The Wesleyans, who were to be included in the plan for public funding, were the "bigoted sect" to which reference was made. Catholics reorganized and in 1847 established the Catholic Poor School Committee, whose original scope was limited to primary education, especially the endowment of training colleges for Catholic teachers. By December 1847 the appropriate government committee authorized grants to Catholic schools, "under certain reasonable conditions," and during the following summer Parliament voted that £125,000 should be allocated for this purpose and "other additional expenses." [25]

Wiseman was quick to take advantage of what had been accomplished. In February 1848 he had already notified the London priests that he wanted to draw up a list of schools requiring assistance. He assured them, moreover, that the government would allow Catholic schoolmasters to be examined before inspectors of their own religion. His interest in the education of the Catholic poor never wavered throughout his life.

In the same circular, sent to the London clergy, Wiseman informed the priests of the district that he was establishing a schedule in order to provide them with ample opportunity of meeting him for the transaction of business. He would be available on Tuesdays, Thursdays, and Fridays between the hours of eleven and three. When longer interviews might be required or when priests living in the country wished to see him at other times, he assured them that if they made the necessary appointments by letter, he would be happy to comply at their convenience. Finally he said that he would be pleased to welcome, every Tuesday evening from seven to ten, "any of the Clergy, who may feel disposed to favour me with their company, and also such gentlemen as I have already the pleasure of knowing, or who may be introduced by any of my acquaintance." [26]

There had been complaints, evidently, that the bishop had been asking people who wished to see him privately to meet him at the home of his friend Bagshawe, and that he often used his secretary as a means of communicating with his priests. Thomas Grant, rector of the English College and agent for the vicars apostolic, was unaware of the arrangement that Wiseman had made and wrote to warn him of the dissatisfaction that had been expressed. [27] Even when Bishop Wiseman tried to meet the demands voiced by his priests, however, his opponents found grounds for criticism. Informed of the arrangement for weekly receptions, Lingard commented: "Am I to send back to you the papers respecting Dr. Wiseman's soirees? I do not like them. There seems to be a wish to transform us into Romans, though manner and circumstances are so different. I dare say that he thinks nothing is so well done as at Rome."

The historian, now seventy years old, identified Wiseman's proposal, then, with the Roman traditions that he considered to be out of place in England.

> I must tell him that when I was at Rome in 1817 I was scandalized at the manner in which things were done. There was nothing like the solemnity and awe to which I had been accustomed in the Netherlands and especially at Douai College. To see the Cardinals at the Papal Mass in St. Peter's talking and taking snuff with each other, and the inferior assistants lolling about, chatting &c. shocked me. . . . According to their notions it is a disrespect not to have a lamp burning before the Eucharist. Whence can that arise? Merely from custom. If I had one here, what would be the use of it? To light robbers to break open the tabernacle &c. One complaint is that a man often turns his back on the sacrament. Can you go out of church without doing so? . . . The best subject for those soirees would be, how to send away those swarms of Italian congregationists which introduce their own customs here, and by making religion *ridiculous* in the eyes of protestants, *prevent it from spreading here.*[28]

Lingard's failure to make any distinctions when he saw what he considered to be Italian influence at work was unfair to Wiseman, but even more so to those Italian missionaries who devoted themselves zealously to work among the English poor.

Wiseman was seriously interested in communicating with his priests and responding to their reasonable requests. He tried to be just, but it would have been impossible for any bishop, most especially one who saw himself as a reformer, to avoid criticism. Even Bishop Griffiths, generally popular among the clergy, had a number of critics. One of these wrote to Wiseman within a week after the bishop had arrived in London.

> Since I have been a priest I have had many difficulties. My first mission was a good school for rum, brandy and whisky drinking & for which the pupils paid dearly. Virginia St. is the name of the mission. At that Virginia St., I established a school of 190 children; also a confraternity of the Rosary, and again, was president of one thousand five hundred teetotalers. At Poplar I got up a choir at Somerstown & established a Guild and tried to establish schools. At West Grinsted, I sold an old horse, missionary property, which has been the cause of my quarrel with Bishop Griffiths at the time. I was in great distress. Consequently I think I committed no fault. I acknowledge I have straid from the subject, which is of congratulation. Yet, I know you

will excuse a broken heart, a heart that has suffered much in silence, a heart that is affraid to make known his supposed wrongs to the public. I fancy you will not be angry with this letter. Indeed if I thought you would, I would not write to you in this stile. In conclusion, I rejoice you are our Bishop and beg to remain your's Obedtly, J. Coyle.

Wiseman discovered in this case, as in others, that a man who poses problems for one bishop is not likely to work more harmoniously with another. Several years later, after the restoration of the hierarchy, the gentleman went public by distributing a printed circular in which he appealed "for the exercise of that humanity and charity which Cardinal Wiseman has refused me."[29]

Bishop Wiseman was especially conscious of the pastoral needs of the poor, a matter that occasionally led to confrontations with his priests. One such instance involved William O'Connor, head priest at the Sardinian Chapel, Lincoln's Inn Fields. The priests assigned to work with O'Connor complained about his failure to respond adequately in opening schools for the poor parishioners or in providing missions and retreats to strengthen their faith. Wiseman's chief source of information was Father Raffaele Melia, member of the Society of the Catholic Apostolate, established by Vincent Pallotti in Rome. Melia, since 1844, had been working among the Italian immigrants who had settled in the area around the Sardinian Chapel. The disagreements among the priests there were due not only to the social and cultural differences among the diverse congregations that worshiped at the chapel but also to the very different styles of the clergymen themselves. O'Connor was representative of an older, clerical mentality, characteristic of priests in England during another era. He seems to have been somewhat autocratic as well.[30]

O'Connor, aware of the complaints that had been carried to the bishop and even of Wiseman's disapproval, ultimately wrote in order to resign: "I have perceived for a long time from many circumstances, that your Lordship has not had that confidence in me, which I should have wished, considering my position of first chaplain. This has evidently been remarked by the other chaplains & hence the constant opposition to my views — hence the almost daily disregard of all respect & authority." He asked, then, to give up his post, adding, "Having now no further control over the chapel, there remain but the books & account which I hope will be found in good order."[31]

The bishop waited for two weeks before responding, and when he did so, the care and prudence with which he dealt with O'Connor, a dedicated priest who had served at one chapel for twenty years, is clear evidence that he was not insensitive to the need for caution in directing those set in their ways. Wiseman acknowledged that the duties of head chaplain were "very important, & his responsibility in proportion." A bishop was also responsible, however, for the administration of the missions in his care: "I have not to answer myself the question 'how will Mr. A. give an account of it,' but 'how shall I do so,' not 'how does Mr. B. discharge his duties,' but 'how do I?'" The salvation of souls was "the first great object to be kept by them and by me," he wrote; "The great, or rather the sole, object of a church or chapel is to effect this grand purpose; it is to enable the people to frequent the Sacraments, comply with the precept of Sunday, & hear the word of God. . . . But if . . . multitudes neglect their duties, & our chapel is empty, the serious question comes, *have I done my utmost to fill it* & have failed?"

Wiseman had investigated church attendance at the Sardinian Chapel and now pointed out that the "galleries" set aside for the poor would hold, if filled, 2,000 people. According to the practice of the day, worshipers were charged a small fee. In the galleries, in this case, the fee was 3d. The "enclosure," reserved for the most prosperous and where the fee was 6d., would hold, if filled 400 worshipers. Then there was the "free space," for which no charge was sought. Over four Sundays, however, there were only 54 persons on an average who attended mass in the galleries and 16 in the enclosure. "Allowing for some miscalculation of room," wrote the bishop, "it is clear that had the chapel been full, a much greater number might have complied with the Sunday precept than did, so far as accommodation goes."

The potential congregation surrounding the chapel was estimated at about 15,000 souls, but the space allotted to the poor, even if filled at each service, could accommodate no more than 2,500. Two different reasons could be offered to account for the lack of worshipers, either lack of means or lack of will. In the first instance, Wiseman suggested that many might give one penny, but could not afford three or six. It seemed clear "that to throw open the galleries to the poor at the lowest possible rate would be profitable." With regard to the second reason, he asked: "How shall I answer for the state of a congregation consisting of 15000 souls, of whom not 3000 (what the free space allows) can be brought to hear Mass on Sundays? Some will say 'that is their look out. I can't help it.' But is it so?" He wrote, "I do not see how we are to answer for a large congregation & an empty chapel, unless we can conscientiously assert that we have tried every means in our power & have failed." He specifically mentioned other poor missions that had achieved noteworthy success by following his advice.

With the exception of the lack of attention to schools, wrote the bishop, he had found no fault previously with O'Connor's work. He pointed out, however, that the priest had obviously not supported his suggestion of "throwing open the greater part of the chapel to the poor, that your fear of dirt prevailed over other considerations when allowing Italian services, that you did not enter into Mr. [John] Kyne's [the second assistant chaplain] views about increasing schools, & that you did not feel with any warmth about the missions among the poor."

Wiseman would not accept O'Connor's resignation until the chief chaplain explained candidly what he considered to be the necessary means of saving the chapel from serious embarrassment, so enabling both men "to answer before God for the salvation of the souls of your poor." He outlined his recommendations:

> I ask you, to look at the plan which I propose fairly, and see if you are dis-posed to work it out. Reserve what is simply sufficient for the better classes that come to the chapel, & throw the rest open to the poor, at the lowest rate possible. Make it the chapel of the poor. Then set to work to make the poor come and fill it; go among them, give them abundant opportunities of instruction, plenty of time for confession, early masses (especially on holi-days) for communion, multiply devotions as the Via Crucis, confraternities &c., make the chapel a home to them; rouse the lukewarm by retreats & awaken sinners by strong & repeated warnings at their very doors; & as one of the most certain means of cooperation & so of success establish *common life* among the clergy of your presbytery, and I will foretell that the chapel will flourish & you will be blessed by God & man. Let us not forget that no District like L[incoln's] Inn F[ields] is exposed to the dangers of bad society & irreligious example. The neighbourhood of the theatres alone would suf-fice to taint its atmosphere with a moral pestilence. Hence our efforts should be redoubled.[32]

O'Connor may have resented the apparent condescension with which Wiseman, relatively inexperienced, addressed him. The bishop, how-ever, had himself lived and worked among the poor of the Sardinian Chapel when visiting London in the previous decade. He mixed his criticism and advice with personal recognition of O'Connor's good qualities, and to his credit, he refused to accept immediately a resigna-tion impetuously and heatedly offered.

O'Connor replied by stating that he knew of no instance of the poor having been refused admittance to the chapel because of the lack of money. He said that Wiseman implied that nothing was being done for the poor. He did not preach in "open courts" or "give missions among them," as his two assistant priests wanted him to do, but, he pointed out, "I hope there are other ways & means of serving them & inviting them to their duties." He complained of the disobedience of the priests assigned to assist him: "If I am to be the *Rector ecclesiae*, I must know my powers. I wish every one to know their position & to keep it." He urged that all head chaplains should be assembled and instructed in this regard, but concluded that he would be obedient to Wiseman's wishes. He added: "I regret to state that the cholera still continues. On

Tuesday last a poor boy was seized with it at our front door! The times are truly awful! God help us!"[33]

O'Connor's assistants were still not satisfied. John Kyne, a native of Roscommon and only thirty years of age in 1849, complained bitterly to Wiseman, "The old, uncatholic, do-nothing system, has it appears, found, if not an able, at least a bold advocate in Mr. O'Connor." He begged for an additional priest, so that the district might be divided into four sections, one assigned to each man: "By this means not only hundreds, but thousands would beyond a doubt be converted." He pleaded persuasively: "If you, my Lord, will only give us the sanction of your authority — if you will open for us the doors of the chapel which are now virtually shut, if you will appoint 4 zealous priests imbued with the right spirit, there is no doubt the result will be such as to more than realize the anticipation of even the most sanguine."[34]

Nothing would have pleased Wiseman more than to accede to the younger man's request. Additional priests were not easily found, however. Not only would they be required to labor among the poor, but, to satisfy the bishop, they would have to be supportive of the kind of devotional life that he considered necessary. At one point he had approached Vincent Pallotti, asking him to bring two other Italian priests to London, where they might provide training for those who would work on the mission. The plan was not immediately practicable. Even when Wiseman attempted to introduce an Italian instructor into St. Edmund's, he encountered stiff opposition. Edward Cox, president of the institution, observed, "It may appear great presumption in me, but I think it is an experiment, to introduce foreigners into our college."[35] The bishop had to bide his time, but he continued to turn more and more to religious orders in the hope that they might provide the kind of work that he considered necessary and for which he could not rely completely on his own priests.

Thomas Griffiths, Wiseman's predecessor, had not been blind to the possibility of making greater use of religious orders to serve the needs of the poor, although he had been accused of opposing the regulars. When the Jesuits applied to him in 1840 for permission to build a chapel in London, he refused to allow them to do so on the site selected. They had proposed building their chapel near the Warwick Street mission, and the priests serving there had told the bishop that the project upon which the Jesuits had embarked would be ruinous to their own endeavors. Instead of a chapel in the West End of London, Griffiths then offered the Jesuits several other locations, including one among the poor in Hackney. When they declined, he complained that they were unwilling to assist him where they were most needed, among the poor. The charge was unjust; the Jesuits were certainly prepared to work among the poor. They understandably wished, however, to maintain at least one establishment in London that might provide sufficient income to finance their other apostolic endeavors and where, as Bernard Ward wrote, "they could get together a congregation of the educated classes, and generally be in touch with men of position and standing."[36]

The Jesuits appealed to Rome, where they received a sympathetic hearing in spite of the fact that Griffiths was in the Eternal City during the spring of 1843 and took advantage of the opportunity to present his objections. The Holy Father himself decided that the society could build its chapel under three conditions: the sacraments of baptism, confirmation, matrimony, and extreme unction were not to be administered by the priests attached to the Jesuit establishment, so that it was not to be considered as a parochial church; the Jesuits were to pay rent of £30 per year to the bishop and another £30 to the Warwick Street mission; and they were to provide a priest to serve in any poor district that the vicar apostolic might name.[37]

Griffiths continued to oppose the construction of the now well known Church of the Immaculate Conception, Farm Street, Berkeley Square. He complained of the way Rome had treated him.

> I am told that I am represented as deficient in zeal for the good of my flock, because I will not receive the proferred help of the Jesuits, and other Regulars. In the first place they have never offered their services and if they had I must have been guided by the . . . principles of justice and charity. But in the second place, do they know the life which the Vicar Apostolic of London leads (for the accusation applies to my office and my predecessors)? He derives no temporal advantage from his chapels, clergy, or any of his duties. His whole time is occupied with his clergy or people. He is devising and executing plans for the education of his clergy, the building of chapels, the erection of schools, the instruction and clothing of the poor. If he seeks any other object but the sanctification and salvation of his flock, he is miserable and foolish, as well as wicked.[38]

Griffiths was perfectly correct in his assessment of the way he was viewed by the authorities in Rome. Many years later Wiseman prepared a report of his own achievement. In it he described an interview with Pope Gregory XVI in which the pontiff had told him that there would one day be a hierarchy in England, "but never during the lifetime of that man, because he is a Gallican for life." Wiseman then identified the man as Bishop Griffiths, who, however, had not been the only one guilty of anti-Romanism, for "such also were the clergy educated under his direction, that is, almost all who were in the district when I arrived in 1847."[39] Griffiths, of course, had been president of St. Edmund's College for a period of sixteen years prior to his elevation to the episcopate.

There is no doubt that the opposition which Bishop Griffiths seemed to display toward the regulars contributed to the pope's opinion of him. In spite of the bishop's protests, in any case, the cornerstone of the Farm Street Church was laid on the feast of St. Ignatius, 1844, although the opening ceremony did not take place until five years later, when Bishop Wiseman participated in the festivities and delivered the sermon.

Shortly after his own arrival in London, Wiseman tried to persuade Newman to establish a house of the Oratory in the English capital. He wrote that he did not want to act otherwise than he would have done had he not been transferred from the Central District and that he "considered Maryvale in every respect the proper place for Noviciate, House of study and retreats, and central house." The bishop simply wanted a branch house in London: "The clergy have been long brought up in dislike of religious institutions; and many prejudices will have to be overcome in consequence. But they are docile, and will be led easily by their Bishop."[40]

Newman returned from Rome to England in December 1847, stopping to visit Wiseman's mother on the way. When the bishop's offer was renewed, however, he found it necessary to decline. He noted, at the same time, "that, if it is the will of Providence that we should be allowed ultimately to proceed to London, and to gain your much desired protection, we shall, by the experience we have had in Birmingham . . . be much better fitted to serve your Lordship in your arduous fields of labour, and to fulfil the expectations of those kind friends who wish us to do so."[41] The opportunity soon came, and in April 1849 Newman divided the Oratorians into two groups: Frederick Faber was placed over the house that opened in King William Street, Strand, on May 31, 1849.

In the spring of 1848 the Passionists established a house in London. Wiseman had been instrumental in bringing the congregation to England under the headship of Dominic Barberi. The following summer the Redemptorists also arrived. Bernard Ward quoted one newspaper account:

At Clapham the Order of Redemptorists, who have lately established themselves there, are putting forth immense exertions to obtain proselytes, and are causing proportionate alarm among the friends of Evangelical truth, who have long made that locality their favourite settlement. . . . The monastery, situated near the Common, is furnished with a large bell, which causes, I hear, much annoyance to the peaceable inhabitants of the vicinity by ringing out at most unseasonable hours for Matins. Parliament is in course of preparation at Clapham against these troublesome intruders; and truly it would be hard to say why Protestants should be annoyed by such

Popish bellringing in a country whose laws confine the right of having and using bells to the National Church.[42]

In October of that year Wiseman ordained the young American convert, then a Redemptorist, Isaac Hecker, who was influenced while in London in his determination to perform mission work by means of a house of American priests who would work among urban, English-speaking Catholics. After his dismissal from the Redemptorists, Hecker founded the Missionary Society of St. Paul the Apostle, or the Paulists, as they are generally known.

Wiseman also appreciated fully the important work that women's religious communities might achieve. Ten years later he expressed his satisfaction at the changes that had been brought about since the seventeenth century, remarking that "the silent steady walk" of the cloister had been exchanged for "the hot and dusty street or lane which lead to the school or hospital." In January 1850 he wrote proudly that in less than two years seven communities of women and three of men had been established in the London District. Among the foundations that he mentioned were "two orphan houses," as well as "an excellent middle school, or grammar school, containing seventy boys already," in addition to "four new missions in the heart of the poor population and at least seven in different parts."[43]

It was under Wiseman's auspices in the Central District that Mrs. Cornelia Connelly founded the Society of the Holy Child of Jesus. After their conversion in 1835, Cornelia and her husband Pierce, an Episcopalian minister in the United States, sought permission to separate in order that he might become a priest while she would devote her life to God as a religious. It was necessary for them to make provision for their three surviving children, but eventually all was settled, and Pierce was ordained in 1845. Wiseman wrote to Cornelia's community in 1846:

> The field which you have chosen for the exercise of spiritual mercies is indeed vast and almost boundless, but it presents the richest soil, and promise of the most abundant return. The middle classes, till now almost neglected in England, form the mass and staple of our society, are the "highest class" of our great congregations out of the capital, have to provide us with our priesthood, our confraternities and our working religious. To train the future mothers of this class is to sanctify entire families, and sow the seeds of piety in whole congregations; it is to make friends for the poor of Christ, nurses for the sick and dying, catechists for the little ones, most useful auxiliaries in every good work. . . . Be not discouraged by present difficulties, but pursue the good course on which you have entered.[44]

The "difficulties" that Wiseman mentioned were, in 1846, to a great extent financial. Mother Cornelia was to encounter more personal problems in the very near future when her husband, living with Lord Shrewsbury at Alton Towers, demanded that his wife should return to him. He carried his case into the courts in an attempt to regain his marital "rights."

In 1848 Bishop Wiseman brought Cornelia Connelly and her sisters to the London District, where they were established at St. Leonards on Sea, near Hastings. Frederick Lucas, in the pages of the *Tablet*, found still another pretext for attacking Lord Shrewsbury, claiming now that Pierce Connelly had exercised undue influence upon his English benefactor. The "eccentricities" of which Shrewsbury was guilty "during the memorable year 1848," wrote Lucas, were "in great part to be credited to the unhappy persecutor of Mrs. Connelly." The "noble Earl" had been the recipient of Connelly's flattery and had been ruled by his chaplain's "own evil purposes." Connelly had taken advantage of his benefactor, "on the strength of Lord Shrewsbury possessing broad acres, an ancient earldom, moderate abilities, and a judgment very liable to be led astray."[45] Shrewsbury, it is true, had at first been sympathetic to Pierce Connelly's determination to interfere in the foundation established by his wife. He soon abandoned his support when Connelly's designs became evident, and it would be absurd to attribute the earl's attitudes toward the Irish and his support of the Diplomatic Relations Bill, the two major matters upon which Lucas took issue, to the influence of his chaplain.

Cornelia Connelly was a strong woman and sufficiently self-willed to stand up to Bishop Wiseman himself when she considered a matter of principle to be at stake, but the work that she and her community took up, most particularly that of education, was, to a great extent, the result of his encouragement and foresight. Her life and achievement evoke greater interest than those of numerous other women engaged in similar works during the nineteenth century, partly, at least, because of the persecution by her husband, who eventually, because of lack of funds, had to abandon his case against her. There were many communities of women performing remarkable work, however, and Wiseman was always prepared to lend them his moral and temporal support. He was not solely responsible for the foundations of sisters in nineteenth-century London, however, as Bernard Ward has made clear in his enumeration of the religious orders established there. Bishop Griffiths deserves some of the credit as well.[46]

In 1847 it was decided that a special church should be built in London to care for the increasing number of Italian immigrants, and early in 1848 the cardinal prefect of the Congregation of Bishops and Regulars issued a circular asking the bishops of Italy for support in obtaining funds for the proposed church in England. Wiseman hoped to secure the assistance of Vincent Pallotti, to whom he had turned when in

Rome for spiritual direction. He later confided to the future Cardinal Herbert Vaughan:

> When I was in Rome before my consecration I had great mental troubles, and I went to a holy man, since dead and declared Venerable (Pallotti). He made me sit on one side of a little table; he sat on the other. A crucifix was on the table between us. After I had opened my mind and laid bare all its troubles to him, he slipped down from his chair to his knees and after a moment's prayer, said, "Monsignor, you will never know the perfect rest you seek until you establish in England a College for the foreign mission." These words fell on me like a thunderbolt; I was in no way prepared for them. I had no interest at the time in foreign missions, nor had the Abbate Pallotti. He gave no other answer to my difficulties. I went home and into retreat previous to my consecration. I then made a resolution to try to form a society of priests who should establish a College for Foreign Missions. On reaching England I at once explained my plans to Dr. Walsh. He opposed them definitively and said that Oscott was to be my Foreign Missionary College.[47]

It is difficult to determine whether the dimmed vision of hindsight later led Wiseman to exaggerate the significance of the incident. He was resolved, in any case, that the mission to non-English-speaking Catholics would not be neglected.

In 1809 Bishop William Poynter, coadjutor in the London District, had opened a German Catholic chapel in Bow Lane, Cheapside. No sooner had Wiseman arrived in the district than he received urgent letters requesting financial assistance to maintain the work being done there by the priest attached to the chapel, James Jauch. By 1849 Jauch had abandoned his post and was living in Switzerland, and the bishop was asked to pay the outstanding debt. James Leachey, the solicitor who contacted Wiseman, stated that the bishop's brother James had resided in the house with Jauch and had "acted as Secretary to the Saint Bonifacius Institution [the German Chapel]."[48] The previous December, Wiseman had attempted to assist his brother in obtaining a post, and it seems that James, whose career remains somewhat elusive, left England at about the same time as Jauch.[49]

One of the high points of Wiseman's first year as bishop in London had been the opening of St. George's, Southwark. The beautiful gothic building, Pugin's work, had been begun in 1840, but the construction proceeded slowly, chiefly because of difficulties in funding. The opening ceremony was eventually held on July 4, 1848, with Wiseman celebrating the mass and preaching. The procession included thirteen other bishops, representatives of at least seven religious congregations, and 240 priests. In the congregation were the earl of Arundel and Surrey, the duke and duchess of Norfolk, the earl and countess of Shrewsbury, Lord and Lady Camoys, Lord and Lady Lovat, Lord and Lady Stafford, Lord and Lady Mostyn, Lord Petre, and others. This was the kind of occasion that Wiseman loved, and its splendor must have seemed a sign pointing to the promising prospects of Catholicism in England.[50]

Wiseman understood full well the difficulties of building churches of this kind. As he wrote to Thomas Grant the following September:

> It is right that you should know how St. George's stands. When I came here I found the debt upon it was far greater than was known. Dr. [Thomas] Doyle [the head priest] had concealed it from his best friends, and all stood amazed at it. And moreover the Church and house were in a state totally unfit for opening, till several thousands were spent on them. I paid £1000 after I came in part of this expense but could not meet all. When the work was nearly finished, the day of opening fixed, and the limitations accepted, the builder's creditors pressed on him, *made him suspend the works*, were going to put a lien on all the property, including things (pulpit or part of it) in his yard, and threatened him with making him a bankrupt if he did not at once give security for his entire debt to *them* by getting it from us. We offered a mortgage on the property, and we strongly suspected that they wanted to ruin us and our church for they said, when asked for a subscription for the Church (they were the tinker-merchants who had supplied the wood) that they would gladly subscribe to pull it down but not to build it.

Ultimately Wiseman borrowed money and paid £4,000 in cash, entering into a joint bond with Lord Arundel and Surrey for the rest. By the time he wrote the letter to Grant, £1,000 had been repaid, and the remainder was to be returned during the following three years: "Such is the load upon my neck, for I cannot think of throwing the burden on good Lord A[rundel]." The debt, altogether, Wiseman wrote, was £10,000.[51] This, of course, was one of his principal concerns when it became clear that Southwark, and so St. George's, would be separated from the archdiocese of Westminster.

As Wiseman had confidently predicted, he gradually won the vast majority of the London District to his cause. Exceptions were to be expected, and lingering resentment remained to dampen his enthusiasm from time to time. His secretary wrote in a private journal several years later that he had just heard of "the change that [had] taken place in the friendly relations between Dr. Maguire & Rev. M. Tierney since the Cardinal's coming to London." The two men had been "like two brothers & paid each other visits without previous notice & in short each one's house & thoughts were the property of the other." Upon the arrival of Wiseman in London, however, Maguire refused to side with the bishop's opposition, and "a coldness commenced ex parte Tierney & on his friend being made V[icar] G[eneral], he wrote him a letter beginning Rev. Sir & requesting that a book lent might be returned; & now if they meet in the street they do not speak." The obvious pettiness in the situation was indicative of the deep resentment with which Wiseman was viewed by some of his priests. Lingard wrote in the summer of 1850:

> I think that you would do well to advise Dr. Wiseman not to undertake so much, not to interfere in matters that do not imperiously require his interference; that he has now more to do than the bodily and mental faculties of any one man is equal to & that he has enemies, ready to catch at every word and action, and misrepresent them at Rome &c. Withdraw him if possible from that state of excitement which he must constantly be in, by seeming to wish the world to look upon him as the only man in the Cath. body calculated to do anything.

A few days later, Lingard wrote: "Dr. W. is to preach at Manchester on the 28th. Why so? has he not enough to do in the London District? He takes too much upon himself, which must keep him in a state of constant excitement."[52]

Wiseman had become a public figure as no Catholic bishop had been since the Reformation, and he felt keenly the responsibilities of his office. He was less than elated, then, when he first heard the rumor that he was to be elevated to the cardinalate. The pope had returned from exile in April 1850, making it possible for the Holy See to proceed with matters pertaining to the church in England. Almost immediately afterward, Thomas Grant informed the bishop of the rumors of his promotion. One of the cardinals had suggested, he informed Wiseman, that "your England would be Rome, he sincerely hoped, after your promotion."[53]

Wiseman's immediate reaction was dismay. His permanent departure from England would interrupt, perhaps forever, the progress toward which he had contributed so much. Bishop Brown of Wales shared his concern: "Such talents, acquirements, & zeal — rare as they are — are, as your Lordship must be convinced, more than ever required in the head of the Catholics of England at this time. Nor is there any one fitted to replace *you*. . . . Your withdrawal from us will overwhelm me with despondency." Bishop Ullathorne was as disturbed as Brown, partially due to the rumor that it would be he who would replace Wiseman in London: "I will not conceal from your Lordship a certain uneasiness which I feel on account of the positive manner in which it is asserted that there is an idea of transferring me once more."[54]

On July 13, 1850, the *Tablet* predicted that the hierarchy was soon to be restored and that Rome's choice for archbishop would be Bishop Briggs of the Yorkshire District, but on August 3 it suggested that Wiseman would be archbishop, with Thomas Grant as his coadjutor. Wiseman himself, however, was convinced that he was now destined for

Rome. He wrote to Newsham: "I have been in great pain, suspense, and lately in deep distress, at being called away from England, to reside permanently in Rome." Similarly, in a letter to Russell of Maynooth, he stated that "the event depresses me, crushes me, nay *buries* me for ever in this life; and so it must be good for me."[55]

The distraught bishop determined to avail himself of the services of George Talbot, who had recently left the London District to serve as papal chamberlain in Rome. Wiseman prepared a confidential memorandum, in which he described the progress of religion since his arrival in London, and the monsignor lost no time in presenting its contents to the authorities. In less than three years noted Wiseman, four communities of men (the Passionists, Oratorians, Redemptorists, and Marists) had been established, and arrangements were being made to welcome more. Six congregations of women had settled there, and two others would soon be added. "It will be easily seen," warned the bishop, "how the nursing of the young communities lately established, as well as the maturing the treaty for the new establishments, must depend upon one who takes a lively interest in the matter, and in whom they have put their confidence."

After listing the new missions and chapels Wiseman added, "Churches which before were empty are now filled, and the devotion of the people gives evidence of the spiritual advantages of the change." He had introduced new devotions, including the *Quarant'Ore* (Forty Hours) and the *Tre Ore dell'Agonia* (a three-hour Good Friday devotion), as well as the *Mese Mariano* (dedication of the month of May to Mary), novenas, and solemn Benediction. He had worked for the poor: "A system of missions among the poor, in their courts & alleys, has been established, by which incalculable good has been done." He claimed that no fewer than fifteen thousand souls had been reclaimed by these missions and Lenten retreats: "This system requires great assistance and encouragement to keep it up."

The report concluded, finally, with "suggestions to Mr. Talbot, to be used prudently":

1. The foregoing statistics may serve to suggest the difficulties of a sudden change, and the danger of falling back into the old state;
2. The state of the Cath. movement at this moment may be explained, & the importance of whoever is in London understanding it;
3. The temporal affairs of the District are undergoing a complete resettlement: new deeds &c. are being made at immense expense, to secure the property from loss. This will have to be done over again most probably;
4. The expenses of the Cardinalship are great; & the Bishop is in no way ready or able to meet them;
5. Should there be no chance of obtaining a change in the Pope's determination, try as follows,

1. Could it not be put off; if not
2. Could not the Bp. continue to administer the District for some time through a Vicar General & a Council? If not
3. At any rate entreat that no successor be named till the Bishop reaches Rome, and explains the whole matter
4. Represent that a different course will be interpreted as proof that he is remanded in displeasure, & that his measures are disapproved.[56]

Even after receiving official word of his impending elevation to the cardinalate, then, Wiseman was unwilling to abandon England without a struggle.

On August 16 Wiseman left for Rome in response to the Holy Father's summons. On August 21 Lingard wrote: "I have been surprised by noticing in letters from London such expressions as these, 'Dr. Wiseman is going to Rome. No great loss.' 'The sooner the better.' I am afraid that he is not in the odour of sanctity there." Two weeks earlier, Lingard, perhaps informed of Wiseman's hope to return to England, predicted: "I will foretell that he will never return." His conclusion was based on his conviction that the Roman cardinals would never permit "the dignity of their estate" to be "treated with disgrace in England" and that the prime minister would not tolerate a cardinal who might threaten the position of the Anglican bishop of London "by residing in London itself."[57] The historian underestimated the persuasive powers of Wiseman and Talbot, although he was nearer the mark in his observation regarding Lord John Russell.

10. The Hierarchy

EVEN BEFORE WISEMAN ARRIVED IN ROME, MONSIGNOR TALBOT WAS seeking information as to the manner in which a cardinal, if appointed to live in England, would be received by the government and by private society. Lord Arundel replied that the government "would advise against it," fearful "of any trouble about it in Parliament or in the papers." He doubted, however, whether "otherwise they would take any pains to prevent it." Arundel added the warning that there would be "no precedence whatever granted to him on account of his rank." In private society the situation would be somewhat different, since "no one would ever invite him without the intention of entertaining him according to his rank & on that head therefore difficulty could scarcely arise." Protocol would be unlike that to which Roman cardinals were accustomed, of course: "I should think English people (*some* Catholics excepted) would hardly leave their company to receive him at the door & have a red carpet spread for him as in the case of Royalty."[1]

Wiseman arrived in Rome on September 5, 1850, having stopped first for a short visit with his sister. A week later he wrote to his friend Henry Bagshawe: "I am sure you will be glad to hear that it is more than probable that before the Consistory the Hierarchy will be proclaimed; and that in the spring I shall return to London, where we shall hold the first Synod (Provincial) since the Reformation."[2]

The apostolic letters establishing the hierarchy and nominating Wiseman as archbishop of Westminster were both dated September 29, 1850. The following day the consistory was held in which he was officially named a cardinal and assigned, according to custom, as titular head of a Roman church, in his case St. Pudentiana. Three days of ceremonial functions and receptions followed. On October 12, finally, the new cardinal began a leisurely journey back to England, stopping at various places on the Continent, where he was received with all of the demonstrations of respect normally accorded to royalty.[3]

Xaviera Wiseman was bursting with pride as she described the events in a letter to her sister: "His third night was most splendid; such they say was without precedent; four cardinals were among the number and these never by any chance show themselves on these occasions." Lord Shrewsbury's daughter, the Princess Doria, arranged and presided over the three receptions following the consistory, and Wiseman was greeted by all of the members of the diplomatic corps in Rome, the dignitaries of the church, and "all the tip top nobility who only mix amongst each other, and are scarcely ever seen at these assemblies."

Wiseman's mother continued, "Who would or could ever imagine that our simple unpretending Colàt (as we used to call him) is actually the *first Sion* of his day." Her joy was less than complete, however, partially for reasons that must have been felt by the cardinal as well. James, it seems, had proved to be a complete failure. "All this is most flattering and gratifying," wrote Xaviera of the honors paid to Nicholas, "but when I view the reverse of the picture, my heart sinks, and I feel as though it could burst asunder when I think of my poor unfortunate James; with such talents and education as he possesses one might hope he would have no difficulty in passing through life, but alas! he has not succeeded." When the boys were at college, James "was always considered to be the more talented of the two . . . , but now nothing succeeds with him that he undertakes." He had been "well off" and living in Germany, "when he must marry, and so brought ruin upon his unfortunate wife and children." Nicholas assisted in so far as possible, "but his own means hitherto have not been sufficient to meet the necessary claims which his position demands." She concluded pathetically: "How I wish that I could finish the remainder of my days with you, for those that remain to me are dull and melancholy. I don't care how soon they finish — and the past ones have been idem. How often it happens that when one has looked forward and expected happiness, they are sure to meet with disappointment."[4] The observation would one day be as applicable to Nicholas as it had been to his mother.

Wiseman was in Vienna when he first became aware of the attack launched by the *Times* upon the Holy See's act of restoring the hierarchy. He immediately wrote to Prime Minister Russell to protest "the erroneous and even distorted views which the English papers have presented of what the Holy See has done in regard to the spiritual government of the Catholics in England." The cardinal reminded Russell that when Lord Minto had been in Rome, he had been shown a copy of the plan drawn up for a hierarchy and had made no objection. Wiseman also stressed the nature of his position: "With regard to myself I beg to add that I am invested with a purely ecclesiastical dignity; that I have no secular or temporal delegation whatever; that my duties will be what they have ever been, to promote the morality of those committed to my charge, especially the masses of our poor; and to keep up those feelings of good-will and friendly intercommunion between Catholics and their fellow-countrymen which I flatter myself I have been the means of somewhat improving."[5] His claim was justified, although he did not yet realize the extent of his own responsibility for the fierce reaction against Catholics in the autumn of 1850.

On October 7 the cardinal had written his famous pastoral letter "From the Flaminian Gate" in order to announce the restoration of the hierarchy. His enthusiasm and the effusiveness of his style resulted in a document that was, to say the very least, unfortunate in its consequences: "Your beloved country has received a place among the fair Churches which, normally constituted, form the splendid aggregate of Catholic Communion; Catholic England has been restored to its orbit in the ecclesiastical firmament, from which its light had long vanished, and begins now anew its course of regularly adjusted action round the centre of unity, the source of jurisdiction, of light and of vigour."

Before the appointment of new bishops, vacant sees were to be administered by those who, as vicars apostolic, had exercised jurisdiction over the counties that comprised them. Wiseman explained his own mandate:

> By a Brief dated the same day [September 29], his Holiness was further pleased to appoint us, though most unworthy, to the Archiepiscopal See of Westminster, established by the above-mentioned Letters Apostolic, giving us at the same time the administration of the Episcopal See of Southwark. So that at present, and till such time as the Holy See shall think fit otherwise to provide, we govern and shall continue to govern, the counties of Middlesex, Hertford and Essex, as Ordinary thereof, and those of Surrey, Sussex, Kent, Berkshire, and Hampshire, with the islands annexed, as Administrator with Ordinary jurisdiction.

Queen Victoria was reported to have asked, "Am I Queen of England or am I not?"[6]

The cardinal had directed that his pastoral should be read from all of the pulpits of the new archdiocese, and Robert Whitty, his vicar general, had complied. Non-Catholic reaction was instantaneous and even violent. Lord John Russell made matters worse by responding sympathetically to the bishop of Durham, who had protested against the "insolent and insidious" action of the pope. On November 4 Lord Russell wrote the letter that appeared in the Times three days later: "I agree with you in considering 'the late aggression of the Pope upon our Protestantism' as 'insolent and insidious,' and I therefore feel as indignant as you can do upon the subject."[7] So was born the "papal aggression" crisis, one of the episodes in Wiseman's life to have received more than adequate attention by historians and biographers.

In spite of the pleas of some that he should remain on the Continent until the storm subsided, Wiseman hurried home, arriving in England on November 11, just a week after the prime minister's commitment to a policy of bold opposition to the hierarchy. The cardinal set to work immediately to answer the charges that were being made. The result was a careful and, for the most part, temperate explanation of the new status of the Catholic church in England and one that even Wiseman's enemies conceded to have done a great deal of good. He denied that the pope's action was an infringement on the Anglican establishment or that Catholics stood in a relationship to their fellow citizens that differed from what had existed previously. He concluded by insisting that the archbishop of Westminster would not interfere with the duties of the dean and chapter of the abbey that stood in the heart of London.

> Close under the Abbey of Westminster there lie concealed labyrinths of lanes and courts, and alleys and slums, nests of ignorance, vice, depravity, and crime, as well as of squalor, wretchedness, and disease; whose atmosphere is typhus, whose ventilation is cholera; in which swarms a huge and almost countless population, in great measure, nominally at least, Catholic; haunts of filth, which no sewage committee can reach — dark corners, which no lighting board can brighten. This is the part of Westminster which alone I covet, and which I shall be glad to claim and to visit, as a blessed pasture in which sheep of holy Church are to be tended, in which a bishop's godly work has to be done, of consoling, converting, and preserving. . . . If the wealth of the Abbey be stagnant and not diffusive, if it in no way rescues the neighbouring population from the depths in which it is sunk, let there be no jealousy of anyone who, by whatever name, is ready to make the latter his care, without interfering with the former.[8]

The implications of the cardinal's remarks may have been unkind to the Anglican clergy, but the clearly limited role that he claimed for Catholic bishops helped to calm the country's hysteria.

Many years later Father Whitty offered an explanation for the success of Wiseman's pamphlet, providing, at the same time, an insight into the cardinal's character.

> I told him [the cardinal] that, so far as I have heard, it was much liked, "in fact some people say that it will outlive all your other writings." "Oh! come," said he, "that is rather too strong," and he seemed a little hurt at the slight thus implied in his other more laboured works. But in truth my an-

swer was not meant as flattery. It was my own belief at the time and the only way in which I could account for the cardinal's different appreciation was that Fabiola cost him little or no labour. It was, as he said, a recreation or rather it was, so to speak, the cream of his own rich Christian imagination. On the other hand most of his other lectures and dissertations required research and labour and he valued them accordingly. (N.B.) Speaking above of his clean & only copy of the "Appeal," I forgot to add that I asked him *how* he managed to write such long documents without a correction or erasure and he said he could not bear to see such blots & gaps in his Mss.! He went on to say somewhat boastingly that if he ever found himself puzzled in the middle of a sentence which he had not fully thought out, he could always manage to devise an ending that would *fit in* somehow. The result however was not always a happy one for his style or his readers. In the "Appeal" he had, as I before observed, fully thought out every word on his journey from Vienna — at least such was my explanation of the success of its style.[9]

Wiseman's pamphlet had been written in four days.

The government, responding to the national outcry, introduced a bill on February 7, 1851, making it an offense, punishable by a fine of £100, for anyone to assume an ecclesiastical title, with the exception, of course, of those appropriated by the Established Church. Wiseman was present in the gallery when the bill was introduced. Gladstone was among those who spoke against the measure, and although it was ultimately passed into law, it was never invoked. Twenty years later, when Gladstone was prime minister, the law was quietly repealed.

Cardinal Wiseman had not expected the offensive measure to be passed. In December he had written confidently, "I doubt if Lord John [Russell] will venture on any new bill, & if he does he will have a hard battle to fight, & no one expects more than a ridiculous law, which will do us more good than harm." In the same letter he observed that "the hubbub" was "nearly at an end. The papers are giving it up, and people on all sides are getting heartily ashamed of it." The reaction had been a mixed blessing, since "the interest and curiosity about us remain unimpaired, or rather increase." After describing a series of three lectures that he had given in St. George's, Southwark, Wiseman wrote, "I now drive about every where with my cardinal's arms on the carriage, & it is known by every one; but I meet with nothing but respect."[10]

Some few Catholics joined those who opposed the restoration of the hierarchy, among them the duke of Norfolk, who, already halfhearted in his profession of faith, now received communion in the Anglican church. Wiseman was heartened, however, by the letters of congratulation and encouragement that he received. Montalembert, with whom he had remained friendly for almost twenty years, wrote, "Here in Paris I have found all honest men, and all conservatives, on your side."

Richard ("Dickie") Doyle, celebrated as a caricaturist and as a water-color painter, resigned his position with *Punch* because of the ridicule and sarcasm that the magazine heaped upon Wiseman, the pope, and Catholics in general. "I know the extent of sacrifice which this involved," wrote the cardinal, "and this greatly enhances the merit of the act. I am sure we shall all feel prouder of you for it, than we do for the genius, and artistic beauty of your performances. But Providence, I am sure, will not allow such noble conduct to go unrewarded."[11]

In the midst of the excitement the cardinal received a blow that wounded him far more than the anti-Catholic demonstrations in England. His mother died in Fano on February 7, 1851. He wrote to Mrs. Bagshawe: "I am sure that, as an old friend, you will sympathise with me in what I feel most severely, the loss of a parent to whom no one but myself can know my obligations."[12] He withdrew very briefly from public activity.

The pressures upon Wiseman when he returned to England were not confined to those resulting from the widespread opposition to the hierarchy's establishment. The step taken by the Holy See did no more than declare that the country would henceforth be under the ordinary jurisdiction of an archbishop and twelve suffragan bishops.[13] John Lingard had written in August 1850: "We shall have a national hierarchy in due order, but the hierarchy will have no power to do anything except according to the fiat of the Propaganda, which will meddle with all things, though their notions and habits are so different from ours that they would shew their wisdom if they never intermeddle at all."[14]

In 1848 Bishop Ullathorne, while negotiating with the Roman authorities on behalf of the vicars apostolic, had recommended that the hierarchy should be established but that the Holy See should leave further implementation of the measure to the bishops themselves. It was his hope that "the institutions of the Church, the multiplication of bishops, and the privileges of the clergy" might "emanate out of the acts of the provincial synod."[15] This was the procedure Rome followed. It was to Wiseman that everyone now turned for direction in the tasks which lay ahead.

The most immediate matter of importance was the nomination of candidates for the five vacant sees. The Sacred Congregation for the Propagation of the Faith, on November 13, asked the English bishops to submit names of those who might be elevated to the episcopate. Two months later Cardinal Wiseman was told to draw up a list of those proposed and send it to his colleagues in order to ascertain the general opinion on the character of each nominee and the diocese for which he might be suited. The following April, Monsignor Talbot complained to Bishop Ullathorne that Rome could not make the appointments because the bishops had still not sent their final observations. Talbot also wrote a pressing letter to Francis Searle, Wiseman's devoted secretary whom he had received into the church and ordained before moving to London: "I hope he [the cardinal] has done something about getting the names for the new five bishops. What we want in England is firmness and zeal and activity. The pope complains that no names have yet been sent; sooner they are sent the better."[16] The list of recommendations had been drawn up when Talbot wrote, in fact, but it had not yet reached Rome. The delay had been due not only to the demands made upon the bishops in countering the public outcry against the hierarchy but also to reasons of a more internal nature.

Wiseman, as we have seen, opposed the division of the London District into two separate sees. When it was done in spite of his protests, he urged that for the time being he should be left in charge of Southwark. He pointed out that Westminster had no church comparable to St. George's, Southwark, to serve as archdiocesan cathedral. It would now be impossible for him to continue the preaching that was drawing enormous crowds. He added what he must have considered an even more compelling reason for not appointing another bishop to the southern part of London: Southwark was the "nest of those traitorous priests" who had supported the ministry in proposing the "infamous law designed to fetter the Church." The clergy of that see were guilty of "Gallicanism," "Febronianism," and "Josephism." Only a strong hand could keep them under control.[17]

Shortly after writing to Propaganda, the cardinal repeated his arguments in a letter to Monsignor Talbot: "What should I do without St. George's? I should have to give up preaching, and I think much good would be lost." He went on to tell Talbot, who had himself lived at St. George's until the previous year, that "the worst anti-Roman clergy in England are in Southwark," men who were "either actively or passively opposed to all progress" and who were "working to get Dr. Cox." Edward Cox, president of St. Edmund's since 1840, was considered by Wiseman to be a weak leader as well as a typical representative of the anti-Roman school in England. The cardinal was convinced that the nomination of such a man to the episcopate would be "fatal." Among the others whom he criticized in his letter were Mark Tierney, the historian, and Daniel Rock. Four of the other bishops, on the other hand, recommended Cox for one of the new dioceses, a fact which could only have confirmed the conviction of Roman authorities that the loyalty of the English episcopate left something to be desired.[18]

Bishop Ullathorne, influential in Rome and respected there for his negotiations in planning for the hierarchy in 1848, argued against Wiseman. He sent his own views to Thomas Grant, rector of the English College and agent for the bishops, who translated the letter into Italian and submitted it for the consideration of Propaganda. The archdiocese was already richer than the suffragan sees, wrote Ullathorne, and, even without the southern half of London, it still had a large Catholic population. The Southwark clergy would be dissatisfied, moreover, if they were left without a bishop of their own, unlike dioceses that were poorer than theirs.[19]

Ullathorne's arguments were conclusive. Perhaps seeing the handwriting on the wall, the cardinal wrote to Talbot, "I should now have no feeling on the subject were it not for St. George's." He still regretted the loss, adding that even Grant failed to appreciate the importance of the lectures which had been given in that church. Grant did understand, however, that the new bishop of Southwark would have to be sympathetic to the cardinal's ideals and plans, as he wrote to Propaganda.[20]

Other factors accounted for the delay in appointing bishops, but none of these could be attributed to Wiseman. The fate of Bishop Hendren posed a serious problem. He was a weak leader who, moreover, was incapacitated by poor health. Formerly vicar apostolic of the Western District, he, like Bishop Ullathorne before him, considered Prior Park to be a drain on the district's resources and sought to close the college. When he was named the first bishop of Clifton, the diocese in which Prior Park was situated, the college authorities decided that his continued presence would be intolerable. They went so far as to send a delegation to Rome to present their case. Grant wrote to Wiseman: "In *confidence.* It would be *cosa grata* if, in suggesting the arrangements for the new bishops, Dr. Hendren could be taken from Clifton." Propaganda at first thought of sending Hendren to Southwark, but, as the cardinal prefect later wrote, it was not known whether Wiseman would have placed his confidence in Hendren, and the proposal never received serious consideration.[21]

Still another problem was the manner in which the old Lancashire District had been divided between the new dioceses of Liverpool and Salford. A minor adjustment was sought, for good reason, so that the Hundreds of Leyland, originally assigned to Salford, might be attached to Liverpool. The requested change was made.[22]

John Henry Newman observed in February 1851: "We are not ripe ourselves for a hierarchy. Now they have one, they can't fill up the sees, positively can't." He was mistaken. The following month Wiseman sent the list of nominations to Rome. Perhaps Newman was influenced in his observation by the fact that Wiseman, on his own authority, had added two suggestions to the list which would not have been included otherwise. The first was Thomas Grant, his protégé and good friend; the second was Newman, who, according to the cardinal, "would be most acceptable to the clergy of Nottingham."[23]

Even the possibility of being a diocesan bishop, remote as it might have been, drove Newman to a state of near panic.

My writings would be at an end, were I a Bishop. I might publish a sermon or two, but the work of a *life* would be lost. For twenty years I have been working on towards a philosophical polemic, suited to these times. I want to meet the objections of infidels against the Church. . . . A fearful battle is coming on and my place seems to lie in it. Make me a bishop, and I am involved in canon law, rubrics, and the working of a diocese, about which I know nothing. It is a very hazardous thing to put a man of 50 on an *entirely new line.* Do think of this. You cannot think how strongly I feel this. Surely my opinion on the subject is of weight.

The letter was written to Monsignor Talbot, and Newman asked him to inform Propaganda of his feeling. His appeal was successful, supported as it was by Ullathorne, his bishop, who pointed out that, however much he respected Newman, he could not close his eyes to the fact that the famous convert had "neither the will nor the tact to manage others."[24]

While waiting for Rome's final selection, Wiseman expressed his concern lest the wrong kind of men should be appointed: "If our body is not strengthened, and if the choice of bishops is not made with regard to local wants and personal claims, not rising higher than being good and *respectable* people, we shall never be equal to the wants of the times." He concluded, "I do not know what will become of us. I know there is little choice, but in that let us have the best."[25]

Propaganda met on June 16 to consider the nominees, and the Holy Father approved the appointments on June 22, 1851. Bishop Hendren was transferred to Nottingham, where he could count on assistance from Ullathorne, who, upon his own transfer from the Western District, had recommended him as his successor. Hendren was replaced in Clifton by Thomas Burgess, one of the Ampleforth monks who had left his monastery and his order to assist Bishop Baines at Prior Park. George Errington was named bishop of Plymouth. Wiseman, in recommending his old friend, stated that Errington was second to none in prudence, business skill, and integrity of life, easily excelling all of the English clergy, moreover, in theology, canon law, and both sacred and profane letters.[26] James Brown, president of Sedgley Park, was the first bishop of Shrewsbury, and William Turner, educated at Ushaw and the English College and, in 1850, a priest of Manchester, was given the see of Salford.

When informing Wiseman of the appointments, Thomas Grant concluded by announcing his own nomination to Southwark: "I need not say that I shall be always more happy to hear your voice than mine in St. George's, and that I trust the sermons which have worked such effects there will not be wanting when the flock has a less able and a less zealous pastor." The cardinal could not have been more relieved: "I am happy that your nomination has come now when large numbers of

Romans are wanted and a cordial cooperation among the bishops. I am indeed pleased to lose Southwark since I shall no longer fear a clash as previously was the case." He spoke too soon. When deciding upon the appointments, Propaganda had considered the possibility of providing for a means of settling the questions that might arise as the bishops divided the temporalities belonging to the former districts. It was determined to defer action on the matter.[27] The lack of clear norms in this regard led eventually to the permanent estrangement of Wiseman and Grant, which, as with later disputes and a similar break with Bishop Errington, was one of the most unhappy episodes in episcopal relations during the first decade of the new hierarchy and a cause of deep personal grief for the cardinal himself.

The majority of the bishops were not well suited for the demanding tasks ahead of them. With the noteworthy exceptions of Ullathorne and Errington, none had demonstrated any evident signs of administrative expertise. Only Wiseman, Errington, and Grant were credited widely with outstanding intellectual acumen, and the new bishop of Southwark was still extremely young (not quite thirty-five years of age) when appointed. Two of the bishops, George Brown of Liverpool and Hendren of Nottingham, suffered from acutely poor health, and few of those named were equipped with leadership qualities of a high degree. Most had been good, hard-working priests who had served the church well either on the missions or in the colleges without alienating those who recommended them for the episcopate. This may be a great deal in itself; it does not necessarily qualify a man to be a bishop. Clearly Wiseman's role would be of paramount importance.

Aside from the prominence of the archiepiscopal see itself, Wiseman's influence would depend largely upon his own personality. An archbishop has little right to interfere in the affairs of his suffragan bishops. Under the ecclesiastical legislation in force before the code of canon law became effective in 1918, it was the right and duty of the metropolitan archbishop to convoke and preside at provincial councils or synods, to see to the residence in their sees of his suffragan bishops, and to act as judge when certain cases might be appealed to him. There was very little left of the extensive power granted to medieval archbishops. Admittedly, he could claim the right of visitation over the sees in his province, but "this was so hedged round with regulations that it was virtually useless."[28] Wiseman's colleagues expected much of him, however, and they were always ready to take advantage of his experience and expertise when it suited their purposes. They were equally ready to criticize him, and even to work against him, when they disagreed with his policies.

The cardinal can hardly be blamed for recognizing his own strengths. There was a certain boastfulness in Wiseman that could be interpreted as arrogance, one of the less savory sides of his character. This was partly the result of a simplicity that led him to direct, outspoken statements, sometimes offensive to others. He tended to act as though he alone knew what was best for the church and nobody else was serving its interests as he was. He wrote to Talbot in December 1850: "Without any personal feelings on the subject, I believe that if I had not been sent back, there would have been serious difficulties in establishing the hierarchy. I have borne the entire brunt of the excitement; the other bishops have escaped almost unnoticed." Wiseman concluded, "As I have broad shoulders and some public estimation and good friendship among the aristocracy, I could stand a great deal."[29]

Wiseman was a man of grand, sweeping plans. As is often the case with those who dare to challenge the status quo, he encountered constant opposition. His biographer maintained that the cardinal was at his best in defending the church from attack and even in carefully framing the statutes of the first two provincial synods. "Where his imagination was fired," wrote Wilfrid Ward, "prolonged labour was not alien to his nature." The difficult sequel to such efforts was another story: "The minute adjustment of the rights of Bishops, a matter requiring tedious and complicated investigations and compromise with colleagues, in some cases devoid of insight; the correlative readjusting of the rights of Presidents of Colleges and the definition of the limits of the powers of Cathedral Chapters, such detailed work showed him almost at his worst."[30] The analysis is not completely accurate: Wiseman, at times, demonstrated a great deal of patience in dealing with administrative details. There can be little doubt, however, that he was easily bored by routine business matters.

Almost thirty years after the cardinal's death, his vicar general Robert Whitty provided some interesting insight into his character: "The Cardinal's Faith was perhaps all the more remarkable because he was not I suppose what could be commonly called a saintly man. His Faith had become a part of himself — so much so that he did not seem to reflect on it or to be conscious of it, no more than one realizes one's breathing." Whitty illustrated his observation by discussing Wiseman's attitude toward the Holy See: "A cold word or even a look from the Pope himself would or could wound him most deeply. And this extended to every authority living and acting under the shadow of the Holy Father." He would be troubled by any word of blame reported to him by the cardinal prefect or the secretary of Propaganda: "Still more, a letter from Propaganda disapproving even in the mildest terms of some step he had taken rankled in his mind for a long time. And this was just as true after he became cardinal — when personally he had nothing either to fear or hope from individuals in Rome, however high in authority, as it was when vicar apostolic."

The same characteristic was evident in the way that Wiseman responded to criticism: "He was utterly indifferent as to what Protestants thought or said of his conduct. Not so with Catholics, especially Priests or Bishops." This was Whitty's explanation of the good humor that the cardinal demonstrated throughout the papal aggression crisis. When Catholics attacked him, however, the story was different. It was on such an occasion that Whitty once said: "Well never mind! They will make a great deal of you when you're dead!" The comment achieved its purpose by prompting Wiseman's laughter: "That is a strange comfort to give me now."[31]

The cardinal loved a show, whether an ecclesiastical function or a spectacle of a more mundane kind. He traveled about London in an "old-fashioned carriage, with its gorgeous trappings . . . to him the natural and right accompaniment of his dignity; and any modification of it in concession to English tastes, was only to yield to No Popery prejudices." He was personally a humble man, however, according to Whitty's account. When told that a lady was asking for a memorial, such as an old zucchetto or a slipper, before he left for Rome in 1850, he was genuinely shocked: "No indeed. I'll do no such thing! I'll give you the relic of a saint for her — but the idea of her keeping any thing I had used!!"[32]

It was remarked that the cardinal had "a lobster salad side as well as a spiritual side." The popular image was captured by the poet, Robert Browning, in his depiction of Bishop Blougram, clearly meant as a caricature of Wiseman. The somewhat skeptical prelate of the poem little resembles the cardinal, however.[33] Whitty admitted that he had often heard "in so many different quarters of his being a great eater and of his fondness for good living, that I feel bound to give my own impressions." Wiseman was not self-indulgent in his use of food or drink. He preferred continental to English dishes and spoke openly of his tastes. Whitty observed, "For I shd. say, his horror of being regarded as a holy man was stronger than his desire of giving edification."

Whitty tried to explain the fact that "a man possessing such qualities of mind and heart should not have been more popular with his priests or even generally with the generation of his Catholic fellow countrymen in the midst of whom he lived and for whom he laboured." Wiseman had "natural defects in his character," but he was also placed in very difficult circumstances, "at least during my part of his London career." He was "an extremely shy man," finding it impossible to maintain a conversation with those "of uncongenial tastes." This was often "mistaken for coldness and want of good will."

The fact that Wiseman never served on the mission or engaged in parochial work was still another reason for criticism by his priests: "Whatever the real explanation was, he too often *seemed* inconsiderate in treating with his priests and unable or unwilling to enter into their difficulties." The vast majority of the London clergy, moreover, had no exposure to the kind of Roman education favored by the cardinal. He was criticized, finally, for failing to persevere "in carrying out a good plan which he himself had conceived and worked out on paper." Whitty stressed the fact that the cardinal acted "*unconsciously* on principle": "Somehow he often did not care to reason out even for himself the principles on which he acted. He was much more inclined to quote some example or some teaching from Rome as his justification." He did not grasp the fact moreover that there was a "deep and wide gulf that separated him (mentally) from some of his most intimate friends on two subjects particularly, viz. on the treatment of religious orders and on the treatment of converts." [34]

The last quality mentioned by Whitty became more evident as the cardinal grew older. Wiseman had increasing difficulty in distinguishing between personal criticism and that which was based upon principle. Even Monsignor Talbot, always loyal to him, issued a warning: "I think you take too much to heart what people say about you." [35]

John Morris, Wiseman's adviser in later years, claimed that "the peculiarity of the cardinal's mind was such that there was no other side possible in his view except that which presented itself to him in the affairs that concerned him." Morris illustrated the observation by describing how Wiseman, at the time of the establishment of the hierarchy, transferred into Southwark those priests "whom he had known to be opposed to himself." [36] Some of them were already living in Southwark, as a matter of fact, but the removal of still others, whom he mistrusted, helps to account for the cardinal's general feelings toward the clergy of the diocese that was now to be governed by Thomas Grant.

Robert Whitty described an incident that tends to support the assertion of Morris. When the names of the new bishops were announced, Whitty suggested that James Bamber, "the chief if not the only person who understood the accounts and all money matters of the bishop, both public and private," should be moved to Southwark. Bamber had been secretary to Bishop Griffiths. Since a division had to be made of the men and money belonging to the old London District, Whitty sensibly pointed out that Bamber, if assigned as secretary to Bishop Grant, could be a great help in preventing "disputes and misunderstandings." "Dr. Grant will not want a secretary," responded Wiseman; "Why he can write more letters himself than we three — you, Searle, and myself can write altogether, i.e. at the same time." Whitty acknowledged the truth of the observation but later pointed out that his real motive in making the suggestion was "to introduce an element of *peace*." There were a number of priests in Southwark opposed to the cardinal, who, nevertheless, "would not yield up a valuable man like canon Bamber." This was the reason, wrote Whitty, that "poor Dr. Grant was forced into a species of opposition, and it showed itself later in the selection of the canons for his chapter."[37]

Since Wiseman tried to surround himself with those who supported him, Grant was left with some whom the cardinal viewed as his "opposition." Grant hoped to heal wounds and avoid anything that smacked of "party spirit" by appointing several of these men to his chapter. Wiseman was offended. When Grant later appointed Edward Cox to be his first vicar general, he anticipated the reaction of the cardinal by writing to Talbot, "We are beginning a new order of things in England, and if we wish to carry it through effectually, we must endeavour, I think, to make no one hostile to it, and to exclude none from its influence who have not been stigmatised for their misdeeds." Grant's policy did him credit, but it resulted in the charge of Gallicanism being leveled at him. He vehemently denied the accusation.[38]

Cardinal Wiseman's sensitivity was an especially tragic flaw when coupled to the fact that he was unduly conscious of the lofty dignity to which he had been called. Whitty may well have been correct when he pointed out that it was not personal pride, but concern for his office, which led the cardinal to value it so highly. If he seemed to flaunt his position publicly, the modest home to which he moved in the middle of the decade, while more spacious than the home in Golden Square that he had inherited from his predecessors, was hardly up to the standard of the splendor to which Roman cardinals were often accustomed.[39]

Archbishop David Mathew concluded that Wiseman's "pompous manner" was a front to veil his sensitivity. Before his elevation to the episcopate, Thomas Grant wrote a number of candid letters to warn of the danger: "Your dignity, as cardinal and archbishop, places you, of course, very much above the other bishops, and as they feel everything you say or do, is it not important at this crisis to attach them very much to yourself personally?"[40]

It was in keeping with his character that the cardinal insisted upon appointing both Whitty, his vicar general, and Searle, his secretary, to positions on the archdiocesan chapter. Realizing that the assignments might easily result in a conflict of interest for the two men, Whitty objected to his own position as chapter provost and to Searle's presence on the chapter in any capacity: "But the Cardinal would not yield and his reasons seem to me characteristic. 'No,' he said, 'if I die I don't want my secretary to fall back into the rank of an ordinary priest, and I don't want my vicar general to be without a permanent dignity in the diocese — for of course my successor may choose another vicar general for himself.'"[41] Cardinal Wiseman had no way of knowing that the day would come when his chapter would question his authority and that his secretary, along with Whitty's successor as vicar general, would side with those opposed to him.

The new archbishop, then, possessed serious weaknesses that the historian cannot ignore. Wiseman was always capable of enormous amounts of labor when inspired by a worthy cause. Although he could be painstaking in drawing up major plans, he was often bored by routine and failed to persevere in seeing projects through to the finish. He was also sensitive to criticism, unable to cope with his friends when they disagreed with him, and anxious, at least in public, to demonstrate the dignity that he felt to be a necessary feature of his office.

Yet Wiseman was head and shoulders above his episcopal colleagues in talent and farsightedness. The very fact that he accepted the kinds of personal criticism made by a young man like Thomas Grant, or by Monsignor Talbot, indicates that he was not unaware of his faults and wanted to correct them. In 1851 Grant wrote a remarkable letter to Wiseman that proved to be prophetic. It is worth quoting as a fitting conclusion to any character study of the cardinal.

> Following the kind permission given to me, I must venture to state that if your Eminence calls George [Errington] to advise you, it may be expedient to be very communicative with him and let him or your other counsellors know your whole mind upon every subject under consideration. It is thought that you do not give your whole confidence . . . and hence your advisors can never really share in your decisions or views. It is likely that the bishops have felt something of the same kind. If I were to state it in other words, it would probably occur to me to say that you are afraid of being opposed in your plans and that you are inclined to seek men who will readily fall in with them and not question their expediency; or you may perhaps seek to act alone. I could not pretend to prove these things by examples, but you will know how to change them if they are truly stated here. It may be answered that no one encourages you to be confidential with him, but it is one of the consequences and troubles of high position and dignity that its possessors must create and seek confidence and afterwards maintain and encourage it. Our poor England is divided sadly into parties, and unless you hear from trusty friends what is said and thought by all, your acts will often be twisted into an approval of the views of particular classes of Catholics. After discussing and determining a course of action, we are tempted to change our resolutions, but do not make these changes without telling those who advised you in the first instance. But whilst I hope you will excuse me for speaking so boldly, do let me entreat you to hear everybody with a cheerful and inviting *accoglienza* [welcome], and to tell your intimate friends and especially the bishops, *everything*. You are too persuasive in argument, and unless you allow men to state their opposition somewhat sturdily, you will at times find the best friends reluctant to oppose your views or timid about entering into a discussion in defence of their own.[42]

Had Wiseman been able to assimilate and to practice what Grant recommended in this letter, one that any person in high office could benefit from reading, he would have avoided much unnecessary and heartbreaking conflict.

11. The First Provincial Synod of Westminster

ECAUSE OF THE UNEXPECTEDLY VIOLENT REACTION TO THE ESTAB-
lishment of the hierarchy, the bishops decided to postpone their
first provincial synod for at least a year rather than risk further
unfavorable notice and criticism. They held a meeting in November
1851, however, and for three days discussed their common difficulties,
along with the possible means of dealing with them synodically.[1] One
of their first concerns was the formation of diocesan chapters, since
church law demanded that members of such bodies should be represented at provincial synods. In addition to serving as advisers to the
bishops, chapter members would also bear the important responsibility
of nominating episcopal candidates in the future.

Wilfrid Ward observed that the establishment of the hierarchy
seemed to increase the influence of the episcopate without offering any
corresponding advantage to the clergy. The bishops, therefore, found
themselves faced with what appeared to be a "constitutional" opposition. Lord Shrewsbury wrote at the time: "I am anxious to know how it
[the hierarchy] is to affect the lower clergy. If they do not get their
rights, they have been scurvily treated."[2] The bishops were only too
aware of the dissatisfaction and took preliminary steps toward responding to it before ending their meeting. They agreed upon a plan
for appointing certain priests in each diocese as "missionary rectors,"
with the canonical rights of pastors.

It was to the new archbishop that the priests turned when seeking
to extend their rights. Early in 1851 the clergy of the southern deanery
of Yorkshire begged Wiseman to use his influence in establishing ecclesiastical laws that would "be in accordance with the free constitution and the equitable laws of their country." They asked for a constitution composed not only of canon law but also of the civil (i.e.,

common and statute) law of England, and they warned against introducing any "mere foreign system of ecclesiastical legislation," which would be "obnoxious to their feelings, and as hateful to the millions by whom they are surrounded, and with whom they are in constant intercourse." They specified ecclesiastical courts, which in England were "held in utter abomination and in all countries condemned by men who have been nurtured in the principles of national freedom." The petition, finally, asked for "a complete change, which may give the governed an efficient affirmative in the nomination of those who are to be their governors [i.e., the bishops]."[3]

The address smacked of the Gallican spirit, abhorred by Wiseman. It clearly confused ecclesiastical institutions with the political structures established to govern a democratic society. Thomas Grant, not yet elevated to the episcopate, prepared a document, "The Practical Consequences of the Restoration of the Hierarchy," in order to answer demands of this kind. He wrote that it would be absurd to alter canon law to incorporate legislation designed for a particular nation. If English Protestants deprecated foreign ecclesiastical systems, he asked, how would they react were the Holy See to establish a code containing the "just and equitable statute laws of England"? The pope, in other words, would have to "constitute himself judge of the justice and equity of our legislation," and by that very fact would have to "abrogate at least a portion of it." There was sound thinking in Grant's conclusion: "As our ecclesiastical government does not interfere with our national laws, will it not be wiser to regulate it by the provisions of the common law of the Church only?"[4]

Grant also commented upon another petition, this one prepared by the deanery of South Northumberland and North Durham. Its framers had demanded that "the second order of the clergy be placed in their proper position and that everything be regulated according to the ordinary canon law." They, too, asked that the bishops might be elected by the general voice of the parochial clergy, that parish priests might be irremovable except for offenses designated by canon law, and that the administration of finances in each diocese might be managed by a board on which the clergy would be justly represented. Grant admitted that it would be beneficial to provide the clergy with security, but permanent sources of income had to be assured for priests assigned to the missions before this could be achieved. He suggested that if they were to be irremovable, their congregations had every right to demand that a means of examining suitable candidates should be instituted "against the possibility of unfit persons being placed over them." Before examiners could be selected, however, it would be necessary to summon diocesan synods, and these could not be convoked until they were provided for by legislation emanating from a provincial synod.[5]

The clergy of the new diocese of Beverley, finally, also petitioned the cardinal for a change in the status of missionaries in England. He replied by acknowledging that the hierarchy would be incomplete if it did not include provision for the organization of the clergy and for the establishment of as much general ecclesiastical law as possible, "without clashing with the law of the land." Wiseman reminded the petitioners, however, that time and labor were necessary for the accomplishment of their objectives, not to mention that "peace which, as yet we have not enjoyed."[6]

Lack of funds was, as predicted, one of the gravest problems facing the bishops. The challenge was greatest in country districts, where the church had relied, in the past, upon the benefactions of a relatively small number of Catholics who, in fact, had often appointed their own chaplains. If a parish system were to be effective, all Catholics had to share the responsibility of supporting their priests. One missionary complained: "The clergy are, for the most part, supported by *endowments*, or by *individuals*, not by their respective congregations; and precisely the same may be said of the schools and other *charitable institutions*." In the Western District twenty chapels were served by "*private* chaplains" who, nevertheless, had to care for "*public* congregations." English Catholics, he complained, "are brought up from their tender infancy with the idea there is no necessity of contributing towards the support of your pastor, your chapel, your school, or anything. *All that is done for you*. When will this proxy system end?" The system had not ended twenty years later, when the Beverley Chapter was asked to solicit from the next provincial synod a statement on the "duties and relations of patrons, chaplains, and congregations."[7]

Wiseman was worried for fear that his income would be insufficient for his needs as a cardinal: "If money is not contributed, I shall be obliged to borrow. . . . But no time must be lost." He observed that he was to be named a cardinal for England, not Rome, so that it was "unreasonable" to expect assistance from the Holy See, "especially in its present embarrassed state of finance." A month later, however, he wrote, "The pope, to whom I have never spoken a word on money matters, has seen, evidently with pain, the apathy of the English Catholics in regard to a dignity which he thought he was highly honouring them by bestowing on one of their bishops." The Holy Father gave him the equivalent of £400, with the promise that he would contribute the same sum annually "*for a few years.*" He wanted "to set the example to the Catholics of England to come forward generously, to support the new dignity conferred on their Church." Wiseman concluded: "But what I feel convinced of is this, that if it is seen that the decorum of the cardinalitial dignity (which is so highly and zealously valued by Rome) is not kept up, I shall soon be recalled to Rome, and there will be an end of the matter. There, I can assure you, I have had such marks, public and private, of regard, confidence, and affection, as have been overpowering, and I believe that an excuse would not be unwelcome for bringing me there." Wilfrid Ward, citing this letter, omitted the last passage and wrote of the cardinal's "simple satisfaction in the state and position attendant on his new dignity."[8] His "simple satisfaction" was less than complete.

Thomas Grant suggested another view of the cardinalitial office, communicated to him by "several thinking men": "The state & splendour of a Cardinal is scarcely attainable with your limited means in London, & even if attainable, is scarcely desirable, whereas a Cardinal, who lives as much as possible for the poor & amongst them is sure to have his weight and consideration even amongst the most unfavourable of our censors." Grant proposed as models St. Charles Borromeo, serving his plague-ridden flock in Milan, and St. Francis of Sales, working in the mountain villages of Geneva: "Excuse me for putting this view, as it is that of very excellent people here [in Rome] and in England."[9]

Although Wiseman did not seek personal comfort, he hoped that the honor shown him would be an encouragement for Catholics and would lead to a greater appreciation of the Holy See. The briefest study of some of the temporal problems facing the new bishops, on the other hand, demonstrates that they were not to be blamed for being less concerned than the Holy See or Wiseman himself in the "niceties of ecclesiastical deportment." Bishop Ullathorne, for example, found it essential, much to his distress, to decrease the already inadequate salaries paid to his priests. Later he was compelled, along with the president of Oscott, to spend a short time in prison because of the outstanding debts for which the two men were legally, but not personally, responsible.[10]

The death of Lord Shrewsbury in 1852 was a catastrophe for Ullathorne. The earl had been providing him with £1,000 a year to cover debts of the old Midland District. In his will Shrewsbury had provided £20,000 in railway debentures for the bishop, but legal battles over the estate resulted in their total loss to the diocese. When the earl's successor died in 1856, the title passed to a Protestant branch of the family, and Ullathorne wrote that "in addition to other difficulties, all the Shrewsbury missions are now thrown on my hands without one penny of endowment."[11]

The western dioceses were particularly poor, both in funds and personnel. The see of Newport and Menevia started with five thousand Catholics and eighteen scattered churches and chapels. It depended upon the Benedictines for its parish priests. Plymouth was composed of three counties served by twenty-four priests, and Clifton had inherited a debt of £60,000 from the former Western District, resulting from the expenditure upon Prior Park. Nottingham and Northampton had far-flung populations, and Bishop Hendren, out of the frying pan into the fire as a result of his transfer from Clifton, complained that the contributions of the faithful in his new see would not even pay his priests the small sums promised by his predecessors. The bishop possessed no more than £20 a year to meet the charge of his own board and lodging, but he maintained surprisingly good humor under deplorable circumstances: "What is to be done? Shall I declare myself insolvent or show my diocese a fair pair of heels? This last would be a difficult feat for a poor old gouty wretch like me."[12]

Liverpool had eight thousand poor Irish in the cathedral city alone, and Philip Hughes, finally, was justified in calling southeast Lancashire, the new see of Salford, "the blackest spot of all this business." Two-thirds of the county was still rural, although the industrial region, between 1801 and 1851, "had increased its population until it was four times as great as that of the rural part; and had increased it at nearly twice the rate at which the population of London had increased."[13] The bishops sometimes considered that Wiseman was insensitive to their particular situations and too forceful in promoting his own schemes for the country, with little understanding of the local peculiarities that made it difficult for his colleagues to implement them.

Few of the bishops were adequately prepared for the financial administration that was now their responsibility. Bishop Wareing of Northampton, when questioned about some important accounts, wrote with apparent unconcern that he had burned whole rooms of papers and documents, "out of a kind of *hatred of* bookeeping and under an idea that they could be of no use in the future." One solicitor, called to assist the bishop, observed in despair, "When I consider how dreadfully our charitable and religious trusts have been mis-managed, I am not surprised that Government should think proper to take into its own hands the management of our trusts as well as those of other religious communions — nor am I much surprised that some of our laity should encourage the Government in its proceedings." Wiseman's books and accounts were kept by Robert Shepherd, one of his priests and later archdiocesan canon. After the cardinal's death, Archbishop Manning's secretary wrote, "Such a labyrinth of errors and confusion as poor Canon Shepherd's ledger I have seldom seen."[14]

Notwithstanding the lack of funds necessary to support the priests already ordained, the bishops were frustrated by the spiritual demands of missions with insufficient numbers of the clergy to serve them adequately. Following their meeting in the autumn of 1851, they asked Thomas Grant to explain to the Holy See their reluctance to release priests who sought entrance into religious orders. Grant asked that such permissions might be withheld by the authorities in Rome. He acknowledged the important work being done by religious orders but pointed out that, in the proper government of a diocese, the bishops had to count on those who were less subject to removal than was the case with those directly under the control of their religious superiors.[15]

John Henry Newman, observing the situation, wrote: "What will the bishops do, if their clergy leave them? Why, they must form seminaries. Seminaries are more wanted than sees; for you cannot fill Sees except from Seminaries."[16] A major decision for the bishops, in fact, was whether or not to establish diocesan seminaries as prescribed by the Council of Trent. In view of the shortage of funds and personnel, the difficulties appeared to render impossible any such plans. Tied to the question, moreover, was the manner to be pursued in distributing funds, students, and administrative personnel among the four colleges in which the diocesan clergy had been educated.

Solutions to all of the above problems and others were sought by the bishops as they prepared, under Wiseman's direction, to assemble for their first provincial synod. Previous episcopal meetings had been informal assemblies, empowered to do no more than make recommendations to the Holy See. Provincial councils or synods, on the other hand, carried far more weight. They could enact disciplinary regulations for the entire province, which in this case included all of England and Wales. Bishop Ullathorne, an important participant in all four of the provincial synods of Westminster, described them as having completed the organization of the hierarchy and having laid the foundations of ecclesiastical discipline for English Catholics.[17] The first three synods were all dominated by the figure of Cardinal Wiseman.

It was decided that the first synod would assemble in July 1852 at Oscott College, more central and with better accommodation than the archdiocesan college of St. Edmund's. Wiseman supervised all of the preparations. He sent each of the bishops an "Epitome Decretorum," a printed summary of proposed decrees, completely his own work with the sole exception of those dealing with the erection and role of cathedral chapters. These were drawn up by Bishops Ullathorne and Grant. The cardinal asked his colleagues for their observations on the various items included in the document.[18]

Wilfrid Ward, writing of the first synod, oversimplified by stating that the bishops occupied themselves to such an extent "with mere elementary questions" that they never came to grips with the important problems confronting them. The synod, it is true, had to deal with some very basic questions in order to establish structures for further action. They deliberately avoided, moreover, issues that could only have led to unnecessary controversy. In the "Epitome Decretorum," for example, Wiseman suggested that the question of the validity of Anglican orders should be discussed and a decision solicited from the Holy See.

Bishop Ullathorne prudently commented: "If the Bishops solicit this decision, will it not be considered a declaration of war against the state? Is it expedient that the Bps. should be the movers of this question at this moment?" The matter was discussed at the synod but no action was taken: "All were unanimous; it wd. have given the gov. a new pretext for persecution."[19]

The bishops avoided another issue that would have been extremely contentious. Bishop Ullathorne, commenting upon the "Epitome Decretorum," wrote that he was dissatisfied with the state of ecclesiastical education and the situation had to be changed. Candidates for the priesthood were not obtaining the proper preparation in biblical studies, theology, pastoral training, or ascetics. Students were also suffering from a lack of personal attention on the part of their superiors. He specifically cited Oscott, where "everything is dry and formal, and except with class, there is no fusion between superiors and subjects." No wonder, he observed, that so many young men were entering religious orders: "I know not what your Eminence's view may be upon this subject, but I presume that you would prefer being nearer the system of the Council of Trent as exemplified in foreign seminaries."[20]

Henry Weedall, whom Wiseman had displaced in 1840, was again serving as president of Oscott, since Ullathorne had dismissed Logan, Wiseman's old friend and his successor at the college. Logan blamed Wiseman, whom he thought to have been responsible, but a series of letters between the two men eventually cleared up what seems to have been a misunderstanding.[21]

The cardinal shared Ullathorne's concern over ecclesiastical education and, in fact, dismissed Edward Cox, president of St. Edmund's. There had been early rumors to the effect that Wiseman and Cox were at odds. "I hear that Dr. Cox has resigned his situation of president of Old Hall," wrote Lingard; "I suspect that Dr. Wiseman and he were never very cordial, but am told that the pretext is that Dr. W. has reduced the pension for ecclesiastical students from £60 to £40 and that Cox declares he will not be responsible for the stability of the college with such a pension."[22]

Wiseman was not one to economize, especially in the formation of future priests. When the blow finally came, his complaints were of another kind. He specified the lack of discipline at St. Edmund's and the inadequate instruction in pastoral theology as primary concerns. The whole system needed revision, he said, noting that "even the professors feel that scholarship is at a low ebb and that great reform is wanting." The cardinal also observed that the material state of the college was "intolerable" and that "the health of every young priest is bad" as a result of "want of care as to diet, ventilation, exercise, etc." He concluded that the seminary was "in no respect what it ought to be and cannot, as now conducted, furnish to this diocese, learned, eloquent, and gifted priests such as the times require." Cox was among those transferred to the diocese of Southwark, where he was given a mission at Southampton. He was replaced by his vice-president, William Weathers. "The college is cleared of its terrible obstruction," wrote Wiseman, predicting that the "whole system will be reformed, and a sound, heightened ecclesiastical spirit will be introduced."[23]

Lingard had also warned that Newsham would be dismissed from the presidency of Ushaw and replaced by Thomas Grant, for "every thing must now be Roman."[24] This prediction was incorrect, of course, but both Ushaw and Prior Park were subject to jurisdictional and financial difficulties. It was clear, therefore, that questions relating to the four ecclesiastical colleges would have to be taken in hand by the bishops.

Wiseman failed to treat the subject adequately in the "Epitome Decretorum." He included brief directives regarding the academic and personal qualifications to be sought in candidates for the priesthood, reports to the bishops by college authorities, the course of studies to be pursued, and the necessity of adequate training in ceremonies and chant. Ullathorne was not satisfied and continued to insist that something should be "thought of and devised which could be accepted as practicable for elevating the ecclesiastical studies." He suggested that a common college for higher studies might be desirable, "if not for all, at least for a certain number of dioceses."[25] The idea was a practical one, but considering the battles that engaged the bishops when they eventually tried to solve the college problems, it was probably wise for them to have approved, as they did, the proposals offered by Wiseman, without attempting anything more ambitious. Admittedly, however, major problems were left unresolved.

The participants of the first synod began their deliberations on July 6, 1852, after a splendid and colorful ceremony in the Oscott College chapel. All but two of the bishops were present, neither George Brown nor William Hendren being well enough to attend. The bishops were joined by the abbots of monasteries in England, major superiors of religious institutes, deputies elected by the chapters, a theologian for each bishop, and specially invited theologians and canonists who might exercise a consultative voice in the proceedings. John Henry Newman and Henry Edward Manning were invited to assist at the synod as special theologians, as were the college presidents.

Newman, at the second session, preached one of his most famous sermons, "The Second Spring": "The English Church was, and the English Church was not, and the English Church is once again. This is the portent, worthy of a cry. It is the coming in of a Second Spring; it is a restoration in the moral world, such as that which yearly takes place in the physical." He described eloquently the vision offered to those who were present: "Priests and Religious, theologians from the schools, and canons from the Cathedral, walk in due precedence," followed by "twelve mitred heads; and last I see a Prince of the Church, in the royal dye of empire and martyrdom, a pledge to us from Rome of Rome's unwearied love, a token that that goodly company is firm in Apostolic faith and hope." The assembly, he said, including the sons of St. Benedict, St. Dominic, St. Bernard, and St. Ignatius, was meant to inaugurate a great act: "What is that act? it is the first synod of a new Hierarchy; it is the resurrection of the Church."[26] All were emotionally moved by the sermon. The cardinal wept openly.

Among the most significant decrees of the synod were those dealing with cathedral chapters and the missionary status of the clergy.[27] Although it was declared that it would be the duty of the chapter to provide a list of candidates for the episcopate after the death or resignation of a bishop, the decree concluded by stating that it would "ever pertain to the free will of the Holy Father, to exercise his own right of election of any other than those recommended as often as he shall deem it necessary."

A temporary solution to the problem of the clergy's status was included in a decree devoted to the government of missions. Each bishop, with the advice of his chapter, was to set aside a certain number of churches as "*quasi*-parishes." Over each of these, he would place a priest with the title of "missionary rector," who would be fixed permanently in his position. In each diocese, moreover, a commission of inquiry would be established to examine any case involving the removal of such a rector. Finally, where two or more priests were assigned to the same mission, one was to be appointed as head of the others, especially responsible for the cure of souls and the management of the church. The decree met some of the problems that had caused dissension previously. Although it was not satisfactory to everyone, England remained without canonical parishes or a parochial clergy until the twentieth century.

There were decrees on the discipline and even the doctrine of the sacraments. They outlined the ceremonial to be followed in their administration and tried, in some cases, to deal with matters of special concern in England. The treatment of baptism, for example, stated that "among Protestants there is no dogma which has been more corrupted in these times." Where there was the least doubt as to the validity of a convert's previous baptism, the sacrament was to be administered conditionally.

The synodical decrees advocated Eucharistic devotions that had been considered by some Catholics as alien to English spirituality. It was still unsafe, in some areas, for the churches to be left unlocked during the day. Yet among the practices demanded by the synod was the Forty Hours devotion, necessitating public worship of the sacramental host for forty consecutive hours in the churches and public chapels of a diocese, each in its turn. When Bishop Briggs commented on the suggestion after reading the "Epitome Decretorum," he objected that the devotion could not be carried out safely at night, "especially in manufacturing towns." Bishop George Brown of Liverpool, when he saw the decree, made a similar observation, and Bishop Hendren said that the proposal would be opposed by "the vast majority of the clergy." He added: "I truly wish such an order or regulation had not *as yet* been made." Wiseman was not impressed by their arguments. He had instituted the practice several years before in London and had written at the time, "We are ripe for anything."[28]

The directives dealing with the life and good conduct of the clergy warned against all spectacles unworthy of an ecclesiastic, specifically including "clamorous hunting with horse and hounds, public dances, unlawful games, and feastings protracted to a late hour of the night." Priests were also forbidden to attend stage plays and public theater, and they were to wear the clerical collar, recently introduced into England, whenever they appeared in public.

A number of embarrassing squabbles had resulted as a result of legacies intended for the church. It was now enacted that priests were not to be guardians or executors of estates without episcopal approval. Bishops were to be consulted if any of the faithful wished to establish a foundation for masses, and rectors were forbidden to assist individuals in drawing up their wills. Trusts and bequests for the purpose of offering masses for the deceased were still legally void in England, where prayers for the dead were regarded by the courts as a "superstitious practice." Various subterfuges, however, were pursued to skirt the law. Normally funds were left outright to an individual priest, who would then execute the wishes of the benefactor. Sometimes there were disputes as to whether the money had been intended for the priest himself, his mission, or religion in general. Edward Cox wrote to Wiseman in 1850, "I am bound to secrecy, but I know of two large sums of money that are intended for the benefit of religion, but which I am sure would be withdrawn or applied elsewhere, if applied at all in religious purposes, if the parties knew that my name had been taken from trusts already existing."[29]

Cardinal Wiseman was questioned by a royal commission as to the truthfulness of a document claiming that "since his arrival here [he] has been very anxious to absorb in his own person all the trusteeships and property within the London mission, as it was formerly called." One property, valued at £200,000, had been vested partially in the names of

Cox and two other priests of the London District. It was asserted that the cardinal's failure to persuade Cox to resign the trusteeship into his own hands resulted in "the loss of the mitre which the clergy of the London District were very anxious that Dr. Cox should receive." One of the other trustees was alleged to have died as a result of "the annoyance and mental anxiety felt at the demand of the surrender of the trust from his hands into those of his Eminence." When asked to comment on the charges, Wiseman replied: "I only wish to say that that statement from the beginning to the end of it is one tissue of untruths, every word of it. Since I came to London I have not transferred to my name solely, one single farthing of property in any form." He had only insisted that whenever he had any connection with property, it was to be "vested in the names of a sufficient number of trustees." All that had been stated with regard to Cox and the others was "untrue."[30] In order to avoid the loss of funds, priests were normally allowed to retain their trusteeships. The first synod did not frame legislation to cover such cases, but it at least provided that the bishops were to be aware of those which existed.

The synod made a tentative step toward resolving the long-standing problems that had arisen among the regular and secular clergy. The decree made it clear that nothing would be done to interfere with the privileges and exemptions properly belonging to religious congregations. Five statutes followed: the bishop was free to make a formal visitation of missionary and public churches served by regulars; provincials and superiors of orders were urged to consult the bishop before removing their priests; faculties, or permission to preach and to hear confessions, were to be granted by bishops only; regulars were encouraged to live as their vocation demanded; and, finally, no new religious houses were to be built without the explicit permission of the ordinary. The members of the communities who were present at the synod offered no objection.

Although Dom Cuthbert Butler was correct in pointing out that "twenty-five years after the Hierarchy the relations of the regulars with the bishops were not yet fully settled, privileges counter to the common law still being claimed,"[31] the synod nevertheless settled the general relationship of the regular clergy with the hierarchy, clearly putting the bishops in control of the missions, without interfering in the internal administration of the communities.

An unfortunate misunderstanding arose, however, almost immediately. It was proposed that an instruction, issued by Propaganda in 1848, should be appended to the decrees, even though it had not been intended for England.[32] The document deplored the fact that the authority of vicars apostolic over religious orders had been called into question. Such priests were commanded to present their credentials to the bishops from whom they were to receive their faculties. They were to render to the vicars apostolic an account of all pious bequests to missions in their control, and whenever controversial questions arose among them, they were to be settled by the bishops, the direct representatives of the Holy See. Finally, and most objectionable, religious missionaries could not be removed from their posts without the consent of the vicar apostolic who exercised jurisdiction over the area.

The superiors of religious congregations in England heatedly opposed the inclusion of this instruction with the synod's decrees. They denied, correctly, that it had been issued for England, where the "painful circumstances" leading to its formulation did not exist. They especially complained of the final provision: "Not to be able under any emergency to remove from a mission one of our subjects would be sometimes very injurious to the body, and seriously impede that freedom of action and arrangement in our communities which is necessary for religious superiors fully to possess in order to provide as well for the government of their houses as for the missions supplied by them."[33]

Wiseman, aware of the complaint, was visiting Rome in 1853 when Bishop Grant wrote: "A few days ago, a regular superior asked me if your Eminence were likely to ask for jurisdiction over the regulars. I gave every reason I could think of to prevent any fresh rumours and annoyance, and I told him if their superiors in Rome would call on your Eminence, they would have the best and fullest account from yourself." The cardinal settled the affair by consulting Propaganda, and the prefect, Cardinal Fransoni, wrote a letter in which he stated that the instruction had been written for China and only with a certain proportionate application was it to be applied in England.[34]

The synod ended on July 17. Wiseman wrote the synodical letter, which was promulgated immediately. The faithful were told that the acts of synods could not be authoritative, nor could they be made public, until they were officially approved by the Holy See. The letter went on to treat a subject of "paramount" importance, the education of the poor. Prior to the synod the Catholic Poor School Committee, formed in 1847, asked the bishops to lend their official support to its work as "the instrument of your Lordships in the religious education of the children of the poor." The bishops readily complied with the request, demonstrating their sincerity by stating that where there seemed to be an opening for a new mission, they preferred the erection of a school "so arranged as to serve temporarily for a chapel, to that of a church without one." Wiseman urged, in the synodical letter, that "the secular part of our education" was to be "as effective as that which others offer," since Catholic schools had to be "equal in every respect to those which are opened to allure away our children."[35]

Newman wrote to a friend on July 18, "We ended the synod yesterday in great triumph, joy, and charity." Much to the cardinal's satisfaction, the decrees were favorably received in Rome. Talbot wrote to Bishop Grant, "The acts of the Oscott synod have arrived in Rome, and all have been very much edified by the beautiful way in which they have been written." They were officially approved, with very minor corrections, the following spring, and in the autumn of 1853, on his way to Rome, the cardinal stopped in Paris to arrange for their publication.[36]

The year 1852 was that in which Cardinal Wiseman's long-cherished dreams were realized. Not only had the hierarchy been restored, but structures were established for the church in England, and the rights and duties of those in authority were clarified. Discipline involving the liturgy and sacraments was made uniform. Regulations were enacted for the clergy, both secular and religious, and the important work of educating the poor, always a special concern for Wiseman, received the united support of the bishops. Most significant of all, however, was the fact that the synod provided a demonstration of unity. Much had been accomplished with very little friction. The popular press would find little upon which it might gloat.

Bishop Ullathorne later observed, "The wisdom of retaining Cardinal Wiseman in England was never rendered more conspicuous than as exhibited in his first Provincial Council; and it may be safely said that his presidency over the assembled fathers, and the Decrees that emanated from the Council were his masterpiece."[37] The first provincial synod was the high point in Wiseman's archiepiscopal career. He knew that the work he hoped to see done was far from complete. The recollection of this achievement, however, would be a source of consolation for him during the difficult struggles that lay ahead.

12. Cardinal Archbishop of Westminster

NEVER DID CARDINAL WISEMAN LOSE SIGHT OF WHAT HAD BEEN one of his major objectives upon first moving to England, that of attracting and converting his countrymen to the Catholic faith. With the cessation of the *Tracts for the Times* and Newman's conversion four years later, many Anglicans, influenced by the Oxford Movement, were left confused and leaderless. Wiseman, concerned now with serving the needs of converts and caught up in administrative activities, had less opportunity than he might have wished to maintain literary and personal relationships with those within the Anglican communion. He continued to publish articles in the *Dublin Review*, however, on a wide variety of subjects, all intended to make Catholicism better understood and respected.

When summoned to Rome in 1850, and afraid that he would not return, he wrote, "Just at this moment too the poor Puseyites are clustering ab[out] me, & almost clinging to me again." He was referring to a state of affairs which had developed when the bishop of Exeter, Henry Phillpotts, refused to institute the Reverend G. C. Gorham to the vicarage of Brampford, Speke. Gorham was accused of denying baptismal regeneration. The court of arches had supported the judgment of the bishop, but its verdict was overturned upon appeal to the privy council. To a large number of Anglicans it seemed as though the state was now claiming the right to speak on matters of doctrine. For some, it was the last straw, and Wiseman found himself again actively welcoming newcomers into the Roman Catholic fold.[1]

The furor over the Gorham verdict was at its height in the summer of 1850. William Maskell, chaplain to Bishop Phillpotts, converted to Rome in June, as did the wife of Newman's longtime friend, Henry

Wilberforce. Others followed, including T. W. Allies, for two years chaplain to the bishop of London and, more recently, vicar of Launton, and Viscount Rudolph William Feilding, a man who had once stood as an antipapal candidate for Cambridge University.

The excitement had not subsided when Cardinal Wiseman returned from Rome. He wrote to Talbot in December: "Conversions are going on, but only just beginning. Even the *Globe* which has been very violent, has just said that the time is setting in our favour, and that conversions are only at their beginning to what they will be." He informed Talbot that Edward Belassis, a distinguished parliamentary lawyer, had sought admittance into the Catholic church, as had William Dodsworth, formerly curate of Christ Church, St. Pancras. Dodsworth told the cardinal that Henry Edward Manning, archdeacon of Chichester, had resigned his living and "is only waiting for a short time, as he is always very cautious." Wiseman guessed that Manning was waiting for William Gladstone to join him, and he anticipated that they would take the step together in the near future.[2] Gladstone remained an Anglican, however, while Manning was received the following spring. Wiseman ordained him to the Catholic priesthood on June 14, 1851, ten weeks after his conversion, much to the astonishment of those who recalled the hasty ordination and later defection of Richard Waldo Sibthorpe.

Once elevated to the cardinalate, Wiseman extended his activities, continuing to speak throughout the country on a wide variety of subjects. Wilfrid Ward observed that he "strove, partly unconsciously, to realise his ideal of the Church in contact with human activity. He wished to learn from the best artists and scholars of his time; he was ready to take his place in all works of importance in the commonwealth." This was the reason for his broad influence: "The ideal Churchman should, he thought, have his interests everywhere, not in order to secure the domination of the Church in secular departments, but to show that the Church is not alien to any human interest, and that the priest can give and take, or if necessary learn, from others, in secular matters, if he claims to teach in religion."[3]

It was the Catholic's duty, Wiseman was convinced, to explain positively and patiently the grounds of his belief and, when attacked, to point out the error of his adversary without rancor. In December 1852 Lord Beaumont, a professed Catholic, addressed the Mechanics Institute of Leeds and criticized the censorship exercised by the church in Catholic countries. His speech was quoted in the newspaper: "Let them never do as other countries had done, and lock up their libraries from the people (Hear Hear). Let them never establish an *Index expurgationis*, and put Newton into the catalog (Loud Cheers)." Wiseman wrote to Beaumont personally, and after quoting the lord's own words, pointed out that Newton's works were not on the *Index* and that, as a matter of fact, two Roman friars had published, between 1737 and 1742, "the best commentary on his *Principia*." While a student at the Roman University, he had studied astronomy, and it was the Newtonian system that was taught there: "Should your Lordship find, that an erroneous impression has been conveyed to your hearers at Leeds, as it certainly has been to other persons, on this subject, I trust your Lordship will take the best means of removing it."[4]

The cardinal himself accepted an invitation from the Leeds Catholic Institute, not in a contentious spirit but as an attempt to undo some of the damage done by Beaumont's speech. He welcomed Protestants to the talk: "Let us show Protestants that we can give the public as good an intellectual treat as they can, and prove as great an interest in the improvement of the people as they can display." His primary object in accepting the invitation was to show that "the Catholic Church does not fear science and does not discourage it." This was not a question of supporting public debate on religious topics, and he forbade his priests to participate in such exchanges. He sternly rebuked one who planned to contravene the directive: "I have long ago come to the resolution of never allowing any priest under my jurisdiction to hold public disputations; and I therefore request you to withdraw your acceptance on this ground, and acting as I do after consulting my ordinary council I shall feel it my duty to enforce this prohibition."[5]

It was a source of dismay for Wiseman that so few priests were capable of complementing the work that he hoped to accomplish through his public appearances. "We are producing no men of great ecclesiastical learning," he lamented. Few continued their literary or theological studies after leaving college, and those who did were "totally wanting in anything approaching to ascetic or even high ecclesiastical feeling." He stated, in confidence, that Daniel Rock and Mark Tierney were examples of what he meant. Although they continued their scholarly pursuits and were undoubtedly learned men, they belonged "to the cold antiquarian school, that never exhibits a spark of devotion, or tries to kindle one."

The cardinal continued the same letter to Charles Newsham by pointing out that when he had first moved to London in 1847, the students at St. Edmund's "were chosen from the cleverest in the poor-schools, and were considered boys of particular abilities." Many had since been ordained, but "not a trace of this cleverness is to be found in them. It seems to have evaporated in their education." Young men who showed promise while in college, "when they have got into the world, and mingled a little in it, become like others, light & foolish in their talk, disrespectful to superiors, worldly and neglectful of piety and religious duties." The bishops had to accept much of the blame "for not providing means of keeping up study and attention to what has been learnt." He suggested a system of conferences that had been followed in Belgium with much success. "Bare theology" was insufficient, and "the two branches of it which we least know in England, are the best enrichers of mere intellectual divinity — the ascetic & the pastoral." [6]

It was still Wiseman's contention that lifelong Catholics should be willing to step aside in order to make way for converts. He was opposed, however, by some of the old Catholics who, after having labored throughout their lives for the church, felt that their efforts were unappreciated. The cardinal obtained an honorary degree for William George Ward in 1854, for example. Ward had been deprived of his Oxford degrees by convocation as a result of the views expressed in his *Ideal of the Christian Church* in 1844. The following year he and his wife were received into the Catholic church. Wiseman appointed him as lecturer in moral philosophy at St. Edmund's College in 1851 and later made him professor of theology. It was unprecedented for a layman, and a married one at that, to hold such a position. [7]

The cardinal also secured a doctorate for Newman and sought to have him elevated to the episcopate early in 1854. The honor would have been a means of enhancing Newman's position as rector of the new Catholic University in Dublin, to which he had been appointed in November 1851. There is no doubt of Wiseman's plan. "I have written a long letter to Dr. Newman," he told Bishop Grant, "the pope having repeated to me his intention of making him a bishop." In his letter to Newman the cardinal had stated that the episcopal office "would at once give you a right to sit with the Bishops in all consultations, would raise you above all other officers, professors, etc. of the University, and would give dignity to this itself, and to its head. The holy Father at once assented." [8]

A year earlier Newman had feared that his name might be among those submitted for the see of Nottingham to replace Bishop Hendren or as coadjutor to Bishop Brown of Liverpool. He had sought to avoid the office: "I feel most deeply and habitually, the office of Bishop is not suited to me. . . . I have not the talent, the energy, the resource, the spirit, the *power of ruling* necessary for the high office of a Bishop. . . . *I have never been in power in my life*." He was willing to accept the office if it were meant to be purely honorary: "It *may* be that no one has an intention except to give me an *honorary* distinction, as that of bishop *in partibus* — which would be a sort of compliment and nothing more. I must not seem, if this is the case, to meet their intentions crossly." [9]

Archbishop Paul Cullen of Dublin opposed the plan to make Newman a bishop, and the matter was dropped. Wiseman has been criticized frequently for his failure to explain the circumstances to

Newman or even to tell him that the appointment would not be made after all. His reluctance to face personal unpleasantness may have been the explanation for his silence. It is also possible that he felt obliged to maintain confidentiality and did not know how to provide the information which common courtesy demanded without giving the reasons for which the appointment was not made. Since the Holy Father's intention had been publicized and letters of congratulation had been received by Newman, it is not easy to absolve Wiseman from blame.[10]

During the three-year period between the first and second synods of Westminster, the cardinal was involved in two embarrassing controversies that were discussed widely. The first resulted when he set out to discredit an apostate priest, Giovanni Giacinto Achilli, an ex-Dominican, whom the Evangelical Alliance had brought to England in order to denounce and publicize Roman corruptions. Achilli claimed that he had been punished unjustly and cruelly for heresy by the Inquisition. His crimes, in fact, were of a far more sensual kind, for he had been found guilty of seducing women on a number of occasions. Wiseman exposed Achilli in the *Dublin Review* in 1850.[11]

Newman, while preparing his *Lectures on the Present Position of Catholics*, delivered the following summer, made use of Wiseman's article in order to illustrate the basis of much of the prejudice against Catholics in England. Achilli was still receiving a hearing throughout the country. Before proceeding, Newman had consulted his friend, James Hope, to find out whether he might be risking libel action. He was told frankly that the possibility was there, but Hope concluded, "I have also been assured that abundant proof is forthcoming of the allegations against Achilli, and if you are satisfied on this point it is an additional security."[12]

Supported by the Evangelical Alliance, Achilli brought suit against Newman. Wiseman, unfortunately, was unable to lay his hands on the documentation upon which Newman was depending and which might have led to a dismissal of the charges. It is clear from the famed convert's own account of the affair that he blamed the cardinal for not lending adequate support when it was so critically needed.[13] The ultimate guilty verdict in January 1853, a notorious miscarriage of justice, resulted in a fine of £100. The expenses, however, amounted to £12,000, met and exceeded by a subscription to which Catholics from around the world contributed. Cardinal Wiseman at last did his best to make amends for his negligence by heartily supporting the subscription, but Newman never again completely trusted him. The cardinal's failure to explain the reasons for which Newman was not elevated to the episcopate a year later only added to an increasing lack of sympathy between the two men.

The second case was even more embarrassing, since it was

Wiseman himself who was found guilty of libel. When he first moved to London, one of the priests in the district who vocally opposed his policies was Richard Boyle, second missioner in Islington. Wiseman eventually succeeded in replacing him, although Boyle demanded compensation for money he had expended on the mission house. The priest published their correspondence and then, early in 1854, was a party to some articles that appeared in the French journal, *Ami de la Religion*, and were insulting to Wiseman and highly critical of his work in London. The cardinal's supporters in France responded in the pages of *L'Univers*, and when he wrote to thank them, after describing the various devotions he had introduced in the archdiocese, he referred to the fact that Boyle, who had been a Jesuit for twenty-two years, had been sent away from the society when he felt unable to take the vow of complete obedience to the Holy See. Although Wiseman wrote his letter in English, he indicated that the word "renvoyé" (sent away) should be used. The translator, however, substituted "expulsé," and Boyle, seizing upon the technicality, pressed charges.

There were two trials. The first, in August 1854, was dismissed because the cardinal had not been called as witness. The second, the following summer, awarded Boyle £1,000 in damages, but upon appeal the court of exchequer set the verdict aside because of the excessive amount demanded. A date was set for still another trial, but at the last minute Boyle agreed to an out-of-court settlement. Wiseman agreed to pay the cost of all three trials, although it was made clear that he offered no apology.[14]

While awaiting the first trial in the Boyle case, the cardinal received word that his brother James had died. It was an unexpected blow, and their sister wrote of her pity for the poor widow who was left "a stranger in a foreign land."[15] James, whose wife Ann was German, had settled in Belgium. Almost a year after his death, when Ann Wiseman wished to return to her native country, the cardinal made arrangements for her to settle in Austria and provided that she be "recommended to the kind care of the ecclesiastical authorities." He offered an annual pension of £25, but said that "she must not expect more, nor are there any funds whatever left by her husband." Should she wish to remarry (provided that the match was approved by her family and ecclesiastical superior), the pension would cease, but he agreed, in such case, to give a dowry of £100. The next clause in this memorandum, in Wiseman's handwriting, is surprising in our age but less so in the nineteenth century and in the circumstances in which James had left his wife and child: "In case of her so marrying, it is my most earnest wish that the girl Sophia should be restored to her father's family, to be educated, as otherwise she may be neglected, from want of means and for other reasons." He added that he earnestly wished that Ann, "seeing the advantages of procuring the child the best education, would consent to allow it to be brought up under my care, even from now. But of course I cannot insist on this, especially at present."

One can only speculate that the cardinal was concerned not only that his niece should have a proper education but that she should receive adequate religious instruction as well. He was at great pains to see that Ann Wiseman should be under the supervision of an ecclesiastic: "If Mrs. Wiseman, after a time should wish to change her place of residence, I will transfer to the Superior of her new abode, the Delegation to act for me given to that of the first. I shall expect, however, that such a change will be made not capriciously, but for good reason, approved by the Parish Priest."[16]

No evidence has thus far turned up to indicate that Sophia ever became her uncle's ward. A few months after making arrangements for his brother's widow and their daughter, however, he received a letter from Frasquita, also widowed, who wrote that her twelve-year-old son, Randolfo, needed the company of other boys and ought to remain at home no longer. However, she was unable to afford the £250 that would be necessary to educate him in England.[17] Wiseman, convinced that Oscott College was in his debt as a result of personal funds that he had expended while serving as its president, made arrangements for the boy to be placed there.

While responding to family demands of this kind, Wiseman still found that unceasing criticism dogged all of his public activities. When he journeyed to Rome in the autumn of 1853, his first visit since the establishment of the hierarchy, his health had again broken down as a result of overwork. Upon his arrival there, he discovered that busybodies, including some priests, had been doing everything in their power to undermine his reputation. John Wallis, a layman who later succeeded Lucas as editor of the *Tablet*, described rumors to the effect that the cardinal would be kept in Rome, where it was felt "that his removal would please many & displease almost none, knowing that after 3 years stay his removal could not be construed into a defeat by the No Popery cry." The vice-rector of the English College in Lisbon wrote: "Well is the Cardinal to return or not? The report here — originating at the Nunciature — is confirmatory of that prevalent in England, viz. that he is to be appointed Prefect of Propaganda."[18]

Wiseman's qualifications might have made him a worthy successor to Cardinal Fransoni as Propaganda prefect, but it was Monsignor Barnabò, the congregation's secretary, who assumed the post. Wiseman soon won the authorities to his cause, however, and devoted his time in Rome to lecturing and preaching, much as he had done when the Eternal City had been his home. He also assisted at the consistory that elevated Vincenzo Gioacchino Pecci, the future Leo XIII, to the cardinalate.

The discovery of the extent to which he had been criticized in Rome was, at first, a deep cause of concern for the cardinal.

> I must sincerely tell you, that the effects of what I have been told since I came here, & what I have found out, of petty attempts to destroy my influence and character here, not merely by misrepresentation but by a system of mean gossip about every trifle, has been to make me disgusted with my position in England, to such a degree, as almost to lead me to seek a withdrawal from it; and it has only been the clear conviction I arrived at, that no unfavourable impression had reached the Holy Father's mind, which prevented it.[19]

Wiseman returned to England in the spring, vindicated by the support he had received in Rome and determined to pursue the policies that he believed to be in the best interests of the church.

No sooner was Wiseman home, however, than he found himself embroiled in the controversy with Boyle. When writing to explain the full circumstances of the case to Monsignor Talbot, he also responded to a new kind of criticism that especially disturbed him. It had been reported to the Holy Father that there were at least 20,000 Catholic children in London without any means of education. He called the charge "a monstrous exaggeration, set out by enemies," and provided statistical information to demonstrate its absurdity. There were already at least 10,000 poor children between the ages of eight and twelve receiving education. Added to those alleged to be neglected, the total number of poor children in London between those ages would have been 30,000. If one supposed an equal number for each preceding four years, there would be 90,000 poor children under twelve years of age in London. If one were then to add to that number those who died during their first eight years, that is, 20,000 more, there would be 110,000 children of the poor born in twelve years, or 8,000 per year: "Multiply this by 30, the usual rate to find population from births, & we have the *poor* population of London to be 270,000. Add middle classes & rich & you will have 300,000 Catholics in London. I repeat that it is a complete exaggeration."

The cardinal was particularly sensitive to the charge that the poor were being neglected: "You are not perhaps aware of what is being done. We are multiplying small schools systematically through all London, and large subscriptions are making for that purpose. I have given £1000 towards beginning a reformatory school, to counteract the operation of the major trades' schools, intended to kidnap our children."[20]

More than a year later the charge was repeated that little was being done to serve the needs of the poor in the archdiocese. Wiseman responded that during the preceding fifteen months a number of new churches had replaced old chapels: Spitalfields, which previously held 100 worshipers, could now accommodate 1,200; Poplar had formerly held 300, but the new church held 1,500; Kingsland, where there had been no mission at all three years earlier, now had two priests and a church for 1,000 worshipers; the church in Commercial Road would hold 2,000 souls and replaced one built for 600. Answering again the reports that Catholics continued to lose thousands of children to Protestant schools, he insisted that there was "plenty of evidence of exaggeration & falsehood." There were more Catholic children educated in London "in proportion to population . . . than in any other city in England," and some of his priests had "gone through the prot[estant] schools in their districts, & not found one cath[olic] in them."[21]

There is sufficient evidence to convince even the most cynical observer that Wiseman was committed to the poor. In June 1851 he published in the *Dublin Review* an analysis of Henry Mayhew's *London Labour and the London Poor* (1851). Wiseman wrote at the outset: "In England at least, where there is more theoretical equality and democracy than elsewhere, there is a natural process of gravitation, by which poverty and suffering sink ever lower and lower, and leave the highest tenants of earthly life floating or gliding on the surface, unencumbered with their annoyance." The accumulation of so much poverty and vice, he noted, "has always been a cause of alarm to statesmen, whose minds are able to rise above political littleness." He cited the examples of ancient Rome and modern Paris in order to illustrate the power and the danger of "proletarianism," which was capable of overturning a state. England was pursuing a course that would be no more successful in averting trouble than had been the case in the historical precedents that he mentioned. "It is . . . perfectly amazing to contemplate, what an immense amount of activity, vigilance, legislation, and force are actually in constant employment, to keep down vice and crime which belong to the poorer class." It was an unhappy fact that "our very compassion embodies itself in a penitentiary form, and our charity confounds relief with incarceration." English justice, while theoretically equal for all, was less so in fact, for "the rich and the high portion of society is represented by judge and bar; the destitute and wretched by the culprit."

Mayhew's book was to be read, urged the cardinal, as "a most appalling lesson of disappointed hopes." He pointed out that religion had failed to deal adequately with the problem of poverty: "In spite of the turned-up eyes of fanatics, or the sneering frown of puritans, we are sure that the religion of the country has much to answer for, in the immorality of the poor." True religion was meant to "work upon the senses, and give them, as well as the soul or rather, the soul through them, their truest and most wholesome gratification." He noted that the Catholic church had the most to offer in this regard: "Processions, paintings, functions, in or about the poorest parish Church, where the poor have all the 'getting up' in their own hands, and in which they have a share and interest, supply the place of court pageants, or lordly entertainments, which the rich find so necessary for their own enjoyment of life."

Wiseman described religion as "the great tamer of man in his wilderness, and in his sullenness; in the deserts, whether of sand, or of peopled cities." Questions naturally arose as to whether enough was being done to provide for the religious needs of "the lower ranges of proletarianism" and whether means could be found "to make religion acceptable to them, or powerful over them, or even known to them." If Wiseman's immediate answers were less than satisfactory, he was nevertheless willing to accept the challenge on behalf of his fellow Catholics: "We take our leave of Mr. Mayhew's instructive volume, and we shall follow his steps with interest, into the haunts of every class of poor. We shall be satisfied if we shall have awakened Catholic sympathies, in favour of a great work which seems committed to our Church, that of evangelizing the poor in London."[22] Wiseman's pastorals and personal correspondence reveal the same constant preoccupation with the anonymous masses, crowded into back alleys and lanes, for whom formal religion was utterly foreign.

The cardinal viewed the education of the poor as an essential element in their self-improvement. He was too much a Victorian to have denied the virtue in "self-help," but he was also realistic enough to recognize the obligation of the more fortunate to assist the needy in acquiring the necessary means for material and spiritual development. Even when poor children were forced to study, he observed, "the education which is given to them in the school is but slightly correlative with what has to form their future occupation in life." There was little opportunity afterward for an underprivileged youth to develop: "During the few years that he was under your tuition, you made him raise his face towards heaven, and the whole remainder of his life his looks will be cast, much like those animals which he has to tend, down upon the earth from which he must work out his daily bread." He urged those with talent to apply themselves to the task of producing literary works that might be understood and appreciated by the poor. To serve them in this way, he wrote, "is the noblest consecration which genius can make of its powers on the altar of society."[23]

Wiseman's frequent excursions throughout the city provided sufficient evidence of the accuracy of reports, provided by his priests, of the deplorable conditions under which large numbers of their people lived. The frequent "begging letters" he received are further proof that whatever criticism may have been made of him, the cardinal was not out of touch with his flock. "Once more I take the liberty of letting your Eminence know that I am still out of employment and I ask, is it not a grievous thing that no one will become instrumental in procuring for me any kind of employment, no matter how small the salary," asked one man, who continued, "What am I to do with myself, or what will become of me and my little family?" Wiseman, contributing to the support and education of his own family and assisting the many charities within the archdiocese, wrote on the back of this letter, which had come from Dublin: "It is useless his continuing to write, as I know of nothing, but will not fail to do what I can if opportunity offers." Still another man wrote that because of "severe illness" he could not find the means "of getting any nourishment." He concluded, "I do most earnest implore your Eminence to grant me your kind assistance *once more* [italics mine] as I am in such need of it as I have not means of getting any food to strengthen me."[24]

Any public figure, *a fortiori* one identified with religion, must expect requests of this kind and must face the inevitable necessity of being unable to respond positively to all of them. The cardinal's pleas on behalf of the poor are, however, a consistent indication of the seriousness with which he viewed them.

Wiseman continued to look especially to religious orders to assist him serving the poor. More and more, however, he considered the plan he had formulated many years before of establishing a community of secular priests who, while drawing spiritual strength from their communal life, might be at the disposal of the bishop to a degree not possible for the traditional religious orders. He had this in mind when he suggested that Newman might establish an Oratory of St. Philip Neri in Birmingham and when he welcomed the establishment of an Oratorian house in London.

In a well-known letter to Frederick Faber the cardinal explained in detail his frustrating attempts to secure the assistance of religious congregations in the work for which they were most needed: "When I first came to London, I saw the neglected part was the poor, and to that I resolved to give immediate attention." He had "spared no pains to secure missionary communities, to help in the work of evangelising the poor." He first of all looked to the Jesuits, since they had a "splendid church, a large house, several priests." Yet, he complained, by 1852 "we have under them only a church which by its splendour attracts and absorbs the wealth of two parishes, but maintains no schools, and contributes nothing towards the education of the poor at its very door." He next encouraged the Redemptorists, but when they were asked to work for the poor, they replied that "this was not the purpose of their institute *in towns*, and that 'another Order would be required for what I wanted.'" Since he had always determined to respect "the plea of rule," he could say no more. The cardinal naturally looked to the Passionists, whom he had encouraged to work in England, but "they have never done me a stroke of work among the poor, and if I want a mission from them, the local house is of no use, and I must get a person from the Provincial, as if it did not exist." The Marists, he admitted, were serving well in the work for which they had come to London, and he continued to look to the Oratory as well.

Wiseman finally mentioned Manning, who had been pursuing his studies in Rome and who, "I think, understands my wishes and feelings, and is ready to assist me; several will, I hope, join him, and I hope also some old and good priests." The cardinal had hit upon the idea that led to the eventual establishment of the Oblates of St. Charles in London: "We shall be able to work together, because there will be no exemptions from episcopal direction, and none of the jealousy on one side, and the delicacy on the other, of interference or suggestion." The "multifarious missionary work" that Wiseman wanted could not be effected "without frequent communication with the bishop." [25]

The cardinal had always recognized the expediency of carefully observing any maneuvers on the part of the government that might affect Catholics. He hoped to avoid, however, associating himself with political causes, except where the interests of the church clearly demanded his interference. In June 1851, for example, he replied to the request that he sanction the formation of an "association for the defence and increase of Catholic liberty": "I feel myself too little acquainted at present with the definite purpose of the proposed Association, and with the means which it intends to employ, to be able to give more than a very general answer: that so far as the title of the Association accurately describes its objects, it seems naturally to claim not only my encouragement, but that of every Catholic." He observed, however, that if the association were to have "a political character & aimed at attaining its object by political means," he would be obliged to leave it in the hands of those who were more familiar with such matters than he was: "I have rigidly adhered through life to the rule of confining my small share of activity to my ecclesiastical and spiritual duties, which are more than sufficient to exhaust my time and strength." As a matter of fact, after the papal aggression demonstrations, Wiseman was less able to communicate effectively with government officials than before, and he was little inclined to risk involvement that might lead to further criticism. In the spring of 1851 he even refused to appear when summoned before a select parliamentary committee on the laws of mortmain. [26]

In 1852 the cardinal became seriously concerned when one of his priests, a Breton named J. J. Mahé, took it upon himself to enter into negotiations with Lord Malmesbury, the foreign secretary, in order to seek concessions for Catholics. Mahé asked to travel to Rome to act as intermediary between the authorities there and those in England. Wiseman said that he could not see "any use of his going with a vague and indefinite purpose" and "was sure the H[oly] S[ee] would make no concessions, & in fact had none to make." Mahé went in any case: "Nobody here knows what he went away for, not even whither he went." In the meantime Lord John Russell became foreign secretary, a position in which, according to the cardinal, he could do little harm.

Upon his arrival in Rome, Mahé gave the impression that he was an official emissary, a claim denied by the cardinal: "He never consulted me at all; he only told me what was taking place between him & Lord M[almesbury]." It was Wiseman's impression that the government wanted to use the priest in an attempt to persuade Pius IX "to advise the Clergy of Ireland to refrain from political agitation &c." According to Mahé, it was the government's intention to repeal the Ecclesiastical Titles Act, to guarantee security for Catholic trusts, and to take steps toward disestablishing the Church of Ireland. The cardinal did not forbid the priest's efforts because if the ministry, in fact, put such intentions in writing, it "would have been at our mercy and could never have attempted to annoy us more. To have had proofs of such offers would have enabled us thoroughly to frustrate all attempts at assaults on us."[27]

Upon his return to England, Mahé continued to deal with the ministry, now negotiating with Lord Clarendon, who had replaced Lord John Russell at the foreign office. He told Wiseman, however, that he was under orders of secrecy and could not reveal the nature of the discussions. Thoroughly exasperated, the cardinal informed him that he "could not employ a priest who had acted as he had done, in making himself the instrument of a prot[estant] govt., interfering with ecclesial affairs, & even asking for a coadj[utor] for his bishop without his knowledge, and then after the H[oly] F[ather] had told him to give up his political pursuits, and become a missionary only, continued still in disobedience, to follow the same course."[28]

Early in 1852 Bishop Grant had a problem similar to Wiseman's: "One of our priests has been carrying on a clumsy correspondence with the admiralty, & I am advised to forbid all correspondence with government offices unless I have first seen it. I do not want to correspond at all but when it is necessary, let us not do it clumsily." A year later, however, Grant himself was preparing to negotiate with the government: "The admiralty have issued an important order that Catholics are to be received equally with others into the navy & that the Faith of the boys in the navy is not to be tampered with. I have requested the clergy never to communicate with govt. until I have seen their letters, and since I sent my circular on this subject, the war office has asked to confer with me upon the means that are to be taken in order to give Catholics fair play." He added, "Of course, I do not intend to undertake any thing without the concurrence of the other bishops." [29]

Cardinal Wiseman, unfortunately, was not consulted when Grant obtained support from the other bishops to deal with the government, and he wrote to ascertain what kind of agreement had been reached. The bishop of Southwark replied with a halfhearted denial, stating that he had not acted in any *official* capacity. Wiseman was hurt: "I never have objected, nor could object, to each bishop acting for himself as he thinks right. And any grievances your Lordship finds in your Diocese, you have a right to get redressed as *you* think right." This, however, was not the case at issue.

> I have said to several persons, that if the Bishops had expressed an opinion (as has often been done at our meetings) that one should be deputed to arrange any given affair, I never should have thought of objecting; for I am glad to get anything put upon another. And if your Lordship had been delegated to undertake army and navy grievances, I should have consented without difficulty. But I do object to anything like an arrangement being made partially, by private consultation, at a meeting called by me, from the determination taken and delegation being made to anyone (in any affair where I have an equal interest) with an understanding that I was not to know it, but was to be left to find it out, and acquiesce tacitly. Confidence will be lost among us, if this new way of transacting business is to be carried on: and I find *several* bishops look upon this result as risked by what has happened. [30]

The complaint was justified, perhaps, but Wiseman's frequent absence from London was a consideration that, along with his personal unpopularity in some quarters, led the bishops to turn to someone else to represent their interests.

When Wiseman was still in Rome in March 1854 and there were rumors to the effect that he would not return to England, Bishop Errington wrote to Monsignor Talbot: "In our new state of organisation, with the feelings of some distrustful of the Cardinal, of others, or the same, opposed in theory to the views of the Cardinal, & in stirring times, our machine won't work well, & will be in danger of permanent damage, if the center wheel is not working normally." Errington urged Talbot to "assist in expediting the return of the Cardinal of Westminster." Wiseman, according to Errington, was "the only man who can keep us in common action, & therefore he ought to come immediately, & remain, at least for some years, till our train gets into the habit of running regularly, & then it will matter less who is the engineer." [31]

Bishop Ullathorne, on the other hand, was among those who felt that Wiseman had damaged the cause of Catholics by the manner in which he announced the hierarchy. When he heard that the cardinal objected to the way in which Grant had been selected to negotiate with the government, the bishop of Birmingham wrote: "The Cardinal has done us enough of injury, and should be gratified that other bishops have been able to aid religion amongst us by ways not open to him." He added, "When we meet, I hope there will not be a general crouching to his title in matters whereon we have a right to our own sentiments."[32]

On his way home in the spring of 1854, the cardinal stopped in Paris, where he was received by Napoleon III and the empress. Wilfrid Ward suggested that his friendship with the French emperor dated from his days in Rome, a fact hardly confirmed by Wiseman's description of their meeting: "On entering the room, he [the emperor] said he had long desired to make my acquaintance." In view of the fact that England, in March of that year, found herself allied with France in a war against Russia, the cardinal thought that his visit might serve a practical purpose. He had become an expert in eastern affairs while still living in Rome, and it now seemed to him that he might have a key role to play. Although his conversation with the emperor, as he admitted, "was of no importance," he admired Napoleon as the great hope of the church in Europe. He was delighted, then, when Napoleon invited him to return to Paris.[33]

In the summer of 1855 the cardinal offered to prepare a report for the Holy Father with "some humble suggestions about the Eastern Churches and the most important crisis in their state, likely to arise." Bishop Louis de Salinis of Amiens, Wiseman's friend, informed him that, according to Napoleon III, "France would take the protectorate of Catholics in the Ottoman Empire, as England would take that of the Protestants at Jerusalem & in the numerous English and American missions established with schools all through Asia, and as in fact she is taking that of the Greek Schismatics, Jacobites, &c." Wiseman opposed such plans to settle the religious instability in the East, convinced that "no civil authority is competent to treat on these subjects without the full intelligence & cooperation of the H[oly] S[ee], the true guardian of religious rights, & the only power competent to make concessions or modifications on eccles[iastical] laws." The church had to be heard on questions relating to her interests, such as "christian marriages, education, charities, the position of bishops, clergy & religion, church property." France was not in a position to take on the duties of a protectorate without first reaching a cordial agreement with Rome. Although Napoleon was reported to be interested in his ideas and even suggested a personal interview to discuss them, the cardinal soon became convinced, like his friend Montalembert, "that the enthusiasm he had felt for the French emperor was misplaced."[34]

In addition to the French emperor, Wiseman was also acquainted with Francis Joseph II of Austria, whom he had met in 1850 when returning to England as newly appointed cardinal archbishop. In 1855 a concordat was signed by Austria and the Holy See, and the news was received in England with prejudiced indignation. The cardinal delivered four lectures on the nature of the agreement and the necessity of repealing the laws that, under Joseph II in the eighteenth century, had subjected the church to state control. When his lectures were published, he reported that the Austrian emperor had read them and "told a person who told me that he was very glad I had not been taken to Rome, and hoped I would continue here." [35]

In spite of the breadth of his interests and activities, Wiseman understood that he had a significant administrative responsibility in his own archdiocese. When in London, he met each week with a board that he had established for the transaction of archdiocesan business. He also appointed two vicars general, Robert Whitty and John Maguire, who, it seems, were unclear as to their specific rights and duties. Maguire complained that "not a few of the clergy look upon him [the vicar general] as an official who goes through the routine of signing and posting certain forms, which they forward [to] him or drop into a servant's hands as the case may be." His role was much like that of "a functionary bearing a close resemblance to a clerk at a foreign consulate or an office of inland revenues, save that he demands no fees." Maguire pointed out that he was often called upon to act in the cardinal's absence, but that his position had not been clarified adequately. When he asked for a list of his responsibilities, he reminded Wiseman, "you seemed surprised and somewhat hurt at a question which you might have thought involved mistrust." He was told that canon law specified the faculties of a vicar general, but Maguire pressed on by observing, not unwisely, that he was not so concerned with what he could do in strict accordance with law but what would be possible "without offence or umbrage to anyone." He also complained that he was obliged to attend the cardinal at least three days a week, but that his salary was "some pounds below that of the most scantily provided-for priest belonging to this diocese," and that he was forced to rely upon friends for lodging, a situation neither "fair" nor "respectable." [36]

Maguire's circumstances were merely an indication that Wiseman, like the other bishops, had little money to spare. There were those in far worse condition, however. The bishop of Salford sought permission to remain as rector of a church in Manchester in order to benefit from the income of the mission. "Actually I work as a missionary anyway," wrote Bishop Turner, "and there is little difference between what I did before being made a bishop and what I am doing now." [37]

It is not surprising that a number of squabbles broke out among the bishops as they attempted to divide the temporalities of the old vicariates. Wiseman, for example, when he was president of Oscott, had borrowed money that he applied to the college and for which he considered it to be liable. When he moved to London he asked the authorities at Oscott to settle its account with him, and investigation there revealed that there were indeed some unsettled financial questions involving also the Central District funds for which he had been responsible. Rumors circulated to the effect that Wiseman had diverted some of these for private purposes. The charge was unjust, and he denied it, insisting that auditors should be called in to examine the accounts. He agreed to "draw up and send to the clergy a full balance sheet of the time of my administration, showing exactly what funds I did receive on coming into administration."[38]

After a delay of more than a year, during which Bishop Ullathorne continued to insist that the accounts should be settled, two documents were sent off as Wiseman had promised. Ullathorne was still not satisfied, stating that he could not do justice to Wiseman's claims "in the twilight of an obscure statement." Henry Bagshawe, answering for Wiseman, replied, "Dr. Wiseman begs me to say that all the monies which constitute the amounts paid by him for the use of the college and mentioned in his account, were paid out of funds which were unconnected whether directly or indirectly with the district or college, and were his private monies for which he was not accountable to any human being." Bagshawe said that he was unaware "of any obscurity or twilight in his Lordship's accounts or statement," and he reminded Ullathorne of the suddenness with which Wiseman was removed from the Central District, "without having any opportunity of adjusting any accounts."[39]

Wiseman's claim, then, was that he had used his private money to pay college debts when in Birmingham and that he expected to be indemnified. Ullathorne suggested that the Birmingham Council of Administration should examine the account and settle the matter, but Wiseman would have none of it: "As a bishop he cannot submit either directly or indirectly to its authority." The objection was reasonable: "Allow me to say, that it is a novel proceeding to constitute a committee of priests in one district to pronounce on the claims of a bishop in another." Ullathorne tried to soothe him, stating that he had not intended to put his fellow bishop on trial. Although Wiseman was placated for the moment, the accounts remained unsettled, and after the restoration of the hierarchy the mutual demands were renewed. In the light of subsequent correspondence, it is clear that no solution had been reached prior to the second provincial synod in the summer of 1855.[40]

The disagreement between Ullathorne and Wiseman did not result from the structural changes that accompanied the restoration of the hierarchy. It paralleled, however, a far more serious and notorious dispute between the cardinal and Bishop Grant, which resulted from the division of the London District. The details of their estrangement have never been fully told. They make tedious reading and out of context fail to do justice to the cause of either man. Yet no study of Wiseman can be considered complete without some discussion of the unfortunate affair. The cardinal's approach to the problem was the same as that which he demonstrated in dealing with Bishop Ullathorne. A single step toward reaching a solution was followed, more than once, by long periods of inaction and apparent indifference. Considering the former intimacy and mutual dependence of Wiseman and Grant, the hostility that developed was all the more deplorable. It is an interesting case study of a situation that, to some degree, arose among other bishops. It was not fully resolved at the time of the cardinal's death in 1865.

As agent of the vicars apostolic in Rome, Grant had been fully aware of Wiseman's reasons for not wanting London divided and for opposing, at first, the appointment of a bishop for the diocese of Southwark. The earliest correspondence concerning the division of temporalities seems to have been lost or destroyed. It is clear that there were six payments made immediately to Southwark which, it was later understood, were part of the old district's common mission fund. Wiseman's books and accounts had been kept by Canon Robert Shepherd. In 1878 Cardinal Manning's secretary, still trying to settle matters with Southwark, wrote, "Canon Shepherd's accounts had been so badly kept (by reason of his unskilfulness in bookkeeping), and contained such grave errors, that, after carefully correcting his books, I find that *no attention is to be paid to his description* (as above written) of the said six payments."[41]

It is not known whether Bishop Grant had reason to doubt Shepherd's competence, but it is clear that he wanted to see all of the books and accounts relevant to the division of temporalities. After he had been bishop for a year, his pleas for action on the part of the cardinal became heatedly pressing. He was "in the disagreeable position," he wrote, "of being obliged to make excuses to myself for borrowing money and to my clergy for not being able to assist them in their wants." There were no funds for his personal maintenance, and his priests considered this to be a reproach to themselves. Yet they would agree to no definite sum until a settlement was reached with Westminster. The cardinal, however, would not proceed further until some agreement was reached over the debts that he had contracted in completing St. George's Cathedral. Grant refused to accept any responsibility: "Your Eminence has probably overlooked the fact that if your diocese has suffered by the money advanced to St. George's, the act was not mine; and there is an equal reason why I should be indemnified for as much of the funds of Southwark as have been spent during the last 20 years on Moorfields [the church serving as Westminster's procathedral]." Grant was a meticulously conscientious man, torn between his obligations to himself and his diocese and his affection for and loyalty to the cardinal: "Why is a quarrel to be created between yourself and me because of a claim, which I surely have, to have the books of the London District examined and its property valued in order that it may be known, by means of fair and impartial men, whether any and what portion of it really belongs to Southwark?" Wiseman, he insisted, would "incur all the blame of an unfair division unless it is effected by means of men equally indifferent to Westminster and to Southwark."[42]

Grant's suggestion was that representatives of the Westminster and Southwark chapters should form a commission for arranging a settlement. Wiseman, however, was offended by the lack of trust implied in the request, insisting that his books should not be examined by priests of another diocese. Although his argument was similar to that which he used in refusing to let a Birmingham commission reach a decision concerning his administration, there was a further consideration in this case. Wiseman knew that a number of the Southwark clergy were unsympathetic to him. He later reported that Pope Pius IX, while discussing the prevalence of the Gallican spirit in England, had once commented: "Yes, it is in the chapter of Southwark that it is chiefly concentrated."[43]

By the summer of 1853 Monsignor Talbot warned the cardinal that letters had been received in Rome complaining of the treatment accorded the bishop of Southwark and that it was likely that a formal complaint would be lodged. Wiseman was already aware of the danger, and when faced with the threat, while acknowledging the pain that it would cause him, he told Grant that he would be content if a solution were reached by "that supreme tribunal to which we have both learnt, in reverence and submission, can cause me no pain but rather satisfaction."[44]

Wiseman was less resigned when writing to Talbot two days later.

Here is a sad business about to happen. The accompanying correspondence should explain it, and I do not wish to do more at present than ask you to read it, and make known its contents to the H[oly] F[ather]. The very idea of a suffragan of the new hierarchy, almost within a year, going off to Rome to carry thither a cause against his Metropolitan, and that that one should be Dr. Grant . . . put at Southwark because he is my friend, is fraught with scandal. But I regret to say it, after the first weeks that he was in England, he became estranged, kept aloof, and made those men his counsellors who had always favoured and headed the old party against me before he came, and finally chose for his chapter those very men who, through the disturbance of the "Papal Aggression," were suspected of being the confederates of Lord John Russell.

Wiseman's next assertion was unjust: "I foresaw all along what would take place. There has been no cordiality, no sympathy, months pass without his calling on me; and every little complaint, every discontent has gone to him." The correspondence shows, in fact, that the estrangement of the two men was a gradual process. Wiseman had relied much on his nearest suffragan, especially in preparing for the first two provincial synods. Grant's willingness to consult with the cardinal's opponents, moreover, was not due to anything except the desire to bring peace to his own diocese, as we have seen, and his own duties in Southwark were sufficient to explain the fact that his visits to Westminster were infrequent.

In the same letter to Talbot the cardinal defended his own conduct. The initial delay in settling the accounts had not been his fault, nor had he been aware of the fact that certain payments had not been made. Some funds had been divided, however, and others such as the London District's poor funds, which only yielded £42 a year, were too small to share. Those established for episcopal maintenance ought not to be divided, and he claimed correctly that there were precedents to support his contention. Legal technicalities, finally, prevented him from exposing the details of certain legacies. "What I hope," he concluded, "is that the scandal of a bishop starting off for Rome on such an errand and dragging his Metropolitan with him, be prevented."[45]

Grant's patience was exhausted by the following autumn, and he sent a formal complaint to Rome. He enclosed it with an explanation to Talbot in which he suggested that a commission might be appointed by the Holy See, consisting of a canon from each of the two chapters, with a third priest to preside over them. These men might then decide upon the principles to be followed in settling the accounts. If Wiseman would not accept the proposal, Talbot was told to present the petition to Propaganda. In case the cardinal were willing to accept it, however, an alternative letter was included for Propaganda, explaining the procedure by which a settlement might be reached.[46] Wiseman, who was in Rome at the time, rejected Grant's suggestions. The bishop of Southwark wrote: "If circumstances have placed me in a painful position towards your Eminence, I hope you will think that I have tried to perform a distasteful duty as respectfully and as late as I could."[47]

In his petition Grant stated that he had never seen the books and accounts of the old London District, and although some funds had been distributed, there was still no plan for the division of income from property that should have benefited both Westminster and Southwark. He added that he was also uninformed as to the number of students whom he could afford to maintain at St. Edmund's, intended as the seminary for both dioceses. Finally he raised the question of the *mensa*, funds for episcopal maintenance that, he claimed, ought to be divided between Wiseman and himself, and, as suggested in his letter to Talbot, he asked Propaganda to nominate a commission.[48]

Commenting upon Grant's letter, Wiseman now admitted that the dispute could be settled only by a superior authority. He refused, however, to submit to a commission of canons: "This is not an expedient which is fitting to my decorum or which has been adopted commonly in similar cases." He added that "in the present circumstances, the members of the chapters of both dioceses are not sufficiently self-possessed to reach an agreement." The major question to be resolved was that of determining the principles upon which a division of funds might be made, and he refused to concede that there was a need for Grant or his delegates to examine accounts or documents.[49]

Propaganda held a general meeting to discuss the case and decided that both prelates should send further details. Grant complied by listing the funds that should be examined. With reference to that established for the support of the bishop, he observed that Wiseman had a furnished house of his own, unlike the bishop of Southwark. Moreover, since most of London's country missions were in the southern diocese, Grant argued that his travel expenses were higher than the cardinal's. He conceded that there was precedent for Wiseman to enjoy such revenues during his own lifetime, but requested that Propaganda determine whether or not at least half of the episcopal maintenance fund should be given to the bishop of Southwark upon the cardinal's death or retirement. He begged, finally, that regardless of the decision reached, the controversy might be settled as quickly as possible.[50]

Wiseman submitted his case a month later, pointing out that he had no sooner been appointed to Westminster than the terrible papal aggression storm had broken out. Even some of the Southwark clergy had supported Lord John Russell. He then argued that if, contrary to custom in such cases, the books and accounts in his possession were to be examined by a bishop of another diocese, Grant would need assistance. If he were to consult a layman for that purpose, as he usually did in financial matters, scandal would result. In the case of some funds, absolute secrecy was necessary, since they were illegal under English law. It should be noted that Wiseman, in his negotiations with Bishop Ullathorne, had used the services of Henry Bagshawe, a layman. At least part of his argument, therefore, was subject to serious question.

With regard to funds for charitable purposes Wiseman argued again that they were too small to divide and that Westminster, in any case, was poorer than Southwark. Resources were not adequate even to provide for the needs of the archdiocese. Lastly he turned to the fund for his personal maintenance: "Am I rich enough to provide for two dioceses?" His position demanded constant travel, and he denied that Grant's expenses exceeded his. The bishop of Southwark, moreover, could live in the fine house attached to the cathedral, a building as large as or larger than those lived in by the bishops of Birmingham, Nottingham, Northampton, and Clifton, not to mention Plymouth, where Bishop Errington occupied one room in a miserable presbytery.[51]

Although he had just been in Rome in the spring of 1854, Wiseman returned there for the definition of the dogma of the Immaculate Conception of the Blessed Virgin Mary on December 8, 1854. Grant also made the trip, as did some of the other English bishops. Before returning to England, Grant further elucidated his arguments in order to answer the cardinal's observations. Wiseman promised that as soon as he returned to England he would comment upon Grant's last letter. More than three years later, however, it was reported that Wiseman had still not complied. On several occasions Cardinal Fransoni and his successor Cardinal Barnabò asked him to do so. No response was forthcoming, in spite of their requests.[52]

Considering all that Wiseman took upon himself and the work thrust upon him in the years immediately after the first synod, it is somewhat astonishing that in the summer of 1854 he completed his famous novel, *Fabiola; or, The Church of the Catacombs* (1855). The work, evidently written in a single year, was widely acclaimed, and translations appeared in at least ten languages. It was not meant as a treatise or even a learned work: it was an attempt to contribute toward what Wiseman so earnestly desired, a popular Catholic literature. He wanted to present an account of the early church as the first volume of a "Popular Catholic Library," and he hoped that others would take up the challenge and prepare similar books to cover other periods. The composition of the novel gave him an opportunity to describe at length many of the remains of ancient Rome as well as the history and the customs with which he was familiar. It was this work which taught many to accept the less-than-accurate idea that the Christians, throughout centuries as a persecuted underground community, sought constant refuge in the labyrinthian corridors of the catacombs, unknown by the imperial authorities. Whatever the merits of the novel, and critics have been divided, it was praised at the time, and its charm is still appreciated by many.[53]

One may well question how the cardinal found the time or could justify writing a novel. He provided the answer himself in a preface to the book.

> It has . . . been written at all sorts of times and in all sorts of places; early and late, when no duty urged, in scraps and fragments of time, when the body was too fatigued or the mind too worn for heavier occupation, in the roadside inn, in the halt of travel, in strange houses, in every variety of situation and circumstances — sometimes trying ones. It has thus been composed bit by bit, in portions varying from ten lines to half a dozen pages at most, and generally with few books or resources at hand. But once begun it has proved what it was taken for, a recreation, and often a solace and a sedative; from the memories it has revived, the associations it has renewed, the scattered and broken remnants of old studies and early readings which it has combined, and by the familiarity which it has cherished with better times and better things than surround us in our age.[54]

It is reasonable to suggest that Wiseman wrote *Fabiola* not in spite of his many other occupations or the burdens that he was carrying but because of them. It was a form of recreation that allowed him, from time to time, to escape the less congenial trials to which he was subjected.

The cardinal, it may be argued, should have confined his efforts to his own archdiocese, or certainly to England. The observation is not without merit. We have seen that he found day-to-day administration tedious, nor did he consider himself to have been placed over the archdiocese for that purpose. He always found it difficult to narrow the scope of his activities and felt that his presence and achievement on a larger scale would ultimately enhance the reputation of English Catholics in general, even when his concern was with religion in the Balkans, or Spain, or Austria, or Spanish America. He sincerely believed, moreover, that when his expertise could be of assistance to the Holy See or could advance the cause of the church, it was his responsibility to offer it.

It was clear that Wiseman would eventually need help in administering the archdiocese, especially if he remained convinced that his larger schemes and efforts should continue. As early as February 1851 he told George Errington, his old friend and assistant, that he wanted him as his coadjutor bishop. Errington refused the offer, pointing out that the two men had worked together twice before, at the English college in Rome and at Oscott, and that they had not been able to do so in complete harmony.[55] Errington, a far more rigid man than Wiseman, and less enthusiastic in his support of the converts as well as somewhat skeptical of the cardinal's more idealistic plans, was recognized as a capable administrator. Wiseman undoubtedly felt that he was the very man who might make up for his own inadequacies.

Monsignor Talbot opposed the appointment of anyone as coadjutor for the cardinal. He recommended an auxiliary bishop instead, a less important position and one that would not involve the right of succession. He did not insist on the point, however, and in February 1855, realizing that the cardinal was overworked and that there were long delays in the transaction of important business (including the settlement with Bishop Grant), Talbot wrote to urge that the Westminster Chapter should hold an election for the coadjutorship as soon as possible, "although the Holy Father has already determined that the Bishop of Plymouth should be the person." Talbot concluded by admitting that he had previously had reservations regarding Errington's suitability, but that these had vanished: "More I hear of him, more I admire him, and he strikes me as being just the man to work under you in London." He saw one obstacle: "The only tendency that I observe in him and which he must be very careful about is not to be vexatious towards his priests, and try to impose on them greater obligations than the canon law sanctions."[56]

Bishop Errington's own reservations remained.

> I shall say nothing of the dangers & ordinary failure of coadjutorships, nor of the still greater danger of the contingency of my having hereafter to supply for the archbishop if he were called to Rome, which would be a kind of work not at all in my way. Either of these considerations would have sufficed to overbalance the natural satisfaction one would feel at having to leave a rocky & desert soil, such as this diocese, to go & work in a far better cultivated & more expansive field. But as you will say that that is the Pope's affair & not mine, I will pass it over & come to what is strictly mine, & for which I must answer also, the statement of reasons why Plymouth should not be vacated.

He then stated the special qualifications that he believed to be his for dealing with the difficulties in Plymouth, including the breadth of his previous experience and the number of his contacts throughout England through whom he could arrange for priests to work in his diocese.[57]

The Westminster Chapter met on February 5, 1855. In compliance with Wiseman's clear wish, all ten votes went to Bishop Errington on the first ballot. It was required that three names should be sent for the consideration of the bishops, however, before recommendations could be forwarded to Rome. Other ballots led to the nominations of Bishop James Brown of Shrewsbury and Canon John Maguire, Wiseman's vicar general. The additional names were all *pro forma*, including that of Newman, who, on all ballots after the first, received votes from three members of the chapter. There was no doubt that Errington would be appointed. The bishops discussed the nominations at a meeting on February 14, and the following month, on March 12, Propaganda confirmed the choice of Errington. The pope ratified the decision six days later. As coadjutor to the archbishop of Westminster, Errington was also named titular archbishop of Trebizond.[58]

Cardinal Wiseman at last had the helper of his choice as he prepared for the second provincial synod, scheduled to meet at Oscott in July 1855. Conditions were not the same as those surrounding the convocation of the first synod. Catholics were no longer receiving the unwelcome attention they had in 1852, but tensions within the episcopal body were far more evident. The unanimity and clear signs of goodwill, noted at the previous assembly, were less apparent than when the onslaught of a common enemy had made a united front imperative.

13. The Colleges

THERE WERE A NUMBER OF CHANGES IN THE COMPOSITION OF THE episcopal body during the period between the first two provincial synods. Bishop Hendren's chronically poor health made it necessary for him to retire, and Bishop George Brown of Liverpool, for the same reason, asked for a coadjutor. Both appointments were made in June 1853. Richard Roskell, the first student whom Wiseman had ordained after his own elevation to the episcopate, was named bishop of Nottingham; a member of the Salford Chapter, he was recognized as a loyal supporter of the cardinal. Alexander Goss, vice-president of St. Edward's College in Liverpool, was appointed to the coadjutorship of that diocese. He had not been Brown's choice: the bishop had asked specifically for Thomas Cookson, a member of his chapter, and that body had supported the recommendation. Cardinal Wiseman, however, opposed the appointment, and his influence in Rome determined the outcome. Cookson, he informed the authorities, was among those northern priests who had demonstrated an unduly independent spirit. His strange opinions never coincided with the sentiments of others. Goss, on the other hand, was decisive, energetic, and persevering.[1] The description was not inaccurate, although Wiseman later had reason to regret his choice when Goss, as bishop of Liverpool in his own right, opposed the cardinal's policies.

In June 1855, a month before the second synod, Propaganda named William Vaughan, member of the Clifton Chapter and uncle of the future archbishop of Westminster, to replace Errington as bishop of Plymouth. He was not consecrated until the following autumn, however, so that a vicar capitular represented that diocese at the assembly in July. In November 1854, finally, Bishop Burgess of Clifton had died.

Prior Park was so badly in debt, and its multiple problems were so pressing that it was resolved to sell it. The Holy See, under the circumstances, decided to postpone the appointment of a new bishop for the see. All of the recommendations for the office had met stiff opposition from the clergy there. Cardinal Fransoni wrote, "Upon reflection that the sale of Prior Park is not effected, it seems necessary to adopt some measure by which to impede the new bishop from encountering the difficulties of his predecessors."[2] The decision was compassionate, since the new bishop, when appointed, would not be held responsible for what was bound to be an extremely unpopular act. Clifton, in the meantime, also sent a vicar captiular to the synod.

There were two instances during the period between the first two synods when suggestions were made for further dividing the sees. The first was a request by Bishop Turner that the Leyland Hundred, originally part of the diocese of Salford and then assigned to Liverpool, should be returned to Salford. Propaganda consulted Wiseman, as was the case whenever major decisions of this kind were to be made. He, in turn, asked the advice of Bishop Grant, and together they decided that no immediate change should take place.[3]

The second case was of greater significance for the cardinal. The Holy Father, during a private audience in which he received Bishop Grant, questioned the wisdom of maintaining the division of London into two separate dioceses. Grant took advantage of the occasion, not to support an alteration of the arrangement by which London was divided but to suggest that Southwark itself might well be made into two dioceses. He drew up a plan in which he pointed out that his see extended from the Thames to France, and he went on to explain the difficulty of ministering to the Catholics who lived on the isles of Guernsey, Alderney, and Jersey. The bishop suggested that the Channel Islands might be united to Berkshire and Hampshire, forming a new diocese of Southampton, over which he was willing to preside.[4]

Fransoni informed Wiseman of the suggestion and asked that the bishops might discuss it at their forthcoming synod. He mistakenly added, however, that the proposal would reunite both parts of London under the authority of a single bishop. Wiseman was delighted. It was only after the synod, when the bishops remained for an extra day and a half to discuss privately a number of nonsynodical questions, that he discovered the real nature of Grant's proposal. He reported to Monsignor Talbot that on the basis of his misunderstanding, he had drawn up a plan of his own. It would have called for adding South London to Westminster along with a portion of Surrey. The rest of Southwark would have been divided into two, with one bishop making his home at Hastings instead of London, and a second assigned to the new see of Southampton. This had all depended upon the Southwark bishop's willingness to divide his own diocese and to reunite London. Grant, however, wrote to Propaganda to explain that he was withdrawing his earlier proposal. He was now convinced that it would be impossible to support an additional diocese, especially since he considered the construction of a seminary to be essential in carrying out his original intention. He had consulted the clergy who would have been affected by the change, moreover, and they opposed it. The confusion did nothing to ease the tension between him and the cardinal.[5]

The participants in the second provincial synod assembled in July 1855 as planned. The decrees were neither as long nor impressive as those of the previous synod.[6] The first seven dealt with routine matters, with the exception of the second, which expressed joyful acceptance of the doctrine of the Immaculate Conception, defined the previous December. The most important decree was the eighth, which consisted of twenty-one articles. It treated of the administration of temporalities and finances related to the English missions and was an attempt to settle, once and for all, the most glaring abuses that had led to litigation in the past.

The general tone of the decree was established at the outset: "Offerings of the faithful for the propagation and ornament of religion, for the support of the clergy, the relief of the poor and other pious uses, are considered as made to God and the Church; and the administrators or guardians of them, whether ecclesiastics or laymen, are to be deemed merely dispensers of them, under obligation of rendering an account to God of their stewardship." The intention of any donor was to be examined carefully. Buildings devoted to religious purposes were to be considered as belonging to the place where they were located, unless it was made very clear that they belonged to a particular religious order. Alienation of church property was prohibited without the bishop's permission, and donations to the parish or mission were not to be considered as belonging to the priests. Various ways of providing income for the church were approved, and clergymen were cautioned to make careful inventories of the material possessions attached to their missions.

A ninth decree provided for a new translation of the Bible into English, a task assigned to the editorship of Newman. Although he accepted the commission and made initial plans for its execution, the project did not receive the support necessary from Wiseman and the other bishops, and it had to be abandoned. It was another instance of initial encouragement, to be followed by neglect and disappointment for Newman, who became more convinced than ever that the word of the bishops was not to be trusted.[7]

The tenth and last decree advised the assistant priest on any mission of his obligation to inform the head missionary before leaving his post, "even for a day."

Cardinal Wiseman prepared all of the decrees, as well as the long synodical letter. It included an explanation of the dogma of the Immaculate Conception and also a summary of the pope's condemnation of rationalism; a plea for support of the English College in Rome; a discussion of the Crimean War, lamenting the horror of the conflict itself but praising the dedication of those priests and sisters who were serving in the Crimea; an urgent appeal for the support of education; and, finally, an exhortation to the faithful, urging them to support their clergy. William Clifford, vicar capitular of Plymouth, was given the task of carrying the decrees to Rome. The decree of approbation by the Holy See was issued on August 16, 1856.[8]

By the end of the second synod the major problem still to be settled was the status and control of ecclesiastical colleges. Late in June, Cardinal Fransoni had written to Wiseman in order to persuade the bishops to examine the questions relating to seminaries and to pass appropriate legislation in their regard.[9] The cardinal later explained that the letter arrived too late to receive adequate attention by the synod. A committee or congregation had been assigned the duty of discussing ecclesiastical education, however, and Bishop Grant, known to be the instigator of Rome's directive, was appointed to preside over the group. Wiseman went on to point out that the English institutions for ecclesiastical education were "colleges" rather than "seminaries" in the strict sense, because lay students attended them along with those preparing for the priesthood. Without such an arrangement, he said, the children of the Catholic nobility and of the "civil class" would have been abandoned to Protestant education.

The synodical congregation produced a long document. It was not a "polished report," wrote the cardinal, but a series of points, written in English, which the secretary read to the synod. There were suggestions regarding the academic, disciplinary, and spiritual formation of those preparing for the priesthood, but the treatment was not detailed. Wiseman pointed out that "after having so lightly treated the most essential parts of the studies and ecclesiastical spirit in the colleges, the congregation passed to their administration, a matter, perhaps, outside of their duty." With regard to college finances, it recommended that two chapter members in each diocese should be assigned to settle seminary affairs, in keeping with a directive of the Council of Trent.

Then, wrote the cardinal, the congregation changed its style. Instead of notes in English, the rest of the report consisted of three Latin decrees. The first provided that chapter deputies should meet with the bishop at least twice a year at the seminary; the second specified that, apart from matters pertaining to the administration of the sacraments, divine worship, preaching, and the formal visitation to encompass external procedures in each college (all of which were the responsibility of the bishop in whose diocese the college was located), all of the bishops whose students were educated there were to share equal responsibility. Finally, the bishops, along with one deputy from each diocese having an interest in a college, were to examine the financial situation of the seminary each year.

Wiseman concluded his report by insisting that no congregation of the synod had a right to present completed decrees to the bishops for approbation. This was the prerogative of the episcopate alone. The congregation, therefore, had gone beyond its commission, and in this case even the bishops could not frame decrees that gave them jurisdiction over colleges outside of their own dioceses. Only the Holy See was competent to approve such an arrangement.[10]

The lines of a first-class battle were being drawn. Those bishops who were responsible for colleges within their own dioceses were understandably jealous of outside interference in their management. Others, however, with no such institutions of their own and without the means necessary to build and support them, were equally convinced that they should be involved in overseeing the seminaries to which they sent their candidates for the priesthood. Neither of the first two synods offered a solution to the problem. Questions related to ecclesiastical education had been discussed informally, even before the first synod, but nothing specific had been accomplished. Wiseman was certainly correct in pointing out that Propaganda's directive regarding the colleges had come too late for serious consideration by the synod, and it was also true that there was not enough time to discuss the report prepared by the synod's special congregation. The bishops were later forced to take the college questions in hand because of disputes demanding immediate solutions. Their failure to reach agreement then split the hierarchy and led to prolonged controversies both in England and Rome.

There was very little precedent in England to assist the bishops in formulating a policy for ecclesiastical colleges. For a period of more than two hundred years after the Reformation, Catholics had been dependent upon colleges established on the Continent to provide for the education of their priests. The French Revolution and its anticlerical aftermath had resulted in the closure of the institutions in Rome, Lisbon, Valladolid, and Douai. Englishmen then found it necessary to establish substitutes in their own country, where obstacles had been removed by the relaxation of the penal laws toward the end of the eighteenth century.[11]

Since it was the aim of the restored hierarchy to introduce normal ecclesiastical organization in England, it is understandable that, along with cathedrals, chapters of canons, and diocesan officialdom, the bishops should have wanted to follow the Tridentine directives by erecting diocesan seminaries.[12] Financial considerations alone would have prevented them from doing so. Students from various dioceses were necessarily sent to a single college. Prior Park, Oscott, Ushaw, and St. Edmund's, then, served those areas formerly attached to the Western, Midland, Northern, and London districts respectively.

The continental colleges had never been considered as seminaries in the strict sense intended by the Council of Trent. In a period when no Roman Catholic educational institutions were permitted in England, lay students had joined those intended for the priesthood in the colleges established elsewhere. The same practice was continued in England. No single vicar apostolic, moreover, exercised jurisdiction over the college authorities, who could, without permission, retain the more promising students to assist with the administration and teaching in the institutions where they had completed their studies. College administrators now made the same demand in England, insisting, quite reasonably, that all of the dioceses had to bear the responsibility of providing teachers and counselors for their students.

The adjustment of the rights of the bishop in whose diocese a college was located, the demands made by the other bishops who made use of the establishment, and the degree of authority permitted to college administrators became major points of controversy. In addition to jurisdictional problems, moreover, the difficulties of financing the colleges resulted in friction among the interested parties. There is no doubt that the questions concerning the status, administration, and financing of the colleges raised the most contentious issues and resulted in more ill will than any other problem faced by the hierarchy. The role of personalities was a significant factor in the various struggles, but the participants were convinced that the principles at stake were crucial.

All four colleges were, at one time or another, of special concern for Wiseman. He had once expected to be named president of Prior Park. Much later he was called upon to assist in settling its affairs. The cardinal was also appointed to assess matters in dispute among the bishops whose students attended Ushaw. He had been president of Oscott College, of course, but by 1850 his involvement there was only indirect, related to the financial problems that were raised by his administration of the college. His primary concern now was St. Edmund's, and it led to open warfare with his coadjutor, his chapter, his secretary, his vicar general, the seminary president, and the chapter and bishop of the neighboring see of Southwark. The battles were seen correctly as similar to controversies concerning Ushaw. The explosive college issues dominated the remainder of Wiseman's life, and they succeeded, to a certain extent, in breaking his spirit. He continued to demonstrate the extraordinary characteristics for which he had always been known and admired, but his increasingly poor health and constant opposition had taken their toll. Following periods of depression, from which he had suffered throughout his life, his resiliency was no longer what it once had been.

By the time that the jurisdictional and financial controversies had reached their climax, only three colleges were of immediate concern to the bishops. In 1856 Prior Park had been closed and its property sold. Considering its eventual collapse, it seems deplorable that so much time, energy, and money should have been thrown into its preservation. From the time of the college's foundation in 1830, the Western District, already poverty stricken, had been severely taxed in order to maintain the ambitious establishment. Bishop Baines had made free use of the district's resources — endowments of mission funds as well as those intended for episcopal maintenance, clergy annuation, and education — and had sunk the capital into the college. Private persons had lent large sums of money for the same purpose. Even under ideal circumstances the challenge of preserving Prior Park would have demanded the attention of the most able and enterprising administrators. Shortly after its establishment its troubles were compounded by a disastrous fire that occasioned further expense. The bitter feuds that may be traced to the foundation of the college continued to plague those responsible for its welfare.

When Bishop Ullathorne was appointed to the Western District in 1846, Prior Park was his greatest challenge. He called it a "bottomless pit, receiving everything and returning nothing." The bishop recommended that it should be turned over to its creditors; but when he established his episcopal residence at Bristol (instead of at the college as his two predecessors had done), he was accused of abandoning his responsibilities to the institution.[13] His successor Bishop Hendren was no more successful in gaining the support of the college authorities or in resolving the problems.

When the hierarchy was established in 1850, Prior Park was still in desperate financial straits. Wiseman was warned to save it if he could, and for that purpose he was appointed apostolic visitor. The task, however, was hopeless. Immediately after the second synod Archbishop Errington, at his own suggestion, was sent to Clifton as apostolic administrator to see what could be done. By the following January, Wiseman wrote, "Prior Park is doomed I fear. . . . The school breaks up for ever this vacation."[14]

Errington's task in Clifton was not a pleasant one, and it took him the greater part of a year. In addition to closing the college he was involved in other diocesan matters. His rigorous enforcement of ecclesiastical discipline, coupled with the unpleasant negotiations regarding the college, made him unpopular with some of the clergy. Wiseman defended his coadjutor: "His firmness, prudence, and patience, seem to me beyond all praise." A month later, however, he was more reserved: "In theory and law I believe Dr. Errington has been right; but I have found fault with him for not leaving many things to the next bishop, instead of doing them while only an administrator."[15]

By November 1856 Errington announced that Clifton was at last "ready for the appointment of a successor to the late Bishop [Burgess]." Wiseman recommended William Clifford, son of Baron Clifford of Chudleigh, and the appointment was made. After a trip to Rome to explain and defend his work, Archbishop Errington returned to Westminster. Clifford was, and remained, Errington's loyal friend throughout all subsequent controversies.[16]

Oscott, like Prior Park, was heavily in debt, but if its financial problems were as serious as those of the other colleges, its jurisdictional conflicts were less so. First founded as a college and seminary in 1794, it was rebuilt on a new site by Bishop Walsh, a venture that was completed at great expense in 1838. Nearly the entire capital of the funds of the Midland District, whether intended for missionary or educational purposes, was used for the construction of the new college. A decade later Bishop Ullathorne, newly installed as vicar apostolic of the Central District, wrote to Wiseman: "We are living at present from hand to mouth at Oscott. Although we have made considerable reforms in management and saving of expenditure, our deficit is still very great, and I shall be compelled to give up one of the half-year collections for its support, although that will put us into immense difficulties in the district."[17] Wiseman was only too familiar with Oscott's financial problems, but he may well have interpreted Ullathorne's remarks as a reflection upon his own administration as president.

At the end of 1855 Bishop Ullathorne again sought from Wiseman an accounting of the use that he had made of district funds when he served as coadjutor to Bishop Walsh. In a polite letter the bishop of Birmingham begged that all differences between them might be settled by arbitration. He received no answer, and when two more letters also failed to elicit a reply, he decided that he would not enter the disputed sum into a report that he was preparing to send to the Holy See but would leave the matter to the cardinal's "consideration."[18]

On the same day that Ullathorne wrote his third letter, Wiseman finally answered the first two requests for information. He explained his delay by stating that Errington, who had assisted him at Oscott and understood thoroughly the temporal affairs of the Central District, was still in Clifton. Since the cardinal intended to give up the temporal administration of the archdiocese to his coadjutor, as Walsh had done, he wanted to consult Errington before responding. He denied, however, that Ullathorne had any right to call upon him to render an account of his administration under a former bishop. The only form in which such a claim could be made upon him was that of "unjust (not imprudent) misapplication of funds, not of reckoning between predecessor and successor." His reaction was characteristic: "My Lord, this is a charge of serious import, not a matter for arbitration, an accusation calling for deprivation as well as restitution. I must look upon it as a criminal charge, for which I must refuse to answer to any one but a superior, and I can own one only, the Sovereign Pontiff. To him I will account for all and everything, and will give reckoning of my Stewardship either here or at Birmingham or elsewhere." He concluded by refusing to submit "any claims you consider yourself justified to make upon me to an arbitration."[19]

Ullathorne, like Grant, found that his repeated requests for an accounting from the cardinal led to a series of explanations, denials, and an ultimate announcement that only the Holy See was competent to pass judgment. After reading Wiseman's long letter, the bishop of Birmingham, who was familiar with the prolonged, complex process that would have resulted from an appeal to Rome, must have regretted having pursued the matter so assiduously. Yet he had not heard the last of it.

The major difficulties related to Ushaw College took their origin in the division that had created three northern vicariates in 1840. Instead of a single bishop with responsibility for the college, there were now three, each demanding administrative rights over the institution upon which he depended for his priests. Newsham observed that when only one bishop had claimed jurisdiction over the college, there had been peace. He was convinced, however, that no institution could be run "with several independent heads."[20]

President Newsham had foreseen the possible instability that a division of authority might create. Although a plan of government was agreed upon by all concerned parties in 1846, there was never general acceptance of the proposals. Moreover, contentious issues were not confined to those of jurisdiction; they extended as well to the division of funds. Newsham finally suggested that Wiseman should be designated as apostolic visitor, and the Holy See made the appointment in 1850. It was Rome's wish that the interested bishops might draw up a plan to end their differences. Grant wrote to Wiseman, "The appointment of a visitor is intended to give full time for preparing and maturing it [a plan]."[21]

The cardinal made his first official visit to Ushaw in 1851. After meeting with the bishops who sent their students to study there, he prepared a report for the Holy See, noting that there had been unanimous and complete agreement among the bishops, a claim that he deleted before sending it to the Holy See.

In his report Wiseman stated that Ushaw should be the episcopal seminary for Hexham, the diocese in which it was situated, as well as for Beverley, Liverpool, and Salford. James Brown of Shrewsbury had a right to educate a number of students there, corresponding to the funds allocated to Cheshire, but he was not to participate in governing the college. Only Bishop Hogarth of Hexham was to exercise spiritual jurisdiction. Each bishop, however, was to nominate two chapter deputies as advisers for college affairs. The secular clergy of each diocese were to elect annually two priests to be added to those chosen by the chapter, and all four would assist the bishops each year in examining the economic state of the college and the administration of its property. They were to have no rights in the government, discipline, or studies of the institution and, in fact, were to have merely a consultative voice even in those matters for which they were elected.

In addition to the annual visitation of the deputies, the bishops were to make triennial visits at the college, accompanied by their chapter deputies. They were then to examine the discipline, moral state, and scholastic progress of their students, and, when abuses were detected, they were empowered to authorize any changes that would not alter the constitution. At least three of the four bishops had to be present for the visitation, but in cases of emergency the bishop of Hexham was to have authority to act alone or to call a special meeting.

The rector was to be nominated by all four bishops, either at their triennial visitation or at a special meeting for that purpose. The bishop of the diocese in which the nominee lived was to give him up willingly, and, once named, the rector or president (the titles were used interchangeably) was to consider himself exempt from the authority of his own ordinary and as subject to the jurisdiction of the bishop of Hexham. He was to have charge of the college's government and economic administration, with full authority in both, subject only to the annual and triennial visitations. He could make no substantial changes, but he was free to introduce improvements in studies or discipline, as circumstances might demand. It was his duty, moreover, to nominate his vice-rector and other administrators and professors, subject to the approval of the bishops. Because of the grave inconvenience suffered when a bishop recalled one of his subjects for missionary purposes, it was asserted that the college had the right to the service of its students, as in Rome and Lisbon, if they were suitable for the college staff. Each year, finally, the president was to send a report to each bishop, including Shrewsbury, on the progress of his students.

The second part of Wiseman's report dealt with the distribution of education funds belonging to the Lancashire District. He concluded this very careful discussion by praising Newsham, who, he said, was responsible for the notable progress of the college.[22]

After the visitation Newsham and Bishop Hogarth discussed the remaining problems. The president urged Wiseman "to obtain from Rome extensive powers applicable to every emergency, for he [Hogarth] is convinced many more cases will arise in which your decision will be wanted." The major concern was Bishop George Brown's refusal to recognize the cardinal's right to settle questions involved in the distribution of the funds of the Lancashire District. Brown had been ill and so unable to attend the meeting at the college. His resistance was due to the fact that in 1850 he had announced his intention of making St. Edward's College, Liverpool, into his diocesan seminary. It was there that he wanted his subjects to prepare themselves for the philosophy and theology that would then be completed elsewhere. He demanded to apply his share of the Lancashire education funds to his own seminary, not to Ushaw. The dispute continued until Brown's death, when it was taken up by his successor.[23]

Propaganda, in assessing the constitution of Ushaw proposed by Wiseman, sought more information on three points: the power of appointing professors, the presentation to sacred orders, and the administration of temporalities. The Holy See took no further action, in spite of pressures from the bishops and the president.[24]

Among the other contentious issues was the right, claimed by the college president and inserted into the proposed constitution, to keep at Ushaw any priests of his choice who had completed their studies. Milburn wrote that after 1851 the president's right in this regard was never discussed, "as though some such decision had been made." Newsham, as a matter of fact, justified in 1852 his practice of retaining students, and in 1854, he wrote to the cardinal of George Brown's "reckless attempt to deprive us of *very* useful professors, without the slightest regard to the wants of the college." He later complained to Talbot that Bishop Briggs was guilty of the same offense. In a letter to Bishop Hogarth in 1856, Newsham stated that there were four members of the college staff who had been ordained after merely four, six, eighteen, and twenty-four months of divinity respectively: "The bishops will say, 'how monstrous to think of such courses of divinity!' So say I, and with quite as intense feelings as they. Let them, then, cooperate with me and assist me in retaining old superiors [teachers] that we may never again be compelled to repeat what has given me as much pain as it can give them."[25]

Because such problems remained unsettled, Cardinal Wiseman's faculties as apostolic visitor were renewed repeatedly throughout the decade. Dom Cuthbert Butler was unjustified in asserting that "this position and power he clung to and sought to perpetuate." Butler also claimed that the president of Ushaw tried to secure the freedom of the college "from such an abnormal position." Certainly Newsham wanted to find a permanent solution to his problems, but he and Bishop Hogarth strenuously urged the cardinal to seek the renewal of his faculties in order to preserve Ushaw from chaos.[26]

Newsham, finally convinced that only a higher authority could resolve the problems, joined with Bishop Hogarth in urging that Ushaw should become a pontifical college. Cardinal Barnabò consulted Wiseman on the request. The Holy See was reluctant to establish the English colleges as pontifical seminaries. Newsham persisted, however, and in 1858 told Talbot, "Only the other day the bishop of Hexham, in his abrupt and terse way, said in a letter to me that 'the struggle is now between Ushaw being a pontifical college and anarchy'; I am quite of this opinion." He added, "Nothing in my mind can be more certain than that neither St. Cuthbert's nor St. Edmund's nor any other college, can be carried on under more than one head."[27]

The other four bishops who sent students to Ushaw were prepared to fight any move to centralize authority. They held a special meeting and wrote to Rome in order to seek an equal voice with Bishop Hogarth in Ushaw affairs. Newsham, informing Monsignor Talbot of the meeting and asking that Ushaw might be made pontifical, noted that Archbishop Errington was in Manchester at the very time that the four bishops were there to prepare their petition to the Holy See. He wondered whether the archbishop of Trebizond might have been "the counsellor and mover in this case at Manchester as in that in London? The coincidence is certainly remarkable."[28]

A series of controversies, similar to those in the North, had arisen over St. Edmund's College, which served Westminster and Southwark. Errington, who opposed the cardinal in his own archdiocese, was playing a major role there, and Newsham's observation was clearly based on substantial evidence. Ushaw's problems were a dress rehearsal for those that Cardinal Wiseman would have to deal with at home, where, however, he was less willing to pursue a policy of compromise than when acting as apostolic visitor for an institution in which his involvement was less personal. Monsignor Talbot later observed, with reference to Ushaw, that the Holy See would have to agree to a compromise "to please all parties."[29] This was easier said than done. The long period during which the disputes dragged on and Wiseman's firm determination to manage St. Edmund's without outside interference provided ample time and opportunity for positions to harden.

After Errington reluctantly took up his position as Wiseman's coadjutor, the first question upon which the two men disagreed involved the position of W. G. Ward at St. Edmund's. William Weathers, the college president, at first supported Ward, who, conscious of the fact that it was unusual for a layman to hold such a position, asked that a priest might attend his lectures. "Mr. Ward has begun today the first of his series of lectures to our divines," wrote Weathers; "It was exceedingly good on the subject of dogmatic theology, being preliminary to the course he is entering upon." A month later the college president was still convinced that Ward was doing the students "a great deal of good."[30]

In 1854, however, Weathers publicly disagreed with Ward on a point of theology, and their cordial relationship ended. Robert Whitty later observed: "It matters little whether Ward was right or wrong on said point. Dr. Weathers might have expressed his dissent and the reasons once and quietly, but to maintain day after day disputes with his own scholars (who for the most part took Ward's side) was to say the least most imprudent for a rector."[31] Whitty was theoretically correct. He overlooked the fact, however, that the president was ultimately responsible for the teaching in the college, a point, at least, that Wiseman had included in the plan he had drawn up for Ushaw. Ward, moreover, was not a man to bow easily to the judgment of others.

Archbishop Errington's first assignment in Westminster was to make an official visitation at St. Edmund's. He sided with those who objected to Ward's position there. Errington would not have objected had Ward been appointed to teach philosophy, but he would not accept him as a professor of theology. Ward, for his part, considered that Errington had so exalted an opinion of his position as bishop "that even were a *priest* dogmatical professor, yet the whole course and order of his lectures, and his mode of teaching, should be marked out even in detail by the bishop." Ward continued: "Now, I am convinced that no man of any power or capacity, even though agreeing substantially with a bishop in his theological views, could ever work on such a principle as this. No one capable of anything beyond mere routine *could* teach as the mere *instrument* of another." Weathers, on the other hand, felt that Ward was a safer guide in theology than in philosophy: "He has so much confidence in his own views and so little respect for the judgment of others, that nothing but express definitions are allowed to stand in his way." He concluded that Ward had "more brilliance than depth."[32]

Errington soon became one of Ward's most vocal opponents, and it was when he saw that the cardinal did not share his view that he asked to be assigned as apostolic administrator of Clifton. He even suggested that he might be removed permanently to another see.[33]

Wiseman wanted his coadjutor to return to Westminster as soon as possible: "I should wish to commit to him the administration, temporal and spiritual, of the diocese, reserving to myself the higher duties of watching over our new institutions, looking to general interests connected with government, parliament, etc., and attending to affairs committed to me by the Holy Father." Wiseman's ambition was to have the "leisure to complete works begun, and to prepare new ones, especially to try to meet the terrible tide of infidelity which is threatening England, under so many forms, and with so much learning and cunning. I have already made considerable progress with materials for the contest."[34]

Monsignor Talbot soon began to play a role that would be a major factor in Errington's ultimate removal from office: "I must now write to you about another matter in strict confidence." Talbot often wrote in strict confidence.

> It is about Monsignor Errington, of whom I saw a great deal when he was in Rome [regarding Clifton affairs], and whom I assisted in every way in my power, according to your desire. I must say in secrecy to your Eminence, that although I like him very much to talk to, and as a companion, yet I fear very much for his future administration in London. The impression he left here is that he has *"una testa piccolare"* [a petty mind]. I do not think he is Roman in spirit. He has a great deal of what they detest so much here, Episcopalianism, that is, thinking that a bishop ought to interfere with everything in his diocese. He also is ultra-parochial in his views. He has a great antipathy to, and want of confidence in, converts, which he shows on every occasion. He is opposed to the Oblates — and to everything new. He did not make a favourable impression by wishing to curtail the devotions at Clifton.

He then repeated, "All this I say to you in confidence."[35]

Errington does seem to have mistrusted converts. One of his admirers wrote, "He [Errington] said with truth that those worthy of being held up for respect and esteem should first of all be the Catholics whose ancestors had abided with the Faith in the days of bitter persecution, and NOT newcomers, quite untried." The writer shared the same sentiment. She was accurate in stating that Errington "had the right head-piece and organising brain to suit a great prelate of the Roman Catholic Church" and that he "was no sort of man to act to any gallery and could not play the sycophant," an obvious reference to his relations with Wiseman.[36] Errington, in fact, was too capable and strong willed to work as the cardinal's alter ego.

The archbishop of Trebizond should have followed his instincts by refusing to return to Westminster. He immediately threw himself, however, into the task of visiting the archdiocese. When announcing the impending visitation, Wiseman proclaimed that his coadjutor's powers extended to "all persons, places, and things, subject to episcopal visitation, according to the laws and constitutions of the holy Catholic Church." For that purpose he had communicated to his coadjutor "all our powers, ordinary and delegated."[37] Less than two weeks later the cardinal informed Talbot that the archbishop had begun the visitation "in earnest" and that "the clergy seem all pleased about it, at least show excellent dispositions." He went on to reply to Talbot's criticism of Errington: "He is very much altered, softer, anxious to raise no obstacle, considerate, and most obliging to the clergy. He comes to me for everything, indeed too much, officiates & preaches much, & I think will answer perfectly in everything." Several months later, when it became apparent that the priests of the archdiocese were not "all pleased" with Errington's visitation, the cardinal still defended him: "I believe Dr. Errington will prove an invaluable bishop."[38]

The day was to come, however, when the cardinal would complain to the pope that his coadjutor had made the visitation "more in the manner and terms of a superior than of a subordinate."[39] If there was truth in the assertion, as there seems to have been, it was Wiseman's own mandate that created the unfortunate situation. Questions related to St. Edmund's College revealed just how incompatible the two men were and later blinded Wiseman to the qualities that he had once admired in Errington.

In 1855, Wiseman assigned Herbert Vaughan, not yet twenty-three years old, to be vice-president of St. Edmund's. After studying at Stonyhurst and at the Jesuit College of Brugellete in Belgium, Vaughan had been enrolled at the Accademia dei Nobili Ecclesiastici in Rome. It was there that he came to know Henry Manning, at whose mass he assisted each day. Only twenty-two years of age at the time of his ordination in 1854, he was far too young and inexperienced for the important post in the diocesan college to which Wiseman appointed him. He encountered immediate opposition within St. Edmund's, intensified by the fact that he was one of the first priests to join the Oblates of St. Charles, established under Manning to provide the kind of community that the cardinal had so long desired for England.[40]

Wiseman was very proud of Manning, who, while in Rome, had also made a favorable impression on the authorities there. The Oblates were a source of even greater pride for the cardinal: "Before winter my Cong[regation] of Oblates of St. Charles will be established; *secular* priests subject to the bishop, to do all works. It is a new feature to have actual communities of priests in a town. This will begin with about 8. The Marists have 8, and the Oratorians 16 priests, and all occupied; 32 priests in 3 houses. Do you think this a bold experiment?" The following month he told Cardinal Barnabò that he had worked with Manning every step of the way in establishing the community.[41]

Errington opposed the Oblates from the beginning, convinced that they would be far more independent of the bishop than Wiseman imagined. His views were shared by many of the clergy, especially disturbed when three members of the community, in addition to Vaughan, were placed at St. Edmund's. It was feared that the administration of the college would be turned over to them, certainly the opinion of Wiseman's nephew William Burke, who had joined the Oblates but later left them, evidently under the influence of Errington. Burke wrote: "I only know that I was always under the impression that the college was to be ultimately under Oblate direction, and that Dr. Weathers retiring, Vaughan was supposed to become president." It is clear, in fact, that Manning was overseeing and even directing his subjects in their work at St. Edmund's, "practically a defiance of the President, or at any rate an attempt to manage the Seminary without reference to him."[42]

The staff and students at the college were soon divided. Weathers sought to have Vaughan replaced in 1858.[43] Wiseman must have regretted the fact that it had been his own recommendation, in his report for Ushaw, that the president, with the consent of the co-interested bishops, should be responsible for selecting his chief assistant. He, in fact, had thrust Vaughan upon Weathers. The young man, earnest in his reforming zeal, was immature in seeking the support of his students and in exercising an imprudent lack of restraint in his utterances. He wrote to the rector of the English College in Rome, for example, to describe the treatment that he had received from Weathers, who, he said, had accused him of "espionage and such like gentle conduct." The president, it seems, had grounds for making the accusations. Vaughan continued, however, by asking: "Can you explain how men, priests possessing certainly some sterling virtues, show themselves continually at enmity with truth and honesty? Is it that with other gifts is vouchsafed to them a special and abundant gift of stupidity, or that there is something *inherently* wicked in truth and honesty themselves? How is this solved in the Roman schools?"[44]

The tension had increased when Talbot, with the cardinal's blessing, succeeded in persuading the pope to appoint Manning as provost or dignitary of the Westminster Chapter in 1857. "It certainly was a happy idea of your Eminence to get Manning made provost of Westminster," wrote Talbot; "It was quite essential in order to give him a position in the diocese." Manning replaced Robert Whitty, who had obtained leave to join the Jesuits. John Maguire, the cardinal's other vicar general, would have been the logical choice, but, as Talbot commented, "he is the greatest Gallican in London *from principle*, and it would not have been an act of loyalty to the Holy See to name him Provost. The Pope having named him [Manning] Provost takes all the odium off your shoulders." Talbot warned Wiseman that Manning would "require your support against Dr. Errington, who is full of all kinds of *idiosyncracies*, as they call his ideas here." He continued: "As for myself, I am very fond of Dr. Errington as a personal friend. I find him a pleasant person to talk *to*, and take a walk *with*, and so forth.

But, nevertheless, I must say, that I never met a man who enters less into the Roman spirit, and has smaller views, both as regards Catholic doctrine and practice. And, such is the general opinion in Rome. Do not tell him that I have told you, because, what I say about him, is in strict confidence."[45]

Not only were the Oblates to be entrenched in the seminary, then, but their superior was to occupy the loftiest position on the archdiocesan chapter, the body specifically designated by the Council of Trent to advise and to assist the bishop in seminary affairs.

In the summer of 1858 the Westminster Chapter, on its own authority, initiated an investigation into the role of the Oblates in the seminary.[46] The members based their interference upon a Tridentine decree which provided that a bishop should appoint two canons to advise him on seminary discipline. The same decree directed that another committee should be established to take charge of diocesan taxation for the seminary's support. It was to be composed of four priests: two canons, one to be appointed by the bishop and the other by the chapter, and two priests of the "city," one to be chosen by the bishop and the other by the clergy of the "city." Finally, a committee of priests, two from the chapter and two from the "city," was to assist annually in the inspection of seminary accounts. It is not at all clear from the text whether the members of the third committee were to be the same as those of the second.[47]

In 1853 Wiseman had appointed John Maguire and Robert Whitty to advise him on seminary discipline. The duration of the assignment was for a single year.[48] The chapter, directed by the cardinal, then elected Canons George Rolfe and James O'Neal "to assist the bishop in drawing up the account of the seminary."[49] Although the number of seminary deputies and the procedure followed in their selection were not in strict accordance with the Tridentine prescriptions, neither were the colleges themselves established as seminaries according to the norms of the Council of Trent. This, at least, was Wiseman's contention.

In 1858, then, Canon John Maguire undertook to question President Weathers, also a chapter member, regarding the administration of the college. He asked specifically whether there was a plan to turn St. Edmund's over to the Oblates, whether professors were, in some cases, subject to the Oblate superior and removable by him, and whether there were differences of feeling, lack of uniformity, and distinctions among the subjects, some responsible to Manning and some to another authority. The provost, present at the meeting, offered to answer the questions himself and denied that any changes were to take place in the college's administration, although he himself had heard rumors to that effect.

In preparation for the next meeting Manning was asked to submit copies of the Oblate constitutions for the inspection of the members. He sought the advice of the cardinal, who refused to admit that the chapter had any authority to launch capitularly an investigation into a community that he himself had established. Copies of the Oblate rules and constitutions were distributed, in any case, and two weeks later the chapter voted to send a deputation with an address to the cardinal. The document specifically requested that the regulations of the Council of Trent concerning seminaries should be implemented, especially urgent in view of the fact that the professorial staff of St. Edmund's, partly formed of the secular priests of Westminster and Southwark, "and partly from members of a congregation standing in a very different relation to the diocese," was quite probably to be "entrusted to the new congregation."

The address then contrasted the Oblates in Westminster with the congregation founded by St. Charles in Milan, insisting that Manning's community, unlike its historical antecedent, was independent of the bishop. The chapter concluded that "to give to the new congregation the management of the seminary or influence in its administration would be, in effect, to withdraw it pro tanto from the control of the ordinary." [50]

Wiseman denied that the chapter had any right to initiate questions on the administration of his seminary, and he wrote to a number of foreign prelates, asking their advice on the matter raised by the chapter's address. The resulting replies, not surprisingly, supported his position. He then announced his intention to preside over a chapter meeting scheduled for December 1, 1858. He asked to see the chapter books in order to prepare himself. The chapter refused, insisting that he had no right to see the minutes, which contained the *secreta causa et motive* of the resolutions. Therefore they presented him with *copies* of the resolutions only. This was too much for Wiseman. He urged the chapter to reverse the course it had taken, and, when the members refused, he declared "all and single, the acts, deliberations, interrogations, and declarations unknown to me, to have been irregular, out of order, and abusive, and all resolutions, including that of presenting me with the address in question, and all decisions on any of these subjects, as null, void, and of none effect." [51]

As a matter of fact, a perusal of the chapter records, still preserved at Westminster, reveals that Wiseman received exact copies of all that was in them. The entire question of a bishop's right to examine the books became far too big an issue, and the chapter's refusal to allow the cardinal to see them was childishly legalistic. At a meeting on December 3, its members decided to present their case to the Holy See.

By now the cardinal had become certain that his coadjutor had taken an active part in all that had gone on. When he expressed his opinion to Talbot, he was warned to avoid a clash. Wiseman was hurt by the advice, and Talbot tried to make amends: "The truth is, that I wrote as strongly as possible, and in a great hurry, in order to prevent anything like a schism between yourself and the Archbishop, and to anticipate his resignation as he threatened to do, nay more, he authorized me, if I thought proper, to give in his resignation." Nothing, according to Talbot, "would have annoyed the Holy Father more." Bishop Grant, after all, with whom the cardinal was involved in litigation, had been named bishop only because of Wiseman's recommendation. There was now the danger that the authorities would be convinced "that it was difficult, or impossible, to please you." Talbot reminded the cardinal "that the Holy Father immediately acceded to your desire to have a coadjutor, allowed you to name him, and would have appointed him even without consulting the chapter of Westminster."[52]

The chapter proceeded to draw up two documents to send to Rome. The first asked whether it was lawful for the chapter to petition formally the bishop of the diocese and also sought a solution to a difference of opinion between the cardinal and the chapter as to his right to examine their books. The second petition asked whether or not the prescriptions of the Council of Trent were to be applied to the English colleges. Manning refused to sign the documents, so that John Maguire affixed his own name, indicating the provost's dissent.

Wiseman wrote to Rome to explain his position. He repeated that the chapter had no right to interfere in matters that touched upon his sole jurisdiction. He acknowledged that he had established a council to assist him with the seminary, but he correctly pointed out that he had done so for a single year, as an experiment, since England had no authorized plan for governing seminaries. Manning, in the meantime, prepared to depart for Rome to defend himself and his congregation. He left London December 27, writing on the previous day: "I do not suppose that they [the chapter's petitions] were written with the intention of delating me to the Holy See. But such is the effect. And I shall be required to account for my conduct as provost."[53]

Matters were further complicated by the fact that Bishop Grant had an interest in St. Edmund's. As early as 1852 he had written to the cardinal, "It would be well to form a plan speedily about the college funds and the administration of the college in general, as I feel like a stranger in the midst of my future clergy, and cannot say a word as to the desirableness or inexpediency of any plans proposed for them"[54] He was still waiting for the cardinal's cooperation in this matter and, in fact, in all financial questions involving the two sees.

In April 1857 Wiseman answered Rome's urgent request that he should settle matters with Grant by declaring that all would be settled quickly now that Errington had completed his work in Clifton. It was proposed that Grant and Errington should form a commission to negotiate the division of funds. The cardinal changed his mind, however, when Errington opposed him on the questions related to St. Edmund's.[55]

When Wiseman found himself at odds with his chapter, Grant wrote and asked that the Southwark Chapter, as well as that of Westminster, might participate in administering St. Edmund's. He suggested that three committees should be formed in accordance with Trent's prescriptions and that both chapters should be represented.[56]

Wiseman denied that "this cumbrous machinery" would be effective, and he was probably correct. He agreed to try it, however, adding: "At present Oscott and Ushaw are in want of a general plan, and I should think the formation of one for all England would be fit matter for our next synod, and can only be taken in hand then. However, if you will put down heads for a plan, we might consider it before petitioning in general terms." A few months later he was no longer agreeable: "I have been studying *seriously* the question of seminary deputies and have collected most important information. I am by no means inclined to complicate government or direction, nor can I, *at this moment, for special reasons* which probably you know, well enter on the subject. When they have passed away, I shall have no objection to do so."[57]

Grant was persistent, and he sent Wiseman a plan that, he suggested, should be forwarded to Propaganda. The cardinal left no room for doubt as to his attitude: "I beg to say that I will write what I have to say in my own sense and fashion. I thought I had explained myself sufficiently in my last note."[58]

Grant then encouraged the Southwark Chapter, which also petitioned Rome, to ask that he and the archbishop of Westminster might be given the faculties necessary to carry out the Tridentine decree concerning college deputies. The chapter further asked that the prescriptions of common law might be followed, whereby the seminary ought not to be entrusted to a congregation of regulars without the approval of the Holy See.[59]

The cardinal described for Newsham, a very interested spectator, the difficulty that he was having with his chapter and the "coincident movement from the Bp. of S[outhwark] to *force* me to give *him* and his chapter equal rights of government." The affair, he wrote, was "partly intended to prepare a precedent etc. for other colleges," and Errington was "the inspirer and counsellor of the entire movement," who had "helped them to draw up the petitions to the Holy See." Two weeks before Wiseman made the accusation, in fact, Errington had written to Bishop Grant, whose chapter was about to send its petition to Rome, "You can mention in your letter, if you think it will add any weight, that I agree with you as to the absolute necessity of some council in the administration of the college, and approve of the particular system you propose."[60] However sympathetic one may be to Errington's position, he was out of order in assisting both the Westminster and Southwark chapters in a course directly opposed to the superior whom he was assigned to represent in an official capacity.

Upon arriving in Rome, Manning discovered that Wiseman's failure to provide Propaganda with further explanations regarding his financial dispute with Bishop Grant was prejudicing the authorities against him. He warned: "I see that the question of the funds of the two dioceses is a difficulty here. . . . If it could be settled, one point of apparent advantage would be taken away by your Eminence's own act." Talbot was even more emphatic: "The great difficulty I have to contend against is his [Wiseman's] not settling the money affairs with Dr. Grant. *That* settled, I will support him through thick and thin. But I cannot take his part in putting off an affair of such importance. It damns his own cause."[61]

What no degree of prodding had been able to achieve over a four-year period was now brought about by the critical situation that had developed by 1859. Wiseman finally sent off his promised report regarding his financial differences with Grant.[62]

In December 1858 the Holy See received *three* petitions on the colleges, since in the same month the four northern bishops had written to ask for their rights in administering Ushaw. They, too, included the request that their chapters might have a role. Wiseman wrote: "I cannot help thinking that these are combined movements. For otherwise it seems strange that the bishop of Southwark, my chapter, the northern bishops, and their chapter should all be making one move by chance."[63]

The Holy See responded to all of the petitions by referring the college questions to a provincial synod. Wiseman realized that a synod would "throw a frightful addition of work on me." He had risen to such occasions in the past, but, as he noted, "in the present state of things, I cannot employ coadjutor, secretary, or vicar general to assist me in drawing up, as I have always had to do, the materials; but further, I suspect no one has studied or will study the questions involved." He could have added that Bishop Grant would be of no help, as he had once been. Even Searle, his devoted secretary, had sided with the other chapter members. Wiseman predicted that Grant and Errington "will of course take against me, and they alone are likely to try to get up a case." He went to work immediately, but so did those who opposed him.[64]

Errington warned Grant, "The card[inal] says the move is a *gallican one* against him etc. — so that great care will be required to meet Roman stories that will be set out etc." With predictable but questionable logic, Talbot was accusing all of Wiseman's opponents of displaying an anti-Roman spirit. Grant replied that the charge could hardly be applied to a group which was asking that the provisions of the Council of Trent might be applied to England. He reminded the monsignor that the appeal was being made *to the Holy See*, certainly not a Gallican maneuver. "Invert the petition," advised Grant, "and let a bishop ask that he may have power to erect a seminary without the machinery prepared and devised by the council, and ask the authorities in Rome whether his request would be entertained for an instant."[65]

Errington was equally vehement in answering Talbot, and the dispute became very personal indeed.[66] The archbishop also wrote to the prefect of Propaganda, asking him to withhold judgment regarding the accusations of Talbot and Wiseman. The charge of Gallicanism was absurd, and the facts cited to substantiate the accusation only demonstrated that Errington was too attached to the observance of discipline and too stubborn in refusing to allow priests to act for the public good in their own way, instead of by rule. "These things may be defects," he admitted, "but they are not Gallicanism or anti-Romanism in the sense that these words are used and in the sense that they convey to the listener."[67]

The controversy was widely discussed throughout the country. Errington was the subject of much gossip and dispute in clerical circles. Some of the tales were irresponsible, including the observations made by Herbert Vaughan, who wrote to Talbot of the different shades of opinion regarding the archbishop: "In some there is timid hesitation and in others the most thorough conviction that he is doing the work of the devil; some are to an extent conciliated by the freedom of his man- ner, his willingness to drink as much wine or spirits as they drink, and a total forgetfulness of his position and dignity, but then they are paid off shortly afterwards, their reasons or sources are smiled at, are not listened to, and go for nothing; and then rises up good rough hatred, i.e. *Xtian hatred!*" He added a postscript: "College as wretched as ever."[68]

Before the third synod Wiseman decided to rid himself of one dif- ficulty by asking Maguire to resign as vicar general. Errington advised his friend not to do so, but dismissal followed in any case. There was also talk of Searle's impending removal.[69] In spite of increased tension between Wiseman and his secretary, however, the step was never taken. The cardinal, perhaps, had come to depend too much on one who had assisted and supported him for so many years.

Wiseman wrote a blistering letter to President Weathers, who had fully supported his fellow chapter members. The cardinal implied that he had rendered useless his future service to the college and that he had betrayed his trust as "the representative of the bishop, his voice, his heart and soul." Wiseman's expectations of his seminary president were extraordinarily high. He then asked, "How could I act, how hold deliberation with *you,* how expect calm and impartial advice, supposing the position of the Oblates required investigation, after, without consulting me, you had made yourself a party to a petition that I would in truth expel them from the college." Weathers, he wrote, had placed himself against him, "and helped to push the sad matter on, to the last, or all but the last extremity, for had you resisted earlier, things would never have reached their last step."[70]

Finally the cardinal determined, once and for all, that he could no longer work with Archbishop Errington. He wrote to the Holy See to ask for his coadjutor's dismissal.[71]

In February 1859 Wiseman issued a preliminary notice to the bishops, advising them that Rome had referred "several urgent matters" to a provincial synod. In spite of inconvenience, the meeting could not be postponed; they would meet at Oscott in July.[72]

At long last, then, the college questions were to be taken in hand by the bishops, but only after matters had been brought to a head by a bitter, even a scandalous, controversy. Without exception, the litigants were good men and dedicated priests. They were also stubborn, unable to bend to any position except their own. Wiseman viewed the colleges as necessary instruments in preparing the kind of clergy demanded by the times. He had long dreamed, moreover, of founding a community like the Oblates to advance the Catholic cause and work among the poor. Now that such a group had been established according to his own plan and headed by one whom he trusted completely, he hoped to use its members in the formation of other priests upon whom he could depend.

Cardinal Wiseman had worked long and hard to bring about so desirable a situation. He was prepared, therefore, to defend his work with all of the vigor that might be necessary. This was far more than a mere test of strength. For him, it was a desperate struggle to defend his plans for his college and for the Oblates of St. Charles, both of which he saw as means for preserving from future attack his achievements for English Catholics.

14. Between Synods, 1855–59

SIX MONTHS AFTER THE SECOND SYNOD, WISEMAN WROTE THAT HE had "got quite knocked up during advent, & was unable for some days at Xmas to do much." He had preached or lectured more than thirty times during the period, and in a single day had delivered retreat conferences for seven hours. In addition to the cardinal's customary activities, he was faced with the disagreeable battles over St. Edmund's. There is no reason to doubt his sincerity when, after hearing of a priest who wanted to be elevated to the episcopate, he wrote: "I should dread seeing any one made a bishop in England who sought it. It shows but a poor estimate of the labour & burthen, not to speak of its responsibility anywhere."[1]

One of Wiseman's most painful burdens was the unceasing complaints, often unjustified, designed to prejudice the Roman authorities against him. In February 1857, for example, he responded to the charge that the English bishops were building small churches, thereby "wasting the money on ornament in preference to size," a practice intended to "make them so rich that the poor cannot go into them." It was further reported that the floors were covered "with rich & magnificent carpets, on which the poor are afraid to tread." Wiseman wrote to Talbot: "You know the falsehood of these charges. . . . As to the carpets, the matter is too laughable, though it gives me the key to the delator." He blamed the lies on an Italian priest whom he had refused to admit into the archdiocese, "for many reasons, some arising from immorality." The man had come to England with letters of commendation from three cardinals, but there had been "bad accounts of his conduct even at Rome." Wiseman added, "These suspended priests from abroad are a plague." He then described a Frenchman, recommended by the late archbishop of Paris, whom the cardinal had recently "been obliged to suspend for *frightful immorality*." He noted, "I have resolved to take no more on any account." [2]

It may have been experiences of the kind described for Talbot that led Wiseman to confine the activities of the priests at the newly constructed St. Peter's Church, Hatton Garden, to Italian-speaking people. He had previously stated "that the benefits to accrue from such a church should not be limited to them, but that all foreigners in London might have access to it." When he changed his mind, it was suggested that he wanted to wrest control of the spacious building from the Italian priests serving there in order to use it as his procathedral. It is far more likely, in fact, that he was attempting to reduce the activities of foreign priests in the archdiocese so that he would have a ready excuse for refusing to accept those of doubtful character who might apply for admission. [3]

Wiseman's reluctance to welcome foreign clergy into the archdiocese must not be interpreted as a loss of zeal on behalf of works that he had previously supported. On the contrary, his increasing awareness of pastoral needs, especially among the poor, made it all the more imperative for him to engage the right kind of people. He urged religious communities to take as their model St. Vincent dePaul, who in the seventeenth century brought about "a complete revolution in the ideas which, till then, had prevailed of the religious life." He praised those who chose active, as distinct from cloistered or monastic, apostolates. Speaking on behalf of the Great Ormond Street Hospital, entrusted to the Sisters of Mercy, Wiseman declared, "The unwholesome court, the narrow, uncleansed staircase, a fit approach to the sick man's garret, those are the only cloisters where the nun can now take her walks and muse of holy things." The sister's community rooms would be "four walls within which 500 children learn to play, or the infected ward with its double row of beds and its 500 sick. She must find it in the infant school, the industrial school, the refuge for penitents, the orphan asylum, or the hospital." Praising the courage of these same nuns during the Crimean War, he now asked rhetorically, "Could there be a more complete overthrow of the monastic life?" [4]

Wiseman established the first Catholic reformatory in England at Hammersmith in 1855 to serve the needs of the increasing number of juvenile delinquents in the country, many of them Catholic. In 1856 he supported a similar foundation begun by the Cistercians at Mount St. Bernard's, Leicestershire, in the diocese of Nottingham. When Abbot Bernard Burder took up this work, he was opposed by the general of the order and some of the monks. Such activities, it was argued, were not in accordance with the contemplative life of a Cistercian. Burder then sought to withdraw his community from the control of the continental Cistercians and to place it under a French Benedictine monastery, but he was faced with near revolt. The cardinal at first sided with the abbot, describing his opponents as "ill advised monks [who] do not care a pin if, to answer their ends, the whole thing be broken up in one day." Three hundred Catholic boys would then be sent to Protestant institutions or to jail. He warned that the result would be "the dreadful scandal given of throwing up a holy work and making Protestants exult that Catholics cannot do what they undertook & that the boasted efficiency of religious orders for great works of charity has been tested & found wanting."[5]

The cardinal was appointed as visitor to Mount St. Bernard's, where he listened to all of the complaints and ultimately directed that the administration of the reformatory should be separated from that of the religious house. He had discovered that there had been serious abuses and that the institution had been subject to gross mismanagement. The abbot resigned in 1858, and in January of the following year Wiseman was able to report that after visiting the place, he had "left all in peace, the Community most happy, with Abbot Bruno [Fitzpatrick] of Mount Melleray in charge to settle all down."[6]

Disagreements among the members of the English hierarchy were not confined to college questions and finances, nor was the cardinal always on the side of the minority. It was Bishop Ullathorne who in 1857 found himself opposed by the majority of his colleagues, including the cardinal. The difficulty concerned the question of government grants for the maintenance and building of elementary schools belonging to various religious denominations. The Catholic Poor School Committee had been dealing with the ministry and ultimately agreed that acceptance of aid had to entail some government supervision over the schools. Its extent was to be determined by the so-called Kemerton Trust, which defined the terms under which schools receiving building grants should be held and administered.

Early in 1857 Ullathorne published a pamphlet in which he urged extreme caution. He followed it up by a letter in the *Tablet* of April 4, where he observed: "It has industriously been stated that the bishops have formally approved the model trust deed. This is incorrect. Points in debate were repeatedly referred to the bishops, but the trust deed itself was never discussed by them." He opposed it on the grounds that religious liberty would be jeopardized, and he argued that building grants under the trust deed should be refused.[7]

The bishops discussed the matter at their annual Low Week meeting, and on May 2 the *Tablet* published a declaration by Wiseman, who in the name of the bishops stated that the trust deed could be accepted safely: "The faithful should not be harassed and perplexed by the raising anew of questions long since solved, after full and deliberate consideration. The whole question of education grants has been reopened, as if the model deed had not been maturely examined till now. Such a view is completely erroneous."[8]

Ullathorne interpreted Wiseman's declaration as a personal rebuke and wrote to his clergy to deny that he had been privy to the resolution of the bishops. Less than a week later he again wrote to the Birmingham clergy, stating that he had been in communication with Wiseman and had discovered that at the opening of the training school at Hammersmith, attended by all of the bishops except Ullathorne and three others, it was resolved that Wiseman should write an open letter to the chairman of the Poor School Committee to express confidence in its work. It had not been the cardinal's intention to allude to Ullathorne's writings.[9]

Fearful that the Birmingham bishop's letters to his clergy would lead to misunderstanding and scandal, the cardinal distributed a questionnaire to all of the bishops asking whether or not, at their Low Week meeting, they had reached the decision that Catholics could safely accept building grants; whether they had agreed that the Kemerton Trust deed might be accepted as the condition of such a grant; and whether they wanted their agreement to be communicated to the public "for their guidance and to put an end to the agitation existing in the Catholic mind on the subject." He considered the answers to the questions "of great importance to my own character, as well as for the regulations of our future meetings," but he assured his colleagues that he had no intention of publishing anything on the subject or of appealing to the public. Wiseman was convinced that Ullathorne's letters had implied that he had gone too far on his own authority by publicly supporting the policy of the Poor School Committee with respect to the grants and by indicating that he was acting on behalf of the other bishops.[10]

Bishop Ullathorne also wrote to his episcopal colleagues, complaining that they had not reached agreement at their Low Week meeting, contrary to the impression given by Wiseman. The bishops had not agreed to support a public resolution, and it was only later, after consulting a group of bishops (four of them having been absent), that the cardinal had acted. Ullathorne now observed that a document of such gravity "should surely have been drawn up and revised with all the care of a Synodal decree." He argued that if Wiseman had submitted his letter for possible revision by the bishops, especially those who had been absent when it was agreed that he should write it, they would have been spared "the distress of this painful controversy." He then concluded, "But if the incident should lead to a stricter adherence to rule and method in our extra Synodal Meetings, I am not alone in thinking that a great good may result."[11] His point was valid: Wiseman had failed to exercise due caution in consulting all of the other bishops and in ascertaining their views before taking action.

The cardinal wrote to Talbot, "A most unfortunate quarrel has arisen between the Bp. of Birmingham & myself, in consequence of his addressing printed circulars to the clergy of Birmingham & the newspapers, denying my right to address Mr. [Charles] Langdale [chairman of the Poor School Committee] in the name of the Bishops, who commissioned me on education." In addition, he wrote, Ullathorne had written "a really insulting letter" to him, as well as another to the bishops: "I have so far been perfectly passive, but the matter must go before Rome or our Synod."[12]

The following year, when a royal commission was established to look into the whole question of popular education, the cardinal, fearful that cooperation with the body might endanger Catholic endowments, proposed that the question of school inspectors should be discussed synodically.[13] The third provincial synod had initially been scheduled for the summer of 1858, but in view of the complex matters that were to be brought before it, the decision to postpone it for a year was probably wise.

Although it was in the summer of 1858 that the Westminster Chapter launched the investigation which caused so much anguish for the cardinal, the subsequent two months were also marked by two extremely pleasant interludes, one of them a virtual triumph. On July 19 Wiseman attended the golden jubilee celebrations of Ushaw College. The dignitaries also included the bishops of Beverley, Hexham, Edinburgh, Nottingham, Clifton, and Northampton; Monsignor Talbot, who came from Rome; and representatives of the colleges in England, including Herbert Vaughan. David Milburn has observed, "It was more the cardinal's jubilee than Ushaw's: for months he had been planning every small detail of the celebrations, arranging the speakers, composing the ode which John Richardson put to music, writing the play which was performed in the college hall."[14] This was the kind of effort that Wiseman loved. The festivities provided amusement and recreation that he sorely needed and that, except for rare occasions of this kind, he had lost when withdrawn from college life more than a decade earlier.

The following month the cardinal traveled to Ireland, where he had been invited to preach at the opening of a new church at Ballinasloe. The visit to his maternal homeland developed into a grand tour during which he was received enthusiastically as he moved from city to city. His sermons, speeches, and the many ceremonial functions to welcome him received widespread coverage in the press. He identified himself with Irish Catholics, telling an audience in Waterford that he had listened to stories by his mother, "whose warmest recollections and most affectionate feelings were connected with this city." She had described for him "what my ancestors had to endure to preserve the faith — how they shared in the confiscations and spoliations of property, which were the heirlooms of every Catholic in those days." [15]

The breadth of Wiseman's interests also won recognition and admiration from Protestants. In Dublin he was invited to dine at the Mansion House, along with Charles Bright, engineer of the Atlantic cable. The lord mayor greeted the cardinal as "a distinguished guest whose name is inscribed upon the roll of illustrious literary celebrities of this age, and whose exertions in the cause of science have met with grateful recognition from men of all creeds in the country of his adoption." Monsignor Talbot accompanied Wiseman throughout the three-week tour, and it is safe to conjecture that their conversations must have touched frequently upon the battles that were taking shape in the Westminster archdiocese. [16]

During his visit to Ireland the cardinal spoke in favor of the conservative parliamentary candidate for Waterford, who, in fact, won the seat. Wiseman was convinced that Catholics, in spite of party loyalties, had to proceed as a united body in supporting those who might advance their cause. He had tried to avoid associating himself publicly with any party, although Catholics were normally identified with the Whigs, from whom, it was felt, they had the most to gain.

Early in 1857 Wiseman had published an unsigned article in which he listed the considerations that should motivate Catholics when offering their support to politicians. He had suggested that the government of Lord Palmerston, formed in February 1855, was preferable to the Tory opposition of Lord Derby, since "knowing Lord Palmerston and all his tricks, his caprices, his waywardnesses, his inconsistencies, it [the Catholic body] will rather have *him* with them all, than one untried whose deficiencies and redundancies when in actual power are as yet unknown." [17] Although he denied that there would be any difference in foreign policy between Palmerston's party and that headed by Derby, he soon changed his mind when the government persisted in supporting Piedmont, which was threatening the very existence of the papal states.

According to Philip Hughes, the fact that English Catholics continued to support the maintenance of the states of the church served "very mischievously, to confirm the general Protestant prejudice that Catholics must defend the indefensible when ordered to do so, and the prejudice, also, that their religious belief was bound up with an allegiance to that whole bad order of things, social and political, which the French Revolution had all but destroyed entirely." [18] It was certainly Wiseman's loyalty to the papacy which ultimately led him to support the Tory ministry that came into power in 1858, but the Tories were themselves turned out a year later. Writing of Wiseman's known prejudice, E. R. Norman has noted that it "had the unfortunate effect of making the new Government look with a jaundiced eye on the Roman Church and its election tactics. They were left prepared to believe anything."[19]

Benjamin Disraeli, chancellor of the exchequer in Derby's ministry, expressed his gratitude to the cardinal, who, he said, had supported them "ungrudgingly, without solicitation, and without condition, and with that true feeling which can only be promoted by a high sense of duty." Wiseman wrote to Talbot in June 1859: "The ministry, I suppose, changes today. It must be owned, we lost by it. Still never has the position of Catholics stood so high in England as now. Our importance even politically is quite recognised." The general public exaggerated Catholic influence, however: "Of course I need not tell you that 'my compact with Lord Derby,' & my sending people to Ireland to stand, were pure lies, and inventions." The cardinal was not unduly concerned by the accusations but remarked that "the imputation of such things shows the strange ideas they entertain of our power."[20]

It was understood, in fact, that the support of the bishops, especially in Ireland, could be valuable for parliamentary candidates. In November 1857 John Acton, only twenty-three years of age, had written to Wiseman to seek his support in obtaining an Irish constituency, through which he might win a seat in Parliament. Acton asserted that "the election will be decided mainly by the influence of the clergy," and he had been advised by the archbishop of Dublin to ask Wiseman to write to the bishop of Waterford on behalf of his candidacy. The young would-be candidate acknowledged the advantage of his relationship with his stepfather, Lord Granville, a member of the cabinet: "But I have no thoughts of ever making use of it to push my own ventures, and I have distinctly stated both to Lord Granville and to Lord Palmerston that though disposed generally in favour of their government, I cannot promise them a definite support and I have mentioned one or two questions upon which I shall most decidedly oppose them."[21]

Acton had been a student at Oscott when Wiseman was president there. Whether or not his assertion of independence was meant to lead the cardinal to the belief that, as a member of Parliament, he would be more willing to support the cause of the papacy than was the government with which his stepfather was identified, nothing came of his attempt in 1857. In the 1859 election, however, he accepted the Liberal nomination for Carlow and was a member of the house that turned out the Derby government.

The cardinal, in fact, would have little cause to place his confidence in the future Lord Acton. The young man had been a student and companion of Wiseman's onetime friend, Döllinger, who was becoming increasingly vocal in opposing the papacy's ultramontane claims regarding its authority. Acton was closely identified with his former mentor and used the pages of the *Rambler*, in which he held an interest, to advance his views. In October 1858 Wiseman wrote: "The *Rambler* unfortunately is getting worse and worse, more anti-Roman, more cynical, more low in moral tone. John Acton is completely in Döllinger's hands, and by no means Roman—but the contrary."

It had appeared for a time that the *Dublin Review* "was on the point of falling into the hands of the *Rambler* people." In fact Acton had entered into preliminary negotiations with a view to fusing the two journals, but Wiseman prevented the merger: "If the Review became the organ of that party, it would rule opinion throughout England, and the consequences would be disastrous." Fearful that the success of one of the two journals would mean the demise of the other, the cardinal worked hard with Frederick Oakeley, an Oxford convert and now a priest of the archdiocese, to give the *Dublin Review* "a new and effective direction . . . , and make it thoroughly a high toned and orthodox superior quarterly." He predicted a battle, however, since he was surrounded by "the old, Dr. Griffiths & half-Gallican party," the Westminster Chapter being "sad proof of it." He noted sadly, "I never felt so lonely as now."[22]

Wiseman anticipated correctly the editorial tone of the *Rambler*, founded in 1848 by John Moore Capes, a convert, and taken over a decade later by Acton and Richard Simpson. It represented the liberal Catholic interest in England, composed of men concerned, above all, with "the task of raising the level of thought and learning amongst English Catholics."[23] Even aside from his identification with Döllinger, Acton's admiration for German scholarship and his own brilliant erudition would have made him a formidable challenge for more cautious Catholics, especially the bishops, who considered ecclesiastical judgments to be their own distinctive preserve. It was unfortunate, however, that Wiseman and Acton could not have cooperated with one another. At one time the cardinal's hopes for the Catholic community resembled, up to a point, those of the young historian, and both men were among the most intellectually enlightened and cosmopolitan Catholics of their day. Wiseman, however, was too thoroughly Roman (and perhaps too paternal) to tolerate the critical stance of Acton and Simpson toward traditional Catholic scholarship and current ecclesiastical issues.

Very soon after Acton and Simpson had become proprietors of the *Rambler* in February 1858, Wiseman realized that he could not count on their support. In June of that year they published an article by Mark Tierney, canon of Southwark and longtime opponent of the cardinal's policies, in which the author found fault with him over a question of historical fact. Tierney had taken it upon himself to defend the reputation of his late friend, John Lingard, which, he felt, had suffered through the cardinal's influence. As Tierney wrote to Newsham: "It is due to him [Lingard] & to us all to set him forth in his true light, to shew what he really effected for religion, and thus to destroy the venom which the satellites of Golden Square [the archbishop's house] are beginning to pour out on his memory." In a memoir on Lingard, Tierney had stated that Pope Leo XII, hoping to retain the historian in Rome, had named him a cardinal *in petto* in 1826. The cardinal, in his *Recollections of the Last Four Popes*, disputed the claim and argued that it was Lamennais, not Lingard, whom the Holy Father had secretly elevated to the cardinalate. After reading the account, Tierney became enraged. "You have no doubt seen the dishonest attempt of Wiseman, in his cumbrous & inflated volume on the Popes, to deprive Lingard of the honour of having been selected by Pope Leo for the purple."[24]

A review of Wiseman's book in the April issue of the *Rambler* made it a point to side with Tierney in the dispute, and in June a letter from Tierney himself was published:

> To Cardinal Wiseman, in his spiritual capacity, I hope I shall always manifest that respectful deference which is due to his exalted position. But the Cardinal Archbishop is one thing, the public writer or lecturer is another. The former, moving in the sphere and surrounded by the legitimate attributes of his authority, may justly claim our respectful regards; the latter, entering the common lists, and prepared to maintain his challenge "against all comers," waives every distinction of rank or place, and meets us as an equal, on an equal field. His talents may be more brilliant, his reputation more extended, his powers more renowned; but he has come down from his sanctuary, he has laid aside the purple, he has assumed the arms of the champion, and the bearing of the assailant; and the contest, therefore, which he has himself provoked, must be conducted on the principles, and decided only by the ordinary rules, of literary warfare.

The cardinal sought verification of his position by writing to Montalembert, who had been associated with Lamennais in seeking the pope's approval of the liberal Catholic movement in France. The Frenchman replied that he had not become acquainted with Lamennais until November 1830: "But during the three years of my intimate intercourse with him, and during his second journey to Rome, where I accompanied him in 1832, I constantly heard his friends and disciples allude to the fact of his intended elevation to the cardinalate by Leo XII. Whether or not he was actually made a cardinal *in petto*, I do not remember."[25] The information was less satisfactory than Wiseman would have hoped.

Both Tierney and Wiseman provided substantial evidence to support their claims for what today seems a purely academic and unimportant dispute. They saw it in another light, however, since Lingard was recognized as representative of what Wiseman and those associated with his views considered to be the old Catholic mentality, mistrustful of Roman interference in their affairs and opposed to devotional innovations in England. If proof were available that he had been elevated to the cardinalate, his reputation and the credibility of his position would have been advanced. Wiseman viewed the support that the *Rambler* gave to Tierney as a sign that its proprietors were among his opponents. He prepared a response in the form of a letter addressed to his chapter, which was printed privately and distributed among some of the clergy. He warned its recipients that he did not want the letter published, in whole or in part. Tierney responded by also preparing a privately printed letter, in which he questioned the cardinal's authorities and repeated the basis of his own view, a letter from Gradwell, who had been rector of the English College in Rome at the time. [26]

Richard Simpson, having sided with Tierney, was not prepared to back out of a battle. Father Isaac Hecker, an admirer and friend of Simpson, once described him as "the long iron snout of the Merrimac, pitching into the sides of all the old hulks she can find." In that spirit Simpson defended himself and the *Rambler* in a letter to the cardinal and then paraphrased its contents for Acton.

> I bestow a reproof on him [Wiseman] for concluding that the R[ambler] had identified itself with Tierney's view. . . . Then proceeding in a friendly way I say that it is the accumulation of such little mistakes that breeds an atmosphere of suspicion against that estimable monthly — that this unhappily creates difficulties in our path, and unjustly hurts us — which is not a small thing to men who with a good conscience make writing their occupation. That I have heard no end of misquotations as well as misrepresentations of what I, lamblike, have innocently said, and that things without guile had been denounced to him by those who knew nothing about the matter — but that he — who knows all things — should attend to such bosh comes only from his foolish misgivings about the R[ambler]. So it came to pass that Aug[ustine] was called the Father of J[ansenism] and the writer of these words was likened to the father of Lies.

The last reference was to a review article in the August issue of the *Rambler*, written by Acton but attributed by Wiseman to Simpson, in which the author had said, "Nor because St. Augustine was the greatest doctor of the West, need we conceal the fact that he was also the father of Jansenism." With reference to the cardinal's dispute with Tierney, Simpson concluded, in an article published in November 1859, "that it seemed probable to him that Lamennais's passion and Lingard's accuracy had ensured that both of them had been awarded the Cardinal's hat."[27]

Wiseman was especially offended when Acton, in February 1859, published an article on the Catholic press in which he commented upon the decline of the *Dublin Review*. He attributed this to the journal's encouragement of "the insane delusion that scientific infidelity is not, like heresy, an antagonist that it behoves Catholics to encounter; that misbelievers and disbelievers must be allowed to fight it out between them, and the dead left to bury their dead; that no danger threatens the Church from that party, and that Catholics have no special duty towards it."[28]

The cardinal and the other bishops were finally goaded into action when S. N. Stokes, a well-known Catholic school inspector, criticized, in the pages of the *Rambler*, the opposition that the bishops had voiced against a Royal Commission on Education set up in 1858. On February 13, 1859, the cardinal met with Archbishop Errington and Bishops Grant and Ullathorne, and together they decided to demand that Simpson should withdraw from the editorship of the journal or risk its episcopal condemnation. As a result of further negotiations, Newman was approached and asked to serve as editor. While not approving of the tone of much that appeared in the *Rambler*, he had wholeheartedly supported its objectives. He reluctantly accepted the position, but in the first issue under his direction he supported Stokes.

> Acknowledging, then, most fully the prerogatives of the episcopate, we do most unfeignedly believe, both from the reasonableness of the matter, and especially from the prudence, gentleness, and considerateness which belongs to them personally, that their Lordships really desire to know the opinion of the laity on subjects in which the laity are especially concerned. If even in the preparation of a dogmatic definition the faithful are consulted, as lately in the instance of the Immaculate Conception, it is at least as natural to anticipate such an act of kind feeling and sympathy in great practical questions, out of the condescension which belongs to those who are *forma facti gregis ex animo.*[29]

It was Newman's turn to be in trouble for implying that the laity were to be "consulted" prior to the definition of Catholic doctrine. At the recommendation of his own bishop, he agreed to give up the editorship. Before doing so, however, he edited one more issue in which he published his famous essay, "On Consulting the Faithful in Matters of Doctrine."[30] Ultimately the article has been viewed as a major contribution in the development of a theology of the laity. Its immediate consequences, however, were extensive criticism from some members of the hierarchy, including Wiseman, and serious mistrust on the part of the ecclesiastical authorities in Rome. The article appeared in the very month that the English hierarchy assembled for the third provincial synod, so that the cardinal, at that moment, had issues with which to contend that were far more personally pressing than the points raised by Newman.

On the eve of the third synod Cardinal Wiseman felt more and more isolated and lonely, in spite of the enthusiasm with which his public appearances had been greeted. His major objectives had not changed throughout the years, but he had not anticipated the extent of the controversies that would surround him, nor had he expected that his closest friends and associates would oppose his policies. He wrote to his nephew: "I never have felt more thoroughly alone than I have been for some months. I feel as if I was living in a frozen atmosphere."[31] Yet it was scarcely two months since he had returned from his triumphant Irish tour.

Feeling the need for close friends, in whom he might confide and from whom he might receive encouragement, the cardinal turned more and more to those who were younger. These young men, however, while lending him the desired support, did little to calm his spirit. In fact, the harshness of their judgments could only have contributed to his sense of despair. Herbert Vaughan, for example, concluded that there was "now a movement . . . evidently designed to drive the Card[inal] out of England: formerly it was the laity who tried to remove him: now it is Dr. Errington, Grant and [the] Westminster Chapter." Vaughan urged his correspondent, Monsignor Talbot, living in Rome, to read an account of events in the archdiocese that he had recently sent him and continued by passing upon Archbishop Errington one of the harshest judgments that can be made upon a priest: "Dr. Errington seems really to care nothing for souls — 'if 1000 souls are damned *by rule* it is God's look out, not mine,' he says — forgetting that if *he* makes the *rule*, it will be *his look out*." Vaughan contrasted the archbishop with Cardinal Wiseman, who had "become much more spiritual." Vaughan added that Searle, the cardinal's secretary, "always did him harm."[32]

Such statements ought not to be taken seriously. Errington, Grant, and Searle had been intimately associated with Wiseman when Vaughan was still a boy and, in Errington's case, before he was born. The cardinal had once been thoroughly devoted to them, and they to him. At a time when relationships had been strained to the breaking point, men like Vaughan should have moderated their rhetoric in the interest of peace; instead they made matters worse by inflammatory judgments and accusations.

Cardinal Wiseman issued the formal summons to the third provincial synod on March 25, 1859. Three days later he directed Bishop

Grant and the Southwark Chapter to submit, for the consideration of the synod, the question of chapter deputies for advising the bishop on seminary affairs, according to their petition to the Holy See. All of the bishops knew that college matters would be the central issue on the agenda, and, accordingly, Bishop Ullathorne had suggested that the participants "should enter into the whole question of clerical education *a fundamentis.*" He was himself reluctant to enter directly into the discussions: "Not being involved personally in the controversy, happily for myself, I feel that my position is one of delicacy towards those who are."[33]

Ullathorne then proposed to Wiseman that the bishops should "take in hand the 18th chapter of the 23rd session of the Council of Trent [relating to seminaries] and consider it article by article with regard to what is and what is not applicable to our state and condition, what is and what is not expedient." He pointed out that they would then be following the plan urged by the Holy See, since they would be making use of the common law of the church as their text and guide. The Tridentine directives would also provide the bishops with a basis for their considerations and would be a means to "accomplish your Eminence's idea of discussing the question of law and right first, and of equity and expediency afterwards."[34]

The bishops devoted the greater part of their annual spring meeting to preparations for the synod. The cardinal wrote that the gathering during Low Week had been "the longest and most full of matter of any I ever remember, having lasted four whole days." Archbishop Errington was there and proposed that the bishops should place the Westminster Chapter dispute on their agenda for the synod. Wiseman objected that his differences with the chapter were not appropriate matter for a synod; he refused to allow Errington to read aloud the chapter's petitions. He conceded, however, that the portions of both the Westminster and Southwark petitions which related to general questions on the condition and government of ecclesiastical seminaries could be discussed and that in fact the Holy See had referred the matter to the synod. The petition of the four northern bishops who requested a role in the government of Ushaw could be treated in the same manner.[35]

Wiseman had hoped that his coadjutor would refrain from participating in the synod itself, and Monsignor Talbot cooperated by urging Errington to accept the archbishopric of Trinidad. The cardinal wrote: "The most important thing is that he should not be in a position entitling him to be in synod. If within reach, the majority of bishops would call him in and give him a vote, unless it was understood that it must not be done." Wiseman had one minor reservation regarding Talbot's suggestion: "One would not like to send him away while unwell or to encounter summer heat, though I suppose every season is about the same in the W[est] I[ndies]." Talbot persisted: "I think that as soon as his health will allow him, it would be desirable for him to go to Trinidad. . . . I sincerely believe him to be just the man for Trinidad, although I am certain he will never do for Westminster."[36]

A delegation of bishops, headed by Turner of Salford, approached the cardinal during the Low Week meeting to see if they could assist in restoring peace between him and his coadjutor. Wiseman informed them that he had already written to the Holy See in order to arrange for Errington's removal, and that nothing could be done to reverse the proceedings. Immediately after the meeting he discovered that Bishop Grant had written to Propaganda on behalf of the archbishop of Trebizond. In his letter Grant stated that at a private conference during the meeting of bishops he had spoken to some of his colleagues regarding the proposed translation of Errington to Trinidad. The loss to the English church would be a major one, argued Grant, since, with the exception of the cardinal, Errington was the most learned of the bishops. In addition he was experienced in mission work and familiar with the system that had existed under the vicars apostolic, as well as that which had been established by the hierarchy. Finally, he was known and trusted by the Holy See, having been assigned several commissions by Propaganda itself.[37]

Wiseman reacted immediately to the news of Grant's action by asking Bishop Roskell for information. Once before, when Grant was designated by the other bishops to deal with the government in matters related to Catholic soldiers and sailors, Roskell had assured the cardinal that hereafter he would act only in union with him. Since Wiseman was convinced that the bishop of Southwark was again representing some of the other bishops, he wrote, "You will . . . confer on me a most signal favour by giving me any information in your power respecting this delegation of Dr. Grant to complain of me at Rome and solicit the rejection of my petition, and if you know, what are its grounds and motives."[38]

Contrary to Wiseman's suspicion, Roskell, known to be Errington's friend, had no information and, in fact, claimed to be shocked by "the want of delicacy in the bishop of Southwark." He suspected that Grant had acted on his own: "I suppose Dr. Grant thinks this petition was the least he could do after helping Dr. Errington into the scrape." The bishop of Nottingham offered to investigate what had been done, as well as when and how it had been accomplished.[39]

In the meantime Wiseman had already written to Cardinal Barnabò, stating that Grant had violated the first principles of ecclesiastical law, not to mention common courtesy, by having failed to provide any intimation of his intention. Unknown to him, however, the cardinal prefect of Propaganda was seeking information from Bishop Ullathorne as to what was behind the Westminster dispute: "This matter is very serious. Therefore I ask your Amplitude, whose prudence I have come to appreciate, to tell me *secretly* what you think has happened between the archbishop and his coadjutor, and what your opinion may be concerning their relationship." Ullathorne demonstrated the prudence that Barnabò so admired by refusing to meddle in a matter confined to a diocese other than his own.[40]

At the Low Week meeting Bishop Grant had proposed that the bishops, in preparing for their synod, should revert to the procedure followed in 1852. Wiseman was asked to draw up the proposed decrees and to circulate them in advance in order to receive the suggestions and comments of his colleagues. He accepted the challenge, but knowing that there would be contradictory opinions on the decrees, instead of expanding them, he thought it wiser to explain in detail the topics to be treated and to outline the various aspects under which they might then be framed.[41]

With care and deliberation the cardinal outlined a manner of procedure that would have covered the various points in dispute concerning the colleges: "It was necessary to give a line and direction to our enquiries," he wrote, "and I cannot but hope that the one I have proposed *forces* every bishop to look the law in the face and either take it, or if the majority decides *against* it, they must *say* that they do so." The document he produced—"Elenchus et Analysis"—was a perceptive summary of the issues to be discussed and a clear analysis of the various possibilities concerning the legislation to be enacted.[42]

Most of the cardinal's document was devoted to colleges or seminaries (*de collegiis seu seminariis*). The section was introduced by the letter which Cardinal Fransoni had written to Wiseman in 1855, when asking that the subject might be treated by the second synod. The cardinal prefect had urged the English bishops "to take into consideration the method followed in the colleges and seminaries for giving young ecclesiastics a thorough training in piety and learning, and to lay down at least the fundamental principles of the improvements to be introduced in order to obtain happier results." He had specifically called to Wiseman's attention "the most wise Tridentine prescriptions on this matter, and . . . the regulations introduced by holy prelates and recommended by happy experience." It would then be up to Wiseman and the other bishops "to make whatever regulations you may consider feasible and opportune, taking into account the state of the ecclesiastical establishments in England and other circumstances."[43]

Wiseman took this letter seriously and endeavored to present, as directed, a report on the state of English colleges and to suggest means of improvement. Faithful to the late cardinal prefect's advice, he examined carefully the prescriptions of the Council of Trent in the light of what was possible or feasible in England.

First of all, the cardinal discussed the means of assessing the state of each college so that the system might be reformed. Bishops who governed dioceses in which the colleges were located were advised to prepare written reports on the studies, religious exercises, and books used by the students. All of the bishops were asked to decide whether those preparing for the priesthood should be separated from the other students and, if so, the manner of bringing this about.

Wiseman then turned to the application of the rules of the Council of Trent, stating that the synod had to decide whether these could be adapted to the purpose and form of the English colleges or whether modifications were necessary. The Tridentine fathers had been concerned with seminaries in the strict sense and, in fact, with their foundation rather than with those already established. It had to be decided, therefore, whether the three English colleges were to be considered as seminaries and, if so, whether they had been constituted as such by reason of the establishment of the hierarchy. Presupposing that the act of 1850 had not, of itself, entitled them to be considered as seminaries, the cardinal listed several alternatives: they could be declared seminaries through legitimate apostolic decrees; they could be treated as colleges, rather than seminaries, in which case the Tridentine rules would not apply; or lastly, the bishops might petition the Holy See, asking that the colleges might remain as they were, but with the application of only those Tridentine regulations suggested by the provincial synod, not as a *right*, but by concession of the Holy See.

The next topic was the most difficult to resolve, that of the role of bishops in governing the colleges. Wiseman noted that according to the common law of the church, all holy places were under the jurisdiction, right of visitation, and supreme government of the bishop in charge of the diocese in which they were located. It was necessary to ascertain, then, whether any special law, decision of the Holy See, or any other factor placed the government of the English colleges in a unique category. The synod had to decide whether or not the colleges were so different from other institutions that the ordinary was not to be allowed his customary administrative role in their case. If it were determined that such was the case, the Holy See had to be asked to repeal the canon law, so that new legislation might be framed to provide for the situation. The cardinal's own position was clear, since he reminded his colleagues that, prior to the establishment of the hierarchy, bishops had no role in administering colleges outside of their own districts. The only right they could claim was that of educating their students there on a basis proportionate to their investment.

Wiseman suggested a compromise. The English colleges of Douai, Rome, Lisbon, and Valladolid had belonged to all of the vicars apostolic, who nevertheless had exercised no personal role in their government. Certain concessions had been made, however, either to individual bishops or to all of them jointly. For example, they were all entitled to nominate the rector of the English College in Rome. The cardinal suggested that the bishops who shared an interest in each college might act together in selecting the rector, nominating students, preparing an annual statement of accounts, and in any other matters that might seem wise to the synod.

He next turned to the question of deputies to advise the bishops on seminary affairs, presenting sections of the Westminster and Southwark chapter petitions that had sought a decision from the Holy See. Even if the prescriptions of Trent were to be applied, Wiseman argued, they were to exercise a consultative voice only. The bishop was never obliged to follow their advice. The Council of Trent, moreover, had presupposed certain facts. It had based its regulations on seminaries in the strict sense, and it had been taken for granted that these institutions were diocesan. It had also been presumed that the seminary would be located in the city where the bishop resided, near the cathedral, so that it would be accessible to all who were to share in its administration. Finally, the Tridentine decrees assumed that a certain and sufficient revenue had been provided for the seminary from the assets of the diocese.

Wiseman contended that the chapter as a whole had no legal grounds for considering itself to have a voice in administering the seminary. On the contrary, it had been excluded deliberately by the provision for specific chapter deputies. Therefore the synod should decree that a diocesan chapter had no authority, in itself and acting as a chapter, over the episcopal seminary, nor could it concern itself with its government and discipline. Neither in its ordinary meetings nor in those not summoned by the bishop could a chapter interfere in these matters, nor could it institute an investigation by asking for explanations from higher authorities. At the Low Week meeting, the cardinal had opposed the introduction of chapter rights into the synod's agenda, a fact he now conveniently overlooked.

In treating the topic of deputies, Wiseman reduced the matter to an absurdity by observing that if the Tridentine regulations were followed in the case of Ushaw, each diocese concerned in its administration would have to provide six deputies to oversee its affairs. Since five sees had some claim on the college, thirty-five men, including the bishops, would be involved. He asked whether such government was possible. Moreover, since English canons had been excused from residence in the episcopal city, some decision had to be reached regarding who was to summon meetings, how travel expenses were to be paid, and who was to provide the funds necessary to lodge thirty-five persons at the college during the annual visitation.

After treating other possible problems that would arise if the

Tridentine rules were to be followed, Wiseman outlined practical modifications that might be implemented. He suggested, for example, that the number of deputies could be lessened by special dispensation from the Holy See, although this would not resolve all of the difficulties. He concluded, finally, by warning that no matter what decisions were reached concerning the colleges, it was imperative that bishops and their chapters should avoid friction regarding their relative rights, usurpation of authority, and neglect of duty.

The "Elenchus et Analysis" was eleven pages long, and almost eight of them were devoted to college questions. The last two major sections of the document dealt with matters referred to the synod by the Holy See and some questions raised by the bishops at their Low Week meeting. Wiseman did not develop these topics, and they may now be left to the next chapter, insofar as they were dealt with by the synod.

The cardinal raised numerous important questions, then, and he was proud of the document. Its composition was an exhausting undertaking, but he was delighted when he received the enthusiastic support of the Abbé Ludovic Chaillot, editor of the *Analecta Juris Pontificii*, who came from Rome to act as his theologian at the synod. As Wiseman informed Talbot: "Abbé Chaillot is arrived and has cheered me much by bringing me the Holy Father's blessings on our labours and assurance of his kind feelings towards myself. He at once read over the papers which I sent you and Cardinal Barnabò the other day (*Elenchus & Analysis*) and has told me it was tres-bien put, and that the alternatives offered throughout were quite correct. To another person he said that the canon law through it was perfectly accurate. This is a further great encouragement."

Wiseman was realistic enough, however, to see that there would be a major struggle: "If I am not greatly mistaken, the wish of the *party* would be, was, & perhaps is yet, not to look at the questions through Canon Law, but just to ask what they liked, & patch up a new system of their own. This would lead to new and endless quarrels. I have therefore sought to give a clue to guide our deliberations, and force all to look the law in the face, and say plainly either we will have the law, or it cannot be applied, and therefore a new law must be framed." It was his conviction that if the entire law were applied to the English colleges, the result would be to "make the Church here completely constitutional, with parliaments or convocations — higher & lower houses — to govern our seminaries." He intended to do his utmost to avoid such a situation, at least in the archdiocese: "When this is over, I intend to apply to have the Metropolitan college put directly under the Holy See as a real Seminary. For thus Roman teaching will be secured, at least at headquarters, & if the metropolitan clergy are sound & zealous, the rest of England will be secured. And thus at least we shall be rid of all influence of Gallican canons." [44]

The deep divisions that surfaced during the third provincial synod were in sharp contrast to the harmony prevailing when the new hierarchy had assembled at Oscott seven years earlier. At that time there were very few changes in the decrees that the cardinal had prepared for the consideration of the assembled fathers. In 1859, however, his carefully worded "Elenchus et Analysis" was almost completely ignored.

15. The Cardinal's Last Synod

O N JULY 11, 1859, THE PARTICIPANTS IN THE THIRD PROVINCIAL synod of Westminster assembled at Oscott for their preliminary meeting. George Brown of Liverpool was the only bishop to have died since the previous synod, although three new bishops had been appointed since then. William Clifford of Clifton had not been present in an episcopal capacity in 1855, and William Vaughan of Plymouth had not been there at all. Wareing of Northampton had resigned in 1857 and been replaced by Francis Kerril Amherst, ordained by Wiseman at Oscott in 1846. Neither Wareing nor Hendren, both retired, assisted at the third synod.[1]

Bishop Briggs of Beverley had been under pressure to retire or to accept a coadjutor. He resisted all such suggestions: "I feel now quite as well in health as I did ten years ago. I have no difficulty in discharging all the duties of my office." He solicited support from his friends. Archbishop Errington wrote to Grant: "I have had a letter from Dr. Briggs about his going to have a coadjutor. Could nothing be done to stop this measure which will be very mischievous to the diocese in all probability as he does not want it?" He added, "I can't speak to the cardinal on this subject, of course."[2] Briggs was active in the synod and continued to govern his diocese unassisted until his retirement in November 1860, two months before his death.

With the exception of the college presidents, who were not invited to the third synod, all of the chief contenders in the various disputes were present in some capacity. The bishops, of course, all participated. John Maguire, whom Wiseman had dismissed as vicar general, came as the elected representative of the Westminster Chapter. The cardinal considered the chapter's selection to have been an insulting gesture, but it was less so than the Southwark Chapter's choice of Mark Tierney. Wiseman observed in a letter to Talbot: "The Duke of Norfolk has *dismissed* him from his chaplaincy for his last libellous attack on me—yet the Chapter send him, though half paralytic, to represent them, and his pamphlet has been allowed to be in theological students' hands at the College, and Dr. Weathers has quite exulted before others in Tierney's foul abuse of me! Are such men to direct our ecclesiastical students?"[3] Tierney became ill and had to excuse himself, but Wiseman could hardly have found consolation in Southwark's second choice, Daniel Rock, whom he had always considered to be a Gallican.

James O'Neal, one of the cardinal's two vicars general, assisted as Archbishop Errington's theologian. Manning attended as one of the preachers, and J. L. Patterson, whom the cardinal had sent to Rome to plead his case when the chapter controversy first arose, was one of the masters of ceremonies. Finally, Wiseman had an ally in John Morris, at that time a canon of Northampton, who served as one of the synod's secretaries.

Much to Wiseman's distress, Errington not only attended the synod but demanded the right to participate as fully as the other bishops. At the second synod he and Goss, both coadjutors, had been allowed the same role in all the proceedings as diocesan ordinaries. Errington feared that this would not be permitted in 1859, and he wrote to Cardinal Barnabò to find out what rights he could claim. Wiseman, in a letter to Talbot, also anticipated the difficulty: "We [he and Errington] had a long but quiet conversation in which he intimated that, though not *de jure*, by concession of the synod he becomes fully independent of me, and is in no way tied by being my coadjutor, but may take his own line without reference to my opinion or wishes. If there is an opposition, he will no doubt be at its head." Talbot replied that church law did not allow a coadjutor "to vote or speak against his principal, which would be tantamount to nullifying the vote of a diocesan bishop." He added, "I cannot conceive how such an idea could enter his head."[4]

In this case Talbot's reasoning was sound. Errington, however, was convinced that he could speak and act fully independently of the cardinal. He later explained that if he had been obliged to defend his superior's policies and position, he could see no reason why he should have had even a consultative voice in the proceedings. That privilege was never in question, in fact, and it was agreed that he should have it. Unlike his role in the second synod, however, he was not allowed a deliberative or voting voice, and a letter from the Holy See stated that the bishops had been within their rights in denying it to him.[5]

Participants were divided into special congregations, as at the other synods. Initially there were two of these, one for the college questions and another for all other topics. The bishops of Newport and Menevia,

Plymouth, and Clifton were on the second congregation since, as a result of Prior Park having been closed, they were no longer directly concerned with the administration of a college. Errington was also assigned to this congregation. Later the congregation for colleges was divided into two sections, one to deal with internal discipline and the other with the questions of government.

The first twelve decrees concerned matters of formality and were passed without debate. The various deliberations then began in earnest on July 13. Instead of following the procedure that Wiseman had outlined in his "Elenchus et Analysis," the congregation on colleges overlooked the first three chapters of the documents and turned immediately to the fourth, which dealt with the episcopal administration of the colleges. They concentrated, however, upon a proposal that had been drawn up and presented independently of Wiseman's suggestions.[6]

The cardinal complained that those who worked on the proposed decree were unwilling to consider canon law or the rights of the ordinary. They offered no explanation for the manner in which they arrived at their final proposals, "leaving them to the sacred congregation without any previous information, except for the fact that it seemed good to them." Considering the various petitions that had been sent to Rome, not to mention the plan which Wiseman himself had prepared for Ushaw College, Propaganda could not have been completely in the dark. On July 18 the cardinal wrote:

> The great endeavour on the part of the opposition is to *derogate* from the common law as much as possible when it is to be applied to the bishops' share in the college question, and to insist on its *application* in the very strictest letter where the chapters are concerned in the same question. In short, having got astride on the *jus commune* and council of Trent as canons, the old Gallicans stand up in their stirrups and run a tilt against diocesan bishops and their hierarchical rights. Their topics are chiefly the *joint endeavours* of the various bishops and their consequent *rights* in a joint government and jurisdiction.[7]

The result of their work may be seen in the fifteenth decree, dealing with college government. A résumé of its provisions will indicate how far it deviated from the cardinal's proposals. It was introduced by a brief explanation stating that the scheme was provisional, to be in force only until abolished by the Holy See and only provided that it did not cause any delay in establishing seminaries, "after the mode prescribed by the Council of Trent, as soon as possible in every diocese."[8]

The first article of the decree gave the ordinary of the see in which a college was located *spiritual* jurisdiction and care over the students. The right and authority to determine and arrange material and temporal matters (i.e., studies, government, and discipline) were to be the responsibility of a "board of bishops who have an interest therein." The bishop of Shrewsbury was assigned to the board for Ushaw, since he had a greater claim on that college than on Oscott.[9] Those bishops who had an interest in any one of the colleges were to nominate one to three proper persons to draw up an account of its assets within a year. The report should list its property of every kind, its sources of income, and the rights that in any way pertained to the college. The document was then to be sent to the Holy See.

The board of bishops for a college was to meet once a year, on a day agreed upon, and the first meeting was to take place within a year from the date of approbation of the synodical decrees. If at any time the majority of bishops should request it, the ordinary of the see in which a college was situated was obliged to summon an extraordinary meeting. The following statement was included with the secretaries' reports: "A strong objection was expressed to giving the power of calling the other bishops for an extraordinary meeting of visitation to the ordinary. It was felt that it would strengthen the notion and feeling that the seminary was *his,* and that an equal share and claim was denied to the other bishops. In the North, many were beginning to feel that the seminary belonged only to the diocese of Hexham." The participants were divided on the wording of the clause, and it remained unaltered.

The ordinary was likewise to preside over each meeting of the co-interested bishops, and, when the votes were equal, he was given the role of casting an additional and deciding one. Where only two dioceses were involved, however, the two bishops were to seek a solution from the Holy See. The last clause of this article was inserted as a result of Archbishop Errington's intervention. The only college limited to the interest of two bishops was St. Edmund's, and Errington observed that the cardinal would have an unwarranted advantage if the deciding vote were to be cast by the ordinary. At this point the cardinal lost his temper. He told the assembled bishops that Errington's interference had gone "beyond the limits of decency."[10]

Throughout the synod J. L. Patterson provided Monsignor Talbot with unofficial reports. Commenting upon the consultative voice that Errington was given, Patterson observed:

This he has had the *good taste* to use from the first moment till now in one undeviating and most vexatious course of opposition to every word and every proposition made by the cardinal. To such a length has this gone, that when a decree was passing on the basis of mutual concessions regarding the colleges on the part of the bishops, and it happened that that decree involved a very slight and unavoidable advantage accruing to the see of Westminster, he actually opposed that arrangement as coming from the cardinal. Thus the cardinal has the mortification to find his own alter ego — his coadjutor, putting himself against him in his own provincial synod.[11]

Patterson was allowing his loyalty to cloud his reason. Without the addition demanded by Errington, the advantage that would have gone to Westminster was not "very slight," nor, as the result proved, was it "unavoidable." Considering the disagreements that had already taken place between Wiseman and Grant, to have allowed the cardinal the final word in all cases of dispute would have been unthinkable. It may reasonably have been argued, however, that the intervention should have come from Bishop Grant, not from the Westminster coadjutor.

The next article assigned a role of vigilance and influence to the ordinary but bound him to adhere to the rules framed for the college and to the decrees agreed upon by himself and the other bishops. To guarantee the stability of college government, the ordinary was to make no essential changes without the approval of the bishops at their annual meeting.

The co-interested bishops were all responsible for appointing the college rector. He, in turn, was to name the vice-rector after obtaining the approval of the ordinary and the concurrence of the other bishops. Professors of theology and philosophy were to be appointed by the ordinary, with the consent of his colleagues, and others could be selected by the rector, with the approval of the ordinary alone. No student could be received into a college without a testimonial letter from his own bishop, and unless the case were one of extreme urgency, the rector could not expel a student without first receiving the approval of his bishop.

Cardinal Wiseman refrained from participation in framing the decree, nor did he vote for its passage. When it became clear that most of the time allotted to the synod would be devoted to this single subject, he set to work, with the encouragement of his colleagues, to prepare a decree on seminary deputies. It was adopted by the synod with little alteration. All of its provisions depended upon the status of the colleges: were it to be decided that they were not seminaries in the strict sense, there would be no need to introduce the Tridentine directives in this regard. The proposed decree, however, never received the approbation of the Holy See. It would have provided for a variation of the councils of deputies described by the Council of Trent's regulations. Each diocese would have had two counselors to advise the bishop on seminary affairs. Both men would have been chapter members: the first, appointed by the bishop, would have counseled him regarding discipline, studies, and other internal matters; the second, elected by the chapter, would have assisted the bishop with the seminary's financial concerns. The deputies would have had a consultative role only. When the bishop met with his colleagues for the annual college visitation, one of the two deputies would have accompanied him, normally the man elected by the chapter. Both deputies were to hold their offices for life. Finally, if the bishop were not able to attend the annual meeting on college affairs, he was to have been permitted to send a procurator, either the elected chapter deputy or the diocesan vicar general. The man appointed, in either case, would have had a deliberative voice in all proceedings.[12]

Wiseman complained that so much time was devoted to framing the fifteenth decree that no report had been prepared on the current state of the colleges, nor had recommendations been made for their improvement. In 1855 Cardinal Fransoni had stated that this should be done, so the cardinal was now urged to take on the task. He complied, and the result of his effort was a special decree on the colleges (decr. xiv, *de collegiis*). Part 1 treated their current state. He raised the difficulty that had persisted by educating clerics along with lay students, although the situation varied from one institution to another. Oscott had more lay students than clerics; the proportion was reversed at Ushaw; and although there were more clerics than lay students at St. Edmund's, the two groups were kept separate. The cardinal relied upon a report submitted to him by President Weathers.[13] Neither man considered the so-called mixed system to be ideal, but financial considerations led them to the conclusion that it could not be altered at that time. Moreover, as Wiseman observed, the scarcity of English colleges for the education of Catholics in higher studies justified the arrangement. Lay students were given the same basic education as those preparing for the priesthood, however, so that when it might have been possible to remove the former from the colleges, no major curricular changes would have been necessary. The rest of the first part of the decree was devoted to the spiritual formation within the colleges.

In the second part of the decree Wiseman listed some of the weaknesses of the English colleges. When nonclerical students were in the majority, as at Oscott, it was "difficult to prevent a worldly spirit from getting by degrees into the house and gaining an ascendancy over it." Second, the lack of priests and the poverty of the colleges made it necessary to appoint senior students for duties connected with administration and discipline. He suggested that an effort should be made to endow chairs and that a full four-year program of uninterrupted theological study should be demanded of those preparing for the priesthood. He also recommended that students should be given a thorough grounding in Hebrew, Latin, canon law, and pastoral theology.

On the second last day of the synod the cardinal noted that the bishops were unanimously agreed upon the necessity of instituting diocesan seminaries as described by the Council of Trent. He therefore suggested that the assembly should make its point by means of a reasoned statement of the objective. Again he was asked to prepare the decree; he worked through the last night, and his work was approved without criticism. It was a long decree which outlined the history of English ecclesiastical education and concluded by stating that all of the bishops would apply themselves carefully and earnestly to the task of founding seminaries, as best they could, in each of their sees (decr. xiii).

Three other decrees were approved by the synod, all of them meant to deal with problems that had been proposed for synodical discussion at the Low Week meeting.[14] One dealt with a problem of mission boundaries, and Wiseman framed the decree intended to solve it. It provided that when Catholics lived so near the church of another diocese that they attended its services and contributed to its support, they were to be considered as belonging to it. The decree's conclusion is its most significant directive and was based on common sense: "The first thing to be looked to is the salvation of souls; the manner of accomplishing this, if a lawful one, need not be too anxiously dwelt upon."

The next decree dealt with the *cathedraticum*, an annual tax paid to the bishop by all churches and benefices subject to his jurisdiction. An explanatory section of the decree stated that some dioceses were in a more favorable financial position than others and so could afford to pay more. Another decree, finally, dealt with the manner of dismissing, when necessary, missionary rectors as instituted by the first synod.[15]

Toward the end of the synod the cardinal raised the question of a chapter's right to interfere in matters outside of its competence. Errington later wrote: "One of the bishops observed that it was strange to enter upon this subject after it had been determined, upon the representation of his Eminence in the Easter meeting, that the subject was not to be treated in the synod." It had been included, however, in the "Elenchus et Analysis." When raising the subject during the synod, the cardinal asked his coadjutor to leave the assembly. Errington refused to do so and stated later that it was well that he had remained, since Wiseman would otherwise have deceived those present on a number of points.

The cardinal told the assembled fathers that his chapter had conducted its inquiry into the college like a trial. Errington denied the charge, insisting that the chapter members had only spoken among themselves, without demanding outside testimony. When Wiseman claimed that Manning had been refused permission to vote during the controversy, the coadjutor interrupted to point out that the members had wanted to proceed capitularly, with the provost's participation, and that it was Manning's own decision to take no part in framing the chapter's petitions. His eminence then observed that the chapter had refused his request that it modify the address which was presented to him. Errington intervened to state that Wiseman had not sought a modification but had demanded that the chapter proceedings should be canceled in their entirety. Finally, when Wiseman said that the Oblates were the same as those established by St. Charles and that he had never intended to place St. Edmund's under their care, his coadjutor denied the accuracy of both claims. The cardinal experienced an indescribable mortification, as he explained in a protest to Propaganda, when his coadjutor disagreed with him on every point, no matter its gravity or insignificance.[16]

The bishops in synod agreed that the chapter had no right to initiate or discuss capitularly questions of episcopal administration. John Maguire, serving as the chapter's elected representative at the synod, offered an immediate apology, bowing to the synod's decision and, in the name of the chapter, declaring "its regret for thus having exceeded its powers." It must be noted, however, that the chapter offered no apology for having addressed the cardinal on the question of implementing Trent's prescriptions but only for the "the addition to their petition," that is, for having entered into the question of the nature and purpose of the Oblates at St. Edmund's, a matter that concerned the cardinal's jurisdiction only.[17]

Archbishop Errington was annoyed that Wiseman should have raised the question of the chapter at all. He was even more distressed that the other bishops should have prepared their statement, making it appear as if they approved "all the cardinal did and condemn all the chapter did." His concern was groundless, however, in view of the fact that the bishops framed and approved another letter which left the major question unsettled: "Having maturely considered the question of the rights of chapters with reference to the administration of colleges, we are unable to determine what those rights precisely are in our peculiar circumstances."[18]

The cardinal prepared the synodical letter addressed to the faithful, although he had begged to be relieved of the task. He praised specifically the readiness of the laity to support the church: "At all times we have found you ready to come openly and boldly forward, to assert the principles of your religion and the claims of the Church. You have readily thrown into the scale, when needed, the weight of your rank, your ancient descent, your social position, and political influence; and, where Providence has not bestowed these, the weight of your numbers, and the unanimity of your voices." He cited, to demonstrate his observation, all that had been done by the Poor School Committee "in maturing and carrying measures which all now acknowledge to have procured most important advantages." Catholics now had "separate reformatories . . . on a footing of equality with those of others," and it was also due to their efforts that they had procured their own chaplains for the army, "honourably appointed, and treated as becomes their sacred office."

In commenting upon the Catholic Poor School Committee, Wiseman passed over in silence, as had the synod, the dispute concerning the acceptance of government grants. He pointed out a number of areas where Catholics were still not treated on an equal basis with their fellow citizens: men in the navy were deprived of the religious instruction and care that had been won for those in the army; Catholic prisoners were not placed on the same footing as Protestants in religious matters; and an equal justice was still to be obtained for those confined in workhouses.

Wiseman then returned to the subject of education for the poor and mentioned "the great negligence, — perhaps a growing negligence, — of parents in sending their children to Catholic schools." He begged that zeal on behalf of this cause might not diminish. He also urged support for the colleges, both in England and on the Continent, and expressed his gratitude to Sir John Sutton, a convert, who had established an English college at Bruges. Wiseman went on to discuss the importance of clerical education and said that the bishops had determined to labor and, "if it please God, to suffer — until we see accomplished the strong desire, or rather fulfilled the wise injunctions of the holy Council of Trent, that each diocese should have its own Seminary, episcopal in name and in character, dear to the Bishop as the apple of his eye, and jealously reserved to his own superintendence and vigilant solicitude (Sess. xxiii. cap. 18, De Reform.)." Of course there was no mention in the synodical letter of the various disputes in which the bishops were engaged.[19]

With the exception of the fifteenth decree, the achievement of the third synod was Wiseman's. Some authors have expressed the opinion that the decrees show the profound influence of Manning. There is no doubt that the cardinal relied on his chapter provost for advice and support. Shortly afterwards he wrote to Manning: "I seize the first moment that I can do anything to thank you for all your kind and valuable assistance and exertions for me at and before the synod." Those services, however, did not include the preparation of the decrees. The cardinal claimed that they were the result of his own efforts, and we have the same testimony from John Morris, a participant in the synod: "The whole of the decrees of the synod were written by Cardinal Wiseman with the exception of one, and the distinction is most remarkable. All run in the full and flowing phraseology of the cardinal's Latin, excepting the decree which makes provision for the joint government of the colleges by the bishops who were respectively interested in them." That particular decree, according to Morris, was prepared by Bishop Grant, assisted by Errington, "and it reads as curtly as a proposition in Euclid." The writer concluded caustically, "The contrast in style is characteristic of the diversities of mind of the writers."[20] There can be little doubt, in any case, that Wiseman deserves the praise or blame for all except one of the decrees.

Monsignor Talbot urged Wiseman to bring the final decrees to Rome personally: "I am afraid that you cannot trust any one of the bishops. I almost think that for many reasons you had better bring them yourself. But do not quote me for God's sake." In the same letter he commented upon the cardinal's plan to ask that St. Edmund's be made a pontifical college. According to Talbot, it would be "the only way of settling the matter," but he observed that Weathers would be "a most unfit person to be at the head of it." He suggested, instead, that Patterson might be appointed, since he was "thoroughly Roman." There was only one difficulty: "Of course there would be a tremendous cry-out, because he is a convert. The poor converts have a sad life of it in England."[21]

Wiseman planned on following Talbot's advice by traveling to Rome: "The acts of the synod must not be examined without my being there." He described the procedure followed by the bishops at the synod, where "everything was determined beforehand, to be carried by majorities — reasoning, canon law, all went for nothing." The results, if applied to the colleges, would be disastrous: "No college can go on three years with them."[22]

There were a number of other unresolved matters for which the cardinal's presence in Rome might be desirable. No decision had yet been reached regarding the financial dispute between him and Bishop Grant or, for that matter, on the less serious controversy with Ullathorne on the same subject; Errington's dismissal was about to be considered; the status of the English colleges had not been determined and the decrees of the synod depended upon a settlement of the question as to whether they were seminaries in the sense of those discussed by the Council of Trent; and finally, the role of the Oblates in St. Edmund's, and even their future as a community, was not secure.

Although the cardinal had planned to leave for Rome in early autumn, the conflicts and excitement of the previous year ultimately led to his serious illness, and he was forced to postpone the trip. It was rumored widely that he would resign, and Archbishop Errington tried to confirm the report. "If this reaches you in time," he wrote to Grant, "learn if possible from Searle or elsewhere if the cardinal does intend to remain in Rome, which would of course include the resignation of Westminster." There were weighty reasons, of course, for his concern: "This would be an important element in regulating the *modus* of my proceedings in Rome and even the time of my going."[23] The archbishop of Trebizond had no intention of remaining in England while the cardinal presented his own side of the case in Rome.

Wiseman ignored the rumors of his possible resignation until the following spring: "Whatever anyone may say, be quite assured that I have not the slightest intention of quitting my post." He was determined to carry on as long as possible: "I do not suppose that I shall have long to work, for my growing infirmities warn me of a brief future; but that shall be spent, with God's help and grace, in doing what I may be capable of in London."[24]

Those who opposed Wiseman made use of the time allowed them by his illness to prepare their case. Errington was more personally involved than anyone else. He urged Bishop Grant to accompany him to Rome to counter the cardinal's activities there: "It appears to me quite necessary for yourself & the college question & others that you should go." Grant had been concerned that Wiseman might make another attempt to reunite the southern part of London with the archdiocese, but Errington doubted that this would be the case, "for he has too many battles to fight, he has lost too much prestige by being defeated in the synod, & as I hear here [Errington was resting in Ireland] has disappointed & annoyed even the Pope by all these affairs considerably."

Errington reminded the bishop of Southwark that his dispute with Wiseman over finances might well be discussed in the near future: "Your finance question which most of all requires your presence may come on any time & will come on soon certainly. If you are away & the Cardinal present in Rome, the same I think about the synod matters. It is much more the wrong impressions which will be unofficially made upon the Congregation & the Pope than the official determinations on which very possibly you will never be consulted nor any of the Bps., that may be usefully encountered." It was above all the matter of the synod's work that motivated Errington, however: "Personally I am interested in this in as much as my defence must depend considerably on the synod decree being shown to be right and being carried through."[25]

Monsignor Talbot encouraged the cardinal on the eve of the battle: "You may be certain that the pope will grant you all you want, and that he will desire your coadjutor, who has been the cause of all your sufferings during the last year, to retire." When initially urging the cardinal to bring the synod's decrees to Rome, Talbot had written to Patterson: "I cannot see how Cardinal Wiseman can avoid coming to Rome to defend himself. Although he will have both the Archbishop and the Bishop of Southwark (who is a most mischievous person) to fight against, he will have no difficulty to carry every thing before him." Talbot went on to describe his opinion of Grant.

The Bishop of Southwark from his long residence in Rome has learnt all the trickiness, and underhand intrigues practised by some persons here, but he has not imbibed the generous, better Spirit, which I look upon as the great characteristic of the Holy See. I have reason to suppose that by means of his letters he has been doing an immense deal of mischief at Propaganda, and especially lately when he has been the great supporter of the Archbishop of Trebizond against Cardinal Wiseman. Besides he is the sworn enemy of all the converts who are active and zealous, although he professes friendship towards them. He is the great supporter of the old high & dry school.[26]

In spite of Talbot's fears and Errington's urgent pleading, Bishop Grant decided against making the trip. Although he lived for ten more years, it seems that he was already suffering from the disease that would end in his death.

Monsignor Talbot's interference in all of the subsequent events reduced the arguments to matters of personality far more than would have been the case had he remained passive. There is no reason to question his motivation; Talbot was willing to go to great lengths to further the cause of the church in England and to support the cardinal, whom he viewed as essential for its welfare: "You know that I can do no more than I have done for the poor cardinal," he wrote. His self-sacrifice became a point of pride: "I took his quarrel on my shoulders and incurred the obloquy of Dr. Errington, the bishop of Southwark, the chapter, etc. — all of whom hate me now, notwithstanding all my past services." He insisted that his support of Wiseman was based on principle, unlike that of others, whose relationship with the cardinal was based only on personal friendship: "When however they have found themselves obliged to act on principles, it has come out that they are almost diametrically opposed to him on all points in question."[27]

In spite of Talbot's self-justification, the trust that Wiseman and some of the Roman authorities, including the pope, placed in him remains an inexplicable factor in the story. Talbot's letters must be read with discrimination, but the effects of his influence cannot be ignored. Even after the most controversial questions had been settled, Wiseman told him, "I trust your friendship as well as your prudence by writing to you unreservedly as I think and feel, leaving it to your discretion how you use anything that I say."[28] The history of nineteenth-century Catholicism in England would have been more peaceful, if less colorful, had it not been for Talbot.

The bishops knew that the aftermath of the third synod would entail struggles and decisions as important as the synod itself. The various combatants busily and hurriedly prepared their cases. The final act in the drama would clearly take place in Rome itself.

16. Roman Armageddon

CARDINAL WISEMAN LEFT ENGLAND IN NOVEMBER AND ARRIVED IN Rome on December 12, 1859. In addition to Monsignor Searle, his secretary, he was accompanied by Robert Cornthwaite, later bishop of Beverley, and John Gillow, who was about to assume the vice-presidency of Ushaw. Archbishop Errington entered the Eternal City two days later, along with bishop Roskell. The cardinal soon summoned Manning, who arrived late in February to defend himself and the Oblates from attacks. Bishop Goss of Liverpool came during the same month in order to uphold the fifteenth decree on behalf of the bishops who sided with Errington and Grant.

As Errington had predicted when urging Grant to travel to Rome, Wiseman's financial dispute with the bishop of Southwark was the first of the contentious issues to be taken in hand by Propaganda. In his last report, written in March 1859, the cardinal had protested that Grant was incorrect in claiming that Southwark needed funds more desperately than the archdiocese. Admitting that the southern see was larger, he argued that the relative size was not as important as the number of Catholics in each. Allowing himself a wide margin of error, the cardinal pointed out that there were four to seven times more Catholics in Westminster than in Southwark. Much of the rural population in Bishop Grant's diocese was Protestant, moreover, so that his travel expenses were less than Wiseman's. Finally, Grant could travel like other bishops, unaccompanied and in second- or third-class carriages, whereas the cardinal had to be accompanied by at least one servant and with a chaplain or secretary as well. Any other procedure would reflect poorly on his position and would shock even Protestants.

After a long discussion on the poverty of the archdiocese, Wiseman concluded by begging Propaganda to consider the following factors: the prerogatives of the metropolitan archbishop, resident in the capital; the large number of Catholics in Westminster; the donations made by wealthy benefactors on behalf of many missions in Southwark; and finally, the maxim, always observed until then, that the fund for episcopal maintenance was not to be divided during the lifetime of the bishop who held it at the time of a territorial division.[1]

Propaganda began its deliberations in December 1860 and reached its decision in February. Bishop Grant was upheld on almost every point in question. Although the cardinal was to be permitted to retain certain funds that he had been administering and was afraid of making public, he was told to present to the Holy See an exact account of all such sources of income, along with their titles and the explicit use made of each. The fund for episcopal maintenance was to be divided immediately, three parts of the capital to be given to Westminster, one to Southwark. The revenues, however, were to be divided in the proportion of two to one. Funds for general charity, poor schools, and ecclesiastical education were to be divided in the same way, unless their use had been specified by the benefactors, whose wishes were to be respected. No decision was reached on the proportion of students from each diocese who might be educated at St. Edmund's, pending Rome's verdict on the decrees of the third synod. The debt on St. George's Cathedral was to be shared by both dioceses, insofar as it had been incurred prior to the division of London. All of its later debts, however, were the sole responsibility of Southwark.[2]

More than a year later Cardinal Barnabò wrote to Wiseman to ask what had been done to implement the directives. The year after Wiseman's death, as a matter of fact, Propaganda was informed that no action had ever been taken, in spite of numerous pleas by Bishop Grant.[3] John Morris later explained that "nothing could induce Cardinal Wiseman to face it, or even to give instructions that it should be done. He did not of course put any hindrance in the way of its being done after his time, but he simply let time go by and did nothing." Morris added, "The very first thing that Dr. Manning did on his appointment to the archbishopric was to give directions that the division should be carried out with the least possible delay."[4]

Even Monsignor Talbot admitted that the cardinal was "in the wrong," although he characteristically blamed Monsignor Searle, Wiseman's secretary, as "the great obstacle in the way of that affair being arranged." The explanation was ludicrous, although it was no more so than that offered by Dom Cuthbert Butler, who claimed that the delay was Propaganda's fault and that the cardinal had wanted a quick decision. Butler wrote, "Englishmen will fight their case determinedly until the decision of authority comes, but will accept the judgment with complete and even effusive loyalty and obedience, once the voice of authority speaks plainly." The cardinal, however, had ignored repeated requests from Grant, Talbot, and Propaganda to prepare a further report. The decision in 1860, moreover, had been sufficiently clear. In spite of his poor health and the complexities of the financial situation, Wiseman cannot be absolved from neglecting his duty not only to Bishop Grant and the diocese of Southwark but to the Holy See as well. Father Morris generously observed that "Dr. Grant, and every one that knew Cardinal Wiseman, fully understood that it was an idiosyncrasy of his nature that prevented him from facing an unpleasant matter, and not any uncharitableness towards the Bishop of Southwark."[5]

Wiseman's prestige in England would depend far more upon his ability to alter the synodical decrees by persuading Propaganda to disapprove of the fifteenth than upon the outcome of his financial dispute with Bishop Grant. He was determined to win the battle; the bishops who opposed him were equally intent upon preserving what they had accomplished. When Bishop Goss of Liverpool arrived in Rome, he was armed with written delegation to act for six of his episcopal brethren in matters concerning the synod.[6] Some also wrote to Talbot to explain their position in detail. Bishop James Brown of Shrewsbury, for example, said that if the cardinal were successful in overturning the synod's decrees, it would be "a death blow to the hierarchy in England." His explanation was exaggerated: "For how, it is asked, can the bishops for the future feel the least security in their synods, if any individual or body of individuals, by extra-synodal proceedings, can nullify all that has been solemnly and canonically done in synod? This is indeed a most grave question."[7] Brown overlooked the fact that the decrees of a provincial synod require the formal approval of the Holy See before they may be promulgated; there is always the chance, therefore, that alterations may be demanded.

Wiseman was distressed to learn that even Canon John Walker, one of his dearest friends and most frequent correspondents, did not fully agree with him. Walker, who had been at the synod as theologian of Bishop Briggs, was forthright in explaining his view to the cardinal: "I see you surrounded and more than surrounded by a belt of suffragans who are unanimously convinced that they are aggrieved and who manifestly prove that they are disaffected and are so bold in both that although they know that your influence is almost all-powerful in Rome, they prefer meeting you there to sitting still any longer at home in their present position." He advised Wiseman "to soften things as much and as speedily as possible and to make all the concessions even, that the principles of your policy will allow you to make." The cardinal had the solid support of President Newsham of Ushaw, however, who observed repeatedly that the college had not been involved in administrative friction until after the division of districts, when its supervision was no longer confined to a single bishop: "Let the fruit decide the character of the tree."[8]

When Propaganda finally examined the synod's decrees in April 1860, the assembled cardinals examined the recommendations of Giovanni Perrone, a well-known Jesuit, who had been appointed consultor for the case.[9] His report tended to support the position that all of the bishops with interests in a particular college should participate in its government, since, as Goss reported to Bishop Grant, "they concur in the expenses and send their students."

In the same letter Goss described a petition to the pope, signed by him and five other bishops, asking that Cardinal Wiseman might be prevented from participating in Propaganda's deliberation on the decrees. Manning, also present in Rome, considered the action as insulting to the cardinal and sought to have it withdrawn. Bishop Ullathorne refused to sign, stating that he "thought the mode of acting excessive, liable to be misunderstood under existing circumstances, and that it might be construed into an act of general hostility against the cardinal." It would appear that they were "instructing the pope in his duty, & that the card[inal] might think it was a strong hint that the Bps. had lost confidence in him." Ullathorne agreed, however, "that no person should sit in judgments on his own case."[10]

Although Cardinal Wiseman was present on the day of Propaganda's crucial meeting, he left the hall, of his own accord, during the discussion of the fifteenth decree. Propaganda approved all of the synod's decrees except those dealing with the government and administration of the colleges. These were referred back to the English bishops, who were told to prepare detailed commentaries on the "Elenchus et Analysis," which Wiseman had provided for them prior to the synod.[11]

The cardinal was unduly encouraged by the decision: "It is all that could be expected or desired. . . . The whole of what I wrote is approved. The decree XV. *De Regim. Collegiorum* is disapproved. Each bishop has separately to write an answer to every question in our *Elenchus*. In the meantime, the colleges to go on as they have till now."

Errington and his allies were reputedly "furious" over the result of Propaganda's deliberation. The cardinal wrote:

The decision is most severe. *They* openly expressed it to be impossible that decrees carried by large majorities should be rejected by Propaganda, and refused to allow any reasons to be added to their propositions. To avoid this, they rejected the Elenchus. And now, instead of taking it as their guide, with a certainty of majorities and with power of joint deliberations, each of them has the tough job imposed upon him of going through the whole *alone*, when the reasoning of each separately, not his silent vote *en masse*, will be discussed *if ever.* Hence, when yesterday afternoon I met Barnabò and five or six other of the Propaganda Cardinals by accident, . . . the others one and all congratulated with me, saying that *nothing* could have been more decisive or complete in my favour (though I consider it as in favour of religion in England.)

He was completely confident: "My only fear," he wrote to President Newsham, "is that you will be anxious about the future, because the matter is not finally settled. It would have been impossible for the Congregation to settle a positive arrangement at one sitting." [12]

Manning was less confident than Wiseman, observing correctly, "We must not I think interpret the decision as favorable or unfavorable." The cardinal was wrong in concluding that the work of the bishops in synod had been "disapproved," as was Talbot, who later wrote that the fifteenth decree had been "annulled by a unanimous vote of the congregation of Propaganda confirmed by the pope." [13] The decree was simply set aside until further information could be obtained, although the fact that the bishops were told to comment upon the cardinal's "Elenchus et Analysis" was an indirect rebuke, a clear reminder that they ought not to have ignored the procedure so carefully laid out by their archbishop.

Throughout all of these proceedings Wiseman remained firm in his determination to rid himself of his coadjutor. Manning supported him wholeheartedly:"The whole of this mischief was the work of two men, Dr. E[rrington] & Searle were the head & the hand & their mere absence makes peace. If they or their spirit were ever again to return & to rule, every free man would ask to go to some other diocese, & the growth of the church in London would be thrown back for 20 years." [14]

Archbishop Errington did not underestimate the extent of his opposition: "The Pope, full of Talbot's notions (he uses their very words and special errors) won't as yet hear of the possibility of not carrying through our cardinal in triumph, as he considers him as the type of Rome and all opposition Gallican and anti-Roman. Besides he thinks any opposition or excitement would kill him. Hence he will, if not changed, shelve me and defer indefinitely the synod." [15] Grant, of course, had written on behalf of his friend, and Bishop Goss would soon lend assistance as well. The bishop of Southwark wrote to Goss in March: "I hope all has gone well & happily with Dr. E[rrington] to whose zeal and clearsightedness we owe everything." [16]

Monsignor Talbot, in the meantime, tried to make use of Bishop Goss for his own purposes: "If you could induce Dr. Errington to *resign*, you will perform a great act of charity, and avert a *terrible scandal.* I pray you for Christ's sake, do all you can to gain this end." Talbot's next observation was a clear sign that he little understood the archbishop of Trebizond: "Even now, if Dr. Errington would throw himself at the feet of the Holy Father, I feel certain all could be arranged to his satisfaction; if he does not, I am afraid he is a lost man for life." Errington would have been the last man to throw himself at anyone's feet, even those of the pope. He had already begun to prepare his written defense, and, following a remarkable argument with Pius IX, during which their raised voices could be heard by those outside the room, he demanded a formal hearing.[17]

Cardinal Wiseman also began a written account of his side of the story, although its progress was slow, partially because of his persistent illness. Attacks of angina had delayed his departure from London the previous autumn and continued to torment him. He was also a victim of diabetes in his later years, and, finally, on two occasions prior to his return to London, it was necessary for him to undergo surgery for carbuncles. In spite of his afflictions, he enjoyed the delights of Rome and regained something of his youthful enthusiasm as he guided others to the sights that had given him so much pleasure in past years.

By spring Talbot was losing patience because of the cardinal's failure to complete his report: "The chief cause of delay is Cardinal Wiseman himself. He is writing a most voluminous *scrittura,* and he is like a child, every amusement interferes with it." It was June before the job was completed. Manning later made an excellent synopsis of its principal assertions. The cardinal, while describing Errington's activities, maintained:

> 1. that he [Errington] has opposed him and formed a party, happily few in number, on the administration of his diocese; 2. that he has alienated from him his secretary, two vicars general, and others intimate with him, and set them in opposition to him; 3. that he advised and directed the chapter of the diocese in a prolonged and organised opposition in which also they invaded his episcopal jurisdiction . . . ; 4. that he wrote or assisted in writing the *supplicas* in appeal to Rome, sent by the chapter in 1858, whereby the canons opposed his decisions and decrees as a bishop; 5. that he defended himself in taking this course in a letter already before the sacred congregation of Propaganda and laid down as a principle that he was at liberty to do the same in any similar case; 6. that he pursued the same course of opposition at the provincial synod; 7. that at this time he has been drawing several of the suffragan bishops into an opposition to him; 8. that in the course of this painful conflict he has manifested such a diversity of principles and distrust as to make it impossible that the cardinal can administer this, the diocese, in union with him or employ him to act as bishop.

Wiseman concluded his *scrittura* by stating that the welfare of the church demanded conciliation, peace, and harmony among the bishops and clergy of every diocese: "Every personal sacrifice is slight that guarantees to England and to its metropolitan see those incomparable gifts of the Holy Spirit of which they have been deprived for two years."[18]

Talbot also submitted a report on the case and described it as "very powerful, so that I do not see how the coadjutor can get out of this affair." As a matter of fact, it was so personal an attack that it is difficult to understand Propaganda's willingness to receive it. Talbot displayed more nerve than sense by claiming that he was Errington's friend. He described the archbishop's character as unusual, so that as a companion he was pleasant, interesting, informative, and attractive. As bishop and superior, however, he was hard, severe, and destructive, animated by a Gallican and Jansenistic spirit, "so different from that generous spirit which distinguishes prelates of the Roman Church."

According to Talbot, Errington exercised more zeal in destroying than in building. Prior Park was cited to support his case, clearly an unfair example since the archbishop had been placed as administrator of Clifton after the second synod for the very purpose of assessing the situation and, if necessary, closing the college. Talbot concluded that it was envy and jealousy that had led Errington to oppose Manning and to turn Wiseman's secretary and vicar general against him. The monsignor then observed, "I am not able to act with duplicity; when I speak, I speak clearly." One could not worry about hurting the feelings of individuals: "Rather, it is a question of a great principle: whether the Church in England ought to be a National, Anglican, Jansenistic Church, or whether it ought to move forward, as it has done under Cardinal Wiseman, on the generous and heroic path by which he has led it, with the direction, more maternal than paternal, of the Roman Church."[19] Talbot was correct in stating that his report was "very powerful," but it also indicated the hysteria that resulted in a mental breakdown eight years later, when it was necessary to place him in an asylum at Passy, near Paris. He remained there until his death in 1886.

Errington's report was longer than the cardinal's. He saw two general reasons for which Wiseman wanted to deprive him of his coadjutorship. The first centered upon the incompatibility of the two men, a situation that Errington insisted was not permanent and, moreover, not sufficient for the deprivation of his office. The second was the cardinal's claim that his coadjutor had committed an ecclesiastical crime, and Errington denied the charge in detail. He carefully outlined his objections to the Oblates and to their position in St. Edmund's College and then moved on to the chapter's right to advise the cardinal on the administration of the seminary and the part that he had played in that endeavor. Errington finally dealt with Wiseman's complaint over the manner in which he had conducted himself during the synod.[20]

The most carefully prepared and best-documented part of Errington's self-justification was his treatment of Manning's Oblates. The cardinal knew that this would be the case and, for this reason, had directed Manning to travel to Rome in order to defend himself. After his arrival Manning prepared a long document, addressed to the pope, in which he answered the charges of those who had opposed his congregation.[21] Edmund Sheridan Purcell, however, had no grounds for claiming that Manning's report was made necessary by the fact that the cardinal would not take the initiative. As a matter of fact, Wiseman prepared a strong defense of Manning, responding to the charge that he had allowed his chapter provost to govern the archdiocese: "To speak the truth, this is an accusation rather against me than against him. It is as much as to say that I allow myself to be led by him and to be governed by him, without perhaps knowing it." This was precisely the accusation that was being made and that has been repeated ever since. The cardinal admitted that he often turned to Manning for advice, but any bishop would have taken advantage of a priest with such fine qualities. Wiseman denied emphatically that he made use of Manning "in the current and daily administration which forms the government of a diocese . . . as though he were my vicar." He continued, "Of the temporal concerns of the diocese, I do not believe that I have ever spoken to him; nor do I believe that he has gained any information concerning them from me."[22]

Errington's attack had not been upon Manning alone, however, but also on the Oblates, who, he insisted, were not truly subject to their bishop in the sense intended by St. Charles when he established his congregation in Milan. The archbishop claimed that their primary loyalty was to their superior. He then turned to his alleged influence over the chapter, pointing out that the cardinal "was not accustomed to consult the Chapter in the administration of the diocese." The canons had been justified in seeking to implement the procedures established by the Council of Trent for the government of seminaries. Errington did not deny his influence over the chapter members. He and Searle had their bedrooms on the top floor of the archbishop's house, and rooms below were used as offices for the archdiocesan officials. He had always spoken freely with these men about matters pertaining to their duties, including the status of the Oblates and Manning's influence. It was he who had encouraged the chapter to address Wiseman in the first place, and he had favored an appeal to the Holy See when the cardinal refused to acknowledge its right to advise him. There was hardly a day, according to Errington, on which one of the canons failed to question him on the legality of a particular course of action, but there had been no violation of canon law.

Archbishop Errington defended his role in the synod, denying that a coadjutor had to abandon his own opinions in order to embrace those of his superior. He included in his defense a letter, written by Talbot in 1855, in which the monsignor claimed to have urged Wiseman to turn over to his coadjutor all of the administrative work and responsibility of the archdiocese.[23]

Manning was appalled by the proceedings: "The history of this case is to me fearful & I am convinced that his [Errington's] mind is not sound, for unreasonableness is unsoundness." At the height of the Westminster disputes, Errington had consulted a physician, complaining of "brain fatigue," and he had then withdrawn from the archdiocese in the winter of 1859 to recuperate.[24] Although the man was exhausted, his report was not the work of one possessed of an unsound mind. Rather it reflected his stubborn self-will, convinced, as he was, that he owed it to himself to prove he had been guilty of no canonical crime.

It was evident that Wiseman and Errington could no longer work together. The Holy See was called upon to resolve an unhappy situation that had been caused initially by the cardinal's persistence in demanding his old friend as coadjutor, in spite of Errington's protests. The archbishop of Trebizond was a conscientious bishop; he was also a legalist. He was, at the same time, one of the most capable members of the new hierarchy, as Wiseman himself admitted. It had been a mistake to place him in a subordinate capacity, even in the archdiocese. Wiseman was not likely to yield to anyone the same freedom of action that Bishop Walsh had conferred upon *him* in 1840, and even in that case the results had not been altogether satisfactory. The cardinal had been in positions of authority since 1828. Although his physical health had deteriorated, he was as mentally acute as ever, and he would not tolerate a subordinate who sought to reverse his own policies or decisions.

Clashes between the two men were perhaps inevitable, although they were exacerbated by the interference of others. The pope still urged Errington to accept the archbishopric of Trinidad or Haiti; the offer was refused. Errington understood that the Holy Father's role was difficult, but he now felt that if he had committed an ecclesiastical crime it was up to the Holy See to specify his errors. If he was considered unfit for one archdiocese, he was surely not suitable for another. Granting that the situation should not have developed in the first place, it is difficult to see how the pope could have avoided the final step. He approved the fatal decree that released Errington from his coadjutorship with the right of succession to the see of Westminster. No reason was given for the action, except the incompatibility of Errington and Wiseman and the necessity of restoring peace to the archdiocese.[25]

Cardinal Wiseman's reputation has suffered from his neglect of an unexpected problem that was placed before him very soon after his arrival in Rome. In view of the state of his health and the demanding issues claiming his personal attention, it must have seemed relatively trivial, although he was surely not without blame. As we have seen, the very month during which the third synod met Newman had published his famous and influential article "On Consulting the Faithful in Matters of Doctrine." There were those who considered some of its passages heretical, and Bishop T. J. Brown of Newport and Menevia went so far as to delate Newman to Rome.[26]

Bishop Brown was advised to send Newman's article to Rome, along with a letter to Cardinal Barnabò, and he complied immediately. Bishop Ullathorne, Newman's bishop, had just arrived in Rome, having been summoned to discuss with the authorities matters related to Australia, with which he was familiar on account of his early assignment there. Cardinal Barnabò took advantage of his presence by seeking his assistance in dealing with Newman's delation. Seven years later Ullathorne prepared a detailed description for Newman of what had taken place: "Cardinal Wiseman was then at the English College at Rome. I told him all that had passed, and spoke to him gravely about the annoyances to which from time to time you had been subjected. . . . At last the Cardinal burst into tears, and said, 'Tell Newman I will do anything I can for him.'"[27]

When he returned to Birmingham, in fact, Ullathorne explained what had taken place to Newman, who then wrote to Wiseman asking for a list of the passages in his article that needed explanation, a copy of the translations that Barnabò had read, and the dogmatic propositions that they contradicted. He promised that when he received the information, he would "accept and profess ex animo in their fulness and integrity the dogmatic propositions implicated." Moreover he would explain his meaning "in strict accordance with those propositions" and would "show that the English text and context of the Article itself are absolutely consistent with them." He added: "I marvel, but I do not complain, that, after many years of patient and self denying labour in the cause of Catholicity, the one appropriate acknowledgment in my old age should be considered to consist in taking advantage against me of what is at worst a slip of the pen in an anonymous un-theological paper. But I suppose it is a law of the world, that those who toil much and say little, are little thought of." He begged to be excused from traveling to Rome to defend himself: "A journey would seriously impair my health and strength and would create great confusion." In 1867 Cardinal Barnabò claimed that he had never read Newman's letter, although in fact a minute preserved in the Propaganda archive indicates clearly that its contents were reported.[28]

Instead of obtaining a list of objectionable passages, as requested, Wiseman had Manning write to Newman from Rome: "The Cardinal desires his kind regards to you, and tells me to say that he has thought it better to wait till his return, when he hopes to bring the matter of your letter to a termination which will be acceptable to you." Several years after Wiseman's death Manning explained to Ullathorne "that the Cardinal fell ill almost at the time he received the letter [from Newman], and that so far as I remember I never heard him again speak of it." [29]

Wiseman had not, in fact, forgotten the matter. More than a year after hearing from Newman he referred to the article in question when writing to Barnabò: "This article caused unspeakable pain, and a learned ecclesiastic, a friend of the writer, undertook to deal with him and to secure explanations and modifications which precluded any subsequent action." [30] The cardinal referred to John Gillow of Ushaw College (not to be confused with his namesake, president of Ushaw when Wiseman was a boy), who had corresponded with Newman over the orthodoxy of his writings in the *Rambler*.

Wiseman hoped, it seems, that Newman would write another article to explain his meaning in the first, but, in that case, he should have provided a list of the passages needing elucidation. Not for the first time, the cardinal chose inaction rather than confront a difficult and complex problem, but in doing so he was unfair to Newman, who for almost a decade was mistrusted by the Roman authorities. Talbot, in 1866, charged that instead of explaining or retracting his statements, Newman had done no more than ask to be excused from traveling to Rome. [31] Talbot ignored the fact that no formal accusations had ever been made, even though Newman had begged Wiseman to obtain a list of charges.

When Wiseman returned from Rome in the summer of 1860, he was a very sick man. Dom Cuthbert Butler wrote that "his health was utterly broken and his nerves shattered." According to the same author, "he was no more the large-minded genial Wiseman of former days, but had grown irritable and morbidly sensitive to opposition." The cardinal had not been successful in persuading the Roman authorities of the rightness of his cause in opposing Bishop Grant, but he was relieved of the interference on the part of Archbishop Errington, and he was convinced that ultimately his position on the college questions would prevail. Butler concluded that "Wiseman's ideas and acts were now inspired by Manning," a fact that the other bishops "greatly resented." [32] It is undeniable that the cardinal relied more and more on his chapter provost, one of the few capable men whom he felt that he could trust, but Wiseman, in fact, remained his own man.

The irritability described by Butler showed itself almost as soon as Wiseman returned to London. The issue was relatively minor, concerning his nephew Randolfo, Frasquita's son, whom Wiseman had placed at Oscott. The cardinal thought that the boy could remain there without charge as a means of settling accounts between him and the institution, since he was still convinced that Oscott was in his debt. When the college president sent a bill for young Gabrielli's tuition and living expenses in the summer of 1860, Searle, on Wiseman's behalf, referred to the mutual demands made by Bishop Ullathorne and Cardinal Wiseman dating from 1847. He stated that the account was settled as far as Wiseman's debt to the diocese of Birmingham was concerned, but that Oscott still owed money to the cardinal. When the college authorities continued to demand payment, Manning blamed the entire situation on Searle, who, he said, had acted without consulting the cardinal. It soon became clear, however, that the cardinal had no intention of backing down, in spite of continued demands by the college president, to whom he finally wrote, "I request you to allow my nephew, the Count Gabrielli, to accompany Mgr. Searle, in order to pass to another college, where I wish him to complete his education." By September 1861 Gabrielli was back in Italy, complaining of his financial dependence upon his uncle and of the fact that his mother, now remarried, had not turned over to him the patrimony that was rightfully his.[33]

On September 29, 1860, Robert Whitty, Wiseman's vicar general at the time of the hierarchy's restoration, wrote: "This is the anniversary of the hierarchy—just now ten years ago. Amid all their troubles, surely it is clear God's cause has advanced considerably." The cardinal never doubted it, but there was much to be done before peace could be restored. One of the major issues still needing attention was the status of the Oblates at St. Edmund's. Errington had not been the only one opposed to Manning and his community. J. L. Patterson described the attitude of two Westminster clergymen: "They . . . in common with every priest to whom I have spoken, say that much as they dislike and disapprove of Dr. Errington and his policy, nothing would induce them to oppose him if the Oblates of St. Charles were put in at St. Edmund's, as they regard that measure as most pernicious and Errington would undo it if he were archbishop."[34]

The Oblates, including Herbert Vaughan, withdrew from the college in the summer of 1861. There is some question as to whether the move was instigated by a request from Wiseman, by order of Propaganda, or voluntarily by Manning himself.[35] Purcell wrote, "Before the decision against Manning and the Oblates was pronounced, the Cardinal received a friendly warning from Propaganda not to appeal to the Pope on their behalf." It was in keeping with his many inconsistencies, however, that Purcell should then have quoted a letter from Manning to Talbot, written on October 4, 1861: "I am going to write to Cardinal Barnabò giving a statement of the reasons of our withdrawal from St. Edmund's; for I can see . . . that it is liable to be misunderstood." He declared that the action was taken as "an act of peace for him [the cardinal] and for ourselves."[36] It is likely that the withdrawal was regarded as a temporary measure to restore a degree of harmony to the archdiocese. Some directive from Wiseman or Propaganda may have been given, but it has not been demonstrated that this was the case. Certainly there was no "decision" made against the community at that time, and, if Propaganda had been behind the withdrawal, it would have made little sense for Manning to write an explanation for the prefect.

Wiseman, in any case, was in no way alienated from the Oblates. On Christmas Eve of 1861 he wrote to the Holy See and asked for final and complete approbation for the community. Barnabò replied that normally a period of ten years was necessary after the foundation of a congregation before it could receive final approval. He asked the cardinal to wait for some little time before expecting it.[37] Shortly after Wiseman's death, Propaganda again discussed the Oblates and granted the decree of final approbation in January 1866.

Monsignor Talbot was convinced that Wiseman would have no peace until Bishop Grant left the neighboring diocese of Southwark. In September 1860 Talbot thought that he had found a way of achieving his objective. He suggested that since Bishop Briggs was about to resign, it might be possible to move Grant to Beverley. Wiseman, however, would not agree to the plan, "merely to get rid of even a grave annoyance." He could not recommend a person whom he conscientiously considered "unfit" to be bishop of a diocese in need of improvements and reforms: "If Dr. Grant were to go there, I believe nothing would be done, and all abuses would be continued."[38]

Having heard the rumor that was circulating, Bishop Grant complained to Cardinal Barnabò, who, in turn, sought an explanation from Talbot. The monsignor's reply was hardly credible in view of the fact that it had been he who had stated explicitly to Patterson that the retirement of Briggs would be "a grand opportunity to translate Dr. Grant to Beverley." Talbot now wrote: "I don't know how such a report can have got abroad. I am afraid that poor Dr. Grant, with all his sanctity, is what they used to call at school a *sneak* and works a great deal too underhand." Grant's sixteen years in Rome had taught him "the cunning and duplicity of the Italian character without the large generosity of the best amongst them, which exists to a great extent."[39]

No fair-minded historian would wish to exaggerate the harmful interference of Talbot, especially in view of his later mental breakdown. Yet he was so undeniably influential that one can hardly understand the pressures upon Wiseman or many of the important factors in his controversies without taking into account the nature of the Talbot correspondence. In this case Bishop Grant effectively stopped the rumors. The provost of the Beverley Chapter sent a letter to the other canons: "Dr. Grant has informed me that the reports respecting his translation to York have greatly annoyed him and disturbed the peace of his diocese." He said that Grant had "no wish to leave his diocese and that for us to think of him would only be, in his opinion, wasting one of the three names to be forwarded to Rome."[40]

When Briggs retired, he was replaced by Robert Cornthwaite, a friend of Wiseman's, who had succeeded Grant as rector of the English College in 1851. In the meantime the cardinal suggested that Beverley might be divided, and he prepared a detailed plan for the division. The diocese was confined to Yorkshire, composed of North, East, and West Ridings. The first two areas were agricultural, but in the West Riding the population was centered about a group of industrial cities, with Leeds as a kind of capital. Since York was the residential city of the bishop, Wiseman suggested that it would be well to place a second bishop in Leeds. Cardinal Barnabò, in announcing the name of Beverley's new bishop, advised Wiseman to discuss the proposed division with his colleagues.[41]

Talbot now saw a new opportunity for further meddling. In January 1862 he suggested to Wiseman that if Beverley were to be divided, Manning would make an excellent bishop for the new diocese: "In the episcopal body you have not one bishop who cordially supports your views. . . . Manning is thoroughly Roman, and I think would be of immense use to you in your episcopal meetings." Canon John Morris, who had moved from Northampton to Westminster at his own request and now assisted Wiseman in a secretarial capacity, wrote to Talbot to oppose the suggestion. Morris admired Manning as "the first priest, not only here, but in England." Yorkshire, he reminded Talbot, "is a long way off and it would be a pity that he should be moved very far from London which is the centre of those movements in which Mgr. Manning takes so great an interest and exercises so useful an influence." He was sorry that Manning had not been appointed to the diocese of Nothampton instead of Bishop Amherst. There was an alternative plan, however. Morris suggested that if Birmingham could be divided, an idea which he had heard attributed to Bishop Ullathorne, Amherst would be "happy as the day is long as Bishop of Stafford." Even Yorkshire might suit the bishop of Northampton. The only hardship in such a situation "would be that poor Dr. Manning would be sent to waste his sweetness on the desert air of Northampton, but this would be in order that he still might be near the cardinal." Morris concluded, "But *if only* he could have half of Southwark — to be really the cardinal's *adlatus* — and that one spirit might prevail in London on both sides of the water."[42]

As it was, Wiseman's plan of dividing Beverley was opposed by its new bishop. Cornthwaite admitted that an eventual change would be necessary, and he offered a plan of his own that would have involved a division not only of Beverley but of Hexham as well, so that the two sees would become three. The cardinal, however, was not easily put off when convinced of the rightness of a particular course of action. He persisted in his efforts, but no change took place during his lifetime.[43]

With the decision on the colleges still pending, another matter arose that divided the bishops until it, too, had to be appealed to the Holy See for a decision. In a letter to Talbot in September 1860 the cardinal complained of the action of Bishop Goss at a meeting of some of the Liverpool and Salford clergy: "Dr. Goss spoke to them for an hour, attacking Ushaw, Rome & me, and telling all that took place in Synod. My health for the first time was not proposed, certainly when it might have been most reasonably & naturally, without party spirit, the clergy were to a man disgusted, but notes were taken of his speech, & I have sent for them." The cardinal threatened to "lay the matter before Propaganda, for it surely cannot be pleasing to the Holy See that a Bishop, after bringing his cases before it (Ushaw, the Synod, the Coadjr.) and while some of them are still pending before it, should appeal to the passions of his clergy, nay to those of the clergy of a neighbouring diocese and through them to the laity, for nothing of this sort is kept secret. How can we have peace or unity while such a course is pursued?" What is the use of synods, he asked, "if there be not in them *secrecy*, the only security of apostolic liberty in a country like England with its constitutional ideas and democratic tendencies. This mode of enlisting popular feeling, to bear on or against the decisions of the Holy See, *must* be stopped at once. Goss is the representative of Englishism as you know." Wiseman's bitterness must have been heightened by the recollection that his three principal opponents among the members of the hierarchy — Grant, Errington, and Goss — had all been elevated to the episcopate following his own recommendations.

In the same letter the cardinal wrote of the newest problem that the bishops had to face: "This national spirit is the worse at this moment, when we have upon us the new Charit[able] Trusts Act, an abominable measure, for which be not surprised if some of us go to prison, an Act which I fear will find in Lancashire favourers & abettors. . . . Depend upon it, they will soon know thoroughly at Rome who are the friends and who are the enemies of the Holy See and of Roman principles."[44]

The government's Roman Catholic Charities Act, intended to supplement the general Charitable Trusts Acts, made it obligatory to register all Catholic charitable or religious trusts with the charity commissioners beginning in 1861. The question had been a long-standing one, and Parliament, for more than a decade, had excluded Catholic trusts from the operation of the law. In May 1847, when a bill concerning charitable trusts had been placed before Parliament, Propaganda judged that it could not "approve that for the regulating & superintending of pious bequests & other such dispositions, lay Tribunals and secular authorities should be constituted, since the direction of such things belongs to the Church alone." It was illegal for such bequests to be applied for prayers and masses for the dead. The directive, referring to that fact, continued, "In like manner, the Sacred Congregation cannot consent that the condition of the above-named pious dispositions should be rendered worse by their being subjected to burthens & to the care of Tribunals not recognized in this behalf by the holy canons of the Church." [45]

There had been numerous complaints, nevertheless, about the careless manner in which Catholics had administered their trusts. It is interesting to note that even before he was a bishop, Thomas Grant had suggested that the directives of the Council of Trent should be followed and that each bishop should be assisted in administering the temporalities of his district by four members of the clergy. Although the Tridentine regulation was meant to apply to seminaries, wrote Grant, "the principle is equally applicable to other cases." In 1853 when the Charitable Trusts Bill was being considered by Parliament, Newman had written to his friend James Hope-Scott, a famed parliamentary lawyer, to ask his opinion. Hope-Scott replied, "For my own part I confess a desire that Catholic Charities should be under some public inspection, both to secure accurate administration in fact; and to give confidence in feeling." [46]

Cardinal Wiseman was correct in anticipating that the bishops would not be unanimous in their view of the law that was passed in 1860. Bishop Ullathorne wrote to Grant: "I am anxious about our Trusts, & what we are to do *apropos* of the Trust Act. There is very little time for consideration, getting all the light we can, deciding what to do, & doing it. Ought we not to take some common counsel, exchange lights, & get what help we can? . . . What will you do? Or what are you doing?" [47] It was known that the cardinal opposed cooperation with the law. Nearly all of the other bishops took the opposite view and favored compliance, except in cases where there was danger of losing their trusts.

Without providing adequate warning beforehand, the cardinal announced that the question of Catholic trusts would be discussed at the annual Low Week meeting of 1861. At the meeting Ullathorne and Clifford were appointed to study the matter and report back at a second meeting to be held in May. It was then that the bishops resolved that they were not bound to offer "unqualified opposition" to the law and did not "consider such opposition expedient." Their resolutions stated, however, that they opposed the principle on which the Charitable Trusts Acts had been founded, that is, the assumption that the state had dominion over trusts. They went on to declare that Propaganda had provided previously adequate norms for each bishop to determine the course of action to be pursued in given cases. They agreed, finally, that "where property would be exposed to danger, either by its confiscation, alienation, or by its being diverted to any purpose different from that determined by the original donor, the Bps. consider themselves bound to prevent, by every means in their power, any information being given in regard to such property, which might lead to such a result."[48] The cardinal was absent from much of the meeting because of illness, but he opposed the resolutions. The others, however, were increasingly resentful of what they considered to be his high-handed manner of treating them.

In the autumn of 1861 Ullathorne and Clifford set out for Rome to explain the position of the majority of the bishops and to complain of the way in which Wiseman conducted provincial affairs. It was their contention that more democratic procedures should be followed and that their opinions should not be disregarded by the cardinal. Wiseman dispatched Manning right behind them in order to present his views. On November 8 Ullathorne wrote to describe for Bishop T. J. Brown the audience that he and Clifford had with the Holy Father.

> The pope was exceedingly kind, entered into the subject, said that all he wished was that truth and justice should be done without favour, and he seemed struck with some of our remarks. From all we have yet heard in official quarters, we see plainly that the question is not understood, and that the first thing we shall have to do will be to show what the Act is not. It gives not our property to Government. It gives not up the administration. It is nothing special to us as Catholics. In short, positive ideas have been entertained that have no existence. Cardinal Barnabò read to us Cardinal Wiseman's letter announcing that Dr. Manning was commissioned on his part, and expressing a hope that the affair will be concluded in peace and charity. I can only say in conclusion that every disposition is evinced to give us a full and fair hearing.

Manning was equally optimistic when writing to the cardinal on December 2.

> I had an audience of a long half-hour to-day, and hope that matters have taken a good beginning. The Holy Father received me with great kindness and spoke with great freedom and openness about your Eminence, and the bishops and England. He spoke of you in the terms he used last year, which were everything you could desire. . . . The following are the heads of what I said: That the present crisis with the bishops was inevitable, con-

sidering the former state of England and the peculiarity of your mission beginning in 1838, which has been of the nature of a *Visita Apostolica* with all its invidiousness and odium in finding fault, correcting, and introducing a new, and that a Roman, order of things. This the Holy Father fully recognized and enlarged upon. That this *sfogo* [outburst] will do good. The Holy Father fully appreciates the personal causes of this feeling, and dwelt upon them. That in the merits of the pending questions your Eminence was beyond all doubt in the right. I gave as examples the colleges at the last Synod, and the trusts now. The Holy Father saw the point of the latter at once. I then said that I believed that no great difficulty would exist in coming to agreement. The Holy Father then spoke very kindly and considerately of the allegations which have been made as to your Eminence's manner in dealing with the bishops, and allowed me to say many things in explanation.

Butler observed that "in Rome every litigant thinks he is winning his case, and most come away in the belief that the case has been won, and the decision will be given in his favour, in a short time — half of them, or more, to be disillusioned at home."[49]

While in Rome Ullathorne offered his resignation. Manning and Wiseman concluded that this was merely an attempt to demonstrate the seriousness with which he considered the issues for which he was fighting and to win sympathy. Manning reported that he had discussed the offer with the Holy Father, to whom he had "said all that is just of Dr. Ullathorne personally and as a bishop, and added that this *rinunzia* would show what infirmities still belong to a man otherwise so good." The pope, in any case, refused to accept the resignation. At a ceremony in St. Peter's, on the Feast of the Purification, His Holiness called Ullathorne to him, and as the bishop later reported to his brother, said: "Monsignor, in the name of St. Peter, I tell you from this holy chair of truth that your demission cannot be accepted. Stand to your place. Persevere until death. You have yet many things to do."[50]

The final decision of the Holy See on the questions raised by Ullathorne and Clifford upheld the view of the majority of the bishops. They were to be free to follow their own individual judgment in each case in registering their trusts. They were also supported in their demand for more democratic procedures at episcopal meetings.[51]

The poor attendance at the Low Week meeting in 1862 was indicative of Wiseman's loss of influence over his suffragans. No decision had yet been reached on the charitable trusts, not to mention the college question, and there was no doubt that the absence of the majority was intended as a direct snub to the cardinal. Bishop Grant claimed that he had presumed there would not be a meeting. He therefore arranged to officiate at a wedding in Plymouth during that time. The bishop of Hexham was ill, a valid excuse in his case. Bishop Goss sent a curt letter, "As circumstances do not allow me to be in London on that occasion, I shall not have the pleasure of meeting my brethren or the honour of dining with your Eminence." The meeting had always opened with dinner, hosted by the cardinal. Bishop James Brown declined the dinner invitation by stating that "as circumstances will prevent me from attending the episcopal meeting this year, I fear that I must not promise myself the pleasure of accepting it." Ullathorne agreed to attend during the first day only, and Clifford said that he would be there, but that "in the present state of affairs" he could not look forward to a meeting "without some degree of apprehension."[52]

The bishops were planning on journeying to Rome for the forthcoming canonization of the Japanese martyrs, and they claimed that they were too busy for a meeting, although they also seemed to feel that it would be inappropriate to have one with the disputed questions still undecided. Wiseman reminded Bishop Grant, however, that "the meetings in Low week have been one of immemorial usage, every bishop has been supposed to keep himself disengaged for it during that week." He warned that while in Rome he would "lay the case before the Holy Father and ascertain his wish about the continuation of our annual meetings, or their suppression, keeping myself totally indifferent to the issue." As it was, only the bishops of Birmingham, Nottingham, Clifton, Northampton, and Beverley appeared.[53]

In May 1862 nearly half of the world's Catholic bishops assembled in Rome for the canonization of the Japanese martyrs. All except two of the English bishops were there. On this occasion the Holy Father spoke to them as a body, lecturing them on their differences. Wiseman described what happened in a letter to Manning.

> As to these [their differences] his wish was — and he added later this must be considered a command — that we should take the highest and largest mountain in the Alps and put it over all past questions and dissensions without any tunnel through to get at them. They were never to be referred to again or brought up under any circumstances. So end the six months' attacks, personalities, etc. Next he said it was his desire that the usual meetings should be held every year as heretofore; and that all matters of a general interest should be discussed, and either settled by a majority of voices or referred to the Holy See, to whose decisions he did not doubt all would submit. Of course he said the subjects for deliberation would be communicated to them beforehand, that each one might study them beforehand. This was all in substance.

The cardinal assured the pope "that it required only a wish of His Holiness to be a command." He went on to ask about the decision of Propaganda on trusts, and was told that it would be communicated to them in writing.[54]

Wiseman was overjoyed, supposing that his own position on the unsettled questions would be fully supported. He ignored the fact that the Holy Father had taken the side of the bishops in their demand for fuller discussion of common issues and for the principle of majority decisions at the annual Low Week meetings. The pope had also taken care to communicate nothing regarding Catholic trusts, although Propaganda had already reached its decision.

As a matter of fact, the response to the Low Week meeting in 1863 was similar to that of the previous year. The disputed decree on the colleges had still not been settled by the Holy See. Bishop Goss wrote to Grant in February: "You don't want to go to Rome, but you can fight the synod at home, if you will refuse to attend an Easter meeting *under existing circumstances.* If two or three of us refuse, he [Wiseman] cannot hold it. . . . Till the synod is settled, we cannot and ought not to meet and we ought to tell Rome and may force a settlement of the synod. . . . Be firm; I will stand by you."[55]

Goss was especially angry because, when President Newsham of Ushaw died on February 1, Bishop Hogarth of Hexham and Newcastle named a successor without consulting the other bishops who had an interest in the college. Even before Newsham's death Hogarth had decided to appoint Robert Tate and had drawn up the necessary documents. Goss of Liverpool, Turner of Salford, and James Brown of Shrewsbury complained bitterly. They were informed that Hogarth had consulted Cardinal Wiseman, who, as apostolic visitor for Ushaw, had full power to permit the ordinary of the diocese to make the appointment without recourse to his colleagues.[56] Others must have shared the opinion of Bishop Goss: "I sincerely hope we shall never have another synod, for it is only a waste of expense and time and ends in nothing but vexation of spirit."[57]

In February 1861 Talbot had condemned the old English clergy and their bishops as "insular, national, narrow-minded, Anglo-Gallican, anti-Roman as they can be." He went on to assert that they were only "kept down during the last twenty years by the talent, the power, the influence, and the high position of Cardinal Wiseman," and he cited the example of the third synod to prove his point.

> The whole history of the third provincial synod of Westminster . . . corroborates this statement. The metropolitan proposes to his suffragan bishops an *Elenchus* which all canonists who have seen it in Rome pronounce to be a masterpiece. They reject it, and make decrees which are annulled by a unanimous vote of the congregation of Propaganda, confirmed by the pope. Written to by the Propaganda, they sulk and refuse to answer. I cannot conceive a greater act of ecclesiastical insubordination and contempt of authority.[58]

The bishops had not refused to answer, and in fact they set to work in order to prepare their comments on Wiseman's "Elenchus et Analysis."

Bishop Hogarth's report was carefully written, but it added nothing to the arguments that he and President Newsham had been offering for a decade. Their position was in complete accord with Wiseman's.[59] More interesting, however, was Bishop Ullathorne's position, since he had not only sided with the majority of the bishops but in fact claimed to have cooperated in composing the fifteenth decree as submitted to Rome. He now changed his mind and concluded that the decree, if implemented, would result in "the transfer of a portion of the jurisdiction and administration of the authority of the ordinary to other bishops" and that it would give them "a share in what is strictly diocesan administration." Now convinced that there was no precedent for a bishop to share joint jurisdiction in the diocese of another, he repented of having been a party to what had been accomplished at the synod. If the decree were approved, he warned, it would lead to divisions, jealousies, and even rivalries for influence and power among bishops, chapters, and college superiors, a spirit that would spread to the students from the various dioceses.[60]

The ordinaries of the three sees in which the colleges were situated (Westminster, Hexham, and Birmingham) were now united. They were not alone, moreover. After 1861 they found an ally in Bishop Cornthwaite, who acknowledged in a letter to Propaganda that he, a canon of Hexham at the time, had been the author of the comments on Bishop Hogarth's copy of the cardinal's "Elenchus et Analysis." He was in perfect agreement with his former bishop and had not changed his mind after his own elevation to the episcopate. Bishop Grant tried to persuade the new bishop to change his position, but the latter coldly declined. Moreover, Bishop Roskell of Nottingham remained publicly neutral and expressed no formal opinion on the disputed decree.[61]

In May 1860 Provost Manning sent his views on the "Elenchus et Analysis" to Rome. Of course he supported the cardinal's contention that the ordinary should have complete control over the institutions in his own diocese. He stressed the importance of seminaries and urged that they should be established in England as soon as possible.[62]

The cardinal waited until 1862 before sending off further comment. He then persisted in maintaining that the English colleges were not seminaries and that the Tridentine regulations did not apply. Like the continental colleges, which had not been seminaries in the strict sense, they did not obtain their main support from ecclesiastical benefices; they were not administered either by clergy or chapters; and when they were founded in England, there were in fact no ordinary bishops, cathedrals, chapters, or benefices. The establishment of the hierarchy had not in itself changed the status of the colleges any more than it had turned missions into canonically erected parishes. Wiseman proposed that the colleges should remain under the jurisdiction and administration of their ordinaries; that the bishops should send their students to them in proportion to their funds; that every six months they should receive an account of those funds, as well as reports on the progress, conduct, ability, and health of their students; that constitutions should be drawn up for each college and sent to Rome; and that when serious disagreements arose, these should be settled by the Holy See.[63]

The bishops of Newport and Menevia, Southwark, Salford, Shrewsbury, Plymouth, Northampton, and Clifton all responded to Propaganda's request for comments on the "Elenchus et Analysis" by supporting in its entirety a report prepared and submitted by Bishop Goss.[64]

By the winter of 1863, when it was evident that Propaganda was preparing to reach its decision, Bishop Clifford hurried to Rome at the expense of the bishops of Salford, Shrewsbury, Liverpool, and Southwark in order to be on hand to present last-minute observations.[65] Manning also made the trip in order to represent the bishops who were in the minority. At Propaganda's request, Clifford and Manning had a series of private meetings to see if they could reconcile their differences. In fact they were able to do so on some points. "We agreed to urge that the colleges should be preserved in their integrity," wrote Manning, "that all the rights of the ordinaries should be preserved inviolate as to all spiritual jursidiction, as to the nomination of rectors and professors and to discipline and internal administration." They did not agree, however, on the fundamental issue, whether all of the bishops with an interest in a particular college should have the right to administer jointly its temporalities.[66]

Propaganda must have tired of the dispute. When the final decision was reached in the summer of 1863, even the compromise that Clifford and Manning were willing to accept was ignored, and the fifteenth decree, with very minor and irrelevant changes in wording, was approved. The decree on seminary deputies was suppressed, an indication that the colleges were not to be considered as seminaries in the canonical sense. Finally, Wiseman was relieved of his post as apostolic visitor of Ushaw.[67]

While Propaganda had supported the cardinal in his view that the colleges were not seminaries strictly speaking, the judgment was substantially a defeat for his position, and he knew it: "I must now give up forever all idea, so long cherished, of true ecclesiastical education for Westminster." He did not see how changes could be made, since Bishop Grant would oppose him every step of the way: "If Dr. Grant differs from me and agrees with the superiors in making no reforms, the least trifle must go to Rome for new contests, of which I am sick, and with every chance of his side being taken." He decided to communicate the approved decree to his colleagues without comment, "and bow my head in sorrowful silence." Wiseman concluded that there would be further disputes: "Numerous questions will yet arise, but none from me. My successor may have to fight it; not I."[68]

The only question that remained undetermined was the right of the chapter to interfere in the administration of the diocese without an invitation from the ordinary. In the summer of 1860 Wiseman had urged Propaganda to define the limitations of the chapters regarding the colleges. Barnabò replied that any such decision would have to wait until the fifteenth decree was considered. Purcell claimed that the competence of the chapter had been resolved in 1863, along with the final decision on the decree. He quoted a document sent to Manning by the secretary of Propaganda stating that the chapter was in no way invested with the "right in office to examine or to discuss any matters relating to the diocese or its administration, much less to initiate any discussion or examination of any acts of the bishop in his administration." Only the bishop could determine when his chapter was to advise him. The Westminster Chapter, therefore, had exceeded its rights. With respect to that body's refusal to exhibit the chapter records for the cardinal, it was declared that "the cardinal archbishop, both in recalling the chapter within the limits of their competence and in requiring not only extracts of the capitular book, but the book itself, to be delivered to him, has acted strictly within his right and duty."[69]

Although Purcell wrote that this letter had been written in 1863, the copy available among Manning's papers, in his own handwriting, is undated. In 1864, moreover, Canon Morris still complained that no decision had been reached on the chapter's rights. Finally, after Wiseman's death, Manning wrote: "I could not help looking at the majority of the chapter to-day and asking myself what one thing have these men done for the Church in all these years. And when have they not crossed everything the cardinal has done." His conclusion was significant: "And he has gone to his grave without a word from Rome."[70] Since Propaganda suppressed the decree regarding chapter deputies, one may safely conclude that the Westminster Chapter had no right to initiate an investigation into the administration of St. Edmund's. The Propaganda secretary's letter, however, could not have been a formal condemnation, since the provost himself did not view it in that light.

While it was evident that Cardinal Wiseman was unwell and felt abandoned and dejected throughout the last five years of his life, he was not inactive, and there were many occasions when he demonstrated his old spirit. His policies more and more coincided with those of Manning, but he was by no means under the control of his chapter provost, at least if this implies that he had abandoned himself into the hands of another. Wiseman trusted Manning, whose influence was clearly evident. Wilfrid Ward wrote, "In critical matters he followed Manning's lead, but with the difference which his fixed habits of mind necessitated."[71] Even this claim was too strong. The two men worked together closely, but the cardinal was never led by others. He saw himself as a lonely warrior almost to the end.

17. Lonely Warrior

●

AS CARDINAL WISEMAN'S HEALTH AND SPIRITS DETERIORATED, THE question of who might succeed him became progressively more critical. It was rumored that Archbishop Errington still claimed his right to the see of Westminster in the event of its vacancy because he had never been "juridically tried and condemned for a fault." Canon Morris argued that the cardinal should nominate another coadjutor, "for that, and apparently that alone, would quite preclude any such application [on behalf of Errington] being made." Morris supported Manning's candidacy for the position. He suggested further that the cardinal might make Rome his place of residence, "coming over to England for acts of higher jurisdiction, such as holding synods etc.," but admitted that Wiseman opposed the plan on the grounds that "it would be a great mortification to him no longer to have under his eyes the progress of the many good works in which he takes so great an interest." Morris also acknowledged that Manning's unpopularity among the London clergy was a drawback. The only other man whom the same correspondent considered to be fit for the coadjutorship was Cornthwaite of Beverley.[1]

Wiseman's reaction to the proposal reveals how isolated he felt himself to be: "I have got into the way of doing my own work (in my head) alone and solitary, for I have never met with anything but opposition when I have mentioned my plans or ideas, and discouragement is the natural result. But when I mature my own plans and then set them to work with God's blessing, they generally prosper. I feel, indeed, that my time is short, but the good I can yet perform will depend on my quiet doing of it my own way." He concluded by stating that the archdiocesan chapter would be unwilling, in any case, to support his choice of a coadjutor. Presumably, he, like Morris, would have supported Manning's candidacy. Soon afterward Bishop Ullathorne's name was raised, but the cardinal would not consider it, especially since he felt "the lack of a certain sympathy with the very worthy person named." He and Ullathorne did not think alike, he wrote, and he "could not in conscience ask for my effective coadjutor a person who could not serve me with faithfulness and love."[2]

Manning was in Rome at the time, and Wiseman told him to inform Cardinal Barnabò, from whom the suggestion of appointing Ullathorne had originated, that there was an additional reason for excluding the Birmingham bishop: "In the two largest properties belonging to London . . . the deeds, above 100 years old, have a condition that if the bishop be a regular, he can have no part in their administration. This is a legal condition and any one could put the charitable trusts commission in motion and you know the possible consequences."[3] Ullathorne, of course, was a Benedictine, and Wiseman's observation was a reminder of the problems that could arise through compliance with the charitable trusts legislation, the very point upon which he and the bishop of Birmingham disagreed. The inference would not have been lost on the Roman authorities. Manning replied, "You may consider the coadjutor question as ended, and as in your hands."[4]

Early in 1862, at the pope's request, the cardinal prepared a report in which he described the progress of religion in Westminster under his direction. He stressed the opposition that he had encountered and the isolation that he had experienced, tracing, at the same time, the history of Gallican sentiment in England. It had originated in eighteenth-century attempts by Catholics to achieve emancipation by claiming their independence from the Holy See, and it persisted to such an extent that before his arrival in London, Gallican tracts had been used for teaching purposes at St. Edmund's. Bishop Bramston, Bishop Poynter's successor in 1827, had been a convert, and although his personal life had been exemplary, he had not been a great bishop. He, in turn, had been succeeded in 1836 by Bishop Griffiths, a man with no love for Rome, of the same stamp as his predecessor, but in a worse sense because of his very limited intelligence and his narrowmindedness.[5]

Wiseman then discussed the rudeness of his fellow bishops, who had never lent him the support that he had expected. For years he had made it a point to send them greetings on major feasts, yet they rarely replied. During the third provincial synod he had retired to his room, anticipating that they would come to him out of respect, but none did so, and during the sessions one of them had been insulting. It was his hope that his last years might now be spent in peace. This first part of his report was the reflection of a tired, lonely man, with a deep feeling of rejection.

Wiseman then went on, however, to describe in detail the progress of religion in the archdiocese. When he had arrived in London in 1847, there were 31 churches; in 1862 there were 80. The number of priests had risen from 58 to 184. There had been only 2 congregations of men in London when he arrived; now there were 13. In addition, the first Catholic hospital had been built, and there were 2 homes for the aged as well. Orphanages, reformatories, and industrial schools had also been established. Wiseman discussed the religious practices and devotions that he had introduced and commented upon the improved state of ecclesiastical discipline. All of this had been achieved in spite of the fact that the whole brunt of the papal aggression crisis had fallen on his head, while the other bishops were tranquil in their own homes.[6]

Wiseman's frequent references to his isolation and the fact that his poor health made it necessary for him to spend more and more time in the country should not lead to the conclusion that his last five years were those of a recluse. He was far from idle. Moreover he never lost interest in the many works to which he had previously devoted himself. There were a number of occasions when his old spirit emerged. Even in the autumn of 1860, immediately after his return from Rome, he described for Talbot the works that were being done.

> Though I have been returned but a few weeks, I have received the following consolations. 1. I have been able to pay off for [William] Kelly above £1000 of the debt on his church [St. Mary of the Angels, Commercial Road]; 2. I have had an offer of £1000 towards a new church in some very poor part of London; 3. I have recd. an offer of endowment of our nuns at the hospital (£300 per an.) . . . ; 4. The establishment has been offered & accepted (of course) of a house of 14 nuns for taking care of the sick in their own homes; 5. We have prepared at Moorfields . . . a dormitory for 50 women, houseless & often in danger. This is due to [Daniel] Gilbert [head priest at St. Mary's, Moorfields], the Cong[regatio]n having subscribed £400. I have put it under the patronage, after Our Lady, of Blessed Benedict Joseph Labre. I think you will agree that all this is something for a few weeks, not actively spent, and I hope for much more as yet.[7]

Numerous examples of charitable works that owed their foundation to Wiseman could be cited. None was dearer to his heart than the care of orphan children. In 1848 he brought the Sisters of the Faithful Virgin from Bayeux to London in order to establish an orphanage for girls at Norwood. They began their work with 2 children under their care; within a month there were 8, and the number increased to 40 within a year. In 1857 there were 143 and more than 200 by 1861. In that year the superior reported, "The number of applications for admission still continues, and one hundred and seventy nine children have been refused during the past three years, for the law will not allow any increase until enlarged accommodation is provided."[8] Wiseman established a similar institution for boys at North Hyde under the Sisters of Mercy.

When the London District was divided, Norwood fell under the care of the bishop of Southwark, as did Mother Cornelia Connelly's establishment at St. Leonards on Sea. The cardinal retained his interest in both institutions, however, although his relationship with Mother Connelly was far less close than had once been the case. This was at least partly the result of her opposition to his plan to establish a marine residence for himself at St. Leonards. In view of the criticism that Pierce Connelly was directing publicly at both his wife and Wiseman, her position was no doubt the proper one, although the cardinal seems to have resented it.[9]

To the very end of his life Wiseman delighted in composing little plays for children. Exactly three months before his death he dedicated and sent a manuscript to St. Leo's Convent, Carlow, to which his cousin belonged. He wrote, "This is the first and only manuscript of the Drama written by the Author, and forwarded to St. Leo's Convent, with his Blessing, and a request for prayers." It was a play for children, in three acts, called "The Witch of Rosenburg." The well-worn plot is not enhanced by Wiseman's crude versification, and yet there is a certain charm in the work. An epilogue, spoken by one of the characters, is striking for what it tells us of the cardinal. It describes the tale of St. Philip Neri, who while walking along the corridor of his church in Rome met one of the fathers rushing to preach to a crowded church. St. Philip advised the priest to obtain a substitute preacher, Father Chrysostom.

> "He's always ready. *Any* one can preach,
>   But very few, like you, can write a play."
> "And fewer can, like you, dear Philip, teach
>   How, than to preach, 'tis better to obey."
>
> Now, you those kindly spirits imitate,
>   Clergy or laity, our good honoured friends,
> Who come our feast to share or consecrate;
>   He highest draws our thanks, who lowest bends.

In a footnote Wiseman directed that the verses should be addressed to the bishop (if present).[10]

A month after sending off his play, the cardinal wrote to his cousin:

My Dear Cousin and Daughter in Christ,
    It has pleased Almighty God to afflict me again with illness, and I write from my bed.
    Many thanks for your kind letter on St. Nicholas' day; soon after this letter you will receive a small box, addressed to the Rev. Mother, from me; it is

intended for the Community, and contains a little Christmas Present, of things from the Tyrol, not indeed of much value.

But my special desire is that it be opened at recreation in presence of all the Community, and you will let me know if they like it.

Prayers if you please — to-day is the anniversary of your foundation.

Your affectionate Father in Christ,
N. Card. Wiseman [11]

The illness described in the letter was Wiseman's last; he died two months later. Letters of this kind and the generous concern that they represent help to explain the affection with which he was viewed by so many recipients of his thoughtfulness. He was like a child in many ways, responding warmly to any sign of appreciation but deeply hurt when neglected.

The cardinal supported a major project during his declining years that had always been one of his dreams and that he did not live to see fully realized. In 1860 Herbert Vaughan approached him and asked to work for the foreign missions. Wiseman replied by describing his own long-standing dream for establishing a mission college: "I determined to wait till the person who should undertake it should be presented to me, and never to pass a day without praying to know God's will and His time for its execution. You are the first person who has offered himself for the purpose. I am now old and cannot hope to do much myself, but I see that God has heard my prayers, and that the work is from Him." [12] In 1863, with the cardinal's blessing, Vaughan sought the approval of the other bishops, and only Goss refused to support the plan. The following August, finally, Vaughan sought even wider approval by raising the subject at an international congress held at Malines, Belgium, where a resolution was passed in favor of the work, and soon afterward he received a special blessing from the Holy Father himself.

In December 1863 Herbert Vaughan set out for America to beg for funds to support the college. On the eve of his departure, the cardinal wrote to him.

My Dear Herbert, — it is only now, when you are on the eve of starting for your noble mission, that I seem to realise the greatness of your devotedness and self-sacrifice in separating yourself from home and friends, and from all that is *naturally* dear to you. I say *naturally*, because I know that *spiritually* the souls of poor heathens, and the most Precious Blood which redeemed them, are infinitely dearer to you. Were I not sure of this, I could not dare to accept such a surrender as you are making of all human comfort and even religious consolation. Health even, of which I hope you will be *most* careful, seems risked in such an undertaking. Indeed, did I not feel an impression which I can scarcely describe of the solemnity, or rather sublimity, of our cause, I would hardly allow you to embark in the double ocean of the work and of the Atlantic. But I feel an inexpressible confidence in the power and goodness of God, that He will prosper this work, such as I have never, perhaps, felt in any other. Especially, while I am myself in so much darkness and depression about myself, this feeling shines brighter and seems given to me to compensate for my past and actual sufferings. I therefore give you a parting, though, I hope, not a final blessing. May God preserve you through all the troubles and dangers of your mission; protect you, support you, and guide you by His wisdom, power, and goodness. May He prosper your work, and crown it with success, and bring you home safe and well, to carry out here to completion what you are so piously beginning at a distance.[13]

Vaughan was begging in South America when he received word of Wiseman's death. He soon returned, and in 1866 founded the College of St. Joseph, Mill Hill.

There were bright moments for the cardinal, then, in spite of the trials that he experienced. He continued to describe the progress of the Catholic cause. In December 1862 he told Talbot that five new churches were under construction in the archdiocese alone, as well as five "new, spacious convents, with schools." He observed "that the coldest and sourest can hardly deny the wonderful change that is gradually taking place. The conversions have increased in a ratio unprecedented."[14]

Wiseman's life had changed radically since he had first given himself to scholarly pursuits in Rome and then set out to provide leadership for the small body of Catholic intelligentsia in England. It was still his ambition to foster the development of a Catholic intellectual community, and in 1861 he founded for that purpose an Academia of the Catholic Religion, based on the Roman society to which he had belonged since 1830. His inaugural address in June 1861 dealt with his favorite themes, the ability of the church to adopt and utilize what is best in the spirit of an age and the alleged conflict between science and religion. He pointed out that "on science seriously and conscientiously conducted, the church looks on fearless, but cautious; fearless of facts, but most cautious on deductions." He referred specifically to the theory of evolution that had been contested so hotly after the publication of Charles Darwin's *Origin of Species* in 1859: "How many human skeletons have been announced in pre-adamitic positions! Yet not one has been admitted as proved. Let any number of new hideous apes be found in Africa, and hailed as a more remote progenitor by enlightened naturalists, I will be satisfied to end my genealogy at the first of the line endowed with reason, . . . and to trace my life to the breath of life inhaled by Adam from the mouth of God."[15]

John Henry Newman had warned Manning that he would not allow his own name to stand as a member of the Academia if the cardinal chose to use the organization as a platform for promoting the temporal power of the pope as dogma to be held by all Catholics.[16] The question of the temporal power was dividing Catholics, with Manning and W. G. Ward in the vanguard of those whose ultramontane views were, as Newman later told Ward, "making a Church within a Church, as the Novatians of old did within the Catholic pale, and as, outside the Catholic pale, the Evangelicals of the Establishment." Wilfrid Ward wrote that the cardinal saw the Academia "as an institution which should keep Catholics abreast of the science and literature of the hour," whereas Manning viewed it "as an engine for infusing the Roman spirit into the cultivated laity." The analysis was essentially accurate. In 1866 Manning stated that the Academia's purpose was "the maintenance and defence of the Catholic religion, both positively in itself, and in its relation to all other truth; polemically as against all forms of erroneous doctrines, principles and thought." Moreover, Manning wanted to broaden the base of the organization and to make it "a society in which *all* Catholic men could meet, if they so desired, for discussion and lectures and which would be a real educative force." The result, almost inevitably, was "a lowering of its intellectual standards" that "may have accounted in some measure for its later decline."[17]

Cardinal Wiseman, though undoubtedly ultramontane in sentiment and conviction, was less likely than Ward or Manning to promote and impose exaggerated claims. Almost thirty years earlier he had raised the subject of the temporal power.

> The supremacy which I have described, is of a character purely spiritual, and has no connexion with the possession of any temporal jurisdiction. The sovereignty of the Pope over his own dominions, is no essential portion of his dignity; his supremacy was not the less before it was acquired, and should the unsearchable decrees of Providence, in the lapse of ages, deprive the Holy See of its temporal sovereignty, as happened to the seventh Pius, through the usurpation of a conqueror, its dominion over the Church, and over the consciences of the faithful, would not be thereby impaired.

However, when it was suggested in November 1861 that Richard Simpson, also a member of the Academia, should read a paper in answer to one by Ward, the cardinal "interposed, & said that the Academy was not to be turned into a mere debating club, & that its forms did not permit of paper against paper."[18] In this, as in all of his projects, Wiseman hoped to unite, not to divide, Catholics. There was too much working against him for his objective to be fully realized.

The cardinal could not remain indifferent, of course, to the loss of the papal states, which, with the exception of Rome itself, was virtually complete by 1860. In March of that year he urged English Catholics to contribute to Peter's pence in order to support the pope. They did so to the extent of £6,340. While returning to England after the canonization of the Japanese martyrs, Wiseman took advantage of his longtime acquaintance with the French emperor to seek his further support on behalf of the Holy Father. He seems to have considered his audience a success but soon learned differently: Napoleon III's policy no longer included a commitment to preserve the pope's temporal power.[19]

In his later years Wiseman was in demand as a public speaker, recognized and accepted as an important figure by both Catholics and non-Catholics. At the beginning of 1863 he described for Talbot a lecture that he had delivered at the Royal Institution, "the highest and most scientific place in London." His topic was "On the Point of Contact between Science and Art," and he wrote that the hall was so crowded "that neither a seat nor a standing place was left vacant." Although he had been suffering from an attack of dyspepsia, he managed to speak for an hour and three quarters to an immense audience. He reported that all could hear him without difficulty and applauded continuously: "The most acceptable criticism which I heard of, was one overheard by Herbert [Vaughan]: 'Why! he will convert the whole place.' Yet there was no controversy of course or theology in the L[ecture]."[20]

The following August, Wiseman was a principal speaker at the Catholic Congress held at Malines, where one of the major topics was the current situation of Catholics in various countries. The cardinal described the constitutional form of government in his own country and the troubled history of Catholicism there. "Justice, as done to their fellow citizens, is all they demand," he said of English Catholics, and he observed that when they were united, they had demonstrated a strength far beyond what might have been expected from their numbers. He listed some of the concessions they had won: separate education for Catholic poor children; their own reformatories and support for Catholic prison chaplains; the appointment of Catholic school inspectors and their own chaplains for both the army and navy, equal in all respects to Protestants. These measures had resulted from special acts of Parliament and had been granted because of the pressures of Catholics upon parliamentary candidates and the various ministries.

The statistics that Wiseman provided for the assembly were impressive. Between 1830 and 1863 the number of priests in England had grown from 434 to 1,240; in 1830 there had been 16 convents, but in 1863 there were 163; there had been very few religious houses of men or monasteries in 1830, but in 1863 there were 55; in 1830 Catholic hospitals or charitable institutions were nonexistent, but there were 34 in 1863. Herbert Vaughan, who was at the congress, later wrote that the address "was delivered fluently in French, though the accent was somewhat English." The cardinal had spoken "at great length, and was enthusiastically applauded." Another observer provided a different account: "Wiseman's speech was a complete fiasco: he read from a paper an account of progress of Church in England; people couldn't hear him, were impatient to hear Montalembert and so tried to 'choke him off' with applause: in vain."[21] It is likely that both Vaughan and Professor T. J. Lamy of Louvain, who provided the unfavorable account, described the reaction of members of the audience with whom they were personally identified.

It was Montalembert who attracted the most attention at the congress. He delivered two addresses that received much criticism from conservative Catholics. One was on "A Free Church in a Free State," the other on "Liberty of Conscience." It was later reported that Wiseman was among those who wished the Holy See to condemn the liberal views expressed by his friend of so many years. Montalembert wrote to Ambrose Phillipps de Lisle, "I have heard from Rome that the Oxford converts and Cardinal Wiseman have been my principal antagonists." Montalembert had urged the principles of democracy and religious toleration upon the assembly, and Wiseman was reported to have said that the count's doctrines "made terrible, though silent confusion." When informed of a rumor that he had complained to the Holy See of one of the Frenchman's speeches, however, the cardinal denied it: "Though I did not and do not agree in its political principles and tendencies, there was no error in it against faith or morals, which could have authorised anyone to denounce it, especially a stranger, in presence of the Metropolitan." He concluded this letter to Phillipps de Lisle, "You may assure the Count of this, and of my undiminished respect and affection for him."[22]

Montalembert upheld political liberalism; Wiseman, however, was faced with a dilemma. He and other Catholics had invoked the principle of political liberalism in demanding that Catholics should be treated as all other citizens. He could not view with indifference, on the other hand, the application of the liberal principle to justify the dismemberment of the papal states or the limitations imposed on the church by the kingdom of Piedmont.

The temporal power of the popes was a major subject treated in the *Rambler*, and the questions raised resulted in complaints from both the bishops and the Holy See itself. When Manning was criticized in the journal for his ultramontanism, Wiseman defended him in a letter to Talbot: "M[anning] is truly the champion of the Pope and his temporality. The R[ambler] gave only garbled extracts to serve its own ends."[23] The cardinal's opposition to the *Rambler* was far deeper, however, than his disagreement with the manner in which its writers treated a single subject, and his attitude was not merely the result of Manning's influence. The other bishops, in fact, were as determined as he was to control Catholic opinion and to limit the influence of liberal Catholics like John Acton and Simpson.

After Newman resigned as editor of the *Rambler* in 1859, Acton and Simpson resumed control. Their continued policy of dealing with sensitive issues and their determination to demonstrate the right of Catholic writers to exercise their independence from ecclesiastical supervision in discussing subjects of a nondoctrinal nature led to further objections and complaints. The *Dublin Review* served as a vehicle of communication for those whom they considered as opponents. By 1862 Acton concluded that the format of his journal did not provide adequate means "to do justice to many important subjects, nor to admit the articles of a large number of contributors." He explained that if he had made the contemplated changes at an earlier time, it would have been interpreted as "an act of aggressive competition with the Dublin Review."[24] He now concluded that the rival journal was in such a "precarious state" that he anticipated no objections. He and Simpson discontinued the *Rambler* and established instead a quarterly, the *Home and Foreign Review*. There was little change in the tone of its contents.

As both men knew, the bishops were becoming increasingly incensed by their editorial policy. The last issue of the *Rambler* was published in May 1862. In the same month Cardinal Barnabò wrote to the English bishops to complain that the *Rambler* was objectionable. Among the criticisms were that "abstruse questions closely connected with the Faith are raised, and one of the principal writers often puts forward temerarious and scandalous propositions; the temporal authority of the Holy See is openly attacked, and the administration of the Pontifical States; it is said that Paul III, Paul IV, Pius V, preferred temporal emolument to the good of souls, and were the cause of England's loss to the Catholic faith." The bishops were told to warn the faithful against the journal.[25]

When it became evident that the new and expanded journal would be as offensive as its predecessor, Wiseman, after his return from Rome in 1862, wrote to his clergy to warn them of the *Home and Foreign* and of "the antecedents of that journal under another name." He mentioned "the absence for years of all reserve or reverence in its treatment of persons or things deemed sacred, its grazing over the very edges of the most perilous abysses of error, and its habitual preference of uncatholic to catholic instincts, tendencies, and motives." His role was not a welcome one: "In uttering these sad thoughts, and entreating to warn your people, and especially the young, against such dangerous leadership, believe me I am only obeying a higher direction than my own impulses, and acting under much more solemn sanctions. Nor shall I stand alone in this unhappily necessary correction."[26] Wiseman's conviction that reverence for religious sensibilities and conformity to the attitudes of the Holy See had to characterize the writings of Catholic authors was far from new. He had used the same arguments many years before in breaking his connection with the *Catholic Magazine*.

Wiseman was supported by his suffragans. Bishop Clifford sent a similar circular to his priests: "We fully concur in the remarks made by his Eminence, and we trust that you will prudently exert your best endeavours, to prevent any of those committed to your care, allowing themselves to be led astray by dangerous teachers." Bishop Ullathorne, always sensitive to possible scandal in the writings of Catholics, took an equally strong stand.[27]

Shortly after the Malines Congress an assembly of German Catholic scholars was held in Munich. Döllinger was its president. In his major address "The Past and Present of Catholic Theology," he criticized traditional scholastic theology with its limitations and argued that Catholic scholars should embrace all of the tools of modern scholarship. They should be allowed complete freedom from the interference of ecclesiastical authority, except for those rare instances when dogmatic error might clearly be an issue. Rome responded in the form of a papal brief, sent to the archbishop of Munich, which repudiated the principle that Catholic scholars might pursue their studies and publish their findings independent of ecclesiastical authority. The Munich brief led directly to the cessation of the *Home and Foreign Review*. Acton wrote: "A conflict with the authorities would not only be a grievous scandal, but would destroy the efficiency and use of the Review, and I have determined not to risk a censure, but to take the significant warning of this document, and to put an end to the Review after the appearance of the next number."[28]

Acton took advantage of the final issue of his review to interpret the Munich brief: "In a word . . . the Brief affirms that the common opinions and explanations of Catholic divines ought not to yield to the progress of secular science, and that the course of theological knowledge ought to be controlled by the decrees of the Index." He went on to state that "one of the essential principles of this Review consists in a clear recognition, first, of the infinite gulf which in theology separates what is of faith from what is not of faith, . . . and next, of the practical difference which exists in ecclesiastical discipline between the acts of infallible authority and those which possess no higher sanction than that of canonical legality." He admitted that the Holy See had not denied the distinction between dogma and opinion, although the aim was "to reduce the practical recognition of it among Catholics to the smallest possible limits." Acton saw no alternative except to cease publication.

> Warned, therefore, by the language of the Brief, I will not provoke ecclesiastical authority to a more explicit repudiation of doctrines which are necessary to secure its influence upon the advance of modern science. I will not challenge a conflict which would only deceive the world into a belief that religion cannot be harmonised with all that is right and true in the

progress of the present age. But I will sacrifice the existence of the Review to the defence of its principles, in order that I may combine the obedience which is due to legitimate ecclesiastical authority with an equally conscientious maintenance of the rightful and necessary liberty of thought.[29]

A modern historian has called Acton's essay "the swan song of English liberal Catholicism." He has further observed, "The cessation of the *Home and Foreign* . . . meant, in effect, the end of the Liberal Catholic movement in England." There is much truth in the observation. At the very least, those who identified themselves with Acton and Simpson were deprived of a vehicle through which their thought might be circulated. On the other hand, W. G. Ward and those who shared his ultramontane sympathies were able to express themselves without fear of serious, public opposition from those Catholics with whom they disagreed. Wiseman officially transferred ownership of the *Dublin Review* to Manning in 1862, and W. G. Ward assumed its editorship in July of the following year.[30]

It has been suggested that the publication of *Essays and Reviews* in 1860 "opened Wiseman's eyes to the theological condition of the Universities and to the heterodox teachings which could with impunity be propagated there." All but one of the seven contributors were clergymen of the established church, and most of them were connected with either Oxford or Cambridge. Their objective was to reconcile the teachings of the church with modern scientific discovery and the methodology of nineteenth-century biblical and historical criticism. Bishop Samuel Wilberforce concluded that the authors could not "with moral honesty maintain their posts as clergymen of the established church."[31] Two of their number were prosecuted for teaching heresy, and the prolonged publicity given to their condemnation by the court of arches, its reversal by the judicial committee of the privy council, and ultimately a condemnation by the convocation of Canterbury made the whole affair one of some notoriety. The seven authors were popularly dubbed "septem contra Christum" (seven against Christ).

The publication of *Essays and Reviews* and Darwin's *Origin of Species*, within two months of each other, and the storm created by both came at a time when Wiseman and his fellow bishops were becoming increasingly concerned with the independence demonstrated by the editors of the *Rambler*. The cardinal had always maintained that the church had nothing to fear from scientific inquiry pursued within its proper sphere. He had been equally insistent in promoting the need for an educated Catholic community. It had never been his contention, however, that the scholar could work in total independence of the church's magisterium. It was not entirely due to Manning then, as some have intimated, that Wiseman ultimately took a position of determined opposition to Catholic youth attending Oxford and Cambridge.[32] The Holy See had not accepted the principle of mixed education in Ireland, nor would it be disposed to support it in England; neither would the cardinal.

Manning later wrote:

> There was no one who ever manifested so large and generous a sympathy with the conversions that issued from Oxford, and with members of the Anglican Communion, than the late Cardinal. His learned and powerful writings in defence of the Catholic faith were studiously directed both in matter and in manner, without sacrifice of jot or tittle of the truth, to attract and to conciliate the members of the Anglican Communion and the writers of the Oxford Movement. . . . If ever, therefore, there was any one who, if it had been possible to sanction it, would have rejoiced over . . . the return of Catholic youth to the Universities which Catholic England had created, it would have been our late Cardinal. But two things forbade him: his unerring Catholic instinct, and his keen intuition of the impossibility of combining fidelity to the divine tradition of the faith with the intellectual developments and contradictions of modern England.[33]

The matter was not resolved until very shortly before Wiseman's death, and Newman was one of the major figures in the ultimate decision of the English bishops to forbid Catholic attendance at the universities.

With the approval of Bishop Ullathorne, Newman had bought land in Oxford for the purpose of establishing an Oratory there. Wiseman, however, was among those who believed that Newman's presence would be a direct invitation for Catholics to enroll in the university. Prompted as much by public debate among Catholics over the question of whether they should send their children to English universities as by Newman's plan to start an Oratory at Oxford, Wiseman prepared a questionnaire and distributed it widely. Its recipients were asked at the outset whether there was anything in English university education that could not be given in the Catholic colleges. The tenth question was especially loaded: "Considering the present condition of belief in the truths of revelation among leading minds in the Universities, do you think that the intercourse natural between the learned and able men of the Universities with younger minds and inexperienced scholars, would not necessarily tend to weaken the faith in these?" The next question was equally weighted: "Would it be possible, not to say expedient, to guard such impressionable minds, especially where there was an ardour for learning, by weakening or destroying all confidence on the part of youth in those whom they were otherwise expected to respect and submit their judgment to?" There were twenty questions in all, and they left no doubt as to Wiseman's own position. Wiseman summoned a meeting of bishops on December 13, 1864, and summarized for his colleagues the replies to the questionnaire: "With only one or two exceptions all the answers given to the Cardinal and to the Bishops show that Catholics ought not to go to the existing Protestant Colleges." All of the bishops then signed a letter to Propaganda stating, "1. that the establishment of Catholic Colleges at the Universities could in no way be approved; and 2. that parents were by all means to be dissuaded from sending their sons to the Universities."[34]

When Newman heard of the decision, he canceled his plan for an Oxford Oratory. He later wrote: "The Cardinal has done a great work and has gone to his reward. Alas! that his last act has been to extinguish a hope of a great future and an opening for a wide field of religious action." To another correspondent he added: "Personally I have not much to thank him for, since I was a Catholic. He always meant kindly, but his impulses, kind as they were, were evanescent, and he was naturally influenced by those who got around him and occupied his ear."[35]

The month before the meeting of the bishops Wiseman sent his views on mixed education to Talbot. Writing in Italian, he showed clearly that his feelings for Newman were not what they once had been. He reported that the famed Oratorian made no secret of his conviction that the Protestant system of education was superior to that of the Catholics. Persuaded by his admirers, wrote Wiseman, Newman had established his school at Edgbaston, modeled on Eton, in which, as he had been told, the religious instruction was insufficient. The cardinal said that he was certain Newman had always viewed Oxford as the place where a boy should conclude his education, although he then observed that nobody for a moment would have questioned the Oratorian's value as a missionary or a priest.[36]

The seven weekly parts of Newman's *Apologia* had been published between April 21 and June 2, 1864. When Newman sent the first part to the cardinal, he received a short note of thanks, stating that he had read it "with great pleasure and admiration." The following autumn Newman heard that the cardinal was surprised and hurt at not having received a further reply to his own note of thanks. He immediately wrote to apologize for any misunderstanding and added: "Our Bishop contemplates putting the Oxford mission into our hands: our view in accepting it would be that of ultimately founding an Oratory there. Some friends wish a subscription opened for a Church there commemorative of the Oxford Movement. In that case I should take the liberty of applying for the aid of your Eminence, whose zeal had so much to do with the direction which it eventually took."[37]

The following November, Newman was persuaded by J. L. Patterson to visit the cardinal while in London. He did so and was treated with some rudeness for the ten minutes that the interview lasted.

I saw him [Wiseman], I suppose, in his usual state—relaxed, feeble, and dejected. On ringing at the door, I had said to P[atterson] "You must bring me off in five minutes, for the Cardinal is so entertaining a talker, that it is always difficult to get away from him." Alas, what I never could have fancied before hand, I was the only speaker. I literally *talked*. He is anxious about his eyes. Patterson calls it "congestion." The Cardinal says that the London fog tries them. He was just down—2 o'clock or 2 1/2.—He listened to the Oxford plan, half querulously—and said that he thought the collection for St. Thomas at Rome would interfere with getting money from the Continent.

Eleven years later Newman added to this letter: "I afterwards had reason for thinking that a deep opposition to my going to Oxford was the cause of the Cardinal's manner. Of this I was quite unsuspicious."[38]

Patterson later substantiated Newman's report and more. The cardinal was only persuaded to see his visitor with some difficulty. Patterson blamed himself for insisting on the meeting, but as he wrote, "I had never heard the Cardinal speak unkindly of Dr. Newman." He went on: "This leads me to say that Cardinal Wiseman was *not* a well-bred man—and he was in such a constant state of bodily suffering from diabetes—which is notoriously a disease that affects the temper almost to the pitch of mania—that at times he was quite unbearable. . . . He was already sickening for his last illness at this time, and lived but 3 months longer." It was shortly after this that Wiseman wrote his views on Newman's planned Oratory. Patterson concluded by referring to a report, heard many years later, that the cardinal had complained to Rome of Newman's "insolence during this visit": "I can only *conjecture* that his mind must have been poisoned against Dr. Newman, and that having nothing of his own to allege he took up some one else's version of Dr. Newman's visit. . . . You will note that I was not present at the interview—but literally there was not time for any irritating (or otherwise) dialogue."[39]

Although the majority of the bishops, not to mention Manning and Talbot, agreed with the cardinal's reaction to the proposed Oxford Oratory, it is improbable that they had "poisoned" him against Newman. The explanation may be more simple, although Patterson was no doubt correct in commenting upon the cardinal's irritability. After all, he was a critically sick man. After reading Newman's *Apologia*, Wiseman started to write a memorandum entitled "Some remarks upon a passage in Dr. Newman's *Apologia*." He completed no more than the following passage, which survives among his papers at Ushaw.

There is a short paragraph in this invaluable work, which appears to me worthy of some elucidation. It occurs at p. 368, and runs as follows.
"Soon" (after Dr. Newman's leaving Littlemore, 1846) "Dr. Wiseman in

whose Vicariate Oxford lay called me to Oscott, and I went there with others; afterwards he sent me to Rome, and finally placed me in Birmingham."

It is possible [wrote Wiseman] that some readers may see in these few lines, even now, a record of three arbitrary sets of episcopal authority, almost simultaneous, or without long intervals, and wholly unconnected with the writer's desires or voluntary concurrence. But it may not be till all the parties interested in this abridged statement have passed away, and no one remains to explain it, that it may be seized on as an evidence of the summary way in which the Church deprives even men of Dr. Newman's genius of any liberty.[40]

The cardinal's reaction was that of an unduly sensitive man. At the same time, he was aware of the nature of much criticism directed at the heavy hand of ecclesiastical authority in dealing with Catholic scholars. Newman himself, during a period of depression, had expressed resentment in his journal at the way in which Wiseman had used him during the period immediately after his conversion.[41] Both men considered themselves to be victims of neglect and outright opposition. They never ceased to admire each other, but they grew mutually suspicious, a feeling that was intensified by their conflicting opinions on mixed education. Their last meeting was memorable only for the cardinal's coldness, an unhappy ending to what had begun twenty years earlier as a promising relationship.

During the last years of his life Wiseman took a position on another matter that has seemed to some observers as reflecting a change from his earlier openness to non-Catholics. In 1857 a group of Roman Catholics, Greeks, and Anglicans met and established a society called the Association for Promoting the Unity of Christendom (APUC). Concerned especially with corporate reunion of the three churches, members were not expected "to compromise any principles which they rightly or wrongly hold dear." They were only "asked to unite for the promotion of a high and holy end, in reliance on the promise of our Divine Lord, that 'whatsoever we shall ask in prayer, believing, we shall receive.' "[42] Ambrose Phillipps de Lisle was active among the founding members.

Wiseman's earlier writings, especially his *Letter on Catholic Unity*, were a clear indication to some that he would support their cause. In 1857, however, he sent a memorandum on the association to the Holy See. He was not especially confident of its immediate prospects and, in fact, saw it as dangerous, insofar as it might be used to argue against individual conversions to Catholicism. He urged, nevertheless, that the Holy See not take action against it, and he raised no objection to Catholic participation in the organization. He opposed explicitly, however, the view held by some members that there were "three great denominations . . . of Christians, i.e. Catholics, Greeks and Anglicans, as though they were all equal, and could treat of religious union upon a footing of equality." [43]

By 1864 Wiseman agreed with those who feared that Catholic orthodoxy was being compromised by the position of many members of the APUC, and he joined the other bishops in asking the Holy See for its condemnation. Catholic members, for one thing, were urging that a hall for Catholics might be established at Oxford, just at the time when the bishops expressed themselves opposed to such a plan. The university question, then, became closely identified with that of the APUC.

Wilfrid Ward and others have written as though Wiseman's position on Catholic attendance at the universities and his opposition to their participation in the Association for Promoting the Unity of Christendom represented a change of view for which Manning was responsible. [44] In spite of his increasing dependence upon Manning in the execution of his affairs, particularly with the Holy See, it is difficult to see where Wiseman had changed his basic approach either to the universities or to Christian unity. His openness to non-Catholics had always been based upon the presumption that union could only be achieved by their acceptance of Catholic truth in its fullness. Moreover, there are few instances throughout his life in which the judgment of the Holy See did not prevail over all other considerations, although he was disappointed on more than one occasion when his own position was not vindicated. Practically speaking, the cardinal had always been an ultramontane, and he remained so until his death. His receptiveness to non-Catholics and his friendly relations with them had never led him to view their religious convictions with favor, except where these indicated an acceptance of Catholic doctrine or practice that, he supposed, would dispose them for eventual conversion.

In 1862 the cardinal was accused of an anti-Irish disposition: he considered it necessary to intervene when London Irishmen took it upon themselves to attack the pro-Garibaldian speakers who had been drawing enormous crowds of supporters in Hyde Park. A recent account of the affair states that "as a major act of identification of Irish cockney violence with Roman Catholicism, the riots of 1862 had neither prelude nor sequal." It has been estimated "that of the 100,000 Londoners who practised the Catholic religion in 1851, some 80,000 were of Irish descent (many of them, one may add, by now rather remotely)." Although Wiseman had no sympathy with those responsible for the loss of the papal states, he felt a special responsibility for the souls of the Irish who had been committed to his spiritual care. In order to prevent further violence, he wrote to his priests and told them to "go into the courts and lanes . . . where the poor Irish dwell, and use every effort, by remonstrance and persuasion, to prevent their going to any public meeting, or forming any gatherings in the street." He also prepared a pastoral letter addressed to his "dear Irish children," which was to be read on Sunday, October 11, in all of the London churches: "Nothing would afflict our Sovereign Pontiff's tender heart more than to hear that you, his most cherished Irish children, have attempted to support his sacred cause by such violence." In the same letter the cardinal acknowledged the righteousness of the indignation felt, an admission which led to the Protestant accusation that he was fanning the flames of further strife.[45]

Wiseman's dilemma was shared by all Catholic priests at the time: "The priest who espoused the political aspirations of his people divided the Church; and the priest who denied the popular voice might destroy the respect which the people paid to him, and risk the salvation of Irish souls." Wiseman explained his own actions in a letter to Talbot: "Now about the Irish news. A Saint died, we are told, 'because he saw God offended in a tumult,' and he was not the Bishop of the place. I am of London and I consider it my first duty to prevent every mortal sin possible. Thank God I hope I have prevented *many*, perhaps murders, certainly many wounds & bloodshed, much misery to families &c. A *second* duty is to prevent scandal to religion and through it loss of souls." Wiseman had been accused in Rome of having acted from an anti-Irish spirit, but he responded warmly:

> The disedification or rather disgust created in the public mind by the conduct of our people in the Park, exaggerated tenfold by the Press, was being painfully used to exasperate the public mind against our religion & the Holy See. Now if preventing sin, misery and scandal be the symptoms of an anti-Irish spirit, I am willing to own it and answer for it. But there is another thing which probably you are not aware of at Rome. It is that we here have no doubt that Govt. connived at the disturbances, and wanted them, to get up a cry before the elections. A writer in the Times said to Sir G[eorge] B[owyer] the other day: "The fact is we are determined to get up a No-Popery cry; and do what you like, we will have it." They are woefully disappointed that an end has been put to the opportunities for mischief: and the "Public Opinion," a moderate paper which collects the sentiments of all others, attributes the stoppage of the riots to my Pastorals. Hence almost all the papers have been furious against it & me.

The cardinal concluded by citing another instance in which he had acted to prevent agitation in England but which had been misunderstood by Cardinal Fransoni and others in Rome: "I wish they wd. give one on the spot & who has not ever committed himself in dealing with public Cath. affairs credit for seeing & knowing more of what is going on under his nose, than they can see at such a distance."[46] Such expressions against the interference of Roman officialdom in local affairs were rare in Wiseman's correspondence, but by then he was thoroughly annoyed by appeals and counterappeals to the Holy See whenever a matter of controversy arose.

The autumn before Wiseman's death, the Royal Institution asked him to prepare a lecture on William Shakespeare in anticipation of the tercentenary of the Bard's death. Too ill to write any longer, Wiseman dictated the lecture in two sessions. The month after his death his executors published the work. In itself it is of little value, but it demonstrates the breadth of Wiseman's interests and even the ideal to which he himself aspired.

> We may compare the mind of Shakespeare to a diamond pellucid, bright, and untinted, cut into countless polished facets, which, in constant movement, at every smallest change of direction or of angle, caught a new reflection, so that not one of its brilliant mirrors could be for a moment idle, but by a power beyond its control was ever busy with the reflection of innumerable images, either distinct or running into one another, or repeated each so clearly as to allow him, when he chose, to fix it in his memory.

It was Shakespeare's genius upon which Wiseman concentrated: "I have spoken of genius as a gift to an individual man. I will conclude by the reflection that that man becomes himself a gift; a gift to his nation; a gift to his age; a gift to the world of all times."[47]

By November 1864 it was evident that Cardinal Wiseman could not live much longer. He had been able to preside over a meeting of the bishops in December, but he did so as an invalid. During those days he was consoled by the return of Richard Waldo Sibthorpe to communion with Rome. Sibthorpe offered his first mass, after a period of twenty years, in the cardinal's chapel.

Wiseman planned his own funeral: "See that everything is done quite right. Do not let a rubric be broken." He later said: "I want to have everything the Church gives me, down to the Holy Water. Do not leave out anything. I want everything." On February 4 he asked for Manning who was in Rome at the time. The provost was notified by telegraph that the end was near, and he hurried home, arriving on February 12. There was some doubt as to whether the cardinal recognized him, but when informed that the Holy Father sent his special blessing, Wiseman responded several times: "I thank him."

The previous week Wiseman had summoned the members of his chapter, and after making a formal profession of faith in their presence, he said:

> I have one word to say, and it is to beg you to cherish peace, and charity, and unity, even though it may be at the price of our occasionally having to give up our own individual opinions for the sake of peace. And if in the past

there has been anything that has made against charity and unity, in God's name let it pass into oblivion; let us put aside all jealousies and let us forgive one another and love one another.

Canon Morris later wrote that when the cardinal was dying, he had suggested to his confessor that he should send for Bishop Grant, "but he was unfortunately dissuaded from doing so." Grant came to him of his own accord and prayed by his bed, but Wiseman was evidently not aware of his presence. This does not mean that Wiseman and Grant were completely estranged until the end. On the contrary, just before his last illness Wiseman wrote to Talbot, "I went the other day to see Dr. Grant, who has sprained his foot."[48]

The cardinal felt his hurts deeply; it was only on the rarest of occasions that he could have been accused of pettiness. More than a year before, he unburdened himself completely to Searle.

> When a man comes to the last possible decade of his life, and looks back to see how short the previous one, though entire, has been, he cannot wish to spend the poor remnant of his life without peace, or to make others, long close to him, unhappy. . . . If anything that I have said or done has inflicted pain on you, I regret it most sincerely, and beg you to forgive it. But I can say from my heart, that it was totally unintentional; and as, I feel sure, must have been anything that has led to erroneous impressions in me, respecting you. I trust, therefore, that in future there will be no more room for misunderstanding: but you must not forget that the infirmities of age have come thick upon me, and that one of the merits of the young and strong and more perfect consists in bearing with the weakness for which in their turn they may have to entreat compassion. God bless you.[49]

Wiseman was anxious to put quarrels behind him, and he proceeded to do so with honesty and humility.

The end came on February 15, 1865. Public expressions of sympathy were immediate and even somewhat staggering for English Catholics, who had grown accustomed to a different kind of publicity. Wilfrid Ward wrote, "The extent of the demonstration took everybody by surprise, and has never been quite adequately explained." Newman, who did not attend the funeral, commented: "What a wonderful fact is the reception given to his funeral by the Population of London! And the Newspapers remark that the son of that Lord Campbell, who talked of trampling on his Cardinal's Hat 14 years ago, was present at the Requiem Mass."[50]

Manning, designated by the cardinal himself to deliver the funeral sermon, offered an eloquent appreciation of Wiseman's achievement. Almost alone among the English bishops, he had foreseen a great future for the church.

Many good and prudent men looked at the same horizon, and saw no signs, no harbinger of the morrow. They treated the Bishop of Melipotamus as sanguine and visionary, one whom hope had distempered. They saw nothing in England but the hard surface of the earth seared by the old storms of religious controversy which had furrowed the land. He saw beneath the surface, and discerned the delicate and vivid lines of new habits of thought, new aspirations after an inheritance which had been forfeited.

Each member of the congregation would picture the cardinal in his own way.

Some of you remember him, as the companion of your boyhood, upon the bare hills of Durham; some, in the early morning of his life, in the sanctuaries of Rome; some see before them now his slender stooping form, on a bright winter's day, walking to the Festival of St. Agnes out of the walls; some again, drawn up to the full stature of his manhood, rising above the storm, and contending with the calm commanding voice of reason against the momentary unreason of the people of England; some, again, can see him vested and arrayed as a Prince of the Church, with the twelve suffragans of England, closing the long procession which, after the silence of three hundred years, opened the first Provincial Synod of Westminster. Some will picture him in the great hall of a Roman palace, surrounded by half the Bishops of the world, of every language and of every land, chosen by them as their chief to fashion their words in declaring to the Sovereign Pontiff their filial obedience to the spiritual and temporal power with which God has invested the Vicar of His Son. Some will see him feeble in death, but strong in faith, arrayed as a Pontiff, surrounded by the Chapter of the Church, by word and deed verifying the Apostle's testimony, "I have fought a good fight, I have finished my course, I have kept the faith." And some will cherish, above all these visions of greatness and of glory, the calm and sweet countenance of their best and fastest friend and father, lying in the dim light of his chamber — not of death, but of transit to his crown. These things are visions; but they are substance. "Transit gloria mundi," as the flax burns in fire. But these things shall not pass away.[51]

Very few would know of the young man, just eighteen years old, who suffered from scruples at the prospect of taking an oath that might remove him forever from serving the church in England. Fewer still would know of his loyal contributions to the support of his mother and sister while he was still a student, or his attempts to assist his brother in later years, or the provision made for his widowed sister-in-law and her child. If it was evident that he provided for the education of his nephews, little was known of the financial need to which he was responding or the generosity that his sacrifice demanded. There was a personal side to Wiseman's character, exposed to few, although he was more open to the young than to those more nearly his equals.

Robert Whitty offered advice on the means of writing Wiseman's biography: "The great difficulty in writing the life of such a man as Card. W. is to represent fairly *both* sides of his character — the darker as well as the brighter side. Even from what I have written, you can see I don't approve of putting forward the bright side only."[52] The cardinal would not have disagreed. One of the problems in treating him is not a lack of information, but rather the vast amount of material available from which to draw. The process of selection and unavoidable omission is not easy. To omit the battles of his later years, even the heated, personal judgments found in the correspondence, would lead to an inadequate picture not only of the man himself but of his determination to pursue the course that he considered right, even at the loss of those whose friendship he valued.

It would be difficult, however, to name anyone who might have been better fitted for the work to which Wiseman devoted himself. He was prepared to meet the demands made by the changing number and condition of English Catholics, and he was farsighted as no other. Those of his accomplishments that contributed to a sense of pride and security among Catholics tend to be overshadowed by the battles in which he was engaged. Controversy did not begin among English Catholics in his time, however, nor were the squabbles that characterized Wiseman's entrance upon the scene more bitter than those of an earlier period. English Catholics were accustomed to a place in society in which, as a body, they were on the defensive. Wiseman encouraged them to be bold, at times even ostentatious, in furthering their cause. He led the way. There was not another man among the English bishops with the personal qualities, the cosmopolitan background and breadth of interests, the depth of learning, and the boldness necessary to seize the opportunities of the hour. When Cardinal Newman died, Manning said of him, "No one who does not intend to be laughed at will henceforward say that the Catholic religion is fit only for weak intellects and unmanly brains."[53] Without in any way taking away from the greatness of Newman, the same could have been said of Wiseman.

In spite of the disputes that had their origin in the altered system of ecclesiastical government after 1850, the achievement of the bishops (and Wiseman in particular) provided a framework that made adaptation to changing conditions easier. The decrees of the first two provincial synods were the result of Wiseman's work. In spite of the controversies surrounding the third synod, Wiseman's colleagues turned to him for the drafting of all but a single decree. The clergy of England, if not completely satisfied with their status after the restoration of the hierarchy, had a more clearly defined position than had been the case before; legislation had been passed to deal with missions and their boundaries; diocesan officialdom had been organized; funds had been distributed (not without controversy); religious orders had been encouraged and had increased dramatically; and the questions surrounding ecclesiastical colleges had at long last been brought into the open, an unavoidable step toward resolving them. Although the numerical growth of the Catholic population and the establishment of their various institutions were not solely Wiseman's work, he took advantage of favorable developments as they arose, and he played a major role in achieving the political and social equality of Catholics with other Englishmen. As a result of the controversies toward the end of his life, the role of the metropolitan archbishop and his relationship with his suffragans were more thoroughly understood. It became increasingly clear that all of the bishops were to participate in shaping ecclesiastical policies in the country. Finally, if the old complaint of anti-Romanism was not completely laid to rest, this was partially due to the worldwide discussions that resulted from the loss of the papacy's temporal power and the proposal that the pope's infallibility should be defined at the First Vatican Council. The loyalty of the body of English bishops to the Holy See was no longer called into question.

It is unlikely that earlier solutions to the problems facing Roman Catholics in England could have been provided had the hierarchy not been restored in 1850. In fact the step forced the bishops to come to grips with situations that could only have become more dangerously divisive had they been further ignored. It was Wiseman's ill fortune that his last years were characterized by so much controversy. He made efforts to remedy the situation before his death and achieved notable success in doing so. By 1864 the bishops again presented a united front. Their policies appeared negative when they agreed that Catholic youth should be forbidden to attend English universities or that Catholics might not belong to the APUC, but they were in harmony with the Holy See. On December 8, 1864, two months before the cardinal's death, Pope Pius IX issued *Quanta cura,* his condemnation of liberalism, and at the same time authorized the distribution of the Syllabus of Errors. The adhesion of the English hierarchy was never an issue.

Cardinal Wiseman's last recorded words as he lay dying were, "I never heard of anyone being tired of the stars."[54] It was to the stars that he had looked throughout his life. At times he stumbled across obstacles in his path, but he quickly recovered, recasting his vision toward the great goals that he desired for English Catholics. There is no reason to question the motives that guided him. His life was characterized by his love for the church and his desire to further its interests in the land that he claimed as his own. He did so with distinction.

Abbreviations

AA   Ampleforth Abbey Archive

ALA   Preston, Public Records Office, Archbishop of Liverpool Archive

BAA   Birmingham, Archdiocesan Archive

BAY   Bayswater, St. Mary of the Angels, Manning Papers

LDA   Leeds, Diocesan Archive

PF   Rome, Archivio della Sagra Congregazione *de Propaganda Fide*

SA   Vatican, Archivio Segreto Vaticano, Spogli Acton

SAA   Southwark, Archdiocesan Archive

UC   Ushaw College Archive

VEN   Rome, Venerable English College Archive

WAA   Westminster, Archdiocesan Archive

Notes

INTRODUCTION

1. *Times* (London), and *Hull Advertiser*, quoted in Wilfrid Ward, *The Life and Times of Cardinal Wiseman*, 2 vols. (London: Longmans, Green, and Co., 1897), 2:522,519; John Norris, "Cardinal Wiseman," *Ushaw Magazine* 8 (1898): 7.

2. Mark Tierney to Charles Newsham, 28 Nov. 1850, UC, President's Archive (hereafter PA), G/la.

3. See John Bossy, *The English Catholic Community*, 1570–1850 (London: Darton, Longman, and Todd, 1975), esp. chap. 13; J. Derek Holmes, *More Roman than Rome: English Catholicism in the Nineteenth Century* (Shepherdstown, W. Va.: Patmos Press, 1978), chap. 1.

4. *Sun*, quoted in Wilfrid Ward, *Wiseman*, 2:518.

5. Brian Fothergill, *Nicholas Wiseman* (London: Faber and Faber, 1963). Ward's biography is described as "highly idiosyncratic, very biassed and distinctly hagiographic" by S. W. Jackman, *Nicholas Cardinal Wiseman: A Victorian Prelate and His Writings* (Dublin: Five Lamps Press, 1977), p. 135 n. 1. I do not concur in the evaluation.

CHAPTER 1

1. Fothergill cites a diary kept by Wiseman's father and a baptismal record by the officiating priest to substantiate 3 Aug. as the date of his birth, whereas Wilfrid Ward had stated that it was 2 Aug. There is evidence to support both claims. An entry in Wiseman's journal, 2 Aug. 1828, begins, "My birthday." Wilfrid Ward, *Wiseman*, 1:71. On the same date in 1819 his mother expressed her regret that it was the "first anniversary for some years" on which she had not enjoyed his company. UC, Nicholas Wiseman Papers (hereafter WP), 675. Wiseman, in fact, used to boast that he was born on 2 Aug., the feast of St. Alphonsus. Mary Teresa Austin Carroll, *Leaves from the Annals of the Sisters of Mercy*, 4 vols. (New York: P. O'Shea, 1881–95), 2:222.

2. Denis Gwynn disputed Ward's contention that Wiseman's father first married the daughter of a Spanish general and stated that Miss Dunphy was from Kilkenny. *Cardinal Wiseman* (Dublin: Browne and Nolan, 1950), pp. 2–3. Most accounts, however, agree with Ward; see T [?]. I. Wiseman to "Very Revd. Sir," Apr.

1865, UC, WP, 1002. The recipient was probably Henry Edward Manning, who was collecting materials for a biography of the cardinal. The writer, whose first initial I cannot decipher, had applied for information on Wiseman to a Mrs. Barry of Ballinacurra, near Cork, who had known Nicholas "in his early days, but only for a short time."

3. T [?]. I. Wiseman to "Very Revd. Sir," Apr. 1865, UC, WP, 1002.

4. Fanny was the daughter of Thomas Tucker and Marianne Wiseman, daughter of Mariana Dunphy and Wiseman's father. Since Marianne was half sister to Xaviera's children, Fanny was more properly their niece, though she was referred to as their cousin. Fanny later married William Burke of Knockmayur. *Dictionary of National Biography*, 21: 714–17. The process of tracing and verifying the family relationships is made even more difficult by the fact that Frances Strange, Xaviera's widowed sister, later married Patrick Wiseman, the brother of the cardinal's father, a union that resulted in the birth of a son, also Patrick. Frances had been married previously to a Mr. Walsh, by whom she had a son, who died witnout issue, and a daughter Isabel. Undated memorandum on Wiseman family, WAA, W3/11.

5. "Morris Manuscript" [fragment], UC, WP, 1025. John Morris served both Wiseman and Manning in a secretarial capacity. He joined the Jesuits in 1867 and, at the time of his death in 1893, was preparing a biography of Wiseman. The fragment to which I have referred, dealing with the cardinal's ancestry and childhood, is at Ushaw, but a longer fragment is in WAA, R79/13.

6. Wilfrid Ward, *Wiseman*, 1:8; Nicholas Wiseman, "A Retrospect of Many Years, Being Verses Which Spontaneously Glided through the Author's Mind on a Sleepless Night, August 25th 1864," WAA, W2/3/8.

7. Wiseman to William Burke, 8 Feb. 1848, UC, WP, 1042.

8. Nicholas Wiseman, *Recollections of the Last Four Popes and of Rome in Their Times* (London: Hurst and Blackett, 1858), p. 329. Lingard's first major work was *Antiquities of the Anglo-Saxon Church* (Newcastle: E. Walker, 1806).

9. Xaviera Wiseman to Robert Gradwell, 8 Feb. 1821, UC, WP, 684.

10. T [?]. I. Wiseman to "Very Revd. Sir," Apr. 1865, ibid., 1002; Wilfrid Ward, *Wiseman*, 1:2.

11. Wilfred Ward, *Wiseman*, 1:9–10; Bossy, *English Catholic Community*, pp. 296–306; Holmes, *More Roman than Rome*, pp. 22–50; David Milburn, *A History of Ushaw College* (Durham: Ushaw Bookshop, 1964), p. 91.

12. Wiseman, *Recollections of the Last Four Popes*, pp. 110–11, 112, 140.

13. The four vicariates were the London, Midland, Northern, and Western districts.

14. Benedict XIV, *Apostolicum ministerium*, 30 May 1763, in W. Maziere Brady, *Annals of the Catholic Hierarchy in England and Scotland, 1585–1876* (London: Thomas Baker, 1877), pp. 496–521.

15. Lynn Hollen Lees, *Exiles of Erin: Irish Migrants in Victorian London* (Manchester: Manchester University Press, 1979); Bossy, *English Catholic Community*, pp. 307–22.

16. Bernard Ward, *The Dawn of the Catholic Revival in England, 1781–1803*, 2 vols. (London: Longmans, Green, and Co., 1909), 1:87–125, and *The Sequel to Catholic Emancipation, 1830–1850*, 2 vols. (London: Longmans, Green, and Co., 1915), 1:221–25. The most recent study of the Cisalpine Movement, with an interesting and plausible thesis, is Joseph P. Chinnici, *The English Catholic Enlightenment: John Lingard and the Cisalpine Movement, 1780–1850* (Shepherdstown, W. Va.: Patmos Press, 1980).

17. Francis Aidan Gasquet, *A History of the Venerable English College, Rome: An Account of Its Origins and Work from the Earliest Times to the Present Day* (London: Longmans, Green, and Co., 1920); Michael E. Williams, *The Venerable English College, Rome; A History, 1579–1979* (London: Associated Catholic Publications, 1979); George Brown to Gradwell, n.d., in Bernard Ward, *The Eve of Catholic Emancipation, Being the History of the English Catholics during the First Thirty Years of the Nineteenth Century*, 3 vols. (London: Longmans, Green, and Co., 1911), 3:11.

18. John Morris stated incorrectly that James moved back to Seville. "Morris Manuscript," UC, WP, 1025.

19. Note added by Xaviera Wiseman to letter from Frasquita Wiseman to Nicholas, 11 Sept. 1818, ibid., 663.

20. James Wiseman to Nicholas, 6 Aug. 1818, ibid., 660.

21. Xaviera Wiseman to Nicholas, 8 Apr. 1819 and 25 Nov. 1822, ibid., 670 (a), 699.

22. Wiseman, *Recollections of the Last Four Popes*, pp. 4–10.

23. Ibid., pp. 14–20.

24. George Heptonstall to his mother, Jan. 1819 [copy], UC, WP, first folder (uncataloged); Gradwell, memorandum, in Wiseman, *Recollections of the Last Four Popes*, p. 20.

25. Wiseman, "A Retrospect of Many Years," WAA, W2/3/8.

26. Wiseman, *Recollections of the Last Four Popes*, pp. 8–13.

27. Williams, *Venerable English College*, p. 85.

28. Frasquita Wiseman to Nicholas, 1 Dec. 1820, UC, WP, 683; Wilfrid Ward, *Wiseman*, 1:28.

29. Wiseman to Burke, 8 Feb. 1848, UC, WP, 1042.

30. James Wiseman to Nicholas, 31 July 1820, ibid., 9.

31. Frasquita Wiseman to Nicholas, 1 Dec. 1820, ibid., 683.

32. Xaviera Wiseman to Nicholas, 22 Feb. 1821, enclosing letter to Gradwell, 8 Feb. 1821, ibid., 686, 684.

33. Joseph Shee to Nicholas, 23 Feb. 1821, and Frasquita Wiseman to Nicholas, with appended note from Xaviera Wiseman, 7 July 1821, ibid., 10, 689.

34. Gradwell to William Poynter, n.d. [1824], in Bernard Ward, *Eve of Catholic Emancipation*, 3:16.

35. Gradwell, writing on 16 Nov. 1826, in ibid., p. 199, n. 2.

36. Xaviera Wiseman to Gradwell, 20 June [1824], UC, WP, 715.

37. Xaviera Wiseman to Nicholas, 5 Sept. 1825, ibid., 725.

38. Frasquita Wiseman to Nicholas, 16–19 June 1826, and James Wiseman to Xaviera Wiseman, 22 June 1826, ibid., 733, 735.

39. Frasquita Wiseman's remarks were added to a letter from Xaviera Wiseman to Nicholas, 23 Feb. 1821, ibid., 687.

40. Frasquita Wiseman to Nicholas, 21 Oct. 1828, 3 Feb. and 30 May 1829, ibid., 764, 767, 768.

41. Frasquita Wiseman to Nicholas, 4 May and 17 July 1828, ibid., 758, 761.

42. Wiseman to George Errington, 8 Sept. 1824, in Wilfrid Ward, *Wiseman*, 1:48.

43. Nicholas Wiseman, *Horae Syriacae, seu commentationes et anecdota res vel Litteras Syriacas spectantia* (Rome: F. Bourl'e, 1827); Wilfrid Ward, *Wiseman*, 1:57.

44. Wiseman described the background to his professorship in *Recollections of the Last Four Popes*, pp. 309–12. The author of the article on Wiseman in the *Dictionary of National Biography* (21:715), states that he was nominated as professor supernumerary in the two chairs of Hebrew and Syro-Chaldaic, with the provisional assignment of 100 scudi until the chairs fell vacant.

45. Thomas Burgess to Wiseman, 20 Nov. 1829, in Wilfrid Ward, *Wiseman*, 1:63–64.

46. Wiseman to Burke, 26 Nov. 1858, UC, WP, 990.

47. Wiseman, "A Retrospect of

Many Years," WAA, W2/3/8; Wiseman to Burke, 1848, in Wilfrid Ward, *Wiseman*, 1:64–65.

48. Wiseman to Burke, 26 Nov. 1858, UC, WP, 990; Wilfrid Ward, *Wiseman*, 1:65–66.

49. George Brown to Wiseman, 7 Apr. 1826, UC, WP, 29.

50. Gradwell to James Yorke Bramston, 9 Feb. 1828, WAA, A.69.

51. T [?]. I. Wiseman to "Very Revd. Sir," Apr. 1865, UC, WP, 1002. Errington's mother was Katherine, daughter of Walter Dowdall of Dublin. *Dictionary of National Biography*, 6:816.

52. Michael Errington to Wiseman, 22 Sept. 1821, UC, WP, 12.

53. Barbara Charlton, *The Recollections of a Northumbrian Lady, 1815–1866*, ed. L. E. O. Charlton (London: J. Cape, 1949), p. 221; Michael Errington to Wiseman, 22 Sept. 1821, UC, WP, 12; Gradwell, quoted in Bernard Ward, *Eve of Catholic Emancipation*, 3:200.

54. Gradwell to Bramston, 12 June 1828, WAA, A.69.

55. Gasquet, *Venerable English College*, p. 223; Williams, *Venerable English College*, p. 93; Frasquita Wiseman to Nicholas, 6 Feb. 1828, UC, WP, 753.

CHAPTER 2

1. Wiseman to Thomas Smith, 2 June 1829, LDA, Thomas Smith Papers (hereafter SP), 380.

2. Wiseman to George Talbot, 27 Oct. 1857, in Gasquet, *Venerable English College*, pp. 254–55.

3. An Act for the Relief of His Majesty's Roman Catholic Subjects was signed into law by King George IV on 13 Apr. 1829. The most significant clauses of the act may be consulted in E. R. Norman, ed., *Anti-Catholicism in Victorian England* (London: Allen and Unwin, 1968), pp. 131–39.

4. Wiseman, *Recollections of the Last Four Popes*, pp. 394–95.

5. Bernard Ward, *Sequel to Catholic Emancipation*, 1:7.

6. Chinnici, *English Catholic Enlightenment*, p. 97; Charles Butler to Wiseman, 22 Apr. 1829, UC, WP, 135.

7. Wiseman to Thomas Penswick, 17 May 1829, LDA, Thomas Penswick Papers (hereafter PP), 53; Thomas Walsh to Smith, 24 Apr. 1829, LDA, SP, 377; minutes of meeting of the vicars apostolic at Wolverhampton, 20 Nov. 1829, WAA, A.70.

8. Bernard Ward, *Sequel to Catholic Emancipation*, 1:12.

9. John Lingard to John Walker, 22 July 1850, UC, John Walker Papers (hereafter WAP), folder 8.

10. Lingard to Walker, 12 Jan. 1850, ibid., folder 7.

11. For accounts of Bishop Baines and his various battles with the Benedictines, see Bernard Ward, *Sequel to Catholic Emancipation*, 1:15–49; J. S. Roche, *A History of Prior Park College and Its Founder Bishop Baines* (London: Burns, Oates, and Washbourne, 1931), pp. 31–159; Vincent Alan McClelland, *English Roman Catholics and Higher Education, 1830–1903* (Oxford: Clarendon Press, 1973), pp. 5–16.

12. Wiseman, *Recollections of the Last Four Popes*, p. 325.

13. The passage is taken from a manuscript Robert Whitty sent to John Morris when the latter was gathering material for a biography of Wiseman, 2 Mar. 1893, WAA, W2/2/1. A letter from Whitty to Morris, also dated 2 Mar. 1893, contains further observations, WAA, R79/16. Whitty had entered the Jesuits in 1856, having considered previously entering Newman's Oratory.

14. Gwynn, *Wiseman*, p. 20; Peter Augustine Baines to Peter Bernardine Collingridge, 14 July 1828, in Bernard Ward, *Eve of Catholic Emancipation*, 3:204, also pp. 4–7; also see Williams, *Venerable English College*, pp. 76–77.

15. Bernard Ward, *Eve of Catholic Emancipation*, 3:20–21; Bramston to Gradwell, 18 June 1828, VEN, 74:1.

16. Gradwell to Poynter, 18 Apr. 1818, in Bernard Ward, *Eve of Catholic Emancipation*, 3:31.

17. Wiseman to Gradwell, 11 Jan. 1829, WAA, A.70. For a description of the various questions involving the vicars apostolic and the Jesuits, see Bernard Ward, *Eve of Catholic Emancipation*, 3:19–56, 205–11, 286–310.

18. Penswick to Gradwell, 19 Aug. 1829, WAA, A.70.

19. Wiseman to Gradwell, 29 Nov. [1829], ibid.

20. Mauro Cappellari to the prior and monks of Downside, 28 July 1829, in Bernard Ward, *Sequel to Catholic Emancipation*, 1:227, also pp. 21–22; Wiseman to Penswick, 17 May 1829, LDA, PP, 53.

21. Wiseman to Penswick, 17 May 1829, LDA, PP, 53. For a discussion of the plan proposed by Baines, see Bernard Ward, *Sequel to Catholic Emancipation*, 1:26–27.

22. Wiseman to Penswick, 17 May 1829, LDA, PP, 53.

23. Baines, quoted in Bernard Ward, *Eve of Catholic Emancipation*, 3:271–72. Wiseman, when discussing the matter in his *Recollections of the Last Four Popes* (pp. 323–28), still seems to have been ignorant of Pius VIII's intention.

24. Walsh to J. A. Birdsall, 17 Nov. 1829, in Bernard Ward, *Sequel to Catholic Emancipation*, 1:27–28.

25. Ibid., p. 23.

26. Ibid., pp. 28–33.

27. Thomas Weld to Bramston, 6 Mar. 1830, Cappellari to Bramston, 23 May 1829, and Wiseman to Bramston, 8 Sept. 1830, WAA, A.71, 70, W1/2; Bernard Ward, *Sequel to Catholic Emancipation*, 1:39–40.

28. Wiseman, *Recollections of the Last Four Popes*, p. 415; Wiseman to Gradwell, 14 Mar. 1831, WAA, A.72.

29. Wiseman to Gradwell, 22 July 1831, WAA, A.72.

30. Charles Baggs to Gradwell, 18 Aug. and 2 Oct. 1831, and Errington to Gradwell, 18 Oct. 1831, ibid.

31. Baines to Wiseman, 14 Nov. 1831, and Walsh to Wiseman, 19 Apr. 1832, VEN, 72:1, 70:3.

CHAPTER 3

1. Leopold Ackermann, quoted in Wilfrid Ward, *Wiseman*, 1:58–59.

2. Nicholas Wiseman, "Two Letters on Some Parts of the Controversy concerning the Genuineness of 1 John v.7," in *Essays on Various Subjects*, 3 vols. (London: Charles Dolman, 1853), 1:5–70; Wilfrid Ward, *Wiseman*, 1:59. Today most biblical scholars agree with Raymond E. Brown that the verses are a "late addition . . . neither canonical nor inspired." *The Gospel of St. John and the Johannine Epistles* (Collegeville, Minn.: Liturgical Press, 1960), p. 116.

3. W. G. Roe, *Lamennais and England: The Reception of Lamennais's Religious Ideas in England in the Nineteenth Century* (Oxford: Oxford University Press, 1966), p. 7; Bernard Reardon, *Liberalism and Tradition: Aspects of Catholic Thought in Nineteenth-Century France* (Cambridge: Cambridge University Press, 1975), p. 89.

4. Frasquita Wiseman to Nicholas, 16–19 June 1826, UC, WP, 733.

5. Wiseman, *Recollections of the Last Four Popes*, pp. 337–38.

6. Roe, *Lamennais and England*, pp. 72–74.

7. Wiseman, *Recollections of the Last Four Popes*, pp. 339–40.

8. William Kyan and Thomas Babington Macaulay, quoted in Wilfrid Ward, *Wiseman*, 1:88, 272.

9. Richard Hurrell Froude and Newman, quoted in ibid., pp. 118, 89.

10. For Newman's account of White's influence, see his *Apologia pro Vita Sua*, ed. Martin J. Svaglic (Oxford: Clarendon Press, 1967), pp. 21, 23, 53–54.

11. Wiseman to F. C. Husenbeth, 10 July 1830, UC, WP, 774.

12. Chinnici, *English Catholic Enlightenment*, p. 136; Wiseman to Husenbeth, 22 Jan. 1831, UC, WP, 776.

13. John Kirk to Wiseman, 30 Apr. 1831, ibid., 169.

14. Chinnici, *English Catholic Enlightenment*, pp. 136–42.

15. Lingard, quoted in ibid., p. 141.

16. Wiseman to William Tandy, 2 Dec. 1833, UC, WP, 787.

17. Kirk to Wiseman, 9 Apr. 1834, ibid., 203.

18. Lingard to Wiseman, 9 Apr. 1834, ibid., 791.

19. Wiseman, writing on 15 Mar. 1834, in Wilfrid Ward, *Wiseman*, 1:123.

20. McClelland, *English Roman Catholics and Higher Education*, pp. 8–9.

21. Claude Leetham, *Luigi Gentili, A Sower for the Second Spring* (London: Burns and Oates, 1965), p. 12, 20; Baines to Wiseman, 21 May 1832, VEN, 72:1. Although this letter is to be located with materials dated 1830 and the date assigned by the archivist is that year, my reading of the script has led me to conclude that it was written in 1832.

22. Baines to Wiseman, 6 Aug. 1828, UC, WP, 762; Wiseman to Thomas Brindle, 27 July 1830, in Roche, *Prior Park*, p. 113. Roche identified Logan as "Thomas."

23. Wilfrid Ward, *Wiseman*, 1:101.

24. Walsh to Wiseman, 9 July 1829, VEN, 70:2.

25. Bernard Ward, *Sequel to Catholic Emancipation*, 1:36–44.

26. Wiseman to Tandy, 15 Mar. 1834, UC, WP, 740.

27. Wiseman to Tandy, 14 Apr. 1834, ibid., 792.

28. Wiseman to Tandy, 6 Aug. 1834, ibid., 793.

29. John Maguire to Wiseman, 13 Dec. 1834, WAA, box 153; Baines to Wiseman, 28 Dec. 1834, VEN, 72:4.

30. Wiseman to Penswick, 20 Dec. 1834 [postmark], LDA, PP, 186.

31. Penswick to Bramston, 21 Dec. 1834 and 18 Feb. 1835, WAA, A.75, W1/2.

32. Wiseman to Penswick, 13 Mar. 1835, LDA, PP, 192.

33. Bossy, *English Catholic Community*, p. 357; E. H. Burton, *The Life and Times of Bishop Challoner, 1691–1781*, 2 vols. (London: Longmans, Green, and Co., 1909), 1:313.

34. Bernard Ward, *Eve of Catholic Emancipation*, 3:33–56, and *Sequel to Catholic Emancipation*, 1:62.

35. Bernard Ward, *Sequel to Catholic Emancipation*, 1:57–64; Bramston to Penswick, 11 July 1834, LDA, PP, 168. For Bramston's side of the controversy, see his letter to Wiseman, 26 May 1834, VEN, 74:1.

36. Baines to Thomas Griffiths, 10 May 1834, WAA, A.75.

37. Baines to Griffiths, 15 Sept. 1834, ibid., W1/2.

38. Wiseman to Bramston, 17 Jan. 1835, and Penswick to Bramston, 24 Oct. 1834, ibid., A.75.

39. Lingard to Bramston, n.d., LDA, PP, 175.

40. Lingard to Bramston, 4 Dec. 1834, WAA, A.74. A copy of the petition may be found with this letter.

41. Bernard Ward, *Sequel to Catholic Emancipation*, 1:63. Walsh stated that he had twice offered mass asking for guidance, that he had studied the Regulae Missionis, the Council of Trent, and the divines, and that he had "taken the advice of confidential, pious, learned & zealous secular clergymen of my District." He concluded that he could not sign the document "in its present shape with the annexed cases." Walsh to Bramston, 20 Jan. 1835, LDA, PP, 188.

42. Lingard to Penswick, n.d., LDA, PP, 169.

43. Bramston to Wiseman, 22 Jan. 1835 [copy], and Andrew Scott to Bramston, 29 Dec. 1834, WAA, A.77, 75.

44. Wiseman to Penswick, 13 Mar. 1835, LDA, PP, 192; Wiseman to Bramston, 14 and 27 Mar. 1835, WAA, A.77.

45. Weld, noted in Bramston to Penswick, 20 Jan. 1835, and Baines to

Penswick, 7 Sept. 1833, LDA, PP, 187, 150.

46. Wiseman to Bramston, 17 Jan. 1835, WAA, W1/2; Bramston to Penswick, 11 Feb. 1835, and Lingard to Penswick, n.d., LDA, PP, 189, 169.

47. Penswick to Griffiths, 13 Apr. 1835, WAA, A.77; Griffiths to Penswick, 11 Apr. 1835, with Baines to Bramston, 6 Apr. 1835 [copy], LDA, PP, 193.

48. Penswick to Wiseman, 20 Apr. 1835, VEN, 70:10; Wiseman to Penswick, 7 May 1835, LDA, PP, 195.

49. Wiseman to Bramston, 10 May 1835, WAA, W1/2; Wiseman to Penswick, 17 May 1835, LDA, PP, 196.

50. Penswick to John Briggs, 11 June 1835, ALA.

51. Gregory XVI to Baines, 20 June 1835 [copy], WAA, A.78.

52. Bramston to Penswick, 3 Aug. 1835, LDA, PP, 198.

53. Wiseman to Griffiths, 15 Feb. 1837, in Bernard Ward, *Sequel to Catholic Emancipation*, 1:125.

CHAPTER 4

1. Wiseman to Tandy, 5 May 1835, UC, WP, 748.

2. Xaviera Wiseman to Harriet Butler, 24 May and 25 July 1835, ibid., 799, 800.

3. Ignaz von Döllinger to Wiseman, 11 Apr. 1835, ibid., 221.

4. Bernard Ward, *Sequel to Catholic Emancipation*, 1:66. The correspondence clearly shows that Wilfrid Ward was incorrect when stating that Wiseman arrived in Sept. 1835. *Wiseman*, 1:214.

5. Griffiths to Briggs, 3 Aug. 1835, LDA, John Briggs Papers (hereafter BP), 94; Bramston to Penswick, 3 Aug. 1835, ibid., PP, 198.

6. H. F. C. Logan to Wiseman, 11 Nov. 1834, VEN, 72:4; Wiseman to Tandy, 16 Mar. 1835, UC, WP, 795.

7. Bernard Ward, *Sequel to Catholic Emancipation*, 1:69.

8. Wiseman to Joseph Bonomi, n.d., ibid., p. 70.

9. Wiseman to Baines, 2 Nov. 1835 [draft], VEN, 73:8. The final copy was probably written on 7 Nov., since it is to that date that Baines referred when acknowledging it.

10. Roche, *Prior Park*, p. 140.

11. Baines to Wiseman, 10 Nov. 1835, VEN, 72:5. Luigi Gentili wrote that clerics at Prior Park were allowed communion only eight times a year. Leetham, *Gentili*, p. 93 n. 1.

12. Baines to Wiseman, 2 Dec. 1835, VEN, 72:5; Bernard Ward, *Sequel to Catholic Emancipation*, 1:45–49; Roche, *Prior Park*, pp. 130–39.

13. Wiseman, *Essays on Various Subjects*, 2:vi–vii.

14. Ibid., 1:vii.

15. Wiseman to R. M. Milnes, Sept. 1835, in Wilfrid Ward, *Wiseman*, 1:215.

16. A. W. N. Pugin, *Contrasts; or, A Parallel between the Noble Edifices of the Fourteenth and Fifteenth Centuries, and Similar Buildings of the Present Day; Shewing the Present Decay of Taste; Accompanied by Appropriate Text*, intro. H. R. Hitchcock, 2d ed. (1841; reprint, New York: Humanities Press, 1969), pp. 8–9.

17. Louis Allen, "Ambrose Phillipps de Lisle, 1809–1878," *Catholic Historical Review* 40 (1954): 1–26.

18. Leetham, *Gentili*, p. 95.

19. Walsh to Wiseman, 6 May 1836, VEN, 70:4.

20. Wiseman to Tandy, 11 Dec. 1835, UC, WP, 801. For the lectures delivered in London, see Nicholas Wiseman, *Lectures on the Principal Doctrines and Practices of the Catholic Church*, 2d ed., 2 vols. in 1 (London: Charles Dolman, 1844).

21. Döllinger to Wiseman, 17 Nov. 1835, UC, WP, 229.

22. Nicholas Wiseman, *The Real Presence of the Body and Blood of Our Lord Jesus Christ in the Blessed Eucharist, Proved from Scripture* (London: James Duffy and Co., 1836), and *Twelve Lectures on the Connexion between Science and Revealed Religion,*

5th ed. (London: Catholic Publishing and Bookselling Co., 1859).

23. Wiseman, *Real Presence*, p. 4.

24. Ibid., Lecture 1, pp. 41–42.

25. Newman, quoted in Wilfrid Ward, *Wiseman*, 1:241–42.

26. NICOLAO WISEMAN, AVITA RELIGIONE FORTI SUAVIQUE ELOQUIO VINDICATA, CATHOLICI LONDINENSES AN. MDCCCXXXVI. See Fothergill, *Wiseman*, p. 38.

27. Husenbeth to Wiseman, 13 Nov. 1836, UC, WP, 806.

28. Husenbeth to William Smith [?], 20 Nov. 1836, ibid., 808.

29. Wilfrid Ward, *Wiseman*, 1:92.

30. Chinnici, *English Catholic Enlightenment*, pp. 148–54.

31. Wiseman to Husenbeth, 17 July 1837, and Peter Kenrick to Wiseman, 30 July 1837, UC, WP, 815, 292.

32. Bernard Ward, *Sequel to Catholic Emancipation*, 1:74.

33. Wilfrid Ward, *Wiseman*, 1: 249–53.

34. Nicholas Wiseman, "The Hampden Controversy," *Essays on Various Subjects*, 2:3–26.

35. *Rambler*, 1st ser., 12 (1853): 225.

36. Wiseman to Husenbeth, 4 Sept. 1836, UC, WP, 804.

37. For a brief history of the journal as well as a list of nineteenth-century contributors, see the invaluable Walter E. Houghton, ed., *Wellesley Index to Victorian Periodicals*, 1824–1900, vol. 2 (Toronto: University of Toronto Press, 1972). See also an interesting printed report by the trustees of the journal, sent to Wiseman by Henry Bagshawe, with a letter from Bagshawe written in the margin, 11 Nov. 1836, UC, WP, 261.

38. Thomas Doyle to Wiseman, 28 Feb. 1837, UC, WP, 277. For more on Doyle, see Bernard Bogan, *The Great Link: A History of St. George's, Southwark*, 1786–1848–1948 (London: Burns, Oates, 1948).

39. J. Chisholm Anstey to Wiseman, 3 Mar. 1837, UC, WP, 280.

40. J. B. Robertson to Wiseman, 5 Mar. 1837, ibid., 281.

41. Wiseman to Tandy, 9 Nov. 1836, ibid., 805.

CHAPTER 5

1. William Riddell to Wiseman, 28 [?] Nov. 1836, VEN, 75:5; Briggs to Griffiths, 30 Dec. 1836, WAA, W1/2.

2. Giacomo Fransoni to Bramston, 16 July 1836, WAA, A.80; Fransoni to Walsh, 2 Mar. 1837, BAA.

3. For the letter, signed "Catholic" and dated 30 Sept. 1833, see the November issue of the *Catholic Magazine and Review* 4 (1833), and for the article cited, the issue for the following month. I consulted the journal in the Ushaw College library.

4. Ibid., 6 (Feb., May, Aug. 1835).

5. For the three petitions, 27 Sept. 1836, 23 Nov. 1836, and 20 Feb. 1837, see LDA, BP, 181, 191, 214 (A).

6. For a statistical analysis of the changes that were taking place, see the detailed study by Jean Alain Lesourd, *Les catholiques dans la société anglais*, 1765–1865, 2 vols. (Paris: H. Champion, 1978), 1:469.

7. Wiseman to Griffiths, 15 Feb. 1837, in Bernard Ward, *Sequel to Catholic Emancipation*, 1:123–26.

8. Weld to Briggs, 26 Mar. 1837, LDA, BP, 230.

9. Briggs to Griffiths, 9 Apr. 1837, WAA, W1/2.

10. Walsh to Briggs, 4 Jan. 1837, LDA, BP, 203.

11. Griffiths to Walsh, 31 Mar. 1837, BAA.

12. Griffiths to Walsh, 14 Mar. 1837 [copy], WAA, B.4.

13. Walsh to Wiseman, 1 Mar. 1837, VEN, 70:5. For a detailed criticism of the policy of arbitrarily transferring priests from one mission to another, see undated, printed letter signed "Clerici," WAA, A.85.

14. Baines to Griffiths, 9 Mar. and 15 May 1837, WAA, W1/2.

15. Bernard Ward, *Sequel to Catholic Emancipation*, 1:127–28.

16. Griffiths to Briggs, 21 June

1837, LDA, BP, 262; Bernard Ward, *Sequel to Catholic Emancipation,* 1:128.

17. For a copy of the petition, 10 July 1837, see BAA.

18. Griffiths to Briggs, 11 July 1837, LDA, BP, 265; Bernard Ward, *Sequel to Catholic Emancipation,* 1:128.

19. Griffiths to Briggs, 18 July 1837, LDA, BP, 267. The bishops were still in Rome when the letter was written, although they were to leave the following day. Bernard Ward was wrong in stating that they left on July 17. *Sequel to Catholic Emancipation,* 1:128.

20. Walsh to Wiseman, 17 July 1838, VEN, 70:5.

21. Wiseman to Briggs, 29 July 1837, ALA.

22. Briggs to Griffiths, 29 Nov. 1837, WAA, W1/2; Griffiths to Briggs, 29 Jan. 1838, LDA, BP, 310.

23. Griffiths to Briggs, 20 Mar. 1838, LDA, BP, 345.

24. For copies of the resolutions, see WAA, Z.46.

25. For the Latin text of the "Statuta Provisoria," see Bernard Ward, *Sequel to Catholic Emancipation,* 1:244–45. They are dated 11 June 1838, when they were sent to Propaganda.

26. Ibid., p. 133; "Monita et Statuta," 4 May 1838, WAA, A.84.

27. Wiseman to Briggs, 20 June 1838 [incomplete], LDA, BP, 386. For Wiseman's letter to Baines, 24 June 1838, see Bernard Ward, *Sequel to Catholic Emancipation,* 1:135–36.

28. Wiseman to Griffiths, 14 July 1838, WAA, W1/2.

29. For text and discussion of the "Statuta Proposita," see Bernard Ward, *Sequel to Catholic Emancipation,* 1:144–45, 246–51. Cardinal Antonino De Luca claimed authorship of the "Statuta Proposita" and said that he had sought advice from both Wiseman and Monsignor Charles Acton. PF, Acta, 202:331.

30. Wiseman to Griffiths, 13 Nov. 1838, WAA, W1/2.

31. Walsh to Wiseman, 25 Aug. 1838, VEN, 70:6.

32. Briggs to Griffiths, 29 Nov. 1837, 3 and 19 Feb. 1838, and Baines to Griffiths, 15 Dec. 1837 and 19 Feb. 1838, WAA, W1/2.

33. Briggs to Griffiths, 19 Feb. 1838 and 24 Jan. 1840, ibid.

34. Baines to Griffiths, 4 Feb. 1840, ibid., Baines to Wiseman, 17 July 1838, VEN, 70:5.

35. Bernard Ward, *Sequel to Catholic Emancipation,* 1:129–31; Tierney to Griffiths, 22 Apr. 1838, WAA, A.83; Griffiths to Wiseman, 20 June 1838, VEN, 74:2.

36. Replies of the vicars apostolic, 20 Nov. 1838, in Bernard Ward, *Sequel to Catholic Emancipation,* 1:252–53.

37. Ibid., pp. 142–44, 258–59.

38. Wiseman to Griffiths, 16 Feb. 1839, WAA, A.85.

39. Bernard Ward, *Sequel to Catholic Emancipation,* 1:149–51.

40. W. B. A. Collier to Thomas Fisher, 31 Aug. 1837, AA, Extravagantes, 262.3.

41. Collier to Fisher, 1 Dec. 1838, ibid., 9.

42. Lesourd, *Les catholiques,* 1:564.

43. Briggs to Wiseman, 23 Oct. 1839, WAA, W1/2.

44. Walsh to John Talbot, sixteenth earl of Shrewsbury (hereafter Shrewsbury), 28 Dec. 1838, UC, Correspondence of Bishop Thomas Walsh with Lord Shrewsbury (hereafter WS). For a treatment of the establishment of the Society for the Propagation of the Faith in England, see Bernard Ward, *Sequel to Catholic Emancipation,* 1:146–53.

45. Griffiths to Walsh, 12 Oct. 1838 [copy], WAA, 120/4. Also see Griffiths to Shrewsbury, 10 Oct. 1838, ibid.

46. Griffiths to Briggs, 12 Dec. 1838, LDA, BP, 453.

47. Robert Tate to Charles Acton, 8 Mar. 1839 [copy], UC, Ushaw Collection of Manuscripts (hereafter UCM), 4:375C.

48. Wiseman to Griffiths, 16 Feb. 1839, WAA, A.85; Bernard Ward, *Sequel to Catholic Emancipation,*

1:149–50; Wiseman to Griffiths, 17 Jan. 1839, WAA, A.85.

49. Wiseman to Briggs, 28 Feb.–2 Mar. 1839, LDA, BP, 495.

50. [Nicholas Wiseman], "State and Prospects of Catholicity in England," *Dublin Review* 8 (1840): 256.

CHAPTER 6

1. Bernard Ward, *Sequel to Catholic Emancipation*, 2:2; Pugin to Wiseman, 1 June 1838, UC, WP, 823.

2. Wiseman to Newsham, Eve of SS. Peter & Paul [28 June] 1838, LDA, BP, 391. The fact that the letter is among the papers of Bishop Briggs indicates that Newsham forwarded it to his bishop.

3. Newsham to Wiseman, 10 Aug. 1838, VEN, 75:6.

4. Bernard Ward, *Sequel to Catholic Emancipation*, 1:163.

5. Wiseman to Newsham, 18 Oct. 1838, UC, PA, H/1.

6. Newsham to Wiseman, 14 May 1839, VEN, 75:7.

7. Walsh to Wiseman, 18 Sept. 1838, ibid., 70:6.

8. Logan to Wiseman, 9 Jan. 1836, UC, WP, 802.

9. Walsh to Charles Acton, 10 Feb. 1840, SA, 3:338.

10. Wiseman, *Essays on Various Subjects*, 2:vii.

11. Newman, *Apologia*, pp. 109–11, and *The Via Media of the Anglican Church, Illustrated in Lectures, Letters, and Tracts*, 2 vols. (London: Longmans, Green, and Co., 1877).

12. "Quapropter SECURUS judicat orbis terrarum, bonos non esse qui se dividunt ab orbe terrarum, in quacumque parte orbis terrarum." Wiseman, "The Catholic and Anglican Churches," in *Essays on Various Subjects*, 2:224.

13. Newman, *Apologia*, pp. 109–11.

14. Wiseman, "Froude's Remains," in *Essays on Various Subjects*, 2:94n. Wilfrid Ward, *Wiseman*, 1:314–19.

15. This note, in Wiseman's hand-writing, is contained in a trunk in the Ushaw College library, in an envelope marked "Cardl. Wiseman's Retreat Notes."

16. Thomas Turton, quoted in Wilfrid Ward, *Wiseman*, 1:243.

17. Wiseman to Husenbeth, 17 July 1837, UC, WP, 815.

18. Edward Cox to Wiseman, 5 June 1838, ibid., 824; Nicholas Wiseman, *A Reply to the Rev. Dr. Turton's "Roman Catholic Doctrine of the Eucharist Considered," Philalethes Cantabrigiensis, The British Critic, and the Church of England Quarterly Review* (London: Charles Dolman, 1839), p. 26.

19. Kyan, quoted in Wilfrid Ward, *Wiseman*, 1:255–56.

20. For the manuscripts of Wiseman's play, see UC, WP, 147 A, B.

21. J. L. Patterson, quoted in Fothergill, *Wiseman*, p. 84; Wilfrid Ward, *Wiseman*, 1:260; Edward Purbrick, quoted in ibid., 2:163, also p. 174.

22. Charlton, *Recollections*, pp. 55–56.

23. Kyan, quoted in Wilfrid Ward, *Wiseman*, 1:260.

24. Wiseman to Frasquita Gabrielli, 27 Apr. 1839, in Fothergill, *Wiseman*, pp. 79–80.

25. Wiseman to Xaviera Wiseman, 11 Oct. 1839, UC, WP, 1041. Wiseman began the entire letter on 2 Oct. and completed it on 13 Oct., dating each section as he wrote. The entire text is in Wilfrid Ward, *Wiseman*, 1:309–14.

26. Richard Thompson to Edmund Winstanley, 26 Sept. 1839, UC, Lisbon Papers (hereafter LP).

27. Wiseman to Xaviera Wiseman, 13 Oct. 1839, in Wilfrid Ward, *Wiseman*, 1:313.

28. Shrewsbury to Phillipps, quoted in Edmund Sheridan Purcell, *The Life and Letters of Ambrose Phillipps de Lisle*, ed. Edwin de Lisle, 2 vols. (London: Macmillan and Co., 1900), 1:105–6.

29. Wiseman to Newsham, 19 Dec. 1839, UC, PA, H/5.

30. This copy of Wiseman's "Sup-

plex Libellus" may be found in BAY, Book of Roman Letters. I have quoted from this source, including the passages in italics. For an Italian copy of the document, in Wiseman's handwriting, see UC, WP, 552 B.

31. Wiseman to Griffiths, 3 Jan. 1840, WAA, W1/2.

32. Griffiths to Briggs, 21 Feb. and 11 Mar. 1840, LDA, BP, 667, 690.

33. Thomas Youens to Briggs, 18 Mar. 1840, ibid., 695.

34. Tate to Briggs, 19 Mar. 1840, ibid., 696.

35. Newsham to Briggs, 15 Mar. 1840, ibid., 691.

36. Wiseman to Newsham, St. Joseph's Day [19 Mar.] 1840, UC, PA, H/6.

37. Baines to Wiseman, 16 Mar. 1840, VEN, 72:6; Fransoni to Walsh, 22 Feb. 1840, with Walsh's reply, n.d., BAA.

38. See PF, Acta, 202:309. For the original letters and manuscripts used in the compilation of the Acta, see PF, Scritture Originali (hereafter SO), 956:275.

39. PF, Acta, 202:324–26. Charles Acton was the son of Sir John Francis Acton, English baronet and prime minister to King Ferdinand IV of Naples. Educated at Magdalen College, Cambridge, Monsignor Acton was unable to take his English degree because of his religion. His younger brother was Sir Ferdinand Acton of Aldenham Hall, Shropshire, father of John Acton, the historian.

40. De Luca's *votum*, 28 Apr. 1839, PF, Acta, 202:328–49; Lingard's arguments in favor of the hierarchy, 16 Feb. 1839, ibid., 358–59.

41. Gentili and Giovanni Battista Pagani, quoted in Leetham, *Gentili*, p. 109.

42. Fransoni to Griffiths, 28 Sept. 1839, WAA, A.86.

43. Wiseman to Griffiths, 3 Jan. 1840, ibid., W1/2; Wiseman to Lingard, 13 Feb. 1840, UC, WP, 433.

44. For the correspondence and discussions of the various candidates,

see PF, Acta, 203:140–60. Fransoni himself served as *ponente* when Propaganda met in May.

45. Walsh to Wiseman, 24 Jan. 1840, VEN, 70:6.

46. Griffiths to Briggs, 28 Jan. 1840, LDA, BP, 643.

47. Baines to Griffiths, 8 Mar. 1839, WAA, A.85.

48. Newsham to Briggs, Sunday [15 Feb.] 1840, LDA, BP, 675.

49. Lingard to Briggs, n.d. [Feb.] 1840, ibid., 652.

50. Lingard to Briggs, 21 Feb. 1840, ibid., 679.

51. PF, Acta, 203:140–60.

52. Wiseman to George Spencer, Ash Wednesday [14 Feb.] 1839, in Purcell, *de Lisle*, 1:176–77.

53. Baines to Wiseman, 16 Mar. 1840, VEN, 72:6.

54. Bernard Ward, *Sequel to Catholic Emancipation*, 1:203–19. Baines later infuriated the Holy Father by printing his explanation of the affair and denying that he had been rebuked by the Holy See. *A Letter Addressed to Sir Chas. Wolseley, Bart., on the Lenten Pastoral of* 1840 (Prior Park: St. Paul's Press, 1840).

55. Wilfrid Ward, *Wiseman*, 1:336. Melipotamus (variously written Mellipotamen, Milopotamen, Milopotamos) was in Crete. See Remigius Ritzler and Pirminus Sefrin, *Hierarchia Catholica Medii et Recentioris Aevi sive Summorum Pontificum – S.R.E. Cardinalium Ecclesiarum Antistitum Series*, vol. 8 (Padua: Il Messaggero di S. Antonio, 1978): 378.

56. Walsh to Shrewsbury, 26 May 1840, UC, WS. The appointments were ratified in May and printed in the *Tablet*, 30 May 1840.

57. Briggs to Griffiths, 3 June 1840, WAA, W1/2. Briggs was now to be vicar apostolic of the Yorkshire District.

58. For descriptions of Henry Weedall's efforts to avoid the episcopate, see Baines to Griffiths, 21 July and 3 Aug. 1840, and Baggs to Griffiths, 6 Aug. 1840, WAA, W1/2; Mil-

burn, *History of Ushaw College*, pp. 181–82; Bernard Ward, *Sequel to Catholic Emancipation*, 2:4–5.

59. William Hogarth to Baggs, 4 Aug. 1840, VEN, 77:2.

60. Petition to Gregory XVI, 12 Feb. 1840, ibid., 70:7; Collier to Charles Acton, Apr. 1839 [copy], AA, Roman Documents, 259.

61. Baines to Griffiths, 5 July 1840, WAA, W1/2.

62. Wiseman to Charles Acton, 2 Sept. 1840, SA, 3:424.

63. Pius IX, cited in Brady, *Annals of the Catholic Hierarchy*, p. 366.

CHAPTER 7

1. Bernard Ward, *Sequel to Catholic Emancipation*, 2:3–5; Wilfrid Ward, *Wiseman*, 1:345–46. Wilfrid Ward cites 16 Sept. as the date of Wiseman's arrival at Oscott, but in that respect as in other aspects of the reception, his brother Bernard's account is more accurate.

2. Walsh's pastoral letter, Feast of the Guardian Angels [2 Oct.] 1840, SA, 3:359–60.

3. Wiseman's memorandum, 7 Mar. 1847, UC, WP, 871.

4. Bernard Smith, quoted in Wilfrid Ward, *Wiseman*, 1:352.

5. [Wiseman], "State and Prospects of Catholicity in England," p. 242.

6. Charles T. Dougherty and Homer C. Welsh, "Wiseman on the Oxford Movement: An Early Report to the Vatican," *Victorian Studies* 2 (1958): 150. The authors consulted a microfilm copy of the letter in the collection of the Knights of Columbus Foundation, Vatican Manuscript Depository, St. Louis University. For a draft of the report, "Cenni sullo stato religioso dell'Inghilterra tratti da lettere particolari scritte di recente," see UC, WP, 819. It is dated 12 Jan. 1838, clearly a mistake on Wiseman's part, as it was written in 1839. For Wiseman's response to the Tractarians, see Wilfrid Ward, *Wiseman*, 1:289–320;

Fothergill, pp. 95–104; Richard J. Schiefen, "The English Catholic Reaction to the Tractarian Movement," *Study Sessions* (Canadian Catholic Historical Association) 41 (1974): 9–31.

7. Josef L. Altholz, "Disputandum Est," *Victorian Studies* 2 (1959): 395–96.

8. "La circolazione di quanti opuscoli poco a poco toglierà delle sue radici la chiesa anglicana," wrote Charles Acton. For a draft of his report, see SA, 2:81.

9. John Henry Newman, *Autobiographical Writings*, ed. Henry Tristram (London: Sheed and Ward, 1956), p. 258.

10. Wiseman to Charles Baggs, 5 Nov. 1840, VEN, 77:2.

11. Baines to Baggs, 30 Nov. 1841, ibid., 72:7.

12. Wiseman to Charles Russell, SS. Cletus & Marcellinus [26 Apr.] 1841, WAA, W.31.

13. Wiseman to Russell, Easter Day [11 Apr.] 1841, WAA, W3/6.

14. Wiseman to Ambrose Phillipps, O[ur] L[ady] of Carmel [16 July] 1841, in Wilfrid Ward, *Wiseman*, 1:393–94.

15. George Spencer, quoted in Denis Gwynn, *Father Dominic Barberi* (London: Burns Oates, 1947), p. 99.

16. Walsh to Wiseman, 24 Jan. 1840, VEN, 70:6.

17. Briggs to Griffiths, 7 Feb. 1840, WAA, W1/2.

18. Wiseman, "The Catholic and Anglican Churches," p. 281.

19. John Henry Newman, "Letter Addressed to the Duke of Norfolk, on Occasion of Mr. Gladstone's Expostulation of 1874," in *Certain Difficulties Felt by Anglicans in Catholic Teaching*, 2d ed., 2 vols. (London: Longmans, Green, and Co., 1892, 2: 171–378.

20. Nicholas Wiseman, *A Letter Respectfully Addressed to the Rev. J. H. Newman upon Some Passages in His Letter to the Rev. Dr. Jelf*, 2d ed. (London: Charles Dolman, 1841), pp. 8–9.

21. Nicholas Wiseman, *A Letter on Catholic Unity, Addressed to the Right Hon. the Earl of Shrewsbury* (London: Charles Dolman, 1841), pp. 13–14, 33–34.

22. Wiseman to Shrewsbury, 21 Aug. 1841, UC, WP, 844.

23. Wiseman to Shrewsbury, St. Francis's Day [4 Oct.] 1841, ibid., 847.

24. Wiseman to Phillipps, Eve of Ascension [19 May 1841], WAA, W3/6; Wiseman to Shrewsbury, SS Peter & Paul [29 June] 1841, UC, WP, 845.

25. Wiseman to Shrewsbury, St. Peter's Chair [22 Feb.] 1842, UC, WP, 850. Also see Owen Chadwick, *The Victorian Church*, 2 vols. (New York: Oxford University Press, 1966–70), 1:189–93.

26. Wiseman to Charles Acton, Ember Friday, Advent [16 Dec.] 1842, SA, 3:429.

27. Joseph Rathborne, *Are the Puseyites Sincere? A Letter Most Respectfully Addressed to a Right Reverend Lord Bishop on the Oxford Movement* (London: T. Jones, 1841), pp. 4–7; *Orthodox Journal*, 18 Feb. 1843, in Bernard Ward, *Sequel to Catholic Emancipation*, 2:92–93, [Frederick Lucas], writing in the *Tablet*, 4 Nov. 1843.

28. Phillips, quoted in Purcell, *de Lisle*, 1:235; Shrewsbury, quoted in Denis Gwynn, *Lord Shrewsbury, Pugin and the Catholic Revival* (Westminster, Md.: Newman Bookshop, 1946), p. xviii.

29. Walsh to Charles Acton, St. Swithin's Day [15 July] 1842, SA, 3:400–401.

30. Walsh to Wiseman, 7 Oct. 1843, BAA. For an account of Richard Waldo Sibthorpe's benefactions, see Wiseman to Shrewsbury, 23 Dec. 1841, and Feast of St. Stanislas [7 May] 1842, UC, WP, 849, 856.

31. Wiseman's memorandum, 7 Mar. 1847, UC, WP, 871.

32. Wiseman to Shrewsbury, St. Mark [7 Oct.] 1843, ibid., 480.

33. Wiseman to Charles Russell, 8 Nov. 1845, in Wilfrid Ward, *Wiseman*, 1:433.

34. Wiseman to Shrewsbury, n.d. [1847], UC, WP, 1015.

35. Wiseman to Walker, St. Thos. Cant. [29 Dec.] 1845, UC, WAP, folder 1; Newman to James Hope, 19 Dec. 1845, in *The Letters and Diaries of John Henry Newman* (hereafter *Letters and Diaries*), ed. C. S. Dessain and others, 26 vols. to date (vols. 11–22, London: Thomas Nelson and Sons, 1961–72; vols. 23–31, 1– , Oxford: Clarendon Press, 1973–), 11:71–72.

36. Newman's memorandum, 10 Jan. 1846, in *Letters and Diaries*, 11:89–90.

37. Newman to Whitty, 10 Jan. 1846, in ibid., p. 88.

38. Newman, *Autobiographical Writings*, p. 255.

39. For a draft of Wiseman's report, written in Italian and undated (probably 1847), see UC, WP, 559 B.

40. Wiseman to Shrewsbury, n.d. [1847], ibid., 1015.

41. Wiseman to Walker, Passion Wed. [5 Apr.] 1843, UC, WAP, folder 1.

42. John Acton, quoted in Wilfrid Ward, *Wiseman*, 1:349.

43. Wiseman's memorandum, 7 Mar. 1847, UC, WP, 871.

44. Arthur S. Barnes, *The Catholic Schools of England* (London: Williams and Norgate, 1926), p. 148.

45. Walsh to Shrewsbury, 14 Oct. 1842, UC, WS.

46. Walsh to Errington, 3 Mar. 1845, BAA.

47. Newman to J. D. Dalgairns, 6 July 1846, in *Letters and Diaries*, 11:195.

48. Wiseman to Shrewsbury, n.d. [1847], UC, WP, 1015; Bernard Ward, *Sequel to Catholic Emancipation*, 2:9.

49. Walsh to Shrewsbury, 24 Dec. 1839, UC, WS.

50. Joseph Ilsley to Winstanley, 13 July 1839, ibid., LP.

51. Wiseman to Shrewsbury, 20 Nov. 1840, UC, WP, 843.

52. Baines to Griffiths, 5 July 1840,

WAA, W1/2. Also see "Statement of the Right Rev. Dr. Walsh with Reference to the Residuary Bequest of the late Charles Robert Blundell, Esq.," n.d. [1841], WAA, St. Edmund's Archive (hereafter SEA), 21/13. For a discussion of the case, see Bernard Ward, *Sequel to Catholic Emancipation*, 1:187–91.

53. Wiseman to Shrewsbury, 2 Sept. 1841, UC, WP, 846.

54. Walsh to Shrewsbury, n.d. [1847], ibid., WS.

55. Francis Searle to Henry Edward Manning, 20 Sept. 1887, BAY.

56. Wiseman to Shrewsbury, 8 Sept. 1846, UC, WP, 864.

57. Thomas M. McDonnell to Midland clergy, 23 Mar. 1840, WAA, A.87.

58. For an account of the episode based on materials now in the Clifton Archive, Bristol, see Bernard Ward, *Sequel to Catholic Emancipation*, 2:15.

59. Wiseman to "Rev. dear Sir," Eve of Ascension [19 May] 1841, WAA, W3/6.

60. Walsh to Charles Acton, 22 Nov. 1839, SA, 3:335–37; Wiseman to Shrewsbury, 20 Nov. 1840, UC, WP, 843; Pugin, quoted in Bernard Ward, *Sequel to Catholic Emancipation*, 1:97.

61. Wiseman to Daniel Rock, 12 May 1840, SAA, Daniel Rock, 1799–1871.

62. Lingard to Walker, 16 Aug. and 8 Oct. 1844, UC, WAP, folder 6.

63. Lingard to Walker, 5 Nov. 1849, ibid.

64. Chinnici, *English Catholic Enlightenment*, pp. 171–75.

65. Newman to Dalgairns, 15 Jan. 1847, and to Wiseman, 17 Jan. 1847, in *Letters and Diaries*, 12:19–20.

66. Wilfrid Ward, *Wiseman*, 1:306–7; J. T. Ward and J. H. Treble, "Religion and Education in 1843: Reaction to the 'Factory Education Bill,'" *Journal of Ecclesiastical History* 20 (1969): 79–110; Bernard Ward, *Sequel to Catholic Emancipation*, 2:49;

G. I. T. Machin, *Politics and the Churches in Great Britain, 1832 to 1868* (Oxford: Clarendon Press, 1977), p. 148; Richard J. Schiefen, "The Crusade of Nicholas Wiseman," in *The View from the Pulpit: Victorian Ministers and Society*, ed. P. T. Phillips (Toronto: Macmillan of Canada, 1978), p. 248.

67. Wiseman, "Memorial Presented to Sir James Graham," "Form of Petition to the House of Commons against the Factories Amended Bill," and to "Rev. and dear Sir," in Festo S. Anselmo D. [21 Apr.] 1843, SA, 3:410.

68. Henry Granville Fitzalan Howard, earl of Arundel and Surrey (hereafter Arundel and Surrey), quoted in Bernard Ward, *Sequel to Catholic Emancipation*, 2:50–51.

69. Wiseman, "Form of Petition against the 'Charitable Trusts' Bill,'" and to "Rev. Dear Sir," 14 May 1846, "Observations on the Charitable Trusts' Bill," WAA, W1/6/2.

70. Walsh to Shrewsbury, 25 Nov. 1844, UC, WS; Lingard to Walker, 24 Nov. 1844, ibid., WAP, folder 6.

71. Wiseman to Charles Russell, 10 Mar. 1845 and n.d. [1846], WAA, W3/6.

72. "Most Humble Supplication and Declaration of the Secular Priests Exercising the Functions of the Apostolic Mission in the London District, in the Year 1840," WAA, A.87. The petition is discussed in Bernard Ward, *Sequel to Catholic Emancipation*, 1:160–63.

73. To the editor, 21 Sept. 1840, *Tablet*, 5 Dec. 1840. The pertinent letters announcing the establishment of the so-called Adelphi Society were published in the *Tablet*, 11 Feb. 1843; see Bernard Ward, *Sequel to Catholic Emancipation*, 2:159–60.

74. Wiseman to Griffiths, 1 Jan. 1843, WAA, W1/2.

75. [Nicholas Wiseman], "Ecclesiastical Organization," *Dublin Review* 12 (1842): 240–51; Wiseman to Walker, Passion Wed. [5 Apr.] 1843, UC, WAP.

76. "Minute Book of Bishops' Meetings, 1844–46," WAA, Z.46.

77. Baggs to Griffiths, 8 Aug. 1845, WAA, W1/2. Dom Cuthbert Butler was uncharacteristically careless in stating that Baggs "was an elderly man and delicate," since Baggs had not yet celebrated his fortieth birthday at the time of his death. *The Life and Times of Bishop Ullathorne, 1806–88*, 2 vols. (London: Burns Oates and Washbourne, 1926), 1:146.

78. "Minute Book of Bishops' Meetings," WAA, Z.46.

79. Walsh to Shrewsbury, 6 July 1847, UC, WS.

CHAPTER 8

1. PF, Acta, 210:714–15, and Congregazioni Particolari (hereafter CP), 157:46. The Acta contain the *ponenza* and *sommario* for 1847, but the material in the volume of the Congregazioni Particolari has correspondence not included in the first source, including letters written the following year. Rather than the Acta, 210:713–44, future references will be to CP, 157:44–199.

2. Bernard Ward, *Sequel to Catholic Emancipation*, 2:163; Leetham, *Gentili*, p. 276.

3. Fransoni to Gentili, 11 Mar. 1847, in Leetham, *Gentili*, pp. 277–78.

4. See summaries of Gentili's letters and reports in ibid., pp. 278–98.

5. William Bernard Ullathorne, *From Cabin-Boy to Archbishop: The Autobiography of Archbishop Ullathorne*, ed. Shane Leslie (London: Burns Oates, 1941), pp. 244–45.

6. A draft of the report, in Wiseman's handwriting, is in UC, WP, 552 A. Someone has written on the manuscript, "Aug. 19, 1848," although it is clearly the draft prepared a year earlier. For the final report, see PF, CP, 157:52–54.

7. Wiseman to vicars apostolic, 19 July 1847, in William Bernard Ullathorne, *History of the Restoration of the Catholic Hierarchy of England* (London: Burns, Oates, and Co. [1871]), pp. 25–26.

8. Walsh to Wiseman, 27 July 1847, WAA, R79/6.

9. Walsh to Wiseman, 3 and 7 Aug. 1847, ibid.; Searle to Wiseman, 8 Aug. 1847, ibid., R79/16.

10. William Wareing to Wiseman, 6 Aug. 1847, ibid., R79/6.

11. Riddell to Wiseman, 7 Aug. 1847, UC, WP, 504.

12. Cox to Wiseman, 3 and 12 Aug. 1847, WAA, R79/16.

13. Gentili, quoted in Leetham, *Gentili*, pp. 311–12.

14. Bernard Ward, *Sequel to Catholic Emancipation*, 2:166; James Sharples to Briggs, 18 Aug. 1847, LDA, BP, 1682.

15. Wiseman to Shrewsbury, n.d., UC, WP, 503; Wiseman to vicars apostolic, 13 Sept. 1847 [draft], WAA, A.101.

16. Wiseman's report, PF, CP, 157:64–66; also draft manuscript, UC, WP, 559 A.

17. Burke to Wiseman, 2 Aug. 1847, UC, WP, 1030; John Acton, quoted in Wilfrid Ward, *Wiseman*, 1:348.

18. Gregory XVI, quoted in Nicholas Wiseman, *Words of Peace and Justice Addressed to the Catholic Clergy and Laity of the London District on the Subject of Diplomatic Relations with the Holy See* (London: Charles Dolman, 1848), p. 6.

19. Wiseman to Henry John Temple, third Viscount Palmerston, 13 Sept. 1847, and memorandum, also in form of letter from Wiseman to Palmerston, 13 Sept. 1847, in Wilfrid Ward, *Wiseman*, 1:571–77. For a draft of the memorandum, see UC, WP, 507. For a discussion of Wiseman's mission, see Wilfrid Ward, *Wiseman*, 1:479–86.

20. Palmerston's directions to Gilbert Elliot, second earl of Minto, quoted in Wilfrid Ward, *Wiseman*, 1:485; Palmerston, quoted in Wiseman to Shrewsbury, n.d., UC, WP, 507.

21. [John Talbot, sixteenth earl of Shrewsbury], *Diplomatic Relations with Rome, Considered Chiefly in Reference to the Restrictive Clause Introduced into the Bill by the House of Lords, in a Letter from John, Earl of Shrewsbury to the Earl of Arundel and Surrey* (London: Charles Dolman, 1848), pp. 9–13, including quotation from Arthur Wellesley, first duke of Wellington.

22. "The Heads of a Proposed Memorial to His Holiness from the Archbishops & Bishops of Ireland & from the Bishops of England & Scotland," LDA, BP, 1693. For a revised version of the document, containing the second passage quoted (omitted from the original proposal), see BAA, 1287. The manuscript is marked "October, 1848," an obvious mistake since it refers to the fact that Lord Minto was in Rome at the time that the memorial was written.

23. Lucas to Ullathorne, n.d., WAA, SEA, 7/4.

24. "To His Holiness, Pope Pius IX, Supreme Pontiff, the Memorial of the Undersigned Catholic Ecclesiastics and Laymen of Great Britain," 20 Mar. 1848, UC, UCM, 434 C. The petition is published in Bernard Ward, *Sequel to Catholic Emancipation,* 2:295–301.

25. Nicholas Wiseman, *Words of Peace and Justice,* pp. 6–16.

26. Wiseman, "Memorial to His Holiness Pius IX," in Bernard Ward, *Sequel to Catholic Emancipation,* 2:301–4.

27. Wiseman to Ullathorne, 13 Apr. 1848, BAA.

28. Ullathorne to Wiseman, 16 Apr. 1848, WAA, R79/3.

29. Walsh to Shrewsbury, 17 Sept. 1847, UC, WS.

30. Wiseman to Briggs, 26 Oct. 1847, LDA, BP, 1689. For the recommendations that Sharples made to Propaganda, see PF, CP, 157:67–71.

31. Walsh to Wiseman, 5 Jan. 1848, UC, Some Correspondence of Bishop Thomas Walsh (hereafter BW). Also

see PF, CP, 157:225; and Ullathorne, *Restoration of the Catholic Hierarchy,* p. 35.

32. Motion of support for Wiseman, 8 Oct. 1847, UC, WP, 880; petition to Pius IX, n.d., WAA, R79/16. For a Latin copy of the second petition, with slightly modified wording and some signatures not included in the English version, see UC, WP, 902.

33. Shrewsbury to Wiseman, 9 Oct. 1847, UC, WP, 881.

34. Thomas Sisk to "Rev. and Dear Sir," 20 Oct. 1847, ibid., 903. The petition to the pope was sent for signatures along with the letter.

35. Peter Collingridge to "Rev. Dear Sir," 28 Oct. 1847, ibid., 905. Father Peter Collingridge is not to be confused with Bishop Peter Collingridge of the Western District, who died in 1829.

36. T. F. Wilkinson to "Rev. Dear Sir," 3 Nov. 1847, ibid., 907. The petition to Briggs for signatures was sent along with the letter.

37. Wiseman to Shrewsbury, 2 Nov. 1847, ibid., 906.

38. Wilkinson to Wiseman, 8 Nov. 1847, ibid., 908.

39. G. J. Caley to Newsham, Feast of St. Andrew [30 Nov.] 1847, ibid., Charles Newsham Papers (hereafter NP).

40. Fransoni to Wiseman, 7 Dec. 1847, WAA, box 140; Thomas Grant to Briggs, 8 Dec. 1847, LDA, BP, 1692.

41. Ullathorne, *Restoration of the Catholic Hierarchy,* p. 32, and *Cabin-Boy to Archbishop,* pp. 249, 258; Bernard Ward, *Sequel to Catholic Emancipation,* 2:205–7, 215.

42. Briggs to Grant, 21 Jan. 1848, and Wiseman to Grant, 5 Sept. 1848, PF, CP, 157:220–21, 189–90.

43. Ullathorne to Wiseman, 12 Aug. 1848, WAA, R79/3.

44. Aubrey de Vere to Mrs. Edward Villiers, Sept. 1848, in Wilfrid Ward, *Aubrey de Vere: A Memoir Based on His Unpublished Diaries and Correspondence* (London: Longmans,

Green, and Co., 1904), p. 147.

45. Walsh to Shrewsbury, 5 Aug. 1848, UC, WS.

46. Bernard Ward, *Sequel to Catholic Emancipation*, 2:233–34.

47. Wiseman to Palmerston, 4 Dec. 1848 [copy], WAA, R79/16; W. A. Addington to Wiseman, 9 Jan. 1849 [copy], LDA, BP, 1802. Also see memorandum outlining the matter, Dec. 1848, VEN, 78:2. Readers may now consult Matthias Büschkuhl, *Great Britain and the Holy See*, 1746–1870 (Dublin: Irish Academic Press, 1982), pp. 83–88, for a discussion of diplomatic relations between Great Britain and the Holy See and for Minto's mission.

CHAPTER 9

1. Wiseman to Shrewsbury, 2 Nov. 1847, UC, WP, 906; Newman to John Bowden, 3 Aug. 1835, in *Letters and Diaries*, 5:114; Newman, *Apologia*, p. 117; Wiseman to Lucas, Feast of SS. Cletus and Marcellinus [26 Apr.] 1842, in Bernard Ward, *Sequel to Catholic Emancipation*, 2:44.

2. [Lucas], writing in the *Tablet*, 30 May 1840, in Bernard Ward, *Sequel to Catholic Emancipation*, 2:31–32.

3. Lucas, quoted in ibid., p. 33.

4. Wiseman to Shrewsbury, Holy Saturday [26 Mar.] 1842, UC, WP, 851.

5. Wiseman to Phillipps, Feast of St. John of Beverley [25 Oct.] 1843, in Wilfrid Ward, *Wiseman*, 1:419. Also see Wiseman to Shrewsbury, Feast of St. Stanislaus [7 May] 1842, UC, WP, 856.

6. Wiseman to Lucas, Feast of SS. Cletus and Marcellinus [26 Apr.] 1842, in Bernard Ward, *Sequel to Catholic Emancipation*, 2:45.

7. Chadwick, *Victorian Church*, 1:272.

8. Arundel and Surrey to John MacHale, 26 Nov. 1847, in Bernard Ward, *Sequel to Catholic Emancipation*, 2:136.

9. MacHale to John Russell, and to Arundel and Surrey, in ibid., pp. 137, 140.

10. For the correspondence, see ibid., pp. 141–44.

11. Shrewsbury to Wiseman, 7 Mar. 1848, UC, WP, 914. On 20 Jan. 1848 Grant had written from Rome to warn Wiseman to "get clear of the Tablet." UC, WP, 510. Wiseman's letter to the cardinal secretary of state was followed by an article in the *Rome Gazette* stating that the London bishop had nothing to do with the weekly journal and that he was far from supporting the extreme positions expressed by its editor. Bernard Ward, *Sequel to Catholic Emancipation*, 2:174–75.

12. Wiseman to bishops, 9 Mar. 1848, WAA, SEA, 15/8; Wareing to Wiseman, 16 Mar. 1848, UC, WP, 516.

13. Phillipps to Wiseman, 14 Mar. 1848, UC, WP, 514.

14. Lucas to Wiseman, 22 Mar. 1848, ibid., 542. For the correspondence between Lucas and Wiseman (including the bishop's message that there would be no further correspondence), printed and circulated by Lucas, see ibid., 520. Also see Josef L. Altholz, *The Liberal Catholic Movement in England: The "Rambler" and Its Contributors*, 1848–1864 (London: Burns and Oates, 1962), p. 13.

15. Shrewsbury to Wiseman, 16 Mar. 1848, UC, WP, 916.

16. Wiseman, "State and Prospects of Catholicity in England," p. 250.

17. [Nicholas Wiseman], "The Industry of the Poor," *Dublin Review* 30 (1851): 512.

18. Griffiths to Baggs, 12 Oct. 1839, WAA, A.86. Also see Griffiths to Shrewsbury, 10 Oct. 1838, in Bernard Ward, *Sequel to Catholic Emancipation*, 1:175.

19. Bossy, *English Catholic Community*, p. 23; Wiseman to Shrewsbury, 29 Mar. 1847, UC, WP, 872.

20. Lucas quoted Thomas Doyle in the *Tablet*, 23 June 1849. Shrewsbury

cited Doyle's statement in a letter to Ullathorne, 25 Feb. 1849, BAA, as did McDonnell to editor, 27 June 1849, *Tablet*, 30 June 1849. Doyle wrote regularly for the *Tablet* as "Father Thomas." Shrewsbury's daughter, Lady Gwendaline Catherine, was married to Marcantonio Aldobrandini, Prince Borghese; Lady Mary Alethea Beatrix married Filippo Andrea, Prince Doria-Pamfili-Landi.

21. Lucas, writing in the *Tablet*, 7 July 1849; Shrewsbury to Wiseman, 9 July 1849 (Shrewsbury wrote two letters on the same day), and Wiseman to Shrewsbury, 12 Sept. 1849, UC, WP, 945, 946, 950.

22. Shrewsbury to Wiseman, 14 Sept. 1849, and Wiseman to Shrewsbury, 26 Oct. 1849, UC, WP, 951, 558.

23. Wiseman to Shrewsbury, 10 Nov. 1849 [copy], ibid., 954 A.

24. B. Hawes to Wiseman, 21 Jan. 1848 and 8 May 1849, WAA, R70/16.

25. Bernard Ward, *Sequel to Catholic Emancipation*, 2:152, 157. For a brief description of the bishops' efforts to promote Catholic primary education, see ibid., pp. 146-48.

26. Wiseman to clergy, 7 Feb. 1848, WAA, SEA, 2/18.

27. Grant to Wiseman, 27 Feb. 1848, UC, WP, 513.

28. Lingard to Walker, 16 Feb. 1850, ibid., WAP, folder 7.

29. John Coyle to Wiseman, 16 Sept. 1847, ibid., WP, 893; Coyle, "To the Benevolent and Charitable," 29 May 1851, WAA, R79/16.

30. John S. Gaynor, *The English-Speaking Pallottines* (Rome: Gregorian University Press, 1962), p. 30.

31. William O'Connor to Wiseman, 12 Aug. 1849, WAA, W2/1/10.

32. Wiseman to O'Connor, 26 Aug. 1849 [copy], ibid.

33. O'Connor to Wiseman, 3 Sept. 1849, ibid.

34. John Kyne to Wiseman, 24 Sept. 1849, ibid. Also see Raffaele Melia to Wiseman, 9 Aug. 1849 and, from the same correspondent, an undated letter marked "Riservatissimo," ibid.

35. Vincent Pallotti to Melia, 26 Feb. 1848, in Gaynor, *English-Speaking Pallottines*, p. 41. Cox to Wiseman, 19 June 1849, WAA, W3/17.

36. Griffiths to Baggs, 26 Sept. 1842, VEN, 77:5; correspondence between Griffiths and the Jesuit provincial, May–July 1840, WAA, A.91; Bernard Ward, *Sequel to Catholic Emancipation*, 2:28.

37. Bernard Ward, *Sequel to Catholic Emancipation*, pp. 28–29; Griffiths to Briggs, 25 Apr. 1843, LDA, BP.

38. Griffiths to Baggs, 12 Oct. 1844, VEN, 77:4.

39. Wiseman, "Relazione Storica e Personale dello Stato passato ed attuale della Diocesi di Westminster," marked "Riservatissimo, con Segreto Pontificio," 18 Jan. 1862, PF, Scritture Riferite nei Congressi (hereafter SR), 16:413. Wiseman, in his *Recollections of the Last Four Popes* (p. 329), described the interview and the pope's reference to an "obstacle" that had to be removed before England would have a hierarchy. Bishop Ullathorne, in his *Restoration of the Catholic Hierarchy* (p. 36), concluded that Griffiths was the "obstacle," but Bernard Ward, in *Sequel to Catholic Emancipation* (2:167), disagreed, having determined that Wiseman's statement better applied to Cardinal Acton. Not only was Ward's logic somewhat faulty in the explanation he offered, but Wiseman's later admission indicates clearly that Griffiths was the man to whom Pope Gregory XVI referred.

40. Wiseman to Newman, 29 Oct. 1847, in *Letters and Diaries*, 12:126.

41. Newman to Wiseman, 15 Jan. 1849, in ibid., 13:9–10.

42. *Oxford Herald*, quoted in Bernard Ward, *Sequel to Catholic Emancipation*, 2:179–80.

43. Wiseman, writing in the *Tablet*, 8 Aug. 1857; Wiseman to Newsham, 25 Jan. 1850, in Bernard Ward,

Sequel to Catholic Emancipation, 2:180.

44. Wiseman to the Society of the Holy Child of Jesus, 19 Oct. 1846, in Mother Marie Thérèse, *Cornelia Connelly: A Study in Fidelity* (London: Burns and Oates, 1963), pp. 82–83.

45. Lucas, writing in the *Tablet,* 12 May 1849.

46. Bernard Ward, *Sequel to Catholic Emancipation,* 1:180–82.

47. Gaynor, *English-Speaking Pallottines,* p. 42; Wiseman, quoted by Herbert Vaughan in his diary, in J. G. Snead-Cox, *The Life of Cardinal Vaughan,* 2 vols. (London: Burns and Oates, 1912), 1:106–7.

48. T. G. Holt, "The German Catholic Chapel in London," *Transactions of the London and Middlesex Archaeological Society* (1977), pp. 323–27; James Jauch to Wiseman, 29 Sept. and 22 Dec. 1847, and James Leachey to Wiseman, 6 June 1849, WAA, W2/2/5.

49. See Wiseman to Newsham, 26 Dec. 1848, UC, PA, 20. Wiseman wrote, "My brother is applying for a situation, and a certificate of his having received a classical education in England is of importance to him."

50. For a description of the opening of St. George's, see Bogan, *Great Link,* p. 128.

51. Wiseman to Grant, 5 Sept. 1848, PF, CP, 157:189–90.

52. Searle's journal, entry for 20 Jan. 1854, SAA, C.2; Lingard to Walker, 17 and 22 July 1850, UC, WAP, folder 7.

53. Grant to Wiseman, 2 July 1850, WAA, 137/1. Grant had already warned Wiseman of the rumors when writing on 24 June 1850, ibid.

54. T. J. Brown to Wiseman, 14 July 1850, and Ullathorne to Wiseman, 16 July 1850, WAA, R79/3.

55. *Tablet,* 13 July 1850; Wiseman to Newsham, 12 July 1850, UC, PA, H/71; Wiseman to Charles Russell, 4 July 1850, in Wilfrid Ward, *Wiseman,* 1:521–22.

56. Wiseman "Confidential Memoranda for Rev. Mr. Talbot," VEN, George Talbot Papers (hereafter TP).

57. Lingard to Walker, 21 and 6 Aug. 1850, UC, WAP, folder 7.

CHAPTER 10

1. Arundel and Surrey to Talbot, 29 Aug. 1850, VEN, TP.

2. Wiseman to Bagshawe, 13 Sept. 1850, WAA, W3/8.

3. Wilfrid Ward, *Wiseman,* 1: 527–37.

4. Xaviera Wiseman to Harriet Butler, 6 Nov. 1850, UC, WP, 965.

5. Wiseman to John Russell, 3 Nov. 1850, in Wilfrid Ward, *Wiseman,* 1:534–36.

6. Wiseman, "From the Flaminian Gate," 7 Oct. 1850 [pastoral letter], in Bernard Ward, *Sequel to Catholic Emancipation,* 2:305–8; Queen Victoria, quoted in Norman, ed., *Anti-Catholicism in Victorian England,* p. 56.

7. John Russell, letter to the *Times,* 7 Nov. 1850, quoted in Norman, ed., *Anti-Catholicism in Victorian England,* p. 158. In addition to Norman's treatment of the papal aggression crisis (pp. 52–79), consult Walter Ralls, "The Papal Aggression of 1850: A Study in Victorian Anti-Catholicism," *Church History* 43 (1974): 242–56; G. I. T. Machin, "Lord John Russell and the Prelude to the Ecclesiastical Titles Bill, 1846–51," *Journal of Ecclesiastical History* 25 (1974): 277–95; Wilfrid Ward, *Wiseman,* 1:538–69, 2:1–37; Walter L. Arnstein, *Protestant versus Catholic in Mid-Victorian England: Mr. Newdegate and the Nuns* (Columbia, Mo.: University of Missouri Press, 1982), esp. chap. 4.

8. Nicholas Wiseman, *An Appeal to the Reason and Good Feeling of the English People* (London: T. Richardson and Son, 1850). See the treatment of the pamphlet in Wilfrid Ward, *Wiseman,* 1:556–69.

9. Whitty to Morris, 2 Mar. 1893, WAA, W2/2/1.

10. Wiseman to Talbot, 30 Dec. 1850, VEN, TP.

11. Charles Forbes de Montalembert to Wiseman, 25 Nov. 1850, and Wiseman to Richard Doyle, 16 Nov. 1850, WAA, W3/47, W2/3/3.

12. Wiseman to Mrs. Henry Bagshawe, 21 Feb. 1851, ibid., W3/8.

13. The new sees and the counties within each were Westminster (Middlesex, Essex, and Hertfordshire); Beverley (Yorkshire); Birmingham, (Oxfordshire, Staffordshire, Somersetshire, and Wiltshire); Hexham (Cumberland, Westmoreland, Northumberland, and Durham); Liverpool (the Hundreds of West Derby, Amounderness, and Lonsdale in Lancashire, and the Isle of Man); Newport and Menevia (Herefordshire, Monmouthshire, and South Wales); Northampton (Bedfordshire, Buckinghamshire, Cambridgeshire, Huntingdonshire, Norfolk, Northamptonshire, and Suffolk); Nottingham (Derbyshire, Leicestershire, Lincolnshire, Nottinghamshire, and Rutland); Plymouth (Devon, Dorset, and Cornwall with the Scilly Isles); Salford (the Hundreds of Salford, Leland [later transferred to Liverpool], and Blackburn); Shrewsbury (Cheshire, Shropshire, and North Wales); Southwark (Surrey, Berkshire, Hampshire, Kent, Sussex, the Isles of Wight, Guernsey, Jersey, and the adjacent isles).

14. Lingard to Walker, 6 Aug. 1850, UC, WAP, folder 7.

15. Ullathorne to Wiseman, 17 [no month] 1848, WAA, R79/3.

16. Grant to Wiseman, written on a letter from Fransoni to Wiseman, 22 Jan. 1851, ibid., box 140; Talbot to Ullathorne, 8 Apr. 1851; BAA; Talbot to Searle, 9 Apr. 1851, SAA, C.2.

17. Wiseman to Fransoni, 23 Mar. 1851, PF, Acta, 213:283.

18. Wiseman to Talbot, 5 Apr. 1851, VEN, TP. For those bishops who recommended Cox, see PF, Acta, 213:281–83.

19. Ullathorne to Grant, 23 Jan 1851, PF, SO, 973:1014–16. Grant's

translation into Italian is in ibid., Acta, 213:285–87.

20. Wiseman to Talbot, 14 Apr. 1851, "Letters to Cardinal Wiseman, with a Commentary by Cardinal Gasquet," *Dublin Review* 164 (1919): 19; Grant, "Cenni Presentati a Monsig. Segretario dall'Agente dei Vescovi," n.d., PF, Acta, 213:288.

21. Grant to Wiseman, 18 Dec. 1850, and Fransoni to Wiseman, 12 Aug. 1851, WAA, R79/8, box 140. For a sympathetic treatment of Joseph William Hendren, see Roche, *Prior Park*, pp. 212–13.

22. For the background to the change, see Sharples to Grant, 22 Aug. 1848, PF, CP, 157:199; Wiseman to Fransoni, 23 Mar. 1851, ibid., Acta, 213:283; Grant, "Cenni Presentati a Monsig. Segretario dall'Agente dei Vescovi," ibid., 287. The matter is discussed briefly by C. A. Bolton, *Salford Diocese and Its Catholic Past* (Manchester: Diocese of Salford, 1950), p. 130, and by Philip Hughes, "The English Catholics in 1850," in George Andrew Beck, ed., *The English Catholics, 1850–1950: Essays to Commemorate the Centenary of the Restoration of the Hierarchy of England and Wales* (London: Burns Oates, 1950), p. 51 n. 2.

23. Newman to J. F. Capes, 18 Feb. 1851, in *Letters and Diaries*, 14:213; Wiseman to Fransoni, 22 Mar. 1851, PF, Acta, 213:281.

24. Newman to Talbot, 3 Feb. 1851, in *Letters and Diaries*, 14:205–6; Ullathorne to Grant, 6 Mar. 1851 [Italian translation], PF, SR, 12:949.

25. Wiseman to Talbot, 14 Apr. 1851, in Butler, *Ullathorne*, 1:195.

26. Wiseman to Fransoni, 22 Mar. 1851, PF, Acta, 213:280.

27. Grant to Wiseman, 23 June 1851, WAA, 137/1; Wiseman to Grant, 10 July 1851, PF, SR, 12:1021; PF, Acta, 213:277.

28. Morgan Sweeney, "Diocesan Organisation and Administration," in Beck, ed., *English Catholics*, p. 124.

29. Wiseman to Talbot, 9 Dec.

1850, in "Letters to Cardinal Wiseman, with a Commentary by Cardinal Gasquet," p. 11.

30. Wilfrid Ward, *Wiseman*, 2:160.

31. Whitty to Morris, 2 Mar. 1893, WAA, W2/2/1.

32. Wilfrid Ward, *Wiseman*, 2:189; Whitty to Morris, 2 Mar. 1893, WAA, W2/2/1.

33. Quoted in Wilfrid Ward, *Wiseman*, 2:189; Robert Browning, "Bishop Blougram's Apology," in *Men and Women* (London: Chapman and Hall, 1855).

34. Whitty to Morris, 2 Mar. 1893, WAA, W2/2/1.

35. Talbot to Wiseman, 20 July 1853, BAY.

36. "Morris Manuscript," WAA, R79/13.

37. Whitty to Morris, 2 Mar. 1893, WAA, R79/16.

38. Grant to Talbot, 1 Feb. and 24 Dec. 1853, VEN, TP.

39. The house on York Place (now York Street) is still standing, but with no indication of the famous occupant who once lived there.

40. David Mathew, *Lord Acton and His Times* (London: Eyre and Spottiswoode, 1968), p. 35; Grant to Wiseman, 18 Dec. 1850, WAA, R79/8.

41. Whitty to Morris, 2 Mar. 1893, WAA, R79/16.

42. Grant to Wiseman, 10 Apr. 1851, ibid., 137/1.

CHAPTER 11

1. The matters discussed by the bishops and the agreements reached may be found in PF, Acta, 214:99–126. For the content of much of this chapter, I have drawn upon the sources included in Richard J. Schiefen, "The First Provincial Synod of Westminster (1852)," *Annuarium Historiae Conciliorum* (1972), pp. 188–213.

2. Wilfrid Ward, *Wiseman*, 2: 54–56; Shrewsbury to Phillipps, n.d., in Purcell, *de Lisle*, 1:327.

3. Robert Hogarth (chairman) to Wiseman, 14 Jan. 1851, WAA W3/29.

4. Grant, "The Practical Consequences of the Restoration of the Hierarchy," 20 Feb. 1851 [postmark], ibid., 137/1. The entire manuscript is in Grant's handwriting. For his explanation of the reasons for writing it, see Grant to Wiseman, 14 Feb. 1851, on inside page of letter from Fransoni to Wiseman, 5 Feb. 1851, ibid., box 140.

5. "Resolutions passed at the Conference of the Clergy of the Deanery of South Northumberland and North Durham," 16 Jan. 1851, ibid., W3/29; Grant, "Practical Consequences of the Restoration of the Hierarchy."

6. The Beverley address, 28 Jan. 1851, and Wiseman's reply, 10 Feb. 1851, were published in the *Tablet*, 22 Feb. 1851.

7. William Vaughan to editor, 14 Aug. 1843, ibid. (the writer was the future bishop of Plymouth); Sweeney, "Diocesan Organisation and Administration," p. 122.

8. Wiseman to Henry Bagshawe, 13 Sept. and 17 Oct. 1850, WAA, W3/8; Wilfrid Ward, *Wiseman*, 1:531. Talbot had already told the cardinal that the pope would assist him financially. Talbot to Wiseman, n.d., SAA, C.1.

9. Grant to Wiseman, 14 Jan. [1851], WAA, 137/1.

10. Hughes, "English Catholics in 1850," pp. 56–57; Ullathorne to Talbot, 7 May 1853, VEN, TP; Ullathorne, *Cabin-Boy to Archbishop*, pp. 290–91; Butler, *Ullathorne*, 1:165–68, 171–74.

11. Ullathorne to Thomas Joseph Brown, 15 Sept. 1856, in *Letters of Archbishop Ullathorne*, ed. Mother Francis Raphael [Augusta T. Drane] (London: Burns and Oates, 1892), pp. 79–80.

12. Hendren to Edgar Estcourt, 3 Apr. 1852, BAA.

13. Hughes, "English Catholics in 1850," p. 61.

14. Wareing to "My dear Sir" [probably Estcourt, Ullathorne's sec-

retary], 7 Aug. 1852, and T. Green to E. Huddleston, n.d. [1852], BAA; W. A. Johnson to James Dannell, 6 July 1878, SAA, Division of Westminster and Southwark.

15. Grant to Alessandro Barnabò, 10 Dec. 1851, PF, SR, 12:1132–34.

16. Newman to J. Spencer Northcote, 28 Feb. 1851, in *Letters and Diaries*, 14:230.

17. Ullathorne, *Restoration of the Catholic Hierarchy*, pp. 108–9.

18. Ibid., p. 109; Ullathorne, *Cabin-Boy to Archbishop*, p. 299. Grant, well grounded in canon law, was of particular help to the cardinal. See Grant to Wiseman, 9 and 11 June 1852, WAA, 116/1. A copy of the "Epitome Decretorum," with the comments of Bishop Ullathorne, may be consulted, along with a letter the Birmingham bishop wrote to Wiseman, 10 June 1852, ibid.

19. Wilfrid Ward, *Wiseman*, 2: 59–60; "Epitome Decretorum," with Ullathorne's comments, WAA, 116/1. The omission of the reference to Anglican orders is explained on a page of corrections prepared at the synod. No heading is provided for the document, although the items are numbered. See ibid., n. 4.

20. Ullathorne's remarks may be found in an undated fragment of a letter included with Ullathorne to Wiseman, 30 Apr. 1852, ibid.

21. Logan's dismissal and Wiseman's part in the affair may be pieced together from the following letters: Logan to Bagshawe, 3 Oct. 1848, UC, Oscott Papers (hereafter OP), 9; Ullathorne to Wiseman, 4 and 8 Oct. 1848, WAA, R79/3; Wiseman to Ullathorne, 8 Oct. 1848, BAA; Ullathorne to Logan, 28 Sept. 1848 [copy], Logan to Wiseman, 9 and 11 Oct. 1848, and Wiseman to Logan, 9 Oct. 1848, UC, WP, 931–35.

22. Lingard to Walker, 31 Dec. 1849, UC, WAP, folder 6.

23. Wiseman to Cox, 20 July 1851, SAA, C.1; Wiseman to Talbot, 3 Aug.

1851, in "Letters of Cardinal Wiseman, with Commentary by Gasquet," p. 22.

24. Lingard to Walker, 21 Aug. 1850, UC, WAP, folder 6.

25. Ullathorne to Wiseman, 10 June 1852, WAA, 116/1.

26. John Henry Newman, "The Second Spring" (1852), in *Sermons Preached on Various Occasions* (London: Longmans, Green, and Co., 1857), pp. 163–82.

27. The most convenient source for the decrees is *Decreta Quatuor Conciliorum Westmonasteriensium, 1852–73: Adjectis pluribus decretis, rescriptis, aliisque documentis* (Salford: John Roberts, [1884]). This edition, however, omits the daily Acta, which are included in Robert E. Guy, ed., *The Synods in English, Being the Text of the Four Synods of Westminster* (Stratford-on-Avon: St. Gregory's Press, 1886).

28. Comments of Briggs on "Epitome Decretorum," 13 June 1852, George Brown to Wiseman, 4 Oct. 1852, and Hendren to Wiseman, 23 Sept. 1852, WAA, 116/1, R79/6, 130/1; Wiseman to Newsham, 22 Apr. 1849, UC, PA, H/21.

29. William Samuel Lilly and John E. E. Wallis, *Manual of the Law Specially Affecting Catholics* (London: W. Clowes, 1893), p. 135; Cox to Wiseman, 24 Feb. 1850, WAA, W3/28.

30. For a transcript of the proceedings, see WAA, W3/17.

31. Butler, *Ullathorne*, 2:187.

32. "Istruzione sulla Dipendenza dei Missionari Regolari dai Vicari Apost. ed Altri Superiori di Missioni," 30 Sept. 1848, WAA, 116/1. The only edition of the first synod's decrees that includes the instruction is *Decreta Quatuor Conciliorum Westmonasteriensium*, pp. 92–94.

33. The letter is addressed to the English bishops and signed by the major superiors of religious communities in England, 25 July 1853, WAA, R91/9.

34. Grant to Wiseman, 17 Dec. 1853, and Fransoni to Wiseman, 21 Sept. 1853, WAA, 130/1, box 140.

35. The synodical letter may be consulted in *Synods in English*, pp. 266–73 (copies may also be found in WAA, 116/1); "To the Cardinal Archbishop of Westminster and to All the Bishops of England and Wales," Visitation of the Blessed Virgin [2 July] 1852, ibid.

36. Newman to Henry Wilberforce, 18 July 1852, in *Letters and Diaries*, 15:126; Talbot to Grant, 12 Oct. 1852, BAY. The decree of approbation, 14 May 1853, precedes all editions of the decrees.

37. Ullathorne, *Restoration of the Catholic Hierarchy*, p. 109. Ullathorne says substantially the same thing in *Cabin-Boy to Archbishop*, p. 299.

CHAPTER 12

1. Wiseman to Charles Russell, 4 July 1850, WAA, W3/6; Wilfrid Ward, *Wiseman*, 1:518–21; Chadwick, *Victorian Church*, 1:250–71.

2. Wiseman to Talbot, 30 Dec. 1850, VEN, TP.

3. Wilfrid Ward, *Wiseman*, 2:153.

4. Wiseman quoted the *Times*, 10 Dec. 1852, in writing to Lord Beaumont, 8th Baron [Miles Thomas Stapleton], 16 Dec. 1852 [copy], UC, WP, 582.

5. Wiseman, quoted in Wilfrid Ward, *Wiseman*, 2:51; Wiseman to Henry Ivers, 10 Jan. 1850 [copy], WAA, A.76.

6. Wiseman to Newsham, Aug. 1853, UC, PA/H.

7. Wilfrid Ward, *William George Ward and the Catholic Revival* (London: Macmillan, 1893), pp. 33–34.

8. Wiseman to Grant, 31 Jan. 1854, SAA, C.1; Wiseman to Newman, 20 Jan. 1854, in *Letters and Diaries*, 16:31–32.

9. Newman to Paul Cullen, 2 Mar. 1853, and to Richard Stanton, 24 Feb. 1853, in ibid., 15:316–17, 310–11.

10. V. F. Blehl, "Newman and the Missing Mitre," *Thought* 35 (1960): 110–23; Fergal McGrath, *Newman's University: Idea and Reality* (Dublin: Browne and Nolan, 1951), pp. 238–46; Meriol Trevor, *Newman: Light in Winter* (Garden City, N.Y.: Doubleday and Co., 1963), pp. 33–34, 45–48; Wilfrid Ward, *The Life of John Henry Cardinal Newman*, 2 vols. (London: Longmans, Green, and Co., 1912), 1:328–31, 356–57.

11. [Wiseman], "Dr. Achilli," *Dublin Review* 28 (1850): 470–511.

12. Newman to Hope, 16 July 1851, and Hope to Newman, 17 July 1851, in *Letters and Diaries*, 14:310–11.

13. Newman's memorandum, 22 Dec. 1851, in ibid., pp. 508–10.

14. Wilfrid Ward, *Wiseman*, 2:82–95; Fothergill, *Wiseman*, pp. 216–18; Bogan, *Great Link*, p. 236.

15. Frasquita Gabrielli to Wiseman, 11 Aug. 1854, UC, WP, 470.

16. Wiseman's memorandum, 3 June 1855, WAA, W3/11.

17. Frasquita Gabrielli to Wiseman, 30 Oct. 1855 and 17 Jan. 1856, UC, WP, 973, 976.

18. John Wallis to Walker, 16 Oct. 1853, UC, WAP, folder 6; Peter Baines to Thomas Barge, 28 Feb. 1854, UC, LP. Peter Baines is not to be confused with Peter Augustine Baines, bishop of Siga, who died in 1843.

19. Wiseman to W. G. Ward, 17 Feb. 1854, WAA, W3/41.

20. Wiseman to Talbot, 15 Sept. 1854, VEN, TP.

21. Wiseman to Talbot, 26 Sept. and 3 Oct. 1856, ibid.

22. [Wiseman], "The Industry of the Poor," pp. 485–86, 505, 513–14, 532.

23. Wiseman, quoted in Schiefen, "Crusade of Nicholas Wiseman," pp. 265–67.

24. Michael Barry to Wiseman, 3 Jan. 1859, and Christopher Ward to Wiseman, 23 Feb. 1859, WAA, W2/3/6.

25. Wiseman to Frederick Faber, 27 Oct. 1852, UC, WP, 581.

26. Wiseman to James Burke, 2 June 1851 [draft], J. T. Headlam to Wiseman, 23 and 24 May 1851, Searle to Headlam [draft] and Headlam to Wiseman, 17 July [1851], WAA, W3/53, W3/29.

27. Wiseman to Talbot, 28 Dec. 1852, VEN, TP.

28. Wiseman to Talbot, 6 Jan. and 21 July 1853, ibid.

29. Grant to Talbot, 11 Feb. 1852 and 1 Feb. 1853, ibid.

30. Wiseman to Grant, 9 Apr. 1853 [copy], and Grant to Wiseman, 18 Apr. [1853], WAA R79/4; Wiseman to Grant, 20 Apr. 1853, SAA, C.2; see Fothergill, *Wiseman*, pp. 206–7.

31. Errington to Talbot, 15 Mar. 1854, VEN, TP.

32. Ullathorne to T. J. Brown, 11 Apr. 1854, BAA.

33. Wilfrid Ward, *Wiseman*, 2:132; Wiseman to Talbot, 18 June 1854, VEN, TP, 1022; also see Wiseman to Frasquita Gabrielli, 29 Apr. 1854, in Fothergill, *Wiseman*, pp. 214–15.

34. Wiseman to Talbot, 25 July and 13 Oct. 1855, VEN, TP; Fothergill, *Wiseman*, p. 216.

35. Wiseman to Walker, 6 Oct. 1856, in Wilfrid Ward, *Wiseman*, 2:147. For a treatment of the entire episode, see ibid., pp. 133–48.

36. Sweeney, "Diocesan Organisation and Administration," p. 132; Maguire to Wiseman, 2 Jan., 3 Feb., and 26 June 1854, WAA, W3/12, R79/16.

37. William Turner to Grant, 19 Jan. 1853 [Italian translation], PF, Acta, 215:65. The Acta state that Turner's request was granted.

38. Wiseman to Ullathorne, 25 Nov. 1847, BAA.

39. "Payments Made by the Rt. Rev. Dr. Wiseman to or on Account of St. Mary's College and Now Owing to Him by the College" and "Statement of Account between the Rt. Rev. Dr. Wiseman and the Central District," with covering letter from Bagshawe, 10 Jan. 1849, UC, OP, 15, 19, 21; Ullathorne to Bagshawe, 22 Jan. 1849, and Bagshawe to Ullathorne, 24 Jan. 1849 [copy], ibid., 16, 17.

40. Wiseman to Ullathorne, 30 Jan. 1849, BAA; Ullathorne to Wiseman, 30 Jan. and 9 Feb. 1849, 30 Dec. 1855, 25 Jan. and 8 Feb. 1856, WAA, R79/3; Ullathorne to Bagshawe, 9 Feb. 1849, UC, OP, 18; Wiseman to Ullathorne, 12 Feb. 1849, and Searle to Ullathorne, 20 May 1853, BAA.

41. Johnson to Dannell, 6 July 1878, SAA, Division of Westminster and Southwark.

42. Grant to Wiseman, 8 Sept. 1852, 18 Apr. [1852], 12 Jan. and 18 Apr. [1853], WAA, R79/4, 130/2. Grant rarely included the year when dating his letters, so it is not always clear to which of his letters Wiseman was responding. The same arguments were often repeated throughout the decade.

43. Wiseman to Searle, 31 Jan. 1854, SAA, C.1.

44. Talbot to Wiseman, 11 Aug. 1853 [postmark], BAY; Wiseman to Grant, 14 Jan. 1853 [draft], WAA, R79/4.

45. Wiseman to Talbot, 16 Jan. 1853, BAY.

46. Grant to Talbot, 14 Nov. 1853, VEN, TP. For the petition to Propaganda, 13 Nov. 1853, see PF, Acta, 223:557–58. Also see Grant to Talbot, 24 Dec. 1853, VEN, TP.

47. Grant to Wiseman, 17 Dec. 1853, WAA, 130/1.

48. Grant's petition to Propaganda, 13 Nov. 1853, PF, Acta, 223:557–58.

49. Wiseman to Propaganda, 3 Dec. 1853, WAA, box 140, and 4 Jan. 1854, PF, Acta, 233:558 (a draft of the latter, dated 3 Jan., is in WAA, box 140).

50. Grant's report, 13 Feb. 1854, PF, Acta, 223:559–60. Also see PF, SR, 13:951–52, 14:147–49, 150–52, 189–90. The report was sent to Wiseman for comment, 10 Mar. 1854, WAA, box 140.

51. Wiseman's report, 26 Mar. 1854, PF, Acta, 223:561–69. Also see

PF, SR, 13:939–50, 14:153–64, 165–76, 192–203.

52. Grant's report, 31 Jan. 1855, and Grant to Propaganda, 6 Feb. 1855, PF, Acta, 223:569–71, 571–78; Fransoni to Wiseman, 28 Feb., 18 May, and 22 Dec. 1855, and Barnabò to Wiseman, 27 Nov. 1856, 31 July and 13 Dec. 1858, WAA, box 140.

53. Wilfrid Ward, *Wiseman*, 2: 95–108.

54. Nicholas Wiseman, *Fabiola; or, The Church of the Catacombs* (London: Burns and Lambert, 1855), preface.

55. Errington reported the background in a report prepared for Propaganda (1860) to defend his position in Westminster. PF, CP, 158:743.

56. Talbot to Searle, 24 Sept. 1854, SAA, C.2; Talbot to Wiseman, 9 Feb. 1855, BAY.

57. Errington to Talbot, 3 Mar. 1855, VEN, TP.

58. See record of bishop's meeting, WAA, 140, and PF, Acta, 219:333.

CHAPTER 13

1. Milburn, *History of Ushaw College*, p. 210; Turner to Newsham, 21 Feb. 1853, UC, PA, L/28; "Informazione particolare dell'Emo. Sig. Card. Wiseman, Riservata," PF, Acta, 215:178–80.

2. Fransoni to Wiseman, 29 Mar. 1855, WAA, box 140.

3. Turner to Propaganda, 17 May 1853, and Wiseman to Propaganda, 20 July 1853, PF, SR, 13:580–81, 671–72.

4. "Proposta di Mons. Grant per la divisione della Diocesi," 23 Dec. 1854, ibid., Acta, 220:264–67. Also see "A notre St. Pére le Pope" (1855), signed by more than two hundred Catholics of Jersey, in which they asked to be placed under the jurisdiction of a French bishop. Ibid., SR, 14:35–39.

5. Fransoni to Wiseman, 29 Jan. 1855, WAA, box 140; Wiseman to Talbot, 20 July 1855, VEN, TP; Wiseman to Propaganda, 9 Nov. 1855, and

Grant to Propaganda, 22 July 1855, PF, Acta, 220:361–64, 367.

6. For the acts and decrees of the second synod, see above, chap. 11, n. 27.

7. Trevor, *Newman: Light in Winter*, pp. 170–73.

8. Propaganda's discussion of the decrees in the spring of 1856, PF, Acta, 220:335–71.

9. Fransoni to Wiseman, 27 June 1855, WAA, box 140.

10. Wiseman to Fransoni, 9 Nov. 1855, PF, Acta, 220:361–64.

11. The most scholarly work on any of the colleges is Milburn's *History of Ushaw College*, although Roche's *Prior Park* is a good, careful history of that institution. Less thorough in its presentation of mid-nineteenth-century events is Bernard Ward's *History of St. Edmund's College, Old Hall* (London: Kegan, Paul, Trench, Trübner and Co., 1893).

12. For the directive of the Council of Trent concerning seminaries, see sess. 23:18. The edition of the decrees that I have consulted is *Canons and Decrees of the Council of Trent*, trans. H. J. Schroeder (St. Louis, Mo.: B. Herder Book Co., 1941).

13. Ullathorne, quoted in Roche, *Prior Park*, p. 200; Ullathorne to Propaganda, 20 June 1848 [draft], BAA. An Italian translation of the letter, dated 21 June 1848, is in PF, SR, 12:109–15.

14. Grant to Wiseman, 1 Dec. 1850, and Wiseman to Walker, 7 Jan. 1856, WAA, 137/1, W3/3/4.

15. Wiseman to Talbot, 22 Aug. and 26 Sept. 1856, VEN, TP.

16. Errington to Wiseman, 21 Nov. 1856, in Roche, *Prior Park*, 240–41. For Errington's mission to Clifton, see the various letters and suggestions to the Holy See, PF, Acta, 223:293–304. Also see Errington to Talbot, 23 Aug. 1855, VEN, TP; a copy of the letter was quoted in its entirety by Wilfrid Ward, *Wiseman*, 2:261–62. The cardinal had suggested that Bishop Alexander Goss might be sent to Clifton as

administrator, but Propaganda felt that he was needed in Liverpool. Fransoni to Wiseman, 18 May 1855, WAA, box 140. Wiseman reluctantly supported Errington's assignment but said that he would miss him and hoped his absence from Westminster would be for a specified, limited period only. Wiseman to Propaganda, 31 Aug. 1855, PF, SR, 14:348–52, Bishop William Clifford again purchased Prior Park for the diocese in 1866. Roche, *Prior Park*, pp. 245–54.

17. Ullathorne to Wiseman, 28 Sept. 1849, WAA, R79/3. For a brief sketch of Oscott's early history and an assessment of its finances prior to 1865, see "Statement Respecting St. Mary's College, Oscott," 10 May 1865, BAA.

18. Ullathorne to Wiseman, 30 Dec. 1855, 25 Jan. and 8 Feb. 1856, WAA, R79/3.

19. Wiseman to Ullathorne, 8 Feb. 1856 [draft], ibid. The sum of money claimed by Ullathorne was £360.

20. Milburn, *History of Ushaw College*, p. 154; also see Newsham to Talbot, 31 Dec. 1858, VEN, TP.

21. Grant to Wiseman, 18 Dec. 1850, WAA, R79/8.

22. "Relazione della visita dell col- legio e seminario di S. Cuthberto nella Diocesi di Hexham addi 29 e 30 agosto 1851 dal Emo. Sig. Card. Wiseman," 24 Dec. 1851 [draft], UC, Ushaw Col- lege History Collection (hereafter UCH), 364. Since the draft of this document was added to the Ushaw ar- chive after Milburn had completed his book, he was unable to consult it. The same document, with an explanatory letter from Wiseman to Fransoni, 20 Jan. 1852, is in PF, Acta, 214:120–26.

23. Newsham to Wiseman, 18 Oct. 1851, WAA, W3/17; Milburn, *History of Ushaw College*, pp. 190–93, 198– 202, 223, 231, 240–41.

24. Fransoni to Wiseman, 17 Apr. 1852, WAA, box 140; Wiseman to Newsham, 8 May 1852, UC, PA, H/30; Newsham to Wiseman, 10 May 1852, WA, W3/17; Hogarth to Wise-

man, 17 Jan. 1854, and Briggs, George Brown, and Turner to Wiseman, 4 May 1855, UC, PA, M/54, N/4.

25. Milburn, *History of Ushaw College*, p. 206; Newsham to Wise- man, 10 May 1852 and 17 Mar. 1854, WAA, W3/17; Newsham to Talbot, 31 Dec. 1858, VEN, TP; Newsham to Hogarth, 11 May 1856, UC, PA, D/34.

26. Butler, *Ullathorne*, 1:255–56; Newsham to Wiseman, 18 Oct. 1851, WAA, W3/17; Robert Cornthwaite to Fransoni, 26 May 1852, PF, SR, 13:218; Cornthwaite to Newsham, 30 Dec. 1854, UC, NP; Wiseman to Newsham, 5 May 1854, UC, UCH, 92; Barnabò to Wiseman, 7 Dec. 1857, and New- sham and Hogarth to Wiseman, n.d. [copy], WAA, box 140, W3/24; Mil- burn, *History of Ushaw College*, pp. 209–10.

27. Barnabò to Wiseman, 19 July 1856, WAA, box 140; Newsham to Talbot, 31 Dec. 1858, VEN, TP. Mil- burn, then, was mistaken in stating that after the discussion of 1856, "of the idea of making Ushaw a pontifical college, we hear no more." *History of Ushaw College*, p. 238.

28. Newsham to Talbot, 31 Dec. 1858, VEN, TP, 535. For the petition of the four bishops, 15 Dec. 1858, see Milburn, *History of Ushaw College*, p. 241. Bishop James Brown signed it and sent a copy to Wiseman, along with a letter explaining its aim, 22 Dec. 1858, WAA, W3/20.

29. Talbot to Newsham, 17 Dec. 1859, UC, UCH, 121.

30. William Weathers to Wiseman, 6 Sept. 1852, and to Searle, 12 Oct. 1852, WAA, W3/17, W1/5/2.

31. Whitty to Talbot, 17 Dec. 1858, VEN, TP. Whitty had still been vicar general and chapter provost when the trouble began in 1854.

32. W. G. Ward to Walker, 4 Jan. 1856, UC, WAP; Weathers to Wise- man, n.d. July 1856, WAA, W3/17. The specific theological questions upon which Ward and Erington dis- agreed are mentioned in W. G. Ward to Walker, 9 Jan. 1856, UC, WAP.

33. Errington to Talbot, 23 Aug. 1855, VEN, TP.

34. Wiseman to Talbot, 22 Aug. 1856, ibid.

35. Talbot to Wiseman, 23 Mar. 1857, BAY.

36. Charlton, *Recollections*, p. 221. It should be noted that although Errington was opposed by Manning, Ward, and Talbot (all converts), he was admired by Canons Searle and Oakeley (also converts).

37. Wiseman's pastoral letter, 1 June 1857, WAA, W2/3/1. This was an announcement of the general archdiocesan visitation, not just that for the seminary.

38. Wiseman to Talbot, 12 June and 27 Oct. 1857, VEN, TP.

39. Wiseman to Pius IX, 3 Mar. 1860 [draft], BAY.

40. The best biography of Vaughan is Snead-Cox, *Vaughan*. Vaughan's missionary career has been more thoroughly examined by Arthur McCormack, *Cardinal Vaughan: The Life of the Third Archbishop of Westminster, Founder of St. Joseph's Missionary Society, Mill Hill* (London: Burns and Oates, 1966).

41. Wiseman to Walker, 19 Oct. 1856, WAA, W2/3/4; Wiseman to Barnabò, 27 Nov. 1856, PF, SR, 14:900–901.

42. Burke to Searle, n.d., SAA, C.2; Manning to Herbert Vaughan, 7 Oct. 1858, in Snead-Cox, *Vaughan*, 1:88–89. The most accurate, detailed biography of Manning is Shane Leslie, *Henry Edward Manning, His Life and Labours* (London: Burns Oates and Washbourne, 1921). It is no substitute, unfortunately, for Edmund Sheridan Purcell, *Life of Cardinal Manning, Archbishop of Westminster*, 2 vols. (London: Macmillan and Co. 1896). Purcell's work is indispensable, in spite of widely publicized errors of fact and interpretation. For a sympathetic study, see Vincent Alan McClelland, *Cardinal Manning: His Public Life and Influence, 1865–1892* (London: Oxford University Press, 1962).

43. Weathers to Grant, [undated fragment], WAA, 137/1. The president described his quarrel with Vaughan and his request that the cardinal should remove him. He also discussed the fact that Wiseman was responsible for a visit that W. G. Ward made to the college to ascertain the feelings of the students toward Vaughan. Grant wrote on this fragment, "Recd. June 14, 1859, T. G." The fragment was most probably sent to Wiseman, along with a letter that the Southwark bishop wrote to the cardinal to complain of Ward's interference, 18 June 1859 [incomplete], ibid.

44. Vaughan to Louis English, 19 Sept. [1858], VEN, TP.

45. Talbot to Wiseman, 7 July, 9 Apr., Easter Monday [13 Apr.] 1857, BAY.

46. For a detailed analysis of the chapter's investigation into the Oblates and the government of the college, see Richard J. Schiefen, "Some Aspects of the Controversy between Cardinal Wiseman and the Westminster Chapter," *Journal of Ecclesiastical History* 21 (1970): 125–48.

47. *Decrees of the Council of Trent*, sess. 23:18. References to the "city" indicate the supposition that the bishop and his seminary were to be located in the major city of the diocese.

48. Whitty and Maguire were appointed on 10 Jan. 1853. WAA, 116/3. The duration of the assignment is significant, since Maguire seems to have presumed that he still held the responsibility later in the decade.

49. Whitty to Wiseman, 12 Jan. 1853, WAA, R79/9.

50. For a discussion of the chapter address to Wiseman, see Schiefen, "Aspects of the Controversy," pp. 128–31.

51. For the decree of censure, see "Resolution Book," 3 Dec. 1858, Westminster Chapter Records.

52. Talbot to Wiseman, 10 Oct. 1858, BAY. The letter has been mistakenly placed among papers marked "1855."

53. Schiefen, "Aspects of the Controversy," pp. 140, 142 n. 5; Manning to Frederick Oakeley, 26 Dec. 1858 [draft], BAY.

54. Grant to Wiseman, 8 Sept. 1852, WAA, R79/4.

55. Wiseman to Propaganda, 26 Apr. 1857, PF, SR, 14:267; Wiseman to Manning, 22 Jan. 1859, in Leslie, *Manning*, p. 502. Errington, at Propaganda's request, had in fact proposed a solution to the financial dispute. Errington to Barnabò, 13 July 1858, PF, Acta, 223:579–80. Barnabò then wrote to Wiseman to suggest that a commission should be formed by Errington and Grant, 21 July 1858, WAA, box 140.

56. Grant to Wiseman, 8 July 1858, WAA, R79/4. Years earlier Grant had suggested a similar means of administering Ushaw. Grant to Newsham, 10 July 1851, UC, NP. There is no reason, then, to believe that Grant, in this regard, was now being led by Errington.

57. Wiseman to Grant, 9 July and 25 Nov. 1858 [drafts], WAA, W3/21.

58. Grant to Wiseman, 28 Nov. 1858, with the plan that begins "Essendosi degnata," Nov. 1858, WAA, 116/3; Wiseman to Grant, 3 Dec. 1858 [draft], WAA, W3/21.

59. Petition of Southwark Chapter, 9 Dec. 1858 [copy], WAA, 116/3.

60. Wiseman to Newsham, 20 Dec. 1858 [copy], WAA, W3/20; Errington to Grant, 5 Dec. 1858, SAA, C.2.

61. Manning to Wiseman, 10 Jan. 1859, in "More Letters of Wiseman and Manning," *Dublin Review* 172 (1923): 112; Talbot to Patterson, 7 Mar. 1859, WAA, 137/5.

62. Wiseman to Propaganda, 25 Mar. 1859, PF, Acta, 223:580–85.

63. Wiseman to Patterson, 28 Dec. 1858, WAA, W3/21.

64. Barnabò to Maguire, 7 Jan. 1859, Wiseman to Patterson, 7 Jan. 1859, and Goss to "My dear Friend," 10 Mar. 1859 [copy], ibid., 116/3, W3/21.

65. Errington to Grant, 5 Dec. 1858, SAA, C.2; Grant to Talbot, 13 Feb. 1859 [incomplete], VEN, TP. For a treatment of the unjust charge of Gallicanism, see Richard J. Schiefen, "'Anglo-Gallicanism' in Nineteenth-Century England," *Catholic Historical Review* 63 (1977): 14–44.

66. For the correspondence between Errington and Talbot, see Wilfrid Ward, *Wiseman*, 2:610–24.

67. Errington to Barnabò, 8 Mar. 1859, PF, SR, 15:799–800.

68. Herbert Vaughan to Talbot, 22 Jan. 1859, VEN, TP.

69. For the correspondence concerning Maguire's dismissal and the rumor that Searle would meet the same fate, see Schiefen, "Aspects of the Controversy," pp. 143–44.

70. Wiseman to Weathers, Whitmonday [13 June] 1859 [incomplete], WAA, W3/17.

71. See Talbot to Errington, 13 and 17 Apr. 1859, in which Wiseman's requests for his coadjutor's dismissal are mentioned, in Wilfrid Ward, *Wiseman*, 2:617–19.

72. Wiseman to bishops, 18 Feb. 1859 [draft], WAA, W3/21.

CHAPTER 14

1. Wiseman to Walker, 7 Jan. 1856, WAA, W2/3/4; Wiseman to Talbot, 26 Sept. 1856, VEN, TP.

2. Wiseman to Talbot, 2 Feb. 1857, VEN, TP.

3. For Wiseman's apparent reversal of his former position, see Gaynor, *English-Speaking Pallottines*, pp. 89–92.

4. *Tablet*, 8 Aug. 1857.

5. Wiseman to Talbot, 8 Sept. 1857, VEN, TP.

6. Wiseman to Talbot, 5 Oct. 1857 and 1 Jan. 1859, ibid. See Bernard Elliott, "Mount St. Bernard's Reformatory, Leicestershire, 1856–81," *Recusant History* 15 (1979): 15–22.

7. Ullathorne to the editor, *Tablet*, 4 Apr. 1857. For a discussion of Ullathorne's pamphlet, *Notes on the Education Question* (1857), see Butler, *Ullathorne*, 1:180–82.

8. Wiseman to Charles Langdale, *Tablet*, 2 May 1857.

9. Ullathorne to Birmingham clergy, 6 and 12 May 1857, BAA.

10. Wiseman to bishops, 21 May 1857, SAA, C.1.

11. Ullathorne to bishops, 30 May 1857, ibid., C.2.

12. Wiseman to Talbot, 12 June 1857, VEN, TP.

13. Wiseman to bishops, 1 Oct. 1858, SAA, C.1.

14. Milburn, *History of Ushaw College*, p. 12. The play Wiseman composed was entitled *The Hidden Gem* (1859). A copy may be found in the Ushaw College library.

15. Nicholas Wiseman, *The Sermons, Lectures, and Speeches Delivered by His Eminence Cardinal Wiseman, Archbishop of Westminster during His Tour in Ireland in August and September* 1858 (Dublin: J. Duffy, 1859), p. 336.

16. Wilfrid Ward devoted an entire chapter to the Irish tour, quoting at length from the sermons and speeches. *Wiseman*, 2:289–320.

17. [Nicholas Wiseman], "State of Catholic Affairs," *Dublin Review* 42 (1857), 213–15.

18. Philip Hughes, "The Coming Century," in Beck, ed. *English Catholics*, p. 17. For the government's policy regarding the papal states and the political activity of Catholics, see C. T. McIntire, *England against the Papacy, 1858–1861: Tories, Liberals, and the Overthrow of Papal Temporal Power during the Italian Risorgimento* (Cambridge: Cambridge University Press, 1983).

19. E. R. Norman, *The Catholic Church and Ireland in the Age of Rebellion, 1859–1873* (Ithaca, N.Y.: Cornell University Press, 1965), p. 36.

20. Benjamin Disraeli to George Bowyer, 25 June 1859, in McIntire, *England against the Papacy*, p. 111; Wiseman to Talbot, 11 June 1859, VEN, TP.

21. John Acton to Wiseman, 23 Nov. 1857, WAA, W3/52.

22. Wiseman to Talbot, 23 Oct. 1858, VEN, TP. For Acton's offer to merge the *Rambler* with the *Dublin Review*, see Acton to Wiseman, 3 Sept. 1858, WAA, W3/52.

23. John Acton to Richard Simpson, 4 Feb. 1859, in Josef L. Altholz, Damian McElrath, and James C. Holland, eds. *The Correspondence of Lord Acton and Richard Simpson*, 3 vols. (Cambridge: Cambridge University Press, 1971–75), 1:149.

24. Tierney to Newsham, 27 July 1857 and 20 Apr. 1858, UC, PA/G1. For Wiseman's observation, see *Recollections of the Last Four Popes*, pp. 331–41. For Lingard's memoir, see John Lingard and Hilaire Belloc, *The History of England, from the First Invasion by the Romans to the Accession of King George the Fifth*, 11 vols. (New York: Catholic Publication of America, 1912), 1:xxxi–xlvi.

25. [Richard Simpson], "Sunny Memories of Rome," *Rambler*, 2d ser., 9 (1858): 274. Tierney to the editors, 1 May 1858, ibid., pp. 425–32; Montalembert to Wiseman, 11 June 1858, WAA, W3/47.

26. The Ushaw College library possesses one of the very rare copies of Wiseman's pamphlet, "A Letter to the Canons of the Cathedral Chapter of Westminster, in Reply to One Published in the "Rambler" for June 1858, Relative to a Passage in the 'Recollections of the Last Four Popes'" (London: [Printed, not published], 1858). Tierney's "A Reply to Cardinal Wiseman's Letter to His Chapter" (London: [Printed, not published], 1858) was based on materials now found among his papers in SAA. Also see Roe, *Lamennais and England*, pp. 127–30.

27. Isaac Hecker, quoted in Damian McElrath, *Richard Simpson, 1820–1876: A Study in XIXth Century English Liberal Catholicism* (Louvain: Publications Universitaires de Louvain, 1972), p. 47; Simpson to John Acton, 13 Nov. 1858, in Altholz et al., eds., *Acton-Simpson Corre-*

spondence, 1:83; [John Acton], writing in the *Rambler*, 2d ser., 10 (1858): 139–40, cited in ibid., p. 74 n. 1; [Simpson], "Dr. Lingard's Alleged Cardinalate," *Rambler*, 3d. ser., 2 (1859): 75–83, in Roe, *Lamennais and England*, p. 129. See, however, Simpson to John Acton, 27 Nov. 1858, in Altholz et al., eds., *Acton-Simpson Correspondence*, 1:98, where Simpson seems to have concluded that Wiseman was indeed correct.

28. [John Acton], "The Catholic Press," *Rambler*, 2d ser., 11 (1859): 73–90, discussed in Hugh A. MacDougall, *The Acton-Newman Relations: The Dilemma of Christian Liberalism* (New York: Fordham University Press, 1962), p. 40.

29. Scott Nasmyth Stokes, "The Royal Commission on Education" and "The Royal Commission and the 'Tablet,'" *Rambler*, 2d ser., 11 (1859): 17–30, 104–113; [John Henry Newman], "Judgement of the English Bishops on The Royal Commission," *Rambler*, 3d ser., 1 (1859): 122–23. In addition to sources already cited, consult V. F. Blehl, "Newman, the Bishops and 'the Rambler,'" *Downside Review* 90 (1972): 20–40; Samuel D. Femiano, *Infallibility of the Laity: The Legacy of Newman* (New York: Herder and Herder, 1967).

30. [John Henry Newman], "On Consulting the Faithful in Matters of Doctrine," *Rambler*, 3d ser., 1 (1859): 198–230.

31. Wiseman to Burke, 26 Nov. 1858, UC, WP, 990.

32. Herbert Vaughan to Talbot, n.d., VEN, 80:4.

33. Wiseman to Grant, 28 Mar. 1859 [copy], and Ullathorne to "My dear Lord," 15 Apr. 1859, WAA, 116/3, W3/10. No indication is given of the recipient. It was not addressed to Wiseman, since Ullathorne discussed him in the letter.

34. Ullathorne to Wiseman, 29 Apr. 1859, ibid., 116/3.

35. Wiseman to Talbot, 7 May 1859, VEN, TP; Errington's descrip-

tion of the meeting, PF, CP, 158:758; minutes, 3 May 1859, SAA, B.13.

36. Talbot to Errington, 23 Feb. and 15 Mar. 1859, PF, CP, 158:833–36; Wiseman to Talbot, 7 May 1859, VEN, TP; Talbot to Wiseman, 13 May 1859, WAA, 137/5. Errington was in poor health at the time, evidently the result of exhaustion. Wiseman to Talbot, 8 Mar. 1859, VEN, TP.

37. Wiseman to Talbot, 7 May 1859, VEN, TP; Grant to Propaganda, 14 May 1859 [extract], PF, CP, 158:591.

38. Wiseman to Richard Roskell, 8 June 1859 [copy], BAY.

39. Roskell to Wiseman, 9 June 1859 [copy], ibid. Incomplete copies of this and the letter above are also in WAA, W3/20.

40. Wiseman to Barnabò, 7 June 1859, and Ullathorne to Barnabò, 7 June 1859, PF, CP, 158:595; Barnabò to Ullathorne, 7 June 1859, BAA.

41. For Wiseman's description of the Low Week meeting and the synod, see "Relazione sul concilio III provinc. West., 1859," 12 Mar. 1860 [copy], WAA, 116/3.

42. Wiseman to Newsham, 7 July [1859], UC, PA, H/60. For a printed copy of the "Elenchus et Analysis," see WAA, 116/3.

43. Fransoni to Wiseman, 27 June 1855, in Guy, ed., *Synods in English*, pp. 224–25.

44. Wiseman to Talbot, 9 July 1859, VEN, TP.

CHAPTER 15

1. Wareing to Wiseman, 26 June 1859, and Hendren to Wiseman, 25 and 26 June 1859, WAA, 116/3.

2. Briggs to Wiseman, 3 June 1858, ibid., 130/1; Errington to Grant, 9 July 1858, SAA, C.2.

3. Wiseman to Talbot, 9 July 1859, VEN, TP.

4. Errington to Barnabò, 8 June 1859, PF, SR, 14:885; Wiseman to Talbot, 9 July 1859, VEN, TP; Talbot

to Wiseman, 18 Mar. 1859, WAA, 137/5.

5. PF, CP, 158:760–63. Also see the Acta of the synod, 12 and 13 July 1859, in Guy, ed., *Synods in English*, p. 15.

6. Wiseman discussed the circumstances under which the decree was framed in his "Relazione sul concilio III provinc. West.," WAA, 116/3. One may follow the discussions in the "Relationes Secretariorum," the lengthiest being that of the *congregatio de collegiis*, where the debates and final voting on each clause are described. Ibid.

7. Wiseman to Talbot, 18 July 1859, VEN, TP.

8. The addition was necessary because of the fact that no agreement had been reached as to whether or not the colleges were seminaries in the Tridentine sense.

9. Bishop James Brown objected to the fact that he was to be cut off from Oscott, "the college towards which I naturally feel the strongest attachment." He vainly appealed to Rome against the decision. James Brown to Ullathorne, 11 Aug. 1859 and 16 July 1860, BAA.

10. PF, CP, 158:678–79.

11. Patterson to Talbot, 15 July 1859, VEN, TP.

12. For a copy of the proposed decree, see WAA, 116/3; it was sent to Rome as the sixteenth decree.

13. For the report on St. Edmund's by Weathers, 4 July 1859, see WAA, 116/3.

14. Minutes, 3 May 1859, SAA, B.13. One may also find among the minutes of the meeting a number of suggestions that were never formulated into decrees, including the possible right of priests who had left their sees to receive remuneration from their former bishops.

15. These final decrees, along with all of the matters discussed at the Low Week meeting, were outlined by Wiseman in his "Elenchus et Analysis," WAA, 116/3.

16. PF, CP, 158:758, 678.

17. For Maguire's apology, on be-half of the chapter, 24 July 1859, see WAA, 116/3.

18. Errington to Grant, 5 Aug. 1859, SAA, C.2; statement by bishops, 22 July 1859, WAA, 116/3.

19. Wiseman's synodical letter, 16 July 1859, in Guy, ed., *Synods in English*, 280–90. Wiseman had at first opposed the establishment of the college in Belgium mentioned in the letter. He wrote his opinion on the back of a circular seeking funds for the college at Bruges, 12 Apr. 1858, VEN, TP. The seminary opened in 1859 and closed in 1873, having sent 110 priests to England during that time. By the autumn of 1858 the cardinal supported the endeavor and traveled to Belgium to discuss the operation with Sir John Sutton. Wiseman to Charles Russell, 10 Nov. 1858, WAA, W3/6.

20. Sweeney, "Diocesan Organisation and Administration," pp. 128–29; Wiseman to Manning, 26 July 1859, BAY; "Morris Manuscript," WAA, R79/13. One of the drafts of the fifteenth decree is in Bishop Grant's handwriting. Ullathorne later claimed responsibility for having drawn up the propositions upon which it was based.

21. Talbot to Wiseman, 18 July 1859, WAA, 137/5. The cardinal never dismissed Weathers. He may have been deterred by the synod's demand that the seminary rector be chosen by all of the bishops who shared an interest in the college, since Bishop Grant would certainly have opposed the change. Patterson finally became president in 1870.

22. Wiseman to Newsham, 2 Aug. 1859, UC, PA, H/61. Wiseman's reference to "three years" was based on the length of time that was supposed to intervene between provincial synods.

23. Errington to Grant, 21 Nov. 1859, SAA, C.2.

24. Wiseman to Searle, 15 May 1860, ibid., C.1.

25. Errington to Grant, 11 and 25 Sept. and 17 Nov. 1859, ibid., C.2.

26. Talbot to Wiseman, St. Charles Day [4 Nov. 1859], and to Patterson,

20 Aug. 1859, WAA, 137/5.

27. Talbot to Patterson, 22 Oct. 1859, ibid.

28. Wiseman to Talbot, 19 Sept. 1863, VEN, TP.

CHAPTER 16

1. For Wiseman's report, 25 Mar. 1859, see PF, Acta, 223:580–85.

2. For the decision, 6 Feb. 1860, see ibid., SO, 984:938.

3. Barnabò to Wiseman, 22 May 1861, WAA, W3/27; PF, Acta, 231:607a. No further pagination is provided for this summary of an oral report, which consists of nearly fourteen folio pages. I am aware of a letter from Manning to Wiseman, 13 Dec. 1861, in Purcell, *Manning*, 2:107, which indicates that the cardinal turned over a portion of the *mensa* to Grant. If such was the case, I have discovered no evidence that any further payments were made until after Wiseman's death.

4. "Morris Manuscript," WAA, R79/13; Manning to Grant, 11 May 1865, SAA, C.2.

5. Talbot to Patterson, 28 June 1860, WAA, 137/5; Butler, *Ullathorne*, 1:243–44; "Morris Manuscript," WAA, R79/13.

6. All of the pertinent materials examined by Propaganda may be found in PF, SO, 985:479–644. Cardinal Ludovico Altieri's *ristretto* was printed separately and may be found in WAA, 116/3. It begins, "Nel mese di luglio del passato anno 1859" and contains a description of the delegation given to Goss.

7. James Brown to Talbot, 7 Dec. 1859, VEN, TP.

8. Walker to Wiseman, 18 Feb. 1860, WAA, R91/9; Newsham to Talbot, 31 Jan. 1860, VEN, TP.

9. Giovanni Perrone's recommendations, 7 Mar. 1860, PF, Acta, 224:134–35.

10. Goss to Grant, 10 Mar. 1860, SAA, B.13; Ullathorne to English, 11 Mar. 1860, VEN, 79:10.

11. For copies of the petition signed by Goss and the bishops of Beverley, Newport and Menevia, Salford, Southwark, and Shrewsbury, 26 Feb. 1860, and for Barnabò's description of Wiseman's conduct at the Propaganda meeting, 23 Apr. 1860, see WAA, 116/3. The decree of approbation (*iuxta modum*), 2 May 1860, precedes all published collections of the synodical decrees. Barnabò wrote an explanation of the conditions to Wiseman, 8 May 1860, and the cardinal announced the results to the bishops in a letter of 12 May 1860, WAA, box 140, 116/3.

12. Wiseman to Patterson, 19 Apr. 1860, in Wilfrid Ward, *Wiseman*, 2:349–50; Wiseman to Newsham, 20 Apr. 1860, UC, PA, H/65.

13. Manning to Newsham, 5 June 1860, UC, UCH, 327; Talbot to Patterson, 15 Feb. 1861 [copy], WAA, W3/20.

14. Manning to English, 27 Dec. 1859, VEN, 29:8.

15. Errington to Grant, 10 Jan. 1860, SAA, C.2. The most complete account of the matters discussed in this chapter, including special emphasis upon the Errington affair, is in Wilfrid Ward, *Wiseman*, 2:321–94, 448–532, 587–637. For a briefer account, but with better balance and more detail in some matters ignored by Ward, see Butler, *Ullathorne*, 1:217–306. To understand Manning's role better, consult the correspondence reproduced in Purcell, *Manning*, 2:75–236, but this should be supplemented by Leslie, *Manning*, pp. 127–70, 498–512. Purcell's many errors of chronology and other details have been discussed in Leslie, pp. ix–xxiii; Ward, 2:631–37; and Butler, 1:238, 271, 273. It is not too strong to say that Purcell's interpretations should be discounted. To conclude, as he does, that Manning was totally responsible for the initiative that Wiseman took in ridding himself of Errington is simply not true.

16. Grant to Goss, 13 Mar. [1860], UC, LP.

17. Talbot to Goss, 16 Mar. 1860, ibid.; Wilfrid Ward, *Wiseman*, 2:376; Leslie, *Manning*, pp. 133–37.

18. Talbot to Patterson, 1 May 1860, WAA, 137/5; Wiseman's *scrittura*, 7 June 1860, PF, CP, 158:642–704. It may also be found among fifty-four pieces of correspondence related to the Errington case in BAY. Wilfrid Ward prepared a detailed summary of the document. *Wiseman*, 2:381–92. Manning's notes against Errington are in a book of Roman Papers, BAY.

19. Talbot to Patterson, 1 May 1860, WAA, 137/5. Talbot's *scrittura*, along with an explanatory letter to the Propaganda secretary, 28 May 1860, may be found in PF, CP, 158:704–22.

20. Errington's *scrittura*, ibid., 724–846. See Wilfrid Ward, *Wiseman*, 2:366–69.

21. Manning to Pius IX, PF, SR, 15:1096–1111. Two copies, one in Italian and the second in Latin, are among the documents relating to the Oblates in BAY, and a fragment is in WAA, 120–37. See Wilfrid Ward, *Wiseman*, 2:366–69.

22. Purcell, *Manning*, 2:91; Wiseman to Barnabò, 22 Feb. 1860, in Wilfrid Ward, *Wiseman*, 2:354–65.

23. Errington's *scrittura*, PF, CP, 158:742–846, with Talbot to Errington, 4 Sept. 1855, fol. 768.

24. Manning to Patterson, 1 June 1860, WAA, R79/5; Fothergill, *Wiseman*, pp. 250–52.

25. Errington to Grant, 7 July 1860, SAA, C.2. The decree, 22 July 1860, and a letter informing Wiseman of what had been done, 24 July 1860, both signed by Barnabò, may be found in Wilfrid Ward, *Wiseman*, 2:392–94.

26. T. J. Brown to Gaetano Bedini, 3 and 30 Oct. 1859, in *Letters and Diaries*, 19:240–41 n. 2.

27. Bedini to T. J. Brown, 17 Nov. 1859, T. J. Brown to Barnabò, 12 Dec. 1859, and Ullathorne to Newman, 9 May 1867, in ibid., pp. 241, 281 n. 2, 276–77 n. 1.

28. Newman to Wiseman, 19 Jan. 1860, in ibid., pp. 289–90. For Barnabò's claim and the minute in Propaganda files, 30 Jan. 1860, see ibid., p. 290 n. 2.

29. Manning's letter is quoted in Newman to Ullathorne, 7 May 1860, in ibid., p. 333; Manning's later explanation to Ullathorne, in ibid., n. 2.

30. Wiseman to Barnabò, 25 Nov. 1861, Blehl, "Newman, the Bishops and 'the Rambler,'" p. 32.

31. Newman described Talbot's charges in a letter to Ambrose St. John, 1 Jan. 1867, in *Letters and Diaries*, 23:3.

32. Butler, *Ullathorne*, 1:220.

33. Searle to Northcote, 16 Sept. 1860, 11 Mar. 1861, Northcote to Searle, 26 Sept. 1860, 23 Jan. and 4 and 20 Mar. 1861, Estcourt to Searle, 19 and 20 Dec. 1860, and Ullathorne to Northcote, 18 Mar. 1861, UC, OP, 25–37; Manning to Talbot, 21 Mar. 1861, in Purcell, *Manning*, 2:103–5; Manning to Wiseman, and explanatory note by Searle, 21 Mar. 1861, UC, OP, 38–39. Also see Wiseman to Ullathorne, 22 Mar. 1861, Wiseman to Northcote, 22 Mar. 1861, and Estcourt to Searle, 11 Apr., 8 June 1861, and 25 Oct. 1863, Northcote to Searle, 27 Sept. 1861, and Searle to Estcourt, 30 Sept. 1863, ibid., 42, 44–50; Randolfo Gabrielli to Wiseman, 6 Feb. and 17 Sept. 1861, UC, WP, 995, 999.

34. Whitty to Wiseman, 29 Sept. 1860, WAA, W3/36; Patterson to Talbot, 5 May 1860, VEN, TP. Patterson later became devoted to Manning and blamed Searle for his previous impressions. See Schiefen, "Aspects of the Controversy," p. 127 n. 5.

35. A letter from Manning to Wiseman, 17 June 1861, implied that the withdrawal was requested by the cardinal upon the advice of Canon Edward Hearn, who had replaced Maguire as vicar general. Wilfrid Ward, *Wiseman*, 2:434–35. Butler

was unable to arrive at an explanation. See *Ullathorne*, 1:254.

36. For Purcell's statement regarding the "friendly warning from Propaganda," see *Manning*, 2:106 n. 1; Manning to Talbot, 4 Oct. 1861, ibid., pp. 125–26.

37. Wiseman to Pius IX, 24 Dec. 1861 [draft], Wiseman to Barnabò, 24 Dec. 1861 [draft], and Barnabò to Wiseman, 5 Feb. 1862, WAA, W3/20, 21, box 140.

38. Talbot to Patterson, 29 Sept. 1860, Talbot to Wiseman, 29 Sept. 1860, and Wiseman to Patterson, 9 Oct. 1860, ibid., 137/5, W3/21.

39. Talbot to Patterson, 29 Sept. 1860, and to Wiseman, 7 Feb. 1861, ibid., 137/5.

40. Joseph Render to Beverley Chapter members, 14 Dec. 1860, SAA, B.13.

41. Wiseman to Barnabò, 14 Dec. 1860 and 1 Jan. 1861, PF, Acta, 225:142–47; Barnabò to Wiseman, 19 Aug. 1861, WAA, box 140. For a draft of Wiseman's proposals, see folder marked "Dec. 1860 & Jan. 1861, Vacancy at Beverley and Division of Diocese," ibid.

42. Talbot to Wiseman, 17 Feb. 1862 [copy], WAA, W3/20; Morris to Talbot, 17 Feb. 1862, VEN, TP.

43. "Estratto di lettera di Mgr. vescovo di Beverley diretta all'Emo. Sig. Card. Prefetto di Propaganda, 22 Dec. 1862," sent to Wiseman by Barnabò, 13 Jan. 1863, and Wiseman to Barnabò, 24 Feb. 1863 [draft], WAA, box 140.

44. Wiseman to Talbot, 1 Sept. 1860, VEN, TP.

45. The subject has been well treated by Butler, who provided much correspondence by those involved. *Ullathorne*, 1:217–56. For a copy of the Charitable Trusts Act, 28 Aug. 1860, and a translation of Propaganda's decision more than a decade earlier, 15 May 1847, see WAA, W3/13, A.101.

46. Grant to Briggs, 26 Oct. 1849

[copy], WAA, SEA, 7/4.70. Newman to James Hope-Scott, 6 Oct. 1853, and Hope-Scott to Newman, 17 Oct. 1853, in *Letters and Diaries*, 15:452–53. In 1847 Hope had married Charlotte Lockhart, grandaughter of Sir Walter Scott, and in 1853 changed his name to Hope-Scott.

47. Ullathorne to Grant, 15 Nov. 1860, SAA, C.2.

48. For Wiseman's summons of the bishops to the second meeting, see Wiseman to Grant, 14 May 1861, ibid., C.1; resolutions of the meeting, signed by Bishop Francis Kerril Amherst, 21 May 1861, ibid., B.13.

49. Ullathorne to T. J. Brown, 8 Nov. 1861, and Manning to Wiseman, 2 Dec. 1861, with Butler's observation, in Butler, *Ullathorne*, 1:229–31.

50. Manning to Wiseman, 7 Feb. 1862, and Ullathorne to his brother, May 1862, in ibid., pp. 234–35.

51. PF, Acta, 228:138. It was reported that the decision was reached on 8 Apr. 1862. Leslie was incorrect in stating that "the Bishops watched uneasily, while Manning won his case." *Manning*, p. 140.

52. The excuses were cited in Wiseman to Manning, Easter [20 Apr. 1862], in Butler, *Ullathorne*, 1:241–42.

53. Wiseman to Grant, 18 Apr. 1862, SAA, C.1; minutes of the meeting, 29 Apr. 1862, WAA, 130/1.

54. Wiseman to Manning, 17 June 1862, in Butler, *Ullathorne*, 1:247–48.

55. Goss to Grant, 25 Feb. 1863, SAA, B.13.

56. Hogarth to Wiseman, 3 Oct. 1862, UC, PA, M/18. By a decree of 23 May 1861, the diocese of Hexham had become that of Hexham and Newcastle. Ibid., M/15.

57. Goss to Grant, 1 June 1863, SAA, B.13.

58. Talbot to Patterson, 15 Feb. 1861 [copy], WAA, W3/20.

59. Hogarth's report, 2 Mar. 1861, PF, Acta, 227:177–85. For a draft of the document, see UC, UCH, 295.

60. Part of Ullathorne's report of 3

Dec. 1861 was omitted from the Acta and should be consulted in PF, SO, 990:332–43. An undated draft of the document is in BAA (1859).

61. Cornthwaite's report, 20 Dec. 1861, PF, Acta, 227:139; Cornthwaite to Grant, 1 Mar. 1863, SAA, B.13; PF, Acta, 227:139.

62. Manning's report, 6 May 1860, PF, Acta, 227:205–11.

63. Wiseman's report, 28 Mar. 1862, ibid., 154–63.

64. For the bishop's letter adhering to the commentary prepared by Goss, 4 Feb. 1862, and Goss's own remarks, 7 Feb. 1862, see ibid., 213–49.

65. Turner to Grant, 3 Mar. 1863, SAA, B.13. The previous day Turner had written to Grant to suggest that the others might pay James Brown's portion of the expenses, since "his signature is of importance, and the expenses of Dr. Clifford going to Rome will not be less if Dr. Brown does not join us." Ibid.

66. Manning to Ullathorne, 27 May 1863, in Leslie, *Manning*, p. 141. Also see Manning to Wiseman, 2 May 1863, in Purcell, *Manning*, 2:129. For the compromise, see William Clifford to Grant, 2 May 1863, SAA, B.13; and Clifford to Barnabò, 30 Apr. 1863, PF, Acta, 227:303–5.

67. The decree of approbation, 14 Sept. 1863, precedes all published editions of the synodical decrees. On 16 Oct. 1863 Wiseman sent a printed circular to the bishops, including a very brief letter announcing the decision. WAA, 116/3.

68. Wiseman to Talbot, 19 Sept. 1863, VEN, TP.

69. Wiseman to Barnabò, 2 Aug. 1860 [copy], and Barnabò to Wiseman, 18 Aug. 1860, WAA, 116/3, box 140; Purcell, *Manning*, 2:114–15, quoting Achille Rinaldini to Manning, n.d.

70. Rinaldini to Manning, n.d. [copy], and Morris to Manning, 27 Feb. 1864, BAY. Manning to Talbot, 14 Mar. 1865, in Leslie, *Manning*, p. 152.

71. Wilfrid Ward, *Wiseman*, 2: 421.

CHAPTER 17

1. Morris to Talbot, 23 June 1863, VEN, TP.

2. Wiseman to Talbot, 26 June 1863, ibid; Wiseman to Barnabò, 12 Jan. 1864 [copy], WAA, box 140.

3. Wiseman to Manning, 12 Jan. 1854, VEN, TP. Manning must have given the letter to Talbot, which would account for its presence among his papers.

4. Manning to Wiseman, 17 Feb. 1864, in Purcell, *Manning*, 2:187.

5. "Dire che non amava Roma, sarebbe dir poco. . . . Questi [Griffiths] fu in tutto e per tutto della medesima pasta dei predecessori, anzi nel senso nostro peggiore, perchè di limitatissima intelligenza, e di testa veramenta fasciata."

6. Wiseman, "Relazione Storica e Personale dello Stato passato ed attuale della Diocesi di Westminster," marked "Riservatissimo, con Segreto Pontificio," 18 Jan. 1862, PF, SR, 16:410–24.

7. Wiseman to Talbot, 24 Sept. 1860, VEN, TP.

8. Circular containing report, 30 Jan. 1861, ibid.

9. Mother Marie Thérèse, *Cornelia Connelly*, p. 128.

10. Nicholas Wiseman, *The Witch of Rosenberg: A Drama in Three Acts, Composed for the Children of St. Leo's Convent, Carlow*, 1864 (London: Thomas Richardson and Son, 1866).

11. The letter, 12 Dec. 1864, was published along with the play itself. Ibid., p. 6.

12. Wiseman, quoted in Herbert Vaughan's diary, in Snead-Cox, *Vaughan*, 1:106–7.

13. Wiseman to Herbert Vaughan, 16 Dec. 1863, in ibid., pp. 121–22.

14. Wiseman to Talbot, 19 Dec. 1862, VEN, TP, 1103.

15. Wiseman's inaugural address, in John D. Root, "The 'Academia of the Catholic Religion': Catholic Intellectualism in Victorian England," *Victorian Studies* 23 (1980): 465.

16. Newman to Manning, 21 June 1861, in *Letters and Diaries*, 19:519. For evidence that Newman, contrary to the assertions of some authors, remained officially a member, see Root, "Academia of the Catholic Religion," p. 468 n. 22.

17. Newman to W. G. Ward, 9 May 1867, in *Letters and Diaries*, 23:217; Wilfrid Ward, *Wiseman*, 2:477; Manning, quoted in Root, "Academia of the Catholic Religion," p. 472, and in McClelland, *Manning*, p. 127.

18. Wiseman, Lecture 9, in *Lectures on the Principal Doctrines and Practices of the Catholic Church*, 1:264; Simpson to John Acton, 27 Nov. 1861, in Altholz et al., eds., *Acton-Simpson Correspondence*, 2:212.

19. Wilfrid Ward, *Wiseman*, 2:410, 447.

20. Wiseman to Talbot, 31 Jan. 1863, VEN, TP, 1103.

21. Nicholas Wiseman, *The Religious and Social Position of Catholics in England: An Address Delivered to the Catholic Congress of Malines, 21 August 1863* (Dublin: J. Duffy, 1864), pp. 18, 46, 49, 58–59; Herbert Vaughan, quoted in Wilfrid Ward, *Wiseman*, 2:458; T. J. Lamy, quoted in Holmes, *More Roman than Rome*, p. 124.

22. Montalembert to Phillipps de Lisle, 9 Mar. 1864, in Purcell, *de Lisle*, 2:257–58; Wiseman, quoted in Holmes, *More Roman than Rome*, p. 124; Wiseman to Phillipps de Lisle, 15 Mar. 1864, in Wilfrid Ward, *Wiseman*, 2:462.

23. Wiseman to Talbot, 15 June 1861, VEN, TP.

24. John Acton to Charles Russell, 25 Mar. 1865, WAA, W3/48. The most detailed study of Acton's journalistic career and the events treated briefly here are found in Altholz, *Liberal*

Catholic Movement in England; my account has drawn from pp. 187–89. Also see Butler, *Ullathorne*, 1:322–29.

25. Barnabò to English bishops, May 1862, cited in Butler, *Ullathorne*, 1:321–22.

26. "Rome and the Catholic Episcopate: Reply of His Eminence Cardinal Wiseman to an Address presented to him by the Clergy, Secular and Regular, of the Archdiocese of Westminster" (1862), in Altholz, *Liberal Catholic Movement in England*, p. 188.

27. Bishop Clifford's circular, 24 Sept. 1862, in ibid., p. 189; Ullathorne to clergy, Oct. 1862, in Butler, *Ullathorne*, 1:322.

28. [John Acton], "The Munich Congress," *Home and Foreign Review* 4 (1864): 209–44; Acton to Newman, 15 Mar. 1864, in Altholz, *Liberal Catholic Movement in England*, p. 225.

29. [John Acton], "Conflicts with Rome," *Home and Foreign Review* 4 (1864): 667–90.

30. Altholz, *Liberal Catholic Movement in England*, p. 228. For Ward's editorship of the *Dublin Review*, see Wilfrid Ward, *William George Ward and the Catholic Revival*, pp. 154–88.

31. McClelland, *English Roman Catholics and Higher Education*, pp. 181–82; Samuel Wilberforce, quoted in Chadwick, *Victorian Church*, 2:78.

32. Purcell, *Manning*, 2:288–89; Butler, *Ullathorne*, 2:4.

33. Manning, quoted in McClelland, *English Roman Catholics and Higher Education*, pp. 189–90.

34. For a discussion of the university question, including Wiseman's questionnaire and summary and the bishops' letter to Propaganda, see ibid., pp. 200–215.

35. Newman to E. S. Ffoulkes, 1 Mar. 1865, and to Charles Russell, 2 Mar. 1865, in *Letters and Diaries*, 21:424, 426.

36. Wiseman to Talbot, 7 Nov. 1864, VEN, TP.

37. Wiseman to Newman, 2 July

1864, and Newman to Wiseman, 28 Sept. 1864, in *Letters and Diaries*, 21:242.

38. Newman to Ambrose St. John, 5 Nov. 1864, in ibid., p. 285. Newman added his note on 4 Nov. 1875, having repossessed the letter, probably after St. John's death the previous May.

39. Patterson to W. P. Neville, 20 Oct. 1893, in ibid., p. 286 n. 2.

40. The memorandum was found in a trunk of unsorted and unclassified papers, primarily transcripts of retreat notes and sermons, in the Ushaw College library.

41. Newman, *Autobiographical Writings*, pp. 249–60.

42. Manifesto of the Association for Promoting the Unity of Christendom, 8 Sept. 1857, in Butler, *Ullathorne*, 1:342–43.

43. Wiseman, "Report on the Party called the 'Union' Party in the Anglican Body," in Wilfrid Ward, *Wiseman*, 2:479–88. Butler devoted an entire chapter to carefully outlining the history of the APUC, including Wiseman's role. *Ullathorne*, 1:334–68.

44. Wilfrid Ward, *Wiseman*, 2:475; Butler, *Ullathorne*, 1:349.

45. Sheridan Gilley, "The Garibaldi Riots of 1862," *Historical Journal* 16 (1973): 731, quotation from Wiseman on pp. 716–17; Bossy, *English Catholic Community*, p. 313.

46. Sheridan Gilley, "Papists, Protestants and the Irish in London, 1835–70," *Studies in Church History* 8 (1971): 263; Wiseman to Talbot, 15 Nov. 1862, VEN, TP.

47. Nicholas Wiseman, *William Shakespeare* (London: Hurst and Blackett, 1865), pp. 50–51.

48. Wiseman, quoted in Wilfrid Ward, *Wiseman*, 2:511–15; "Morris Manuscript," WAA, R79/13; Wiseman to Talbot, 7 Nov. 1864, VEN, TP. A firsthand account of Wiseman's last illness may be found in the diary of Mother Mary Gonzaga Barrie of the Sisters of Mercy who nursed him throughout the ordeal. She was completely devoted to the cardinal, and he to her. See Carroll, *Annals of the Sisters of Mercy*, 2:227–48.

49. Wiseman to Searle, 3 May 1863, in Fothergill, *Wiseman*, p. 272.

50. Wilfrid Ward, *Wiseman*, 2:522; Newman to Charles Russell, 2 Mar. 1865, in *Letters and Diaries*, 21:426.

51. For a summary, with long excerpts of Manning's sermon, see Wilfrid Ward, *Wiseman*, 2:524–31.

52. Whitty to Morris, 2 Mar. 1893, WAA, R/79.

53. Manning, quoted in Purcell, *Manning*, 2:751.

54. Wiseman, quoted in Wilfrid Ward, *Wiseman*, 2:515.

Select Bibliography

MANUSCRIPT SOURCES

Ampleforth Abbey Archive.

Bayswater, St. Mary of the Angels. Henry Edward Manning Papers.
Cardinal Manning left his personal papers to the Oblates of St. Charles, who deposited them at their Bayswater residence. No catalog was available when I consulted them there, but where possible I have identified collections in the notes.

Birmingham, Archdiocesan Archive.
All manuscripts have been arranged in folders in chronological order, and complete lists are available. No designation other than the date is required to locate specific manuscripts.

Bristol, Clifton Diocesan Archive.
This collection has now been transferred from the bishop's house to the Bristol City Records Office.

Leeds, Diocesan Archive.
Chronologically arranged lists are available for the collections I consulted: John Briggs Papers, Thomas Penswick Papers, Thomas Smith Papers.

Preston, Public Records Office. Archbishop of Liverpool Archive.

Rome, Archivio Storico della Sagra Congregazione *de Propaganda Fide*. Acta Sacrae Congregationis, Congregazioni Particolari, Scritture Originali, Scritture Riferite nei Congressi.

———, Venerable English College Archive.
Various collections of scritture, George Talbot Papers.

Southwark, Archdiocesan Archive.
B.13, Hierarchy 1850; C.1, Cardinal Nicholas Wiseman; C.2, Henry Edward Manning, William Bernard Ullathorne, George Errington, Francis

Searle, George Talbot, and John Henry Newman; S.74, Provincial Synods; Mark Tierney Papers; Daniel Rock, 1799–1871; Division of Westminster and Southwark, Properties, Rents, etc., Pre-1882.

Ushaw College Archive.
The collection is rich in nineteenth-century materials. Lists of the various collections are available, but the process of organization is ongoing, and the researcher should not rely completely on their accuracy. Among the collections consulted are Diocese of Liverpool Archive, John Lingard Papers, Lisbon Papers, Oscott Papers, Charles Newsham Papers, President's Archive, Some Correspondence of Bishop Thomas Walsh, Ushaw Collection of Manuscripts, Ushaw College History Collection, John Walker Papers, Correspondence of Bishop Thomas Walsh with Lord Shrewsbury, Nicholas Wiseman Papers.

Vatican, Archivio Segreto Vaticano, Spogli Acton.
Cardinal Charles Acton's papers were gathered together in four folio volumes by Cardinal Francis Aidan Gasquet.

Westminster, Archdiocesan Archive.
Elisabeth Poyser, Westminster archivist, has been responsible in recent years for organizing and cataloging the masses of relevant materials in this valuable archive. Lists of documents are provided, and as various collections are reclassified, records of former classifications are maintained. In some instances my references may be outdated, but there will be no difficulty in locating particular manuscripts from my citations. I made use of at least sixty collections in the archive; the notes provide sufficient information to locate them.

——, Chapter Records.
Resolution Book, 30 June 1852–4 Dec. 1877; Minutes Book, 24 Apr. 1855–30 Nov. 1858.

PUBLISHED WORKS

[Acton, John]. "Conflicts with Rome." *Home and Foreign Review* 4 (1864): 667–90.

[——]. "The Munich Congress." *Home and Foreign Review* 4 (1864): 209–44.

Allen, Louis. "Ambrose Phillipps de Lisle, 1809–1878." *Catholic Historical Review* 40 (1954): 1–26.

Altholz, Josef L. "Disputandum Est." *Victorian Studies* 2 (1959): 395–96.

——. *The Liberal Catholic Movement in England: The "Rambler" and Its Contributors, 1848–1864.* London: Burns and Oates, 1962.

——. "Political Behavior of the English Catholics, 1850–1867." *Journal of British Studies* 3 (1964): 89–103.

——, Damian McElrath, and James C. Holland, eds. *The Correspondence of Lord Acton and Richard Simpson,* 3 vols. Cambridge: Cambridge University Press, 1971–75.

Arnstein, Walter L. *Protestant versus Catholic in Mid-Victorian England: Mr. Newdegate and the Nuns.* Columbia, Mo.: University of Missouri Press, 1982.

Baines, P. A. *A Letter Addressed to Sir Chas. Wolseley, Bart., on the Lenten Pastoral of 1840.* Prior Park: St. Paul's Press, 1840.

Barnes, Arthur S. *The Catholic Schools of England.* London: Williams and Norgate, 1926.

Beck, George Andrew, ed. *The English Catholics, 1850–1950: Essays to Commemorate the Centenary of the Restoration of the Hierarchy of England and Wales.* London: Burnes Oates, 1950.

Blake, Robert. *Disraeli.* New York: St. Martin's Press, 1967.

Blehl, Vincent F. "Newman and the Missing Mitre." *Thought* 35 (1960): 110–23.

———. "Newman, the Bishops and 'the Rambler.'" *Downside Review* 90 (1972): 20–40.

———. "Newman's Delation: Some Hitherto Unpublished Letters." *Dublin Review* 204 (1960–61): 296–305.

Bogan, Bernard. *The Great Link: A History of St. George's, Southwark, 1786–1848–1948.* London: Burns, Oates, 1948.

Bolton, C. A. *Salford Diocese and Its Catholic Past.* Manchester: Diocese of Salford, 1950.

Bossy, John. *The English Catholic Community, 1570–1850.* London: Darton, Longman, and Todd, 1975.

Boyle, Richard. *Boyle versus Wiseman: A Full Statement of the Causes Which Necessitated the Action, and a Complete Refutation of All the Allegations of the Libel.* London: Partridge, 1855.

Brady, W. Maziere. *Annals of the Catholic Hierarchy in England and Scotland, 1585–1876.* London: Thomas Baker, 1877.

Browning, Robert. "Bishop Blougram's Apology." In *Men and Women.* London: Chapman and Hall, 1855.

Burton, E. H. *The Life and Times of Bishop Challoner, 1691–1781.* 2 vols. London: Longmans, Green, and Co., 1909.

Buschkühl, Matthias, *Great Britain and the Holy See, 1746–1870.* Dublin: Irish Academic Press, 1982.

Butler, Cuthbert. *The Life and Times of Bishop Ullathorne, 1806–88.* 2 vols. London: Burns Oates and Washbourne, 1926.

Canons and Decrees of the Council of Trent. Translated by H. J. Schroeder. St. Louis, Mo.: B. Herder Book Co., 1941.

Carroll, Mary Teresa Austin. *Leaves from the Annals of the Sisters of Mercy.* 4 vols. New York: P. O'Shea, 1881–95.

Catholic Magazine and Review. Birmingham, 1831–36.

Chadwick, Owen. *The Victorian Church.* 2 vols. New York: Oxford University Press, 1966–70.

Charlton, Barbara. *The Recollections of a Northumbrian Lady, 1815–1866.* Edited by L. E. O. Charlton. London: J. Cape, 1949.

Chinnici, Joseph P. *The English Catholic Enlightenment: John Lingard and the Cisalpine Movement, 1780–1850.* Shepherdstown, W. Va.: Patmos Press, 1980.

Decreta Quatuor Conciliorum Westmonasteriensium, 1852–73: Adjectis pluribus decretis, rescriptis, aliisque documentis. Salford: John Roberts, [1884].

Dictionary of National Biography. London, 1885–1901.

Dougherty, Charles T., and Homer C. Welsh. "Wiseman on the Oxford Movement: An Early Report to the Vatican." *Victorian Studies* 2 (1958): 149–54.

Dublin Review. 1836–1963.

Elliott, Bernard. "Mount St. Bernard's Reformatory, Leicestershire, 1856–81," *Recusant History* 15 (1979): 15–22.

Femiano, Samuel D. *Infallibility of the Laity: The Legacy of Newman.* New York: Herder and Herder, 1967.

Fothergill, Brian. *Nicholas Wiseman.* London: Faber and Faber, 1963.

Gasquet, Francis Aidan. *A History of the Venerable English College, Rome: An Account of Its Origins and Work from the Earliest Times to the Present Day.* London: Longmans, Green, and Co., 1920.

Gaynor, John S. *The English-Speaking Pallottines.* Rome: Gregorian University Press, 1962.

Gilley, Sheridan. "The Garibaldi Riots of 1862." *Historical Journal* 16 (1973): 693–732.

——. "Heretic London, Holy Poverty and the Irish Poor." *Downside Review* 89 (1971): 64–89.

——. "Papists, Protestants and the Irish in London, 1835–70." *Studies in Church History* 8 (1971): 259–66.

Guy, Robert E., ed. *The Synods in English, Being the Text of the Four Synods of Westminster.* Stratford-on-Avon: St. Gregory's Press, 1886.

Gwynn, Denis. *Cardinal Wiseman.* Dublin: Browne and Nolan, 1950.

——. *Father Dominic Barberi.* London: Burns Oates, 1947.

——. *Lord Shrewsbury, Pugin and the Catholic Revival.* Westminster, Md.: Newman Bookshop, 1946.

Holmes, J. Derek. "English Catholicism from Wiseman to Bourne: I." *Clergy Review* 61 (1976): 57–69.

——. *More Roman than Rome: English Catholicism in the Nineteenth Century.* Shepherdstown, W. Va.: Patmos Press, 1978.

——. "Some Unpublished Passages from Cardinal Wiseman's Correspondence." *Downside Review* 90 (1972): 41–52.

Holt, T. G. "The German Catholic Chapel in London." *Transactions of the London and Middlesex Archaeological Society* (1977), pp. 323–27.

Home and Foreign Review. 1862–64.

Houghton, Walter E., ed. *Wellesley Index to Victorian Periodicals, 1824–1900*. Vol. 2. Toronto: University of Toronto Press, 1972.

Jackman, S. W. *Nicholas Cardinal Wiseman: A Victorian Prelate and His Writings*. Dublin: Five Lamps Press, 1977.

Lees, Lynn Hollen. *Exiles of Erin: Irish Migrants in Victorian London*. Manchester: Manchester University Press, 1979.

Leetham, Claude. *Luigi Gentili: A Sower for the Second Spring*. London: Burns and Oates, 1965.

Leslie, Shane. *Henry Edward Manning, His Life and Labours*. London: Burns Oates and Washbourne, 1921.

Lesourd, Jean Alain. *Les catholiques dans la société anglais, 1765–1865*. 2 vols. Paris: H. Champion, 1978.

Lilly, William Samuel, and John E. E. Wallis. *Manual of the Law Specially Affecting Catholics*. London: W. Clowes, 1893.

Lingard, John, and Hilaire Belloc. *The History of England, from the First Invasion by the Romans to the Accession of King George the Fifth*. 11 vols. New York: Catholic Publication of America, 1912.

Lucas, Edward. *The Life of Frederick Lucas, M.P.* 2 vols. London: Catholic Truth Society, 1887.

McClelland, Vincent Alan. *Cardinal Manning: His Public Life and Influence, 1865–1892*. London: Oxford University Press, 1962.

———. *English Roman Catholics and Higher Education, 1830–1903*. Oxford: Clarendon Press, 1973.

McCormack, Arthur. *Cardinal Vaughan: The Life of the Third Archbishop of Westminster, Founder of St. Joseph's Missionary Society, Mill Hill*. London: Burns and Oates, 1966.

MacDougall, Hugh A. *The Acton-Newman Relations: The Dilemma of Christian Liberalism*. New York: Fordham University Press, 1962.

McElrath, Damian. *Richard Simpson, 1820–1876: A Study in XIXth Century English Liberal Catholicism*. Louvain: Publications Universitaires de Louvain, 1972.

McGrath, Fergal. *Newman's University: Idea and Reality*. Dublin: Browne and Nolan, 1951.

Machin, G. I. T. "Lord John Russell and the Prelude to the Ecclesiastical Titles Bill, 1846–51." *Journal of Ecclesiastical History* 25 (1974): 277–95.

———. *Politics and the Churches in Great Britain, 1832 to 1868*. Oxford: Clarendon Press, 1977.

McIntire, C. T. *England against the Papacy, 1858–1861: Tories, Liberals, and the Overthrow of Papal Temporal Power during the Italian Risorgimento*. Cambridge: Cambridge University Press, 1983.

Marie Thérèse, Mother. *Cornelia Connelly: A Study in Fidelity.* London: Burns and Oates, 1963.

Mathew, David. *Lord Acton and His Times.* London: Eyre and Spottiswoode, 1968.

Milburn, David. *A History of Ushaw College.* Durham: Ushaw Bookshop, 1964.

"More Letters of Wiseman and Manning." *Dublin Review* 172 (1923): 106–29.

Newman, John Henry. *Apologia pro Vita Sua.* Edited by Martin J. Svaglic. Oxford: Clarendon Press, 1967.

——. *Autobiographical Writings.* Edited by Henry Tristram. London: Sheed and Ward, 1956.

——. *Certain Difficulties Felt by Anglicans in Catholic Teaching.* 2d ed. 2 vols. London: Longmans, Green, and Co., 1892.

[——]. "Judgement of the English Bishops on The Royal Commission." *Rambler.* 3d ser., 1 (1859): 117–23.

——. *The Letters and Diaries of John Henry Newman.* Edited by C. S. Dessain and others. 26 vols. to date. Vols. 11–22, London: Thomas Nelson and Sons, 1961–72; vols. 23–31, 1– , Oxford: Clarendon Press, 1973–

[——]. "On Consulting the Faithful in Matters of Doctrine." *Rambler.* 3d ser., 1 (1859): 198–230.

——. *Sermons Preached on Various Occasions.* London: Longmans, Green, and Co., 1857.

——. *The Via Media of the Anglican Church, Illustrated in Lectures, Letters, and Tracts.* 2 vols. London: Longmans, Green, and Co., 1877.

Norman, E. R., ed. *Anti-Catholicism in Victorian England.* London: Allen and Unwin, 1968.

——. *The Catholic Church and Ireland in the Age of Rebellion, 1859–1873.* Ithaca, N.Y.: Cornell University Press, 1965.

Norris, David. "Cardinal Wiseman: The Diocesan Bishop." *Dublin Review* 237 (1963): 158–67.

Norris, John. "Cardinal Wiseman." *Ushaw Magazine* 8 (1898): 1–19.

O'Connell, Marvin R. *The Oxford Conspirators: A History of the Oxford Movement, 1833–45.* London: Macmillan Co., 1969.

Pugin, A. W. N. *Contrasts; or, A Parallel between the Noble Edifices of the Fourteenth and Fifteenth Centuries, and Similar Buildings of the Present Day; Shewing the Present Decay of Taste; Accompanied by Appropriate Text.* Intro. H. R. Hitchcock. 2d ed. 1841. Reprint. New York: Humanities Press, 1969.

Purcell, Edmund Sheridan. *The Life and Letters of Ambrose Phillipps de Lisle.* Edited and finished by Edwin de Lisle. 2 vols. London: Macmillan and Co., 1900.

——. *Life of Cardinal Manning, Archbishop of Westminster.* 2 vols. London: Macmillan and Co., 1896.

Ralls, Walter. "The Papal Aggression of 1850: A Study in Victorian Anti-Catholicism." *Church History* 43 (1974): 242–56.

Rambler. 1848–62.

Rathborne, Joseph. *Are the Puseyites Sincere? A Letter Most Respectfully Addressed to a Right Reverend Lord Bishop on the Oxford Movement.* London: T. Jones, 1841.

Reardon, Bernard. *Liberalism and Tradition: Aspects of Catholic Thought in Nineteenth-Century France.* Cambridge: Cambridge University Press, 1975.

Reynolds, E. E. *Three Cardinals: Newman – Wiseman – Manning.* London: Burns and Oates, 1958.

Ritzler, Remigius, and Pirminus Sefrin. *Hierarchia Catholica Medii et Recentioris Aevi sive Summorum Pontificum – S.R.E. Cardinalium Ecclesiarum Antistitum Series.* Vol. 8. Padua: Il Messaggero di S. Antonio, 1978.

Roche, J. S. *A History of Prior Park College and Its Founder Bishop Baines.* London: Burns, Oates, and Washbourne, 1931.

Roe, W. G. *Lamennais and England: The Reception of Lamennais's Religious Ideas in England in the Nineteenth Century.* Oxford: Oxford University Press, 1966.

The Roman Catholic Question: A Copious Series of Important Documents of Permanent Historical Interest on the Re-Establishment of the Catholic Hierarchy in England, 1850–51. London: J. Gilbert, 1850–51.

Root, John D. "The 'Academia of the Catholic Religion': Catholic Intellectualism in Victorian England." *Victorian Studies* 23 (1980): 461–78.

Schiefen, Richard J. "'Anglo-Gallicanism' in Nineteenth-Century England." *Catholic Historical Review* 63 (1977): 14–44.

——. "The Crusade of Nicholas Wiseman." In *The View from the Pulpit: Victorian Ministers and Society,* edited by P. T. Phillips. Toronto: Macmillan of Canada, 1978.

——. "The English Catholic Reaction to the Tractarian Movement." *Study Sessions* (Canadian Catholic Historical Association) 41 (1974): 9–31.

——. "The First Provincial Synod of Westminster (1852)." *Annuarium Historiae Conciliorum* (1972), pp. 188–213.

——. "Some Aspects of the Controversy between Cardinal Wiseman and the Westminster Chapter." *Journal of Ecclesiastical History* 21 (1970): 125–48.

Snead-Cox, J. G. *The Life of Cardinal Vaughan.* 2 vols. London: Burns and Oates, 1912.

Tablet. 1840–65.

[Talbot, John, sixteenth earl of Shrewsbury]. *Diplomatic Relations with Rome, Considered Chiefly in Reference to the Restrictive Clause Introduced into the Bill by the House of Lords, in a Letter from John, Earl of Shrewsbury to the Earl of Arundel and Surrey.* London: Charles Dolman, 1848.

Tierney, Mark. "A Reply to Cardinal Wiseman's Letter to His Chapter." London: [Printed, not published], 1858.

Trevor, Meriol. *Newman: Light in Winter.* Garden City, N.Y.: Doubleday and Co., 1963.

——. *Newman: The Pillar of the Cloud.* Garden City, N.Y.: Doubleday and Co., 1962.

Ullathorne, William Bernard. *From Cabin-Boy to Archbishop: The Autobiography of Archbishop Ullathorne.* Edited by Shane Leslie. London: Burns Oates, 1941.

——. *History of the Restoration of the Catholic Hierarchy of England.* London: Burns, Oates, and Co., [1871].

——. *Letters of Archbishop Ullathorne.* Edited by Mother Francis Raphael [Augusta T. Drane]. London: Burns and Oates, 1892.

Ward, Bernard. *The Dawn of the Catholic Revival in England, 1781–1803.* 2 vols. London: Longmans, Green, and Co., 1909.

——. *The Eve of Catholic Emancipation, Being the History of the English Catholics during the First Thirty Years of the Nineteenth Century.* 3 vols. London: Longmans, Green, and Co., 1911.

——. *History of St. Edmund's College, Old Hall.* London: Kegan Paul, Trench, Trübner and Co., 1893.

——. *The Sequel to Catholic Emancipation, 1830–1850.* 2 vols. London: Longmans, Green, and Co., 1915.

Ward, J. T., and J. H. Treble. "Religion and Education in 1843: Reaction to the 'Factory Education Bill.'" *Journal of Ecclesiastical History* 20 (1969): 79–110.

Ward, Wilfrid. *Aubrey de Vere: A Memoir Based on His Unpublished Diaries and Correspondence.* London: Longmans, Green, and Co., 1904.

——. *The Life and Times of Cardinal Wiseman.* 2 vols. London: Longmans, Green, and Co., 1897.

——. *The Life of John Henry Cardinal Newman.* 2 vols. London: Longmans, Green, and Co., 1912.

——. *William George Ward and the Catholic Revival.* London: Macmillan, 1893.

——. *William George Ward and the Oxford Movement.* London: Macmillan, 1889.

Williams, Michael E. *The Venerable English College, Rome: A History, 1579–1979.* London: Associated Catholic Publications, 1979.

Wiseman, Nicholas. *An Appeal to the Reason and Good Feeling of the English People.* London: T. Richardson and Son, 1850.

[——]. "Ecclesiastical Organization." *Dublin Review* 12 (1842): 240–51.

——. *Essays on Various Subjects.* 3 vols. London: Charles Dolman, 1853.

——. *Fabiola; or, The Church of the Catacombs.* London: Burns and Lambert, 1855.

——. *Home Education of the Poor: Two Lectures Delivered by Cardinal Wiseman at St. Martin's Hall, Long Acre.* London, 1854.

——. *Horae Syriacae, seu commentationes et anecdota res vel Litteras Syriacas spectantia.* Rome: F. Bourl'e, 1827.

[——]. "The Industry of the Poor." *Dublin Review* 30 (1851): 484–532.

——. *Lectures on the Principal Doctrines and Practices of the Catholic Church.* 2d ed. 2 vols. in 1. London: Charles Dolman, 1844.

——. *A Letter on Catholic Unity, Addressed to the Right Hon. the Earl of Shrewsbury.* London: Charles Dolman, 1841.

——. *A Letter Respectfully Addressed to the Rev. J. H. Newman upon Some Passages in His Letter to the Rev. Dr. Jelf.* 2d ed. London: Charles Dolman, 1841.

——. "A Letter to the Canons of the Cathedral Chapter of Westminster, in Reply to One Published in the "Rambler" for June 1858, Relative to a Passage in the 'Recollections of the Last Four Popes.'" London: [Printed, not published], 1858.

——. "Letters of Cardinal Wiseman, with a Commentary by Cardinal Gasquet." *Dublin Review* 164 (1919): 1–25.

——. *The Real Presence of the Body and Blood of Our Lord Jesus Christ in the Blessed Eucharist, Proved from Scripture.* London: James Duffy and Co., 1836.

——. *Recollections of the Last Four Popes and of Rome in Their Times.* London: Hurst and Blackett, 1858.

——. *The Religious and Social Position of Catholics in England: An Address Delivered to the Catholic Congress of Malines, 21 August 1863.* Dublin: J. Duffy, 1864.

——. *Remarks on a Letter from the Rev. W. Palmer, M.A. of Worcester College, Oxford.* London: Charles Dolman, 1841.

——. *A Reply to the Rev. Dr. Turton's "Roman Catholic Doctrine of the Eucharist Considered," Philalethes, Cantabrigiensis, The British Critic, and the Church of England Quarterly Review.* London: Charles Dolman, 1839.

——. *The Sermons, Lectures, and Speeches Delivered by His Eminence Cardinal Wiseman, Archbishop of Westminster during His Tour in Ireland in August and September 1858.* Dublin: J. Duffy, 1859.

[——]. "State and Prospects of Catholicity in England." *Dublin Review* 8 (1840): 240–71.

[——]. "State of Catholic Affairs." *Dublin Review* 42 (1857): 211–30.

———. *Three Lectures on the Catholic Hierarchy*. London: Thomas Richardson, [1850].

———. *Twelve Lectures on the Connexion between Science and Revealed Religion*. 5th ed. London: Catholic Publishing and Bookselling Co., 1859.

———. "Unpublished Letters of Cardinal Wiseman to Dr. Manning." *Dublin Review* 169 (1921): 161–91.

———. *William Shakespeare*. London: Hurst and Blackett, 1865.

———. *The Witch of Rosenburg: A Drama in Three Acts, Composed for the Children of St. Leo's Convent, Carlow, 1864*. London: Thomas Richardson and Son, 1866.

———. *Words of Peace and Justice Addressed to the Catholic Clergy and Laity of the London District on the Subject of Diplomatic Relations with the Holy See*. London: Charles Dolman, 1848.

Index

Cornthwaite, Robert, 294, 307–8, 312, 314, 318
Cox, Edward, 148, 157, 177, 193, 200, 208–9, 211
Coyle, John, 173–74
Crimean War, 243, 264
Cullen, Paul, 218

Darwin, Charles, 323, 329
De Luca, Antonino, 81, chap. 5, n. 29, 105–6
Derby, 14th earl of (Edward George Geoffrey Smith Stanley), 268–69
de Salinis, Louis, 229
Digby, Kenelm, 63
Diplomatic Relations Bill, 153–56
Disraeli, Benjamin, 269
Dodsworth, William, 216
Döllinger, Johann Joseph Ignaz von, 34, 54, 65–66, 270, 328
Doria-Pamfili-Landi, Prince Filippo Andrea, 170, chap. 9, n. 20
Doria, Princess (Mary Alethea Beatrix Talbot), chap. 9, n. 20, 188
Douai, College of, 4, 278
Downside Abbey, 25, 29–31, 111
Doyle, Richard ("Dickie"), 192
Doyle, Thomas, 70, 170, chap. 9, n. 20, 183
Dublin Review, 91, 97, 163, 329; editorship of, 70–71; foundation of, 68–69; and *Rambler*, 270, 273, 327; Wiseman's articles in, 69, 95, 140, 215, 219

Ecclesiastical Titles Act, 191, 227
Education Committee, 171
Elenchus et Analysis, 277–80, 284, 297–98, 313–15
English bishops, *see* Hierarchy, Vicars apostolic
English Catholics, 6–7, 35–36, 38–39, 62, 65, 75, 204; described by Briggs, 85–87; legal restrictions on, 131, 137–38, 159, 170–72, 290; opposed to Oxford Movement, 122–23; old versus new, 38–39, 135–36; opposition to, xii, 6, 18–19, 65, 82, 86–87; Wiseman's views on, 90–91, 145–46, 268–69
Epitome Decretorum, see Provincial synods
Errington, George, 19–20, chap. 1, n. 51, 32, 44–45, 104, 196, 201, 228, 236, 240, 247, 253, chap. 13, n. 36, 257–59, 261, 273–75, 291–94, 297, 304–5, 308; and

Ushaw College, 251; apostolic administrator in Clifton, 246–47, chap. 13, n. 16, 252; at 3d synod, 283, 285–86, 288–90; bishop of Plymouth, 195; claims right of succession to Westminster, 318; coadjutor of Westminster, 251–54; defends role in archdiocese, 300–2; opposes Oblates, 254–55, 300–1; removal sought from Westminster, 262, 275–76, 292, 298–302; responds to charge of Gallicanism, 260–61; sought by Newsham for Ushaw, 94; Wiseman's assistant: in Rome, 19–20, 22, 32, 44–45; at Oscott, 127–30
Errington, Michael, 20
Essays and Reviews, 329
Established Church, *see* Anglican Church

Faber, Frederick, 179, 225
Fabiola, 10, 191, 236–37
Fano, 53, 71, 192
Fathers of Charity, *see* Rosminians
Feilding, Rudolph William, 216
Fitzpatrick, Bruno (abbot of Melleray), 265
Forty hours devotion, 185, 211
Fothergill, Brian, xiii
France, 16, 152, 229, 325
Francis Joseph II, 230
Francis of Sales, Saint, 205
Fransoni, Giacomo, 106–10, 112, 213, 221, 236, 241, 243, 277, 287, 335; critical of vicars apostolic, 72–73; seeks Gentili's advice, 142
Froude, Richard Hurrell, 36–37, 61

Gabrielli, Andrea, 53
Gabrielli, Francesca Wiseman (sister), 3–4, 8, 19, 53–54, 99, 305; letters to Nicholas, 10–12, 15–16, 21, 35, 220–21
Gabrielli, Randolfo, 221, 304–5
Gallicanism, 35, 203, 260–61, 298, 300; charge against: English clergy, 22, 278, Grant, 200, 260–61, Maguire, 255, Southwark clergy, 193; Wiseman on its history in England, 319
Gallini, Luisa and Jesse, 47
Gasquet, Francis Aidan, 20
Gentili, Luigi, 135; opposes restoration of hierarchy, 106, 144; and Prior Park, 40–41, 55, 57, 63–64, chap. 4, n. 11; reports to Propaganda, 142–44, 148–49
Gilbert, Daniel, 320
Gillow, John (2d president of Ushaw), 5, 13

Prior Park College, 31, 33, 40–46, 54–64, 94, 169, 194, 206, 209, 241, 246–47, 300. *See also* Baines, Peter Augustine

Propaganda, *see* Sacred Congregation for the Propagation of the Faith

Protestants, English: their view of Catholics, 6, 18–19, 35, 45, 73, 86–87, 116, 133–34, 136, 150, 179–80, 189–92, 203, 216–17, 265

Provincial synods, 146, 202–3, 207, 234; the first (1852): decrees, 210–12; *Epitome Decretorum*, 207–9, 211; on education of poor, 213–14; preparations for, 207–9; the second (1855): 241; decrees, 242–43; on colleges, 243–44, 277; the third (1859): 282–93, 313–15; decree on colleges, 284–86; postponement of, 267; preparations for, 277–81; proposed decree on seminary deputies, 286–87; synodical letter, 289–90; Wiseman's defeat, 315–16

Pugin, Augustus Welby, 63, 90, 100, 116, 127–28, 133–34, 182

Purcell, Edmund Sheridan, 301, 305, 316, chap. 16, n. 15

Pusey, Edward, 116, 121

Puseyite, 17, 109, 215

Quin, Michael, 68, 70

Rambler, 69, 270–74, 326–27, 329

Redemptorists, 135, 179–80, 185, 225–26

Regular clergy, *see* Religious orders

Religious orders, 73, 100–1; and 1st provincial synod, 212–13; excluded by Catholic Emancipation Act, 23; opposition to, 46–52, 108–9, 111–12, 134–36, 177–79; regular versus secular clergy, 27–28, 46–50, 74, 145–46, 206–7; strengthened by decrees on indulgences and right to construct chapels, 83–84; supported by Wiseman, 135–37, 185; Wiseman's hopes for, 225–26

Richardson, John, 267

Riddell, William, 72, 143, 147–49, 160

Rio, Alexis-François, 34

Robertson, J. B., 70

Rock, Daniel, 63, 116, 134–35, 139, 157, 193, 217, 283

Rolfe, George, 256

Roskell, Richard, 240, 276, 314

Rosmini-Serbati, Antonio, 40, 55

Rosminians, 101, 126

"Rules of the Mission" (1763), 6, 46

Russell, Charles, 70, 138, 185

Russell, John, (1st earl), 152–53, 166, 186, 188–91, 227, 235

Sacred Congregation for the Propagation of the Faith, 6, 42–43, 48, 72–73, 80–81, 83, 109, 192, 195; approves of Wiseman's approach to Anglicans, 121; considers reorganization of ecclesiastical structures (1839) and restoration of hierarchy (1848), 105–7, 160; on charitable trusts, 309–11; on decrees of 3d synod, 296–98, 315; on Grant versus Wiseman, 294–96; on Oblates of St. Charles, 305–6; receives Wiseman's report on Oxford Movement, 116; refuses to name Wiseman Baines's coadjutor, 43

St. Chad's, Birmingham, 133

St. Cuthbert's, *see* Ushaw College

St. Edmund's College, Old Hall, Ware, 4, 24, 28, 130, 168–69, 208–9, 217, 235, 285, 287, 295, 319; Oblates at, 254–62, 289, 305–6; Talbot's views on, 291; Vaughan's position at, 254–55; W. G. Ward's lectures at, 251–52

St. Edward's College, Liverpool, 250

St. George's Southwark, 131, 160, 182–83, 191, 193–95, 232–33, 295

St. John's Wood, 47–48, 52, 77

St. Mary's Moorfields, 65, 233, 320

St. Paul's College, 55, 58. *See also* Prior Park

St. Peter's College, 58. *See also* Prior Park

St. Peter's Church, Hatton Garden, 264

Salford, diocese of, 206, 241

Sardinian Chapel, 64–65, 174–77

Scholz, J. M. A., 34

Searle, Francis, 98, 193, 199–200, 260, 274, 294–95, 298, 305, 337

Seminaries, diocesan, 207, 242, 244–45. *See also* Colleges, ecclesiastical; Oscott; Prior Park; St. Edmund's; Ushaw

Sharples, James, 9–10, 140, 142–43, 148; in Rome with Wiseman (1847), 142, 144, 146–49; recommends Bp. Walsh as archbishop, 156–57

Shee, James, 13–14

Shepherd, Robert, 206, 232

Shrewsbury, 16th earl of (John Talbot), 51, 56, 60, 63–64, 111, 120–23, 125, 128–32, 134, 141, 145, 155–58, 161; attacked by Lucas, 164–66, 169–71, 180–81; death of, 205; entertains Wiseman in Rome, 53;

interferes in ecclesiastical affairs, 56, 168–71; on Diplomatic Relations Bill, 153; on hierarchy, 157–58; on Irish clergy, 166–68; on religious orders, 100–1; on rights of clergy, 202; relations with Pierce Connelly, 181

Sibthorpe, Richard Waldo, 123–25, 216, 336

Siga, bishop of, *see* Baines, Peter Augustine

Simpson, Richard, 270, 272–73, 324, 326–27, 329

Sisters of the Faithful Virgin, Norwood, 320

Sisters of Mercy, 264, 321

Smith, Thomas, 22

Society of the Catholic Apostolate, *see* Pallottines

Society of the Holy Child of Jesus, *see* Connelly, Cornelia

Society of Jesus, 10, 26, 28, 42, 45, 72, 82, 91, 98, 114, 135, 225; and chapel at Wigan, 46–47; and construction of Farm Street church, 177–79; excluded by Catholic Emancipation, 23; opposed by vicars apostolic, 46–52, 72, 109; restoration of, 27–28; Wiseman's view of, 98–99, 144

Society for the Propagation of the Faith, 87–88

Southwark, diocese of, 189, 296; chapter of, 233, 259–60, 275, 283; clergy of, 193, 199–200, 232–33; Grant and Wiseman suggest divisions of, 241–42; Wiseman seeks to control, 193, 232

Spencer, George (Father Ignatius), 41, 109–10, 116, 118–19, 124, 127, 136

Spencerite, *see* Spencer, George

Spiritual Exercises of St. Ignatius, 91, 144

"Statuta Proposita," 81, 83, 85, 87

"Statuta Provisoria," 79–81

Stokes, S. N., 273

Sutton, John, 290

Tablet, 123, 139, 153, 164–67, chap. 9, n. 11, 69–71, 184, 221. *See also* Lucas, Frederick

Talbot, George, 193–95, 197, 199–200, 214, 216, 222, 228, 233–34, 241, 250–51, 255–56, 258, 260–61, 263, 267–68, 274, 283, 285, 292–93, 296, 305, 308, 320, 323, 326, 331, 337; assists Wiseman to remain in England (1850), 185–87; obtains chapter dignity for Manning, 255; on ap-

pointment of bishops (1851), 192–93; on character of English bishops, 313; on Errington as coadjutor, 237–38, 253–56, 300; on Grant, 292–93; on Newman's delation, 304; on 3d synod, 291–92, 298; seeks Errington's removal, 275, 292, 298–99; suffers mental breakdown, 300; suggests Manning as bishop of Beverley, 307

Talbot, John, *see* Shrewsbury, 16th earl of

Tandy, William: Wiseman's letters to, 39–40, 42–43, 53, 55, 65, 71

Tate, Robert, 103, 109, 313

Temple, William, *see* Palmerston, 2d viscount

Thirty-nine articles, 117, 120

Tholuck, Friedrick Augustus, 34

Tierney, Mark, 70–71, 157, 183, 193, 270–72, 283

Tract XC, 117, 119–20

Trebizond, archbishop of, *see* Errington, George

Trench, Richard, 37

Trent, Council of, 36; on seminaries, 207, 244–45, 256, 258–59, 275, 277–80, 284, 286–87, 290–91, 301, 309

Tridentine, *see* Trent, Council of

True Tablet, 165

Tucker, Fanny, 4, chap. 1, n. 4

Turner, William, 195, 230, 241, 276, 313

Turton, Thomas, 96–97

Ullathorne, William Bernard, 143, 148–49, 184, 192, 194–96, 207–8, 214, 273, 276–77, 291, 297, 307, 312, 328; advises Wiseman on relations with bishops, 155–56; changes position on 15th decree, 314; critical of Wiseman, 229; dissatisfied with ecclesiastical education, 208–9, 275; lack of funds, 205, 247; mission to Holy See (1848), 160; on Gentili, 144; on Prior Park, 246; opposes Wiseman on charitable trusts, 265–67, 309–11; proposed as Wiseman's coadjutor, 319; quarrels with Wiseman over finances, 231–32, 235, 247–48, 305; seeks to resign, 311; supports Newman, 303–4; urges division of London, 193–94

Ultramontanism, 35, 324; and Wiseman, 134, 155

Ushaw College, 4, 12, 24, 28, 37, 57, 92–94, 96, 104, 129–30, 209, 248–51, 259, 267, 275, 279, 287, 296–97, 315

Vatican Council, First, 120
Vaughan, Herbert, 182, 254–55, chap. 13,
n. 43, 261, 267, 274, 305, 322–23, 325–26
Vaughan, William, 240, 282
Vavasour, Edward, 62
Venerable English College, Rome, 7, 10,
71–72, 91, 110, 114, 130, 243; Baines cari-
catures Wiseman's rectorship of, 59–60;
Weld appointed protector of, 49–50;
Wiseman advises successor at, 117
Via media, 95–96
Vicars apostolic, English, 6–7, 22, 24, 30,
72–89, 105; and Jesuits, 27–28; and
"Statuta Provisoria," 79–80; and selection of episcopal candidates (1839–40),
107–11; dissatisfaction with Wiseman,
49–52, 72, 75, 84, 88–89, 102; Gentili's
judgment of, 143–44; lack of funds of,
79; on Catholic Emancipation, 23; on
restoration of hierarchy, 139–40, 146–48;
oppose decrees on regulars, 46–52,
83–84; oppose Wiseman's plan for missionary community, 102–3; oppose Wiseman's plan for Newman, 125–26; Rome's
dissatisfaction with, 80–81, 84; Wiseman's advice to Baggs regarding, 117
Vicars apostolic, Scottish, 48
Victoria, Queen, 189
Vincent de Paul, Saint, 264

Walker, John, 296
Walsh, Thomas, 30, 33, 41, 65, 72, 74–75,
81–82, 84, 105–9, 112, 114, 130–33, 135,
138–39, 141–42, 147, 160, 182, 247, 302;
advises Wiseman, 123–24; and archbishopric of Westminster, 156–61; and Blundell legacy, 131; concerned with Wiseman's administration of Oscott, 128–29;
death and Bernard Ward's appreciation
of, 161; discusses Spencer, 119; encourages Pugin, 133–34; Gentili on, 143–44;
objects to restoration of hierarchy,
146–47; refuses to sign petition against
regulars, 48, chap. 3, n. 41; regrets loss
of Weedall and Wareing, 111; seeks
Wiseman as coadjutor, 64, 77–78,
93–94; shares Wiseman's views on Oxford Movement, 95; supports Society for
the Propagation of the Faith, 87–88;
turns administration of district over to
Wiseman, 114; visits Rome with Bp.
Griffiths, 75–78

Ward, Bernard, 23–24, 56, 68, 90, 93, 130,
161, 178–79, 181
Ward, Wilfrid, xi, xiii, Intro., n. 5, 4, 11,
18, 35, 41, 67, 137, 197, 202, 205, 207,
216, 229, 317, 324, 337; and biography of
Wiseman, xiii, Intro., n. 5
Ward, William George, 123, 218, 324, 329;
at Oscott, 121; at St. Edmund's, 218,
251–52; receives honorary degree, 218
Wareing, William, 110–11, 143, 149, 167,
206, 282; on hierarchy, 147
Weathers, William, 157, 209, 251–52,
255–56, chap. 13, n. 43, 261–62, 283,
287, 291, chap. 15, n. 21
Weedall, Henry, 38–39, 61, 107, 109,
111–12, 148, 208
Weld, Thomas, 31, 49–53, 74–76, 142
Wellington, 1st duke of (Arthur Wellesley),
xi, 153
Western District, 24, 29–30, 204, 246
Westminster, archdiocese of, 183, 189, 230,
237; Wiseman's concern for poor of,
190, 222–26
Westminster, chapter of, 200, 233, 267,
270, 274–75, 282, 288–89, 301; and elec-
tion of Errington, 238–39; and St. Ed-
mund's, 256–58, 316; Wiseman's last
words to, 336–37
White, Blanco, 37, 125
Whitty, Robert, Chap. 2, n. 13, 189–91,
230, 252, 255, 305, 339; description of
Wiseman, 26, 197–201
Wilberforce, Mr. & Mrs. Henry, 215–16
Wilberforce, Samuel, 329
Williams, Michael, 20
Windischmann, Karl Joseph, 34
Winstanley, Edmund, 100
Wiseman, Ann, 220–21
Wiseman, Francesca (Frasquita), *see*
Gabrielli, Francesca
Wiseman, James (grandfather), 3
Wiseman, James (father), 3
Wiseman, James (brother), 3–4, 53–54;
death of, 220; discussed by mother, 15,
53–54; instability of, 15–16, 54, 182,
chap. 9, n. 49; letters to mother, 8, 15;
on deficiencies of Ushaw education, 12;
returns to Spain, 8, chap. 1, n. 18
Wiseman, Mariana Dunphy, 3, chap. 1,
n. 2
Wiseman, Nicholas Patrick Stephen: ad-
ministration of Central District, 114–15,
231, 274–75; advised by Pallotti, 181–82;

agent of vicars apostolic, 27–28, 46–52, 72–73, 75, 80–81, 84, 87–88; and Achilli case, 218–19; and Baines, 26–28, 40–46, 55–62, 110; and Blundell legacy, 131–32; and *Catholic Magazine*, 38–40; and diplomatic mission (1847), 151–53; and Ecclesiastical Titles Act, 191–92; and education, 171–72, 222, 224; and Errington, 19–20, 22, 44–45, 127–29, 195, 237–39, 246–47, 252–53, 297–302; and first three synods of Westminster: 1st synod, 207–14; 2d synod, 497–99; 3d synod, 274–98, 315–16, 319; and Lamennais, 35–36; and London Oratory, 179; and Mt. St. Bernard, 264–65; and Newman, 36–37, 119–20, 125–27, 194, 218–19, 302–4, 331–33; and Oblates of St. Charles, 226, 254–59, 262, 301, 305–6; and *Rambler*, 270–74, 326–29; and restoration of hierarchy, xi–xii, 139–41, 146, 149, 159, 187–92; and selection of first archbishop, 157–59; and Tierney, 70–71, 270–72, 283; and women's religious communities, 180–81, 185, 264, 320–21; anticipates Newman on doctrine of development, 96, 103; apostolic visitor of Ushaw, 248–51, 315; as administrator in Westminster, 197, 206, 230–31, 237; at Malines Congress, 325–26; at opening of St. George's, 182–83; birth and early childhood, 3–4, chap. 1, n. 1; bishop and president of Oscott, 111–16; character of, 3–4, 7, 26, 115–16, 150, 196–201; contribution of, xi–xiii, 199–200, 210–11, 265, 351–54, 368–74, 380–85, 441–42, 445–51, 656, 691, 694; criticized by Gentili, 143–44; death of brother and care of family, 220–21; defends position on colleges, 314–15; defends Shrewsbury, 165–68; delays hierarchy (1847), 159; describes Blanco White, 37; descriptions of, 26, 36–37, 97–99, 150, 197–200; disassociates self from *Tablet*, 166–67, chap. 9, n. 11; dismisses Cox, 208–9; disputes with Grant over finances, 232–36, 258–60, 294–96; disputes with Ullathorne, 231–32, 235, 247–48, 305; establishes *Dublin Review*, 68–69; family connections of, chap. 1, nn. 2,4; final illness, death and funeral xi–xii, 321–22, 336–38; founds Academia of the Catholic Religion, 323–24; health, 8, 10, 32–33, 138–39, 141, 299, 304; his house, 200, chap. 10, n. 39; interest in English affairs while in Rome, 18–19, 23–24, 37–38, 40–42, 44, 46, 71–72, 90–105; letter "from the Flaminian Gate," 189–91; *Letter on Catholic Unity*, (1841), 120, 333; letters to nephew, 4–5, 11–12, 17–18; mental trials in Rome, 17–18; moves to London, 149; offers suggestions on Eastern churches, 229; on Association for Promoting the Unity of Christendom, 333–34; on Austrian concordat, 230; on Catholic attendance at universities, 329–31, 334; on Catholic devotions and ceremonial, 133–34, 198; on communism, 168; on charitable trusts, 138, 308–11; on conversions to Roman Catholicism, 117–19, 121–27, 215–16; on Diplomatic Relations Bill, 153–56; on ecclesiastical education, 217–18, 208–9, 243–44; on elevation to cardinalate and restoration of hierarchy, 184–88; on foreign priests in London, 263–64; on government grants for education, 265–67; on Oxford Movement and Anglicanism, 61–62, 69, 95–96, 116–25, chap. 7, n. 6, 127, 215–16, 330; on politics, 171–72, 226–27, 268–69; on public prayers for England's conversion, 110; on repeal of union with Ireland, 165; on restoration of Jesuits, 27; on Shakespeare, 336; opposed by Lingard, 25, 95, 173, 184, 186; opposes division of London, 159, 193–94; opposes 15th decree of 3d synod, 296–98; opposes Graham's education bill, 137–38; opposes Irish violence in London (1862), 334–35; opposition to, xii, 94–95, 99, 102–4, 113, 115, 123–24, 128, 143–44, 153–56, 163–64, 183–84, 189–92, 197, 199, 218, 221–22, 229, 274, 308–9; ordination of, 16; plan for community of secular priests, 93–94, 100–4, 115, 125–26, 143; playwrite, 97–98, 267; presidency at Oscott, 114–15, 127–31, 150, 231–32, 247–48; professor and preacher in Rome, 16–17, chap. 1, n. 44; proposes division of Beverley, 307–8; proposes division of Southwark, 241–42; proposes Newman and Grant for episcopate, 194; provides solution to dispute between Baines and Benedictines, 31; rebukes Shrewsbury, 169–71; recommended as rector of English college, 19–20; recommends Gentili to Baines, 40–41; rectorship in Rome, 20–21, 71, 91, 97–98; refuses 2d coadjutor, 318–19; refuses to allow Grant's transfer to Beverley, 306; relations with family, 16, 53–54, 182, 188, 220–21, 304–5; relations with fellow bishops, 227–29, 308–13, 319; relations with his priests, 172, 174–77, 183–84, 198–99; relationship to Manning, 301, 304, 316–17, 334; relationship with four colleges, 245–61; reports to pope on archdiocese (1861), 319–20; responds to attacks, 190–91, 216–17, 263–64; responds to Lord John Russell, 188–89; rumored as prefect of Propaganda, 221; scholarship, 10–12, 14, 16–17, 34–35, 41, 65–68, 96–97, 216–17, 325; seeks protection of British property in Rome, 161–62; sends Logan to Prior Park, 41; sensitivity of, 19, 197–98, 200, 274; sermons and lectures in London, 65, 67–68, 90, 191; sought by Walsh as coadjutor, 64, 77–78, 93, 108; student at Ushaw, 4–6, 8–9; student in Rome, 7–14; subject to depression, 17–18, 99, 123–24, 129, 245–46, 304; sued by Richard Boyle, 220; supports establishing hierarchy, 139–40; supports religious orders, 85, 108, 135–37, 179–82, 199, 213, 264; supports Vaughan's efforts for foreign missions, 322–23; tour of Ireland, 267–68; treatment of converts, 124–27, 216, 218; visits England: (1832), 33, 38; (1835–36), 52, 55–71; (1839), 100; visits family in France, 14–15; visits Germany, 54; visits Rome with Sharples (1847), 140–42, 145–50; work for the poor, 99, 168, 174–77, 180, 185–86, 190, 222–26, 264, 289–90; writes *Fabiola*, 10, 236–37

Wiseman, Patrick, 8

Wiseman, Sophia, 220–21

Wiseman, Xaviera Strange (mother), 5–6, 15–16, 19, 53–54, 99–100, 188, 267–68; death of, 192; financial worries of, 8, 15–16, 54; marriage and loss of husband, 3; opposes Nicholas's reception of orders, 12–14

Wright's Bank, failure of, 131

Youens, Thomas, 103

Zurla, Giacinto Placido, 22, 28, 50

A Note on the Type

The text of this book was set in Caledonia, one of the
most popular book typefaces of our century. Created
by the late W. A. Dwiggins of Boston, the eminent
American graphic artist, the typeface immediately
found favor among prominent book designers.
There were several reasons for this, the most
important of which is that the basic design is at
home in all the printing processes. Upon close
examination, one finds the basic design appropriate
not only for books, but for advertising and periodicals
as well.

This book was composed and printed by the
Wickersham Printing Company, Inc. and bound
by the Short Run Bindery.

This edition was first published in July 1984.

Book design is by Howard N. King.